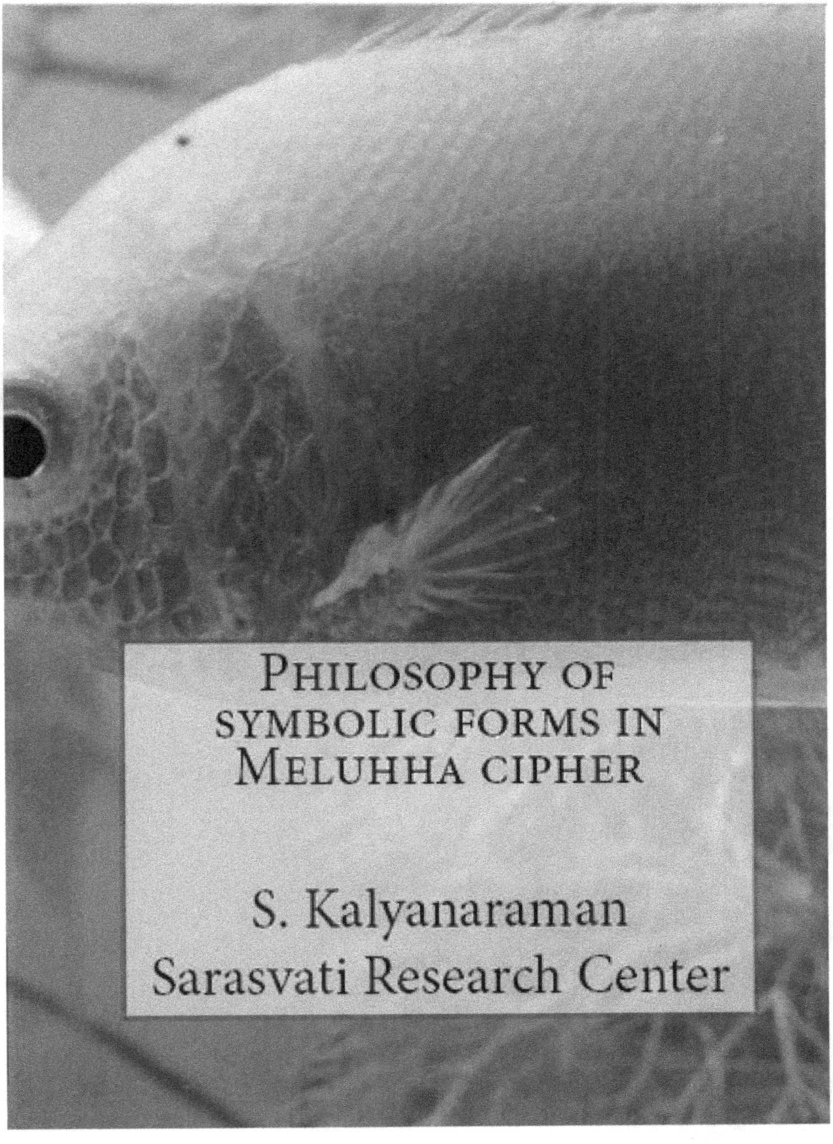
PHILOSOPHY OF SYMBOLIC FORMS IN MELUHHA CIPHER
S. Kalyanaraman
Sarasvati Research Center

ISBN: 9780991104826

ISBN 10 digits: 099110482X

Library of Congress Control Number: 2014906634

Table of Contents

life are Meluhha sacred carvings. So are many carvings relate to specific varieties of plants, buds, flowers which are associated with sacredness because they connote -- rebus -- metal artifacts of a *kole.l* 'smithy/forge' which is, *kole.l* 'temple'. Archaeological evidences from Ancient Near East point to the practice of worship in temples of divinities associated with these hieroglyphs. *Kabbalah* of the Ancient Near East tradition is a synonym of *āgama* of Indian tradition with the roots found in Meluhha as a visible language. Both traditions venerate altars as models of temples. Many metal artifacts are shown as *āyudha* 'weapons' in the hands of *pratimā* in Indian iconographic tradition with an intimation of memories of smithy traditions of ancestors. In Indian tradition, *Pratimā* is a *bimba* a reflection in a tranquil pool of consciousness. Hence, evolved a science called study of *Pratimā lakṣaṇa* for representation of such reflections translated into stone or metal or wood in a temple. '*Pratimā*' or '*mudrā-s*' are not mere abstractions but firmly premised on language sememes. The identification of these sememes in Meluhha is one of the objectives of this philosophical inquiry using the evidence of plain texts and cipher texts of Meluhha language.

Deogarh. Viṣṇu temple. Āyudha puruṣa-s relief panel ca. 6th century.[4] Srinivasa Rao provides an overview.[5]

cedar'denoting western limit of the empire. The text indicates that Meluhha was situated to the east of Sargon's empire. Potts has reviewed the evidence related to Baza and discusses the two locations, mentioned at different periods, of two Meluhhas – one in the vicinity of Baluchistn and the other in Africa (possibly a location in Nubia or Ethiopia).[8] Shrinivas Tilak[9] notes that King Śālivāhana demarcated Sindhu *rāṣṭra* as the nation of the Aryas that lay east of the Sindhu river (*sthāpita tena maryāda mlecchāryānām pṛthak pṛthak. Sindhu sthānam iti jñeyam rāṣṭram āryasya ca uttamam. Mleccha sthānam param sindhoh kritam tena mahātmanā*: Pratisarga Adhyāya 2). Commenting on *Jaiminisutra* (1:3.10), Śabara discusses whether meaning of some Vedic words like pica, nema (not common among the Aryas but well preserved by *mleccha*-s) should be derived from Sanskrit roots or from their actual usage by mlecchas. Śabara advocates the use of such words as used and understood by mlecchas and recommends their incorporation at the Prākṛt (*lokavāṇi*) level. In *Tantravārttika* (#150, 153 on *Jaiminisutra* 1:3.10), Kumarila discusses mlecchas in detail and recommends learning from their professions and skills in agriculture, building houses, producing silk products, making harnesses, astrology and drama – and related terminology and words used by mlecchas. Prabhakara also rejects parochial efforts to derive all mleccha words from Sanskrit roots and notes the need for recognizing the actual usage by mlecchas.[10] In Baudhayana, there is an intimation of deviant behavior in the beef-eating habits of mlecchas: *gomāmsa khādako yastu, viruddham bahu bhāṣate, sarVākāra vihīnasya mleccha iti abhidhīyate*).

Unraveling Meluhha cipher is an exercise in hermeneutics. Hermeneutics is the science of discovering new meanings and interpretations in 'all those situations in which we encounter meanings that are not immediately understandable but require interpretive effort'.[11] The philosophical hermeneutics attempted in this work provides evidence from the lexical repertoire languages which are cognate with Meluhha; and thus, 'discovery of new meanings' is related to re-statement or 'interpretive effort' of identifying meanings in the context of life-activities of Meluhha speakers of the Bronze Age and the cultural context of their lives.

Invention of bronze-age technologies – *cire perdue* casting, alloys: tin-, zinc- bronzes/ brasses/ pewter complementing arsenical copper, alloying ore stones (including carbonate-, sediment-hosted lead-zinc-copper stones) -- necessitated the invention and development of a writing system of Meluhha cipher evidenced in corpora of about 7000 inscriptions. This constitutes a penultimate stage, before syllabic writing evolved. Meluhha cipher continued to be used together with cuneiform syllable symbolic forms in Ancient Near East and Fertile Crescent. These archaeo-metallurgical inventions enabled the production of goods surplus to the requirements of the artisan guilds. These inventions also created the imperative of and necessity for a writing system which could represent about about 1000 specific categories of activities related to the artisanal repertoire of a smith. Such a large number of categories could not be handled by the limited number of geometric shapes used in the token system of accounting and documenting – goods, standard measures of grains, liquids and surface areas. Around 7500 BCE, tokens appeared and represented perhaps the early deployment of a writing system to count objects. Many geometric shapes were used for the tokens. Tracing the evolution of a writing system, Schmandt-Besserat evaluates the next stage of keeping tokens in envelopes with markings abstracting the tokens inside and calls these abstract numbers are 'the culmination of the process…' This evaluation is the starting point for identifying another stage before 'the culmination' represented by the use of syllabic representation in glyphs of sounds of a language as in *kharoṣṭī* and *brāhmī.*
Many samples of results from an enquiry into *mleccha Vācas* as distinguished from *ārya Vācas* (Manu) are presented. Listing 64 arts to be learnt by youth, Vātsyāyana, ca. 6th cent. BCE, attests three types of symbolic forms: 1. *mlecchita vikalpa* as a cipher, 2. *deśabhāṣā jnānam* as symbolic forms of spoken, meaningful sememes and *vākya* 'sentences'; and 3. *akṣaramuṣṭika kathanam* as symbolic forms for narrative rendered by finger- and wrist-signals

or gestures. Patanjali elaborates on *mleccha* (language embedded in *mlecchita vikalpa*) as a dialect.

Divinity Vāk belonged to the mleccha, says Śathapathabrāhmaṇa (3,2,I, 18ff.) Rigveda has a hymn 10.125 addressed to Vāk. Mleccha in Pali is milakkha or milakkhu to describe those who dwell on the outskirts of a village.[12]

mlech 'to utter indistinctly' (Skt.S'Br.) *mlecchayati* id. (Dhātup. xxxii , 120)

Language-speakers -- both *mleccha* and *ārya* are *dasyu* (cf. OIr. *daha* 'people') and mleccha speakers are *dwīpavāsinah* 'island dwellers'.

In Kautilya's *ArthaŚāstra mleccha* is used as a suffix to describe aṭavi or forest people.[13] *Mlecchadeśa* is an area where the four varṇas were not known (VS LXXXIV.4) It is 'that land where the black antelope naturally roams, one must know to be fit for performance of sacrifice; (the tract) different from that (is) the country of the Mlecchas.'[14]

According to the great epic, *Mahabharata*, *mleccha*-s lived on islands: "*sa sarvān mleccha nṛpatin sāgara dvīpa vāsinah, aram āhāryàm àsa ratnāni vividhāni ca, andana aguru vastrāṇi man.i muktam anuttamam, kāñcanam rajatam vajram vidrumam ca mahādhanam*: (Bhima) arranged for all the mleccha kings, who dwell on the ocean islands, to bring varieties of gems, sandalwood, aloe, garments, and incomparable jewels and pearls, gold, silver, diamonds, and extremely valuable coral… great wealth." (*MBh.* 1933-1966: 2.27.25-26). The reference to gems, pearls and corals evokes the semi-precious and precious stones, such as carnelian and agate, of Gujarat traded with Mesopotamian civilization. According to Sumerian records from the Agade Period (Sargon, 2373-2247 BC), Sumerian merchants traded with people from (at least) three named foreign places: Dilmun (now identified as the island of Bahrain in the Persian Gulf); Magan (a port on the coastline between the head of the Persian Gulf and the mouth of the Sindhu river); and

Meluhha. Mentions of trade with Meluhha become frequent in Ur III period (2168-2062 BCE) and Larsa dynasty (2062- 1770 BCE). By Ur III Period, Meluhhan workers residing in Sumeria had Sumerian names, leading to a comment: '…three hundred years after the earliest textually documented contact between Meluhha and Mesopotamia, the references to a distinctly foreign commercial people have been replaced by an ethnic component of Ur III society' This is an economic presence of Meluhhan traders maintaining their own village for a considerable span of time.[15]
A reference also to the salty marshes of Rann of Kutch in Gujarat (and also, perhaps, the Makran coast, south of Karachi), may also be surmised, where settlements and fortifications such as Amri Nal, Allahdino, Dholavira (Kotda) Sur-kota-da, and Kanmer have been excavated – close to the Sarasvati River Basin as the River traversed towards the Arabian ocean.
Kathāsaritsāgara[16] associates mleccha with Sind. Mleccha kings paid tributes of sandalwood, aloe, cloth, gems, pearls, blankets, gold, silver and valuable corals.

Nakula conquered western parts of Bhāratavarṣa teeming with mleccha (MBh.V.49.26: *yah pratīcīm diśam cakre vaśe mlecchagaṇāyutām sa tatra nakulo yoddhā citrayodhī vyavasthitah*). Bṛhatsamhitā XIV.21 refers to lawless mleccha who inhabited the west: *nirmaryādā mlecchā ye paścimadiksthit āsteca*. A Buddhist chronicle, *āryaManjuśrī Mūlakalpa* [ed. Ganapati Śāstri, II, p. 274] associates pratyanta (contiguous)with mlecchadeśa in western Bhāratavarṣa: *paścimām diśīm āsṛtya rājāno mriyate tadā ye 'pi pratyantavāsinyo mlecchataskara jīvinah*. [Trans. 'Then (under a certain astrological combination) the kings who go to the west die; also inhabitants of pratyanta live like the mlecchas and taskara.')

According to Matsya Purāṇa (10.7), King Veṇa was the ancestor of the *mleccha*; according to Mahābhārata (MB. 12.59, 101-3), King Veṇa was a progenitor of the *Niṣāda* dwelling in the Vindhya mountains. Nirukta 3.8 includes Niṣāda among the five peoples mentioned in the Ṛgveda 10.53.4, citing Aupamanyava; the five peoples are: brāhmaṇa, kṣatriya, vaiśya, śūdra and Niṣāda. Niṣāda gotra is mentioned in the gaṇapāṭha of Pāṇini (Aṣṭādhyāyī 4.1.100). Niṣāda were mleccha. It should be noted that Pāṇini associated yavana with the Kāmboja (Pāṇini, *Gaṇapāṭha*, 178 on 2.1.72).

Various terms are used to describe mleccha social groups and communities: *pratyantadeśa* (*Arthaśāstra*VII.10.16), *paccantimā janapada* (*Vinaya Piṭaka* V.13.12, vol. I, p. 197), *aṭavi, aṭavika* (DC Sircar,*Selected Inscriptions*, vol. I, 'Thirteenth Rock Edict Shābhāzgaṛhī, text line 7, p.37; 'Khoh Copper Plate Inscription of Saimkshobha', text line 8; *Arthaśāstra* VII.10.16; VII.4.43: *mlecchaṭavi* who were considered a threat to the state; *Arthaśāstra* IX.2.18-20 mentions *aṭavibala*, troops from forests as one of six types of troops at the disposal of a ruler). Some mleccha lived in border areas and forests, e.g. *pratyanta nṛpatibhir* (frontier kings: JF Fleet, CII, vol. II, 'Allahabad Posthumous Pillar Inscription of Samudragupta, text line 22, p. 116) cf. Arthaśāstra– a 4th century BCE text — I.12.21; VII.14.27; XIV.1.2; *mleccha jāti* are: *bheda,kirāta, śabara, pulinda*: *Amarakośa* II.10.20, a fifth century CE text).

In many Persian inscriptions Yauna, Gandhāra and Saka occur together. [For e.g., DC Sircar, *Selected Inscriptions*, no.2 'Persepolis Inscription on Dārayavahuṣ (Darius c. 522-486 BCE),' lines 12-13, 18, p.7; no. 5, 'Perseplis Inscription of Khshayārshā (Xerxes c. 486-465)', lines 23, 25-6, p. 12]. Thus, *yavana* may be a reference to people settled in the northwest Bhāratavarṣa (India).
There are references to Mleccha (that is, *śaka, Yavana, Kamboja, Pahlava*) in Bāla Kāṇḍa of the *Valmiki Rāmāyaṇa* (1.54.21-23; 1.55.2-3). *Taih asit samvrita bhūmih śakaih-Yavana miśritaih | | 1.54-21 | | taih taih Yavana-Kamboja barbarah ca akulii kritaah | | 1-54-23 | | tasya humkaarato jātah Kamboja ravi sannibhah | udhasah tu atha sanjatah Pahlavah śastra panayah | | 1-55-2 | | yoni deśāt ca Yavanah śakri deśāt śakah tathā | roma kupeṣ u Mlecchah ca Haritah sa Kiratakah | | 1-55-3 | |.Kāmboja Yavanān caivaśakān paṭṭaṇāni ca |*

Anvīkṣya Varadān caiva Himavantam vicinvatha || *12* || — (*Rāmāyaṇa* 4.43.12)

The Yavanas here refer to the Bactrian Yavanas (in western Oxus country), and the Sakas here refer to the Sakas of Sogdiana/Jaxartes and beyond. The Vardas are the same as Paradas (*Hindu Polity*, 1978, p 124, Dr K. P. Jayswal; *Goegraphical Data in Early Purana*, 1972, p 165, 55 fn, Dr M. R.Singh). The Paradas were located on river Sailoda in Sinkiang (MBh II.51.12; II.52.13; VI.87.7 etc) and probably as far as upper reaches of river Oxus and Jaxartes (Op cit, p 159-60, Dr M. R.Singh).

Vanaparva of Mahābhārata notes: "......Mlechha (barbaric) kings of the śaka-s, Yavanas, Kambojas, Bahlikas etc shall rule the earth (i.e India) un-rightously in Kaliyuga..." *viparīte tadā loke purvarūpān kṣayasya tat* || *34* || *bahavo mechchha r\ājānah pṛthivyām manujādhipa* | *mithyanuśāsinah pāpa mṛṣavadaparāṇah* || *35* || *āndrah śakah Pulindaśca Yavanaśca narādhipāh* | *Kamboja Bahlikahśudrastathābhīra narottama* || 36|| MBH 3/188/34-36). Anushasanaparava of Mahābhārata affirms that Mathura, was under the joint military control of the Yavanas and the Kambojas (12/102/5). *Tathā Yavana Kambojā Mathurām abhitaś ca ye ete niyuddhakuśalā dākshiinātyāsicarminah.* Mahābhārata speaks of the Yavanas, Kambojas, Darunas etc as the fierce mleccha from Uttarapatha : *uttaraścāpare mlechchha jana bharatasattama.* || *63* || *Yavanashcha sa Kamboja Daruna mlechchha jatayah.* | — *(MBH 6.11.63-64) They are referred to as papakritah (sinful): uttara pathajanmanah kirtayishyami tanapi.* | *Yauna Kamboja Gandharah Kirata barbaraih saha.* || *43* || *ete pāpakṛtāstatra caranti pṛthivīmimām.* | *śvakakabalagridhraṇān sadharmaṇo narādhipa.* || *44* || — (MBh 12/207/43-44).[17]

In the Mahābhārata, sons of Anu are noted as mleccha. Yavana are descendants of Turvaśu, one of the four sons of Yayāti. The sons were to rule over people such as Yavana, Bhoja and Yādava (MBh. 1.80.23-4; Matsya Purāṇa 34.29-30). Yavana, descendants of Turvaśu are noted as meat-eaters, sinful and hence, anārya. [MBh. trans. PC Roy, vol. I, p. 179] These people were brought over the sea safely by Indra (RV 6.20.12). Ṛgveda notes that Yadu and Turvaśa are dāsa (RV 10.62.10):

sanema te vasā navya indra pra pūrava stavanta enā yajnaih
sapta yat purah śarma śāradīr dadruiśa dhan dāsīh purukutsāya śikṣan
tvam vrdha indraprvyarja bhūr varivasyann uśane kāvyāya
parā navavāstvam anudeyam mahe pitre dadātha svam napātam
tvam dhunir indra dhunimtrṇor āpah sīrā na sravantīh
pra yat samudram ati śūra parśi pāraya turvaśam yadum svasti

RV 6.020.10 (Favoured) by your proection, Indra, we solicit new (wealth); by this adoration men glorify you at sacrifices, for that you have shattered with your bolt the seven cities of śarat, killing the opponents (of sacred rites), killing the opponents (of sacred rites), and giving (their spoils) to Purukutsa. [Men: puravah = manuṣyah; śarat = name of an asura].
RV 6.020.11 Desirous of opulence, you, Indra, have been an ancient benefactor of Us'anas, the son of Kavi; having slain Navavāstva, you have given back his own grandson, who was (fit) to be restored o the grandfather.
RV 6.020.12 You, Indra, who make (your enemies) tremble, have caused the waters, detained by Dhuni, to flow like rushing rivers; so, hero, when, having crossed the ocean, you have reached the shore, you have brought over in safety Turvas'a and Yadu. [*samudram atiprapar*ṣ*i* = samudram atikramya pratirṇo bhavasi = when you are crossed, having traversed the ocean, you have brought across Turvaśa and Yadu, both standing on the future shore, *samudrapāreti*ṣṭ*hantau apārayah*].

Mullaippāṭṭu (59-66) (composed by kāvirippūmpāṭṭinattuppon vāṇigaṇār mahanārṇ.appūḍanār) are part of Pattuppāṭṭu, ten Tamil verses of Sangam literature; these refer to a chief of Tamil warriors whose battle-field tent was built by Yavana and guarded by mleccha who spoke only through gestures. (JV Chelliah, 1946, *Pattuppāṭṭu; ten Tamil idylls, translated into English verse*, South India Saiva Siddhanta Works Publishing Society, p. 91).

Mahābhārata notes that the Pāṇḍava army was protected by mleccha, among other people (Kāmboja ,śaka, Khasa, Salwa, Matsya, Kuru, Mleccha, Pulinda, Draviḍa, Andhra and Kāñci) (MBh. V.158.20). Sūta laments the misfortune of the Kaurava-s: 'When the Nārāyaṇa-s have been killed, as also the Gopāla-s, those troops that were invincible in battle, and many thousands of mleccha-s, what can it be but Destiny?' (MBh. IX.2.36: *Nārāyaṇā hatāyatra Gopālā yuddhadurmahāh mlecchāśca bahusāhasrāh kim anyad bhāgadheyatah*?)

The thesis demonstrates that rebus memories are retained by Meluhha language speakers in Ancient Near East, Fertile Crescent and India from ca.5th millennium BCE, dawn of bronze-age, as evidenced by examples of hieroglyhs and related glosses from Indian *sprachbund*. It is clear that many nomadic settlements attested in proto-history of the region relate to Meluhha speaker settlements principally working in stone, ores and metals.

"A *Sprachbund*...in German, plural "Sprachbünde" IPA, from the German word for "language union", also known as a linguistic area, convergence area, or diffusion area, is a group of languages that have become similar in some way because of geographical proximity and language contact. They may be genetically unrelated, or only distantly related. Where genetic affiliations are unclear, the *sprachbund* characteristics might give a false appearance of relatedness...In a classic 1956 paper titled "India as a Linguistic Area", Murray Emeneau laid the groundwork for the general acceptance of the concept of a *Sprachbund*. In the paper, Emeneau observed that the subcontinent's Dravidian and Indo-Aryan languages shared a number of features that were not inherited from a common source, but were areal features, the result of diffusion during sustained contact." _Common features of a group of languages in a *Sprachbund* are called 'areal features'. In linguistics, an areal feature is any typological feature shared by languages within the same geographical area. An example refers to retroflex consonants in the Burushaski, Nuristani, Dravidian,

Munda and Indo-Aryan language families of the Indian

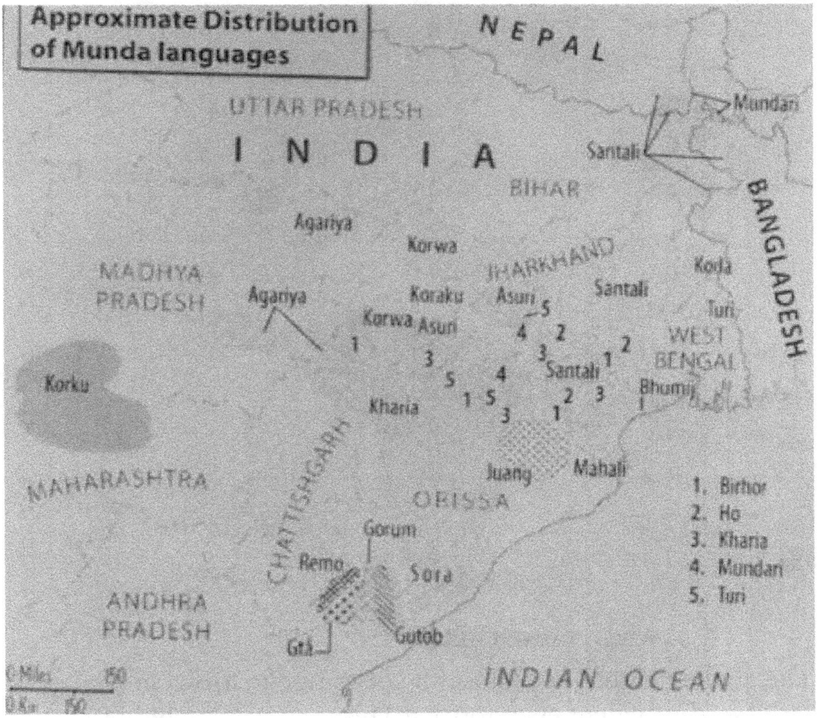

subcontinent.[18]

At the 2004 annual meeting of the Southeast Asian Linguistic Society held in Bangkok, David Stampe reiterated the view that "India may be the homeland of Austroasiatic, and Mon-Khmer reflects an offshoot that migrated eastward". And, more recently on Monday, 16th July 2007, Gerard Diffloth has in a lecture presented some fresh arguments suggesting that "the origins of the Austroasiatic family are more likely to be found somewhere on the shores of the Bay of Bengal.

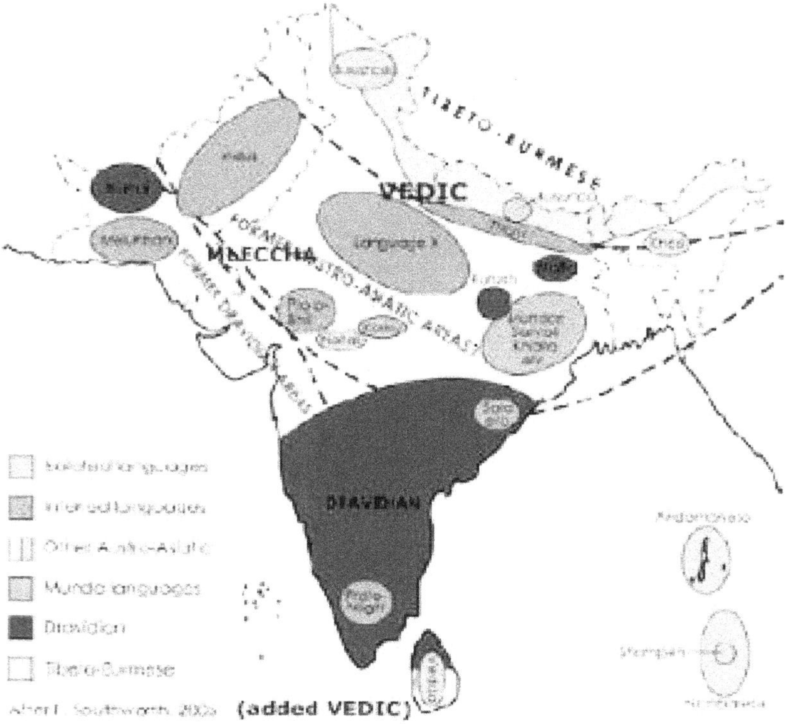

The abiding nature of philosophy of symbolic forms in Indian *sprachbund* is evident even today.[19] This is a resource base for further studies in the formation and evolution of most of the Indian languages. Identifiable substrata glosses include over 4000 etyma of Dravidian Etymological Dictionary and over 1000 words of Munda with concordant semantic clusters of Indo-Aryan. That the substrata glosses cover three major language families – Dravidian, Munda and Indo-Aryan -- is a surprising discovery. There are over 1240 semantic clusters included in the *Indian Lexicon* from over 25 languages which makes the work very large, including cognate entries of CDIAL (Indo-Aryan etyma), together with thousands of lexemes of Santali, Mundarica and other languages of the Austro-Asiatic linguistic group, and, maybe, Language X. . Most of the lexical archives relate to the bronze-age cultural context and possible entries are relatable rebus to Indian hieroglyphs. (See Appendix M: Rebus as dream, as literacy). Many

are found to be attested as substratum lexemes only in a few languages such as Nahali, Kashmiri, Kannada or Telugu or lexical entries of Hemacandra's *deśī nāmamālā (Prākṛt)*; thus, many present-day Indian languages are rendered as dialects of an Indus language or proto-Indic *lingua franca* or gloss. The identification of a particular Indian language as the Indus language has presented some problems because of the received wisdom about grouping of language families in Indo-European linguistic analyses.
About 3500 BCE, Meluhha cipher was developed to use hieroglyphs to represent the 'spoken words' identifying each of the goods and processes. A rebus method of representing similar sounding words of the lingua franca of the artisans was used. Evidence is provided by over 2,000 rebus lexical glosses of mleccha (meluhha) and over 1,000 unambiguously written-down engraved or incised or sculpted hieroglyphs in the corpora. The written symbolic forms are demonstrated to relate to many languages of Indian *sprachbund.* In vogue as *parole* of many living languages (including Deśi or Prākṛts) are glosses which continue to be used – for generations -- by speakers of many Indian languages, their vernacular). The *sprachbund* is proximate to the area where most of the Meluhh cipher deploying Meluhha hieroglyphs were discovered, as documented in the corpora. That hundreds of Indian hieroglyphs continued to be used in metallurgy is evidenced by their use on early punch-marked coins.

Indian linguistic area: pre-aryan, pre-Munda and pre-dravidian in India

Mleccha was the *lingua franca* of Bhāratam, of the 'linguistic area' called Sarasvati civilization. Meluhha may be interpreted as the *parole*, or *vāk* symbolic form of bhāṣā. In Indian tradition, diction takes the symbolic forms of chandas (Ṛgveda) and mleccha (meluhha); the superset gloss is: भाषा bhāṣā *f.* speech , language (esp. common or vernacular speech , as opp. to Vedic or in later times to Sanskrit) (Nirukta. Pāṇini.Manu.MBh.); any Prākṛt dialect or a partic. group of 5 of them (viz. माहाराष्ट्री, शौरसेनी, मागध, प्राच्या, and अवन्ति , also called पञ्च-विधा भाषा (Monier-Williams lexicon, p.703, 755). A hypothesis has been posited, central to the identification of Meluhha (mleccha): Language X (cf. Masica 1991) + Proto-Munda = Proto-mleccha (vernacular of Sarasvati hieroglyphs). The hypothesis has been tested by identifying the borrowings into the Indian languages which can explain, rebus, the Meluhha hieroglyphs in a Proto-Vedic continuum of Indian linguistic area (*sprachbund*).

Sources of OIA agricultural vocabulary (based on Masica 1979: 55-152) are identified as follows:

	Percentage
• IE/IIr	40%
• Drav	13%
• Munda	11%
• Other	2%
• Unknown	34%
• **Total**	100%

It will be a hasty claim to make that Old Tamil or Proto-Munda or Santali or Prakṛt or Pali or any other specific language of the Indian linguistic area, by itself (to the exclusion of other languages in contact), explains the language of the Sarasvati civilization.

Some hieroglyphs of the writing system are yet to be decoded. Tentative, provisional readings of such glyphs yet to be validated by the cipher code key of Meluhha hieroglyphs have been detailed (including decipherment of inscriptions from scores of small sites).[20]

"The toponym Meluhha is found in cuneiform texts of the mid- to late third millennium BCE. An inscription of King Sargon of Akkad states that the boats of Dilmun, Magan, and Meluhha docked at the quays of Akkad. The names always occur in this sequence, and Meluhha is therefore thought to have been the farthest away.

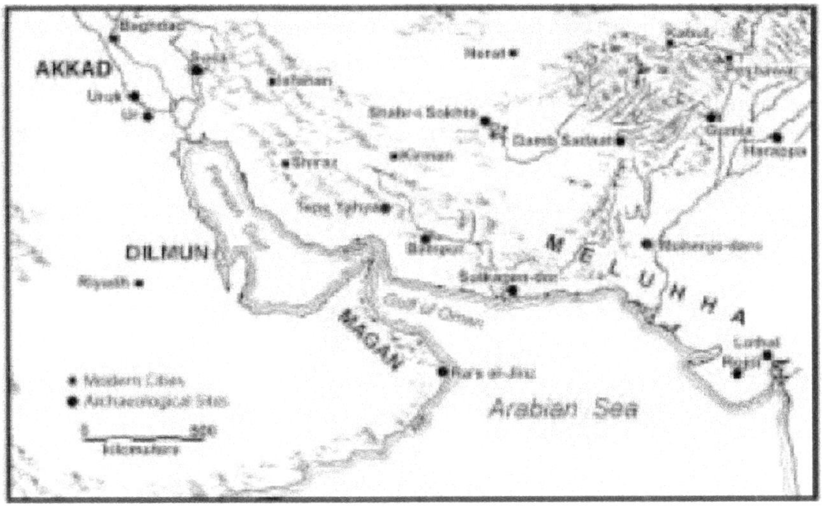

It is usually identified with the Indus valley, Gujarat, and the Harappan culture. The identification is strengthened by the nature of the commodities brought from Meluhha. These included special woods such as ebony, gold, ivory, carnelian, and lapis. Most arrived in Mesopotamia in an unworked state, but etched carnelian beads and long tubular beads of the same material were undoubtedly made in the Indus. Many of the materials originated in the Indus, but others such as lapis were traded on from further afield. It is not clear what was received in return, as few goods of Mesopotamian origin have been found in the Indus. Some Meluhhan merchants apparently lived in a special settlement near Lagash, suggesting that the trade was not exclusively in the hands of Mesopotamian merchants. A seal of the Agade period identifies its owner, who bears the Akkadian name Šu-ilišu, as a Meluhhan interpreter. The name Meluhha disappears from the texts after the third millennium, when the Indus civilization declined and direct contact apparently ceased. However, in the Neo-Assyrian period the name reappears, now used to denote Nubia and Ethiopia, which supplied some of the same goods previously obtained from the Indus."[21]

Close to Caspian Sea is the site of Altyn-tepe which was an interaction area with Meluhha and where three Indus seals with inscriptions were found, including a silver seal showing a composite animal which can be called a signature glyph of Meluhha cipher.

Intimations of casting, soldering, riveting work, working with zinc (pewter), ivory

खोंड [khōṇḍa] *m* A young bull, a bullcalf (Marathi). kōḍiya, kōḍe young bull (Telugu) Rebus: *kõdā* 'turn in a lathe'; koḍ 'workshop' (Kuwi) *mẽḍha* 'antelope' Rebus: *meḍ* 'iron' (Ho.) *ḍangar* 'bull' Rebus: *ḍhangar* 'blacksmith'.

Altyn depe finds: Two seals found at Altyn-depe (Excavation 9 and 7) found in the shrine and in the 'elite quarter'.

A shell seal, Bet Dwaraka uses the same hieroglyph composition as on Altyn Depe silver seal.

Archaeologically attested date for shell bangle (of turbinella pyrum) is 6500 BCE – ornaments found in a burial in Mehergarh. 6500 BCE. Date of the woman's burial with ornaments including a wide bangle of shankha.

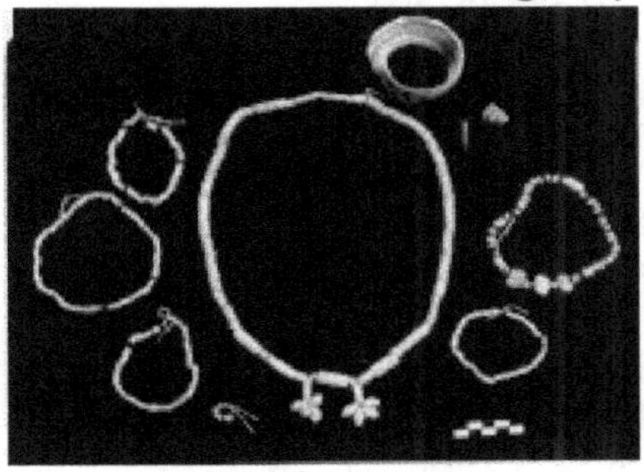

Mehergarh. Burial ornaments made of shell and stone disc beads, and turbinella pyrum (sacred conch, s'an:kha) bangle, Tomb MR3T.21, Mehrgarh, Period 1A, ca. 6500 BCE. The nearest source for this shell is Makran coast near Karachi, 500 km.

South. [After Fig. 2.10 in Kenoyer, 1998]. S'ankha wide bangle and other ornaments, c. 6500 BCE (burial of a woman at Nausharo). Seven shell bangles from burial of an elderly woman,

Harappa. Glyph: 'shell-cutter's saw' Glyph: *svastika*; rebus: *jasta* 'zinc' (Kashmiri). *sathiyā* (G.); satthia, (H.), sāthiyo sotthia (Pkt.) Rebus:

svastika pewter (Kannada) Hieroglyph: *kolom* 'three' Allograph: *kolmo* 'sprout' Rebus: *kolami* 'smithy, forge'.

Altyn Depe seal hieroglyphs.

dula 'pair' Rebus: *dul* 'cast metal' *ṭaṅka* 'hoe' (Sanskrit) *ṭŏnguru* m. ' a kind of hoe (Kashmiri)(CDIAL 5427).
Rebus: *ṭā̃knā* ' to stitch, join, rivet, solder' (Hindi)(CDIAL 5432).
Rebus: Kho. (Lor.) danākār ' borax, alum ' prob. ← Ir., cf.
Pers. *tangār* (CDIAL 5437). Rebus: T*a.* taṅkam pure gold, that which is precious, of great worth. *Ma.* taṅkam pure gold. / ? < Skt. ṭaṅka- a stamped (gold) coin. (DEDR 3013).

This hieroglyph is remarkable, for the unique two-pronged ligatures superscripted. Mahadevan has indicated that this 'sign' may signify a bandicoot looked at from the back, based on a variant which is noticed in the corpora.

Hieroglyph sequence on Altyn Depe seal.

Seal impression; UPenn; steatite; bull; dia. 2.4cm.; Gadd, PBA 18 (1932), p. 13, Pl. III, no. 15; Legrain, MJ (1929), p. 306, pl. XLI, no. 119; found at Ur in the cemetery area, in a ruined grave .9 metres from the surface, together with a pair of gold ear-rings of the double-crescent type and long beads of steatite and carnelian, two of gilt copper, and others of lapis-lazuli, carnelian, and banded sard. The first sign to

the left has the form of a flower or perhaps an animal's skin with curly tail; there is a round spot upon the bull's back.

goṭa 'numerative particle' (Maithili) *gōṭī* 'round pebble. Rebus: *khoṭ* f 'alloy (Lahnda) Hence खोटसाळ [khōṭasāḷa] *a* (खोट & साळ from शाला) Alloyed--a metal. (Marathi) खोट [*khōṭa*] 'ingot, wedge'; A mass of metal (unwrought or of old metal melted down). (Marathi) M.*khoṭā* 'alloyed' (CDIAL 3931) Rebus 2: kōṭhī] f (कोष्ट S) A granary, garner, storehouse, warehouse, treasury, factory, bank.

Hieroglyph: blazing pot: *kuṭṭhita* 'molten'  *kāḍ* काड् 'the stature of a man' Rebus: *meḍ khaḍā* 'iron stone' *kola* 'bandicoot Rebus: 'koles, iron smelters'; *kol* 'working in iron, alloys' (Tamil). kuṭṭakam, kuṭṭukam = cauldron (Ma.); *kuṭṭuva* = big copper pot for heating water (Kod.)(DEDR 1668). gudgā to blaze; guḍva flame (Man.d); gudva, gūdūvwa, guduwa id. (Kuwi)(DEDR 1715). kuṭṭhita = hot, sweltering; molten (of tamba, cp. uttatta)(Pali) uttatta (ut + tapta) = heated, of metals: molten, refined; shining, splendid, pure (Pali) Alterntive: sangatarāśū = stone cutter; sangatarāśi = stone-cutting (Telugu) రాజు [rāzu] rāḍzu. [Tel.] v. n. To take fire, flame, begin to burn.(Telugu) రాచ (adj.) Pertaining to a stone. (Telugu) sang 2 संग् m. a stone (Rām. 199, 143, 1412; YZ. 557).

kāḍ काड़ 'the stature of a man' Rebus: खडा [khaḍā] *m* A small stone, a pebble (Marathi) *meḍ* 'body' *meḍ* 'iron'.

 Ligatured hieroglyph: *baṭhu* 'large pot' Rebus: *baṭa* = a kind of iron (Gujarati) *bhaṭa* 'furnace' (Gujarati) *ḍab bhaṭa* 'ingot furnace'. Rebus: *ḍab, ḍhimba, ḍhompo* 'lump (ingot?)'.

Alternative: *meṛgo* = rimless vessels (Santali) Rebus: *meḍ* iron (Ho.) Alternative: కుండ [kuṇḍa] *kunḍa.* [Tel.] n. An earthern pot. A pot. కుండము [kuṇḍamu] *kunḍamu.* [Skt.] n. An earthen pot. A pit or pot for receiving and preserving consecrated fire. A fire pit నిప్పుల గుండము. *Ka.* kuṇḍa, koṇḍa, kuṇṭe pit, pool, pond.

kuṇḍ 'pot used for oblation with fire' Rebus: *kẽṛẽ kõṛẽ* an aboriginal tribe who work in brass and bell-metal (Santali) *teben:ko kuṭhi yet kana*, they are working (or building) the furnace to-day (H. koṭhī) (Santali.lex. Bodding)

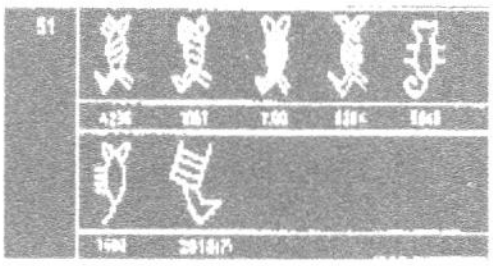

Hieroglyph Variants of 'Sign 51'. Seal impression.

This superscript ligaturing  elements to two hieroglyphs: 1. Bandicoot; and 2. Ficus leaf seems to signify meaning 'person' performing the function. Superscripted 'bandicoot' hieroglyph *kola* performs the functions of a *kole* 'smelter'. Superscripted 'ficus leaf' *loa* performs the functions with *lo* 'copper'.

Thus the pair of hieroglyphs on Ur seal 159845  read rebus: *ayo kola* 'alloy metal smelter'. This reading is together with reading of other hieroglyphs on the circular Ur seal impression: *goṭa* 'numerative particle' Rebus: *khoṭ* 'alloy'. Hieroglyph: *ḍhangra* 'bull'. Rebus: *ḍhangar* 'blacksmith'. Thus, the complete message conveyed by the symbolic forms in Meluhha hieroglyphs:

Blacksmith smelted ironstone alloy; *kuṭṭhita* 'molten' *meḍ khaḍā* 'iron stone'.

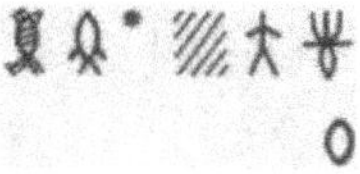

urseal159845 Ur [The last glyph on top line looks like an animal with a long tail – as seen from the back and may have been the model for the orthography of Sign 51 as noted in Mahadevan corpus]. Hieroglyph: *kola* [*kōla*] f. The bandicoot rat, *mus malibaricos* (Rajasthani) Rebus: *kolhe* 'koles, iron smelters'; *kol* 'working in iron, alloys' (Tamil).

**kōlhuvagāra* ' mill house '. P.*kolhār* m. 'oil facory '; Bi. *kolhuār* ' sugarcane mill and boiling house house '(CDIAL 3537). G. *kohlu* m. ' sugarcane press '. -- Deriv.: B. Or. *kalu* ' oil -- man (by caste) ', H. *kolū* m. (CDIAL 3536). Allographs: కోలె [kōle] *kōle.*

[Tel.] n. Stubble, a stamp of corn. వెన్నుకోసినకాడ, కోసె.

கோலாரிக்கம் kōlārikkam , *n.* perh. T. *kolārakamu.* Duel; **இருவர் இடும் சண்டை.** (R.)

kollāra, kollāri, kollāru, kol = kolike-āru 'a cart to which oxen etc. are yoked; kolārubaṇḍi id. (Telugu)

கோலாள் kōl-āḷ, *n.* < **கோல்**[1] +. Charioteer; **தேர்ப்பாகன்.** **அங்கவன்றன் கோலாளைக் கொன்று** (**பாரதவெண்.** 799).

Similar two-pronged ligaturing occurs on 'ficus leaf' hieroglyph. (Example taken from Segment 3 of Dholavira sign-board).

loha-

kāra (metalsmith). Glyph 'leaf, petal': A 'leaf' glyph has to be distinguished from a 'petals' glyph because the leaf orthography is clearly representative of the *ficus* genus which attains sacredness in later historical periods in the Indian linguistic area. Allograph: *kamaḍha* 'ficus religiosa' (Skt.) *kamaṛkom* 'ficus' (Santali) Rebus: *kampaṭṭam* coiner, mint (Tamil) *kammaṭa* = portable furnace for melting precious metals (Telugu) Glyph: *loa* = a species of fig tree, ficus glomerata, the fruit of ficus glomerata (Santali) Rebus: *lo* 'iron' (Assamese, Bengali); *loa* 'iron' (Gypsy) *lauha* = made of copper or iron (Gr.S'r.); metal, iron (Skt.) *loha-kāra* a metal worker, coppersmith, blacksmith Miln 331 (Pali) Glyph 'fig, ficus glomerata': మేడి [mēḍi] *mēḍi.* [Tel.] అత్తి, ఉదుంబరము. మేడిపండు the fruit of this tree. *Ka.* mēḍi glomerous fig tree, *Ficus racemosa*; opposite-leaved fig tree, *F. oppositifolia. Te.* mēḍi *F. glomerata. Kol.* (Kin.) mēṛi id. [*F. glomerata* Roxb. = *F. racemosa* Wall.](DEDR 5090). Rebus: *meḍ* 'iron' (Ho.)

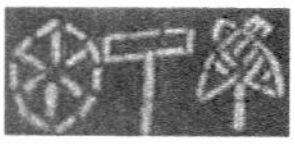

Segment 3: *āra eraka* 'brass, copper'; *kamaṛkom, kamaḍha* 'ficus' (Santali) Rebus: *kammaṭa* 'mint, coiner'. Alternative: *loa* 'ficus religiosa' + *kār* ligature Rebus: *lohār, lohāra* 'coppersmith, blacksmith' (Lahnda. Prākṛt).

Seal impression; Dept. of Antiquities, Bahrain.

 *kāḍ* काड़् 'the stature of a man' Rebus: *meḍ khaḍā* 'iron stone'. खांडा [khāṇḍā] *m* A jag, notch, or indentation (as upon the edge of a tool or weapon). Rebus: khāṇḍa 'tools, pots and pans, and metal-ware'. sangatarāśi = stone-cutting (Telugu) రాజు [rāzu] rāḍzu. [Tel.] v. n. To take fire, flame, begin to burn.(Telugu) రాచ (adj.) Pertaining to a stone. (Telugu) sang 2 संग् m. a stone (Rām. 199, 143, 1412; YZ. 557). *kāmṭhā* 'bow'Rebus: *kammaṭa* 'coiner' (Kannada).

Archaeological evidence attests to use of iron during the bronze age.[22]

Evidence from Vālmīki Rāmāyaṇa

Slokas 5.30.16 to 21 in the 29th sarga of Sundara Kandam, provide an episode of Hanuman introspecting on the language in which he should speak to Sita. This evidence refers to two dialects: Sanskrit andmānuṣam vākyam (lit. jāti bhāṣā). In this narrative mānuṣam vākyam (spoken dialect) is distinguished from Sanskrit of a Brahmin (or, grammatically correct and well-prounced Sanskrit used in yajña-s).

1. "antaramtvaha māsādya rākṣasīnam iha sthitah"

2. "śanairāśvāsaiṣyāmi santāpa bahulām imām"

(Staying here itself and getting hold of an opportunity even in the midst of the female-demons (when they are in attentive), I shall slowly console Sita who is very much in distress.)

3. "aham hi atitanuścaiva vānara śca viśeṣata"

4. "Vākam ca udāhariṣyāmi mānuṣīm iha samskṛtām"

(However, I am very small in stature, particularly as a monkey and can speak now Sanskrit, the human language too.)

5. "yadi Vākam pradāsyami dwijātiriva samskṛtām"

6. "rāvaṇam manyamānā mām sītā bhītā bhavi ṣyati"

7. vānarasya viśeṣena kathamsyādabibhāṣaṇam

(If I use Sanskrit language like a llsde, Sita will get frightened, thinking that Rāva ṇ a has come disguised as a monkey. Especially, how can a monkey speak it?)

8. "avaśyameva vaktavyam mānuṣam vākyam arthavat"

9. "mayā śāntvayitum śakyā"

10. "nānyathā iyam aninditā"

(Certainly, meaningful words of a human being are to be spoken by me. Otherwise, the virtuous Sita cannot be consoled.)

11. "sā iyam ālokya me rūpam jānakī bhāṣitam tathā | |
rakṣobhih trāsitaa pūrvam bhuūah trāsam gamiṣyati | "

(Looking at my figure and the language, Sita who was already frightened previously by the demons, will get frightened again.)[23]

Milakkhu refers to copper. Theragāthā in Pali refers to a banner dyed the colour of copper: *milakkhurajanam* (The Thera and

Theragāthā, PTS, Verse 965: *milakkhurajanam rattam garahantā sakam dhajam; tithiyānam dhajam keci dhāressanty avadātakam*; K.R. Norman tr., Theragāthā: Finding fault with their own banner which is dyed the colour of copper, some will wear the white banner of sectarians. In *Abhidhāna Cintāmaṇi* of Hemacandra, twelve synonyms are given for tāmram, 'copper' including the words: *mleccha, mlecchaśāvarabhedā, mlecchamukha*. The full list is: *tāmram mlecchamukham śulvam raktam dvaṣṭamudumbaram mlecchaśāvarabhedākhyam markatāsyam kanīyasam brahmavarddhanam variṣṭham sīsantu sīsapatrakam*.

A Pali text, *Uttarādhyayana Sūtra* 10.16 notes: *ladhdhaṇa vimānusattaṇṇamāriattam puṇrāvi dullaham bahave dasyū milakkhuyā*; trans. 'though one be born as a man, it is rare chance to be an *ārya*, for many are the *dasyu* and *milakkhu*'. Milakkhu and *dasyu* constitute the majority, they are the many. *Dasyu* are *milakkhu* (*mleccha* speakers). *Dasyu* are also *ārya Vācas* (Manu 10.45), that is, speakers of Sanskrit. Both *ārya Vācas* and *mleccha Vācas* are *dasyu* [cognate *dahyu, daŋ́ha, daha* (Khotanese)], 'people', in general. दाशः A fisherman; इयं च सज्जा नौश्चेति दाशाः प्राञ्ज- लयो$ब्रुवन् Rām.7.46.32; Ms.8.48,49;1.34. दासः 'a fisherman' (Apte. Sanskrit). Such people are referred to in Ṛgveda by Viśvāmitra as 'Bhāratam janam.' Mahābhārata alludes to 'thousands of mlecchas', a numerical superiority equaled by their valour and courage in battle which enhances the invincibility of Pāṇḍava (MBh. 7.69.30; 95.36). Excerpt from Encyclopaedia Iranica article on cognate *dahyu* country (often with reference to the people inhabiting it): DAHYU (OIr. *dahyu-*), attested in Avestan *dax́iiu-*, *daŋ́hu-* "country" (often with reference to the people inhabiting it; cf. *AirWb.*, cot. 706; Hoffmann, pp. 599-600 n. 14; idem and Narten, pp. 54-55) and in Old Persian *dahyu-* "country, province" (pl. "nations"; Gershevitch, p. 160). The term is likely to be connected with Old Indian *dásyu* "enemy" (of the Aryans), which acquired the meaning of "demon, enemy of the gods" (Mayrhofer, *Dictionary* II, pp. 28-29). Because of the

Indo-Iranian parallel, the word may be traced back to the root *das-*, from which a term denoting a large collectivity of men and women could have been derived. Such traces can be found in Iranian languages: for instance, in the ethnonym Dahae (q.v., i) "men" (cf. Av. ethnic name [fem. adj.] *dāhī*, from *dåŋ́ha-*; *AirWb.*, col. 744; Gk. Dáai, etc.), in Old Persian *dahā* "the Daha people" (Brandenstein and Mayrhofer, pp. 113-14), and in Khotanese *daha* "man, male" (Bailey, *Dictionary*, p. 155).
In Avestan the term did not have the same technical meaning as in Old Persian. Avestan *dax́iiu-*, *dańhu-* refers to the largest unit in the vertical social organization. See, for example, Avestan *xᵛaētu-* (in the Gathas) "next of kin group" and *nmāna-*"house," corresponding to Old Persian *taumā-* "family"; Avestan *vīs-* "village," corresponding to Avestan *vərəzə̄na-* "clan"; Avestan *zantu-* "district"; and Avestan*dax́iiu-*, *dańhu-* (Benveniste, 1932; idem, 1938, pp. 6, 13; Thieme, pp. 79ff.; Frye, p. 52; Boyce, *Zoroastrianism* I, p. 13; Schwartz, p. 649; Gnoli, pp. 15ff.). The connection *dax́iiu*, *dańhu-* and *arya-* "Aryans" is very common to indicate the Aryan lands and peoples, in some instances in the plural: *airiiå daŋ́hāuuō,airiianąm dax́iiunąm*, *airiiābiiō daŋ́hubiiō*.
In *Yašt* 13.125 and 13.127 five countries (*dax́iiu-*) are mentioned, though their identification is unknown or uncertain; in the same *Yašt* (13.143-44) the countries of other peoples are added to those of the Aryans: *tūiriia*, *sairima*, *sāinu*, *dāha*.

In Achaemenid inscriptions Old Persian *dahyu-* means "satrapy" (on the problems relative to the different lists of *dahyāva* [pl.], cf. Leuze; Junge; Walser, pp. 27ff.; Herzfeld, pp. 228-29; Herrenschmidt, pp. 53ff.; Calmeyer, 1982, pp. 105ff.; idem, 1983, pp. 141ff.) and "district" (e.g., Nisāya in Media; DB 1.58; Kent, *Old Persian*, p. 118). The technical connotation of Old Persian *dahyu* is certain and is confirmed—despite some doubts expressed by George Cameron but refuted by Ilya Gershevitch—by the loanword *da-a-yau-iš* in Elamite. On the basis of the hypothetical reconstruction of twelve "districts" and twenty-nine "satrapies," it has been suggested that the formal identification of the Old Persian numeral 41 with the ideogram *DH*, sometimes used for *dahyu* (Kent, *Old Persian*, pp. 18-19), can be explained by the fact that there were exactly forty-one *dahyāva* when the sign *DH*was created (Mancini).

From the meaning of Old Persian *dahyu* as "limited territory" come Middle Persian and Pahlavi *deh* "country, land, village," written with the ideogram *MTA* (*Frahang ī Pahlawīg* 2.3, p. 117; cf. Syr. *mātā*), and Manichean Middle Persian *dyh*(MacKenzie, p. 26). At times the Avestan use is reflected in Pahlavi *deh*, but already in Middle Persian the meaning "village" is well documented; it appears again in Persian *deh.*

The vernacular in ancient India was *Meluhha* also called *Mleccha*[24].

In another Northern dialect of India, it is *milakkha, milakkhu.* Close to it are *milech, malech* (Punjabi); *milis* (Sindhi). hh-kh-cch variant sound shifts are unexplained in Indian *sprachbund.* *mlēch* 'speak indistinctly ': Pk. *maleccha* -- , *milíccha* -- , *meccha* -- , *miccha* -- m. ' barbarian '; K. *mīˇch*, dat. *mīˇcas* m. ' non -- Hindu ' (loss of aspiration unexpl.); P. *milech*, *mal*° m. (f.*milechṇī*, *mal*°) ' Moslem, unclean outcaste, wretch '; WPah.bhad, *məle_ch* ' dirty '; B. *mech* ' a Tibeto -- Burman tribe ' ODBL 473; Si. *milidu*, *miliñdu* ' wild, savage ' (< MIA. **mlēcha* -- or with H. Smith JA 1950, 186 X pulindá --), *milis* (<MIA. *milíccha* --). -- Paš. *mečə* ' wretched, miserly ' rather < *mēcca -- 'defective '. -- With unexpl. -- *kkh* -- : Pa. *milakkha* -- , °*khu* -- ' non -- Aryan ', Si. *malak* ' savage ', *malaki* -- *dū* ' a Väddā woman '. -- X piśācá -- : Pa. *milāca* -- m. ' wild man of the woods, non -- Aryan '; Si. *maladu* ' wild, savage '. (CDIAL 10389). *mrēcchati ~ *mlḗcchati* ' speaks indistinctly ' ŚBr. [MIA. *mr* -- < *ml* -- ? See Add. -- √mlēch] K. *bričhun*, pp. *bryučhu* 'to weep and lament, cry as a child for something wanted or as motherless child'.(CDIAL 10384). Mleccha is a synonym of म्लिष्ट 'spoken indistinctly or barbarously' (Pāṇini 7-2) Patañjali outlines the characteristics of mleccha: *mlecchaḥ ha vai eṣah yat*

apaśabdaḥ 'mleccha deploys ungrammatical forms of words'; *mlecchitavai na apabhāṣitavai* 'mleccha has dialectical variants or unrefined sounds in words'; *mlecchāḥ mā bhūma iti adhyeyam vyākaraṇam* 'in order to avoid reaching down to level of mleccha speech one must learn rules of (Sanskrit) grammar'; *mlecchitam vispaṣṭena iti eva anyatra . tasmāt brāhmaṇena na* 'mleccha (is) with unintelligible/incorrect utterances unlike the perfection needed for expressing mantra-s'. In some respects *apaśabda* is vulgar speech (unpolished, unrefined), also a synonym of *apabhramśa* 'corruption of words', for e.g., घर is an अपभ्रंश or corruption of गृह; (hence) considered an incorrect word whether formed against the rules of grammar or used in a sense not strictly Sanskrit. Thus, mleccha has all the attributes of a vernacular, of *parole* while Sanskrit gains the status of a 'literary, grammatically perfect, using semantically correct forms'. Thus, *apaśabda* is considered a corrupt language, a form of Prākṛita dialect used by, say, cowherds etc. in kāvyas. The word *apabhramśa* also signifies, in Śāstras,a language other than Sanskrit such as *ābhīra.*
An ancient text record the nature of speech of at least some of the speakers in the following terms: *te 'surā āttavacaso he lavo he lava iti vadantah parābabhūvuh tatraināmapi Vākamūduh upajijñāsyā sa mlecchastasmānna brāhmaṇo mlecchedasuryā haiṣā vāg* "The Asuras, deprived of (correct) speech, saying *he lavo, he lavah*, were defeated. This is the unintelligible speech which they uttered at that time. Who speaks thus is a mleccha. Therefore a brāhmaṇa should not speak like a mleccha, for that is the speech of the Asuras." (*śatapatha brāhmaṇa* 3.2.1.23-24). Mleccha-speakers failed to articulate *arava(h)* correctly. *śatapatha brāhmaṇa* 3.2.1.18-24 speaks of *asuryā vāk*. After the Asura were deprived of speech (vāk) which was offered to fire for purification while reciting *anuṣṭubh* (*chandas* 'speech').

The *he 'lavo he'lavah* is a refrain of boatman's song. Cognate glosses in Indian sprachbund: *elava* 'a wave' (Kolāmī); *helva* id., flood (Gondī) (DEDR 830). *Ka. elā, ele, elē, elo, elō* excl. of a familiar and friendly character, used in calling or directly addressing any person; elage ho! used in calling to females (Kannada). *elā* interj. of surprise (Tulu) *Kui ēla* companionship (Kui)(DEDR 831). *Te. elũgu* voice; elĩgincu, elũgincu, elũgiccu to make a noise, cry, roar, sound, resound. Pa. *ilunẹ* voice (Parji) *lēnẹ* a tune (Gadba)(DEDR 835). ఏల *ēla*, ఏలా *ēlā* [Tel.] n. A hurrah, or hoop. A carol or catch used by rowers of boats శృంగారపు పాట. ఏల *ēla*. [Tel.] n. Name of a stream in the Godavery District ఏలేరు. ఏలపదము [ēlapadamu] or **ఏలపాట** *ēla-padamu*. [Tel.] n. A carol or ballad. (Telugu)

Evidence from *Śatapatha Brāhmaṇa* for *mleccha Vācas*

An extraordinary narrative account from *Śatapatha Brāhmaṇa* is cited in full to provide the context of the yajña in which Vāk (speech personified as woman) is referred to the importance of grammatical speech in yajña performance and this grammatical, intelligible speech is distinguished from mlecccha, unintelligible speech. The example of the usage of phrase 'he 'lavo is explained by Sayana as a pronunciation variant of: 'he 'rayo. i.e. 'ho, the spiteful (enemies)!' This grammatically correct phrase, the Asuras were unable to pronounce correctly, notes Sayana. The ŚB text and translation are cited in full because of the early evidence provided of the mleccha speech (exemplifying what is referred to Indian language studies as 'ralayo rabhedhah'; the transformed use of 'la' where the syllable 'ra' was intended. This is the clearest evidence of a proto-Indian language which had dialectical variants in the usage by asuras and devas (i.e. those who do not perform yagna and those who perform yagna using vaak, speech.) This is comparable to mleccha Vācas and ārya Vācas differentiation by Manu. The text of ŚB 3.2.1.22-28 and translation are as follows:

yoṣā vā iyaṃ vāgyadenaṃ na yuvitehaiva mā tiṣṭhantamabhyehīti brūhi tām tu na āgatām pratiprabrūtāditi sā hainaṃ tadeva tiṣṭhantamabhyeyāya tasmādu strī pumāṃsaṃ saṃskṛte tiṣṭhantamabhyaiti tāṃ haibhya āgatām pratiproVākeyaṃ vā āgāditi tāṃ devāḥ |
asurebhyo 'ntarāyaṃstāṃ svīkṛtyāgnāveva parigṛhya sarvahutamajuhavurāhutirhi devānāṃ sa yāmevāmūmanuṣṭubhājuhavustadevaināṃ taddevāḥ svyakurvata te 'surā āttavacaso he 'lavo he 'lava iti vadantaḥ parābabhūvuḥ atraitāmapi Vākamūduḥ |
upajijñāsyāṃ sa mlecastasmānna brāhmaṇo mlecedasuryā haiṣā vā natevaiṣa dviṣatāṃ sapatnānāmādatte Vākaṃ te 'syāttavacasaḥ parābhavanti ya evametadveda o 'yaṃ yajño Vākamabhidadhyau |
mithunyenayā syāmiti tāṃ saṃbabhūva indro ha vā īkṣāṃ cakre |

mahadvā ito 'bhvaṃ janiṣyate yajñasya ca mithunādVākaśca yanmā tannābhibhavediti sa indra eva garbho bhūtvaitanmithunam praviveśa sa ha saṃvatsare jāyamāna īkṣāṃ cakre |
mahāvīryā vā iyaṃ yoniryā māmadīdharata yadvai meto mahadevābhvaṃ nānuprajāyeta yanmā tannābhibhavediti tām pratiparāmṛśyaveṣṭyācinat |
tāṃ yajñasya śīrṣanpratyadadhādyajño hi kṛṣṇaḥ sa yaḥ sa yajñastatkṛṣṇājinaṃ yo sā yoniḥ sā kṛṣṇaviṣāṇātha yadenāmindra āveṣṭyācinattasmādāveṣṭiteva sa yathaivāta indro 'jāyata garbhobhūtvaitasmānmithunādevamevaiṣo 'to jāyate garbho bhūtvaitasmānmithunāt tāṃ vā uttānāmiva badhnāti |

Translation: 22.The gods reflected, 'That Vaak being a woman, we must take care lest she should allure him. – Say to her, "Come hither to make me where I stand!" and report to us her having come.' She then went up to where he was standing. Hence a woman goes to a man who stays in a well-trimmed (house). He reported to them her having come, saying, 'She has indeed come.' 23. The gods then cut her off from the Asuras; and having gained possession of her and enveloped her completely in fire, they offered her up as a holocaust, it being an offering of the gods. (78) And in that they offered her with an anushtubh verse, thereby they made her their own; and the Asuras being deprived of speech, were undone, crying, 'He 'lavah! He 'lavah!' (79) 24. Such was the unintelligible speech which they then uttered, -- and he (who speaks thus) is a Mlekkha (barbarian). Hence let no Brahman speak barbarous language, since such is the speech of the Asuras. Thus alone he deprives his spiteful enemies of speech; and whosoever knows this, his enemies, being deprived of speech, are undone. 25. That Yajna (sacrifice) lusted after Vaak (speech [80]), thinking, 'May I pair with her!' He united with her. 26. Indra then thought within himself, 'Surely a great monster will spring from this union of Yagna and Vaak: [I must take care] lest it should get the better of me.' Indra himself then became an embryo and entered into that union. 27. Now when he was born after a year's time, he thought within himself, 'Verily of great vigour is this womb which has contained me: [I must take care] that no great monster shall be born from it after me, lest it should get the better of me!' 28. Having seized and pressed it tightly, he tore it off and put it on the head of Yagna (sacrifice [81]); for the black (antelope) is the sacrifice: the black deer skin is the same as that sacrifice, and the black deer's horn is the same as that womb. And because it was by pressing it tightly together that Indra tore out (the womb), therefore it (the horn) is bound tightly (to the end of the garment); and as Indra, having become an embryo, sprang from that union, so is he (the sacrifice), after becoming an embryo, born from that union (of the skin and the horn). (ŚB 3.2.1.23-25). (fn 78) According to Sayana, 'he 'lavo' stands for 'he 'rayo' (i.e. ho, the spiteful (enemies)!' which the Asuras were unable to pronounce correctly. The Kaanva text, however, reads te hātavāko 'su hailo haila ity etām ha Vākam vadantah parābabhūvuh (? i.e. he p. 32 ilaa, 'ho, speech'.) A third version of this passage seems to be referred to in the Mahā bhāṣya (Kielh.), p.2. (p.38). (fn 79) Compare the corresponding legend about Yagna and Dakṣiṇā (priests' fee), (Taitt. S. VI.1.3.6. (p.38) (fn 79) 'Yagnasya sīrṣan'; one would expect 'kṛṣṇa(sāra)sya sīrṣan.' The Taitt.S. reads '*tām mṛgeṣu ny adadhāt.*' (p.38) (fn81) In the Kanva text 'atah (therewith)' refers to the head of the sacrifice, -- *sa yak khirasta upasprisaty ato vā enām etad agre pravisan pravisaty ato vā agre gāyamāno gāyate tasmāk khirasta upasprisati.*[25]

A *brāhmaṇa* for the first time refers to Mleccha NOT in terms of referring to a group of people but to their linguistic distinctiveness. The allusion is to asura who had lost speech or Vāk, since they utter incomprehensible words similar to those deployed by Mleccha-speakers. It is noted that there is a linguistic variation in the utterance by Asura of: *he 'lavo he'lavah*. One linguistic explanation is that these are mispronunciation of words, rather than some examples of hostile speech, noting that the correct pronunciation of the intended meaning should be: *he 'ari h'ari* (O! spiteful enemies), interchanging *l* with *r* sound which is a common feature in Prākṛt dialects. Thus, the Mleccha speakers are simply speakers of Indo-Aryan but with tendency to deploy dialectical phonetic variations. In *Aṣṭādhyāyi* (VII.2.18), *mleccha* gets semantically associated with indistinct speech. Patañjali (*Mahābhāṣya* I.14) uses the same *Śathapathabrāhmaṇa* example to cite indistinct speech forms of Mleccha dialects, calling them apaśabda (corrupt pronunciation). *Brāhmaṇa* learning grammar and language were asked to be cautious about corrupt pronunciations so as not to lead to the type of downfall which has befallen asura. It should be noted that the semantics of asura in early texts refer to their being possessed of wonderful power. Even Sarasvati is referred to *āsurī* sarasvatī linked to the root *asu* , lit. 'spiritual, divine'.

Jayaswal notes that mleccha was the Samskṛtam representation of Hebrew melekh meaning, 'king' and that the utterance: he lavah! he lavah! in the *śatapatha brāhmaṇa* was a specimen of mleccha speech; that this spoken phrase is cognate with Hebrew ēloāh (plural ēlōhim) meaning, 'God'. Paton discusses the term *milcom* which was the name of an Ammonite god, notes that Phoenician equivalent *milk* means 'king' and that *melek* as the divine name is found in all branches of the Semitic language. Rejecting all theories about *melek*, Paton notes that *melakim* of the Semitic groups probably bore a family resemblance to each other as the Baalim did. Is the term *mleccha* derived from Akkadian *malik* (Hebrew *molech*; Phoenician *milk*) given the resemblance of the Pali terms *milakkhu* and *milakka* ? "The most conspicuous of the Phoenician Milkim was Melkart = Milk-kart, 'king of the city', the chief god of Tyre."[26]

Ur seal (showing a person holding an antelope by its neck).Two

figures carry between them a vase, and one presents a goat-like animal (not an antelope) which he holds by the neck. Human figures wear early Sumerian garments of fleece. *melkhā* throat, neck (Kur.); melque throat (Malt.)(DEDR: 5080). This glyph of holding by the throat of the animal is a phonetic determinant of the animal itself: *mēlh* goat (Brahui); *mṟēka* (Te.); meque to bleat (Malt.); mēke she-goat (Ka.); goat (Nk.) mē~ka, mēka goat (Te.); me.ke (Kol.); mēge goat (Ga.); mekā, mēka (Go.); mēxnā to call, hail (Kur.)(DEDR: 5087). *meḍa* = neck (Telugu) meṭe = the throat (Ka.); meṉṉa, meṉṉi (Ta.); menne (Ma.); miḍaṛu = the neck, the throat (Ta.Ma.); meṭregaṭṭu = a swelling of the glands of the throat (Kannada) [The dotted circle connoting the eye: khan:gar 'full of holes'; rebus: kan:gar 'furnace' (Kashmiri)] Rebus: *milakkhu* 'copper' Rebus: *meḍ* 'iron'. Rebus: *melukkha* 'Meluhha'.

"Mleccha were those who could not pronounce Samskṛta (*vāk*) appropriately as prescribed in Svaravidhāna of the grammatical treatises. Mostly the mleccha were the Kirata, the Savara, the Pulinda (*Amarakośa*, Sundaravarga)." Akkadian *maliku(m)* means god, king, lord. This anecdote clearly notes mleccha as a grammatical entity, a language.

In summary, Meluhha is cognate of Sanskrit mleccha (Sememe variants: Sindhi *milis*, Panjabi *malech*, Pali *milakkhu.*). Sargon of Akkad (c. 2200 BCE) had 'dismantled the cities, as far as the shore of the sea. At the wharf of Agade, he docked ships from Meluhha, ships from Magan.'

Bharata's *Nāṭyaśāstra* refers to *mleccha* as language, bhāṣā: XVIII. 80 : RULES ON THE USE OF LANGUAGES 827 The Common Language

Nāṭyaś'āstra XVII.29-30):*dvividhā jātibhāṣā ca prayoge samudāhṛtā mlecchaśabdopacārā ca bhāratam varṣam āśritā* 'The jātibhāṣā (common language), prescribed for use (on the stage) has various forms. It contains words of *mleccha* origin and is spoken in *Bhāratavarṣa* only...

28. The Common Language prescribed for use [on the stage] has various forms 1 . It contains [many] words of Barbarian {mleccha) origin and is spoken in Bharata-varsa [only] Note: 28 (C.26b-27a; B.XVII.29b-30a). 'Read *vividha-jāti bhāṣā* ; vividha (ca, da in B.) for *dvividhā*. 'The common speech or the speech of the commoners is distinguished here from that of the priests and the nobility by describing it as containing words of Barbarian (mleccha) origin. These words seem to have been none other than vocables of the

Dravidian and Austric languages. They entered Indo-Aryan pretty early in its history.'[27]

Beyond the Mahābhārata incident in which Vidura is said to have alerted Yudhiṣṭira in Mleccha bhāṣā, evidence is provided on mleccha (cognate meluhha) language from ancient texts.

MBh describes mleccha as sāgara dvīpavāsinah 'island dwellers' *Amarakośa* defines mleccha as a reference to forest people while categories of people such as niṣāda (of Vindhya mountains), ābhīra (reed-workers), kirāta, śabara, pulinda, āndhra, puṇḍra, drāviḍa, lāṭa, oḍra, darada, kāmboja, khasa, kalinda, uṣinara, mahiska, mekala, barbara, pahlava, śaka, yavana, sinhala also get designated as mleccha, milakkha or milakkhu in early texts. The collective phrase used is: nānāmlecchagaṇa (MBh I.165.35-37). The narratives accout for mlecchas with haihaya and tālanangha vanquished the regime of Bāhu of Ikṣvāku dynasty. Bauddham piṭaka texts place mleccha in paccantima (pratyanta) janapada (i.e. border territories). Samantapāsādikā on VinP I:255 refers to '*milakkhakam nāma yo koci anāriyako andhadamḷādi.*'

Vidura speaks to Yudhishthira in mleccha language (*mleccha Vākā,* MBh. 1.135.6b). Khanaka, a dear friend of Vidura is sent to help the Pāṇḍava in confinement to report on how Purocana would put fire in the door of Pāṇḍava's house .

" kṛṣṇa *pakṣe caturdasyām rātrāv asya purocanah, bhavanasya tava dvāri pradàsyati hutāsanam, mātrā saha pradagdhavyàh pāṇḍavāh puruṣarṣabhā, iti vyavasitam pātha dhārtarāṣṭrāsya me śrutam, kiñcic ca vidurenokto mleccha-Vākāsi pāṇḍav, tyayā ca tat tathety uktam etad visvāsa kāraṇam*: on the fourteenth evening of the dark fortnight, Purocana will put fire in the door of your house. 'The Pandavas are leaders of the people, and they are to be burned to death with their mother.' This, Pārtha (Yudhiṣṭira), is the determined plan of Dhṛtarāṣṭra's son, as I have heard it. When you were leaving the city, Vidura spoke a few words to you in the dialect of the mlecchas, and you replied to him, 'So be it'. I say this to gain your trust. (*MBh.* 1.135.4-6). This passage shows that there were two categories of Aryans distinguished by language and ethnicity, Yudhiṣṭira and Vidura. Both are aryas, who could speak mlecchas' language; Dhṛtarāṣṭra and his people are NOT aryas only because of their behavior.

Evidence related to proto-Indian or proto-Indic or Indus language

A proto-Indic language is attested in ancient Indian texts. For example, Manusmṛti refers to two languages, both of dasyu (daha): ārya Vācas, mleccha Vācas. This distinction between *lingua franca* and literary version of the language, is elaborated by Patañjali as a reference to 1) grammatically correct literary language and 2) ungrammatical, colloquial speech (*deśī*). Ancient text of Panini also refers to two languages in *śikṣā*: Sanskrit and Prākṛt. Prof Avinash Sathayeprovides a textual reference on the earliest occurrence of the word, 'Sanskrit' :

triṣaṣṭiścatuh ṣaṣṭirvā varṇāh ṣambhumate matāh |
prākṛite samskṛte cāpi svayam proktā svayambhuvā | | *(pāṇini's śikṣā)*

Trans. There are considered to be 63 or 64 varṇā-s in the school (mata) of *śambhu*. In Prākṛt and Sanskrit by swayambhu (manu, Brahma), himself, these varṇā-s were stated.

This demonstrates that pāṇini knew both samskṛta and prākṛita as established languages. (Personal communication, 27 June 2010 with Prof. Shrinivas Tilak.)

Chapter 17 of Bharatamuni's *Nāṭyaśāstra* is a beautiful discourse about Sanskrit and Prākṛt and the usage of *lingua franca* by actors/narrators in dramatic performances. Besides, Raja Shekhara, Kalidasa, Shudraka have also used the word Sanskrit for the literary language. (Personal communication from Prof. TP Verma, 7 May 2010). *Nāṭyaśāstra* XVII.29-30: *dvividhā jātibhāṣāca prayoge samudāhṛtā mlecchaśabdopacārā ca bhāratam varṣam aśritā* 'The jātibhāṣā (common language), prescribed for use (on the stage) has various forms. It contains words of mleccha origin and is spoken in Bhāratavarṣa only…'

Manu (10.45) underscores the linguistic area: *mleccha Vācas* distinguished from ārya *Vācas* (*lingua franca* or deśi distinguished from literary Sanskrit):

mukhabāhurūpajjānām yā loke jātayo bahih
mlecchaVākaś cāryaVācas te sarve dasyuvah smṛtāh

"All those people of the world which are excluded from the (community of) those born from the mouth, the arms, the thighs and the feet (of Brahman) are called Dasyu, whether they speak the language of the mleccha or that of the ārya." (Buhler). Alt. Mleccha dialect speakers and ārya dialect speakers are all remembered as dasyu. Thus, it is clear that there were two dialects in the linguistic area: *mleccha Vācas* and *ārya Vācas*. Dasyu is a general reference to people. Dasyu is cognate with dasa, which in Khotanese language means 'man'. It is also cognate with *daha*, a word which occurs in Persepolis inscription of Xerxes...[28]
"While Prof. Thomson maintained that a Munda influence has probably been at play in fixing the principle regulating the inflexion of nouns in Indo-Aryan vernaculars, such influence appeared to be unimportant to Prof. Sten Konow… Prof. Przyluski in his papers, translated here, have tried to explain a certain number of words of the Sanskrit vocabulary as fairly ancient loans from the Austro-Asiatic family of languages. He has in this opened up a new line of enquiry. Prof. Jules Bloch in his article on Sanskrit and Dravidian, also translated in this volume, has the position of those who stand exclusively for Dravidian influence and has proved that the question of the Munda substratum in Indo-Aryan cannot be overlooked…In 1923, Prof. Levi, in a fundamental article on *Pre-Aryen et Pre-Dravidian dans Vinde* tried to show that some geographical names of ancient India like Kosala-Tosala, Anga-Vanga, Kalinga-Trilinga, Utkala-Mekala and Pulinda-Kulinda, ethnic names which go by pairs, can be explained by the morphological system of the Austro-Asiatic languages. Names like Accha-Vaccha, Takkola-Kakkola belong to the same category. He concluded his long study with the following

observation, " We must know whether the legends, the religion and the philosophical thought of India do not owe anything to this past. India has been too exclusively examined from the Indo-European standpoint. It ought to be remembered that India is a great maritime country... the movement which carried the Indian colonization towards the Far East... was far from inaugurating a new route...Adventurers, traffickers and missionaries profited by the technical progress of navigation and followed under better conditions of comfort and efficiency, the way traced from time immemorial, by the mariners of another race, whom Aryan or Aryanised India despised as savages." In 1926, Przyluski tried to explain the name of an ancient people of the Punjab, the Udumbara, in a similar way and affiliate it to the Austro-Asiatic group. (cf. *Journal Asiatique*, 1926, 1, pp. 1-25, Un ancien peuple du Pendjab — les Udumbaras: only a portion of this article containing linguistic discussions has been translated in the Appendix of this book.) In another article, the same scholar discussed some names of Indian towns in the geography of Ptolemy and tried to explain them by Austro-Asiatic forms...Dr. J. H. Hutton, in an interesting lecture on the Stone Age Cult of Assam delivered in the Indian Museum at Calcutta in 1928, while dealing with some prehistoric monoliths of Dimapur, near Manipur, says that " the method of erection of these monoliths is very important, as it throws some light on the erection of prehistoric monoliths in other parts of the world. Assam and Madagascar are the only remaining parts of the world where the practice of erecting rough stones still continues....The origin of this stone cult is uncertain, but it appears that it is to be mainly imputed to the Mon-Khmer intrusion from the east In his opinion the erection of these monoliths takes the form of the lingam and yoni. He thinks that the Tantrik form of worship, so prevalent in Assam, is probably due to " the incorporation into Hinduism of a fertility cult which preceded it as .the religion of the country. The dolmens possibly suggest distribution from South India, but if so, the probable course was across the Bay of Bengal and then back again westward from further Asia. Possibly the origin was from Indonesia whence apparently the use of supari (areca nut) spread to India as well as the Pacific." (From the Introduction by PC Bagchi and SK Chatterjee, 1 May 1929).

Kuiper notes: " ...a very considerable amount (say some 40%) of the New Indo-Aryan vocabulary is borrowed from Munda, either via Sanskrit (and Prākṛt), or via Prākṛt alone, or directly from Munda; wide-branched and seemingly native, word-families of South Dravidian are of Proto-Munda origin; in Vedic and later Sanskrit, the words adopted have often been Aryanized, resp. Sanskritized. "In view of the intensive interrelations between Dravidian, Munda and Aryan dating from pre-Vedic times even individual etymological questions will often have to be approached from a Pan-Indic point of view if their study is to be fruitful. It is hoped that this work may be helpful to arrive at this all-embracing view of the Indian languages, which is the final goal of these studies."[29]

Emeneau notes: "In fact, promising as it has seemed to assume Dravidian membership for the Harappa language, it is not the only possibility. Professor W. Norman Brown has pointed out (The United States and India and Pakistan, 131-132, Cambridge, Harvard University Press, 1953) that Northwest India, i.e. the Indus Valley and adjoining parts of India, has during most of its history had Near Eastern elements in its political and cultural make-up at least as prominently as it had true Indian elements of the Gangetic and Southern types. [M.B.Emeneau, India as a Linguistic Area [Lang. 32, 1956, 3-16; LICS, 196, 642-51; repr. In Collected papers: Dravidian Linguistics Ethnology and Folktales, Annamalai Nagar, Annamalai University, 1967, pp. 171-186.] The passage is so important that it is quoted in full: 'More ominous yet was another consideration. Partition now would reproduce an ancient, recurring, and sinister incompatibility between Northwest and the rest of the subcontinent, which, but for a few brief periods of uneasy cohabitation, had kept them politically apart or hostile and had rendered the subcontinent defensively weak. When an intrusive people came through the passes and established itself there, it was at first spiritually closer to the relatives it had left behind than to any group already in India. Not until it had been separated from those relatives for a fairly long period and had succeeded in pushing eastward would I loosen the external ties. In period after period this seems to have been true. In the third millennium B.C. the Harappa culture in the Indus Valley was partly similar to contemporary western Asian civilizations and partly to later historic Indian culture of the Ganges Valley. In the latter part of the next millennium the earliest Aryans, living in the Punjab and composing the hymns of the Rig Veda, were apparently more like their linguistic and religious kinsmen, the Iranians, than like their eastern Indian contemporaries. In the middle of the next millennium the Persian Achaemenians for two centuries held the Northwest as satrapies. After Alexander had invaded India (327/6-325 B.C.) and Hellenism had arise, the Northwest too was Hellenized, and once more was partly Indian and partly western. And after Islam entered India, the Northwest again was associated with Persia, Bokhara, Central Asia, rather than with India, and considered itself Islamic first and Indian second. The periods during which the Punjab has been culturally assimilated to the rest of northern India are ew if any at all. Periods of political assimilation are almost as few; perhaps a part of the fourth and third centuries B.C. under the Mauryas; possibly a brief period under the Indo-Greek king menander in the second century B.C.; another brief period under the Muslim kingdom of Delhi in the last quarter of the twelfth century A.D.; a long one under the great Mughals in the sixteenth and seventeenth centuries A.D.; a century under the British, 1849-1947.'

"Though this refers to cultural and political factors, it is a warning that we must not leap to linguistic conclusions hastily. The early, but probably centuries-long condition in which Sanskrit, a close ally of languages of Iran, was restricted to the northwest (though it was not the only language there) and the rest of India was not Sanskritic in speech, may well have been mirrored earlier by a period when some other language invader from the Near East-a relative of Sumerian or of Elamitic or what not-was spoken and written in the Indus Valley-perhaps that of invaders and conquerors-while the indigenous population spoke another language-perhaps one of the Dravidian stock, or perhaps one of the Munda stock, which is now represented only by a handful of languages in the backwoods of Central India.

"On leaving this highly speculative question, we can move on to an examination of the Sanskrit records, and we find in them linguistic evidence of contacts between the Sanskrit-speaking invaders and the other linguistic groups within India…the early days of Indo-European scholarship were without benefit of the spectacular archaeological discoveries that were later to be made in the Mediterranean area, Mesopotamia and the Indus Valley… This assumption (that IE languages were urbanized bearers of a high civilization) led in the long run to another block-the methodological tendency of the end of the nineteenth and the beginning of the twentieth century to attempt to find Indo-European etymologies for the greatest possible portion of the vocabularies of the Indo-European languages, even though the object could only be achieved by flights of phonological and semantic fancy… very few scholars attempted to identify borrowings from Dravidian into Sanskrit…The Sanskrit etymological dictionary of Uhlenbrck (1898-1899) and the Indo-European etymological dictionary of Walde and Pokorny (1930-1932) completely ignore the work of Gundert (1869), Kittel (1872, 1894), and Caldwell (1856,1875)… It is clear that not all of Burrow's suggested borrowings will stand the test even of his own principles…'India' and 'Indian' will be used in what follows for the subcontinent, ignoring the political division into the Republic of India and Pakistan, and, when necessary, including Ceylong also… the northern boundary of Dravidian is and has been for a long time retreating south before the expansion of Indo-Aryan… We know in fact from the study of the non-Indo-European element in the Sanskrit lexicon that at the time of the earliest Sanskrit records, the R.gveda, when Sanskrit speakers were localized no further east than the Panjab, there were already a few Dravidian words current in Sanskrit. This involves a localization of Dravidian speech in this area no lather than three millennia ago.

It also of course means much bilingualism and gradual abandonment of Dravidian speech in favor of IndoAryan over a long period and a great area-a process for which we have only the most llsd of evidence in detail. Similar relationships must have existed between Indo-Aryan and Munda and between Dravidian and Munda, but it is still almost impossible to be sure of either of these in detail... The Dravidian languages all have many Indo-Aryan items, borrowed at all periods from Sanskrit, Middle Indo-Aryan and Modern Indo-Aryan. The Munda languages likewise have much Indo-Aryan material, chiefly, so far as we know now, borrowed rom Modern Indo-Aryan, thogh this of course llsdes items that are Sanskrit in form, since Modern Indo-Aryan borrows from Sanskrit very considerably. That Indo-Aryan has borrowed from Dravidian has also become clear. T. Burrow, The Sanskrit Language, 379-88 (1955), gives a sampling and a statement of the chronology involved. It is noteworthy that this influence was spent by the end of the pre-Christian era, a precious indication for the linguistic history of North India: Dravidian speech must have practically ceased to exist in the Ganges valley by this period... Most of the languages of India, of no matter which major family, have a set of retroflex, cerebral, or domal consonants in contrast with dentals. The retroflexes include stops and nasal certainly, also in some languages sibilants, lateral, tremulant, and even others. Indo-Aryan, Dravidian, Munda and even the far northern Burushaski, form a practically solid bloc characterized by this phonological feature... Even our earliest Sanskrit records already show phonemes of this class, which are, on the whole, unknown elsewhere in the Indo-European field, and which are certainly not Proto-Indo-European. In Sanskrit many of the occurrences of retroflexes are conditioned; others are explained historically as reflexes of certain Indo-European consonants and consonant clusters. But, in fact, in Dravidian it is a matter of the utmost certainty that retroflexes in contrast with dentals are Proto-Dravidian in origin, not the result of conditioning circumstances ... it is clear already that echo-words are a pan-Indic trait and that Indo-Aryan probably received it from non-Indo-Aryan (for it is not Indo-European)... The use of classifiers can be added to those other linguistic traits previously discussed, which establish India as one linguistic area ('an area which includes languages belonging to more than one family but showing traits in common which are found not to belong to the other members of (at least) one of the families') for historical study. The evidence is at least as clear-cut as in any part of the world... Some of the features presented here are, it seems to me, as 'profound' as we could wish to find... Certainly the end result of the borrowings is that the languages of the two families, Indo-Aryan and Dravidian, seem in many respects more akin to one another than Indo-Aryan does to the other Indo-European languages. (We must not, however, neglect Bloch's final remark and his reasons therefor: *'Ainsi donc, si profondes qu'aient ete les influences locales, Ils n'ont pas conduit l'aryen de l;inde... a se differencier fortement des autres langues indo-europeennes.'*)"[30]

The profundity of these observations by Emeneau and Bloch will be tested through clusters of lexemes of an *Indian Lexicon*, which relate to the archaeological finds of the civilization.

Tamil and all other Dravidian languages have been influenced by Sanskrit language and literature. Swaminatha Iyer [Swaminatha Iyer, 1975, Dravidian Theories, Madras, Madras Law Journal Office] posits a genetic relationship between Tamil and Sanskrit. He cites GU Pope to aver that several Indo-European languages are linguistically farther away from Sanskrit than Dravidian. He cites examples of Tamil and Sanskrit forms of some glosses: hair: mayir, śmaśru; mouth: vāya, vā c; ear: śevi, śrava; hear: kēḷkeṇ (Tulu), karṇa; walk: śel, car; mother: *āyi, yāy* (Paiśāci). Evaluating this work, Edwin Bryant and Laurie Patton note: "It is still more simple and sound to assume that the words which need a date of contact of the fourth millennium BCE on linguistic grounds as loan words in Dravidian might be words originally inherited in Dravidian from the Proto-speech which was the common ancestor of both Dravidian and Indo-Aryan...It will be simpler to explain the situation if both Indo-Aryan and Dravidian are traced to a common language family. In vocables they show significant agreement. In phonology and morphology the linguistic structures agree significantly. It requires a thorough comparative study of the two language families to conduct a fuller study. " Bryant, Edwin and Laurie L. Patton, 2005, The Indo-Aryan controversy: evidence and inference in Indian history, Routledge, p.197.

The influence of Vedic culture is profoundly evidenced in early sangam texts.31

Proto-Munda continuity and Language X

Hence, a Language X is postulated; Language 'X' to explain a large number of agriculture-related words with no IE cognates.32

Since there is cultural continuity in India from the days of Sarasvati civilization, it is possible to reconstruct Language X by identifying isoglosses in the linguistic area. (About 80% of the ca. 2600 archaeological sites of the so-called Indus Valley civilization are on the banks of the Vedic river Sarasvati, hence justifying the rechristening as Sarasvati civilization). Resemblances between two or more languages (whether typological or in vocabulary) can be due to genetic relation (descent from a common ancestor language), or due to borrowing at some time in the past between languages that were not necessarily genetically related. When little or no direct documentation of ancestor languages is available, determining whether a similarity is genetic or areal can be difficult. Meluhha cipher is a superset which subsumes *Indus script cipher.*[33] Manu 10.43-45 considered Coda, Dravida, Persian etc. as former kshatriya who sank to the level of *śūdra*, whether they speak the language of the *mleccha* or the language of ārya. Kane *History of Dharmaśāstra* Vol. II, p. 383 gives the impression that these groups were bilingual, speaking both 'mleccha' language and 'ārya' language. In *Mahabharata*, Pahlava, śabara, śaka, Yavana, Pundra, Kirāṭa, Dramiḷa, Simbhala, Barbara, Darada and Mleccha are collectively summed up as mleccha (1.165.35-37).

McAlpin[34] proposes that 20% of Dravidian and Elamite vocabulary are cognates and 12% are probable cognates. Elamite civilization was centered in Khuzestān province (Old Persian *Hūjiya* "Elam," in Middle Persian *Huz* "Susiana", modern Persian *Xuz*, compounded with *-stån* "place".) and Ilam in prehistoric times. Kushasthali is the old name for Dwaraka. Devibhagavata Saptamaskanda and Shrimadbhagavata Dashamaskanda locate this west of Gujarat.

Vocabulary of Brahui is substantially of non-Dravidian origin and has cognates in Balochi and Sindhi languages, derived from Iranian and Indo-Aryan languages. It is likely that the present-day languages of India evidence a *dialect continuum* from the days of Sarasvati civilization.

Fuller et al[35] note that some crops such as sorghum (sorhum bicolor), pearl millet (pennisetum glaucum) and finger millet (eleusine coracana) originated in Africa and arrived in India at some point in prehistory. One conjecture is that this happened perhaps ca. 2600-2000 BCE brought by Harappan seafarers. Movement of zebu cattle from India to Yemen and East Africa might also have occurred in the Harappan era. A corollary pointer is the presence of cloves from Malacca in Terqa (Tell Asmar).

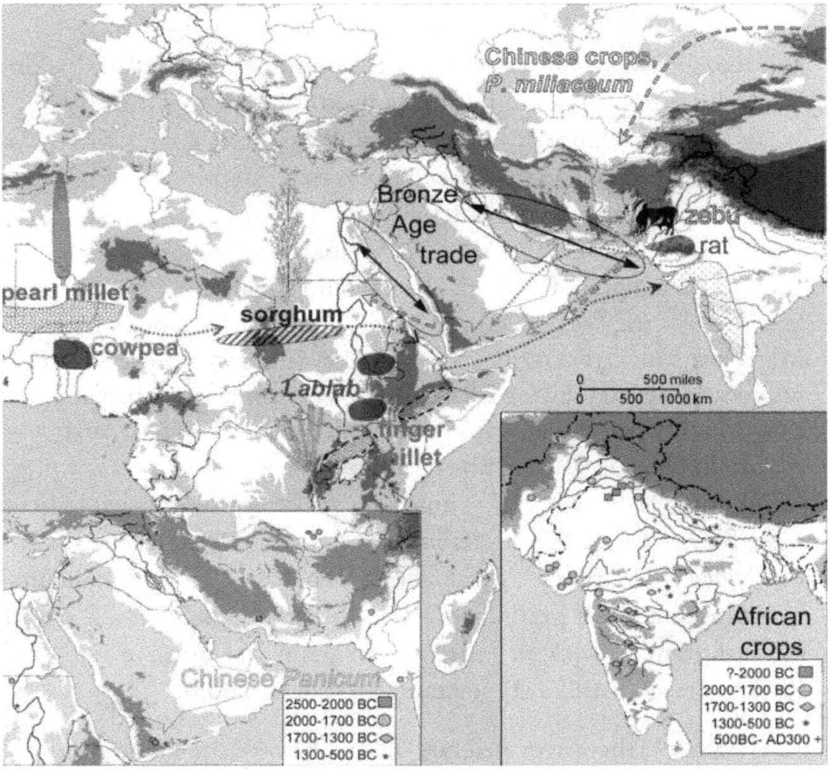

Shematic map of major Bronze Age translocations between South Asia, Arabia and Africa. Inset lower left: map of the distribution of archaeobotanical evidence of broomcorn millet (*Panicum miliaceum*) of Chinese origin, suggesting dispersal from South Asia to Arabia and Nubia via the sea. Inset lower right: map of the distribution of sites in South Asia with archaeobotanical evidence for one or more crops of African origin. (After Fig. 1 in Fuller et al. 2011).

Ψ   A frequently deployed Meluhha hieroglyph. kāsa 'millet' ;
    kāɔ 'millet'Rebus: *kaṁsa--* m. (?) ' bronze '(Pali).

cinna -- *Panicum miliaceum* , °*aka* -- m. BHSanskrit ii 231(CDIAL 4842). kā´śa m. ' a grass used for mats, Saccharum spon- taneum ' Kauś. Pa. Pk. *kāsa* -- m.; Kt. *kāɔ* ' millet ', Wg. *kāi̊*; S. *kā̃hu* m. ' S. spontaneum ', °*hī* f. ' a species of grass '; L. *kā̃h* f. ' S. spontaneum '; P. *kā̃h* m., *kāhī* f. ' S. spontaneum ', *kāh*m. ' a kind of reed '; Ku. *kās* ' a kind of grass used for religious purposes '; N. *kās* ' S. spontaneum ', A. *kā̃huwā*, B. *kās*, Or. *kāsa*, *kāiśa*, *kāĩca*, Bi. Mth. *kās*, *kāsī*, OAw.*kāṁsa*; H. *kās* m. ' S. spontaneum ', *kās* f. ' id., the tall grass Imperata spontanea '; G. *kās* m. ' a kind of white grass ' (CDIAL 3112). 2605 kaṅku m. ' a panic seed ' VarBr̥S. 2. kaṅgu -- f. ' Panicum italicum ' VarBr̥S., °*gū* -- f. lex. °*guka* -- m., °*gukā* -- f., *gaṅkuka* -- m. Suśr. [A word of the Mlecchas for Aryan *yava* -- according to Gotama Nyāya -- sūtra 2, 56,quoted by Mayrhofer EWA i 138, who comparing priyáṅgu -- as a pop. etymology of a form with initial*p*<->suggests Austro -- as. origin. This is further borne out by the form *ṭaṅgunī -- s.v. *kaṅkunī --]1. L. *kaṅgrī* f. ' millet '; Or. *kaṅku* ' Panicum italicum ' (← Sk.?); H. *kā̃k* m. ' P. italicum ', *kā̃kṛā* m. 'cotton seed '. 2. Pa. *kaṅgu* -- f. ' millet ', Pk. *kaṁgu* -- f. n.; Or. *kaṅgu* ' P. italicum ', *kāṅgu* ' a kind of grain or pulse ' = *kāṅgurā*, °*gula;* G. *kā̃g* m. ' a kind of grain ', *kā̃grɔ* m. ' dish of this grain and pulse '; M. *kā̃g*, °*gū* m. ' millet, P. italicum '.(CDIAL 2605).

"...Ganga, on the lower reaches of which were the kingdoms of Anga, Vanga, and Kalinga, regarded in the Mahabharata as

Mleccha. Now the non- Aryan people that today live closest to the territory formerly occupied by these ancient kingdoms are Tibeto-Burmans of the Baric branch. One of the languages of that branch is called Mech, a term given to them by their Hindu neighbors. The Mech live partly in Bengal and partly in Assam. B(runo) Lieblich remarked the resemblance between Mleccha and Mech and that Skr. Mleccha normally became Prākṛt Meccha or Mecha and that the last form is actually found in Sauraseni. 1 Sten Konow thought Mech probably a corruption of Mleccha.* I do not believe that the people of the ancient kingdoms of Anga, Vanga, and Kalinga were precisely of the same stock as the modern Mech, but rather that they and the modern Mech spoke languages of the Baric division of Sino-Tibetan...Now the non-Aryan people that today live closest to the territory formerly occupied by these ancient kingdoms (Anga, Vanga, Kalinga) are Tibeto-Burmans of the Baric branch. [For the easy access of the Baric people to the area occupied by these three kingdoms, see the introduction to my 'Classification of the Northernmost Naga Languages' *JBRS* 39 (1953), 225-264.] One of the languages of that branch is called Mech, a term given to them by their Hindu neighbours. The mech live partly in Bengal and partly in Assam. B(runo) Lieblich (1918: 286-7) remarked the resemblance between *mleccha* and *mech* and that Skr. *mleccha* normally became Prākṛt *meccha* or *mecha* and that the last form is actually found in śaurasenī. Sten Konow thought *mech* probably a corruption of *mleccha*. (*Linguistic Survey of India* 3, pt.2, p.1) I do not believe that the people of the ancient kingdoms of Anga, Vanga and Kalinga were precisely of the same stock as the modern Mech, but rather that they and the modern Mech spoke languages of the Baric division of Sino-Tibetan…I suspect that skr. *mleccha*, referring to the indistinct speech of some non-Aryans, is taken from proto-Bodish (proto-Tibetan) **mltśe* 'tongue', Old Bodish ltśe, Kukish generally **mlei*, the combination of initial consonants *(*mltś-)* being simplified in various ways in different Tibeto-Burmic languages. Aspiration cannot occur after *l* in Old Bodish, and the proto-Bodish form may have been **mlts'e* for all we know, so the *cch* of

Skr. *Mleccha* may come nearer the primitive affricate than anything preserved in the Tibeto-Burmic languages."[36]

Meluhha speech areal map of the Bronze Age spread over an extensive Fertile Crescent, Ancient Near East and India.

"Meluhha, it is now generally agreed, was the name by which the Indus civilization was known to the Mesopotamians. Meluhha was the most distant of the trio of foreign lands, and the imports from Meluhha mentioned in Sumerian and Akkadian texts, such as timbers, carnelian, and ivory, match the resources of the Harappan realms. The Meluhhans were said to have had large boats, and indeed substantial, seaworthy craft would have been a prerequisite for trade over the distances involved. By the time of Sargon, therefore, if not before, the Indus people were plying the Gulf sea lanes and anchoring in Mesopotamian ports…Gudea (2141-2122 BCE), who made use of the established trade networks to acquire exotic materials, including wood and 'translucent carnelian from Meluhha,' for a great temple he was building in his capital city, Girsu. Southern Mesopotamia was again united in 2112 BCE by Ur-Nammu, who founded the Third Dynasty of Ur (Ur III), the second Mesopotamian edmpire…It is probable that Harappan merchants were resident in Mesopotamia by this time, but one should not underestimate the difficulty of archaeologically identifying their presence: In a comparable situation in nineteenth-century BCE Kanesh in Anatolia, the presence of a substantial Assyrian merchant quarter in the town was known only from the cuneiform tablets found in the merchants' houses detailing their trading and other activities…Small objects that have been occasionally found, such as dice, frequently in a worn or broken condition, might have been the personal possession of Indus merchants, as would be the Harappan seal that have been found. The Akkadian levels in the city of Eshnunna yielded Harappan material, including a cylinder seal with a design of Harappan animals (an elephant, a rhino, and a gharial), carnelian beads, and Harappan period…During the Ur III period, there are a number of references to Meluhhan people or sons of Meluhha (du-mu me-luh-ha) in various contexts. Evidence of the presence of Harappan merchants in Sumer at this time comes from a number of major cities, including Lagash and Girsu in the territory of Lagash, Ur, Kish, Eshnunna and Umma. A village of Meluhhans (e-duru me-luh-ha), presumably a trading colony managing the Sumerian end of the Indus trde network, existed on Lagash land in the twenty-first century BCE…A clay sealing, probably found in the city of Umma, bore the impression of a seal with a bull and manger motif and a six-sign Harappan inscription. The sealing had been placed over the knot in a cord that fastened a piece of cloth to the neck of a jar. The city had direct trading connections with Meluhha, Dilmun, and Magan. A text from Umma recorded that a ship's agent from Meluhha had received rations of oil, while another of the period recorded an advance of silver (used, in effect, as currency) to a Meluhhan man. Around forty-five seals with Harappan connections were found in Sumerian cities, beginning in the Akkadian period, though the majority were of Ur III date. These included standard square Harappan seals and cylinder seals with Indus animal designs and inscriptions in the Harappan script, known from Ur, Susa, and Eshnunna. An unusual seal from Ur had a design of a bull without a manger and an inscription in cuneiform…Tin was a rare commodity in the ancient world, but one to which Sumer and Meluhha both had access. Its sources are uncertain. On reference, in an inscription of Gudea, suggests that some of Sumer's tin came from Meluhha. The Harappans may have obtained tin from the Aravallis, but more probably it came from Afghanistan, where it occurred close to the Indus outpost of Shortugai, along with gold."[37]

Maybe, some Meluhha nomads who left behind *cire perdue* arsenical copper metal artifacts of 5th millennium BCE in a Nahal Mishmar cave included Meluhha *kācahārā* scepter-bearers in *kole.l* 'temple, smithy' announcing the dawn of the Bronze Age.

Further researches in language studies of the *sprachbund* will further unravel the structure, form and evolution of the Meluhha-mleccha *parole* sustaining the unified cultural framework of India from ancient times. The polemics of Aryan Invasion/Migration or Out of India Theories need not detain us here, in this enquiry related to identification of glosses of mleccha (meluhha), the most likely Indus language, and the underlying sounds used on Indus writing of metalware catalogs. The direction of 'borrowings' is a secondary component of the philological excursus; there is no universal linguistic rule to firmly aver such a direction of borrowing. Certainly, more work is called for in delineating the structure and forms of meluhha (mleccha) language beyond a mere list of metalware glosses.

Reconstructing mleccha of 5th millennium BCE Indian

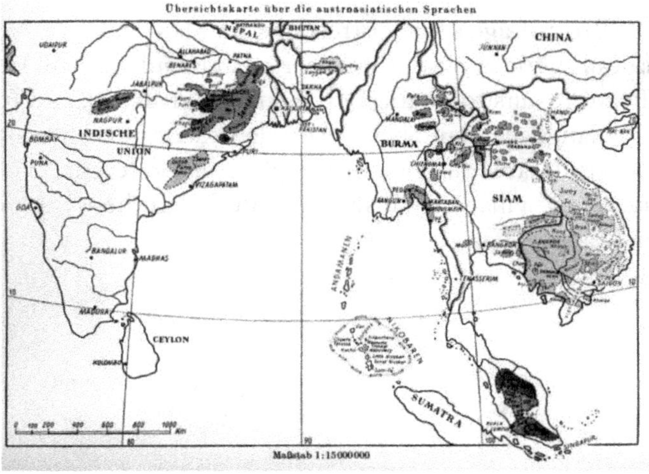

Pinnow-map of Austro-Asiatic language speakers[38]

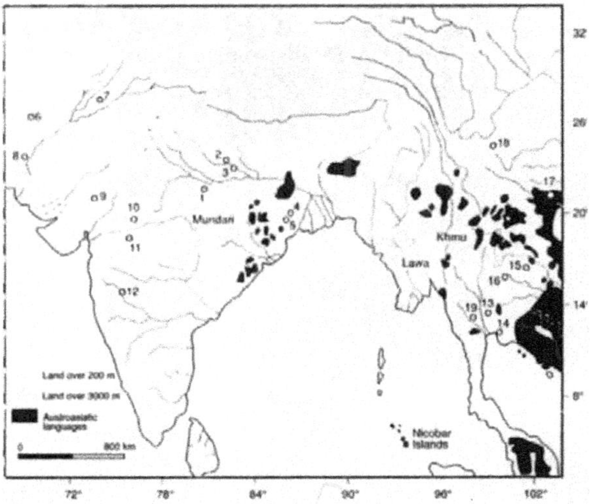

Bronze Age sites of eastern Bha_rata and neighbouring areas: 1. Koldihwa; 2. Khairdih; 3. Chirand; 4. Mahisadal; 5. Pandu Rajar Dhibi; 6. Mehrgarh; 7. Harappa; 8. Mohenjo-daro; 9. Ahar;

10.Kayatha; 11. Navdatoli; 12. Inamgaon; 13. Non Pa Wai; 14. Nong Nor; 15. Ban Na Di and Ban Chiang; 16. Non Nok Tha; 17. Thanh Den; 18. Shizhaishan; 19. Ban Don Ta Phet[39]

Map 1 (Bronze-age sites) correlates with Map 2 (Austro-Asiatic languages). A focus on this area for areal linguistics will yield significant results to delineate the ancient structure and form of mleccha language. Santali and Munda lexicons and literature will be of considerable relevance with particular reference to cultural traditions and village festivals associated with the work on minerals and metals.

"The term mleccha occurs often in collocation with bhāṣā 'speech' and deśa 'country, region'. It is probable that in the OIA Brahminical sources, the lands designated as mleccha-deśa included not only areas in which non-Aryan languages were spoken, but also those Indo-Aryan-speaking areas which were regarded as religiously unorthodox.)." This may explain why Magadha was known as mleccha-deśa (whether the language of that area was a form of Indo-Aryan or not), 'whereas to the Buddhists the term meant primarily those lands in which non-Aryan languages were spoken.'..It seems probable, on the basis of this evidence, that there was a good deal of bilingualism and diglossia in ancient India, with those of non-Aryan groups who dealt with the Aryan Brahmans being obliged to learn some form of Indo-Aryan (Sanskrit or Prākṛt) for day-to-day communication. On the other hand, the presence of many words of foreign origin in Vedic from the earliest times indicates that this was not a one-sided process."[40]

A good indication of the mleccha-speaker community is also provided by the locations of Ashoka's edicts which included territories crossing the Vindhya mountains. Adding Dravida (andha damilādi), the mleccha was apparently the *lingua franca,* the spoken tongue which enabled the use of Prākṛts to convey Ashoka's messages through the edicts.

Since 1956 when Emeneau referred to an ancient linguistic area in India, there has been a paradigm shift in IE linguistics as applied to the area called 'India' using terms such as areal linguistics, *sprachbund*, linguistic area.

The credit for using the term 'linguistic area' goes to MB Emeneau, even though he used the term as a translation of 'sprachbund' invented by HV Velton in 1943. Linguistic areas are areas in which 'languages belonging to more than one family show traits in common which do not belong to the other members of (at least) one of the families'.The methodology used to recognize a linguistic area is a bifurcate one. First, a typological feature is established as pan-Indic and at the same time not extra-Indic. Second, the historical diffusion of features throughout the languages of the linguistic area are investigated through questions of lexical lists, phonology, syntactic, morphological and semantic development and sociolinguistic questions. Emeneau recognizes (1956: 1,2) that '…it is rarely possible to demonstrate this (Indo-Aryan to Dravidian) direction (except for diffusion of lexical items).

The term *sprachbund* was used in 1931 by Nikol Trubetzkoy and Roman Jakobson when they discussed the long-recognized linguistic areas such as the languages of the Caucasus or of the Balkans. In this context, a number of researches have been referenced.[41]

The conclusions of Southworth about 'Indus' language, Proto-Munda and Language X are consistent since the assumption made about the arrival of Indo-Aryan languages is not relevant for and do NOT upset his hypotheses. The *mleccha* Southworth refers to is more extensive in areal usage than suggested by his analyses. Mleccha-speaker areas according to Mahābhārata and Patañjali are extensive areas covering the *lingua franca* of many regions outside of Kurukshetra – ranging from Gandhāra in the west to Kosala in the East, from Kashmir in the north to Coda in the South. Mleccha, *lingua franca* (deśī -- vernacular) " a very considerable amount (say some 40%) of the New Indo-Aryan vocabulary is borrowed from Munda, either via Sanskrit (and Prākṛt), or via Prākṛt alone, or directly from Munda; wide-branched and seemingly native, word-families of South Dravidian are of Proto-Munda origin; in Vedic and later Sanskrit, the words adopted have often been Aryanized, resp. Sanskritized. "In view of the intensive interrelations between Dravidian, Munda and Aryan dating from pre-Vedic times even individual etymological questions will often have to be approached from a Pan-Indic point of view if their study is to be fruitful. It is hoped that this work may be helpful to arrive at this all-embracing view of the Indian languages, which is the final goal of these studies."[42]

"...recent archaeological researches in East Arabia have brought to light many finds which are related to the presence of Indus valley people. In the settlements of Hili 8 and Maysar-1, both of which have been investigated, Indus valley pottery is frequently found. Seals with Indus valley script and typical iconography indicate influences in Makkan down to the level of business organization. Marks identifying pottery in Makkan were taken from those used in the Indus valley, including the use of the signs on pottery used in the Indus valley. The discovery of a sea-port-- which may be ascribed to the Harappans-- at Ra's al-Junayz on Oman's east coast by an Italian expedition would seem to indicate that trade routes should be viewed in a more differentiated fashion than has been done upto now." Simo Parpola et al report[43] on the Meluhhan village in the late third millennium Mesopotamia, where tablets and envelopes apparently of Harappan traders, were found. 'If the tablets and their sealed envelopes had not been found, in fact, we might never have suspected the existence of a merchant colony.' [44]

The trans-continental journey of mleccha-speakers and bronze-age mine-workers/smiths of Sarasvati civilization during the historical periods has to be narrated. An indication is provided by Bnei Menashe, descendants of one of the ten lost tribes of Israel. Also known as the Shinlung, the Bnei Menashe have a memory of their history of movement from the Northern Kingdom of Israel in 721 BCE. across the silk route finally ending up in Mizoram, India. Devala noted that anyone who had visited the Sindhus or Sauvīras should be initiated afresh – an apparent reference to mleccha as settlers in Sindh. Buddhaghosa specifies *milakkha bhāsas* or mleccha languages as those of: Andhra, Dami*ḷa,* kirāta, yonaka (yavana) (*Manorathapuraṇī* on *Ang. N* II: 289) and lauds the superiority of Māgadhabāsa over these dialects. (*Sammohavinodanī*: 388). "The Jaimini Dharmashastra lists some (sanskritized) Dravidian words as characteristic of mleccha speech, and Panini makes reference to the onomastic suffix –an (a Dravidian form) in the names of members of the Andhaka, Vṛṣṇi and Kuru tribes." (Southworth, opcit., fn. 30, p. 61) *śatapatha brāhmaṇa* includes in mleccha territories: Saurashtra, Gujarat and Maharashtra, but also the eastern areas (Bihar and Bengal). Mahabharata regards Anga, Vanga, Kalinga as mleccha kingdoms and that the sons of Turvasu are the Yavanas and that the sons of Anu were the Mlecchas. (*Cr. Ed.* I.80.26; Roy I.85). cf. Dharmasūtra I.1.32-33: ca. 4th cent. BCE, according to Bhandarkar. Deshpande (1979: 48) observes: "The Baudhayana Dharmasūtra (1.1.32-33) gives us a clear idea of how the 'Vedic Aryans' viewed the 'mixed Aryans' of the outer regions: The inhabitants of ānartta, of Anga, of Magadha, of Saurāṣṭra, of the Deccan, of Upavṛt, of Sind, and the Sauvīras are of mixed origin. He who has visited the countries of the ārattas, Kāraskaras, Puṇḍras, Sauvīras, Vangas, Kalingas [or] Pranūnas shall offer a Punastoma...sacrifice [for purification]." Deshpande (1979: 48) underscores the fact that speakers of Indo-Aryan who belonged to regions other than Aryavarta considered themselves as āryas, not mlecchas. This indicates that language was the criterion for distinguishing Aryan-speakers – ārya Vācas-- and mleccha-speakers – mleccha Vācas.

Mahābhārata lists people and their characteristics of comprehension -- linguistic in particular:
ingitajnāś ca magadhāh prekṣitajnāś ca kosalāh
ardhoktāh kuru-pāncālāh śālvāh kṛtnānuśāsanāh
pārvatāyāśca viṣamaāyathaiva girayas (sibayas) tathā
sarvajnāyavanārājan śūrās caiva viśeṣatah
mlecchāh svasamjnāniyataānānukta itaro janāh

'The magadhas comprehend gestures, the kośalas understand at a glance; the kuru-Pāncālas a speech half-uttered, the śālvas only when the whole sentence is spoken; mountaineers, like the śibi, understand with difficulty. The yavanas, O king, are omniscient, the śūras especially so. The mleccha rely on their own knowledge; 'other people cannot understand.'[45]

One resource for recontruction of mleccha is a work which dealt with *Prākṛit* forms. The work is Simharaja, 1909, *Prākṛti*

Rupavatara -- A Prākṛt grammar based on the Valmikisutra, Vol. I, Ed. by E. Hultzsch, Albermarle St., Royal Asiatic Society.[46]

Name of Himalayas is given as dāruṇa mleccha (Mārkandēya Purāṇa). Bhagadatta the ruler of Prāgjyotiṣa was a mleccha heading a large number of yavanas. In *Mahābhārata* (XVI.7.63) *ābhīra*-s are called mleccha; kings regarded as *vrātya*. Garuda Purana refers to *madraka* (Capital śākala, modern Siālkot) as mleccha.

Prākṛitarūpāvatāra literally means 'the descent of *Prākṛit* forms'. Pischel noted: "…the *Prākṛitarūpāvatāra* is not unimportant for the knowledge of the declension and conjugation, chiefly because *Simharāja* frequently quotes more forms than Hēmachandra and Trivikrama. No doubt many of these forms are theoretically inferred; but they are formed strictly according to the rules and are not without interest." (Pischel, 1900, *Grammatik der Prākṛit-Sprachen*, Strassburg, p.43). Pischel also had written a book titled, *Hēmachandra's Prākṛit grammar*, Halle, 1877. The full text of the *Vālmīkisūtra*, with *gaṇas, dēśīyas, and iṣṭis*, has been printed in Telugu characters at Mysore in 1886 as an appendix to the *ṣaḍbhāṣachandrikā.*

A format to determine the structure of *Prākṛit* is to identify words which are identical with Sanskrit words or can be derived from Sanskrit. In this process, *dēśīyas* or *dēśyas,* 'provincialisms' are excluded. One part of the work of Simharja is *samjñāvibhāga* 'technical terms'. Another is *pari bhāṣāvibhāga* 'explanatory rules'. Dialects are identified in a part called *śaurasēnyādivibhāga*; the dialects include: *śaurasēni, māgadhī, paiśācī, chūḷikā paiśācī, apabhramśa.* Additional rules are identified beyond those employed by Pāṇini: *sus*, nominative; *as*, accusative; *ṭās*, instrumental; *nēs*, dative; *nam*, genitive; *nip*, locative.

Mahābhārata (XII.5.13.2) lists duties of mleccha (*yavana, shaka, tushāra, pahlava, cina*): obedience to parents, preceptors, kings and

hermits; performance of vedic and *pāka yajña*-s; digging of wells; absention from violence; absence of wrath; adherence to purity, truthfulness, peace; maintenance of family; veneration of *pitṛ*-s (ancestors). *Gargi Samhita* evidences the respect shown to mleccha stating that Yavana have knowledge of astronomy: 'The yavana are mleccha, but among them this science is duly established; therefore even though they are mleccha they are honoured as rishis;much more than an astrologer who is a brāhmaṇa'
Other resources available for delineation of mleccha are: *The Prākṛita-prakāśa; or the Prākṛt grammar of Vararuchi.* With the commentary Manorama of Bhamaha. The first complete ed. of the original text... With notes, an English translation and index of Prākṛit words; to which is prefixed a short introd. to Prākṛit grammar.[47]

On these lines, and using the methods used for delineating *Ardhamāgadhi* language, by *Prākṛita* grammarians, and in a process of extrapolation of such possible morphemic changes into the past, an attempt may be made to hypothesize morphemic or phonetic variants of mleccha words as they might have been, in various periods from ca. 4th millennium BCE. There are also grammars of languages such as Marathi (William Carey), Braj bhāṣā grammar (James Robert), Sindhi, Hindi, Tamil (*Tolkāppiyam*) and Gujarati which can be used as supplementary references, together with the classic *Hemacandra's Dēsīnāmamālā, Prākṛt Grammar of Hemachandra* edited by P. L. Vaidya (BORI, Pune), Vararuchi's works and Richard Pischel's *Comparative Grammar of Prākṛt Languages.*(Repr. Motilal Banarsidass, 1957). Colin P. Masica's *Indo-Aryan Languages*, Cambridge University Press, 1993,"... has provided a fundamental, comparative introduction that will interest not only general and theoretical linguists but also students of one or more languages (Hindi, Urdu, Bengali, Punjabi, Gujurati, Marathi, Sinhalese, etc.) who want to acquaint themselves with the broader linguistic context. Generally synchronic in approach, concentrating on the phonology, morphology and syntax of the modern representatives of the group, the volume also covers their historical development,

writing systems, and aspects of sociolinguistics." Thomas Oberlies' Pali grammar (Walter de Gruyter, 2001) presents a full description of Pali, the language used in the Theravada Buddhist canon, which is still alive in Ceylon and South-East Asia. The development of its phonological and morphological systems is traced in detail from Old Indic (including mleccha?). Comprehensive references to comparable features and phenomena from other Middle Indic languages mean that this grammar can also be used to study the literature of Jainism. Madhukar Anant Mehendale's *Historical Grammar of Inscriptional Prākṛts* is a useful aid to delineate changes in morphemes over time. A good introduction is: Alfred C. Woolner's *Introduction to Prākṛt*, 1928 (Motilal Banarsidass). "*Introduction to Prākṛt* provides the reader with a guide for the more attentive and scholarly study of Prākṛt occurring in Sanskrit plays, poetry and prose--both literary and inscriptional. It presents a general view of the subject with special stress on Sauraseni and Maharastri Prākṛt system. The book is divided into two parts. Part I consists of I-XI Chapters which deal with the three periods of Indo-Aryan speech, the three stages of the Middle Period, the literary and spoken Prākṛts, their classification and characteristics, their system of Single and Compound Consonants, Vowels, Sandhi, Declension, Conjugation and their history of literature. Part II consists of a number of extracts from Sanskrit and Prākṛt literature which illustrate different types of Prākṛt--Sauraseni, Maharastri, Magadhi, Ardhamagadhi, Avanti, Apabhramsa, etc., most of which are translated into English. The book contains valuable information on the Phonetics and Grammar of the Dramatic Prākṛts--Sauraseni and Maharastri. It is documented with an Index as well as a Students'. "
It may be noted that Hemacandra is a resource which has provided the sememe *ibbo* 'merchant' which reads rebus with *ibha* 'elephant' hieroglyph.

Sir George A. Grierson's article on The Prākṛt Vibhasas cites: "Pischel, in §§3, 4, and 5 of his Prākṛt Grammar, refers very briefly to the Vibhāṣās of the Prākṛt grammarians. In § 3 he quotes Mārkaṇḍēya's (Intr., 4) division of the Prākṛts into *Bhāṣā,*

Vibhāṣā, Apabhraṁśa, and *Paiśāca*, his division of the Vibhāṣās into *Śākārī, Cāṇḍālī, Śābarī, Ābhīrikā*, and *Ṭākkī* (not *Śākkī*, as written by Pischel), and his rejection of *Auḍhrī* (Pischel, *Oḍrī*) and *Drāviḍī*. In § 4 he says, "Rāmatarkavāgīśa observes that the *vibhāṣāḥ*cannot be called Apabhraṁśa, if they are used in dramatic works and the like." He repeats the latter statement in § 5, and this is all that he says on the subject. Nowhere does he say what the term *vibhāṣā* means. The present paper is an attempt to supply this deficiency."[48]

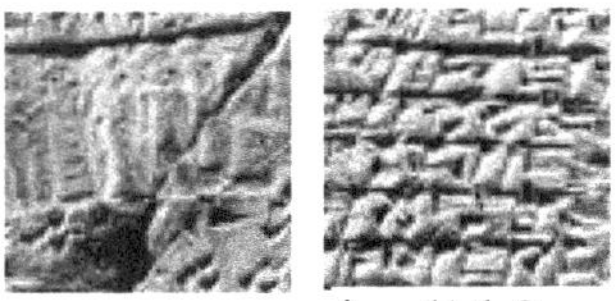

Metmuseum. Cuneiform tablet case, 1920–1840 BCE; Old Assyrian Trading Colony period. Central Anatolia, Kültepe (Karum Kanesh) Clay; L. 6 5/8 in. (16.8 cm) Record of a lawsuit. Two cylinder seal impressions on tablet case. "The records of the Assyrian trading colonies, of which Kültepe (ancient Karum Kanesh) was one, provide detailed information about one part of a lively international trade in the early second millennium B.C. that extended from Egypt to the Caucasus to Central Asia and the Indus Valley. The Assyrian tablets describe the exchange of tin and textiles from Ashur for silver from Anatolia as well as detail the specifics of contracts and lawsuits, and tell about bandits and other misfortunes. The tablet contained in this case (MMA 66.245.5a) is the record of court testimony describing an ownership dispute of a business firm. The case is sealed with two different cylinder seals rolled across the front and back of the envelope in five parallel rows separated by plain clay. Both seals illustrate presentation scenes in which worshippers approach a larger seated figure holding a cup. The obverse, shown here, is also inscribed in cuneiform."[49]

Three cylinder seal impressions. Relate to loan of silver. Envelope. "The texts on the

tablets, written in the Old Assyrian dialect of Akkadian, describe the Assyrians bringing textiles and tin to Anatolia on the backs of donkeys, and trading it with the locals for silver and gold. This letter is from Ashur-malik to his brother Ashur-idi complaining that, although winter has already come, he and his family have been left in Ashur without food, clothes or fuel. Lack of space obliged him to finish his letter on a small supplementary tablet. Often, as in this case, the tablet was encased in a clay envelope. These were sometimes inscribed with a summary of the contents and sealed by witnesses, using the traditional Mesopotamian cylinder seal rather than the local Anatolian stamp seal. Here the sender's seal shows figures approaching a seated king with a bull-man at the end of the scene."[50] The bull-man shown on the line-drawing of the seal impression is an emphatic Meluhha expression. Overflowing water from the shoulders of the bull-man: *kāṇḍa* 'water'; lo 'overflow' Rebus: *lokhāṇḍā* 'copper metalware'. Hieroglyph: *ḍangra* 'bull' Rebus: *ḍangar* 'blacksmith' (Meluhha) *damgar* 'merchant' (Akkadian).

Cuneiform tablet case impressed with four cylinder

seals[51]

Cuneiform tablet case impressed with three cylinder seals, for cuneiform tablet 66.246.18a: quittance for a loan in copper[52]

"The Early Bronze Age of the 3rd millennium BCE saw the first development of a truly international age of metallurgy… The question is, of course, why all this took place in the 3rd millennium BCE… It seems to me that any attempt to explain why things suddenly took off about 3000 BCE has to explain the most important development, the birth of the art of writing… As for the concept of a Bronze Age one of the most significant events in the 3rd millennium was the development of true tin-bronze alongside an arsenical alloy of copper…" (J.D. Muhly, 1973, *Copper and Tin*, Conn.: Archon., Hamden; *Transactions of Connecticut Academy of Arts and Sciences*, vol. 43, p. 221f.)

Tin road caravan documentation

Fresco on the wall of the Ankara Museum of Anatolian Civilization showing a scribe writing on clay tablets.[53] Hieroglyph (decorating the head of the girl): *khāḍ* n. ' piece ', f. ' break, fissure '(Marathi) (CDIAL 3792). *gaṇḍa*-- m. ' piece, part '(Buddhist Hybrid Sanskrit) 'four' (Munda) Rebus: *khāṇḍā* 'metalware'. Hieroglyph (phonetic determinant): *kanā'* -- f. ' girl ' RV. kanyā` f. ' maiden ' RV., °*yakā* -- f. MBh. Pa. *kaññā* -- f., Pk. *kaṇṇā* -- , °*ṇagā* -- , ś. *kajjaā* -- , paiś. *kaṁcā* -- f., S. *kañā* f., L. *kanj* f. -- A. *kanāi* ' bundle of seven figs, rice and dūrvā grass placed in a girl's lap at puberty ceremony ' P. ludh. *kanneā* f. ' girl ' (B. D. Jain PhonPj 116) ← Sk. (CDIAL 2737). *sā̃go* m. ' caravan '; *sangu* 'body of pilgrims' (Sindhi) (CDIAL 12854). *saṅghvī* m. ' leader of a body of pilgrims, a partic. surname '(Gujarati)(CDIAL 12857). Sanga 'priest' (Sumerian) Rebus: khar 'blacksmith' (Kashmiri) Hieroglyph: khara1 m. ' donkey ' KātyŚr., °*rī* -- f. Pāṇ. NiDoc. Pk. *khara* -- m., Gy. pal. *ḳăr* m., *kắri* f., arm. *xari*, eur. gr. *kher*, *kfer*, rum. *xerú*, Kt. *kur*, Pr. *korū'*, Dm. *khar* m., °*ri* f., Tir. *kh**lr, Paš. lauṛ. *khar* m., *khär* f., Kal. urt.*khār*, Phal. *khār* m., *khári* f., K. *khar* m., *khürü* f., pog. kash. ḍoḍ. *khar*, S. *kharu* m., P. G. M. *khar* m., OM. *khari* f.; -- ext. Ash. *kərəṭék*,

Shum. *xareṭá*; <-> L. *kharkā* m., °*kī*f. -- Kho. *khairánu* ' donkey's

foal ' (+?). Bshk. Kt. *kur* ' donkey ' (for loss of aspiration Morgenstierne ID 334).(CDIAL 3818). Khot. *khaḍara* ' mule '(CDIAL 3820a). *kharapāla ' donkey -- driver'. Paš. *kharwāl*.(CDIAL 3822).

By 1960 BC, Assyrian merchants had established Karum Anadolu Medeniyetleri Müzesi, Ankara (, Seton Lloyd, 1998, *Ancient Turkey* (Translation: Ender Verinlioğlu) Tubitak, Ankaro.) Assyrian merchants used gold for wholesale trade and silver for retail trade. Gold was considered eight times more valuable than silver. But there was one more metal, *amutum*, which was even more valuable than gold. Amutum is thought to be the newly discovered iron and was forty times more valuable than silver. The most important Anatolian export was copper, and the Assyrian merchants sold tin and clothing to Anatolia. (Ekrem Akurgal, 2000, *Anadolu Kültür Tarihi*,Tubitak, Ankara,2000).

karum 'harbor, quay' (Anatolian). "*Karum*...a foreign merchants' colony enjoying an autonomous sttus with rights to self-government granted by the local city-state (*alum*); and *wabartum*, a trading factory. The center that organized all foreign trading communities was located in the *karum* of Kanesh. There were also native traders among the merchants of the foreign trading colonies. Most traders, however, were from Asshur. The Assyrians were the ones who brought with them the first writing system and literary language used in Asia Minor—the Old Assyrian dialect of the Akkadian language. Though Asshur greatly influenced the commercial activities of these trading communities through its own agreements with the local rulers. The primary task of the trading colonies was to organize the export of silver-lead and gold...In exchange for silver and copper ore the merchants imported to Asia Minor woolen and linen textiles and also great amounts of the metal *annakum*, which has been identified both as tin and lead. It abounded in Asshur on the Tigris, but its origin is still a subject of contention. Goods were transported by donkey caravans...*Annakum* served as money at Asshur; there its price in relation to silver was 15:1; in Asia Minor it was 7.5:1."[54]

Çorum, Boğazkale or Bogazköy, Hattuşaş, Yazılıkaya – Hattusa, Inscribed Rock. Meeting of processions with Meluhha hieroglyphs. Two language groups are identified by the hieroglyphs of meeting of two processions: babbara, mlecha. Hieroglyph: *babhru* 'ichneumon' (CDIAL 9149). Rebus: *babhruśá* -- Pāṇ.gaṇa, *babhluśá* – Vajasneyi Samhita. What Hemachandra calls deśi seems to aptly describe this linguistic area as a continuum from the days of Sarasvati hieroglyphs. The word *mlecchati* of Vedic, means 'speaks indistinctly'. mliṣṭa is referred to by Panini meaning 'spoken indistinctly or barbarously' [Monier-Williams 1899; Pali milakkha, Pkt. Milicchа; <PD *muṟi/miṟi 'say, speak, utter'; *muzankk 'make noise, speak' (DEDR 4989); probably connected with tamiṟ (Tamil)]. Patanjali's Mahābhāṣya refers to asura (OIr ahura) who substitute *l* for *r* an apparent reference to poor speakers of Indo-Aryan. Dāsa are pre-Vedic Indo-Aryan speaking people; dāsavarṇa a reference to all the indigenous peoples. Balbūtha Tarukṣa, presumably a Dāsa, is referred to as a patron of a Vedic seer. Combatants of 'Battle of Ten Kings' include those with Aryan-sounding names (such as Vasiṣṭha and Bharata) and

those with non-Aryan-sounding names (such as the Sṛnjayas and śimyu).

Variants of the *śrivatsa* hieroglyph on Jaina *āyāgapaṭa* of Kankali Tila, Manoharpura. [Vedic ārya, Metathesis for ariya as diaeretic form of ārya, of which the contracted (assimilation) form is ayya. See also ariya] (n.) ariyan, nobleman, gentleman (Pali)]

Mollusc: *hangi* 'snail'; *hõgiñ* f. a pearl-oyster shell (Śiv. 1551, 1755; Rām. 1142); the shell of any aquatic mollusc (cf. **kŏla-hõgiñ**, s.v. **kŏl** 2); ? a snail (L. 157, 464, *hāngi*)(Kashmiri) Rebus: *sangi* 'caravan of pilgrims' (Gujarati). *kola sangi* 'metalworkers' caravan'. Leading the procession is a lady on a panther showing something like a *śrivatsa* symbolic form. *karaḍa* 'panther' Rebus: *karaḍa* 'hard alloy of gold, silver etc.' (Marathi) She is leading a *sangi* 'caravan of pilgrims'. This composite hieroglyph has been shown to be formed by entwined, inverted pair of fishes with fish-tails tied together by a cord (shown with molluscs on Mathura Lion Capital and on Sanchi stupa torana).

This is an announcement of puja for prosperity of *ariya sangha, ariya dhamma* (ayire 'fish'; Rebus ayas 'metal'); dula 'pair' Rebus: dul 'cast metal'. Pali. dāma a bond, fetter, rope; chain; Telugu. దారము [dāramu]n. A thread, cord, string, rope. dāman rope RV. (CDIAL 6283). Rebus: OB. *dhāma* 'religious conduct' (CDIAL 6753).

Following the lady is a person with conical cap leading a tiger. The conical cap is comparable to the cap shown on Shahdad standard – of a Meluhha merchant. Hieroglyph: *potṛka* 'trefoil' Rebus: *pot* ' jeweller's polishing stone ' (CDIAL 8403). *kola* 'tiger' Rebus: *kol* 'working in iron', 'working in 5 alloys'. *pajhaṛ* 'eagle' Rebus *pasra* 'smithy, forge'.

Procession Bogazkale. A drawing of rock-carved reliefs of a procession of Hittite deities in Yazilikaya, Turkey. (Mitchell, Wright, 1883, *A History of Ancient Sculpture*. Dodd & Mead).

Proto-Indo-Aryan is evidenced in Mitanni inscriptions/treaties (pace review by Paul Thieme) or Kikkuli's horse-training manual (ca. 1400 BCE). "Thus speaks Kikkuli, master horse trainer of the land of Mitanni" (*UM.MA Ki-ik-ku-li* LÚ *A-AŠ-ŠU-UŠ-ŠA-AN-NI ŠA* KUR URU *MI-IT-TA-AN-NI*) (The Kikkuli Text, Lines 1-4).[55] The assimilation of dissimilar plosives (*sapta* > *satta*), and the break-up of consonant clusters by interpolation of vowels (anaptyxis, *Indra* > *Indara*) are indications of early Middle Indo-Aryan features in Mitanni.[56]

Tin Road was from Meluhha to ancient Near East and beyond upto Haifa (Levant or Fertile Crescent): the route was: via Elam, Susa, Persian Gulf, Ashur to Kanesh/Nesh (Kultepe, Anatolia or modern Turkey), close to Mitanni with evidence of Indo-Aryan superstrate which evidences the presence of speakers of Meluhha, Indian *sprachbund*.

"For approximately two thousand years, beginning in the mid-third millennium BCE, ancient Sumerians and Akkadian cuneiform sources frequently mention two foreign lands, Makkan and Meluhha....Makkan is the southern shore of the Persian Gulf and of the Arabian Sea; it denotes Arabia, extending east of ancient Sumer up to and including Oman. Meluhha is the northern shore of the Persian Gulf and of the Arabian Sea; it denotes Iran and India, extending east of ancient Elam and Anshan up to and including the Indus Valley...Four pieces of evidence based on conquests place Meluhha close to Mesopotamia, specifically in Iran east of Elam and Anshan. The evidence concerning the lapis lazuli, the sissoo-tree, and the black people of Meluhha, corresponding to the Aithiopes of classical times, place Meluhha between Iran and Afghanistan. The farthest extent of Meluhha in India is indicated by the imports. I know of no evidence favoring the location of Meluhha in Arabia, south of the Persian Gulf."[57]

Historical background

"...twentieth century BCE...A building inscriptionof Ilu-Shumma from Ishtar Temple at Ashur links the copper trade with the inhabitants of southern Mesopotamian cities, who mediated in the exchange of copper coming from the region of Oman. At the same time, textiles from Mesopotamia and tin from Iran or beyond were traded for silver in Anatolia, where Ashur's traders had established permanent trading colonies in a number of princedoms with the consent of the local rulers and carried on trade with Anatolian merchants. Thousands of cuneiform texts discovered in these settlements known as karums, especially in Kultepe (Kanesh), not far from Kayseri, provide a glimpse into the business practices of merchants from Ashur and their relations with Anatolian princes as well as with their home city. At the time when Assyrian merchants were trading in Anatolia, a certain Erishum I, son of Ilushumma, ruled in Ashur. Several of his building inscriptions are preserved. One example also turned up in Kanesh, which may indicate that it was probably during his reign that trading colonies were established in Anatolia. The year-officials (eponyms) listed in Old Assyrian clay tablets in Anatolia seem to confim this date. Other rulers of Ashur who governed the city-state during the period when trading centers were established in Anatolia were Ikunum, Sargon I, Puzur-Ashur II, Naram-Sin, and Erishum II. Since ther\se were followed by the 'interregnum' of Shamshi-Adad, they must date from the nineteenth century BCE. Iknum and Sargon I are not only attested in the Assyrian king list but also in inscriptions they left behind in Ashur. The latter is also known from impressions of his seal found at Kanesh...Shamshi-Adad, son of Ila-kabkabu, apparently came from seminomadic roots; the list of his ancestors includes the names of tribes. He managed to incorporate Ashur into his realm and to govern the city in the name of the city god. He did not call himself 'king' of Ashur and did not make the city his residence. Inscriptions found in Ashur speak of him as a builder but also point to his military successes...He was followed by his son, Ishme-Dagan I (1782-1742 BCE), who had previously seen to his father's interests in Ekallatum, on the Tigris not far from Ashur. But soon Ashur was again ruled by representatives of the local aristocracy. The first of these, Puzur-Sin (late eighteenth century BCE), stressed in an inscription discovered in Ashur that he occupied the throne of Shamshi-Adad, who 'was not flesh of the city of Ashur'. These 'regents of the god Ashur' were unable to proclaim any military successes in their texts, and ultimately they fell under the supremacy of the Hurrian state of Mitanni, which had come into being in upper Mesopotamia...A new phase in the history of Ashur (Middle Assyrian period) began at the time of Ashur-uballit I (1363-1328 BCE). During his reign the Hurro-Mitannian empire collapsed under attack from the Anatolian Hittites...Adad-nirari I (1305-1274 BCE), a great-grandson of Ashur-uballit, made Assyria a military power. He fought against the upper Mesopotamian city Hanigalbat, which was still largely supported by the Hittites, and he penetrated as far as the vicinity of the fortress of Carchemish on the Euphrates. He was also able to subject the valleys of the Balikh and Habur rivers to his control...Shalmaneser I (1273-1244 BCE) incorporated the region of Hanigalbat into his realm, establishing an Assyrian administration there. Assyria and the Hittites now confronted one another on the Euphrates, and Tukulti-inurta I (1243-1207BCE) even claimed to have fought successfully against the Hittites to the west of the river. Tukulti-Ninurta led campaigns not only into the mountains of Nairi, northeast of Ashur, but also against Babylonia, whih suffered a heavy defeat. The city of Babylon itself was conquered and destroyed, and its king, Kashtiliash IV, accompanied by a portion of the populace, was taken captive to Assyria. The same fate befell Marduk, the city god of Babylon, for his statue was removed to Assyria. Tukulti-Ninurta ruled Babylon for 'seven' years. It was perhaps the opposition of the Ashur aristocracy that led him to establish his residence in Kar Tukulti-Ninurta, a city quickly constructed within sight of Ashur. According to a late Babylonian chronicle, he was murdered during a palace conspiracy in which his own son partiipated...Ashur-resha-ishi I (1132-1115 BCE) was the first to mention conflicts with mountain dwellers in the east and Aramaic groups in the west. Tiglath-pileser I (1114-1076 BCE), who led Assyrian forces as far as Lake Van in the northeast and the coast of the Mediterranean in the west, was once again able to report greater successes."[58]

Mohenjo-Daro seal m1186.

In the context of documentation for languages, writing systems occur during the Bronze Age. Viable writing systems arose in Meluhha hieroglyphs [*mũh* 'face'. *mũhe* 'ingot' *mũhã* 'the quantity of iron produced at one time in a native smelting furnace' (Santali)], China (oracle bone script), Near East (cuneiform – related to Sumerian, Akkadian or Elamite or Hittite or Ugaritic), Egypt (hieroglyphs Determinative hieroglyph for copper/bronze), and the Mediterranean (Linear B 'bronze'). This is a remarkable hieroglyph component signifying a human face and ligatured with parts of some animals such as trunk of elephant, forelegs of tiger, hindpart of a bovine and horns of a ram to create a hieroglyph composition conveying meaning in detailed, precise symbolic

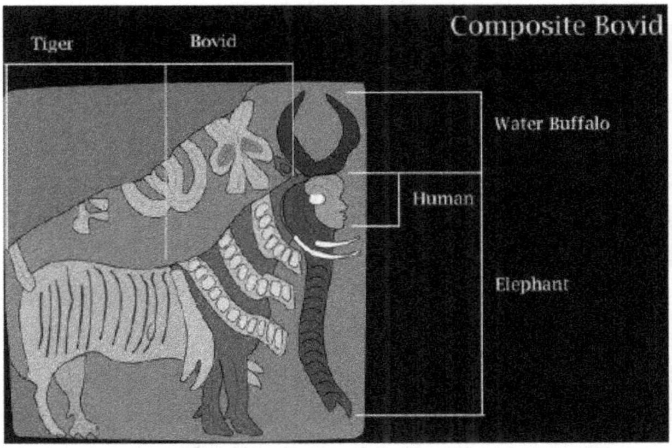

expression read rebus.

Composite bovid with a combination of hieroglyphs. Mohenjo-daro Seal m0304. (After Huntington 2007): two profile faces, bovine ears. Probable bristles like the bristles on a tiger's mane. The face profiles do not match with other faces profiled on other inscribed objects. The profiles of two faces however, can be compared with the profile of human face shown on this seal of a composite animal (elements: human, tiger, tiger's mane, markhor horns). The 'face' hieroglyph is the superset signifying 'ingot'. The contributing subsets are: ibha 'elephant' Rebus: ib 'iron'; ibbo 'merchant'. *dhaṭu* 'scarf' Rebus: *dhatu* 'metallic ore'. *paśu* 'bovid' Rebus: *pās* 'silver ingot'. *kola* 'tiger' Rebus: *kol* 'alloy, pañcaloha'. *kaṭái* ' buffalo calf '(Gaw.) *kāṭo* ' young buffalo bull ' (Kumaoni) (CDIAL 2645). *kāṛā* 'buffalo' bull (Tamil) Rebus: *khaḍā* 'nodule (ore), stone'. Variant horn-style indicates: *ṭagara* 'ram' Rebus: *tagara* 'tin'.

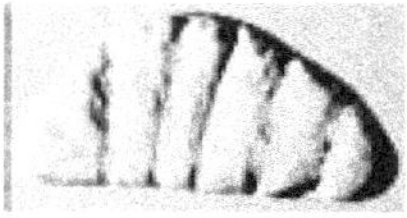

Musée du Louvre. A complex token shaped like a bun-ingot denoted metal ingot, Susa, ca. 3300 BCE. Bronze inscriptions (金文, i.e. "text on metal") preceded by a century the oracle bone script. Mleccha-speaking artisans invented alloying of metals, *cire perdue* techniques of metal-casting and a writing system which became necessary because of the metallurgical inventions.

Like the postman in *Father Brown*, the linguistic area (*sprachbund*) of India formed *circa* 6500 years ago and continued to the present day has gone unnoticed. This failure to notice is simply because evidence of symbolic forms is all around us. As a dialectical continuum stretching from Kanyakumari to Kashmir, from Dholavira to Dacca, symbolic forms have left hundreds of traces in India, in the Fertile Crescent and Ancient Near East and along the coastline Magan, Dilmun settlements of Persian Gulf. "Although a Meluhhan village (e-duru me-luh-ha) integrated under the jurisdiction of Girsu/Lagash in southern Mesopotamia has been known since Sargonic times, it has never previously been identified with a specific place name. In this article the Meluhhan village has now, for the first time, been connected in a Ur III text with the well-known village/town of Guabba (Gu-ab-ba-ki) based on the (twice) published text MVN 7 420 = ITT 4 8024 from Ur III Girsu."[59] Citing a cuneiform tablet inscription of Sargon of Akkad (2370-2316 BCE), Dhavalikar notes that the boats of Dilmun, Magan and Meluhha were moored at the quay in his capital (Leemans, WF, 1960, *Foreign Trade in the Old Babylonian Period as revealed by texts from Southern Mesopotamia*, EJ Brill, Leiden, p. 11). The goods imported include agate, carnelian, shell, ivory, varieties of wood and copper. Dhavalikar cites a reference to the people or 'sons' of Meluhha who had undergone a process of acculturation into Mesopotamian society of Ur III times cf. Parpola, S., A. Parpola and RH Brunswwig, Jr., 1977, The Meluhha Village: evidence of acculturation of Harappan traders in the late Third Millennium Mesopotamia, *JESHO*, 20 , p.152. Oppenheim describes Meluhha as the land of seafarers. (Oppenheim, AL, 1954, The seafaring merchants of Ur, *JAOS*, 74: 6-17). Dhavalikar notes the name given to a rāga of classical Indian (Hindustani) music – maluha kedār – which may indicate maluha as a geographical connotation as in the name of another rāga called Gujarī Todi. Noting a pronunciation variant for meluhha, melukkha, the form is noted as closer to Prākṛt *milakkhu* (Jaina Sūtras, *SBE* XLV, p. 414, n.) cognate Pali *malikkho* or *malikkhako* (Childer's *Pali Dictionary*). Prākṛt *milakkhu* or Pali *malikkho* are cognate with the Sanskrit word *mleccha* (References cited include Mahabharata, Patanjali). Jayaswal (Jayaswal, KP, 1914, On the origin of Mlechcha, *ZDMG*, 68: pp. 719-720) takes the Sanskrit representation to be cognate with Semitic melekh (Hebrew) meaning 'king'.

According to Geiger and Kern, the Pali term, milāca meaning 'forest dweller' was the original variant of milakkhu and was used in Jatakas and Digha Nikaya (Wilhelm 1956: 524). [Pali lexicon: Milāca [by -- form to milakkha, viâ *milaccha>*milacca> milāca: Geiger, *P.Gr.* 622; Kern, *Toev.* s. v.] a wild man of the woods, non -- Aryan, barbarian J iv.291 (not with C.=janapadā), cp. luddā m. ibid., and milāca -- puttā J v.165 (where C. also expls by bhojaputta, i. e. son of a villager).]

A milakkhu is disconnected from Vāk [refined speech, for e.g. samskṛtam, as distinguished from the natural (spoken dialect or *lingua franca*) Prākṛt] and does not speak Vedic; he spoke Prākṛt. [Pali lexicon: milakkha [cp. Ved. Sk. mleccha barbarian, root mlecch, onomat. after the strange sounds of a foreign tongue, cp. babbhara & mammana] a barbarian, foreigner, outcaste, hillman S v.466; J vi.207; DA i.176; SnA 236 (°mahātissa -- thera Np.), 397 (°bhāsā foreign dialect). The word occurs also in form milakkhu (q. v.).] Samskṛta (refined speech) is distinguished from asura, pisaca, mleccha as dialects with incorrect pronunciation of *Samskṛtam.*

Mleccha in Sanskrit is milakkhu in Pali, and the term describes those who dwell on the outskirts of a village. [Shendge 1977, pp.389-390: "Mleccha first occurs in śB III.2.1.24...The point made towards the end of the passage is that those who speak like Asuras are the mlecchas...But from the usage of the word milakkhu (as in Dīghanikāya III.264, Samyuttanikāya V.466, Vinaya III.28 etc.), it seems to be more a generic term used to describe all those who lived in the outskirts of the village (*paccantimesu janapadesu pacc*ājāyanti aviññātāresu milakkhesu, i.e., born on the outskirts of the janapada amongst the unknown milakkhus)."]. [Pali lexicon: Milakkhu [the Prk. form (A -- Māgadhī, cp. Pischel, *Prk. Gr.* 105, 233) for P. milakkha] a non -- Aryan D iii.264; Th 1, 965 (°rajana "of foreign dye" trsl.; Kern, *Toev.* s. v. translates "vermiljoen kleurig"). As milakkhuka at Vin iii.28, where Bdhgh expls by "Andha -- Damil' ādi."] Śathapatha Brāhmaṇa [3.2.1(24)], a Vedic text (ca. 8th century BCE) uses the word mleccha as a noun referring to Asuras who ill-pronounce or speak an imprecise language: *tatraitāmapi Vākamūduḥ | upajijñāsyāṃ sa mlecastasmānna brāhmaṇo mlecedasuryāhaiṣā vā natevaiṣa dviṣatāṃ sapatnānāmādatte Vākaṃ te 'syāttavacasaḥ parābhavanti ya evametadveda.* This is a remarkable reference to mleccha (meluhha) as a language in the ancient Indian tradition. Pali texts *Digha Nikāya* and *Vinaya*, also denotes milakkha as a language (*milakkha bhāsā*). Comparable to the reference in Manu, a Jaina text (*Pannavana*, 1.37) also described two groups of speakers (people?): *ārya* and *milakkhu.* Pāṇini also observes the imprecise nature of mleccha language by using the terms: *avyaktayam* Vāk*i* (X, 1663) and *mleccha avyakte śabde* (1.205). This is echoed in Patanjali's reference to *apaśabda.*

The term, mleccha, should be differentiated from another term, pāṣaṇḍa, who were opposed to the doctrines of the times. There is no indication whatsoever in any text that *mleccha* were pāṣaṇḍa; the *mleccha* were in fact an integral and a dominant part of the community called in the Ṛgveda *bhāratam janam* – the people of the nation of Bhārata (RV 3.53.12).

The *ṛṣi* of the *sūkta* is *Viśvāmitra Gāthina.*
Ya ime rodasī ubhe aham indram atuṣṭavam
viśvāmitrasya rakṣati brahmedam bhāratam janam
RV 3.53.12 I have made Indra glorified by these two, heaven and earth, and this prayer of viśvāmitra protects the people of Bhārata. [Made Indra glorified: *indram atuṣṭavam* — the verb is the third preterite of the casual, I have caused to be praised; it may mean: I praise Indra, abiding between heaven and earth, i.e. in the firmament].

Mleccha as *bhāratam janam*

The evidence is remarkable that almost every single glyph or glyptic element of the Indus script can be read rebus using the repertoire of artisans (lapidaries working with precious shell, ivory, stones and terracotta, mine-workers, metal-smiths working with a variety of minerals, furnaces and other tools) who created the inscribed objects and used many of them to authenticate their trade transactions. Many of the inscribed objects are seen to be calling cards of the professional artisans, listing their professional skills and repertoire and/or repertoire of *karṇī,* supercargo for a boat shipment.

Similarly, there is no indication whatsoever that mleccha were a distinct linguistic entity. The only differentiation indicated in the early texts that mleccha is 'unrefined' speech, that is, the *lingua franca* (as distinct from the dialects used in mantra-s or Samskṛtam).

Thus mleccha is a reference to a common dialect, the spoken tongue in the Indic language family.

Dhavalikar notes: "Sengupta (1971) has made out a strong case for identifying mlecchas with the Phoenicians. He proposes to derive the word mleccha from Moloch or Molech and relates it to Melek or Melqart which was the god of the Phoenicians. But the Phoenicians flourished in the latter half of the second and the first half of the first millennium when the Harappan civilization was a thing of the past." (MK Dhavalikar, 1997, Meluhha, the land of copper, *South Asian Studies*, 13:1, p. 276).

Worterbuch (St. Petersburg Dictionary), Hemacandra's *Abhidāna Cintāmaṇi* (IV.105), lexicons of Monier Williams and Apte give 'copper' as one of the meanings of the lexeme *mleccha.*

Gudea (ca. 2200 BCE) under the Lagash dynasty brought *usu* wood and gold dust and carnelian from Meluhha. Ibbi-Sin

(2029-2006 BCE) under the third dynasty of Ur "imported from Meluhha copper, wood used for making chairs and dagger sheaths, *mesu* wood, and the multi-coloured birds of ivory."

Dhavalikar argues for the identification of Gujarat with Meluhha (interpreted as a region and as copper ore of Gujarat) and makes a reference to *Viṣṇu Purāṇa* (IV,24) which refers to Gujarat as *mleccha* country.[60] The word me-la-hha may also be cognate with: meṛh, meḍh, 'copper merchant' (G.). Another example of a substrate term: Sumerian tibira, tabira (Akkadian. LU2 URUDU-NAGAR =. "[person] copper-carpenter"); a word indicating borrowing from a substrate. In Pkt. tambira = copper. According to Gernot Wilhelm, the Hurrian version of tabira is: tab-li 'copper founder'; tab-iri 'the one who has cast (copper)'.

Meluhha was also a region from which traded many types of stones. Lipshur litanies state: 'Melukkha...is the land of carnelian' (Sumerian NA4.GUG, Akkadian sa_mtu). In the 17th century BC, the Neo-Assyrian king Esarhaddon called himself, 'king of the kings of Dilmun, Magan, and Melukkha'. The Sumerian myth Enki and the World Order has Enki exclaiming: 'Let the magilum-boats of Melukkha transport gold and silver for exchange!' Enki and Ninkhursag (lines 1-9, Tr. by B. Alster) has references to the products of Melukkha: 'The land Tukrish shall transport gold from Kharali, lapis lazuli, and bright...to you. The land Melukkha shall bring carnelian, desirable and precious, sissoo-wood from Magan, excellent mangroves, on big-ships! The land Markhashi will (bring) precious stones, *dušia*-stones, (to hand) on the breast, mighty, diorite-stones, u-stones, *śumin*-stones to you!' [The cuneiform characters meluh-ha should be read with an alternative phonetic value: *me-la-h-ha* who are a clan from a Sindhi seafarers called Mohāna.] The city-state of Lagash (ca. 2060: king Shulgi) records a toponym about the presence of a 'Melukkhan village'. The word 'Melukkha' also appears, occasionally, as a personal name in cuneiform texts of the Old Akkadian and Ur III periods. Seals of the Indian civilization have been found in Mesopotamia and Iran at Kish (modern Tell Ingharra), Ur, Tell

Asmar, Nippur (modern Nuffar), and Susa; a shard with an inscription has been found at Ras al-Junayz, the southeastern extremity of the Oman Peninsula; seal impressions of the civilization have been found at Umma (Tell Jokha) and Tepe Yahya.

Harappan control over the Oman Sea

"Oman peninsula/Makkan lies half way between the two main civilization centres of the third millennium Middle East: Mesopotamia and the Indus valley... an increasing influence of Harappan civilization on Eastern Arabia during the last two centuries of the third millennium. This influence seems to strengthen during the early second millennium where proper Harappan objects are found all over the Oman peninsula: a cubic stone weight at Shimal, sherds of Harappan storage jars on several sites including Hili 8 (period III). Maysar and Ra's Al-Junayz bears a Harappan inscription and Tosi (forth.) has emphasized the importance of this discovery for knowledge of Harappan control over the Oman Sea."[61]

It is also possible to locate Meluhha (mleccha) in the region around Gandhāra. *pracetasah putraśatam rājānah sarva eva te // mleccharāṣṭrādhipāh sarve udīcīm diśam āśritāh* (Trans. 'all these 100 kings, sons of pracetās (a descendant of a 'druhyu'), kings of mleccha kingdoms, are 'adjacent' (āśrita) to the 'northern direction.' This signifies Gandhāra.[62] This can be construed as a reference to a migration of the sons of Pracetas towards the northern direction to become kings of the mleccha states. The son of Yayati's third son, Druhyu, was Babhru, whose son and grandsons were Setu, Arabdha, Gandhara, Dharma, Dhṛta, Durmada and Praceta. It is notable that Pracetas is related to Dharma and Dhṛta, who are the principal characters of the Great Epic, the Mahābhārata. It should be noted that a group of people frequently mentioned in the Great Epic are the mleccha, an apparent designation of a group within the country, with Bhāratam janam (Bhārata people). This is substantiated by the fact that Bhagadatta, the king of Pragjyotiṣa is referred to as mleccha and he is also said to have ruled over two yavana kings (2.13). Nandana, another commentator of *Mānava Dharma śāstra.* 10.45, defines *āryaVāk as samskṛtaVāk*. Thus, according to Medhātithi, neither habitation nor mleccha speech is the ground for regarding

groups as Dasyus, but it is because of their particular names Barbara etc., that they are so regarded. These people were brought over the sea safely by Indra, as noted by this ṛca. This ṛca also notes that Yadu and Turvaśa (are) dāsa; and that Turvaśu is a son of Yayāti. The sons of Yayāti were to rule over people such as Yavana, Bhoja and Yādava. Turvaśu and Yadu crossed the oceans to come into Bhāratavarṣa. In this ṛca., 'samudra' can be interpreted only as an ocean. The ocean crossed by Indra, may be not too far from Sindhu. Sindhu is a 'natural ocean frontier' in Ṛgveda. Given the activities of the Meluhha along the Makran Coast (300 km. south of Mehergarh, in the neighbourhood of Karachi), Gulf of Kutch and Gulf of Khambat, (evidence? *Turbinella pyrum* —śankha-bangle found in a woman's grave in Mehergarh, dated to c. 6500 BCE, yes 7th millennium BCE; the type of shell found nowhere else in the world excepting the coastline of Sindhu sāgara upto to the Gulf of Mannar).
The ocean referred to may be the ocean in the Gulf of Kutch and was situated with a number of dvīpas. In places north of Lamgham district, i.e. north bank of river Kabul, near Peshawar were regions known as Mi-li-ku, the frontier of the mleccha lands.[63] *Harivamśa* 85.18-19 locates the mleccha in the Himalayan region and mleccha are listed with yavana, *śaka, darada, pārada, tuṣāra, khaśa* and *pahlava* in north and north-west Bhāratavarṣa: *sa viv ṛddho yad ā rāj ā yavan ānām mah ābalāh tata enam nṛpā mlecch āh sams'rity ānuyayaus tad ā śakās tuṣār ā daradāh pāradās tan:gaṇāh khasśāh pahlavāh śataśaścānye mlecch ā haimavat ās tathā. Matsya Purāṇa* 144.51-58 provides a list. Pracetā had a hundred sons all of whom ruled in mleccha regions in the north. [Matsya Purāṇa 148.8-9; Bhāgavata Purāṇa IX.23.16.] Bhīṣma Parvan of Mahābhārata notes that mleccha jāti people lived in Yavana, Kāmboa, Dāruṇā regions and are listed together with several other peoples of the northern and north-western parts of Bhāratavarṣa (MBh. VI.10.63-66: *uttarāścāpare mlecchā janā bharatasattama yavanāśca śaka, kāmbojā dārun.ā mlecchajātayah*).
In *Rāmāyaṇa* IV.42.10, Sugrīva is asked to search for Sītā in the northern lands of mleccha, pulinda, sūrasena, praṣalā, bhārata, kuru, madraka, kamboja and yavana before proceeding to

Himavat: *tatra mlecchān pulindāmśūrasen āmś tathaiva ca prasthalān bharatāmścaiva kurūmsśca saha madraih*. Mlecchas came from the valley adjoining the Himalaya. [Rājatarangiṇī , VII. 2762-64.] When Sagara, son of Bāhu, was prevented from destroying śaka, Yavana, Kāmboa, Pārada and Pāhlava after he recovered his kingdom, Vasiṣṭha, the family priest of Sagara, absolved these people of their duties but Sagara commanded the Yavana to shave the upper half of their heads, the Pārada to wear long hair and Pahlava to let their beards grow. Sagara also absolved them of their duty to offer yajna to agni and to study the Veda. [Vāyu Purāṇa 88.122. 136- 43; Brahmāṇḍa Purāṇa 3.48.43-49; 63.119-34.] This is how these Yavana, Pārada and Pahlava also became mleccha. [Viṣṇu Purāṇa 4.3.38-41.] The implication is that prior to Sagara's command, these kṣatriya communities did respect Vasiṣṭha as their priest, studied the Veda and performed yajna. [Harivamśa 10.41-45.] Śaka who were designated as kings of mleccha jāti by Bhaṭṭa Utpala (10th century) in his commentary on Bṛhatsamhitā, were defeated by Candragupta II. That the mleccha were also adored as ṛṣi is clear from the verse of *Bṛhatsamhitā* 2.15:

mlecchā hi yavanās teṣu samyak śāstram kadam sthitam ṛṣivat te 'pi pūjyante kim punar daivavid dvijāh

(The yavana are mleccha, among them this science is duly established; therefore, even they (although mleccha) are honoured as ṛṣi; how much more (praise is due to an) astrologer who is a brāhmaṇa'). *Bṛhatsamhitā* 14.21 confirms that the yavana, śaka and pahlava lived on the west. Similarly, Konow notes that Sai-wang (Saka King) mentioned in Chinese accounts should be interpreted as Saka Muruṇḍa and the territory he occupied as Kāpiśa. [Sten Konow, *CII*, vol. II, pp. xx ff; Sten Konow, EI, no. 20 'Taxila Inscription of the Year 136', vol. XIV, pp. 291-2.] Śaka migrated to Bhāratavarṣa through Arachosia via the Bolan Pass into the lower Sindhu, a region called Indo_Scythia by Greek geographers and called śaka-dvīpa in Bhāratiya texts.[64] Another view expressed by Thomas is that the migration was through Sindh and the valley

of the Sindhu River. [FW Thomas, 'Sakastana', JRAS, 1906, p. 216.] Kalhaṇa notes that Jalauka, a son of Aśoka took possession of Kāśmīra, advanced as far as Kanauj, after crushing a horse of mleccha. [Rājatarangiṇī, 1.107-8.] Greek invasions occurred later, during the reign of Puṣyamitraśunga (c. 185-150 BCE). The regions inhabited by the 'milakkha' could be the Vindhyan region. The term, 'mleccha' of which 'milakkha' is a variant, could as well have denoted the indigenous people (Nahali?) or of Bhāratavarṣa who had lived on the Sarasvati River basin and who moved towards other parts of Bhāratavarṣa after the gradual desiccation of the river, over a millennium, between c. 2500 and 1500 BCE. Medhātithi, commenting on the verse of Manu, defines a language as mleccha : *asad avidyam ān\ārthās ādhu śabdatayā vāk mleccha ucyate yathā śabarāṇām kirātānām anyeyām va antyānām*: Medhātithi on*Mānava Dharmaśāstra* X.45 – 'Language is called mleccha because it consists of words that have no meaning or have the wrong meaning or are wrong in form. To this class belong the languages of such low-born tribes as the śabara-s, Kirāta and so forth…'… He further proceeds to explain that āryaVāk is refined speech and the language of the inhabitants of āryāvarta, but only of those who belong to the four varṇa-s. The others are called Dasyus.: ibid. – *āryaVāka āryāvartam vāsinas te cāturvarṇy ādanyajātīyatvena prasiddhas tadā dasyava ucyante* 'Arya (refined) language is the language of the inhabitants of āryāvarta. Those persons being other than the four varṇa-s are called Dasyus.'
In Dhammapada's commentary on Petuvathu, Dwaraka is associated with Kamboja as its Capital or its important city.[The Buddhist Concepts of Spirits, p 81, Dr B. C. Law.] See evidence below:

"*Yasa asthaya gachham Kambojam dhanharika/ ayam kamdado yakkho iyam yakham nayamasai// iyam yakkham gahetvan sadhuken pasham ya/ yanam aaropyatvaan khippam gaccham Davarkān iti* " [Buddhist Text *Khudak Nikaya* (P.T.S)]

Mleccha who came to the Rājasūya also included those from forest and frontier areas (MBh. III. 48.19: *sāgarān ūpagāmścaiva ye ca paṭṭaṇavāsinah simhal ān barbarān mlecchān ye ca jān:galavāsinah*). Bhīmasena proceeded east towards Lohitya (Brahmaputra) and had conquered several mleccha people who bestowed on him wealth of various kinds (MBh. II.27.23-24:

suhmānāmādhipam caiva ye ca sāgaravāsinah sarvān mlecchagaṇāmścaiva vijigye bharatarṣabhah evam bahu vidhān deśān vijitya pavanātmajah vasu tebhya upādya lauhityam agad balī.[65]

Celebrations at the Kalinga capital of Duryodhana were attended by preceptors and mleccha kings from the south and east of Bhārata (MBh. XII.4.8: *ete cānye ca bahavo dakṣinām diśām āśritah mlecchā āryāśca rāj ānah prācyodicyāśca bhārata*).

Bhāgadatta, the great warrior of Prāgjyotiṣa accompanied by mleccha people inhabiting marshy regions of the sea- coast (*sāgarānūpavāsibhih*), attends the Rājasūya of Yudhiṣṭhira (MBh. II.31.9-10:*prāgjyotiṣaśca nṛpatir bhagadatto mahāyaśāh saha sarvais tathā mlecchaih sāgarānūpavāsibhih*). This is perhaps a reference ot the marshy coastline of Bengal. *Amarakośa* II, Bhūmivarga – 6: pratyanto mlecchade śah syāt; Sarvānanda in his commentary, ṭīkāsarvasva, elaborates that mleccha deśa denotes regions without proper conduct such as Kāmarūpa: *bhāratavarṣasyāntadeśah śiṣṭācārā rahitah kāmarūpādih mlecchadeśāh* [Nāmalingānuśāsana, with commentary ṭīkāsarvasva, of Sarvānanda (ed. Ganapati śāstri)]; he also cites Manu that where four varṇa-s are not established that region is mlecchadeśa. A contemporary of Harṣavardhana was Bhāskaravarman of Kāmarūpa; this king was supplanted by another dynasty founded by śālastambha who was known as a mleccha overlord.[66]

The adjective ārya is used to differentiate the language from mleccha. Both ārya speech and mleccha speech constitute the prākṛta, the ancient form of the *lingua franca* of India. A term for speech was bhāratī (vāk) which is also related to the language of the Bharatas, giving the name bhāratavarṣa for India. "The vocabulary (of Sanskrit) was further enriched from outside Indo-Aryan itself. The pre-existing vernaculars made a sizeable contribution to the Sanskrit vocabulary…Even when all these new words have been accounted for there remains a considerable number of words in classical Sanskrit whose origin is unknown. Most were no doubt originally deśī words in the Indian terminology, and since the linguistic complexity of pre-Aryan India must have been greater than anything that now appears, we should not be surprised to find so many words whose origin remains unexplained. Such in brief are the main changes which took place in Sanskrit between the early Vedic and the classical period…The Sanskrit of the Jains is influenced by the language of the earlier Prākṛt literature in the same way as the Sanskrit of the Buddhists. In vocabulary it draws more extensively than contemporary classical Sanskrit on vernacular sources, and words familiar later in Modern Indo-Aryan are often first recorded here…(Dravidian languages) were earliest influenced by Prākṛt, which was the administrative language of the Sātavāhanas and their immediate successors…The Prākṛt influence in these languages, dating from the earlier period, is rapidly overlaid by extensive borrowings from the Sanskrit vocabulary. In their early classical form these languages draw on Sanskrit wholesale, and the process was continued in the succeeding periods."[67]

Meluhha, Mleccha areas: Sarasvati River Basin and Coastal Regions of Gujarat, Baluchistan, Ancient Near East

Meluhha referred to in Sumerian and old Akkadian texts refers to an area in Sarasvati Civilization; Asko and Simo Parpola add: '...probably, including NW India with Gujarat as well as eastern Baluchistan'.[68]

The prehistory of the civilization is also all around us emphasizing the cultural continuity for over 6500 years to the present day. Our ancestors have delivered the messages in unambiguous, clearly identifiable glyphs which compose over 7,000 epigraphs anchored on lexemes of the linguistic area of the civilization. The sounds represented by the hieroglyphs relate to the sounds of a language called mleccha -- *Milakkha bhāsā* !

We had somehow not noticed the postman for the last 150 years, ever since the first seal was discovered close to the Sarasvati river basin. It is possible to identify both the *mleccha/ meluhha* messenger and the *mleccha/ meluhha* symbolic forms. To quote, Tolkāppiyam, "ellāc collum poruḷ kuṟittanavē" (Tol. Col. Peya. 1), i.e. all words are semantic indicators. Hence, the use of rebus to denote *res* 'things'.

Three stakes shown on Sit Shamshi bronze compare with three stakes on a cylinder seal:

This large bronze platform shows a religious ceremony. In the center are two men in ritual nudity, surrounded by religious furnishings: vases for libations, perhaps bread for offerings, steles; in a stylized urban landscape: a multi-tiered tower, a temple on a terrace, a sacred wood. Middle-Elamite period (15th-12th century B.C.)

Three stalks are shown next to the large storage jar on Sit Shamshi bronze which narrates a Meluhha offering to the sun divinity and ancestors. This hieroglyph composition is the signifier of a sacred smithy. *kolom* 'three' Rebus: *kole.l* 'smithy, temple'; *kolami* 'smithy, forge'. *kaṇḍa* -- m.n. ' joint of stalk, stalk (Pali) *kāṇḍá* काण्डः m. the stalk or stem of a reed, grass, or the like, straw. In a compound with dan 5 (p. 221*a*, l. 13) the word is spelt *kāḍ*. Rebus: *kaṇḍa* 'stone (ore)(Gadba)' Ga. (Oll.) *kanḍ*, (S.) *kanḍu* (pl. kanḍkil) stone (DEDR 1298). *gaḍa*-- n. 'large stone' (Prākṛt) *kāṭha* m. 'rock' (Sanskrit) The two polished pillars are *kunda* 'pillar' *dula* 'pair' Rebus: *dul* 'cast metal'. *kunda* 'turner's lathe'. *kũdnu* 'to shape smoothly, smoothe, carve, hew'(Nepali)(CDIAL 3295).

Allograph: *khaḍḍu* -- 'ram'. [Cf. words listed under **kaḍḍa* --] P. *khāḍū* m. 'hill goat'; WPah.J. *khāḍū* m. 'ram', kṭg. (kc.) *kháḍḍu* m., poet. *khaṛu* m. (Him.I 31 all prob. conn. K. *kaṭh*, stem *kaṭ* -- , < *kaṭṭa -- 2). (CDIAL 3790a). **kaḍḍa* 'young male animal'. Or. *kaṛā* 'castrated male buffalo, *kaṛāi* 'young buffalo cow that has not calved', *kaṛhi* 'lamb that has not borne'; Bi. *kāṛā* m., °*ṛī* f. 'buffalo calf', H. *kāṛā* m.(CDIAL 2658). Bi. *kaṛrū* 'buffalo calf'. (CDIAL 2659). Rebus: *gaḍa*-- n. 'large stone' (Prākṛt)

The argument: The Khafaje seal hieroglyphs signify a catalog of a smithy/forge.

Provenience: Khafaje Kh. VII 256 Jemdet Nasr (ca. 3000 - 2800 BCE) Frankfort, Henri: *Stratified Cylinder Seals from the Diyala Region.* Oriental Institute Publications 72. Chicago: University of Chicago Press, no. 34. Mythological scene: tailless lion or bear standing erect behind tree; two goats feeding at other side of tree; another tree, with bird in branches, behind monster; three-lowered buildings with door at left side; watercourse along bottom of scene. Gray limestone. 4.1x3.5cm.[i]

The cylinder seal is a catalog of a smithy: copper, iron alloy smith, turner, hard alloy metal tools, pots and pans.

Frame of a building: *sā̃gāḍā* m. ' frame of a building ' (M.)(CDIAL 12859) Rebus: jaṅgaḍ 'entrustment articles' *sā̃gaṛh* m. ' line of entrenchments, stone walls for defence ' (Lahnda).(CDIAL 12845) Allograph: *saṅgaḍa* 'lathe'. *sang* 'stone', *gaḍa* 'large stone'.

The two animals are: markhor, antelope. *miṇḍāl* 'markhor' (Tōrwālī) *meḍho* a ram, a sheep (Gujarati)(CDIAL 10120); rebus: *mẽṛhẽt, meḍ* 'iron' (Munda.Ho.) *mr̤eka, melh* 'goat' (Telugu. Brahui) Rebus: *melukkha* '*milakkha*, copper'. *khāḍū* m. 'hill goat' (Punjabi) Rebus: *gaḍa* n. 'large stone' (Prākṛt)

करडणें or करंडणें [karaḍaṇē or ṅkaraṇḍaṇēṃ] v c To gnaw or nibble; to wear away by biting (Marathi). Rebus: *karaḍa* 'hard alloy'. करडा [karaḍā] Hard from alloy--iron, silver &c. (Marathi)

karaḍa *'duck'* karaṇḍa 'duck' (Sanskrit) karaṛa 'a very large aquatic bird' (Sindhi) Rebus: *karaḍa* 'hard alloy' *karaḍa* 'wave' *Rebus: karaḍa* 'hard alloy' *karaḍa* 'panther' Rebus: *karaḍa* 'hard alloy'. *khōṇḍa* a stock or stump (Marathi); *khōṇḍa* 'leafless tree' (Marathi). *Rebus: kõdār* 'turner' (Bengali) *kõdā* 'to turn in a lathe' (Bengali). *kāṇḍa* 'flowing water' Rebus: *kāṇḍā* 'metalware, tools, pots and pans'.

Alternative: kul 'tiger' (Santali); kōlu id. (Telugu) kōlupuli = Bengal tiger (Te.) *कोल्हा [* kōlhā] *कोल्हें [*kōlhēṃ] A jackal (Marathi) Rebus: kole.l 'temple, smithy' (Kota.) kol = pañcalōha, a metallic alloy containing five metals (Tamil): copper, brass, tin, lead and iron (Sanskrit); an alternative list of five metals: gold, silver, copper, tin (lead), and iron (dhātu; Nānārtharatnākara. 82; Mangarāja's Nighaṇṭu. 498)(Kannada) kol, kolhe, 'the koles, iron smelters speaking a language akin to that of Santals' (Santali) Skanda Purāṇa refers to *kol* as a mleccha community. (Hindu *śabdasagara*).

kolhe, 'the koles, are an aboriginal tribe of iron smelters speaking a language akin to that of Santals' (Santali) kōla m. name of a degraded tribe Hariv. Pk. Kōla — m.; B. kol name of a Muṇḍā tribe (CDIAL 3532). A Bengali lexeme confirms this: কোল[1] [kōla[1]] an aboriginal tribe of India; a member of this tribe. (Bengali) That in an early form of Indian linguistic area, *kol* means 'man' gets substantiated by a Nahali and Assamese glosses: kola 'woman'. See also: Wpah. Khaś.kuṛi, cur. kuḷī, cam. kŏḷā ' boy ', Sant. Muṇḍari koṛa ' boy ', kuṛi ' girl ', Ho koa, kui, Kūrkū kōn, kōnjē). Prob. separate from RV. kṛ́tā -- ' girl ' H. W. Bailey TPS 1955, 65; K. kūrü f. ' young girl ', kash. kōṛī, ram. kuṛhī; L. kuṛā m. ' bridegroom ', kuṛī f. ' girl, virgin, bride ', awāṇ. kuṛī f. ' woman '; P. kuṛī f. ' girl, daughter ', (CDIAL 3295). कारकोळी or ळ्या [kārakōḷī or ḷyā] a Relating to the country कार-country कार- कोळ--a tribe of Bráhmans (Marathi). *kole.l* 'temple' Rebus: kole.l 'smithy'. khōṇḍa A tree of which the head and branches are broken off, a stock or stump: also the lower portion of the trunk—that below the branches. (Marathi) Rebus 1: kõdā 'to turn in a lathe' (Bengali) Rebus 2: koḍ 'workshop' (Gujarati) Glyh of flowing water: kāṇḍa 'flowing water' ***खांडा*** [khāṇḍā] A division of a field. (Marathi) Rebus: kāṇḍā 'metalware, tools, pots and pans'.Thus, the entire hieroglyphic composition of the cylinder seal is a smithy catalog:

karaḍ 'nibbling' karaḍa 'duck' *karaḍa* 'wave' *karaḍa* 'panther' करडी [karaḍī] f (See करडई) Safflower -- all connoting reinforcing, Rebus: *karaḍa* 'hard alloy' and work of kõdār 'turner' in kole.l 'smithy, temple' producing: kāṇḍā 'metalware, tools, pots and pans'.

British Museum No. 89147 Akkadian 2400-2200 BCE. Chalcedony. Ruler: Puzur-shullat. Brown and white quartz var chalcedony cylinder seal, contest scene; two antithetical groups, each consisting of a bearded hero (full face - one of which is possibly Gilgamesh) who is naked except for a belt and who is kneeling on one knee and wrestling with a lion; one arm is round the lion's neck, thus bending it right back, while the other is reaching round the lion's body to grasp it's tail. Terminals, a frame which must have contained two lines of inscription, now erased. The lines framing the inscription have been changed into three fronds. At the bottom are two shapes which were probably added to convert the design into a sheaf of corn. Terminal also contains an inscription; edges of seal bevelled; seal is slightly chipped.

Sumerian Inscription Transliteration: [P]U-SA -PA / saga BAD / sag-gul-lum dub-sar / ir-zu
Inscription Translation: Puzar-Shullat, priest of Duram: Shakullum,scribe is your servant.
Inscription Comment: 5 ll.; identifies the seal owner as Shakullum, a servant of Puzur-Shullat, priest of the city of Duram.

According to the catalogue this seal has probably been published more than any other seal. A great many of the early drawings of it are inaccurate, however, particularly as regards the hero's arm that clasps the lion around the neck. Frankfort, Henri, The art and architecture of the Ancient Orient, Harmondsworth, Middlesex, Penguin Books, 1954. Pl. 45A.

A line drawing of the seal impression is presented:

Sumerian cylinder seal.[69]

kāṭhī काठी (काष्ट S) The stalk, stem, or trunk of a plant. *khātī* 'wheelwright' (Hindi) *āra* 'six hair curls'. *kolom* 'three' Rebus: *kolami* 'smithy, forge'. *arye* 'lion' Rebus: *āra* 'brass'. *dula* 'pair' Rebus: *dul* 'cast metal'. If the panther is also signified, *karaḍa* 'panther' Rebus: *karaḍa* 'hard alloy'. Thus, the message is: cast brass smithy of *ārakāṭi* 'sailor'. *khāti dul āra karaḍa kolami* 'wheelwright cast brass hard alloy smithy'.

Shahdad cylinder seal: copper turner, smith- artisan, merchant. *khōṇḍa* 'leafless tree' (Marathi). Rebus: *kõdār* 'turner' (Bengali) [Allograph: खोंड [khōṇḍa] m A young bull, a bullcalf. (Marathi)] *kola* 'woman' (Nahali) Rebus: *kol* 'working in iron' (Tamil) *kolom* 'sapling' Rebus: *kolami* 'smithy, forge'. Tagaraka 'tabernae montana' tulip flower Rebus: *tagara* 'tin (cassiterite)' *khāḍū* m. 'hill goat' (Punjabi) Rebus: *gaḍa*-- n. 'large stone' (Prākṛt) krammara 'turn back' Rebus: kamar 'artisan'. *kūdī, kūṭī* bunch of twigs (Sanskrit) Rebus: *kuṭhi* 'smelting furnace' (Santali)

The motif of nine twigs is comparable to Mohenjo-Daro seal impression m0296: lo, no 'nine' (B.); loa 'ficus religiosa' (Santali); rebus: loh 'metal' (Skt.); loa 'copper' (Santali)

Bull on the field, bottom left:Hieroglyph: *ḍhangar* 'bull' Rebus:

dhangar 'blacksmith' (Maithili) *ḍangar* 'blacksmith' (Hindi) *ārakāṭi* 'sailor' *khāti* 'wheelwright' arye 'lion' Rebus: *āra* 'brass' 'oxide of iron' (Kannada); *malla* 'wrestler' *malla, mallā-malli* pugilistic encounter. Rebus A ملاح *mallāḥ*, s.m. (5th) (adj. sup. of ملح) A sailor, a boatman, a mariner, a waterman. Pl. ملاحان *mallāḥān*. See مانګي and مهانه (Pashto) *āṟa* 'to make' as in: *uppāṟa, kammā ṟa* 'salt-maker, artisan'(Kannada) *āṟṟu* 'to make' (Tamil) *kaṭi* 'to cut a stone with chisel' (Kannada. Marathi) *kāṭi* 'name of a Golla' (Kannada).

Top register, centerpiece: *kōlu 'tiger' Rebus: kol* = pañcalōha, a metallic alloy; *meḍha* 'polar star' (Marathi). *meḍ* 'iron' (Ho.Mu.) *pāsa* -- m. ' spear '(Prākṛt) Rebus: *pās* 'silver ingot, iron share of harrow '.(Marathi) Alternative Hieroglyph: īthī, īṭī ' spear ' Rebus: ఇటిక [iṭika] or ఇటికె or ఇటుక *iṭika*. [Tel.] n.

Brick. ఇటికెలుకోయు or ఇటుకచేయు to make bricks. వెయ్యి యిటుక కాల్చిరి they burnt 1000 bricks.

British Museum No. 113871 Third Dynasty of Ur (inscription) Ur-Nammu. Akkadian. Ca. 2100 -2000 BCE. Quartz var crystal cylinder; contest scene; two antithetical groups consisting of two inverted lions in the centre, facing each other. Each is being attacked by a bearded hero…who is naked except for a belt. The hero on the left grasps one of the lions by the off hind leg and plunges a dagger into it's entrails, while that on the right grasp both the other lion's hind legs. Between the two groups is a standard consisting of a spear surmounted by a lion pacing towards the right, with a six-pointed star on either side. Terminal, inscription in a frame above a bull which is pacing towards the right. The inscription is continued in the field between the figures of the second group of contestants. The perforation flares out the end. The seal is chipped. Inscription Transliteration:mes-lam-ta-e-a / lugal a zi-da / lagasa / digir-ra-ni / sur -ama-na-zadim / dumu sur-gish gigir (a)-ka-ge / mu-na-dim Inscription Translation: For Meslamtaea, the king, the true might of Lagash, his god: Sur-amana, stone-cutter, son of Sur-Gigira, has made (this seal).70

kul 'tiger' (Santali); *kōlu* id. (Telugu) kōlupuli = Bengal tiger (Te.) कोल्हा [kōlhā] कोल्हें [kōlhēṃ] A jackal (Marathi)
Rebus: *kole.l* 'temple, smithy' (Kota.) *kol* = pañcalōha, a metallic alloy containing five metals (Tamil): copper, brass, tin, lead and iron (Sanskrit); an alternative list of five metals: gold, silver, copper, tin (lead), and iron (dhātu; Nānārtharatnākara. 82; Mangarāja's Nighaṇṭu. 498)(Kannada) *kol, kolhe*, 'the *koles*, iron smelters speaking a language akin to that of Santals' (Santali) íṣṭakā f. ' brick ' VS., iṣṭikā -- f. MBh., iṣṭā -- f. BHSk. [Av. ištya -- n. Mayrhofer EWA i 94 and 557 with lit. <-> Pk. has disyllabic iṭṭā -- and no aspiration like most Ind. lggs.]Pa. iṭṭhakā -- f. ' burnt brick ', Pk. iṭṭagā -- , iṭṭā -- f.; Kho. uṣṭū ' sun -- dried brick, large clod of earth ' (→ Phal. iṣṭū́ m. NOPhal 27); L. iṭṭ, pl. iṭṭã f. '

brick ', P. iṭṭ f., N. ĩṭ, A. iṭā, B. iṭ, ĩṭ, Or. iṭā, Bi. ī˜ṭ, ī˜ṭā, Mth. ī˜ṭā, Bhoj. ī˜ṭi, H. ī˜ṭh, īṭ, ī˜ṭ, ĩṭā f., G. ĩṭi f., M. īṭ, vīṭ f., Ko. īṭ f. -- Deriv. Pk. iṭṭāla -- n. ' piece of brick '; B. iṭāl, °al ' brick ', M. iṭhāḷ f. ' a piece of brick heated red over which buttermilk is poured to be flavoured '. -- Si. uḷu ' tile ' see uṭa -- .S.kcch. eṭṭ f. ' brick ', Garh. ī˜ṭ; -- Md. īṭ ' tile ' ← Ind. (cf. H. M. īṭ).*iṣṭakālaya ' brick -- mould '. [íṣṭakā -- , ālaya --] M. iṭāḷẽ n. 'brick-mould' (CDIAL 1600).

īṭhī, īṭī ' spear ' (Hindi)(CDIAL 14298). A. zāṭhi ' lance, spear '; yaṣṭí f. ' stick, pole ' ŚBr.Or. jāṭhi ' iron rod used as a weapon '(CDIAL 10444).

kunta1 ' spear '. 2. *kōnta -- . [Perh. ← Gk. konto/s ' spear ' EWA i 229]1. Pk. kuṁta -- m. ' spear '; S. kundu m. ' spike of a top ', °dī f. ' spike at the bottom of a stick ', °diṛī, °dirī f. ' spike of a spear or stick '; Si. kutu ' lance '.2. Pa. konta -- m. ' standard '; Pk. koṁta -- m. ' spear '; H. kõt m. (f.?) ' spear, dart '; -- Si. kota ' spear, spire, standard ' perh. ← Pa.(CDIAL 3289).
prāsa m. ' throwing ' Br., ' barbed missile ' MBh. [√as2]Pa. pāsa -- m. ' a throw, spear '; Pk. pāsa -- m. ' spear '; K. prās m. ' customary return of a certain portion of gift sent by bride's father to husband's family on certain festive occasions, the portion so returned '; N. pāso ' anything unwanted that is left or deposited '; A. pah ' weapon, arrow '. (CDIAL 8969).

Allograph: pāśa1 m. ' die, dice ' MBh., °aka -- m. Mr̥cch. [Poss. with Lüders PhilInd 120 hyper -- sanskritism from MIA. pāsa(ka) -- < prāsaka -- m. ' die ' lex. (cf. prāsyati ' lays a wager ' TāṇḍBr. and prāsa --). It does not appear in any language differentiating pr -- from p -- or -- s -- from -- ś -- . Moreover the meaning ' lump of metal ' in N. H. M. may indicate a different origin] Pa. pāsaka -- m. ' die ', Pk. pāsaga -- m., Ku. pā̃so, N. B. pāsā; Or. pasā, (Bastar) pāsā ' game of dice ', OAw. sāri -- pāṁsā; H. pāsā m. ' die ' (→ P. pāsā m.), G. pāsɔ m., M. phāsā m. (infl. by forms of pāśa -- 2 ~ *spāśa -- with p -- ~ ph -- ?), Si. pasa -- äṭa. -- N. pāso

' head of an iron instrument (such as axe or spade) ' rather than < parśvadha -- ; Or. pasā ' iron ring through which plough iron is thrust '; H. pāsā m. ' lump, cube, lump of metal '; M. pās f. ' silver ingot, iron share of harrow '.(CDIAL 8132).

kṣurá m. ' razor ' RV., ' sharp barb of arrow ' R., °rī -- f. ' knife, dagger ' lex., °rikā -- f. Rājat. [√kṣur]ch -- forms, esp. in sense ' knife ', are wide -- spread outside dial. bounds: -- Sk. chūˇrī -- f. ' knife, dagger ' lex., churikā -- f. Kathās., chūr° lex., Pa. churikā -- f., NiDoc. kṣura; Pk. chura -- m. ' knife, razor, arrow ', °rī -- , °riā -- f. ' knife '; Gy. pal. číri ' knife, razor ', arm. čhuri ' knife ', eur. čuri f., SEeur. čhurí, Ḍ. čuri f., Kt. ̣curī´, ̣cuī; Dm. ̣chúri ' dagger '; Kal. ̣chū´ŕi ' knife '; Bshk. ̣chur ' dagger, knife ', Tor. ̣chū, Phal. ̣chūr f.; Sh. (Lor.) ̣cūr ' small knife '; S. churī f. ' knife with a hooked blade '; L. churī f. ' knife ', awān. churā m.; P. churā m. ' large knife ', °rī f. ' small do. ', Ku. churo, °rī; N. churā ' razor ', °ri ' knife '; A. suri ' knife ', B. churi; Or. churā ' dagger ', °rī ' knife '; Bi. chūrā ' razor '; Mth. chūr, °rā ' dagger, razor ', °rī ' small knife '; Bhoj. Aw. lakh. chūrā ' razor '; H. churā m. ' dagger, razor ', °rī f. ' knife '; G. charo m. ' large knife ', °rī f. ' small do. ' (Bloch LM 415 wrongly < tsáru -- : churī ← H. or M.), M. surā m., °rī f.; Si. siriya ' dagger '; -- Woṭ. čir ' dagger ' ← Psht. ← IA. Buddruss Woṭ 96.kh -- forms: Pa. khura -- m. ' razor '; Pk. khura -- m. ' knife, razor '; K. khūru m. ' razor '; S. khuryo m. ' grass -- scraper, tip of silver at the bottom of a scabbard '; WPah. bhal. khuro m. ' razor '; Ku. khuro -- muṇḍo ' the shaving of heads '; N. khuro ' head of a spear, ferrule of a stick, pin at the top or bottom of a door; A. B. khur ' razor ' (whence A. khurāiba ' to shave '), Or. khura; Bi. khūr ' razor ', khurā, °rī ' spiked part of the blade of a chopper which fits into the handle '; H. khurā m. ' iron nail to fix ploughshare '; Si. karaya ' razor '.WPah.kṭg. ċhúrɔ m. ' dagger ', Garh. khur, churī ' knife ', A. spel. churī AFD 216. (CDIAL 3727). kṣurapra ' sharp -- edged like a razor ' BhP., m. ' sharp- edged arrow ' MBh., ' sharp -- edged knife ' Pañcat., ' a sort of hoe ' lex. [Cf. *prakṣurikā -- . -- kṣurá+?] Pa. khurappa --

m. ‘ arrow with a horseshoe head ’; Pk. khurappa -- , °ruppa -- m. ‘ a kind of arrow, knife for cutting grass ’; S. khurpo m. ‘ a pot -- scraper ’; P. khurpā m., °pī f. ‘ pot -- scraper, grubber for grass ’; N. khurpo ‘ sickle ’, °pi ‘ weeding knife ’; B. khurpā ‘ spud for grubbing up grass ’ (X khanítra -- q.v.), Or. khurapa, °pā, °pi, °rupā, °pi;; Bi. khurpā ‘ blade of hoe ’, °pī ‘ small hoe for weeding ’; Mth. khurpā, °pī ‘ scraper ’; H. khurpā m. ‘ weeding knife ’, °pī f. ‘ small do. ’; G. kharpɔ m. ‘ scraper ’, °pī f. ‘ grubber ’ (X kāpvũ in karpī f. ‘ weeding tool ’); M. khurpẽ n. ‘ curved grubbing hoe ’, °pī f. ‘ grub -- axe ’. -- Deriv. H. khurapnā, °rupnā ‘ to scrape up grass ’; G. kharapvũ ‘ to cut, dig, remove with a scraper ’; M. khurapṇẽ ‘ to grub up ’. kṣuráti ‘ cuts, scratches, digs ’, churáti ‘ cuts off, incises ’ Dhātup. [√kṣur]Pa. khurati ‘ scrapes ’, Pk. churaï ‘ breaks ’; G. chɔrvũ ‘ to dig up with a sharp spade ’. -- Ext. with -- ḍ -- : S. khurṛaṇu ‘ to scrape ’, khurṛi f. ‘ scrapings ’; -- with -- kk -- : S. khurka f. ‘ itching ’; L. khurkaṇ ‘ to scratch ’, P. khurkṇā; N. khurkanu ‘ to scrape ’; -- with -- cc -- : P. khurcṇā ‘ to scrape (a pot) ’; G. khurcā m. pl. ‘ scrapings ’. -- X trōṭayati: M. khurtuḍṇẽ ‘ to nip off ’.(CDIAL 3729, 3730).

kūṭa1 n. ‘ iron mallet ’ MBh. [J. Bloch BSOS v 738 and T. Burrow TPS 1945, 93 connect with √kuṭṭ as ← Drav.]Pa. kūṭa -- n. ‘ sledgehammer ’, Pk. kūḍa -- n. ‘ a kind of stone hammer ’; Si. kuḷu -- geḍiya ‘ sledgehammer ’; -- A. kurā ‘ handle of a spear ’?(CDIAL 3391).

*chaṭa ‘ stick, cane ’1. S. chaṛaha f. ‘ thin pole ’, °hī ‘ walking-stick ’; L. chaṛī f. ‘ rod, switch ’ (→ K. chīrü f. ‘ switch ’); P. chaṛ f. ‘ bamboo spear -- shaft ’, °ṛī f. ‘ stick, cane ’, Ku. chaṛ ‘ shoot ’, °ṛī ‘ stick ’; A. sari ‘ bamboo punting pole ’; B. chaṛ ‘ spearshaft ’, °ṛī ‘ switch, cane ’; Or. chaṛa ‘ spear -- shaft ’, °ṛī ‘ switch, cane ’;J. chaṛi f. ‘ gold -- or silver -- mounted stick kept by a gatekeeper ’; Garh. chaṛ ‘ iron bar ’. G. chaṛ m. ‘ reed, bamboo, spearshaft ’, °ṛī f. ‘ switch, cane ’; M. saḍ m. ‘ piece of stubble, stump of sugarcane ’, °ḍī f. ‘ splinter, piece of stubble ’.(CDIAL 4966).

chaṭā f. ' mass, lump ' Śiś.Pk. chaḍā -- f. ' mass, collection '; Si. saḷāva ' mass, crowd '; -- H. chār, °rī f., °rā m. ' mass, lump, clod '?(CDIAL 4967).

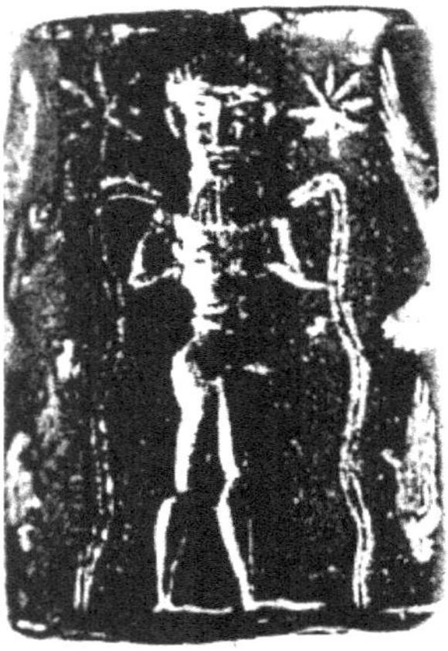

meḍha 'polar star' (Marathi). *meḍ* 'iron' (Ho.Mu.) *nāga* 'snake' Rebus: *nāga* 'lead'; *dula* 'pair' Rebus: *dul* 'cast metal'. Cast metals: lead, iron; Hieroglyphs: *lo* 'overflowing pot' *kāṇḍa* 'water' Rebus: *lokhaṇḍā* 'copper tools, weapons, metalware'. Thus, alloys of copper, lead and iron cast metals are the repertoire of this *kāṭhī* 'stature of person' . *kāṭi* 'sailor' *kāti* 'wheelwright'. [See Appendix O: Eagle and snake hieroglyphs.]

A person with a vase with overflowing water; sun sign. C. 18th cent. BCE. [E. Porada,1971, Remarks on seals found in the Gulf states, Artibus Asiae, 33, 31-7].

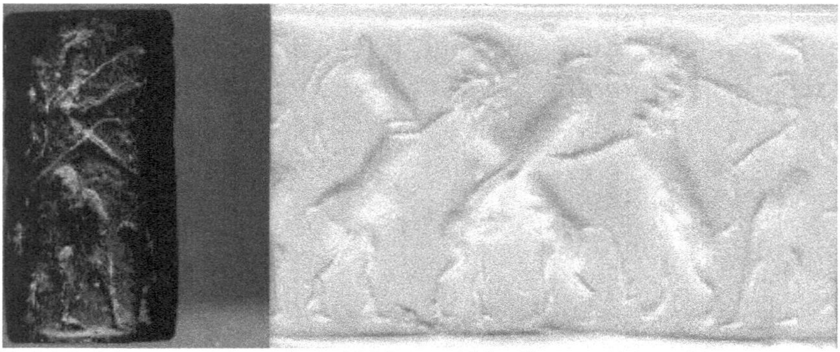

British Museum No. 2012,6003.11. Akkadian. 2400-2200 BCE. Dark grey stone cylinder seal. Engraved with design showing contest scene. A long-horned antelope is attacked by a lion crossed with another animal (also an antelope?) attacked by a second lion. A nude figure grasps the mane and tail of the second lion.

British Museum No. 116720. Proto-elamite. ca. 2800 BCE. Pale green tuff cylinder seal; engraved; shows two types of antelope, stylised plants and crosses between their legs; repaired from several fragments. Wiseman, Donald J, Catalogue of the Western Asiatic Seals in the British Museum: Cylinder Seals I: Uruk - Early Dynastic Periods, London, British Museum, 1962, p.8, pl.7a.

British Museum No. 2012,6003.3. Old Babylonian? Old Assyrian? 2000-1600 BCE Dark grey stone cylinder seal. Engraved design shows two rows of horned animals (antelope or goats). The upper row has two walking animals and one couchant. The lower row has three walking animals. In the background there are a goatfish, crescent, hedgehog, bat/bird and flying bird. there is a line border along the bottom edge of the scene.

British Museum No. 89303. Old Babylonian. ca. 1900 BCE.

Hamilton Collection. Hematite cylinder seal; presentation scene; a bearded god and a bald, clean-shaven worshipper, both wearing fringed robes and standing with hands clasped, face a deified king behind whom, instead of an inscription are a lion and a bull-man (full-face with a horned head-dress) in conflict. In the field are a small figure in a cap, upside down, and a ball-and-staff; a couchant lion set at right-angles and a small suppliant goddess; two ostriches (?) on either side of a star-disc and crescent below which are four drill-holes round the hand of the king, with a fourth behind him, a small star behind his head and a monkey facing him; a merman (?) wearing a crested cap. Line border round the bottom of the seal.

British Museum No. 134849. Akkadian 2400-2200 BCE. White, mottled calcite (limestone) cylinder seal; a seated, bearded god, wearing a flounched skirt, holds a staff or curved blade behind him; his other arm is missing owing to damage but was probably stretching towards the foremost of the two bulls which face him.

The first of these is small and rampant while the second is larger and paces towards the deity with two birds, one of them a spread eagle on it's back. Above the bulls are a crouching figure (damaged) before a framed panel containing eight circles (cheeses?), a lion crouches on two horizontal lines. Behind the bulls, and also facing the god, stands a bearded god wearing a striped skirt, who holds a crook or curved blade over his left shoulder and raises his right hand. Terminal, a doorway framed by two gate-posts. From the lintel hang four small objects, probably dried cheeses, and in the doorway stands a large, flat-bottomed jar. Collon, Dominique, Catalogue of the Western Asiatic Seals in the British Museum: Cylinder Seals II: Akkadian, Post Akkadian, Ur III Periods, II, London, BMP, 1982, pl. XXII.

British Museum No. 89337. Neo-elamite. 6th cent. BCE. Chalcedony cylinder seal: showing a double combat scene. The pair to the left consists of a personage (royal hero?) who stands facing right with torso presented frontally with his unmarked, square-tipped beard shaped to the contours of his jaw and his faintly striated hair bunched at the nape of the neck with a row of round curls outlining the hairline; his prominent nose, fleshy lips, large full eye and high cheekbone are carefully modelled; he wears a dentate crown set on a wide base and is dressed in a so-called Persian robe worn hitched up at the belt, with long sleevespushed back at the shoulders, decorated along the sleeve and hem borders with rows of dots. This personage carries at his side, in his right hand, a dagger with pommel, straight guard and ridged leaf-shaped blade, while his other arm is slightly raised and he lifts by a hind leg an inverted, snarling lion. The lion has its head turned backwards, its mane depicted by four rows of fine, overlapping lines, and its tail in double curls upwards.

The second pair consists of a bare-headed personage (royal hero?) leaping forward, also to the right with his torso shown frontally; his beard and hair are similar to those of the first figure but with a double row of round curls outlining his face; he wears a fringed calf-length robe, reminiscent of Neo-Assyrian dress, with the upper half making a long 'V' down the chest with all of the borders fringed and fringe extending round the thigh; he holds a two-strand whip at his side, in his right hand, slightly raises the left arm and seizes a rampant, regardant bull by its angled horn. The bull has undulating lines across its neck and a long, tufted tail that curls up and round.

The facial and bodily features of all the figures are very carefully detailed with fine and, in the main, naturalistic modelling, emphasized by well-intergrated large andsmall drill-holes used for the hair curls, eyes, noses, dress decorations, jaw and berry-like paws (but note the more realistic lion's second hind paw with one claw).

The battling pairs are placed on a ground line and the scene is bordered above by a narrow double line.
Both edges are worn and chipped; small chip below the hem of the figure in Persian dress. Frankfort, Henri, The art and architecture of the Ancient Orient, Harmondsworth, Middlesex, Penguin Books, 1954, p.190 b&c.

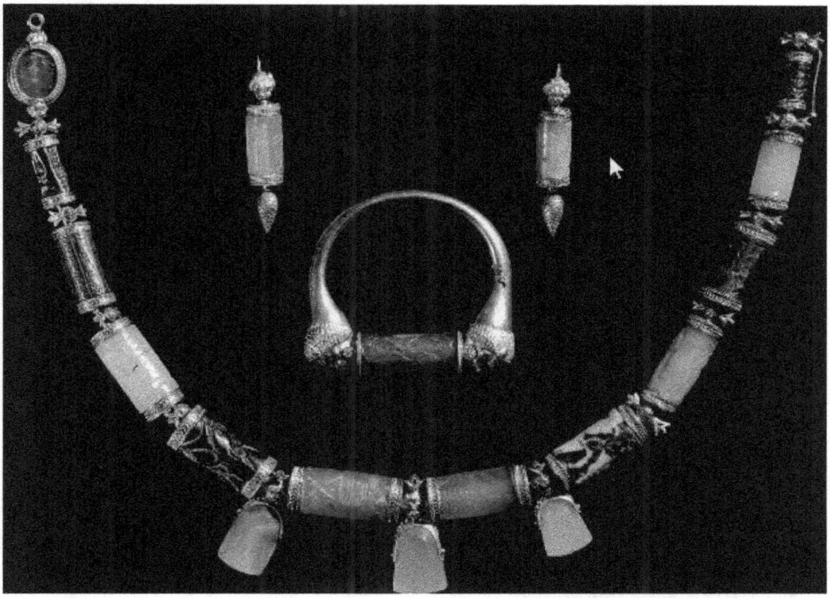

British Museum No. 105113. Late Babylonian (?seal). Neo-Assyrian (?seal) gold, chalcedony. Agate or carnelian are also chalcedony silica mineral. Find spot: Kouyunjik (probably) or Palace of Esarhadden in Nimrud. Chalcedony cylinder seal; pale-grey, clouded; a beardless, proabably female worshipper (or priest?), wearing a head-scarf or fillet over her hair, which is in a bun, extends both hands, palm up, and stands facing right. Facing her is a beardless deity, probably a goddess, who wears a globular (? - chipped), horned head-dress and a vertically striated, tiered skirt which hangs open over a fringed kilt; she raises her right hand and holds a double ring of small and large drill-holes which encircles her. Behind her stands a bearded scorpion-man, who wears a globular, horned head-dress with a tassel or necklace counterweight hanging down behind, and has a double belt, below which his legs are those of a bird of prey (or perhaps a lion), indicated by drill-holes, with more drill-holes for his scorpion's tail; he carries a cone in his right hand and a bucket in his left. In front of the goddess are a crescent and a cross-legged table with a horizontal line above it; in front of the scorpion-man is a horizontal fish, swimming towards the right, and behind him are a centre-dot circle and a dagger with an ornamented hilt (or the wedge or stylus of Nabu?). A line border is visible along the bottom of the seal, and originally the seal probably had a line border round the top as well. This seal is mounted as an ear-ring (to match necklace) in a gold setting whose chevron design can be seen at the top and bottom of the seal impression. The seal may have been filed down to match the other ear-ring but the caps obscure the ends. Collon, Dominique, Catalogue of the Western Asiatic Seals in the British Museum: Cylinder Seals V: Neo-Assyrian and Neo-Babylonian Periods, V, London, BMP, 2001, pl. XXII. maṇí1 m. ' jewel, ornament ' RV.

Pa. *maṇi* -- m. ' jewel ', NiDoc. *mani*, *maṁni*, Pk. *maṇi*<-> m.f.; Gy. pal. *máni* ' button '; K. *man* m. ' precious stone ', *muñu* m., *müñü* f. ' pupil of eye '; S. *maṇi* f. ' jewel ', *maṇyo* m. ' jewels '; P. *maṇī* f. ' jewel ', N. *mani*, Or. *maṇī*, Mth. *manī*, H. *man* m., *manī* f., *maniyā̃* m.; M. *maṇī* m. ' pearl, jewel '; Si. *miṇa*, pl. *miṇi* ' jewel '; -- ext. -- *kk* -- : Gy. gr. *minrikló* m. ' ornament ', rum. *mərənkló*, hung. *miriklo* ' pearl, coral ', boh.*miliklo*, germ. *Merikle* ' **agate** ', eng. *mérikli* ' bead '; Kal.rumb. *mŕãŕik* ' bead necklace '; K. *manka* m. ' snake -- stone '; L. *maṇkā* m. ' bead ', awāṇ. *miṇkā*; P. *maṇkā* m. ' bead, jewel '; G. *maṇkɔ* m. ' gem, bead '; M. *maṇkā* m. ' large gem or bead '.(CDIAL 9731).

British Museum No. 89765. Akkadian. 2400-2200 BCE. Black serpentine cylinder seal; contest scene of three separated groups-bearded sun-god with rays, standing sideways but with face turned in front, wearing a skirt and grasping a long-haired bull-man from behind by the hair and tail; the bull-man holds a mace in his left hand and grasps the sun-god's left arm. Antithetical group consisting of two-human-headed bulls in the centre (full-face) being protected by a bearded hero (full-face) naked except for a belt, and by a bearded hero who is wearing his hair in a bun, an outward flaring cap decorated with fluting, and a skirt. N.B the sun-god has replaced the lion as the bull-man's opponent. For over 8000 years in the Middle East people have used small purpose-made objects to seal packages, mark ownership, witness transactions or confirm signatures. The earliest of these seals were small square, rectangular or triangular stamps with geometric designs carved on the face with a small handle on the reverse which was perforated for suspension by a cord around the wrist or neck of the owner. At about 3,000 BC in Mesopotamia (modern Iraq), these were replaced by cylindrical seals which carried longer and more complex figural compositions. Different stones were preferred at different periods, perhaps because of a combination of changing patterns of fashion, availability and drilling technologies. Harder stones were preferred as they were the least susceptible to wear but cheaper locally available materials such as clay were used by poorer individuals. The name of the owner was sometimes added on the seal but most are uninscribed. The seals are broadly datable according to their style, and there has been much research into their iconography. Seals are occasionally found in excavated graves, thus proving how they were worn. Unsurprisingly, owing to their attractive appearance they have also been widely collected. Cullimore, A, Oriental Cylinders, Impressions of ancient oriental cylinders, or rolling seals of the Babylonians, Assyrians, and Medo-Persians, London, G.W. Nickisson, 1842, no. 98.

British Museum No. 1930, 1213.407. Early Dynastic III. 2650-2500 BCE. Ur. Clay door peg sealing; elaborate design on the cylinder seal is divided into registers; above, a lion attacking a stag between two reclining human headed bulls, little figures, a bird, a crescent and a scorpion; below a man in a chariot, accompanied by attendants and dog (?), and a scene of men fighting.

British Museum No. 116719. Ruler: Shulgi. Third Dynasty of Ur. ca. 2075 BCE. Dolomite (magnesium limestone) cylinder seal; a bald, clean-shaven worshipper (seal owner?), wearing a fringed robe, stands with his right hand raised. He faces a standard which is planted in a mountain, whose upper extremity terminates in a triple mace-head. A rampant lion-griffin stands to the left of this, grasping it with both forelegs and placing one talon on the mountain. A bearded god stands on other side of the standard and grasps it in his right hand while resting his right foot on the mountain; he wears a robe with a striped skirt and a a multiple-horned head-dress and he holds a fenestrated axe in his left hand; inscribed. Frayne, Douglas R, Ur III Period (2112-2004 BC), 3/2, Toronto, University of Toronto Press, 1997 RIME 3/2 RIM.E.3/2.1.2.2038.

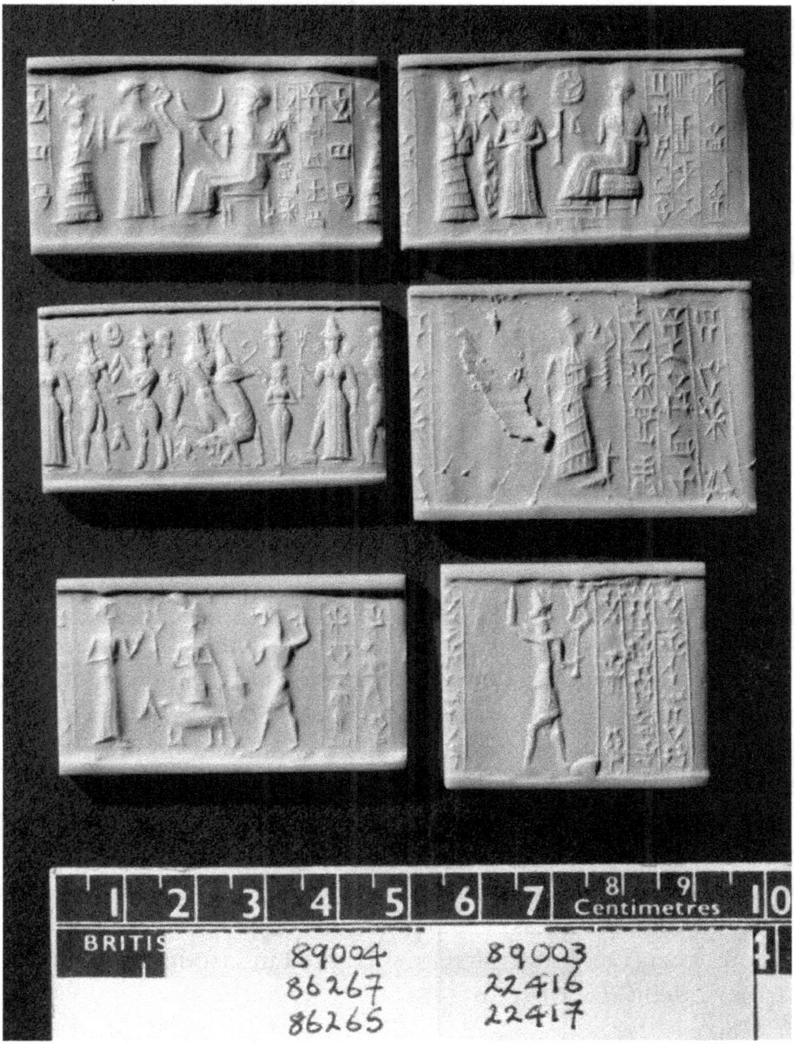

British Museum No. 86265. Old Babylonian. Impressions of six cylinder seals. Black, calcite and quartz (siliceous limestone) cylinder seal; a figure wearing a crested cap and a long striped robe raises one hand towards a god in ascending posture who stands on a quadruped (probably a bull). It seems that the seal-cutter was in some doubt as to the attitude to be adopted by the god: normally he holds the lightning-fork in his right hand and his left arm is folded; here both arms were folded, possibly holding a vessel, but have been recut to hold the lightning fork and a "harpe"-sword. Behind the god stands a kilted lion-demon facing left, in the smiting posture and brandishing a knife (recut). In the field are a fly; a fish. Inserted in the first line of the inscription is a small kilted figure in a cap, facing right and raising one hand; the second line is a small nude goddess (full-face); two-line inscription. Collon, Dominique, Catalogue of the Western Asiatic Seals in the British Museum: Cylinder Seals III: Isin-Larsa and Old Babylonian Periods, III, London, BMP, 1986, pl. XXXIII.

Inscription Script Cuneiform Inscription Transliteration ishkur, sha-l[a].Inscription Translation Adad, Shala.

British Museum No. 89538. Early Dynastic II. Abu Habba (Sippar). ca. 2700 BCE. Aragonite cylinder seal; contest scene; in the centre - a bearded, nude hero, with a crested head-dress, holds a bull in each hand (possibly to protect them); to the left - bull-man (in profile) fights rampant lion. A bird in between them; to the right - the bull-man, full faced, fights two lions; an ibex or small goat between them. Terminal an ibex head; slightly chipped at edges. Frankfort, Henri, Stratified Cylinder Seals from the Diyala Region, LXXII, Chicago, University of Chicago Press, 1955, pl.XIb-d (cf:) Named in inscription: Enzi (Dedicator of statue) Named in inscription: Amar-Kiku (son of dedicator of statue)

British Museum No. 2010,6025.5. papier mâché Cylinder seal,impression. Made of Middle Eastern packaging, newpapers and glue. It represents an object stolen from Iraq following the US led invasion of 2003 and that was placed on a list by the University of Chicago, (Inv# 10197) The most important missing objects were placed on the University of Chicago's Lost Treasures from Iraq database and only a small proportion have been subsequently recovered. Each of the objects made of packaging and newspapers is referred to by its database number.

British Museum No. 129480 Akkadian. 2400-2200 BCE. Dark green serpentine cylinder seal, possibly showing the ascent to heaven of Etana. Two lions, one on each side of a tree; that on the left is standing on its hind legs while that on the right is pacing towards the left. In the branches of the tree is a spread eagle holding a small animal, probably a lion-cub, in its right talon. To the right of the tree is a vertically hatched square which may represent the byre to which a shepherd is leading his flock. The shepherd wears a skirt, holds a staff and raised his right arm towards the eagle in the tree, or possibly, by analogy with other seals in this group, towards the eagle who is carrying away "Etana" on the side of the tree. His flock consists of one markhor-type goat and of three sheep, all long-haired; another shepherd follows it who also wears a skirt, carries a whip over his left shoulder and raises his right hand. In the field above are a seated figure facing left, holding a large pot by the handle and raising his right arm (the pot, probably a churn, has a stopper in its neck which is fastened to the handle by a piece of string); a kneeling figure facing right before a rectangular shape; a kneeling figure facing left a higher level with ten drill-holes (cheese moulds?) before him into which he seems to pouring some liquid from a flask (?). "Etana" is being carried off by the eagle while two seated dogs face each other on the ground and bark in the direction of the eagle. Between them are a bucket and a rectangular object with a handle (?). Representation of Etana. Aruz, Joan; Wallenfels, Ronald, Art of the First Cities: The Third Millennium B.C. from the Mediterranean to the Indus, New York, Metropolitan Museum of Art, 2003, no. 148, p. 219.

British Museum No. 130865. Neo-Assyrian 700 BCE. Nimrud (Kalhu). Excavated/Findspot: Governor's Palace, In Room B, adjoining the bathroom, in ashy fill used to raise the floor level in the course of repairs. Violet or mauve chalcedony cylinder seal in the modelled style; antithetical group consisting of a winged disc, with divine torso and short streamers, above a kneeling Atlantid figure (hero?) facing left, flanked by supporting bull-men, a beardless worshipper before an altar on the left and a rampant lion-griffin on the right; helmets (?) and a cock in the upper field. The very top and bottom of the seal are missing. As a result, the head-dress and most of the head of god rising from the beaded circle of the winged disc are lacking, he faces left, is bearded and raises his left hand. The wings and tail are tripartite and they and the quadripartite streamers consist of many short, flaring feathers; there is also a group of short lines rising from the top of each wing, but because they are fragmentary, it is impossible to say whether these were beards of gods or an ornate appendage, though the angle would favour the latter. The Atlantid figure kneels on one knee, with hands raised and long fingers touching the ends of the streamers. He wears a beaded band above his brow and the undulations of his shoulder-length hair are indicated with short, close wheel-cuts, ending with rows of very fine drill-holes, and there are equally fine drill-holes over the cheek and chin; two more rows of fine wheel-cuts form the end of a band hanging down his back. His muscles and sinews are beautifully modelled and his whole body, from just above his biceps down to his ankles in the front and to mid-calf at the back, is covered with rows of small wheel-cuts, probably indicating hair some of which look almost like drill-holes. The long, thin toes of one foot are carefully cut. The bull-men were certainly carved by the same craftsman was the Atlantid figure and they have the same long fingers, musculature, hairy bodies down to mid-haunch and tassle down the back, but their hair is indicated by fine horizontal lines. Although both hands are raised, they only touch the wings of the winged disc with one hand. They have the legs and hanging tail of a bull but the bull-man on the right stands at a higher level; the tassles of the tails are carved with thicker wheels to produce constrasting fluffy effect. The worshipper looks youthful and stands straight; he has hair like that of the Atlantid figure, but without the beaded band; he wears a short-sleeved, long, fringed robe patterned with dot-filled hexagons, with a fringed shawl wrapped around the upper part, he extends his left hand palm uppermost and raises his clenched right hand with his long index finger extending towards the centre scene (note that the indication of the bone at the heel of his hand makes it clear that we are seeing his hand in a twisted perspective from the front and not, as we should, from the back); his feet are totally missing and he was evidently standing at a lower level than the other figures. Before him is an altar or table shaped like a bull's hind leg turned towards the right, but there are traces at the bottom of it, and probably to the right of the top, of some previous cutting in the form of very short, vertical wheel-cut lines. The ithyphallic lion-griffin has a lion's snarling head with wrinkled muzzle but a mule's long pointed ears and a lion's forepaws, one of which is raised to grasp the elbow of the right-hand bull-man, while the other is extended towards the small of his back; it has a bird's tail and talons on its hind legs, and its body, from the head to haunch, and the leading edges of its wings are covered with an even closer patterning of wheel-cuts than the bodies of the bull-man and Atlantid figure, in this case representing feathers. The figure has been carefully inserted between the bull-man and worshipper, but its avian hind-legs are unfinished and its talons are at a higher level than the feet of the other figures, overlapping the bull-man's tail and leg. Inserted in the upper field in front of the worshipper is a large cock with somewhat eagle-like eye and beak; its crest was removed when the seal was cut down, but its wattle is indicated by a cluster of drill-holes and its body-and-wing feathers are executed with rows of short wheel-cuts as for the winged disc, with the addition of arcs of diagonal and chevron lines for the tail; one foot could not be completed for lack of space. Above the right-hand bull-man, the lion-griffin and the worshipper are three irregular shapes, each with a vertical projection and 'handles' on either side, probably representing crested helmets although they might be water-pots and the cock could be a bringer of rain. The helmets or water-pots were probably not part of the original design but would suggest that this seal had metal (probably gold) caps; while these caps were being removed the ends of the seal became badly chipped and had to be ground down, thus obliterating the parts of the design closest to the top and bottom. Some of the chips extended beyond this, however and to mask them they were deepened (there are traces of the use of the drill in the lowest corners of each, linked by a cut line) to form the helmets or water-pots; this would explain their irregular positioning and angle and careless execution compared to the remainder of the design. The worshipper, cock and offering table may have been cut over an abraded area as the seal is flattened on this side and the tail of the left-hand bull-man has been recut but the same craftsman executed the whole design with the probably exception of the helmets / water-pots. Edges chipped; seal ends reground in antiquity and now convex; very straight and narrow.

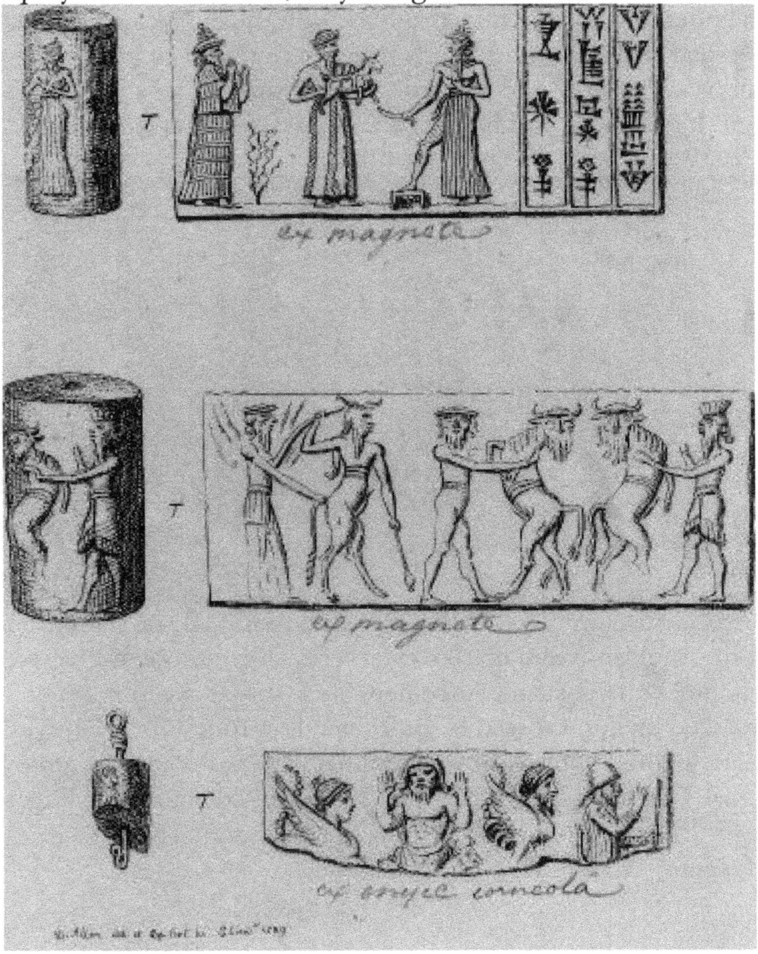

British Museum No. 2010,5006.1541.Cylinder seal with a suppliant goddess and the robed king holding an animal offering, facing the sun god who rests his foot on a trapezoidal chequer-board mountain and holds a knife (BM ME 1814,0705.1). Cylinder seal with a bearded sun-god with rays, grasping a bull-man from behind by the hair and tail, and two-human-headed bulls, each being protected by a bearded hero (BM ME 1814,0705.2).

Cylinder seal with a winged sphinx with the tail of a scorpion, a bearded figure with his hands raised, a mythical creature with the tail of a scorpion, and a bearded figure wearing a cap, with his right hand raised and holding a rod or staff in his left hand (BM ME 1814,0705.3). Engraving, 1789.

British Museum No. 119427. Early Dynastic III. ca. 3000 BCE. Large, pinkish-white marble cylinder seal with orange-brown patches; contest scene; nude hero with curved weapon holds bull attacked by lion crossed by bull-man; lion fought by bull-man. Note feathered head-dress. Terminal - space for inscription over figure fighting goat. Gadd, Cyril John, Mesopotamian cylinder seals, British Museum Quarterly, 3, 2, London, The British Museum, 1929, p.39, pl.XXIb (1).

British Museum No. 89769. Neo-Assyrian. 720-700 BCE. Pale green grossular garnet cylinder seal in the modelled style; a beardless male worshipper stands facing right, points with his right hand and extends the other towards the warrior-goddess Ishtar who stands on the back of a couchant lion, raises her right hand and holds a bow and two arrows in her left. Behind the two figures are a date-palm and two rearing crossed ibexes or mountain goats. In the upper field, behind the worshipper's head is an earring. The worshipper has shoulder-length hair and wears a short-sleeved, hexagaon-patterned, fringed robe with a webbing belt, and sandals. A row of dots above his forehead may indicate the hairline but could be a jewelled circlet; he has a necklace of square plaques, in which dots probably indicate jewels, with a tasselled necklace counterweight hanging behind, and bracelets on each wrist (that on the right wrist has a star pattern); at his waist is a sword with a lion's head decorating the hilt. Ishtar wears a tall, cylindrical, feathered and horned head-dress decorated with dots. Her hair is slightly longer than the worshipper's. She wears a short-sleeved, hexagon-patterned, fringed robe with a webbing belt, which hangs open to reveal a hexagon-patterned, fringed kilt; she also wears sandals. She may have a plain band around her neck but this could be the edge of her robe; a tasselled band hanging behind may be attached to her head-dress or it may be a necklace counterweight; she has triple bracelets on each wrist, single armbands above the elbow and a triplet anklet is visible on her right ankle (the left ankle is hidden by her robe). She has crossed quivers on her back which are tipped by stars and decorated with dots, she also has a dot-decorated bow-case and sickle-sword on her back. A sword at her waist has hilt made up of three drill-holes; small lines near the end of the star-tipped scabbard probably stand for the pair of lion or volutes with which the scabbards were often decorated. She holds her arrows close to the feathers, point upwards and her bow is decorated with ducks' heads. Her lion turns its head back towards her; its jaws are closed and its body is decorated with minute drill-holes to indicate fur on the mane and belly. The palm-tree has eleven branches and triple bunches of dates hang down on each side. The crossed male ibexes or mountain goats twist their heads backwards over their shoulders. Both ears are shown and the tips of both notched horns. The animals are bearded and three rows of chevrons mark the hair along the underside of their necks and across their flanks; their tufted tails curl upwards. The musculature is carefully indicated. The earring is crescent-shaped with three bell-like arms. Minute details such as the patterning of the robes, the crossed quivers on Ishtar's back and her sickle, sword, bow and two arrows are beautifully cut. Line borders at top and bottom. Slight chipping at the ends. A very narrow, straight perforation. Collon, Dominique, Catalogue of the Western Asiatic Seals in the British Museum: Cylinder Seals V: Neo-Assyrian and Neo-Babylonian Periods, V, London, BMP, 2001, pls.XIX, XXXIII, XXXVIII.Representation of Ishtar.

British Museum No. 120529. Third Dynasty of Ur. Akkadian. Royal cemetery. 2100 BCE. Quartz var crystal cylinder seal; lead tube? painted with a chevron design in red and white stripes, which are visible through the design, inserted in the perforation to add colour; seal has ornamental copper or bronze caps over a bitumen core; edges of seal are bevelled; contest scene; antithetical group consisting of two bearded, naked? heroes (full-face) each grasping the tail and one foreleg of, respectively, a water buffalo and a lion. The hero on the left is astride the water buffalo. In the field between the two pairs of contestants is an ibex lying down; two lines of inscription. Woolley, Charles Leonard, The Royal Cemetery, II, London, British Museum, 1934 p. 526, pl. 205, no. 178 and p. 314 for inscription. Inanna named in inscription. Inscription Script cuneiform Inscription Language Akkadian Inscription Transliteration "ip-hur" shita -AB.DI / inana-[ka]. Inscription Translation Iphur, ...-priest of Inanna.

British Museum No. 89046. Akkadian. 2400-2200 BCE. Serpentine cylinder seal; contest scene; bearded hero (Chaldean

Hercules?), wearing a skirt, in conflict with a water buffalo. His right arm is poised in a manner characteristic of the period. The group is repeated. Terminal, a knotted pole in the space left for an inscription. In the field between the last two figures, an inscription: geme-e, Amat-bitim or Amat-E<a>.Translation: Slave-girl of the house? (Possibly added at a later date to the seal) Blurton, T Richard, The Enduring Image, Treasures from the British Museum, London, The British Council, 1997, no. 49, pl.64-65 (article by D.Collon).

British Museum No. 121566.d Akkadian. Royal cemetery. 2400-2200 BCE. Lapis lazuli cylinder seal; contest scene - bull-man (full-face) in conflict with a lion. Antithetical group consisting of two bearded heroes (full-face) in the centre, who are naked except for a triple belt and who are protecting or are in conflict with, respectively, a human-headed bull (full-face) and a bull. One side has been filed down so that part of the bull-man and one leg of the bull are no longer visible. At the top the perforation is surrounded by a deep groove. Woolley, Charles Leonard, The Royal Cemetery, II, London, British Museum, 1934, p. 549, pl. 212, no. 313.

Seal of Ibni-Sharrum, the scribe of King Sharkali-Sharri son of Naram-Sin - 2,250 B.C.

khaṇṭi 'buffalo bull' (Tamil) Rebus: *khãḍ* '(metal) tools, pots and pans' (Gujarati)

Lyre-player, from one of the steles of king Gudea of Lagash. The lyre has eleven strings. Around 2150 BCE

Louvre, Departement des Antiquites Orientales, Paris, France Glyph: *tambura* 'harp'; rebus: *tambra* 'copper' (Pkt.) *ḍangar* 'bull' (Hindi) Rebus: *ḍhangar* 'blacksmith' (Hindi).

 This hieroglyph , a symbolic form, takes on about 70 ligatures to make the meanings 'definitive'. The hieroglyph signifies, in Meluhha rebus readings of hieroglyph: *kāṭhī* the make of the body; the stature of a man (Gujarati) Rebus: *khātī* 'wheelwright' (Hindi) *meḍ* 'body' Rebus: *meḍ* 'iron' (Ho.) Together, the meaning is:

khātī meḍ 'wheelwright iron'.  Further embellished with *āra* 'six' 'curls' on his hairstyle, he reads rebus: *ārakāṭi.* [Tel.] n. A boatman, a sailor. ఓడనడపువాడు, నావికుడు. (Telugu). This symbolic form becomes a cultural continuum signifying *harosheth hagoyim* 'smithy of nations' (Judges 4.2) -- Cognate: *kharoṣṭī goya* lit. 'blacksmith lip, very close friend' [*khara* 'blacksmith' (Kashmiri) + *ṓṣṭha* m. 'lip' (Ṛgveda)] Pk. *guttiya* -- m. 'kinsman'; S. *goṭrī* 'related', P. *gotī*; N. *goti, gotiyā bhai* 'kinsman', N. *goyā, gūyā bhai* 'very close friend', H. *goiyā̃, guiyā* m.f. ' companion '(CDIAL 4281). *kharoṣṭī* signifies a writing system starting from ca. 5th cent. BCE in Gāndhāra between Ancient Near East and India.

Sphōṭavāda, theory of bursting forth

Bhartṛhari anticipates propositional calculus and number as a class of classes: *samkhyeya samgha samkhyānasamghah samkhyeti kathyate* (3.11.19) and *so 'yam ity abhisambandho buddyā prakramyatē yadā vākyārthasya tadaiko 'pi varṇah pratyāyakah kvacit* (2.40) What is the process of representing a network of classes as a class? The process seems to involve some mental activity by which one representation is 'pictured' to represent another 'artifact'. *sphōṭa* accoding to VS Apte's Sanskrit lexicon is: 1. Breaking forth, bursting or disclosure; and 2. The idea which bursts out or flashes on the mind when a sound is uttered.[71] This thesis presents evidence of such flashes of the mind expressed as Meluhha hieroglyph symbolic forms.

sphōṭa is that from which the meaning bursts or shines forth; and as an entity which is manifested by the spoken letters or sounds.[72]

Significative Power (*Śakti*)

(1-13). Sphōṭa can be classified into eight varieties: *varṇasphōṭa, padasphōṭa, vākyasphōṭa* (each divided into the universal or the particular), *akhaṇḍa padasphōṭa*, and *akhaṇḍa vākyasphōṭa.* Of these types the *vākyasphōṭa* is the most important, for the sentence is the unit of speech in worldly usage. The division of the sentence into words, and further into the stems and suffixes, is only a grammatical device for analysis and has no reality…

(37). Meaning (*vṛtti*) is of three kinds, primary significative power (śakti), secondary meaning (*lakṣaṇā*), and suggestion (*vyanjanā*)…

(43). The identity and the superimposition of word and meaning are in the mind. Strictly speaking, the existence of the meaning, as well as that of the word, is only in the mind. The word is the integral *sphōṭa.* The meaning is a vikalpa, a mental construct that comes along with the knowledge of the word and has nothing to do with the actual existence...One cannot say that meaning is got from corrupt words through an erroneous notion of the meaningfulness. Meaning is known without any doubt (from corrupt words), hence no confusion is to be assumed. That is why women, uneducated people, and children have to be told the corrupt words, when they have doubts on hearing the correct words. The *Mahābhāṣya* passage, 'although meaning is known from correct as well as corrupt words, grammar gives the rules about meritorious usage', and Bhartṛhari's line 'Although there is no difference in meaningfulness, the grammatical rules are for merit and demerit in usage,' are in favor of this view. The discussion regarding the Āryan and Mleccha usages in Mīmāmsā also shows this view. This discussion itself shows that both the Āryan and the Mleccha usages are valid; the Āryan usage is preferred as far as the Vedic terms are concerned."[73]

For Bhartṛhari, Brahman precedes the conveyance of meaning through words. Thus, individual words do not matter but the complete thought which precedes as a sentence. *Sphōṭa* of Vākyapadīya breaks down to *pada-sphōṭa.* It is the idea which results in sound.

Sphōṭasiddhi of Mandana Misra (KA Subramania Iyer trans., 1966, Poona, Deccan College) maintains that individual phonemes (*varṇa*-s) convey no meaning. It is the word which bears meaning. "As for the definition that a word is what is cognized by the auditory sense-organ, it is vitiated by serious defects. The auditory organ aso apprehends qualitative differences of pitch and modulation and such universals as wordhood and the like. These attributes though known through the organ of hearing are not words. Morevover, word is not known only by the auditory organ but also the mind. So the definition proposed by Kumarila is misleading and apt to create confusion. The verdict of unsophisticated common sense that 'cow' is a whole word which yields meaning, ought not to be brushed aside as an uncritical appraisal. The unity of the significant word is a felt fact and no amount of quibbling can conjureit away."[74]

Three Samarra bowls: *morakkhaka loha, pisācī loha*

Elaborating on Denise Schmandt-Besserat's observation that "art became narrative and went beyond accounting to become a comprehensive medium of communication," three artifacts – Samarra bowls dated ca. 4000 BCE – use Meluhha cipher to demonstrate the use of hieroglyphs to communicate substantive information on the life-activities of artisans of the bronze age.

Sammara is on the east bank of Tigris river, 125 kms. from Baghdad. Ancient toponyms (Samarra Archaeological Survey) are Greek Souma (Ptolemy V.19, Zosimus III, 30), Latin Sumere, a fort mentioned during the retreat of the army of Julian the Apostate in 363 CE (Ammianus Marcellinus XXV, 6, 4).[75]

Three prehistoric bowls from Samarra are surmised to relate to the period (ca. 3500 - 3000 BCE).[76] The first image is discussed in Denise Schmandt-Besserat, When writing met art, p.19. "The design features six humans in he center of the bowl and six scorpions around the inner rim. The six identical anthropomorphic figures, shown frontally, are generally interpreted as females because of their wide hips, large thighs, and long, flowing hair…Six identical scorpions, one following after the other in a single line, circle menacingly around the women."

美索不達米亞Hassuna時期陶器上的「卍」紋圖案，約公元前5000年(網絡圖片)[77] Mesopotamia "svastika" patterns on pottery Hassuna period, about 5000 BC (network picture)

Image 1. Eight fish, four peacocks holding four fish, slanting strokes surround

The Samarra bowl (ca. 4000 BC) at on exhibit at the Pergamon museum, Berlin. The bowl was excavated as Samarra by Ernst Herzfeld in the 1911-1914 campaign, and described in a 1930 publication. The design consists of a rim, a circle of eight fish, and four fish swimming towards the center being caught by four birds. At the center is a swastika symbol.[78] Svastika!! The bowl was broken, part of the rim is missing, and one crack ran right across the central symbol, so that the swastika symbol should be considered a reconstruction. The 'svastika' hieroglyph on a Samarra bowl is a reconstruction.[79]

dhāḷ 'a slope'; 'inclination of a plane' (G.); *dhāḷako* 'large metal ingot' (G.) gaṇḍa set of four (Santali) Rebus: kaṇḍ 'fire-altar, furnace' (Santali) *kāṇḍā* 'tools, pots and pans, metalware' (Marathi). *ayo* 'fish' Rebus: *ayas* 'metal'; *mora* peacock; *morā* 'peafowl' (Hindi); rebus: *morakkhaka loha*, a kind of copper, grouped with *pisācaloha* (Pali). *moraka* "a kind of steel" (Sanskrit) 'svastika' hieroglyph: *sathiyā* (Hindi), *sāthiyo* (Gujarati); *satthia, sotthia* (Prākṛt) Rebus: *satthiya* 'zinc'; jasta id. (Kashmiri) *satva* 'zinc' (Prākṛt) *svastika* pewter (Kannada).

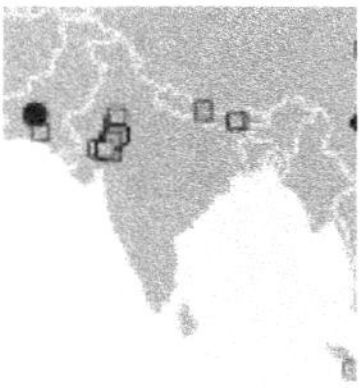

This is portion of a map which depicts the world-wide distribution of Mississippi Valley-Type and clastic-dominated sediment-hosted lead-zinc deposits as documented in Open-File Report 2009-1297 of the United States Geological Survey authored by By Ryan D. Taylor, David L. Leach, Dwight C. Bradley, and Sergei A. Pisarevsky[80]. This means that the sediments carried by River Sarasvati could be subjected to placer mining both for cassiterite and zinc-lead deposits which are hosted by the river sediments. Clastic sequences are also seen in Dharwar Basin zinc-lead deposits, India where sulfides are hosted in shears within dolomite sequences. These are concentrations of lead and zinc sulfide ores within copper metal or carbonate formations such as dolomite. Dolomite is used as a flux for smelting of iron.

"Carbonate-hosted lead-zinc deposits of the Mississippi Valley-type (MVT) appear to be at one of a spectrum of base-metl ore deposit types which form in sediments some time during the lifetime of a sedimentary basin. The spectrum of deposits includes red-bed copper, shale-hosted lead, as well as MVT deposits. As in the case of petroleum and natural gas, these ore deposits are now generally viewed as being a normal part of the evolution of a sedimentary basin."[81]

Carbonate hosted deposits: Limestone and dolomite are the most common host rocks. The zinc lead content usually ranges from 5%-10% with zinc usually predominating over lead. Concentrations of copper, silver and barite of fluorite may also be present.

Sediment hosted (sedex deposits) The host rocks are mainly shale, siltstone, and sandstone. Sedex deposits represent some of the world's largest accumulations of zinc, lead and silver. The mineral has a high silver content. The lead/zinc content ranges from 10-20%.

The host rocks are mainly shale, siltstone, and sandstone. Sedex deposits represent some of the world's largest accumulations of zinc, lead and silver. The mineral has a high silver content. The lead/zinc content ranges from 10-20%.

"Centuries before zinc was recognized as a distinct element, zinc ores were used for making brass. A prehistoric statuette containing 87.5% zinc was found in a Dacian archaeological site in Transylvania (modern Romania). Palestinian brass from the 14th to 10th centuries BC contains 23% zinc. The primitive alloys with less than 28 per cent zinc were prevalent in many parts of the world before India. Brass in Taxashila has been dated from third century BC to fifth century AD. A vase from Taxashila is of particular interest because of its 34.34 percent zinc content and has been dated to the third century BC. Recently two brass bangles belonging to the Kushana period are discovered from Senuwar (U.P.), which also shows 35 percent zinc.

Indians were the first to know about metal zinc, the bluish-white, lustrous metal and smelt on a large scale. The testimony to it is the presence of huge numbers of retorts and ruins spread over a large area in old Zawar village in southeastern Rajasthan. References to medicinal uses of zinc are in the Charaka Samhita, which is believed to have been written as early as 300 BC in India.
Zinc was rediscovered in Europe by Marggraf in 1746. It got its name after German word 'zinke' for this metal. In English and French it became 'zinc', in German and Dutch 'zink', in Spanish 'cinc' and in Welsh 'sinc' (pronounced "shink"). The Greek word for zinc is 'pseudargyros', literally meaning "pseudo-silver" for its silvery lustre. In Russian, it is 'tsink'. In India it is known as 'Yashad', Jasta, Jast, Naag in Hindi/ Sanskrit, Tunga in Tamil and Naagam in Malyalam.

Zinc is a bluish-white, lustrous, diamagnetic metal. In nonscientific contexts zinc is known as 'spelter'. It is covered by a protective transparent layer of basic carbonate, hence, show a dull finish...Sphalerite or zinc blende is the most important zinc ore as it contains 64.06% zinc. It occurs mostly as veins. It shows brown, yellow, red, green and black colour, has uneven fracture and occur as colloform, euhedral crystals and granular masses. It has 3.5 to 4 hardness, brownish white streak, 3.9 to 4.2 density and adamantine lustre. It is fluorescent and triboluminescent. It occurs in isometric-hextetrahedral crystal system, which is analogous to diamond. Sphalerite is a polymorph (many shapes but same chemistry) and has two minerals i.e. wurtzite and matraite...In ancient India, production of zinc metal was common... Process of the production of metallic zinc has been described in several Sanskrit works e.g. 'Rasarnavam Rastantram' (500-100 BC), 'Rasratnakar' (2nd century AD), 'Rasprakash Sudhakar' (12th century AD) and 'Rasaratna Samuchchaya' (13th century AD). The ingredients for zinc production mentioned in the last book include lac, bark of 'pipal' tree, 'harad', 'haldi', resin, salt, borax and 'kharpar' (zinc ore); and grinding them with cow milk and purified butter to prepare balls to put into the retorts.

Spharlite, the purplite ore mineral of zinc.

Walls of houses built by spent retorts at old Zawar - a notable example of re-using the

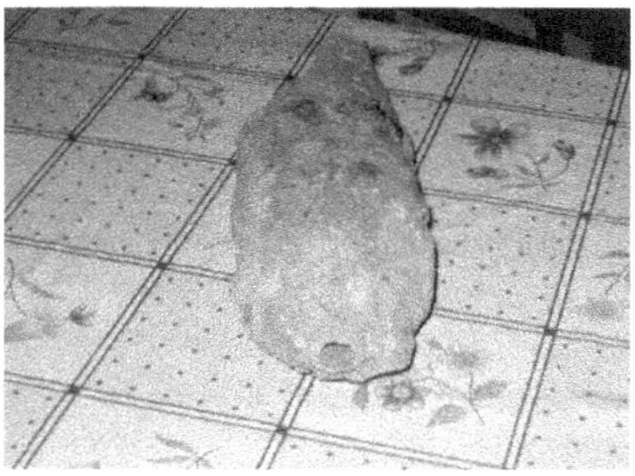

industrial waste by ancient Indians

Cross-section through a zinc-smelting retort, 14–16th centuries,

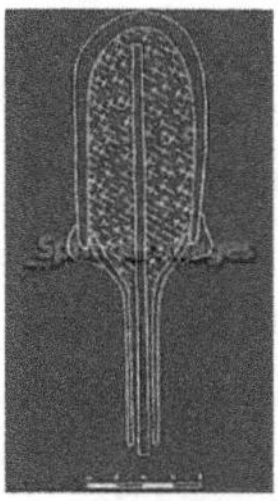

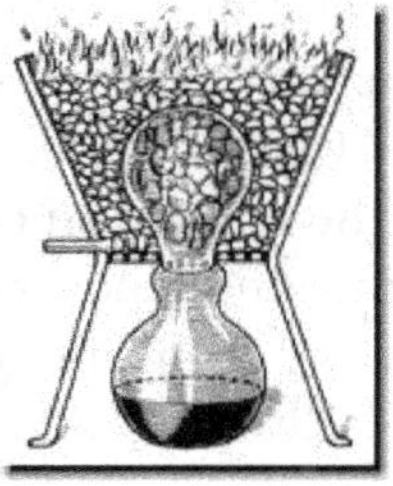

Zawar. "A conical clay condenser tube was securely luted to the end of the retort and a then open stick was inserted to stop the charge from falling out when inverted and to create a central channel

down which the zinc vapour could pass." Craddock, Paul Terence, 2009, The origins and inspirations of zinc smelting, Journal of Material Science, May 2009, Vol. 44, Issue 9, pp. 2181-2191.

In the 13th century Marco Polo described the manufacture of zinc oxide in Persia.

Ancient zinc retorts

A team of scientists from British Museum (London), HZL (Udaipur) and Baroda University (Gujarat) unearthed this ancient Indian technique of zinc smelting at old Zawar, Udaipur district, Rajasthan, which is now considered to be the oldest site of industrial zinc production in the world. During the process, typical slag is not produced because of small-sized retorts. Ore was roasted to convert zinc sulphide to zinc oxide; mixed with reducing agents and fluxes (dolomite/ salt) and filled-in cylindrical retorts (brinjal-shaped, tapering at one end). The retorts are about 20 to 35 cm long and 8 to 12 cm in diameter with about 1 cm thick walls. A small diameter tube was fixed onto the open end of the retort for condensation of zinc vapours through this. The retorts are fitted upside down in perforated plate, to be fired in-situ, in a closed furnace. By controlled-firing the zinc gets evaporated, condensed and collected at the bottom. Assuming 20-25% losses of zinc, the quantity obtained was about 300 to 400 g of zinc metal per retort or 10 to 15 kg per smelt of the furnace of 36 retorts. Over 130,000 tons of residues remain at Zawar which indicates the extraction of the equivalent of 1,000,000 tons of metallic zinc and zinc oxide. Radiocarbon age determinations of launder wood from the old lead-zinc mines of Zawar Mala yielded an age of 2180+/- 35 years.[82]

The *pisācaloha* referenced as a Pali gloss may refer to such lead, zinc, copper stone-ores which occur together – these are referred to metallurgical literature as carbonate-hosted lead-zinc ore deposits. The presence of svastik hieroglyph points to the zinc as the center-piece in the composition of the image on sammara bowl, surrounded by fishes and peacocks: ayo 'fish' Rebus: ayo 'allloy metal'; moraka 'peacock' Rebus: *morakkhaka loha*, a kind of copper, grouped with *pisācaloha* (Pali). Thus, the Samarra bowl signifies the smelting of a type of copper named *morakkhaka loha* and the artist had realized that the carbonate-hoted copper ore complex contains zinc.

Two sides of Harappa tablet (h182A, B) are an Account of entrustment articles -- cast metal stones of *morakkhaka loha*, a kind of copper, grouped with *pisācaloha* (Pali) *moraka* 'a king of steel'

h182A

h182B  4306Tablet in bas-relief

h182A Pict-107: Drummer and a tiger. h182B Five svastika signs alternating right- and left-handed.  har609 terracotta tablet, bas-relief [The drummer is also shown on h182B tablet with a comparable epigraph and five svastika glyphs alternating right-

and left-handed arms. Hieroglyph 'count of five': *mõṛẽ* = five (Santali) Rebus: *moraka* 'a kind of steel' *morakkhaka loha*, a kind of copper, grouped with *pisācaloha* (Pali). Thus, five svastika hieroglyphs may be read as: *satthiyā mora* 'a kind of copper-zinc-lead ore complex – sediment-hosted lead-zinc deposits together with copper'.

See chapters elaborating on morakkhaka loha 'a composite metal':

> Three Samarra bowls: *morakkhaka loha, pisācī loha*
> *morakkhaka loha* 'a kind of copper'
> *pisācī loha*, 'a kind of copper'

Sanskrit lexicon provides a synonym for Piśāca as a personification of *ignis fatuus* indicating a link with fire-workers. Pāṇini refers to Piśāca as a warrior clan (Aṣṭādhyāyi). Citing Mahābhārata, the "Piśāca people" (equivalent to the modern day Nuristani people) are said to live in northwest India, and they are descendants of Prajāpati Kaśyapa, Grierson discusses Piśāca languages.[83] Since both *pisācī loha* and *morakkhaka loha* are referred to as metallic ores, the indications are that the *pisācī loha* refers to a carbonate-host ore complex containing *sathiya* 'zinc' (together with other minerals such as copper or lead) to create *karaḍa* 'hard alloy'. Hence, the hieroglyph of drummer: *karaḍa* 'drum'.

 Meaning: *sangaḍa* 'pair' Rebus: 'entrustment articles'. *kaṇḍa kan-ka* 'rim of jar' Rebus: *kaṇḍa karṇīka* 'supercargo account (scribe)'.

 Hieroglyph: dula 'pair' Rebus: dul 'cast metal'. Hieroglyph: Phal. *kāṛa* ' bracelet ' (Phal) Rebus: Rebus: *kāḍ* 'stone'. Ga. (Oll.) kanḍ, (S.) kanḍu (pl. kanḍkil) stone (DEDR 1298).

खडा [khaḍā] *m* A small stone, a pebble (Marathi) kāṭha m. ' rock ' (Sanskrit) Bshk. *kōr* ' large stone ' AO xviii 239. kānta -- ' stone ' (CDIAL 3018).

Hieroglyph: *karaḍa* 'double-drum' *Rebus: karaḍa* 'hard alloy'. *Ta.* karaṭi, karaṭi-pparai, karaṭikai a kind of drum (said to sound like a bear, karaṭi). *Ka.* karaḍi, karaḍe an oblong drum beaten on both sides, a sort of double drum. / Cf. Skt. karaṭa- a kind of drum.(DEDR 1264).

Hieroglyph: *kola* 'tiger' Rebus: *kol* 'working in alloys, iron' 'smelter'.

Hieroglyph: Phal. *kāṛa* ' bracelet ', káṭa1 m. ' twist of straw, mat ' TS., *káṭaka* -- m.n. ' twist of straw ' Kād., ' bridle ring ' Suśr., ' bracelet ' Kālid., *kaṭikā* -- f. ' straw mat ' KātyŚr. com. Pa. *kaṭa* -- m. ' mat ', °*aka* -- m.n. ' ring, bracelet '; Pk. *kaḍaya* -- m.n. ' ring ', *kaḍā* -- f. ' chain '; Gy. wel. *kerō* m. ' bracelet ', gr. *koró*; Dm. *kaŕai*; Paš. *kāṛa* ' snare (made of horsehair) ' IIFL iii 3, 98 with (?);Sh. *kāvu̯* m., (Lor.) *kāo*, K. *karu* m.; S. *kaṛo* m. ' ring, chain or hasp to fasten door, buttonhole ', °*ṛī* f. ' metal ring, anklet '; L. *kaṛā* m. ' bracelet, magic circle drawn round person or garden produce to keep off jinni ', °*ṛī* f. ' anklet '; P. *kaṛā* m. ' bracelet, tyre of wheel ', °*ṛī* f. ' ring, manacle '; WPah. bhal. *kaṛu* n. ' link of a chain '; Ku. *kāṛo* 'bangle '; N. *karo*, pl. °*rā* ' rings of a vessel by which it is lifted '; B. *kaṛ* ' lac bracelet worn by women with living husbands ', *kaṛā* ' metal ring ', °*ṛi* ' ring, bracelet '; Or. *kaṛā* ' metal ring, link '; Bi.*karā* ' handle of a vessel '; H. *kaṛā* m. ' ring, bracelet, anklet ', °*ṛī* f. ' metal ring ' (→ Bi. Mth. *kaṛī* ' iron ring '); Marw. *kaṛo* m. ' bracelet '; G. *kaṛo* m. ' large mat ', °*ṛũ* n. ' circular ring of gold or silver ', °*ṛī* f. ' link, hook, chain '; M. *kaḍẽ* n., °*ḍī* f. ' metal ring '. -- Ext. with -- *ḍa* -- : G. *kaṛṛɔ* m. ' toe ring ', °*ṛī* f. ' ear -- ring '; -- with -- *la* -- : N. *kalli* ' anklet '; G. *kaḍlũ*, *kallũ* n. ' bracelet, anklet ', *kaḍlī*, *kallī* f. ' ring, armlet '. (CDIAL 2629).

Image 2. Six women, curl in hair, six scorpions

Harappa potsherd shows four women with comparable disheveled hair, together with signifiers of peacock (stars with dots in the center).

Women with flowing hair and scorpions, Samarra, Iraq. ca. 5000 BCE. After Ernst Herzfeld, Die Ausgrabungen von Samarra V: Die vorgeschichtischen Topfereien, Univ. of Texas Press, pl. 30. Courtesy Dietrich Reimer. This image is discussed in Denise Schmandt-Besserat, When writing met art, p.19. "The design features six humans in he center of the bowl and six scorpions around the inner rim. The six identical anthropomorphic figures, shown frontally, are generally interpreted as females because of their wide hips, large thighs, and long, flowing hair…Six identical scorpions, one following after the other in a single line, circle menacingly around the women."

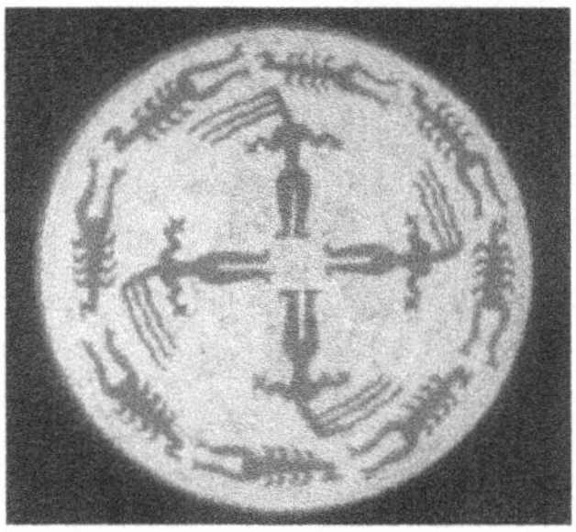

Image 3: Four women, disheveled hair, 8 scorpions The entire hieroglyphic composition is about *rāca* 'pertaining to a stone'. The sone referenced and signified is Hieroglyph: *bicha* 'scorpion' Rebus: *bica* 'stone ore'. The gloss for Hieroglyph: *kola* 'woman' Rebus: *kol* 'working in iron', 'smelters'. Thus the composition indicates smelting of bica 'stone ore'.

<raca>(D) {ADJ} ``^dishevelled'' (Munda) *rabca* 'dishevelled' Rebus 1: రాచ *rāca* (adj.) Pertaining to a stone. cf. Use of a morpheme related to రాచ *rāca* in the compound gloss: *sangatarāśi* = stone-cutting (Telugu)

Rebus 2: *rasāṇẽ* n. ' glowing embers '(Marathi). of kuṭhi 'smelter'.

bicha ‘scorpion’ (Assamese) Rebus: bica ‘stone ore’ (Munda). Thus, the glyphic of ‘dishevelled hair’ (*rāca* ‘pertaining to a stone’) is a semantic reinforcement of the nature of ‘stone’ ore represented by the ‘scorpion’ glyph, *bica.*

kola ‘woman’ Rebus: *kol* ‘working in iron’.

mī˜ḍhī f., °ḍho m. ‘ braid in a woman's hair ’, L. mē̃ḍhī f.; G. mīḍlɔ, miḍ° m. ‘braid of hair on a girl's forehead ’ (CDIAL 10312). meṛha M. meṛhi F.’twisted, crumpled, as a horn’; meṛha deren ‘a crumpled horn’ (Santali) मेंढा [mēṇḍhā] A crook or curved end (of a stick, horn &c.) and attrib. such a stick, horn, bullock. मेढा [mēḍhā] A twist or tangle arising in thread or cord, a curl or snarl (Marathi). Rebus: mē̃ḍ ‘iron’ (Mu.)

meṛed-bica = iron stone ore, in contrast to *bali-bica*, iron sand ore (Munda)

morakkhaka loha 'a kind of copper'

The cult of Isis is thought to arrived, with Hellenitic sailors, in Pompeii.[84] Temples of Isis and Serapis in Rome were built around 220 BCE. A temple of Sarapis (or Roman Serapis) in Egypt is mentioned in 323 BC by Plutarch (*Life of Alexander*, 76) and by Arrian (*Anabasis*, VII, 26, 2). "One of the most used forms of communication in the ancient world was by river or sea.In the time of the Roman Empire half of the sailors in the imperial fleet were recruited inEgypt and in the Hellenistic East. They travel all over the "Old world" as soldiers and sailorsof merchant ships. Egyptian cults for example diffused from the sea ports into the mainlandthrough the major ports."[85]

Sommer, Giorgio (1834-1914) - n. 1216 - Pomepi - Tempio di Iside.jpg The small, walled enclosure on the left is for a pool containing water used in the ritual of Isis.

The temple of Isis at Pompeii. Engraved by Francesco Piranesi, 1788. London. British Museum. Pompeii.

The bronze pine cone, about 4 meters high. Water flowed from the top of the cone, making it a water-fountain that resided in the Temple of Isis in Campo Martius next to the Pantheon. "The fountain is described as having water gushing from the holes in the scales of the cone similar to the Meta Sudans (the sweating rock that was also topped by a pine cone according to some) that still stands outside the Coliseum."[86] The bronze peacocks on either side of the fountain are copies of those decorating the tomb of the Emperor Hadrian, now the Castel Sant'Angelo. The original peacocks are in the Braccio Nuovo Museum.

Both the pine cone and the flanking pair of bronze peacocks now adorn (since ca. 1st century) the Vatican City in a place called Fontana della Pigna facing the Cortile della Pigna.

Vatican Museum: giant pine cone. Description: Vatican City: Vatican Museum: giant pine cone (gilt bronze, originally a Roman fountain dating from 1st or 2nd century AD) (Cortile della Pigna, Courtyard of the Pine Cone).[87]

Bronze peacock now in Braccio Nuovo Museum
Link with the Assur group of 'metal smelters, metal workers'.

Assyrian Ashurnasirpal Relief from Nimrud, 865 B.C., can now be found at the British Museum. This section of wall relief was behind the king's throne and depicts a ritual involving a tree. Another panel with the same scene was opposite the center doorway of the throne room. The king is shown twice, on either side of a symbolic tree. On the left and on the right is an apkallu. Hieroglyphs: *eraka* 'wing' Rebus: *erako* 'moltencast copper'; dhokra 'bag' Rebus: dhokra '*cire perdue*/lost-wax casting'; karaḍa 'safflower' Rebus: karaḍa 'hard alloy'.

A pine cone comparable to this Vatican model is held on the right hand of Ashurnasirpal who is an 'Ashur, Assur':

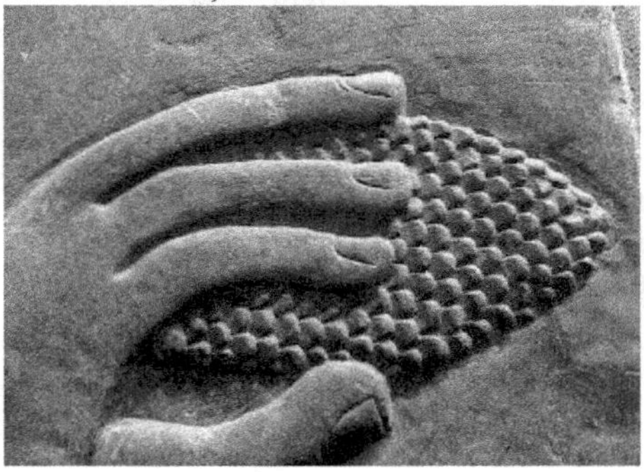

[quote] Detail of pine cone. Standard Inscription.Palace of Ashurnasirpal, priest of Ashur, favorite of Enlil and Ninurta, beloved of Anu and Dagan, the weapon of the great gods, the mighty king, king of the world, king of Assyria; son of Tukulti-Ninurta, the great king, the mighty king, king of Assyria, the son of Adad-nirari, the great king, the mighty king of Assyria; the valiant man, who acts with the support of Ashur, his lord, and has no equal among the princes of the four quarters of the world; the wonderful shepherd who is not afraid of battle; the great flood which none can oppose; the king who makes those who are not subject to him submissive; who has subjugated all mankind; the mighty warrior who treads on the neck of his enemies, tramples down all foes, and shatters the forces of the proud; the king who acts with the support of the great gods, and whose hand has conquered all lands, who has subjugated all the mountains and received their tribute, taking hostages and establishing his power over all countries.

When Ashur, the lord who called me by my name and has made my kingdom great, entrusted his merciless weapon to my lordly arms, I overthrew the widespread troops of the land of Lullume in battle. With the assistance of Shamash and Adad, the gods who help me, I thundered like Adad the destroyer over the troops of the Nairi lands, Habhi, Shubaru, and Nirib. I am the king who had brought into submission at his feet the lands from beyond the Tigris to Mount Lebanon and the Great Sea [the Mediterranean], the whole of the land of Laqe, the land of Suhi as far as Rapiqu, and whose hand has conquered from the source of the river Subnat to the land of Urartu.

The area from the mountain passes of Kirruri to the land of Gilzanu, from beyond the Lower Zab to the city of Til-Bari which is north of the land of Zaban, from the city of Til-sha-abtani to Til-sha-Zabdani, Hirimu and Harutu, fortresses of the land of Karduniash [Babylonia], I have restored to the borders of my land. From the mountain passes of Babite to the land of Hashmar I have counted the inhabitants as peoples of my land. Over the lands which I have subjugated I have appointed my governors, and they do obeisance.

I am Ashurnasirpal, the celebrated prince, who reveres the great gods, the fierce dragon, conqueror of the cities and mountains to their furthest extent, king of rulers who has tamed the stiff-necked peoples, who is crowned with splendor, who is not afraid of battle, the merciless champion who shakes resistance, the glorious king, the shepherd, the protection of the whole world, the king, the word of whose mouth destroys mountains and seas, who by his lordly attack has forced fierce and merciless kings from the rising to the setting sun to acknowledge one rule.

The former city of Kalhu [Nimrud], which Shalmaneser king of Assyria, a prince who preceded me, had built, that city had fallen into ruins and lay deserted. That city I built anew, I took the peoples whom my hand had conquered from the lands which I subjugated, from the land of Suhi, from the land of Laqe, from the city of Sirqu on the other side of the Euphrates, from the furthest extent of the land of Zamua, from Bit-Adini and the land of Hatte, and from Lubarna, king of the land of Patina, and made them settle there.

I removed the ancient mound and dug down to the water level. I sank the foundations 120 brick courses deep. A palace with halls of cedar, cypress, juniper, box-wood, meskannu-wood, terebinth and tamarisk, I founded as my royal residence for my lordly pleasure for ever.

Creatures of the mountains and seas I fashioned in white limestone and alabaster, and set them up at its gates. I adorned it, and made it glorious, and set ornamental knobs of bronze all around it. I fixed doors of cedar, cypress, juniper and meskannu-wood in its gates. I took in great quantities, and placed there, silver, gold, tin, bronze and iron, booty taken by my hands from the lands which I had conquered. [unquote][88]

Image of apkallu, winged 'sage'i n Mesopotamia carrying a pot? Two hieroglyphs are carried. 1. Pine cone; and 2. Wallet. *kaṇḍe* 'pine cone' Rebus: *kaṇḍ* 'stone' *dhokra* 'wallet' Rebus: *dhokra* '*cire perdue* cast'.

Assyrian Eagle Protective Spirit.Also known as Apkallu griffin. Originally from 865 B.C., it can now be found at the New York Metropolitan Museum. *eruvai* 'eagle, kite' Rebus: *eruvai* 'copper'. eraka 'wing' Rebus: erako 'moltencast copper'. *kaṇḍe* 'pine cone' Rebus: *kaṇḍ* 'stone'. *dhokra* 'wallet' Rebus: *dhokra* '*cire perdue* cast'. This hieroglyphic composition signifies a cire perdue casting of copper stone (perhaps carbonate-hosted ores with a mix of copper, lead and zinc).

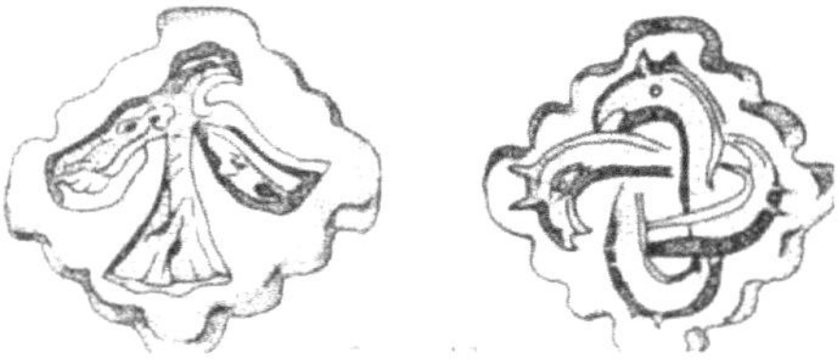

Two seals from Gonur 1 in the Murghab delta; dark brown stone,[89] eagle engraced on one face. *eruvai* 'eagle' Rebus: *eruvai* 'copper'. *nāga* 'serpent Rebus: *nāga* 'lead'. Thus a copper-lead carbonate (perhaps sediment-based) ore is indicated.

New York city Art museum. Ashurnasirpal. Kalhu Ear-ring and pendant with a pine cone glyph

Pine cone hieroglyphs adorn the side stools and is atop the 'altars' or 'standards'. [quote]Description: The 'Garden Party' relief from the

North Palace of Ashurbanipal at Nineveh. This carved stone picture hides a gory secret. King Ashurbanipal and his Queen are enjoying a party in their garden. Can you see the Queen sitting down facing her husband? A harpist on the left plays music while they eat and drink. But in the tree beside him is the severed head of King Teumann, a local ruler who had tried to fight against Ashurbanipal. The picture was on the wall in the royal palace, to warn any visitors not to try the same thing. It should also be noted that depictions of women are rare in Assyrian art. c.645 BCE90 [unquote]

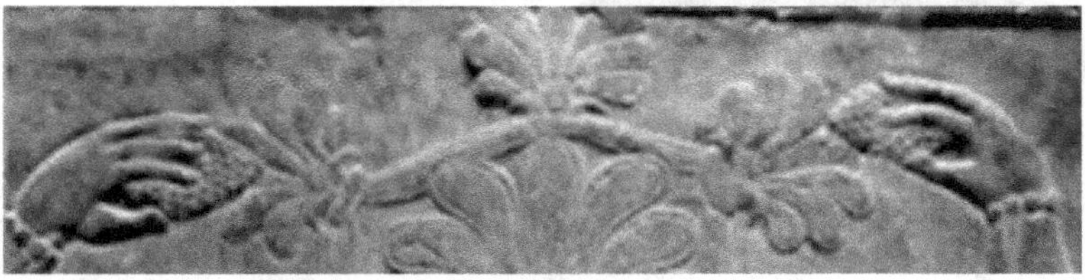

Assyrian Period, reign of King Ashurnasirpal 11 (883 -- 859 BCE) Alabastrous Limestone Height 110.5 cm. Width 183 cm. Depth 6.4 -- 9.6 cm. Miho Museum91

Assyrian) alabaster Height: 236.2 cm (93 in). Width: 135.9 cm (53.5 in). Depth: 15.2 cm (6 in). This relief decorated the interior wall of the northwest palace of King Ashurnasirpal II at Nimrud. On his right hand, he holds a pine cone. Examples of reliefs of king ashur-nasir-pal II

The Egyptian Staff of Osiris, dating back to approximately 1224 BC, depicts two intertwining serpents rising up to meet at a pinecone. (Photo: Egyptian Museum, Turin, Italy)

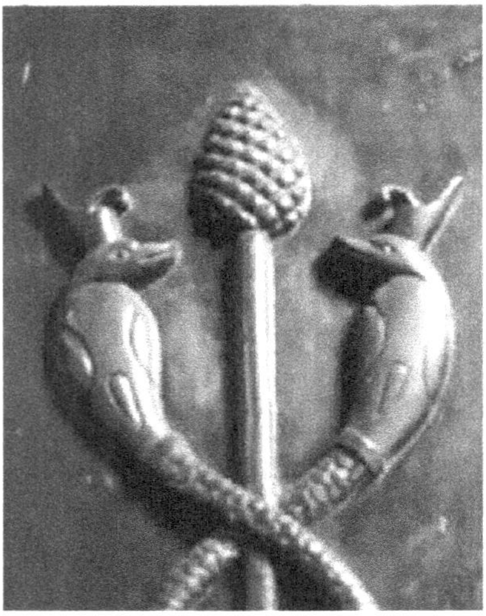

Hieroglyphs read rebus: pine cone as water fountain *kāṇḍa* 'flowing water'
Rebus: Ku. *lokhaṛ* 'iron tools '; H. *lokhaṇḍ* m. ' iron tools, pots and pans '; G. *lokhāḍ* n. 'tools, iron, ironware'; M. *lokhāḍ* n. ' iron '(CDIAL 11171).

The object carried by the Ashurbanipal may be a pine-cone. Rebus readings are: Ash. piċ -- kandə ' pine ', Kt. pūc̣i, piċi, Wg. puċ, püċ (pūc̣ -- kəŕ ' pine -- cone '), Pr. wyoċ, Shum. lyēwič (lyē -- ?).(CDIAL 8407). Cf. Gk. peu/kh f. ' pine ', Lith. pušìs, OPruss. peuse NTS xiii 229. The suffix –kande in the lexeme: Ash. piċ-- kandə ' pine ' may be cognate with the bulbous glyphic related to a mangrove root: Koḍ. kaṇḍe root-stock from which small roots grow; ila·ti kaṇḍe sweet potato (ila·ti England). Tu. kaṇḍe, gaḍḍè a bulbous root; Ta. kaṇṭal mangrove, Rhizophora mucronata; dichotomous mangrove, Kandelia rheedii. Ma. kaṇṭa bulbous root as of lotus, plantain; point where branches and bunches grow out of the stem of a palm; kaṇṭal what is bulb-like, half-ripe jackfruit and other green fruits; R. candel. (DEDR 1171). Rebus: *kaṇḍa* 'tools, pots and pans of metal'. Alternative: Paš. lauṛ. kayā´ ' edible pine cone '.

Rebus: *kaṇḍa* '(mineral) stone', Rebus: *kaṇḍa* 'stone (ore)(Gadba)' Ga. (Oll.) *kanḍ, (S.) kanḍu* (pl. *kanḍkil*) stone (DEDR 1298). *khaḍā* 'circumscribe' (M.); Rebus: *khaḍā* 'nodule (ore), stone' (M.) *kāṇḍā* 'metal tools, pots and pans'. kaṇḍa = a furnace, altar (Santali)

Allograph: *kaṇḍe* head or ear of millet or maize (Telugu) [Tel.]

Since Isis and Serapis were divinities adored by seafaring merchants, the hieroglyphs associated with the fountain near the temple of Isis in Pompeii may relate to mineral ore stones of a special type: *morakkhakaŋ* or *pisāca lohaŋ* recognized in early metallurgy. This *morakkhaka* ore stone is depicted by the hieroglyph: *moraka* 'peacock'. A pair of peacocks: dula 'pair' Rebus: dul 'cast metal'. Thus the hieroglyphic composition, in bronze, of two peacocks flanking a pine cone is read rebus: *morakkhaka kaṇḍa* 'moraka ore complex stone'.

pisācī loha, 'a kind of copper'

The Prākṛt Vibhāṣās . Pischel quotes Mārkaṇḍēya's division of the Prākṛt-s into *Bhāṣā, Vibhāṣā, Apabhraṁśa*, and Paiśāca, his division of the Vibhāṣās into *Śākārī, Cāṇḍālī, Śābarī, Ābhīrikā*, and *Ṭākkī*), and his rejection of *Auḍhrī* (Pischel, *Oḍrī*) and *Drāviḍī.* He says, "Rāmatarkavāgīśa observes that the *vibhāṣāḥ* cannot be called Apabhraṁśa, if they are used in dramatic works and the like.[92] In dramas, Dramili was the language of "forest-dwellers", Sauraseni was spoken by "the heroine and her female friends", and Avanti was spoken by "cheats and rogues".

A synonym of *morakkhaka loha* is *pisācī loha*, 'a kind of copper': pisācī J v.442. -- 2. [like pisāca – loha referring to the Paiśāca district, hailing from that tribe, cp. the term malla in same meaning and origin] a sort of acrobat, as pl. *pisācā* 'tumblers' Miln 191. -- nagara town of goblins (cp. yakkha -- nagara) Vism 531. -- loha [connected with the tribe of the Paiśāca's: Mhbh vii.4819; cp. Paiśācī as one of the Prākrit dialects: Pischel, *Prk. Gr.* § 3] a kind of copper of copper VbhA 63 (eight varieties).

Hieroglyph: *pisācā* 'tumblers' Rebus: *pisācī loha*, 'a kind of copper'

Is the artisan attempting to signify – deploying Meluhha symbolic forms -- a Mississippi Valley-Type and clastic-dominated sediment-hosted copper-lead-zinc deposit stone ore, prospected by panning identified as *pisācī loha* or *morakkhaka loha* ?

Paiśāca were metalworkers connected with *pisācī loha.* Like *morakkhaka loha*, the hieroglyphs may signify *pisācī loha* which was copper-lead-zinc ore aggregate, perhaps sediment deposits of ore stones. Rebus: *kāḍ,* kanḍ 'stone' Hieroglyph: *kaṇḍ, kaḍā* 'buffalo'

m0312 Persons vaulting over a water-buffalo.

A seal from Banawali shows women tumblers, acrobats leaping over a water-buffalo:

Impression and line-drawing of a steatite stamp seal with a water-buffalo and leapers. Buffalo attack or bull-leaping scene, Banawali (after UMESAO 2000:88, cat. no. 335). A figure is impaled on the horns of the buffalo; a woman acrobat wearing bangles on both arms and a long braid flowing from the head, leaps over the buffalo bull. Two Indus script glyphs in front of the buffalo. Glyphs: '1. arrow, 2. jag/notch':

1. *kaṇḍa* 'arrow' (Skt.) H. *kā̃ḍerā* m. ' a caste of bow -- and arrow -- makers (CDIAL 3024). Or. *kāṇḍa, kā̃ṛ* 'stalk, arrow '(CDIAL 3023). *ayaskāṇḍa* 'a quantity of iron, excellent iron' (Pāṇ.gaṇ)
2. खांडा [khāṇḍā] *m* A jag, notch, or indentation (as upon the edge of a tool or weapon). (Marathi) Rebus: *khāṇḍā* 'tools, pots and pans, metal-ware'.

The message of stone ore is reinforced by the glyphics of buffalo and overthrow of an acrobat woman (*kola* 'woman'; rebus: *kol*'smithy'): கண்டி kaṇṭi buffalo bull (Tamil) kaṇḍ 'buffalo'; rebus: kaṇḍ 'stone (ore)'. *kiḍāvu*. He-buffalo; எருமைக்கடா (Malayalam) *Colloq.*கடவு[3] kaṭavu , *n.* < கடா. 1. Male buffalo; எருமைக்கடா. முதுகடவு கடவி (அழகர்கல. 33). *kaḍawan hoṛ* 'a man who has buffaloes'. (George L. Campbell, Compendium of the World's Languages, Routledge, London, 1991, p. 1199).Rebus: khāḍ 'trench, firepit' (G.) khāṛo 'pit, bog' (Nepali)

Rebus: kāḍ 'stone'. Ga. (Oll.) kanḍ, (S.) kanḍu (pl. kanḍkil) stone (DEDR 1298). mayponḍi kanḍ whetstone; (Ga.)(DEDR

4628).(खडा) Pebbles or small stones: also stones broken up (as for a road), metal. खडा [khaḍā] *m* A small stone, a pebble. 2 A nodule (of lime &c.): a lump or bit (as of gum, assafœtida, catechu, sugar-candy): the gem or stone of a ring or trinket: a lump of hardened fæces or scybala: a nodule or lump gen. CDIAL 3018 kāṭha m. ' rock ' lex. [Cf. *kānta* -- 2 m. ' stone ' lex.]

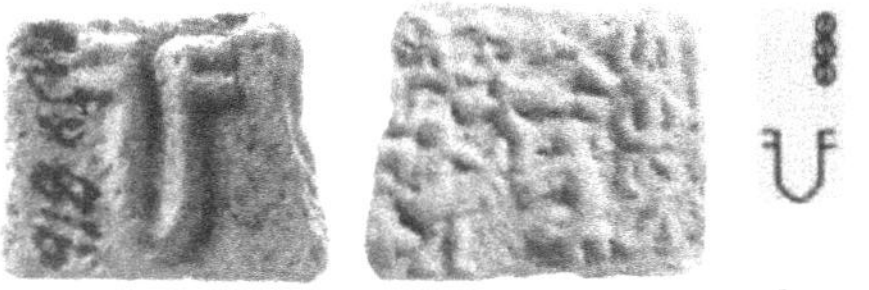

m1406At m1406B 2827 Pict-102: Drummer and people vaulting over? An adorant?

karaḍa 'double-drum' *Rebus: karaḍa* 'hard alloy'. Rebus: kāḍ 'stone'. Ga. (Oll.) kanḍ, (S.) kanḍu (pl. kanḍkil) stone (DEDR 1298). mayponḍi kanḍ whetstone; (Ga.)(DEDR 4628). (खडा) Pebbles or small stones: also stones broken up (as for a road), metal. खडा [khaḍā] *m* A small stone, a pebble. 2 A nodule (of lime &c.): a lump or bit (as of gum, assafœtida, catechu, sugar-candy): the gem or stone of a ring or trinket: a lump of hardened fæces or scybala: a nodule or lump gen. CDIAL 3018 kāṭha m. ' rock ' lex. [Cf. *kānta* -- 2 m. ' stone ' lex.] Bshk. *kōr* ' large stone ' AO xviii 239. கண்டு[3] kaṇṭu , *n.* < *gaṇḍa.* 1. Clod, lump; கட்டி. (தைலவ. தைல. 99.) 2. Wen; கழலைக்கட்டி. 3. Bead or something like a pendant in an ornament for the neck; ஓர் ஆபரணவுரு. புல்லிகைக்கண்ட நாண் ஒன்றிற் கட்டின கண்டு ஒன்றும் (S.I.I. ii, 429). (CDIAL 3023) kāṇḍa cluster, heap ' (in *tṛṇa -- kāṇḍa* -- Pāṇ. Kāś.). [Poss. connexion with gaṇḍa -- 2 makes prob. non -- Aryan origin (not with P. Tedesco Language 22, 190 < *kṛntáti*). Pa. *kaṇḍa* -- m.n. joint of stalk, lump. काठः A rock, stone. kāṭha m. ' rock ' lex. [Cf. *kānta* -- 2 m. ' stone ' lex.] Bshk. *kōr* ' large stone ' AO xviii 239.(CDIAL 3018). অয়স্কঠিন [ayaskaṭhina] as hard as iron; extremely hard (Bengali)

Rebus message: alloying (mixing) zinc (sattiya). Casting (metal, iron, bronze, bell-metal); big stone mason. kaḍī a chain; a hook; a link (G.); kaḍum a bracelet, a ring (G.) Rebus: kaḍiyo [Hem. Des. kaḍaio = Skt. sthapati a mason] a bricklayer; a mason; kaḍiyaṇa, kaḍiyeṇa a woman of the bricklayer caste; a wife of a bricklayer (G.) A pair of chain-links may be read rebus: *dul kaḍī* 'cast stone (ore)'.

Loha (nt.) [Cp. Vedic loha, of Idg. *(e)reudh "red"; see also rohita & lohita] metal, esp. copper, brass or bronze. It is often used as a general term & the individual application is not always sharply defined. Its comprehensiveness is evident from the classification of loha at VbhA 63, where it is said lohan ti jātilohaŋ, vijāti°, kittima°, pisāca° or natural metal, produced metal, artificial (i. e. alloys), & metal from the Pisāca district. Each is subdivided as follows: jāti°=ayo, sajjhaŋ, suvaṇṇaŋ, tipu, sīsaŋ, tambalohaŋ, vekantakalohaŋ; vijāti°=nāga -- nāsika°; kittima°=kaŋsalohaŋ, vaṭṭa°, ārakūṭaŋ; pisāca°= morakkhakaŋ, puthukaŋ, malinakaŋ, capalakaŋ, selakaŋ, āṭakaŋ, bhallakaŋ, dūsilohaŋ. The description ends "Tesu pañca jātilohāni pāḷiyaŋ visuŋ vuttān' eva (i. e. the first category are severally spoken of in the Canon). Tambalohaŋ vekantakan ti imehi pana dvīhi jātilohehi saddhiŋ sesaŋ sabbam pi idha lohan ti veditabbaŋ."

ఆరకూటము [ārakūṭamu] *āra-kūṭamu.* [Skt.] n. Steel or brass. ఉక్కు, ఇత్తడి. ఆరకూటచ్ఛాయ the hue of steel or brass.

vekantakalohan 'mercury'? Perhaps related to: कान्त kānta A kind of iron. A precious stone (in comp. with सूर्य, चन्द्र and अयस्). -लोहम् the loadstone. -लौहम् steel.

Kaŋsa [cp. Sk. kaŋsa; of uncertain etym., perhaps of Babylonian origin, cp. hirañña] 1. bronze Miln 2; magnified by late commentators occasionally into silver or gold. Thus J vi.504 (silver) and Ji.338; iv.107; vi.509 (gold), considered more suitable

to a fairy king. -- 2. a bronze gong Dh 134 (DhA iii.58). -- 3. a bronze dish J i.336; āpānīya° a bronze drinking cup, goblet M. i.316. -- 4. a "bronze," i. e. a bronze coin worth 4 kahāpaṇas Vin iv.255, 256. See Rhys Davids, *Coins and Measures* §§ 12, 22. -- "Golden bronze" in a fairy tale at Vv 54 is explained by Dhammapāla VvA 36 as "bells." -- It is doubtful whether *brass* was known in the Ganges valley when the earlier books were composed; but kaŋsa may have meant *metal* as opposed to earthenware. See the compounds. -- upadahārana (n. a.) metal milk -- pail (?) in phrase: dhenusahassāni dukūla -- sandanāni (?) kaŋsūpadhāraṇām D ii.192; A iv.393; J vi.503 (expld at 504). Kern (*Toev.* p. 142) proposes correction to kaŋs'ûpadohana (=Sk. kāŋsy'opodohana), i.e. giving milk to the extent of a metal pailful. -- kaṇṭaka metal thorns, bits of sharp metal, nails J v.102 (cp. sakaṇṭaka) -- kūta cheating with false or spurious metal D i.5 (=DA i.79: selling brass plates for gold ones). -- tāla bronze gong DhA i.389; DhsA 319 (°tāḷa); VvA 161 or cymbals J vi.277. 411. -- thāla metal dish, as distinguished from earthenware D i.74 (in simile of dakkho nahāpako=A iii.25) cp. DA i. 217; Vism 283 (in simile); DhA iii.57 (: a gong); DA i.217; DhA iv.67 =J iii.224; reading at Miln 62 to be °tāla (see *J.P.T.S.* 1886, 122). -- pattharika a dealer in bronze ware Vin ii.135. -- pāti & pātī a bronze bowl, usually for food: M i.25; A iv.393; Sn 14; PvA 274. -- pūra full of metal J iv.107. -- bhaṇḍa brass ware Vin ii.135. -- bhājana a bronze vessel Vism 142 (in simile). -- maya made of bronze Vin i.190; ii.112; -- mallaka metal dish, e. g. of gold J iii.21. -- loha bronze Miln 267.
Vaṭṭa -- kāra a worker in brass. The meaning of vaṭṭa in this connection is not clear.

Loha -- kaṭāha a copper (brass) receptacle Vin ii.170. -- kāra a metal worker, coppersmith, blacksmith Miln 331. -- kumbhī an iron cauldron Vin ii.170. Also N. of a purgatory J iii.22, 43; iv.493;v.268; SnA 59, 480; Sdhp 195. -- guḷa an iron (or metal) ball A iv.131; Dh 371 (mā °ŋ gilī pamatto; cp. DhA iv.109). -- jāla a copper (i. e. wire) netting PvA 153. -- thālaka a copper bowl Nd1226. -- thāli a bronze kettle DhA i.126. -- pāsāda "copper terrace," brazen palace, N. of a famous monastery at Anurādhapura in Ceylon Vism 97; DA i.131; Mhvs passim. -- piṇḍa an iron ball SnA 225. -- bhaṇḍa copper (brass) ware Vin ii.135. -- maya made of copper, brazen Sn 670; Pv ii.64. -- māsa a copper bean Nd1 448 (suvaṇṇa -- channa). -- māsaka a small copper coin KhA 37 (jatu -- māsaka, dāru -- māsaka+); DhsA 318. -- rūpa a bronze statue Mhvs 36, 31. -- salākā a bronze gong -- stick Vism 283.

sīsa (lead)

Tipu [cp. Sk. trapu, non-- Aryan?] lead, tin Vin i.190 (°maya); S v.92; J ii.296; Miln 331 (°kāra a worker in lead, tinsmith); Vism 174 (°maṇḍala); DhA iv.104 (°parikhā)

Ayo & Aya (nt.) [Sk. ayaḥ nt. iron & ore, Idg. *ajes -- , cp. Av. ayah, Lat. aes, Goth. aiz, Ohg. ēr (= Ger. Erz.), Ags. ār (= E. ore).] iron. The *nom.* ayo found only in set of 5 metals forming an alloy of gold (jātarūpa), viz. ayo, loha (copper), tipu (tin), sīsa (lead), sajjha (silver) A iii.16 = S v.92; of obl. cases only the *instr.* ayasā occurs Dh 240 (= ayato DhA iii.344); Pv i.1013 (paṭikujjita, of Niraya). -- Iron is the material used -- In compn. both ayo° & aya° occur as bases. I. ayo°: -- kapāla an iron pot A iv.70 (v. l. °guhala); Nd2 304 iii. d 2 (of Niraya). -- kūṭa an iron hammer PvA 284. -- khīla an iron stake S v.444; M iii.183 = Nd2 304 iii. c; SnA 479. -- guḷa an iron ball S v.283; Dh 308; It 43 = 90; Th 2, 489; DA i.84. -- ghana an iron club Ud 93; VvA 20. -- ghara an iron house J iv.492. -- paṭala an iron roof or ceiling (of Niraya) PvA 52. -- pākāra an iron fence Pv i.1013 = Nd2 304 iii. d 1. -- maya made of iron Sn 669 (kūṭa); J iv.492 (nāvā); Pv i.1014 (bhūmi of N.); PvA 43, 52. -- muggara an iron club PvA 55. -- sanku an iron spike Siv.168; Sn 667. II. aya°: -- kapāla = ayo° DhA i.148 (v. l. ayo°). -kāra a worker in iron Miln 331. -- kūṭa = ayo° J i.108; DhA ii.69 (v. l.). -- nangala an iron plough DhA i.223; iii.67. -- paṭṭaka an iron plate or sheet (cp. loha°) J v.359. -- paṭhavi an iron floor (of Avīci) DhA i.148. --

saṅghāṭaka an iron (door) post DhA iv.104. -- sūla an iron stake Sn 667; DhA i.148.

Sajjha (nt.) [cp. Sk. sādhya] silver D ii.351 (v. l.); S v.92 (v. l.); A iii.16. Cp. sajjhu. -- kāra silversmith Miln 331.

Illustrated London News 1936 - November 21st. A 'Sheffield of Ancient India: Chanhu-Daro's metal working industry 10 X photos of copper knives, spears, razors, axes and dishes.

Bronze statue of a woman holding a small bowl, Mohenjo-daro; copper alloy made using cire perdue method (DK 12728; Mackay 1938: 274, Pl. LXXIII, 9-11)

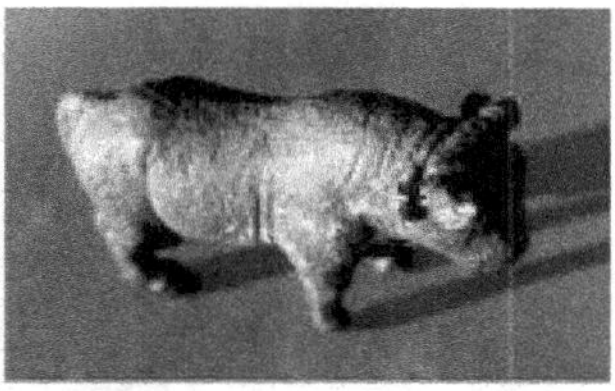

The 'Dancing Girl' (Mohenjo-daro), made by the lost-wax process; a bronze foot and anklet from Mohenjo-daro; and a bronze figurine of a bull (Kalibangan). (Courtesy: ASI) "Archaeological excavations have shown that Harappan metal smiths obtained copper ore (either directly or through local communities) from the Aravalli hills, Baluchistan or beyond. They soon discovered that adding tin to copper produced bronze, a metal harder than copper yet easier to cast, and also more resistant to corrosion.

Whether deliberately added or already present in the ore, various 'impurities' (such as nickel, arsenic or lead) enabled the Harappans to harden bronze further, to the point where bronze chisels could be used to dress stones! The alloying ranges have been found to be 1%–12% in tin, 1%–7% in arsenic, 1%–9% in nickel and 1%–32% in lead. Shaping copper or bronze involved techniques of fabrication such as forging, sinking, raising, cold work, annealing, riveting, lapping and joining. Among the metal artefacts produced by the Harappans, let us mention spearheads, arrowheads, axes, chisels, sickles, blades (for knives as well as razors), needles, hooks, and vessels such as jars, pots and pans, besides objects of toiletry such as bronze mirrors; those were slightly oval, with their face raised, and one side was highly polished.

The Harappan craftsmen also invented the true saw, with teeth and the adjoining part of the blade set alternatively from side to side, a type of saw unknown elsewhere until Roman times. Besides, many bronze figurines or humans (the well-known 'Dancing Girl', for instance) and animals (rams, deer, bulls...) have been unearthed from Harappan sites. Those figurines were cast by the lost-wax process: the initial model was made of wax, then thickly coated with clay; once fired (which caused the wax to melt away or be 'lost'), the clay hardened into a mould, into which molten bronze was later poured. Harappans also used gold and silver (as well as their joint alloy, electrum) to produce a wide variety of ornaments such as pendants, bangles, beads, rings or necklace parts, which were usually found hidden away in hoards such as ceramic or bronze pots. While gold was probably panned from the Indus waters, silver was perhaps extracted from galena, or native lead sulphide...While the Indus civilization belonged to the Bronze Age, its successor, the Ganges civilization, which emerged in the first millennium BCE, belonged to the Iron Age. But recent excavations in central parts of the Ganges valley and in the eastern Vindhya hills have shown that iron was produced there possibly as early as in 1800 BCE. Its use appears to have become widespread from about 1000 BCE, and we find in late Vedic texts mentions of a 'dark metal' (krṣnāyas), while earliest texts (such as the Rig-Veda) only spoke of ayas, which, it is now accepted, referred to copper or bronze.

Damaged circular clay furnace, comprising iron slag and tuyeres and other waste materials stuck with its body, exposed at lohsanwa mound, Period II, Malhar, Dist. Chandauli.[93]

Harappa. kiln.Figure 9. Harappa 1999, Mound F, Trench 43: Period 5 kiln, plan and section views.[94]

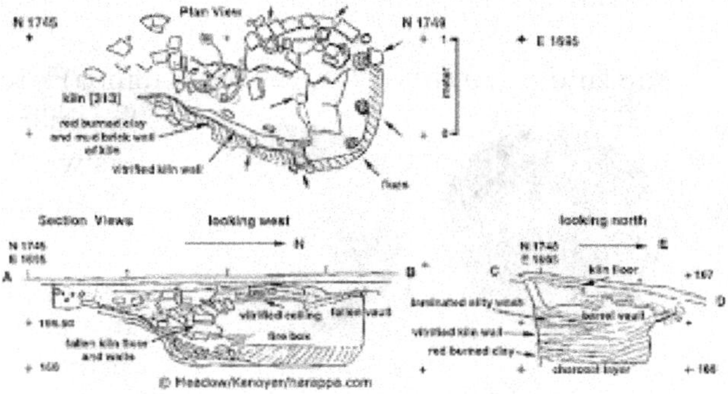

Tin Road: Ashur-Kultepe and Meluhha hieroglyphs

Presence of Meluhha artisans -- of mints and metalwork -- back in time from c. 150 BCE to 3rd millennium BCE is attested by the use of Meluhha hieroglyphs, in an extensive contact/trade area stretching from foothills of the Himalayas to Pontic mountains of Turkey.

The land of Kuninda (also called Kulinda) stretched along the foothills of the Himalayas eastwards from the borders of Audumbara (c. 150-100 BCE) temporarily independent of the Punjab area in the Pathankot region of the Beas river valley to the borders of Nepal.

Legend in Prākṛt (Brahmi script, from left to right):: "Rajnah Kunindasya Amoghabhutisya maharajasya." Obverse: Kharoshti legend. AIC pg. 146, 1; MACW 4442; Senior pg. 233. Legend in Kharoshti script, from righ to left: Rana Kunidasa Amoghabhutisa Maharajasa, ("Great King Amoghabhuti, of the Kunindas").
The hieroglyphs on the Kuninda/Puninda silver coin of ca. 2nd century BCE are : on the obverse a deer to the right of a female figure (facing) and holding a flower in right hand and her left hand rests on the thigh with inscriptions written around. On the reverse a five-arched hill in the centre surmounted by a Nandi-pada symbol, on the right is a tree in a railing and on the left two symbols: svastika and 'standard device'*sangaḍa* 'lathe, portable furnace'.

kola 'woman' Rebus: kola 'working in iron'.
melh 'goat' (Brahui) Rebus: *milakkhu* 'copper' (Pali)
kāṇḍa 'flowing water' Rebus: Ku. *lokhaṛ* 'iron tools '; H. *lokhaṇḍ* m. ' iron tools, pots and pans '; G. *lokhãḍ* n. 'tools, iron, ironware'; M. *lokhãḍ* n. ' iron '(CDIAL 11171).
ḍangar 'bull', *ḍā̃g* mountain-ridge (H.)(CDIAL 5476). Rebus: *dhangar* 'blacksmith' (Maithili)

satthiya 'svastika glyph' Rebus *satthiya, jasta* 'zinc' (Kashmiri. Kannada); *sattva* 'zinc' (Prākṛt)

Rebus: *khōṇḍa* 'leafless tree' (Marathi). Rebus: *kõdār* 'turner' (Bengali) Ka. kōḍu horn, tusk, branch of a tree (DEDR 2200). खोट [khōṭa] alloyed ingot (Marathi). *koḍ* 'artisan's workplace'.

Function served by the 'standard device' in Meluhha cultural, life-activities

The 'standard device' frequently deployed as a hieroglyph is associated with the process of 'alloying'. Something comparable to the making of crucible steel to create 'hard alloys'. A pointer of this semantic, cultural significance is seen on a tablet showing 'standard device' flanked by columns of 'circles' or 'round pebbles'.

Hieroglyph: *gōṭī* 'round pebble Rebus: L. *khoṭ* f 'alloy, impurity', °*ṭā* 'alloyed', awāṇ. *khoṭā* 'forged'; P. *khoṭ* m. 'base, alloy' M.*khoṭā* 'alloyed' (CDIAL 3931).
m0008, m0021, h228B

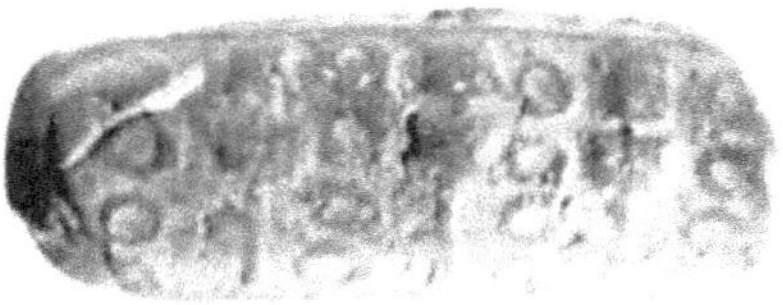

Carved Ivory

Standard in the middle

har501 Harappa 1990 and 1993.
Standard device, model reconstructed after

Mahadevan

? The dotted circles on the bottom portion of the device connote *ghangar ghongor*; rebus: *kangar* 'portable furnace'. Rebus: *kangar kandi* 'bead (out of crucible,furnace)'. A good example is dull olive-brown colour carnelian stone, which is turned red artificially and color designs on the beads added in special ceramic containers and kilns by the Meluhha artisans.

The standard device thus connotes: *sangaḍa* 'lathe, furnace' (for) *khāṇḍa* 'tools, pots and pans and metal-ware'; and *kandi* 'beads'. Syena-citi: A Monument of Uttarakashi District[95]

Excavated site – Purola

Geo-Coordinates-Lat. 30° 52'54" N Long. 77° 05'33" E

Notification No& Date;2742/-/16-09/1996 The ancient site at Purola is located on the left bank of river Kamal in District Uttarkashi. The excavation carried out by Hemwati Nandan Bahuguna University, Srinagar Garhwal. The site yielded the remains of Painted Grey Ware (PGW) from the earliest level along with other associated materials include terracotta figurines, beads, potter-stamp and the dental and femur portions of domesticated horse (Equas Cabalus Linn). The most important finding from the site is a brick alter identified as Syena chitti by the excavator. The structure is in the shape of a flying eagle Garuda, head facing east with outstretched wings having a square chamber in the middle yielded the remains of pottery assignable to circa first century B.C. to second century AD along with copper coin of Kuninda , bone pieces and a thin gold leaf impressed with a human figure identified as Agni.

A good background article is Subhash Kak, Ancient religion in ancient Iran and Zarathushtra,(2003). The article notes common cultural concepts including: Saena (Syena): the eagle; also Saena meregh (mr.ga), Simurg.

"The Zoroastrian innovations did not change the basic Vedic character of the culture in Iran."

śyena of Rgveda gets exemplified in ancient Iranian glyphics matching the cultural traditions.

"Ahura Mazda, the god who created High Hara, also built palaces on it for the greatest gods: Mithra, Sraosha, Rashnu, Ardvi-sura Anahita, and Haoma, all of whom ride in special chariots. While humans could not live on the holy mountain, the greatest mythical heroes made sacrifices there. The way to the other world, a special abode of the blessed (where the largest and most choice specimens of plants and animals were found) lay through the foothills of Hara/Meru. The Chinvat bridge of Zoroastrian mythology, over which the souls of the dead had to pass was on or near High Hara. The motif of birds dwelling near the summit is shared by Iranian and Indian accounts, as is the theme of the theft of the intoxicating plant haoma/soma from the mountain's summit by a magical bird (Syena/Garuda/ Simurgh); and the slaying of a multi-headed, multi-eyed dragon nearby (1). In the Indian tradition, Agni, the rock-born god of fire with tawny hair and iron teeth is connected with the sacred mountain. In the Iranian tradition, High Hara is also associated with metallurgy. Fire and metals were introduced to humanity after the hero Hoshang (Haoshyangha) sacrificed on the mountain (2). High Hara was also the locale of many of the most memorable contests in Iranian mythology."[96]

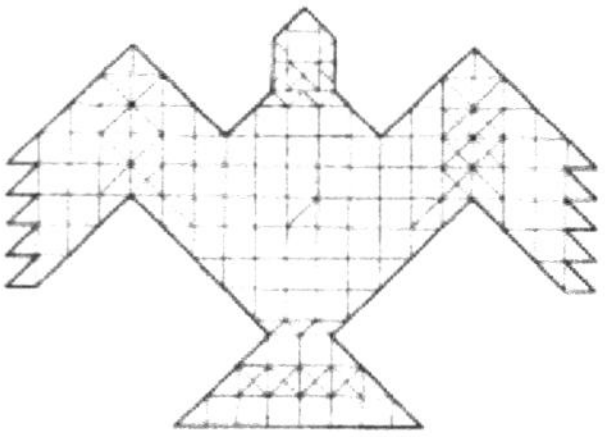

Figure 7. The syena citi: layers 1, 3, and 5

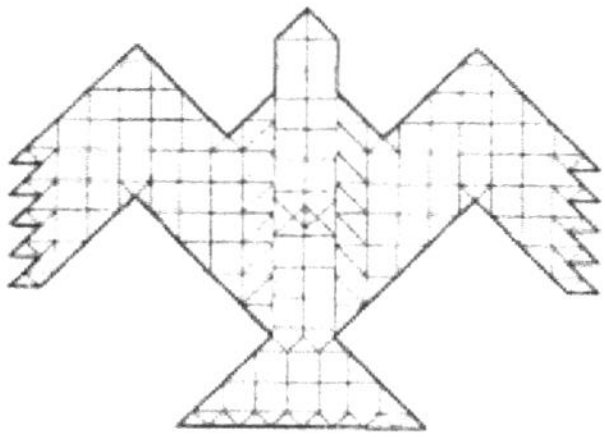

Figure 8. The syena citi: layers 2 and 4.

Syena Chiti, Garuda shaped Chiti Schematic as described by John F Price. Context: Panjal Atiratra yajnam (2011). cf.The paper of John Price: Applied geometry of *śulbasūtra*s.

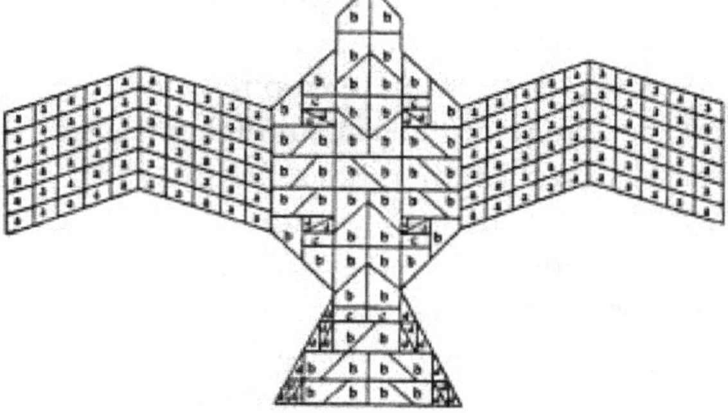

First layer of vakrapakṣa śyena altar. The wings are made from 60 bricks of type 'a', and the body, head and tail from 50 type 'b', 6 of type 'c' and 24 type 'd' bricks. Each subsequent layer was laid out using different patterns of bricks with the total number of bricks equalling 200.

"Sênmurw (Pahlavi), Sîna-Mrû (Pâzand), a fabulous, mythical bird. The name derives from Avestan mərəγô saênô 'the bird Saêna', originally a raptor, either eagle or falcon, as can be deduced from the etymologically identical Sanskrit śyena." See: discussions in the appended, embedded document.

Senmurv on the tomb of Abbess Theodote, Pavia early 8th c.

"Griffin-like . Simurgh (Persian: سيمرغ), also spelled simorgh, simurg, simoorg or simourv, also known as Angha (Persian: عنقا), is the modern Persian name for a fabulous, benevolent, mythical flying creature. The figure can be found in all periods of Greater Iranian art and literature, and is evident also in the iconography of medieval Armenia, the Byzantine empire , and other regions that were within the sphere of Persian cultural influence. Through cultural assimilation the Simurgh was introduced to the Arabic-speaking world, where the concept was conflated with other Arabic mythical birds such as the Ghoghnus, a bird having some mythical relation with the date palm, and further developed as the Rukh (the origin of the English word "Roc")."[97]

Sassanid silk twill textile of a simurgh in a beaded surround, 6-7th c. CE

"The simurgh was considered to purify the land and waters and hence bestow fertility. The creature represented the union between the earth and the sky, serving as mediator and messenger between the two. The simurgh roosted in Gaokerena, the Hōm (Avestan: Haoma) Tree of Life, which stands in the middle of the world sea Vourukhasa. The plant is potent medicine, is called all-healing, and the seeds of all plants are deposited on it. When the simurgh took flight, the leaves of the tree of life shook making all the seeds of every plant to fall out. These seeds floated around the world on the winds of Vayu-Vata and the rains of Tishtrya, in cosmology taking root to become every type of plant that ever lived, and curing all the illnesses of mankind. The relationship between the simurgh and Hōm is extremely close. Like the simurgh, Hōm is represented as a bird, a messenger and as the essence of purity that can heal any illness or wound. Hōm - appointed as the first priest - is the essence of divinity, a property it shares with the simurgh. The Hōm is in addition the vehicle of farr(ah) (MP: khwarrah, Avestan: khvarenah, kavaēm kharēno) "[divine] glory" or "fortune". Farrah in turn represents the divine mandate that was the foundation of a king's authority."[98]

The ancient site at Purola is located on the left bank of river Kamal. The excavation yielded the remains of Painted Grey Ware (PGW) from the earliest level alongwith other associated materials include terracotta figurines, beads, potter-stamp, the dental and femur portions of domesticated horse (Equas Cabalus Linn). The most important finding from the site is a brick alter identified as Syenachiti by the excavator. The structure is in the shape of a flying eagle Garuda, head facing east with outstretched wings. In the center of the structure is the chiti is a square chamber yielded remains of pottery assignable to circa first century B.C. to second century AD. In addition copper coin of Kuninda and other material i.e. ash, bone pieces etc and a thin gold leaf impressed with a human figure tentatively identified as Agni have also been recovered from the central chamber.

Note: Many ancient metallic coins (called Kuninda copper coins) were discovered at Purola. cf. Devendra Handa, 2007,*Tribal coins of ancient India*, ISBN: 8173053170, Aryan Books International.

Kuninda

"In the Visnu Purana, the domain of Kunindas is especially defined as the Kulindopatyaka, i.e., the bounding foothills demarcating the Kuninda territory (NSWH, p. 71)...According to Ptolemy (McCrindle's Ptolemy, p. 110), the country of the Kulindrine, Kulindas, was located somewhere in the mountainous region around the sources of Vipasha (the Beas), the Shatadru (the

Satluj), the Yamuna and the Ganga...Kulindas emerged as a powerful warrior community...upgrade them as the vratya kshatriya...(Manusmriti, 10.20.22)"(Omacanda Handa, 2004, Naga cults and traditions in the western Himalaya, Indus publishing, p.76.)

In Dyuta parva (Sabhaparva, Mahabharata) Duryodhana said: "I describe that large mass of wealth consisting of various kinds of tribute presented to Yudhishthira by the kings of the earth. They that dwell by the side of the river Sailoda flowing between the mountains of Mer and Mandara and enjoy the delicious shade of topes of the Kichaka bamboo, viz., the Khashas, Ekasanas, the Arhas, the Pradaras, the Dirghavenus, the Paradas, the Kulindas, the Tanganas, and the other Tanganas, brought as tribute heaps of gold measured in dronas (jars) and raised from underneath the earth by ants and therefore called after these creatures." [cf. Section LI, Kisari Mohan Ganguli's translation (1883-1896)].

The Kuninda warrior clan is mentioned in ancient texts under the different forms of its name: Kauninda, Kulinda, and Kaulinda. Their coins have been found mostly in the Himalayan foothills, between the Rivers Sutlej and Yamuna. The Kuninda were therefore neighbors of the Kuluta and Trigarta clans.

Their coins have the figure of Bhagwan Shiva holding a trident, with the legend: Bhagwatah Chatresvara-Mahatmanah, translating to Bhagwan Shiva, tutelary deity of Ahichhatra, the Kuninda capital. On the obverse the coins portray a deer, six-arched hill, and a tree-in-railing.

These coins are made of copper, silver, and bronze, and are found from the 1st century BCE to the 3rd century CE. This suggests that the Kuninda gained independence from both the Indo-Greek and Kushan invaders. A Raja named Amoghabhuti features prominently in the later coins, which bear a striking resemblance to the coinage of the Yaudheya clan. It seems that the Kunindas in alliance with the latter ejected the Kushans in the 3rd century CE.

By the 5th century the clan-state of the Kuninda disappeared, or more accurately, broke-up into tiny fragments under the families of Ranas and Thakkuras just as their neighbors the Kuluta. The region of Simla Hills, down to the 20th century, was littered with tiny entities ruled by such petty chieftains, which were grouped by the British Empire into the Simla Hill States.

It is important to note that Pulinda were mleccha: पुलिन्दा नाहला निष्ट्याः शबरा वरुटा भटाः । माला भिल्लाः किराताश्च सर्वे$पि म्लेच्छजातयः ॥ Abh. Chin.934. (cited in Apte lexicon: म्लेच्छः [म्लेच्छ्-घञ् = mountaineer; -देशः, -मण्डलम् = कृष्णसारस्तु चरति मृगो यत्र स्वभावतः । स ज्ञेयो यज्ञियो देशो म्लेच्छदेशस्त्वतः परः ॥ Ms.2.23.)pulindá m.pl. ' name of a barbarous tribe ' AitBr. Pk. pulimda -- m.; Si. pulindā (st. pulindu --) ' a barbarian, a Väddā '. -- X mlēcchá -- q.v.(CDIAL 8297). పుళిందు [puḷinda] puḷinda. [Skt.] adj. Barbarian, savage, rude. పుళిందదేశము a certain country inhabited by savages. Bulinda Devi is the goddess of the Bheels. Tod's Rajasthan. i. 506. పుళిందుడు puḷinduḍu. n. A barbarian, savage, cannibal. புலிந்தம் pulintam , n. < Pulinda. A country, one of 56 tēcam, q.v.; ஐம்பத்தாறு தேசங்களுள் ஒன்று. (திருவேங். சத. 97.) புலிந்தன் pulintaṉ , n. < pulinda. Hunter; வேடன். (யாழ். அக.)Gāma : Ārāmika°, Pilinda° Vin i.28, 29 (as Ārāmikagāmaka & Pilinda-- gāmaka at Vin iii.249)(Pali) पुलिंद [pulinda] m (S) A barbarian, a savage or mountaineer; one who uses an uncultivated or a barbarous dialect.(Marathi) परंद or parinda परिंद m. a winged creature, a bird (Rām. 545, 779); a kind of long light boat with forty or fifty paddlers. (In the front is a raised seat covered with a canopy in which four persons can sit) (El.; L. 381, 382).(Kashmiri)

This is a *khāṭī* wheelwright's seal working kole.l 'smithy, temple' on iron, as a turner (producing) 'tools, pots and pans, metalware'.
Sumerian white marble cylinder seal. Early Dynastic, Circa 3200-3000 B.C. Engraved with a temple facade with a gateway, a gatepost to the left -- a reedpost with a scarf atop as flag -- together with a standing nude hero with a *kāṭī* ' knife ', 'sword' in one hand, holding a small quadruped (young bull?) in the other, to their left a stag (markhor?). *kole.l* 'smithy' Rebus: *kole.l* 'temple';
काँड् । काण्डः *kāḍ kāṇḍa* 'reed, stalk'; Rebus: *kāṇḍā* 'tools, pots and pans, metalware'.
Hieroglyph 'young bul': *kondh* 'young bull'. Rebus: *kũdār* 'turner, brass-worker'.
Hieroglyph: 'markhor': *miṇḍāl* markhor (Tor.wali) *meḍho* a ram, a sheep (G.)(CDIAL 10120)
Hieroglyph: *kāṭī* f. ' large knife or dagger ' (Sindhi) Rebus: *khāṭī* 'wheelwright' (Hindi) ఆరకాటి [ārakāṭi] *ārakāṭi*. [Tel.] n. A

boatman, a sailor. ఓడనడపువాడు, నావికుడు. (Telugu)

*karta3 ' knife '. [Cf. Av. *karəta* -- , °*ti* -- ' knife ': √kr̥t1]
B. *kāti* ' shell -- cutter's saw ', *kātān* ' large sacrificial knife '; Or. *katā* ' small billhook ', *kātī* ' knife '; Bi. Mth. *kāt* ' brazier's cutters '; H. *kāt* m. ' shears for shearing sheep, cock's spur ', °*tā* m. ' knife for cutting bamboos ', (*kattā* m. ' small curved sword ', *kattī* f. ' knife ', *kaṭṭī* f. ' small sword ' ← EP.); G. *kāt*ũ n. ' knife ', °*tī* f. ' knife, saw '; M. *kātī* f. ' cleaver '. -- Or < *kārti -- .(CDIAL 2853). *kārti ' knife '. [Cf. Bal. *kārč* < **kārti* -- , Pahl. *kārt* < **kārti* -- or °*ta* -- . For the series kr̥tí -- 2: *karta -- 3 or °*ti* -- : *kārti -- cf. Gk. kardi/a: Goth.*haírtō*: Gk. kh=r and Sk. *hr̊d* -- : *hā´rdi.* -- √kr̥t1]Ash. *kāṭa* f. ' knife ', Kt. *kṭå*,

Wg. *kaṭā´*; S. *kātī* f. ' large knife or dagger ', °*tu* m. ' large knife, tool for cutting edges of books '; L. mult. khet. *kātī* f. ' knife '; WPah. bhal.*kāt*, pl. °*tā̃* f. ' shears for shearing sheep '; Si. *kätta*, pl. *käti* ' billhook ' (early loan with *t*, not *ṭ*). <-> Forms of B. Or. Bi. Mth. H. G. M. alternatively < *kartá -- 3.[Cf. Shgh. *čād* ' knife ', EVSh 25, 40](CDIAL 3069).
Cylinder seal impression. Iraq museum.99

āra 'six curls' Rebus: ఆరకాటి [ārakāṭi] *ārakāṭi*. [Tel.] n. A boatman, a sailor. ఓడనడపువాడు, నావికుడు. (Telugu) Rebus 2: *khātī* 'wheelwright' (Hindi) eraka 'wing' Rebus: erako 'moltencast copper'. *kaṭā* கடவு[3] kaṭavu , *n.* < கடா .1. Male buffalo 'buffalo' *kāṛā* young buffalo (Go.) *kaṭā, kaṭamā* 'bison' (Ta.)(DEDR 1114) Rebus 1: *kā̃ṭhāḷ* 'maritime'; *kaṭalar, n.* < seamen, inhabitants of maritime tracts. Rebus 2: *khaḍā* 'nodule (ore), stone' (Marathi). Thus, the message relates to a seafaring merchant dealing in copper and stone.

āra 'six' Rebus: *āra* 'brass'.

Alternative: *kaṇḍe* A head or ear of millet or maize.
కందళము [Skt.] n. A germ or shoot, a sprout.

కొత్తమొలక. కందళించు *kandaḷinṭsu.* v. n. To sprout, germinate, shoot. (Telugu) काँड् | काण्डः m. the stalk or stem of a reed, grass, or the like, straw. In the compound with dan 5 (p. 221*a,* l. 13) the word is spelt *kāḍ.*

Sumer reed hut.

A pair of reeds on Warka vase top register. The rebus reading of the pair of reeds in Sumer standard is:

dhatu dul kāṇḍā 'mineral-orecast metal tools, pots and pans and metal-ware'. Hieroglyph: *mund or mudif* 'Toda hut, or reed hut or Iraqi marches'. Rebus: मुण्ड *muṇḍa* 'iron'. Thus, together, the rebus reading is: *āra muṇḍa dul khāṇḍā* 'brass, iron cast metalware'. *kaṇḍe.* [Tel.] n. Rebus: rebus: *kaṇḍa* '(mineral)stone', *kāṇḍā* 'metal tools, pots and pans'. The goats coming out of the kole.l 'smithy, temple' signify: *mlekh* 'goat' (Br.) Rebus: *milakku* 'copper' (Pali). Thus, the entire hieroglyphic composition signifies a smithy/forge working in copper, brass, iron, producing tools, pots and pans. What is being delivered to Inanna as signified on the Warka vase are storage jars containing metal ingots -- *mũh,* 'face' Rebus: *mũh,* 'ingots' as signified on the second register from top showing a bull face between two storage jars of ingots -- of copper and iron (alloys): (goat, *mlekh* and tiger, *kola*).

Close-up of top register Warka Vase.[100] Face of bull show between two large storage jars is a hieroglyph rebus semantic symbolic form providing 'meaning' of the contents of the jars: *mũh* *'face'* Rebus: *mũh* 'ingot'.

Read together with the 'ram' hieroglyph, as a signifier of the specific metal of the ingots in the accompanying two conical storage jars: Hieroglyph tagara 'ram' Rebus: tagara 'tin'. Thus, read together as *tagara mũh* 'tin ingots'.

Plus a hieroglyph which describes the superset: Kur. *xolā* tail. Malt. qoli id. (DEDR 2135). Rebus: *kol* 'working in iron', 'working in alloys' 'iron smelter' *kholī* = a metal covering; a loose covering of metal or cloth (Gujarati)

miṇḍāl markhor (Toṛwali) *meḍho* a ram, a sheep (G.)(CDIAL 10120) Rebus: मेढ 'merchant's helper' *meḍ* 'iron' (Munda). *mlekh* 'goat' (Br.) Rebus: *milakku* 'copper' (Pali); *mleccha* 'copper' (Skt.) Meluhha ! Mleccha ! tagara 'antelope' Rebus: tagara 'tin'. [The 'short-tail' is a hieroglyph which is ligatured to an 'antelope' – as a hieroglyph read rebus. Such a ligatured-tail evolved into a 'sign' of the Indus script which appears on inscribed copper-tablets.] Rebus: kol 'working in iron (metal), blacksmith (in this case, tin-smith)'. baṭa 'six' (hence six short strokes)(G.); rebus: bhaṭa 'furnace, smelter' (Santali). The stalk in front of the antelope is explained rebus: kolmo 'rice-plant'(Santali); rebus: kolami 'smithy/forge' (Te.) The antelope orthography shows a 'ram': tagara 'ram'; if the plant is tabernae montana, tagaraka 'tabernae montana'; rebus: tagara 'tin'. The seal shows an artisan-merchant who has a smelter to produce tin ingots.Antelope: meḷh 'goat' (Br.) Rebus: meṛha, meḍhi 'merchant's clerk; (G.) meḍho 'one who helps a merchant' vi.138 'vaṇiksahāyah' (deśi. Hemachandra). Cf. meluhha-mũh > mleccha-mukha 'copper (ingot)'.

Meluhha people of maritime tracts, mariners
Hieroglyph: *gṛālu* 'calf'; ḍālu, dālu calf. *khāḍū* m. 'hill goat'; *Kur. kaṛā* young male buffalo; Rebus: *kãṭhāḷ* 'maritime' (Gujarati) கடலர் *kaṭalar, n.* < id. Fishermen inhabitants of maritime tracts; நெய்தனில மாக்கள். (திவா.) கடலோடி kaṭal-ōṭi, n. < id. +. Mariner, seaman; சமுத்திரப்பிரயாணி. (சிலப். 2, 2, அரும்.)

Greenstone seal Akkadian, about 2250 BCE From Mesopotamia Belonging to the servant of a prince. This seal dates to a time when much of Mesopotamia was united under the control of the rulers of Agade (Akkad). The inscription records the name of the owner but it is not clear; it possibly reads Amushu or Idushu. He is described as the servant of Bin-kali-sharri, a prince. The depiction of buffalos in combat may suggest a signifier: mariner. Hieroglyph: *gr̥ālu* 'calf' *kaṭā* கடவு[3] kaṭavu , *n.* < கடா. 1. Male buffalo 'buffalo' Rebus: *kā̃ṭhāḷ* 'maritime'; *kaṭalar, n.* < seamen, inhabitants of maritime tracts. *malla* 'wrestler' (Kannada); Rebus: *malla* m. pl. ' name of a people' (Sanskrit). *malah* 'sailor' (Akkadian) *māluti* 'sailor' (Tamil) A ملاح *mallāḥ*, s.m. (5th) (adj. sup. of ملح) A sailor, a boatman, a mariner, a waterman. Pl. ملاحان *mallāḥān*. See مانگي and مهانه (Pashto) *malla, mallā-malli* pugilistic encounter.

Hieroglyph: Kt. *kŕū, kuŕuk* 'young of animals'; L. *kuṛā* m. 'bridegroom', *kuṛī* f. ' girl, virgin, bride ', awāṇ. *kuṛī* f. ' woman ';(CDIAL 3245)

Hieroglyph: *kolo, koleā* jackal (Konkani) kul tiger; kul dander den of tiger; an.d.kul to become tiger; hudur. to growl as tiger; maran. d.at.kap kul a big-headed tiger (Santali.lex.) kōlupuli = a big, huge tiger, royal or Bengal tiger; kōlu = big, great, huge (Telugu) Rebus: Pk. *kōla* -- m.; B. *kol* ' name of a Muṇḍā tribe '(CDIAL 3532). kol metal (Ta.) kol = pañcalōkam (five metals) (Ta.) pañcaloha = a metallic alloy containing five metals: copper, brass, tin, lead and iron (Sanskrit); an alternative list of five metals: gold, silver, copper, tin (lead), and iron (dhātu; Nānārtharatnākara.[82]; Mangarāja's Nighaṇṭu. 498)(Ka.) *kol, kolhe*, 'the koles, an aboriginal tribe if iron smelters speaking a language akin to that of Santals' (Santali) kol = kolla ṉ, kammāḷan- (blacksmith or smith in general)(Tamil)

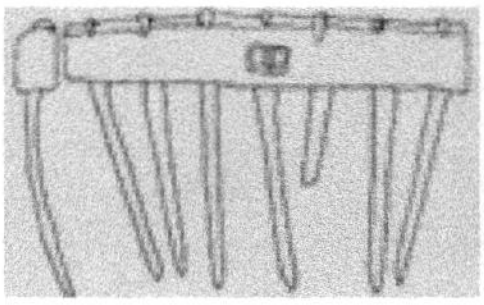

Wooden rake (source: Rees, S. 1981. *Ancient Agricultural Implements.* Shire Archaeology.) Types of metal rakes found in a 20th cent. Railroad construction.

Hieroglyph: *kaṇṭhāla* 'a hoe , spade' (Sanskrit)

Hieroglyph/Rebus: †*kaṇṭhāla* कण्ठाल -- *m.* a boat , ship (Sanskrit) [kaṇṭhá --] G. *kā̃ṭhāḷ* 'maritime'(CDIAL 2682a).

Ta. kaṭal sea; kaṭalar fishermen. *Ma.* kaṭal sea. *Ka.* kaḍal id. *Koḍ.* kaḍa id. *Tu.* kaḍalů id. *Te.* kaḍali id.; kaḍalu a wave; kaḍalu-konu to swell, rise, increase (or the latter with 1350 Ta. kaṟal).(DEDR 1118).

P. *khāḍū* m. ' hill goat '; WPah.J. *khāḍū* m. ' ram ', kṭg. (kc.) *kháḍḍu* m., poet. *khaṛu* m. (Him.I 31 all prob. conn. K. *kaṭh*, stem *kaṭ* --(CDIAL 3790). *Ta.* kaṭavu, kaṭā, kaṭāy male of sheep or goat, he-buffalo; kiṭā buffalo, bull, ram kiṭāy male of sheep; kaṭāri, kiṭāri heifer, young cow that has not calved; kaṭamai female of the goat. *Ma.* kaṭā, kiṭā, kiṭāvu male of cattle, young and vigorous; child, young person; kaṭacci heifer, young cow, calf; kiṭāri a cow-calf, heifer; female buffalo. *Ko.* kaṛc na·g buffalo calf between two and three years; kaṛc kurl cow calf between two and three years; ? ke·v calf of buffalo or cow, under one year (? <*kṛe·v); ? ke·n im, ke·no·ṛ im buffalo with its calf; ke·n a·v, ke·no·ṛ a·v cow with its calf. ? *To.* kaṛ pen for calves from 6 months to 1-2 years. *Ka.* kaḍasu young cow or buffalo that has not yet calved. *Koḍ.* kaḍïci id. *Tu.* gaḍasů id. *Te.* krēpu calf (? or with 1594 Ta. ciṟu). *Go.* (Ph.) kāṛā young buffalo (*Voc.* 648). *Koṇḍa* (BB) gṛālu calf. *Kui* (K.) grāḍu, (W.) ḍrāḍu (*pl.* ḍrāṭka) id.; (W.) gāṛo a bullock or buffalo not trained to the plough; kṛai young female buffalo or goat. *Kuwi* (Su.) ḍālu, (F. S.) dālu calf. *Kur.* kaṛā young male buffalo; kaṛī young female buffalo; kaṛrū, kaḍrū buffalo calf (male or female). *Br.* xarās bull, bullock; xaṛ ram. Cf. 1114 Ta. kaṭamā. / Cf. Turner, *CDIAL*, no. 2645 *kaṭṭa- (also Skt. [*lex.*] kaṭāha- a young female buffalo whose horns are just appearing), and no. 2658 *kaḍḍa-. (DEDR 1123). *Ta.* kaṭamā, kaṭamāṉ bison; kaṭamai, kaṭampai elk. *Ma.* kaṭamān elk, fallow deer. *Ka.* kaḍave, kaḍava, kaḍaba, kaḍabe, kaḍavu, kaḍaha elk; Indian stag,*Rusa aristotelis*; kaḍiti, gaṇaje a kind of deer or elk; (Gowda) kaḍE stag. *Koḍ.* kaḍamë sambur.

Tu. kaḍama stag, elk. *Te.* kaḍāti, kaṇāti musk deer; kaḍãju, kaḍiti, kaṇãju, kaṇiti nilgao, a species of antelope; (B.) kaṇuju sambur deer. *Kol.* kaḍas id. *Nk.* kaṛas id. *Kur.* kāṛsā, (Tiga, Bleses) kãṛsā male of the bādō-deer. (DEDR 1114). *kaṭṭa2 ' young male animal '. [Cf. *kaṭāha* -- 2 m. ' young male buffalo with horns just appearing ' prob. ← Drav. T. Burrow BSOAS xii 368; *kaḍḍa -- , *kēṭṭa --] Gaw. *kaṭái* ' buffalo calf ', Bshk. *kaṭṓr*, Sh. (Lor.) *k**l*tu* (*ṭ*?); K. *kaṭh*, °*ṭas* m. ' ram, sheep in general, (contemptuous) son '; L. *kaṭṭā* m., °*ṭī* f. ' buffalo calf '; P. *kaṭṭā* m., °*ṭī* f. ' yearling buffalo ', *kaṭṭū* m. ' young buffalo bull ', *kaṭṛā* m., °*ṛī* f. ' young buffalo '; WPah. khaś. rudh. marm. *kaṭṛu* ' buffalo calf ', bhal. *kaṭṭā* m., °*ṭī* f. ' buffalo calf ', *kaṭru* n. ' bear cub '; Ku. *kāṭo* ' young buffalo bull ', *kaṭyāro* ' young buffalo '; H. *kaṭiyā* f. ' buffalo heifer ', *kaṭrā* m. 'buffalo calf', *kaṭhṛā* m. ' young buffalo bull '; -- WPah. bhal. *sakaṭṭ* f. ' she -- bear with young ' prob. WPah. cmpd. (CDIAL 2645). Or. *kaṛā* ' castrated male buffalo ', *kaṛāi* ' young buffalo cow that has not calved ', *kaṛhi* ' lamb that has not borne '; Bi. *kāṛā* m., °*ṛī* f. ' buffalo calf ', H. *kāṛā* m. (CDIAL 2658).

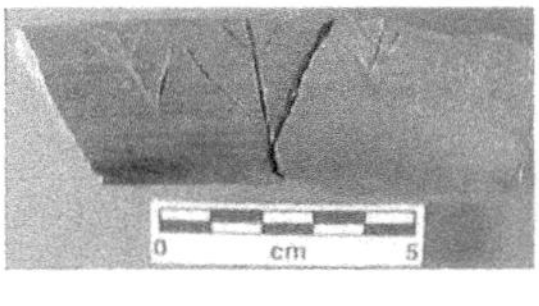

Harppa. Potsherd with incisions of three glyphs. "The earliest (Indus) inscriptions date back to 3500 BC." h1522A sherd. Inscribed Ravi sherd. The origins of Indus writing can now be traced to the Ravi Phase (c. 3300-2800 BCE) at Harappa. Some inscriptions were made on the bottom of the pottery before firing. Other inscriptions such as this one were made after firing. This inscription (c. 3300 BCE) appears to be three plant symbols arranged to appear almost anthropomorphic. …"

http://news.bbc.co.uk/2/hi/science/nature/334517.stm This is the citation attributed to the HARP Project member, Meadow. The image posted by BBC was later replaced by Meadow.

There are three hieroglyphs on the potsherd. Each hieroglyph denotes a five-petaled flower making it a set of three. *kolom* 'three' Rebus: *kolami* 'smithy,forge'. Based on the evidence from Tell Abraq comb, axe and vase which bore a hieroglyph with five petaled flower identified as *tabernae montana*, each of the three hieroglyphs on the potsherd are read rebus: *tagaraka* 'tabernae Montana, tulip fragrance flower' Rebus: *tagara* 'tin (ore)'. Thus, the set of three tagaraka flower hieroglyphs on the potsherd read rebus: *tagara kolami* 'tin smithy/forge'.

śyēná m. 'hawk, falcon, eagle' RV.Pa. sēna -- , °aka -- m. 'hawk ', Pk. sēṇa -- m.; WPah.bhad. śeṇ 'kite'; A. xen ' falcon, hawk ', Or. seṇā, H. sen, sẽ m., M. śen m., śenī f. (< MIA. *senna --); Si. sen 'falcon, eagle, kite'. (CDIAL 12674) Rebus: Senaka a carter ThA 271 (=sākaṭika of Th 2, 443) (Pali) *kola* 'woman' (Nahali). *kola* 'tiger' Rebus: *kol* 'working in iron'; *pañcaloha*, alloy of five metals (Tamil). Adar *ḍangra* 'zebu: Rebus: *aduru ḍhangar* 'native metal smith'. *tamar* 'palm tree, date palm' Rebus: *tam(b)ra* = copper (Pkt.) *tamar* 'tin'. खांडा [*khāṇḍā*] A division of a field. (Marathi) Rebus: *khāṇḍā* tool, pots and pans, metalware (Marathi) *kaḍī* a chain; a hook; a link (Gujarati) Rebus: kaḍiyo [Hem. Des. kaḍaio = Skt. sthapati a mason] a bricklayer; a mason (Gujarati).

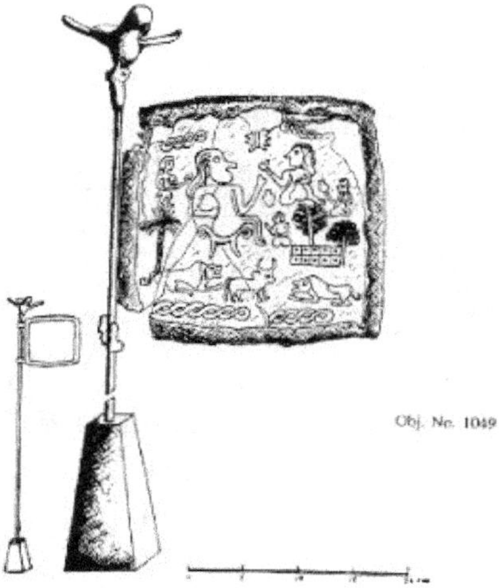

Chanhudaro2  6128

koḍiyum 'young bull'(G.) koḍe 'young bull' (Telugu) खोंड [khōṇḍa] m A young bull, a bullcalf. Rebus: कोंडण [kōṇḍaṇa] f A fold or pen. (Marathi) koḍ 'workshop' (G.) *kõdā 'young bull' Rebus: kõdā 'turn on a lathe'; kõdār* 'turner' sangaḍa 'lathe' (G.) Rebus: *jangaḍ* 'entrusment articles'. ranku 'liquid measure'. Rebus: ranku 'tin' (Cassiterite) tagaraka *tabernae montana* (Skt.) Rebus: t*agara* 'tin' (Ka.) *kanka* 'rim (of jar, *kaṇḍ*)' (Santali) *kárṇa*— m. 'ear, handle of a vessel' RV., Glyph: kaṇḍ kanka, kaṇḍ karṇaka 'rim of jar' (Santali. Sanskrit). Rebus: furnace account (scribe). khanaka m. one who digs , digger , excavator Rebus: karṇaka 'scribe, accountant'. *karṇika* 'supercargo'.

m0516Atm0516Bt 3398 [Copper tablet; side B perhaps is a graphemic representation of an antelope; note the ligatured tail.

The pictograph on m516 B (antelope) appears on a tin ingot found in Haifa, Israel. The antelope may be connoted by *ranku*, deer. Rebus: *ranga* = tin. Kur. *xolā* tail. Malt. *qoli* id. (DEDR 2135). Rebus: *kol* 'working in iron' (Tamil)

takaram tin, white lead, metal sheet, coated with tin (Ta.); tin, tinned iron plate (Ma.); tagarm tin (Ko.); tagara, tamara, tavara id. (Ka.) tamaru, tamara, tavara id. (Ta.): tagaramu, tamaramu, tavaramu id. (Te.); ṭagromi tin metal, alloy (Kuwi); tamara id. (Skt.)(DEDR 3001). Trapu tin (AV.); tipu (Pali); tau, taua lead (Pkt.); tu~_ tin (P.); ṭau zinc, pewter (Or.); tarūaum lead (OG.); tarvu~ (G.); tumba lead (Si.)(CDIAL 5992).

Banawali 009 markhor (*capra falconeri heptneri*). *gaṇḍa* 'four' (Santali) Rebus: *kaṇḍ* fire-altar, furnace' (Santali) tagaraka 'tabernae montana' Rebus: tagaram 'tin'.

Banawali10 9204 xolā = tail (Kur.); qoli id. (Malt.)(DEDR 2135). Rebus: kol 'pañcalōha' (Ta.) கொல் kol, n. Iron. (Tamil) Dm. *mraṅ* m. 'markhor' *Wkh. merg f. 'ibex'* (CDIAL 9885) Tor. *miṇḍ* 'ram', *miṇḍā́l* 'markhor' (CDIAL 10310) Rebus: meḍ 'iron' (Ho.) kolom 'sprout' Rebus: kolami 'smithy/forge'. eae 'seven' (Santali); rebus: *eh-ku* 'steel' (Tamil)

Hieroglyphs on Warka vase read rebus as epigraphs

The Indus hieroglyphic writing system had a significant role in advancing cultural interactions with the Ancient Near East. The context provides for a review of development of glyptic art, adaptation of metallurgical practices, trade in minerals and metals by seafaring merchants traversing an expansive cultural area from Rakhigarhi in Sarasvati river basin to Haifa in the Levant. Trade loads were conveyed to trade agents across a vast area extending from Rakhigarhi in the east to Altyn-tepe in the northwest, using caravans and from Daimabad in the southwest to Susa in the northwest, navigating the Persian Gulf using the famed Meluhha boats. Susa in Khuzistan province of southwestern Iran is located on Karkeh river which converges with Tigris-Euphrates river system at the Shatt al-Arab. Susa was continuously occupied from around 4000 BCE until the end of the 13th century CE and was in contact with Dilmun and Meluhha between 4th and 2nd millenniums BCE. Use of hieroglyphs for tablets was a revolution in the mode of thought of early inventors of the bronze age. Using the rebus method of the type used on Narmer palette, use of hieroglyphs together with their rebus rendering provided the facility for accounting for a large number of types of transactions (mining, smelting, ingot-making, forging, turning, i.e. re-processing used metal). Hieroglyphs of writing systems were also improvised. Sets of hieroglyphic ligatures were created to communicate messages involving multiple transaction types. For example, when a bronze-age smith's role had to be described, three hieroglyphs were ligatured to communicate that the smith was also a merchant and a turner (with a forge/workshop).

Tabernae montana as a hieroglyph

Warka stone (alabaster) vase dated to c. 3000 BCE, has relief decoration in four registers.[101] On top register are glyphs of a goat and a tiger/jackal above two glyphs (which may denote bun-ingots out of a furnace). On bottom register are shown *tabernae montana* sprouts. The second and third registers of the vase seem to show a procession of metal workers and animals bringing alloyed metal ingots in pots.

Tell Abraq axe102 with epigraph ('tulip' glyph + a person raising his arm above his shoulder and wielding a tool + dotted circles on body). tabar = a broad axe (Punjabi). Rebus: tam(b)ra 'copper' tagara 'tabernae montana', 'tulip'. Rebus: tagara 'tin'.

[quote] The site of Uruk, modern Warka, is located in southern Iraq about 35 kilometers east of the modern course of the Euphrates river. Settlement at the site began in the Ubaid period (5th millennium BC). In the Uruk period (4000-3000 BC) the site was the largest in Mesopotamia at 100 hectares. Uruk continued to grow in the Early Dynastic period (2900-2350 BC), reaching a size of about 400 hectares. After the end of the Early Dynastic period, the city declined in size and significance until the Ur III period (2100-2000 BC), when the ruling dynasty pursued new building projects in the Eanna precinct. It is to this period that the massive ziggurat still visible today dates. Uruk declined again after the Ur III period, and was resettled in the Neo-

Assyrian (883-612 BC) and Neo-Babylonian periods (612-539 BC). [unquote] [103]

These flowers are identified as tulips, perhaps Mountain tulip or Boeotian tulip (both of which grow in Afghanistan) which have an undulate leaf. There is a possibility that the comb is an import from Bactria, perhaps transmitted through Meluhha to the Oman Peninsula site of Tell Abraq.

kand 'fire-altar' (Santali) The pair of composite glyphs together with ram and tiger glyphs may read as: tin ingot, *tagara kand mũh* and *kol kand khōṭ*, 'alloyed ingot'. An allograph for kand: kŏnḍ क्वंड् or kŏnḍa क्वंड । कुण्ड m a deep still spring (El., Gr.Gr. 145); (amongst Hindūs) a hole dug in the ground for receiving consecrated fire; cf. agana-kŏnḍ (p. 16*b*, l. 34) (Rām. 631). kọ̆nḍu or konḍu । कुण्डम् m. a hole dug in the ground for receiving consecrated fire kō̃da कोँद । कुलालादिकन्दुः f. a kiln; a potter's kiln (Rām. 1446; H. xi, 11); a brick-kiln (Śiv. 133); a lime-kiln. (Kashmiri)

A pair of *khōṭ* 'alloyed ingots' are shown atop the fire-altars. An allograph for mũh 'ingot' (Santali) : kōḍ कोड् m. a kernel (Kashmiri) खोट [khōṭa] A lump or solid bit (as of phlegm, gore, curds, inspissated milk); any concretion or clot. (Marathi) Rebus: L. *khoṭ*f. ' alloy, impurity ', °*ṭā* ' alloyed ', awāṇ. *khoṭā* ' forged '; P. *khoṭ* m. ' base, alloy ' M.*khoṭā* ' alloyed ', (CDIAL 3931)

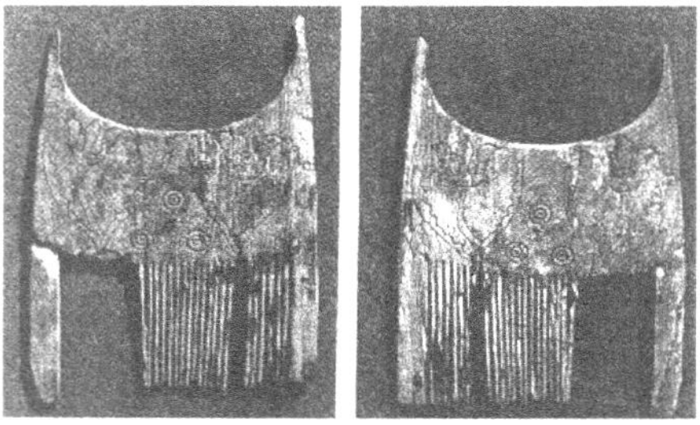

kol 'tiger' (Kon.) Rebus: kol 'iron' (Ta.)

tagara 'ram' (Ta.) Rebus: *damgar* 'merchant' (Akk.) (Top register, ahead of the two storage jars with ingots).

pasaramu, pasalamu =

quadrupeds (Telugu); pasra 'smithy, forge' (Santali) (Third register).
tagaraka *tabernae montana* (Skt.) Rebus: tagara 'tin' (Ka.) (Fourth register).
Thus, the vase describes two types of metal ingots being carried into the treasury: ingots of tin, ingots of iron.

That a metal ingot is being carried is reinforced by the head of an ox shown together with a pellet between its horns.

This depiction may be seen between the two storage jars filled with the ingots.[104]

On the top register, a scarf atop a post is shown behind two adorants standing on two 'frames of buildings' and atop a ram. The male adorant carries in his hands a glyphic comparable to the glyptic shown on the Susa ritual basin flanked by two antelope-goat composite hieroglyphs. If this glyphic denotes tamar, 'palm tree, date palm' the rebus reading would be: tam(b)ra, 'copper' (Pkt.)

The frames of buildings used in the glyphic composition are hieroglyphs: *sā̃gāḍā* m. ' frame of a building ' (M.)(CDIAL 12859) Rebus: *jangaḍiyo* 'military guards who accompanies treasure into the treasury" (G.)

tagara 'ram' (Ta.) Rebus: *damgar* 'merchant' (Akk.) (Top register, ahead of the two storage jars with ingots).

dhatu 'scarf'; rebus: dhatu 'mineral' (Santali) dhātu 'mineral (Pali) dhātu 'mineral' (Vedic); a mineral, metal (Santali); dhāta id. (G.) H. dhāṛnā 'to send out, pour out, cast (metal)' (CDIAL 6771).
A pair of reeds as standard. *sangaḍa* 'pair', *kāḍ* काँड् । काण्डः m. 'the stalk or stem of a reed, grass, or the like, straw', *khōṭ* 'blob atop standard' *dhatu* 'scarf'.

The rebus reading of the pair of reeds in Sumer standard is: *khāṇḍa* 'tools, pots and pans and metal-ware', *khōṭ* 'alloyed ingots', dhatu 'mineral (ore)'.

Ko. goṇḍ knob on end of walking-stick, head of pin (DEDR 2081). Rebus: kọ̆nḍu or konḍu । कुण्डम् m. a hole dug in the ground for receiving consecrated fire (Kashmiri) H. *gõṛā* m. 'reservoir used in irrigation '. (CDIAL 3264). अग्निकुण्डम्. A pool, well; especially one consecrated to some deity or holy purpose. (Sanskrit) *Kur.* xoṇḍxā, xõṛxā deep; a pit, abyss.

Malt. qonḍe deep, low lands. (DEDR 2082).
The glyphs in the composition of a pair of scarved posts are:

sangaḍa 'pair' (Marathi) Rebus: jaṅgaḍ 'entrustment articles'. The pair of pegs denote the pair of minerals dealt with: *tagara,*'tin' and *kol,* 'iron'. The pair of reed stalks read rebus: *sangaḍa kāṇḍa* 'entrustment articles' of 'tools, pots and pans, metal-ware'.

goṇḍ 'knob on end of walking-stick, head of pin' (Ko.); *khū̃ṭ* peg, post'. Allograph: *kõdā* खोंड [khōṇḍa] m A young bull, a bullcalf. (Marathi) Rebus 1: kọ̆nḍu or konḍu । कुण्डम् m. a hole dug in the ground for receiving consecrated fire (Kashmiri) Rebus 2: A. *kundār*, B. *kũdār*, °*ri*, Or. *kundāru*; H. *kũderā* m. ' one who works a lathe, one who scrapes ', °*rī* f., *kũdernā* ' to scrape, plane, round on a lathe '.(CDIAL 3297).

dhatu 'scarf'; rebus: 'cast mineral' (Santali); (cf. H. dhāṛnā 'to send out, pour out, cast metal)

The pegs or posts may be joints of stalk or reeds: *kaṇḍa* -- m.n. ' joint of stalk, stalk (Pali); *kā̃ḍ* m. ' stalk of a reed, straw ' (Kashmiri); *kā̃ḍ* n. ' trunk, stem ' (Marathi); Or.*kāṇḍa*, *kā̃ṛ* ' stalk (Oriya); *kā̃ṛā* 'stem of muñja grass (used for thatching) (Bihari); *kānā̃* m. ' stalk of the reed Sara ' (Lahnda)(CDIAL 3023). Rebus: *kāṇḍa* 'tools, pots and pans, metal-ware'.
Thus the combined glyphs of *goṇḍ* knob, *kā̃ḍ* reed, *dhatu* scarf read rebus: *kũdār* 'turner'; *koṇḍu* 'consecrated fire'; furnace' (Santali); *kāṇḍa* 'tools, pots and pans, metal-ware'; *dhatu* 'mineral ore'.

medhi (f.) [Vedic methī pillar, post (to bind cattle to); BSk. medhi Divy 244; Prk. meḍhi Pischel *Gr.* § 221. See for etym. Walde, *Lat. Wtb.* s. v. meta] pillar, part of a stūpa [not in the Canon?].(Pali) What are often referred to as 'temple poles' of Inanna may thus connote: the following glyphic readings:

sangaḍa 'pair' [A word associated with the pair of storage jars, pair of 'reed' glyphs, pair of vases – glyphs shown on Warka vase.]
meḍhi 'pillar'.
dhatu 'scarf'

The rebus readings for these glyphs are:

jangaḍa 'entrustment articles' (of) *dhatu* 'iron ore'.

dhatu 'minerals' (cast in) *kaṇḍa*, furnace (fire-altar, consecrated pit). khondu id. (Kashmiri) kŏnḍ क्वंड् 'a hole dug in the ground for receiving consecrated fire' (Kashmiri) kunḍa 'consecrated fire-pit'. Allograph: koṇḍi knot of hair on the crown of the head (Telugu) Allograph: konḍu spine (Kashmiri) *kaṇḍa* 'nodule of stone ore'.

The pair of 'reed' glyphs can thus be read rebus: *sangaḍa* 'entrustment articles': *dhatu.kũdār kāṇḍa* 'iron ore turner tools, pots and pans, metal-ware'.

The word *kole.l* has two meanings: smithy, temple. Thus, the pair of 'reeds' signify sacredness associated with a temple.

mēḍhā मेढा A twist or tangle arising in thread or cord, a curl or snarl (Marathi) कांड [*kāṇḍa*] Thrashed or trodden stalks of leguminous plants, pulse-straw. Rebus: *meḍ* 'iron' *kaṇḍa* 'tools, pots and pans, weapons', *meḍh* 'merchant'. The Warka vase top register is recording receipts of storage vases containing ingots' into merchant's warehouse *karum* or artisan's smithy, signified by the pair of curled reeds. The next register documents other storage vessels with perhaps tools, weapons, pots and pans and jars containing liquids?

kunḍa 'pot; rebus: 'consecrated fire-pit'. The 'U' glyphic is a semantic determinant to emphasize that this is a temple with a smithy furnace and a consecrated fire-pit. The structural form (*sangaḍa* 'frame of a building') within which this sign is enclosed may represent a temple: kole.l 'temple, smithy' (Ko.); kolme smithy' (Ka.) The ligatured sign may thus be read: *sangaḍa kunḍ* to mean 'entrustment articles (of) consecrated fire-altar or furnace'. The naked person is offering a large storage jar with ingots of smithy to a person who carries on the left hand face of a bull. ḍangar 'bull' ḍāṅgar 'cattle'; rebus: *ṭhākur* ' blacksmith ' (Maithili) [The bull head carried by the person is a phonetic determinant of the identification of the person's title or profession.]
Allograph: damgar 'merchant' (Akkadian).

The person stands in front of two poles surmounted by two scarves.

Thus, the scarfed composition denotes the *damgar* 'merchant' and female (*kola*, smithy) attendant, offering *dhatu,* 'mineral', and *tam(b)ra* 'copper' from *kand*, 'furnaces (consecrated fire-altars)'. The top register of the vase records this offering on a tall storage jar containing ingots and a cob. The cob is kolmo 'seeding, rice-plant'(Munda) rebus: kolami 'smithy'; (Telugu) mũh ' ingot' (Santali).

Allograph of Maithili. *ṭhākur* 'blacksmith' : Pk. *ṭhakkura* -- m. 'Rajput, chief man of a village'; P. *ṭhākar* m. landholder, ludh. *ṭhaukar* m. ' lord '; Ku. *ṭhākur* m. ' master, title of a Rajput '; N. *ṭhākur* ' term of address from slave to master ' (f. *ṭhakurāni*), *ṭhakuri* 'a clan of Chetris' (f. *ṭhakurni*); A. *ṭhākur* 'a Brahman', *ṭhākurānī* 'goddess'; B. *ṭhākurāni, ṭhākrān,* °*run* ' honored lady, goddess '; Or. *ṭhākura* ' term of address to a Brahman, god, idol ', *ṭhākurāṇī* ' goddess '; Bi. *ṭhākur* ' barber '; Maithili. *ṭhākur* ' blacksmith '; Bhoj. Aw.lakh.*ṭhākur* ' lord, master '; H. *ṭhākur* m. ' master, landlord, god, idol ', *ṭhākurāin, ṭhākurānī* f. ' mistress, goddess '; G. *ṭhākor,* °*kar* m. ' member of a clan of Rajputs ',*ṭhakrāṇī* f. ' his wife ', *ṭhākor* ' god, idol '; M. *ṭhākur* m. ' jungle tribe in North Konkan, family priest, god, idol '; Si. mald. "*tacourou*" ' title added to names of noblemen '; Garh. *ṭhākur* ' master '; A. *ṭhākur* also ' idol ' (CDIAL 5488).

sangaḍa 'pair' (Marathi) Rebus: jaṅgaḍ 'entrustment notes' indicates entrustment into the treasury by *jangaḍiyo* 'military guards who accompanies treasure into the treasury" (G.)
Vedi as fire-altar denoted by vēdha 'hole'

vēdha m. 'hitting the mark ' MBh., ' penetration, hole ' VarBr̥S. [√vyadh] Pa. vēdha -- m. ' prick, wound '; Pk. vēha -- m. ' boring, hole ', P. veh, beh m., H. beh m., G. veh m. karṇavēdha --

.(CDIAL 12108) வேதிதம் vētitam , n. < vēdhita. (யாழ். அக.) 1. Perforating, drilling; துளைக்கை. 2. Tube; துளையுடைப் பொருள். வேதை[3] vētai , n. < vēdha. 1. Drilling, boring; துளைக்கை. (Tamil) Vedhin (adj.) [fr. vidh=vyadh] piercing, shooting, hitting (Pali) Rebus: vḗdi f. ' raised piece of ground serving as an altar and usu. strewed with kuśa grass ' RV., ' stand, bench ' MBh., ' platform for wedding ceremony ' Kāv., vēdika<-> m. ' bench ' R., °kā -- f. MBh. [Cf. vēdá -- m. ' bunch of kuśa grass used as broom ' AV.] Pa. vēdi -- , °dī -- , °dikā -- f. ' cornice, ledge, rail '; Pk. vēi -- , vēiā -- f. ' platform '; A. bei ' quadrangular frame of greenery forming platform on which ceremonial bathing of bride and bridegroom is performed'.(CDIAL 12107).

There are three glyptic elements in the composition:1. + shape denoting: kaṇḍ = a furnace, altar (Santali.lex.); khaṇḍaran, khaṇḍrun 'pit furnace' (Santali) 2. (.dot) infixed circle (dotted circle): khaṇḍa 'tools, pots and pans and metal-ware'; 3. raised large-sized dot: गोटी [gōṭī] f (Dim. Of गोटा) A roundish stone or pebble. Rebus: *khoṭ* m. 'alloy' (Punjabi)

Ta. katu a scar. *Ka.* gadu, gaduvu a swelling (as from a blow), a tumour; gaddarisu to swell (as the face or limbs); gādari weal. *Tu.* gadarů a lump. *Te.* kadumu a swelling, bump; kanti excrescence, lump, wen, swelling. (DEDR 1196).

गोदा [gōdā] m A circular brand or mark made by actual cautery (Marathi)गोटा [gōṭā] m A roundish stone or pebble. 2 A marble (of stone, lac, wood &c.) 2 A marble. 3 A large lifting stone. Used in trials of strength among the Athletæ. 4 A stone in temples described at length under उचला 5 fig. A term for a round, fleshy, well-filled body. 6 A lump of silver: as obtained by melting down lace or fringe. गोट्ळा or गोटोळा [gōṭuḷā or gōṭōḷā] a (गोटा) Spherical or spheroidal, pebble-form. (Marathi) Rebus 1: खोट [

khōṭa] *f* A mass of metal (unwrought or of old metal melted down); an ingot or wedge. Hence खोटसाळ [khōṭasāḷa

] *a* (खोट & साळ from शाला) Alloyed--a metal. (Marathi) Bshk. *khoṭ* 'embers', Phal. *khūṭo* 'ashes, burning coal'; L. *khoṭ*f 'alloy, impurity', °*ṭā* 'alloyed', awāṇ. *khoṭā* 'forged'; P. *khoṭ* m. 'base, alloy' M.*khoṭā* 'alloyed', (CDIAL 3931) Rebus 2: kṛvṛi f. 'granary (Wpah.); kuṛī, kuṛo house, building'(Ku.)(CDIAL 3232) कोठी [kōṭhī] f (कोष्ट S) A granary, garner, storehouse,

warehouse, treasury, factory, bank. (Marathi) कोठी The grain and provisions (as of an army); the commissariat supplies. Ex. लशकराची कोठी चालली-उतरली- आली-लुटली. कोठ्या [kōṭhyā]

कोठा [kōṭhā] m (कोष्ट S) A large granary, store-room, warehouse, water-reservoir &c. 2 The stomach. 3 The chamber of a gun, of water-pipes &c. 4 A bird's nest. 5 A cattle-shed. 6 The chamber or cell of a hunḍí in which is set down in figures the amount. कोठारें [kōṭhārēṃ] n A storehouse gen (Marathi)

Ceramics and Meluhha word signs for glass

The earliest ceramics made by humans were pottery objects, including 27,000 year old figurines, made from clay, either by itself or mixed with other materials, hardened in fire.

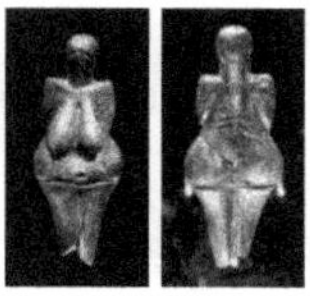

29,000 BCE – 25,000 BCE Ceramic. Front and back views. Paleolithic settlement of Moravia. If a similar artifact was presented to a Meluhha speaker of Indian *sprachbund*, what glosses would have burst forth in his or her mind? Some possibilities:

<kacO>(M),,<kac>(K) {N} ``drinking ^glass''. *Kh.<ka:~c>(B), H.<??>. %15591. #15481. kācá1 m. ' glass ' ŚBr., °*aka* -- m. W. 2. *kācca -- .1. Pa. *kāca* -- m. ' crystal, glass ', Pk. *kāya* -- m.;

S. *kāo*, *kāyo* m. ' glass, glass tumbler '; Si. *kadā* ' silicious earth used in making glass, beads, &c. '2. Pk. *kacca* -- n. ' glass, crystal '; K. *kăċh*, abl. *kăċa* m. a species of pottery made of a kind of fine clay '; S. *kacu* m. ' glass ' and L. *kacc* m. both with *a* ← E; P. ludh. *kañc* m. ' glass '; N. *kāc*, *kā̃c* ' glass,quartz '; A. *kās* ' glass ', *kā̃s* ' a kind of clay from which china is made '; B. *kāc*, *kā̃c* ' glass, crystal ', Or. *kāca*, *kā̃c*, Bhoj. *kā̃c*, H. *kāc*, *kā̃c* m., G. *kāc* m., M. *kāċ*, *kā̃c* f. WPah.kṭg. *kəccẹṭi* f. ' white pebble, quartz, crystal '.(CDIAL 3007).

I am suggesting this class because Meluhha speech chose to signify bronze an alloy of tin and copper as *kā̃sī*. Invention of words to signify a new artifact or new metal is dictated by the socio-cultural context of the language repertoire, say of a Meluhha speaker or listener or writer or reader. If this gloss, *kā̃sī* is to be signified by a hieroglyph, the choice is likely to be: *kā̃gsī* f. ' comb ' (Gujarati); *kāgśī*, śeu. *kāśkī* 'a comblike fern' (*Western Pahāṛī*)(CDIAL 2599).

Rebus readings of Meluhhan hieroglyphs attest to the tin trade at Ashur and at Susa of the Middle Bronze Age. This is consistent with the hypothesis that tin of the Middle Bronze Age arrived from Meluhha, mostly mediated by Meluhha artisans and merchants who recorded the Meluhha hieroglyphs -- a legacy which continued in the example of the overflowing pot which reads rebus: *lo* 'overflowing pot' Rebus: *loh* 'copper'.

sphōṭa as a hieroglyph reveals two things simultaneously: it manifests the word-sound or s'abda and simultaneously, it revels the word-meaning. Thus, *sphōṭa*, by definition, is rebus.
Rebus is a cipher, a means by which word knowledge is manifested and communited in ordinary vocal conversations. Since hieroglyphs are picture-forms, the conversations can also occur in writing.

Rebus uses two words with the same form but different senses. Such a pair of words are homonyms and ideal candidates for building up rebus as a cipher.

For Hegel language is a mediation of the subjective spirit with the being of objects. For Ernest Cassirer, criteria for truth and meaning are found within language itself. (Ernst Cassirer, 1946, Trans. Suzanne K. Langer, *Language and Myth*, New York and London, Harper & Bros., pp. 8-9). The error in Cassirer's reasoning is that art and knowledge are forms of representation which occur within the idealistic notion of natural language taken from Aristotle and expounded by Herder and von Humboldt.

In Indian philosophy of language, *Vāk* is a continuum of cognition, starts internally, gets externalized by speech and reinforced by the heard sound.

All speech, *Vāk* is identified with Brahman, a unique medium of human consciousness to perceive and transmit human knowledge. *Vāk* descends to various levels of a thesis, chapter, paragraph, sentence, word.

Vāk is more than word forms outwardly expressed orally or in written form.

There is an enormous body of literature in Indian tradition related to language. Each dars'ana (viewpoint) has presented specific perspectives on language as revelation.

Patañjali starts with popular language using words for communication purposes.

Proof 1:

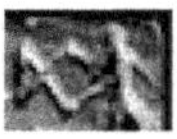

'Body, stature of person' hieroglyph ligatured to 'pincers' hieroglyph is a phonetic determinant of the nature of ore - *kanḍ* 'stone': *dhaṛu* 'body' (Sindhi), *ḍato* 'claws or pincers of crab' (Santali) rebus: *dhatu* 'ore' (Santali) The ligatured hieroglyph is read rebus: *khātī meḍ dhatu* 'wheelwright iron stone (ore)'. (See Appendix K: Metals trade catalog on a seal).

The first set of three glyphs on a broken

seal m0304 (reconstructed) Mohenjo-Daro are read rebus:

dhatu kuṭi 'mineral (ore) smelter furnace' (Santali) *koṭil* tongs (Malayalam) Rebus: *kuṭila, katthīl* = bronze (8 parts copper and 2 parts tin).

Proof 2:

Meluhha symbolic forms for sailor, metalsmith, seafaring merchant

Mohenjo-Daro seal m0308 provides a detailed representation of the *kāṇa* 'one-eyed' *kola* 'woman' wrestling (*malla*) with two tigers/jackals. [See Appendix D: *kola, kolum* 'a jackal' (Gujarati) *kolhuyo* (Dh.Des.); *kōlupuli* 'a big, huge tiger (Telugu).] On this symbolic form, the woman is shown with *āra* 'six curls' or knobs circumscribing her hairdo, yielding rebus meaning: *kaṇṇahāra* 'helmsman, sailor' (Prākṛt). Rebus meaning of hieroglyph *malla* 'wrestler': *malah* 'sailor' (Akkadian) *māluti* 'sailor' (Tamil) A ملاح *mallāḥ*, s.m. (5th) (adj. sup. of ملح) A sailor, a boatman, a mariner, a waterman. Pl. ملاحان *mallāḥān*.
See ماڼ كي and مهاڼه (Pashto). Most of the 'wrestling' or 'combat' hieroglyphs on cylinder seals of Ancient Near East are related to this cipher, thus denoting *malla* 'wrestler' Rebus: *malah* 'sailor' (Akkadian).

m0308 Pict-105: Person grappling with two tigers standing on either side of him and rearing on their hindlegs. Text 2075

ayo 'fish' Rebus: *ayas* 'metal'. *kaṇḍa* 'arrow' Rebus: *khāṇḍa* 'tools, pots and pans, and metal-ware'. *ayaskāṇḍa* is a compounde word attested in Panini. The compound or glyphs of fish + arrow may denote metalware tools, pots and pans.
[The third sign from left may be a stylized 'standard device'?]

Hieroglyph: *sangaḍa* 'lathe/portable furnace' (Marathi) Rebus 1: *jangaḍa* 'products entrusted for approval'; jangaḍ 'courier' (Gujarati. Marathi); *jangaḍiyo* 'military guard accompanying treasure into the treasury' (Gujarati) *sangaḍa* 'association' (guild). Rebus 2: *sangatarāsu* 'stone cutter' (Telugu). Rebus 3: *sangar* 'fortification wall' (Pushto).

kola 'tiger' Rebus: *kol* 'working in iron, alloy of 5 metals - pancaloha'. The terminal sign read from r. is a 'ladder' hieroglyph (which is comparable to the curved step-ladder *senī* f. ' ladder' (Hindi) Rebus 1: *seniya* 'soldier' Rebus 2: *seṇi* 'a guild'

The 'ladder hieroglyph' unites six hieroglyphs of 'animal' heads on Mohenjo-Daro Seal m0417:

Th hieroglyphic composition of six animals on the Mohenjodaro seal m0417.

A pun on the word *seniya* 'soldier' relates it to *seṇi* 'a guild' Vin iv.226; J i.267, 314; iv.43; Dāvs ii.124; their number was *eighteen* J vi.22, 427; VbhA ; *seṇipamukha* 'the head of a guild' J ii.12 (Pali) An allograph: śyēná m. ' hawk, falcon, eagle ' RV. Pa. *sēna* -- , °*aka* -- m. ' hawk ', Pk. *sēṇa* -- m.; WPah.bhad. *śeṇ* ' kite '; A. *xen* ' falcon, hawk ', Or. *seṇā*, H. *sen, sẽ* m., M. *śen* m., *śenī* f. (< MIA. **senna* --); Si. *sen* ' falcon, eagle, kite '. (CDIAL 12674) Thus, the use of 'falcon, eagle' as

Meluhha hieroglyph is read rebus: *seṇi* 'guild'. *śyēnácit* श्येन--चित् *mfn.* piled in the shape of a hawk (Śulbasūtras).

seniya [fr. senā] belonging to an army, soldier J i.314.; *seṇimokkha* ' the chief of an army J vi.371' (Pali) Supplementary: *bhaṭa* 'warrior' The presence of a 'warrior' Rebus: *bhaṭa* 'furnace'. This 'warrior' hieroglyph points to the possibility of semantics related to 'ladder or stepped chain' hieroglyph uniting the six animal heads signifying smelting/smithy/forge operations. The composition of symbolic forms, is semantically a representation of a *śrḗṇi*, 'guild', a *khũṭ* , 'community' of smiths and masons. This guild, community of smiths and masons evolves into Harosheth Hagoyim, 'a smithy of nations'. *śrēṇikā* -- f. ' tent ' lex. and meanings. ' house ~ ladder ' in *śriṣṭa -- 2, *śrīḍhi -- . -- Words for ' ladder ' see śrití --śri] H. *sainī, senī* f. ' ladder '; Si. *hiṇi, hiṇa, iṇi* ' ladder, stairs ' (GS 84 < *śrēṇi* --).(CDIAL 12685). Woṭ. Šen ' roof ', Bshk. Šan, Phal. Šān(AO xviii 251) Rebus: seṇi (f.) [Class. Sk. Śreṇi in meaning "guild"; Vedic= row] 1. A guild Vin iv.226; J i.267, 314; iv.43; Dāvs ii.124; their number was eighteen J vi.22, 427; VbhA 466. ° -- pamukha the head of a guild J ii.12 (text seni-) 2. A division of an army J vi.583; ratha -- ° J vi.81, 49; *seṇimokkha* the chief of an army J vi.371 (cp. Senā and seniya)(Pali).

The core is a glyphic 'chain' or 'ladder'. Alternative/supplementary rebus reading of hieroglyph: *kaḍī* a chain; a hook; a link (Gujarati); kaḍum a bracelet, a ring (Gujarati) Rebus: *kaḍiyo* [Hem. Des. *kaḍaio* = Skt. sthapati a mason] a bricklayer; a mason; *kaḍiyaṇa, kaḍiyeṇa* a woman of the bricklayer caste; a wife of a bricklayer (Gujarati)

The six animals are:

1.Hieroglyph: *kondh* 'young bull'. *kũdār* 'turner, brass-worker'.

2. Hieroglyph: *ḍhangra* 'bull'. *Rebus: ḍhangar* 'blacksmith'. Alternative: Hieroglyph: <*barad*>(D) {NA} ``^bullock used for carrying or dragging carts''. #2631.Kh<*barad*>(D) {NA} 'bullock used for carrying or dragging carts'.Rebus 1: *baran, bharat* (5 copper, 4 zinc and 1 tin) (Punjabi. Bengali) Rebus 2: *barada, barda, birada* = a vow (Gujarati)

3. Hieroglyph: *khũṭ* 'zebu'. Rebus: *khũṭ* 'guild, community' (Semantic determinant of the 'jointed animals' glyphic composition). *kūṭa* joining, connexion, assembly, crowd, fellowship (DEDR 1882) Pa. *gotta* 'clan'; Pk. *gotta, gōya* id. (CDIAL 4279) Semantics of Pkt. lexeme *gōya* is concordant with Hebrew *'goy'* in *ha-goy-im* (lit. the-nation-s)˙ Pa. *gotta* -- n. ' clan ', Pk. *gotta* -- , *gutta* -- , amg. *gōya* -- n.; Gau. *gū* ' house ' (in Kaf. and Dard. several other words for ' cowpen ' > ' house ': gōṣṭhá -- , Pr. *gū ́ṭu* ' cow '; S. *g̠oṭru* m. ' parentage ', L. *got* f. ' clan ', P. *gotar, got* f.; Ku. N. *got* ' family '; A. *got* -- *nāti* ' relatives '; B. *got* ' clan '; Or. *gota* ' family, relative '; Bhoj. H. *got* m. ' family, clan ', G. *got* n.; M. *got* ' clan, relatives '; -- Si. *gota* ' clan, family ' ← Pa. (CDIAL 4279). Alternative: adar ḍangra 'zebu or humped bull'; rebus: aduru 'native metal' (Ka.); ḍhangar 'blacksmith' (H.)

4. kol 'tiger'.Rebus: *kol* 'worker in iron'. Alterntive: *karaḍa* 'panther' (Prākṛt) Rebus: *karaḍa* 'hard alloy'.

Seafaring metal merchants

Hieroglyphs from a vase in Tell Asmar (29-27th cent. BCE). Pair of tigers, pair of zebu; a person holding two hooded-snakes; eagle and lion attacking a zebu. In the bottom register, right corner of the composition, a palm tree is also seen.

The hieroglyphs are: zebu, lion, tiger, snake, one-eyed woman impeding two rearing hoods of snakes; palm fonds as a field hieroglyph. Motif is combat or impedence or thwarting.

malla 'wrestler' (Kannada); Rebus: *malla* m. pl. ' name of a people' (Sanskrit). *malah* 'sailor' (Akkadian) *māluti* 'sailor' (Tamil)

A ملاح *mallāḥ*, s.m. (5th) (adj. sup. of ملح) A sailor, a boatman, a mariner, a waterman.

Alternative (if the impeding of attacking tigers signifies obstinacy): S. *aṭaru* 'obstinate'; L. *aṭṭ* m. 'sediment in a well, silt'; Or. *aṭāi* 'enclosure for cattle' Rebus: *aduru* 'native metal'.

tamar 'palm tree, date palm' the rebus reading would be: *tam(b)ra* 'copper' (Prākṛt)

nāga 'snake' Rebus: *nāga* 'lead' anakku 'tin'.
kāṇa 'one-eyed' Rebus: *kanḍ* 'stone'; *kāṇḍā* 'tools, pots and pans and metal-ware'. *tagar* 'to impede'Rebus: *tagaram* 'tin'.
arye 'lion' Rebus: *āra* 'brass'.
adar ḍangra 'zebu or humped bull' Rebus: *aduru* 'native metal' (Kannada); *ḍhangar* 'blacksmith' (Hindi)

kol 'tiger'.Rebus: *kol* 'worker in iron'. Alterntive: *karaḍa* 'panther' (Prākṛt) Rebus: *karaḍa* 'hard alloy'.

paṭam , *n.* < *phaṭa.* 'cobra's hood' phaṭa n. ' expanded hood of snake ' MBh. 2. *phēṭṭa -- 2. [Cf. *phuṭa* -- m., °*ṭā* -- f., *sphuṭa* -- m. lex., °*ṭā* -- f. Pañcat. (Pk. *phuḍā* -- f.), *sphaṭa* -- m., °*ṭā*-- f., *sphōṭā* -- f. lex. and phaṇa -- 1. Conn. words in Drav. T. Burrow BSOAS xii 386]1. Pk. *phaḍa* -- m.n. ' snake's hood ', °*ḍā* -- f., M. *phaḍā* m., °*ḍī* f.2. A. *pheṭ*, *phẽṭ*. (CDIAL 9040). Rebus: 'sharpness of iron': *padm* (obl.*padt-*) temper of iron (Kota)(DEDR 3907); *patam* 'sharpness, as of the edge of a knife' (Tamil)

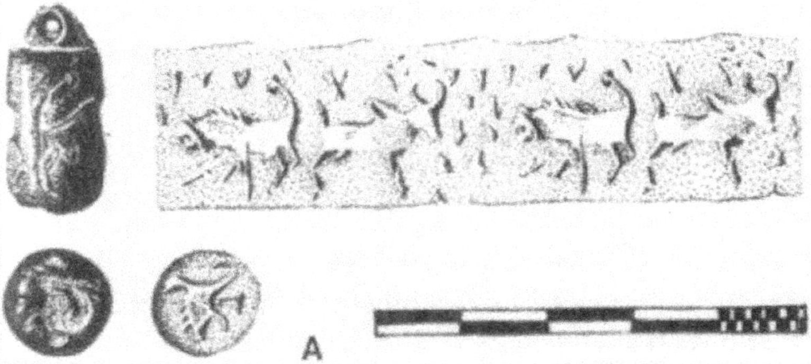

Sibri cylinder seal with Indus writing hieroglyphs: notches, zebu, tiger, scorpion?. Each dot on the corner of the + glyph and the short numeral strokes on a cylinder seal of Sibri, may denote a notch: खांडा [khāṇḍā] *m* A jag, notch, or indentation (as upon the edge of a tool or weapon). (Marathi) Rebus:*khāṇḍā* 'tools, pots and pans, metal-ware'.

Go. (A.) khaṛyal tiger; (Haig) kariyāl panther (Voc. 999). Kui kṛāḍi, krānḍi tiger, leopard, hyena. Pkt. (DNM) *karaḍa* Rebus 1: kharādī ' turner, a person who fashions or shapes objects on a lathe' (Gujarati) *karaḍo –kār* : an artisan-turner who works on a lathe – on hard alloys (Gujarati)Rebus 2: करड्याची अवटी [karaḍyācī avaṭī] f An implement of the goldsmith. Rebus: करडा [karaḍā] Hard from alloy--iron, silver &c. (Marathi)

Alterntive rebus readings of zebu and 'tiger'? on the cylinder seal shown on 7.31d: *khũṭ* m. ' Brahmani or zebu bull ' (G.) Rebus:*khũṭ* 'community, guild' (Santali) kola 'tiger' Rebus: kol 'working in iron'; pañcaloha, alloy of five metals (Tamil). *aṭar* 'a splinter' (Ma.) *aṭaruka* 'to burst, crack, sli off,fly open; *aṭarcca* ' splitting, a crack'; *aṭarttuka* 'to split, tear off, open (an oyster) (Ma.); *aḍaruni* 'to crack' (Tu.) (DEDR 66) Rebus: *aduru* 'native, unsmelted metal' (Kannada) *aduru'gaṇiyinda tegadu karagade iruva aduru'*, that is, ore taken from the mine and not subjected to melting in a furnace (Kannada)

The numerical strokes on the seal may denote the number of 'ingots?' of iron made for the guild by the artisan who owned the cylinder seal. It may also denote that he was a worker in 'iron' for the smithy guild. An allograph to denote a guild is: footprint shown on some seals discussed in previous section.

Animal heads 5 and 6 are assumed to be (consistent with such sets of animals in processions on other artifacts): rhinoceros and antelope. (See: Appendix G: Processions of metalware competence)

5. Hieroglyph: *gaṇḍa* 'rhinoceros' Rebus:*khaṇḍ* 'tools, pots and pans and metal-ware'.
6. Hieroglyph: 'antelope': *mṛeka* 'goat'. Rebus: *milakkhu* 'copper'. *meṛh* 'helper of merchant'. Vikalpa : *meluhha* '*mleccha*' 'copper worker'.

One-eye + 6 hair curls (+ stretched hands impeding two tigers) are read rebus in Meluhha language to signify Meluhha gloss: *kanahār* m. ' helmsman, fisherman ' (Hindi); phonemic variant: *kaṇṇahāra* 'helmsman, sailor' (Prākṛt) This is a composite of two symbolic forms: *kaṇ* 'one eye' + *āra* 'six curls'. Rebus: *kāṛṇī* 'supercargo of a ship' (Marathi) A hieroglyphic composition of crocodile + fish – read rebus: *ayakara*, 'alloy metal smith' occurs on the obverse side of two molded tablets. She wrestles with two tigers/ jackals: *malla* 'wrestler' (Kannada); *malah* 'sailor' (Akkadian)

māluti 'sailor' (Tamil) A ملاح *mallāḥ*, s.m. (5th) (adj. sup. of ملح)
A sailor, a boatman, a mariner, a waterman. Pl. ملاحان *mallāḥān*. See ماڼ کي and مهاڼه (Pashto) مهرنړه *mahaṟṟṉah*, s.m. (5th) A boatman, a sailor, a mariner. Pl. مهرنړګان *mahaṟṟṉa-gān*. (Panjābī). (Pashto). The obverse of 5 molded tablets has two hieroglyphic sequences with a common hieroglyph: *kāru* 'crocodile' Rebus: *khār* 'blacksmith' (Kashmiri). *khār* 1 खार् । लोहकारः m. (sg. Abl. Khāra 1 खार; the pl. dat. Of this word is khāran 1 खारन्, which is to be distinguished from khāran 2, q.v., s.v.), a blacksmith, an iron worker (cf. bandūka-khār, p. 111b, l. 46; K.Pr. 46; H. xi, 17); a farrier (El.). This word is often a part of a name, and in such case comes at the end (W. 118) as in Wahab khār, Wahab the smith (H. ii, 12; vi, 17)(Kashmiri). The rebus reading of Meluhha hieroglyphs of a woman wrestling with two tigers is completely represented in Meluhha cipher: *dul kol malla kaṇṇahāra* 'cast alloy metalsmith, helmsman, sailor'. *kola* 'woman' Rebus: *kol* 'working in iron', 'working in alloys', 'smelter'.

Five molded tablets: Obverse h1970A to h1974A are tokens to be handed over as consignments for boat cargo to *malla kaṇṇahāra* 'helmsman, sailor'. It is possible that the helmsman, sailor is the Meluhha sea-faring merchant whose *kāṃī* supercargo included other consignments of metal, metal ingots on a famed *magilum* Meluhha boat (cognate: *bagala* 'boat'). The function of the Such cargo loads included moltencast copper ingots signified by hieroglyphs 'pair of palm trees', 'pair of ox-hide type ingots': *dul tam(b)ra ḍhālako*; *ayo* 'alloy metal', *khaḍā* 'stone-ore nodule' (Marathi) (may be stone beads). If the date palm denotes tamar (Hebrew language), 'palm tree, date palm' the rebus reading would be: tam(b)ra, 'copper' (Pkt.) But in one Indian language -- Kannada --, tamara means: tagarm tin (Ko.); tagara, tamara, tavara id. (Kannada.) Based on this reading, the two ox-hide ingots shown between two palm tree hieroglyphs may signify tin ingots as supercargo on the Meluhha *magillum* boat.

The ligatured hieroglyph composition connotes: *kaṇḍe* A head or ear of millet or maize (Telugu) *kāṟ* 'stack of stalks of large millet' (Maithili) Rebus: *kaṇḍa* 'stone (ore)(Gadba)' Ga. (Oll.) *kanḍ, (S.) kanḍu* (pl. *kanḍkil*) stone (DEDR 1298). *khaḍā* 'circumscribe' (M.); Rebus: *khaḍā* 'nodule (ore), stone' (M.)

Hieroglyph 1: *kan-ka* 'rim-of-jar'; Hieoglyph 2: *kāṇá* ' one -- eyed ' (RV.Pali.Prākṛt) *kāṛa*, *°ṛī* f. ' blind ' (Ash.)(CDIAL 3020). Rebus: *kan-ka*, *karṇaka*, *kārṇī* m. 'super cargo of a ship '(Marathi) *kaṉ* 'copper work, copper, workmanship' (Tamil) Thus, the 'eye' glyph, 'six spokes' glyph connote: *kaṉṉār* 'brass-workers'. *kola* 'woman' Rebus: kol 'working in iron' kola 'tiger' Rebus: *kol* 'working in iron'. *kolhe* (iron-smelter; kolhuyo, jackal) Rebus: *kol, kollan-, kollar* 'blacksmith' (Tamil)

Proof 3:
Meluhha symbolic forms for sailor, metalsmith, seafaring merchant

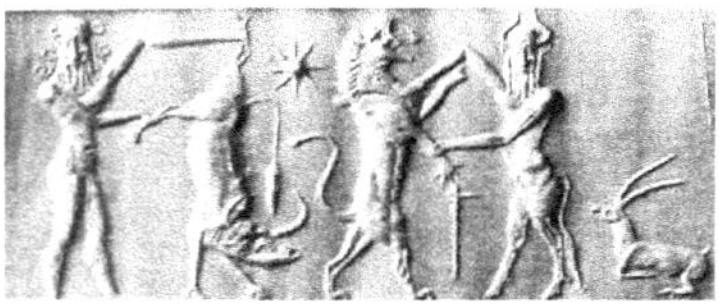

Cylinder seal with contest scene, 2350–2150 B.C. Mesopotamia Albite H. 15/16 in. (3.4 cm), Diam. 7/8 in. (2.3 cm) Gift of Nanette B. Kelekian, 1999 (1999.325.4). The man with six hair curls wrestles with a buffalo. The man with a horn,ligatured to a bovine hindpart wrestles with a lion. An antelope watches the narrative. Hieroglyph: *ran:gā* 'buffalo' Rebus: *ran:ga* 'pewter or alloy of tin (ran:ku), lead (nāga) and antimony (*añjana*)' (Santali) Hieroglyphs: *āra* 'six', 'curls'. arye 'lion' Rebus: *āra* 'brass'. Hieroglyph composition: *ḍhangar* 'bull'; *ḍhagaram* 'buttock'. *ḍhangar* 'blacksmith'. *malla* 'to wrestle, wrestler' Rebus: *malla* 'sailor'. Hieroglyph: *meḍha* 'polar star' (Marathi). Rebus: *meḍ* (Ho.); *mẽṛhet* 'iron' (Munda.Ho.) Hieroglyph: ṭagara 'antelope'; rebus: ṭagara 'tin'. Cf. cognate: *tamkāru, damgar* 'merchant' (Sumerian. Akkadian). Supplementary readings: Hieroglyph: *grālu* 'calf' *kaṭā* கடவு[3] kaṭavu , *n.* < கடா .1. Male buffalo 'buffalo' *kāṛā* young buffalo (Go.) *kaṭā, kaṭamā* 'bison' (Ta.)(DEDR 1114)

Rebus: *kãṭhāḷ* 'maritime'; *kaṭalar, n.* < seamen, inhabitants of maritime tracts. *malla* 'wrestler' (Kannada); Rebus: *malla* m. pl. ' name of a people' (Sanskrit). *malah* 'sailor' (Akkadian) *māluti* 'sailor' (Tamil) A ملاح *mallāḥ*, s.m. (5th) (adj. sup. of ملح) A sailor, a boatman, a mariner, a waterman. Pl. ملاحان *mallāḥān*. See مانگي and مهانه (Pashto) *malla, mallā-malli* pugilistic encounter. [For a hieroglyph signifier of *añjana* ,'arsenic' (Sb) as an alloying element, see: Appendix R: *ran:ga* 'pewter or alloy of tin (*ran:ku*), lead (*nāga*) and antimony (*añjana*)'].

"...Contests between heroes and animals first appeared in cylinder seals in the late fourth millennium B.C., and by the middle of the third millennium B.C., the combatants, which might include mythological opponents, had assumed heroic status...A standing nude bearded hero with five visible sidelocks of hair (the traditional sixth curl is hidden by his raised right arm) grasps a water buffalo that is rearing on its hind legs. The head of the water buffalo is pushed back by the hero's right hand... Such imagery demonstrates cultural interaction resulting from trade and possibly diplomatic connections between the Akkadian empire and the Indus Valley (Harappan) civilization. Between the hero and the water buffalo is a small female in a long robe, perhaps holding a vessel. The hero's ally in the contest scene is a bull-man, shown full-face with the horns, ears, and lower body of a bull. In Akkadian-period contest scenes, the bull-man is almost invariably, as here, in conflict with a lion. A horned animal lies between the two combatants. A two-column cuneiform inscription names the seal owner as Ishri-ilum."[105]

Enki and the world order, a philosophical treatise referred to seaborne trade conducted from Dilmun and Makkan sailing farther into the Persian Gulf: "The lands of Magan and Dilmun looked up at me, Enki, moored the Dilmun-boat to the ground, loaded the Magan-boat sky high; The magilum-boat of Meluhha transports gold and silver, brings them to Nippur or Enlil, the king of all the lands." (Silver, Morris, Economic structures of Antiquity, Wesport: Greenwood Press, p.19).

One Meluhhan village in Akkad (3rd millennium BCE)

Mohenjo-daro three-sided Prism tablet m1429 shows a boat + crocdile + fish hieroglyphs + Text 3246 on the third side of the prism. .

The *bagala, magillum* Meluhha boat has an inlaid hieroglyph of two ox-hide shaped ingots.

bagalo = an Arabian merchant vessel (Gujarati) *bagala* = an Arab boat of a particular description (Ka.); bagalā (M.); bagarige, bagarage = a kind of vessel (Kannada) Alternative: *Ta.* mañci cargo boat with a raised platform; vañci canoe. *Ma.* mañci a large sort of boat, single-masted Pattimar in coasting trade, holding 10-40 tons; vañci a large boat. *Ka.*mañji a large boat with one mast used in coasting trade; (Bark.) maccïve a kind of boat. *Tu.* mañji a long boat, a single-masted country vessel. / Possibly < IA; Turner, *CDIAL*, no. 9715, mañca- stage, platform (DEDR 4638).

tamar, 'palm tree, date palm' (Hebrew) Rebus: *tam(b)ra*, 'copper' (Prākṛt) [Two palm trees flank two ox-hide shaped ingots]

Alloy ingots
A pair of ingots with notches in-fixed as ligatures.

ḍhālako 'large ingot'. खोट [*khōṭa*] 'ingot, wedge'; A mass of metal (unwrought or of old metal melted down)(Marathi) *khoṭ* f 'alloy (Lahnda) Thus the pair of ligatured oval glyphs read: *khoṭ ḍhālako* 'alloy ingots'.

kāḍ काड् 'the stature of a man' Rebus: खडा [khaḍā] *m* A small stone, a pebble (Marathi) dula 'pair' Rebus: dul 'cast (metal)'shapes objects on a lathe' (Gujarati) *kanka, karṇaka* 'rim of jar' Rebus: *karṇaka* 'account scribe'. *kārṇī(ka)* m. 'super cargo of a ship '(Marathi)

Forge: stone, minerals, gemstones

khaḍā 'circumscribe' (M.); Rebs: *khaḍā* 'nodule (ore), stone' (M.) *kolom* 'cob'; rebus: *kolmo* 'seedling, rice (paddy) plant' (Munda.) kolma hoṛo = a variety of the paddy plant (Desi)(Santali.) kolmo 'rice plant' (Mu.) Rebus: *kolami* 'furnace, smithy' (Telugu) Thus, the ligatured glyph reads: *khaḍā* 'stone-ore nodule' *kolami* 'furnace,smithy'. Alternatives: 1. *koṛuŋ* young shoot (Pa.) (DEDR 2149) Rebus: *kol* iron, working in iron, blacksmith (Tamil) kollan blacksmith, artificer (Malayalam) kolhali to forge.(DEDR 2133). 2. *kaṇḍe* A head or ear of millet or maize (Telugu) Rebus: *kaṇḍa* 'stone (ore)(Gadba)' Ga. (Oll.) kanḍ, (S.) kanḍu (pl. kanḍkil) stone (DEDR 1298).

Alternative: kolmo 'three' Rebus: *kolami* 'furnace, smithy'. Thus, the pair of glyphs may denote lapidary work – working with stone, mineral, gemstones.

ayo 'fish' Rebus: ayas 'metal'. kāru 'crocodile' Rebus: kāru 'artisan'. Thus, together read rebus: ayakara 'metalsmith'.

karaṇḍa 'duck' (Sanskrit) *karaṛa* 'a very large aquatic bird' (Sindhi) Rebus: करडा [karaḍā] Hard from alloy--iron, silver &c. (Marathi) *kāṃī* m. 'super cargo of a ship '(Marathi)
Meluhha lay to the east of Magan and linked with carnelian and ivory. Carnelian! Gujarat was a carnelian source in the ancient world. Possehl locates meluhha in the mountains of Baluchistan and meluhhan use magilum-boat (Possehl, Gregory. Meluhha. in: J. Reade (ed.) *The Indian Ocean in Antiquity.* London: Kegan Paul Intl. 1996a, 133–208 sinda refers to date-palm. (cf. Landsberger, Die Welt des Orients 3. 261).

Hieroglyph: *malla, mallā-malli* pugilistic encounter. Rebus: Akk. *Magillu* "type of boat, barge". *malah* 'sailor' (Akkadian) Cognate: *malla* m. pl. ' name of a people' (Sanskrit). kol 'tiger' Rebus: kol 'smelter' 'working in iron (metal)'. dula 'pair' Rebus: dul 'cast (metal)'. Thus, the centerpiece hieroglyph composition reads rebus: *dul kol malla kaṇṇahāra* -- m. 'helmsman, sailor'.

The reverse of the 5 molded tablets shows hieroglyph *karā* 'crocodile' (Telugu). Rebus: *khar* 'blacksmith' (Kashmiri).
Reverse h1970 to h1972B Harappa.

Reverse h1973B. h19744B
Subset 1: person kicking, spearing buffalo: *kol* 'to kill' Rebus: *kol* 'working in alloys'. Hieroglyph: ran:gā 'buffalo' Rebus: *ran:ga* 'pewter or alloy of tin (ran:ku), lead (nāga) and antimony (*añjana*)'(Santali) మేడెము [mēḍemu] or మేడియము *mēḍemu.* [Tel.] n. A spear or dagger. Rebus: *meḍ* 'iron'. Supplementary reading: Hieroglyph: *grālu* 'calf' *kaṭā* கடவு[3] kaṭavu , *n.* < கடா .1. Male buffalo 'buffalo' *kāṛā* young buffalo (Go.) *kaṭā, kaṭamā* 'bison' (Ta.)(DEDR 1114) Rebus: *kãṭhāḷ* 'maritime'; *kaṭalar, n.* < seamen, inhabitants of maritime tracts.
Subset 2 tiger (looking back), rhinoceros in file (procession): spy (*heraka*); leafless tree (*khōṇḍa*) *erako* 'moltencast copper'; *kōdār* 'turner'.

krammara 'turn back' *kammara* 'artisan'; *kol* 'tiger' Rebus: *kol* 'working in iron, alloy of 5 metals - pancaloha'. *kāṇḍa* 'rhinoceros' Rebus: *khāṇḍa* 'tools, pots and pans, and metal-ware'.
Similar hieroglyphic composition of crocodile + fish – *ayakara*, 'alloy metal smith' occurs also in the context of another hieroglyph signifying a boat with ingots on a prism tablet. This

context reinforces the unique signifier cipher as rebus symbolic form with the meaning *karṇika* कर्णिक 'helmsman, sailor' (using a boat for trade by a sea-faring merchant AND alloy metalsmith). Details of the supercargo conveyed using Meluhha hieroglyphs read rebus. (Appendix C: काण *kāṇa* 'one-eyed', *āra* 'six', 'six rings of hair' symbolic forms)

A frequently deployed symbolic form kan-ka 'rim of jar' is also relatable to the symbolic form *karṇika* कर्णिक 'having a helm, *m.* a steersman'. Thus, all the epigraphs deploying this 'rim-of-jar' hieroglyph signify a cargo account scribe.

Daimabad1 Sign342 as a terminating a string of other hieroglyphs can relate to the meaning *karṇika* कर्णिक 'having a helm, a steersman' uttered in parole as word *kan-ka* 'rim of jar' (Santali) Rebus 1: *karṇika* 'having a helm, *m.* a steersman'. Rebus 2: *karaṇika* 'scribe, account (of) *karṇī* 'boat cargo'.

Most of the epigraphs in Indus writing corpora[106] are thus consignments carried by Meluhha sea-faring helmsmen or steersmen. The writing system is a catalog of the cargo carried. This also explains the finds of Meluhha hieroglyphs on seals and seal impressions called Dilmunite seals, along the Persian Gulf which links Dholavira settlement (at the mouth of Rivers Sarasvati and Sindhu), with Failaka, Uruk and further beyond into Tigris-Euphrates rivers, into Ashur-Kanesh TinRoad journey and upto Haifa into the Fertile Crescent -- linking settlements of Meluhha-Magan-Dilmun-Elam-Mesopotamia of Ancient Near East.

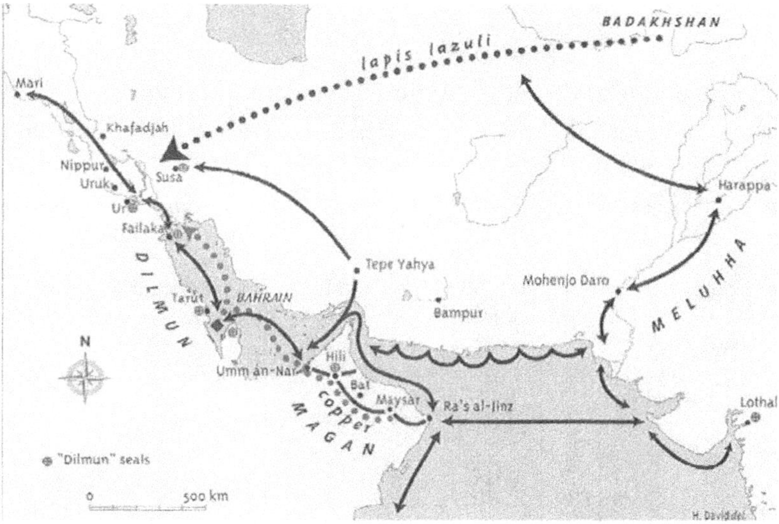

Trade interactions of bronze age[107]

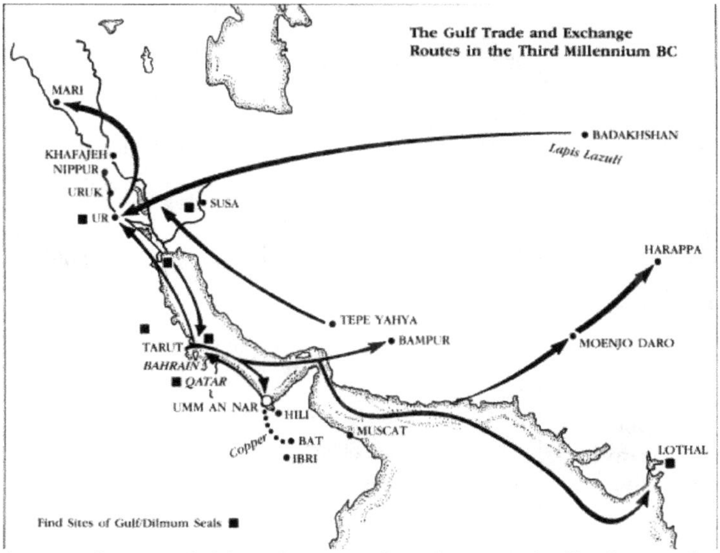

Appendix J Meluhha glosses related to symbolic forms: helmsman, cargo *karaṇi* account.

Mesopotamian trade with Dilmun, Magan and Meluhha[108]

Products imported into Ur from Dilmun	Products imported into Ur from Magan	Products imported into Ur from Meluhha
Late third and early second millennium BC	Late third millennium BC	Mid-third to mid-second millennium BC
lapis lazuli	timber and wooden objects	Timber and wooden furniture
cornelian	a type of onion (?)	Copper
semi-precious stones	copper	Gold dust
ivory and ivory objects	ivory	Lapis lazuli
copper	gold dust	Cornelian
silver	cornelian	Birds (including peacock)
'fish-eyes'	semi-precious stones	Multi-coloured ivory birds
red gold	diorite	Cornelian monkey
white corals	red ochre	Red dog
various woods	goats	(Ratnagar, 1981: 66ff.)
dates	[Cornelian and ivory were being shipped from further east; copper and diorite were local].	Texts refer to it as the land of seafarers.
[Except for the dates and 'fish-eyes', all the commodities came to Dilmun from elsewhere for onward shipment; cf. Tilmun: Edzard et al., 1977, p. 157-8; Groneberg, 1980: 237).	Akkadian kings claimed to have campaigned in Magan and taken boody. (Potts, D., 1986).	

Hypothesis: Philosophy of speech is perceived as representation – by *sphōṭa*, 'bursting forth'; reality finds expression in symbolic forms of language words and language writing.

Argument: Meluhha symbolic forms range from glosses *karaḍa* to *kan-ka*, from hieroglyphs of *kol* to *karā* – from fire venerated as divine, kole.l as smithy and also a temple, from rim-of-jar, from tiger looking back, from crocodile holding fish in its jaws. Māyā a Kolia woman sees rebus as a dream of elephant entering *kola*, her womb; she sees elephant rebus as *ibha* meaning *ib* 'iron', *ibbo* 'merchant' of Kolia parole, Meluhha. [There is a Railway station, a village called *Ib* near Bokaro (with a steel plant in the iron ore belt) on the Howrah-Mumbai rail-route]. So it is, that Meluhha language of Māyā exemplified *sphōṭa*, 'bursting forth' as symbolic forms of Meluhha glosses and rebus Meluhha hieroglyphs which were Māyā's life-experiences, coming from a community with competence in smelting *ib*, 'iron'. So, Māyā perceives *ibha* 'elephant' image in her consciousness network which is evoked by the word *ib* 'iron', a life-activity. This is why *sphōṭa* found expression in the dream as 'elephant'. A Meluhha writing system is reinforced, the way the birth of Gautama, the Buddha is narrated in Indian *sprachbund* tradition. The entire Indus script corpora bursts forth a set of hieroglyphs as symbolic forms signifying a meaningful catalog of a smithy/forge and lapidary work. Advancement from tokens/bullae to incised speech

Philosophy of Speech in the reality of cultural context of Meluhha V*ā*k has a subset, philosophy of symbolic forms and 'meanings'. The evidence of Meluhha hieroglyphs is related to the reality of life-activities of Meluhha speakers of the Bronze Age. The hypothesis is that writing system of Meuhha hieroglyphs (also called Indus writing) is based on language. What language, what speech sounds what life-activities and what spatial knowledge (say, stones or ores) were associated with this language are determined in the context of Bronz Age archaeology and validated by the rebus readings of hieroglyphs.

Meluhha hieroglyphs constitute a linguistic rebus engine to communicate information about the life-activities of artisans and merchants engaged in Bronze Age trade by signifying material and process categories principally in shell- stone- and metal-work. Sankara's commentary on Brihadaranyaka Upanishad, 1.iii.1 notes: "The Devas and the Asuras are the organs of speech and the rest. They become Devas when they shine under the influence of thoughts and actions as taught by the scriptures. Those very organs become Asuras when they are under the influence of their natural thoughts and actions, based only on perception and inference, and directed merely towards the attainment of worldly ends".

  m1493B copper tablet. Glyph:

kulai 'a hare' (Santali) Rebus: *kolhe* 'smelter'. S. *kā̃ḍo* 'thorny' (CDIAL 3022). Rebus: *kaṇḍ* 'tools, pots and pans and metal-ware'.

Person kneeling under a tree facing a tiger. 

[*Chanhudaro Excavations*, Pl. LI, 18] 

6118  Seal T-A-T ID 1743

Hieroglyphs: tiger (*kol*), offering (*eragu*), cross over (*dā̃ṭu*), slanted three (*gaṇḍe kolom*), water-carrier (*kuṭi),* leafless tree (*khōṇḍa* Marathi). Rebus meaning: Alloy of five metals (*kol*), moltencast copper (*erako*), mineral (*dhatu*), smelter-furnace (*kuṭhi*), fire-altar (ka*ṇḍa), smithy (kolami)* metal tools (*kāṇḍa*) turned in a lathe: turner (*kõdār* Bengali) *kõdā* ' to turn in a lathe.' (Marathi)

dā̃ṭu = cross over; daṭ- (da.ṭ-t-) to cross (Kol.)(DEDR 3158) Rebus: dhātu 'mineral'; rebus: dhatu = a mineral, metal (Santali)

gaṇḍe 'to place at a right angle to something else, cross, transverse'; *gaṇḍ* gaṇḍ 'across, at right angles, transversely' (Santali) [Note: A slanted line Lahn.d.a writing of accounts connotes a quarter; a straight line connotes 'one'.] Rebus: kaṇḍa 'fire-altar' (Santali) *kāṇḍa* 'iron' as in *ayaskāṇḍa* 'excellent iron' (Pan.Skt.)

kolmo 'three' (Mnda); rebus: *kolimi* 'smithy' (Telugu)
This is a remarkable example of Indus script epigraphs where the pictorial motifs and signs coalesce to convey a message.

The tree glyph shown on this Chanhudaro seal is vividly depicted on a side of a Harappa tablet occupying the entire field: *khōṇḍa* 'leafless tree' (Marathi). *khōṇḍa* A tree of which the head and branches are broken off, a stock or stump: also the lower portion of the trunk—that below the branches. (Marathi) Rebus 1: *kōḍā* 'to turn in a lathe' (Bengali) 2. *kõdār* 'turner' (Bengali)

Molded terracotta tablet showing a tree with branches; the stem emanates from a platform (ingot?). Harappa. (After JM Kenoyer/Courtesy Dept. of Archaeology and Museums, Govt.

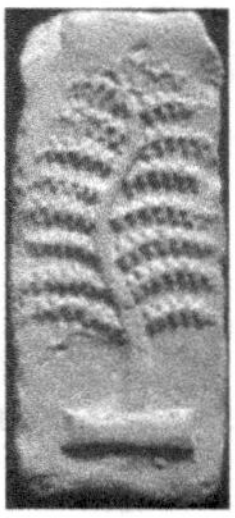

kuṭi, kuṭhi, kuṭa, kuṭha a tree (Kaus'.); kuḍa tree (Pkt.); kuṛā tree; kaṛek tree, oak (Pas;.)(CDIAL 3228). kuṭha, kuṭa (Ka.), kudal (Go.) kudar. (Go.) kuṭhāra, kuṭha, kuṭaka = a tree (Sanskrit) kut., kurun: = stump of a tree (Bond.a); khuṭ = id. (Or.) kuṭamu = a tree (Telugu)

Rebus: kuṭhi 'a furnace for smelting iron ore to smelt iron'; *kolheko kut.hieda* koles smelt iron (Santali) kuṭhi, kuṭi (Or.; Sad. koṭhi) (1) the smelting furnace of the blacksmith; kut.ire bica duljad.ko talkena, they were feeding the furnace with ore; (2) the name of ēkuṭi has been given to the fire which, in lac factories, warms the water bath for softening the lac so that it can be spread into sheets; to make a smelting furnace; kuṭhi-o of a smelting furnace, to be made; the smelting furnace of the blacksmith is made of mud, cone-shaped, 2' 6" dia. At the base and 1' 6" at the top. The hole in the centre, into which the mixture of charcoal and iron ore is poured, is about 6" to 7" in dia. At the base it has two holes, a smaller one into which the nozzle of the bellow is inserted, as seen in fig. 1, and a larger one on the opposite side through which the molten iron flows out into a cavity (Mundari.lex.) kuṭhi= a factory; lil kuṭhi= an indigo factory (H.kot.hi)(Santali.lex.Bodding) kuṭhī = an earthen furnace for smelting iron; make do., smelt iron; *kolheko do kut.hi benaokate baliko dhukana*, the Kolhes build an earthen furnace and smelt iron-ore, blowing the bellows; *tehen:ko kuṭhi yet kana*, they are working (or building) the furnace to-day (H. koṭhī) (Santali.lex. Bodding) kuṭṭhita = hot, sweltering; molten (of tamba, cp. uttatta)(Pali) uttatta (ut + tapta) = heated, of metals: molten, refined; shining, splendid, pure (Pali) kuṭṭakam, kuṭṭukam = cauldron (Ma.); kuṭṭuva = big copper pot for heating water (Kod.)(DEDR 1668). gudgā to blaze; guḍva flame (Man.d); gudva, gūdūvwa, guduwa id. (Kuwi)(DEDR 1715).

This is Sign 12 kuṭi = a woman water-carrier (Te.) kuṭi = to drink; drinking, beverage (Ta.); drinking, water drunk after meals (Ma.); kud.t- to drink (To.); kuḍi to drink; drinking (Ka.); kuḍi to drink (Kod.); kuḍi right, right hand (Te.); kuṭī intoxicating liquor (Skt.)(DEDR 1654).
Hieroglyph: 'archer': kamāṭhiyo = archer; kāmaṭhum = a bow; kāmaḍ, kāmaḍum = a chip of bamboo (G.) kāmaṭhiyo a bowman; an archer (Skt.lex.) Rebus: kammaṭi a coiner (Ka.); kampaṭṭam coinage, coin, mint (Ta.) kammaṭa = mint, gold furnace (Te.)
Allograph: kamaṛkom = fig leaf (Santali.lex.) kamarmaṛā (Has.), kamaṛkom (Nag.); the petiole or stalk of a leaf (Mundari.lex.) kamaṭha = fig leaf, religiosa (Skt.)

Cultural context specific reasoning may explain elephant in Māyā's dream because of the following glosses and traditional meanings of a community of people called Kolia; Māyā was a Kolia whose lingua franca was Meluhha of Indian *sprachbund*: *kola* 'woman'; *kol* 'working in iron'. *kolhe* (iron-smelter; *kolhuyo*, jackal) Rebus: *kol, kollan-*, kollar = blacksmith (Tamil) *kū́ṛə* 'child, foetus' (Ashkun (Aṣkū̃ — Kaf.) *kola* m. ' foetus (Old Mārwārī) Hindi. *kor* f. 'womb' (Hindi). *koḷ* m. 'lap' (Marathi) (CDIAL 3607). *wol* व्वल् ।

कललम् f. the undeveloped foetus with its surrounding membrane (Kashmiri) *kalala* 'foetus' (Pali) *kūl* belly, stomach, womb; *kūlas* offspring, descendant (Kurku). *kóli* abdomen. *Br.* *xōl* womb, offspring, entrails, woof, weft; *xōlaxū, xōxū* entrails, woof and warp (Maltese) / ? < IA. Cf. *kol* breast, bosom; *kaulā, kolā, kaulī* id., lap (Hindi) (DEDR 2244).

Representations of these symbolic forms also occur as hieroglyphs in Indus script corpora.

Meluhhans had travelled, traded and settled in Ancient Near East

Raw nodules of large-sized stones (of carnelian) might have been represented by a symbolic form:

 This symbolic form, a hieroglyph has about 70 ligatured constructions in Indus writing corpora.

This symbolic form has a Meluhha hieroglyph rebus reading relatable to the 'meaning' of 'stone nodule':

 Hieroglyph: *kāḍ* 2 काड़् । पौरुषम् m. a man's length, the stature of a man (as a measure of length) (Rām. 632, *zangan kaḍun kāḍ*, to stretch oneself the whole length of one's body. So K. 119) (Kashmiri).

A variant of this symbolic form or a semantic expansion of word *kāḍ* occurs in a ligatured representation on a Mohenjo-daro seal m1162:

  m1162 Text 2058 Ligatured glyph of three sememes: 1. *meḍ* 'body'(Mu.); rebus: 'iron' (Ho.); *kāḍ* 2 काड़् a man's length, the stature of a man (as a measure of length); rebus: *kāḍ* 'stone'; Ga. (Oll.) *kanḍ* , (S.) *kanḍu (pl. kanḍkil)* stone; 2. *aḍar* 'harrow'; rebus: *aduru* 'native metal'. *ibha* 'elephant'; rebus: *ibbo* 'merchant' (Gujarati) ibha 'elephant' Rebus: ib 'iron', ibbo 'merchant'. Thus, this merchant on Seal m1162 is trading in nodules of stone and nodules of native metal 'iron' (perhaps, meteoric, unsmelted iron rocks). Alternative reading for the ligaturing element, if interpreted as hoe or spade: Hieroglyph: *kaṇṭhāla* 'a hoe , spade' (Sanskrit)

Hieroglyph/Rebus: †*kaṇṭhāla* कण्ठाल -- *m.* a boat , ship (Sanskrit) [kaṇṭhá --] *kā̃ṭhāḷ* 'maritime'(Gujarati) (CDIAL 2682a). Thus, an alternative reading rebus: *kā̃ṭhāḷ* 'boat' with *meḍ kāḍ* 'iron stone (ore)'.

Another ligatured variant occurs on another seal denotating metal tools, pots and pans subjected to furnace action but relatable to *meḍ kāḍ* 'body, stature' Rebus: 'iron, stone (ore) nodule'

Listed by Koskenniemi and Parpola and cited by Diwiyana109. Ligatured glyph of three sememes: 1. *meḍ* 'body' (Mu.); rebus: 'iron' (Ho.); 2. *kuṭi* 'water carrier' (Te.) Rebus: *kuṭhi* 'smelter furnace' (Santali); 3. खांडा [*khāṇḍā*] *m* a jag, notch, or indentation (as upon the edge of a tool or weapon); rebus: *khāṇḍā* 'metal tools, pots and pans'. In parole, this reads: *kolheko kuṭhieda* 'koles smelt iron' (Santali)

Thus the symbolic form, hieroglyph: *kāḍ* signifies the underlying *sphōṭa* 'bursting forth' referring to the life-activity of trade in stone ore nodules.

Hieroglyph: *kāḍ* 2 काड् । पौरुषम् m. a man's length, the stature of a man (as a measure of length) (Rām. 632, *zangan kaḍun kāḍ*, to stretch oneself the whole length of one's body. So K. 119). Rebus: *kaṇḍa* 'nodule of stone ore'. *kāḍ* 'stone'. Ga. (Oll.) *kanḍ*, (S.) *kanḍu* (pl. *kanḍkil*) stone (DEDR 1298). maypoṇḍi kanḍ whetstone; (Ga.)(DEDR 4628). *khaḍā* (खडा) Pebbles or small stones: also stones broken up (as for a road), metal. खडा [*khaḍā*] *m* A small stone, a pebble. 2 A nodule (of lime &c.): a lump or bit (as of gum, assafœtida, catechu, sugar-candy): the gem or stone of a ring or trinket: a lump of hardened fæces or scybala: a nodule or lump gen. (CDIAL 3018). *kāṭha* m. ' rock ' lex. [Cf. *kānta* -- 2 m. ' stone ' lex.] Bshk. *kōr* ' large stone ' AO xviii 239. கண்டு[3] kaṇṭu , *n.* < *gaṇḍa.* 1. Clod, lump; கட்டி. (தைலவ. தைல. 99.) 2. Wen; கழலைக்கட்டி. 3. Bead or something like a pendant in an ornament for the neck; ஓர் ஆபரணவுரு. புல்லிகைக்கண்ட நாண் ஒன்றிற் கட்டின கண்டு ஒன்றும் (S.I.I. ii, 429). (CDIAL 3023) *kāṇḍa* cluster, heap ' (in *tr̥ṇa* -- *kāṇḍa* -- Pāṇ. Kāś.). [Poss. connexion with gaṇḍa -- 2 makes prob. non -- Aryan origin (not with P. Tedesco Language 22, 190 < *kr̥ntáti*). Pa. *kaṇḍa* -- m.n. joint of stalk, lump. काठः A rock, stone. kāṭha m. ' rock ' lex. [Cf. *kānta* -- 2 m. ' stone ' lex.]Bshk. *kōr* ' large stone ' AO xviii 239.(CDIAL 3018). অয়স্কঠিন [aẏaskaṭhina] as hard as iron; extremely hard (Bengali)

tāna m. ' tone ' MBh., ' fibre ' Suśr. [√tan]Pk. *tāṇa* -- m. ' tune '; K. *tān* m. ' thread, fibre, rigid bar, beam of a house '; S. *tāṇo* m. ' warp '; L. *tāṇā* m. ' woof ', °*ṇī* f. ' prepared woof ' (both in error for ' warp '?), awāṇ. *tāṇā* ' warp '; P. *tāṇ* m. ' strength ', f. ' tune ', *tāṇā* m., °*ṇī* f. ' warp '; WPah.bhal. *tāṇi* f. ' unsewn woollen cloth '; Ku. *tāṇo* ' tape or string for fastening clothes '; N. *tān* ' warp ', *tānā* ' tune '; B. *tān* ' expanse ', *tānā* ' warp '; Bi. *tān* ' string braces to keep awning of litter steady ',*tānā* ' warp ', *tānī* ' warp, strings of a balance '; Mth. *tānī* ' warp '; Bhoj. *tān* ' tune '; H. *tānā* m. ' warp ', *tānī* f. ' warp, price paid for weaving ', *tānā* -- *bānā* m. ' warp and woof ' (→ N. *tānā* -- *bānā* ' apparatus '); G. *tāṇi* f. ' strain ', *tāṇɔ* m. ' warp '; M. *tāṇ* m. ' strain ', *tāṇā* m. ' warp '.(CDIAL 5761).

Tanana mleccha. A Jaina text, *Avasyaka Churani* notes that ivory trade was managed by *mleccha*, who also traveled from Uttaravaha to Dakshinapatha. Guttila Jataka (ca.4th cent.) makes reference to itinerant ivory workers/traders journeying from Varanasi to Ujjain.110 The phrase, *tanana mleccha* may be related to: (i) tah'nai, 'engraver' mleccha; or (ii) tana, 'of (mleccha) lineage'. 1. See Kuwi. *tah'nai* 'to engrave' in DEDR and Bsh. *then, thon*, 'small axe' in CDIAL: DEDR 3146 *Go.* (Tr.) *tarcana* (Mu.) *tarc-* to scrape; (Ma.) *tarsk-* id., plane; (D.) *task-*, (Mu.) *tarsk-/tarisk-* to level, scrape (*Voc.*1670).

kāḍ 2 काड् a man's length, the stature of a man (as a measure of length); rebus*: kāḍ* 'stone'; *meḍ* 'body'(Mu.) Rebus: 'iron' (Ho.); *kāḍ meḍ* 'stature of person, body'.

See a hieroglyph of 'body' of a standing person on a Banawali seal 17: A unique hieroglyphic form also ligatures 'tiger' hieroglyph with zebu horns, possibly rendering 'meaning' that 'tiger horned' refers to an artisan shown in front of the 'standard device', *sangaḍa*. Rebus reading may relate to: *sagaḍa* 'cart, waggon, cartload' (Prākṛt). Thus, two types of consignments are recorded as hieroglyphs:

1. *sangaḍa* 'lathe, portable furnace' Rebus: *sagaḍa* 'cartload'.
2. *karṇaka, kan-ka* 'rim-of-jar' Rebus: *karṇī* 'supercargo for boatload'.
3. A ligatured hieroglyph denotes a 'person standing' atop two spoked wheels. This may be read rebus: *kāṭhī* = body, person; *kāṭhī* the make of the body; the stature of a man (Gujarati) Rebus: *khātī* 'wheelwright' (Hindi) *meḍ* 'body' Rebus: *meḍ* 'iron' (Ho.) dula 'pair' Rebus: dul 'cast (metal)' śakaṭa 'wheel' Rebus: *sagaḍa* 'cartload'. *khātī* m. ' member of a caste of wheelwrights '(Hindi); Pa. *khattar* -- m. 'attendant, charioteer'; (CDIAL 3647).

 Thus, the ligatured hieroglyph may be read as: *khātī dul meḍ sagaḍa* (lit. wheelwright cast iron cartload).

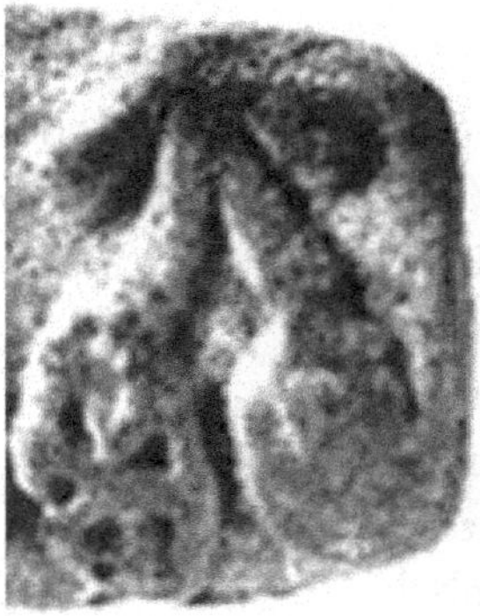

Harappa seal h212A, B

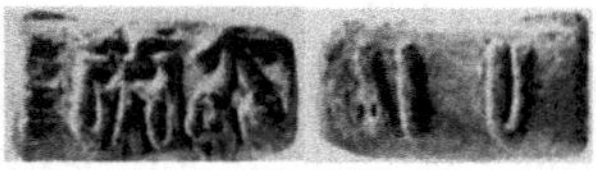

h212A

h212B

Text 4357
Lothal 221A Potsherd
The hieroglyph sequence which appears on Harappa seal h212A

occurs on this potsherd, subject to stylistic variation caused by incision on a potsherd.

Th two hieroglph compositions on the potsherd Lothal 221A can be read rebus from r. to l.: 1. *khātī dul meḍ sagaḍa* (lit. wheelwright cast iron cartload).

2. *kuṭhi kaṇḍa kaṃīka* 'smelting furnace supercargo account (scribe)'.

Consistent with this rebus reading, the Text 4357 on Harappa Seal with two lines of epigraphs on h212A, h212B on two sides, can be read:

The meaning of message of 5 hieroglyphs: wheelwright cast iron, bronze cartload; smelting furnace supercargo account scribe. engraved entrustment articles of metal-turner:

Line 2 is read rebus*:* U | | Meaning: *sangaḍa kõdā* 'metal-turner, engraved entrustment articles'.

Line 1: First two hieroglyphs from r.

1. *khātī dul meḍ sagaḍa* (lit. wheelwright cast iron cartload).

2. *kuṭhi kaṇḍa kaṃīka* 'smelting furnace supercargo account (scribe)'.

kā̃gsī f. ' comb ' (Gujarati), Rebus: *kā̃sī* 'bronze' (Punjabi); kā̃so ' bronze, pewter, white metal ' (Nepali) WPah. khaś. *kā̃gśī*, śeu. *kā̃śkī* 'a comblike fern'(CDIAL 2599). Rebus: *kāṁsako, kāṁsiyo* = a large sized comb (G.) Rebus: *kaṁsa*= bronze (Te.) *kā̃sāri* 'pewterer' (Bengali) kā̃sārī; H. kasārī m. ' maker of brass pots' (Or.); Pa. kaṁsa -- m. ' bronze dish ' (CDIAL 2756). kāṁsya ' made of bell -- metal ' KātyŚr., n. ' bell -- metal ' Yājñ., ' cup of bell -- metal ' MBh., aka -- n. ' bell -- metal '. 2. *kāṁsiya -- .[kaṁsá -- 1] 1. Pa. kaṁsa -- m. (?) ' bronze ', Pk. kaṁsa -- , kāsa -- n. ' bell -- metal, drinking vessel, cymbal '; L. (Jukes) kā̃jā adj. ' of metal ', awāṇ. kāsā ' jar ' (← E with -- s-- , not ñj); N. kā̃so ' bronze, pewter, white metal ', kas -- kuṭ ' metal alloy '; A. kā̃h ' bell -- metal ', B. kā̃sā, Or. kā̃sā, Bi. kā̃sā; Bhoj. kā̃s ' bell -- metal ',kā̃sā ' base metal '; H. kās, kā̃sā m. ' bell -- metal ', G. kā̃sũ n.,

M. kā̃sẽ n.; Ko. kā̃śẽ n. ' bronze '; Si. kasa ' bell -- metal '. 2. L. kā̃ihā̃ m. ' bell -- metal ', P. kā̃ssī, kā̃sī f., H. kā̃sī, A. kā̃h also ' gong ', or < kaṁsá -- . (CDIAL 2987) *kāṁsyakara ' worker in bell -- metal '. [See next: kāṁsya -- , kará -- 1] L. awāṇ. kasērā ' metal worker ', P. kaserā m. ' worker in pewter ' (both ← E with -- s --); N. kasero ' maker of brass pots '; Bi. H. kaserā m. ' worker in pewter '. (CDIAL 2988). kāṁsyakāra m. ' worker in bell -- metal or brass ' Yājñ. com., kaṁsakāra -- m. BrahmavP. [kā´ṁsya -- , kāra -- 1] N. kasār ' maker of brass pots '; A. kãhār ' worker in bell -- metal '; B. kā̃sāri ' pewterer, brazier, coppersmith ', Or. kãsārī; H. kasārī m. ' maker of brass pots '; G.kãsārɔ, kas m. ' coppersmith '; M. kā̃sār, kās m. ' worker in white metal ', kāsārḍā m. ' contemptuous term for the same '. (CDIAL 2989). *k̠ǒṅḍu* m. ' large cooking pot '(Kashmiri) Rebus: *kõdā* 'to turn in a lathe' (B.) कोंद *kōnda* 'engraver, lapidary setting or infixing gems' (Marathi)

U | | Two long linearstrokes: *sangaḍa* 'a pair, two' Rebus: *sangaḍa* 'fortification' or *jangaḍa* 'entrustment article' + *kõdā* 'engraver, to turn in a lathe'. (That is, artifacts turned in a lathe to be inventoried in fortification or inscribed on seal as 'entrustment articles' for onward trade consignment). Alternative 1: Hieroglyph: *dula* 'pair' Rebus: *dul* 'cast metal' + *kõdā* 'engraver, to turn in a lathe'. Meaning: Cast metal turned in lathe. Alternative 2: dula 'pair' Rebus: dul 'cast metal' + baṭhu large cooking fire' baṭhī f. 'distilling furnace'; L. bhaṭṭh m. 'grain—parcher's oven'. Rebus: bhrāṣṭra = furnace (Skt.) baṭa = a kind of iron (G.) bhaṭa 'furnace' (G.) baṭa = kiln (Santali). bhaṭṭha -- m.n. ' gridiron (Pkt.) baṭhī f. 'distilling furnace'; P. bhaṭṭh m., ṭhī f. 'furnace', bhaṭṭhā m. 'kiln'; S. bhaṭṭhī keṇī 'distil (spirits)'. (CDIAL 9656)

U | | Meaning: *sangaḍa kõdā* 'metal-turner, engraved entrustment articles'. Alternative: dul *kõdā* Cast metal turned in lathe + *baṭa* = a kind of iron (Gujarati) bhaṭa 'furnace' (Gujarati).

U| Meaning: *koḍ kõdā 'metal-turner workshop' koḍa* 'one' Rebus: *koḍ* 'workshop' *kõdā* 'metal-turner' Alternative: *koḍ baṭa* = furnace for a kind of iron (Gujarati) *koḍ* bhaṭa 'furnace workshop' (Gujarati).

U||| Meaning: *kolami kõdā 'metal-turner smithy' kolmo* 'three' Rebus: *kolami* 'smithy, forge' + *kõdā* 'to turn in a lathe'. Alternative: *kolami baṭa* = smithy for a kind of iron (Gujarati) *kolami* bhaṭa 'smithy furnace' (Gujarati).

U|||| Meaning: *kaṇḍa kõdā* 'metal-turner furnace' *gaṇḍa* 'four' Rebus: *kaṇḍa* 'furnace, fire-altar' + *kõdā* 'to turn in a lathe'. (that is, artifacts turned in a lathe to be subjected to furnace firing in a furnace). Alternative: *kaṇḍa baṭa* 'fire-altar, furnace'.

khondu 'small ditch or moat' (Kashmiri) WPah.kṭg. *kv́ṇḍh* m. ' pit or vessel used for an oblation with fire into which barley etc. is thrown '; H. *gõṛā* m. 'reservoir used in irrigation '. (CDIAL 3264). अग्निकुण्डम्. A pool, well; especially one consecrated to some deity or holy purpose. (Sanskrit) *Kur.* xoṇḍxā, xō̃ṛxā deep; a pit, abyss. *Malt.* qonḍe deep, low lands. (DEDR 2082). kŏnḍ (p. 16*b*, l. 34) (Rām. 631). *kọ̆nḍu or konḍu* । कुण्डम् m. a hole dug in the ground for receiving consecrated fire (Kashmiri) kō̃da कोँद । कुलालादिकन्दुः f. a kiln; a potter's kiln (Rām. 1446; H. xi, 11); a brick-kiln (Śiv. 133); a lime-kiln. -bal -बल् । कुलालादि कन्दु स्थानम् m. the place where a kiln is erected, a brick or potter's kiln (Gr.Gr. 165). -- khasüñü – कुलालादि कन्दु यथावद्भावः f.inf. a kiln to arise; met. to become like such a kiln (which contains no imperfectly baked articles, but only well-made perfectly baked ones), hence, a collection of good ('pucka') articles or qualities to exist. Cf. Śiv. 133, where the causal form of the verb is used. (Kashmiri)(CDIAL 2726) 1669 *Ta.* kuṭṭam depth, pond; kuṭṭai pool, small pond; kuṇṭam deep cavity, pit, pool; kuṇṭu depth, hollow, pond, manure-pit. *Ma.* kuṇṭam, kuṇṭu what is hollow and deep, hole, pit. *Ka.* kuṇḍa, koṇḍa, kuṇṭe pit, pool, pond; guṇḍa hollowness and deepness; guṇḍi hole, pit, hollow, pit of the stomach; guṇḍige pit of the stomach; guṇḍitu, guṇḍittu that is deep; guṇpu, gumpu, gumbu depth, profundity, solemnity, secrecy. *Koḍ.* kuṇḍï pit; kuṇḍitere manure-pit. *Tu.* kuṇḍa a pit; koṇḍa pit, hole; guṇḍi abyss, gulf, great depth; gumpu secret, concealed. *Te.* kuṇṭa, guṇṭa pond, pit; kuṇḍu cistern; guṇḍamu fire-pit; (Inscr.) a hollow or pit in the dry bed of a stream; gunta pit, hollow, depression. *Kol.* (Pat., p. 115) gunḍi deep. *Nk.* ghuṇḍik id. *Pa.* guṭṭa pool. *Go.* (A.) kunṭa id. (*Voc.* 737). *Konḍa* guṭa pit, hollow in the ground. *Kui* kuṭṭ a large pit (Chandrasekhar, *Trans. Linguistic Circle Delhi* 1958, p. 2). *Kuwi* (S.) guntomi pit; (Isr.) kuṇḍi pond. Cf. 1818 Ta. kuṟal and 2082 Kur. xoṇḍxā. / Cf. Skt. kuṇḍa- round hole in ground (for water or sacred fire), pit, well, spring. (DEDR 1669).

కుండ [kuṇḍa] *kuṇḍa.* [Tel.] n. An earthern pot. A

pot. కుండము [kuṇḍamu] *kuṇḍamu.* [Skt.] n. An earthen pot. A pit or pot for receiving and preserving consecrated fire. A fire pit నిప్పుల గుండము.

Hieroglyph: *dula* 'pair' Rebus: *dul* 'cast metal' meḍha 'polar star' (Marathi) *kāṭhī 'stature of person' Rebus: kāthī* wheelwright. *meḍ* 'body' Rebus: *meḍ* 'iron' (Ho.) Thus, *kāṭhī meḍ* 'wheelwright iron'. Seal impression, Ur (UPenn; U.16747); dia. 2.6, ht. 0.9 cm.; Gadd,

PBA 18 (1932), pp. 11-12, pl. II, no. 12; Porada 1971: pl.9, fig.5; Parpola, 1994, p. 183; water carrier with a skin (or pot?) hung on each end of the yoke across his shoulders and another one below the crook of his left arm; the vessel on the right end of his yoke is over a receptacle for the water; a star on either side of the head (denoting supernatural?). "The whole object is enclosed by 'parenthesis' marks. The parenthesis is perhaps a way of splitting of the ellipse. An unmistakable example of an 'hieroglyphic' seal."111

This hieroglyph is normalized as a 'sign' (Glyph 12) on Indus Writing corpora.
kuṭi 'water carrier' (Te.) Rebus: *kuṭhi* 'smelter furnace' (Santali) *kuṛī* f. 'fireplace' (Hindi); krvṛI f. 'granary' (Wpah.); *kuṛī, kuṛo* house, building'(Ku.)(CDIAL 3232) *kuṭi* 'hut made of boughs' (Skt.) guḍi temple (Telugu)

Ligatured glyph 15. Thus, the 'rim-of-jar' glyph connotes: furnace account (scribe). Together with the glyph showing 'water-carrier', the ligatured glyphs of 'water-carrier' + 'rim-of-jar' can thus be read as: *kuṭhi kaṇḍa kan-ka* 'smelting furnace account (scribe)'. Alternate reading: *kuṭhi kaṇḍa karṇīka* 'smelting furnace supercargo account (scribe)'

h215A 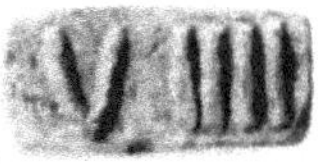 h215B5271  The ligatured hieroglyph on Line 2 is read rebus: *kāṭhī 'stature of person' Rebus: kāthī* wheelwright. *meḍ* 'body' Rebus: *meḍ* 'iron' (Ho.) Thus, *kāṭhī meḍ* 'wheelwright iron' + Hieroglyph: Ash. *kuṭä´* ' heel ', Wg. *kūṭewī´* NTS ii 263; Dm. *khuṭṭa* ' knee ', Paš. *kōṭa*, Bshk. *kuṭ*, *kuṭh*, Tor. *kūṭh*, Kand. *kūṭhu*, Phal. *kuṭho*, *khūṭu*, Sh. gil. *kŭṭo* m. (→ Ḍ. *kuṭá* prob. pl.), pales. koh. *kūṭhu*, jij. *kuṭh*, K. *koṭhu* m. (CDIAL 3243). Rebus: kuṭṭa1 in cmpd. ' breaking, cutting ', °*aka* -- ' id. ', m. ' cutter, breaker, grinder '; Ku. *kuṭo*,°*ṭī*, °*ṭlo* ' hoe ' Or. *kuṭa* ' small hammer for breaking stones ', °*ṭā* ' act of beating or pounding or husking '; M. *kuṭā* -- *kuṭī* f. ' fighting '.(CDIAL 3236). Thus, the ligatured hieroglyph is read rebus: *kāṭhī meḍ kuṭa* 'wheelwright iron hammer'.

There are two segments with two hieroglyphs each on Line 2 of Harappa tablet h213 and h214; read rebus:

kāgsī f. ' comb ' (Gujarati), Rebus: *kãsī* 'bronze' (Punjabi) *kāṇḍa* 'arrow' Rebus: *kāṇḍā* 'tools, pots and pans, metalware' (Marathi) That is, read together *kãsī kāṇḍā* 'bronze tools'.

kāgsī f. ' comb ' (Gujarati), Rebus: *kãsī* 'bronze' (Punjabi) Ligatured hieroglyph: *ḍabu* 'an iron spoon' (Santali) Rebus: *ḍab, ḍhimba, ḍhompo* 'lump (ingot?)' (Mu.) Rebus: *baṭa* = a kind of

iron (Gujarati) *bhaṭa* 'furnace' (Gujarati) That is, read together *kā̃sī ḍab bhaṭa* 'bronze ingot furnace'. Alternative: *kā̃sī ḍab kõdā* 'bronze ingot turner'.

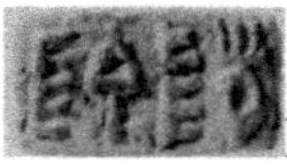h213A  h213B 5270

h214A 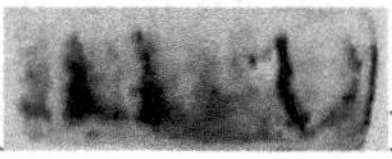h214B

 4684

Harappa seal h506 Text 4097 *kõda* 'young bull' Rebus: *kõdā* 'lathe-turner' *koḍa* 'horn' *koḍ* 'workshop'; *sangaḍa* 'lathe, portable furnace' Rebus: *jangaḍ* 'entrustment articles'.

 *eraka āra* 'nave of wheel, spokes' Rebus: *erako āra* 'moltencast copper, brass'. खांडा [*khāṇḍā*] *m* a jag, notch, or indentation (as upon the edge of a tool or weapon). *khāṇḍā* 'tools, pots and pans, metal-ware'.

 *ranku* 'liquid measure' rebus: *ranku* 'tin'.

 *eraka āra* 'nave of wheel, spokes' Rebus: *erako āra* 'moltencast copper, brass'.

 *ḍab bhaṭa* 'bronze ingot furnace'. Rebus: *ḍab, ḍhimba, ḍhompo* 'lump (ingot?)'.

 *tān* 'fibre, warp' Rebus: *tanana mleccha, tah'nai*, 'engraver' mleccha, *tanana mleccha*.

Lothal021 Seal Text 7047

kõda 'young bull' Rebus: *kõdā* 'lathe-turner' *koḍa* 'horn' *koḍ* 'workshop'; *sangaḍa* 'lathe, portable furnace' Rebus: *jangaḍ* 'entrustment articles'.

 *eraka āra* 'nave of wheel, spokes' Rebus: *erako āra* 'moltencast copper, brass'. **கண்டம்**[3] kaṇṭam , *n.* < *khaṇḍa.* 1. Piece, cut or broken off; fragment, slice, cutting, chop, parcel, portion, slip; **துண்டம்**. **செந்தயிர்க் கண்டம்** (கம்பரா. நாட்டுப். 19). *khāṇḍā* 'tools, pots and pans, metal-ware'. *erako āra khāṇḍā* 'moltencast copper, brass, tools'.

 *khāṭī meḍ koḍa* 'stature of person, body one' Rebus: *kāṭī meḍ koḍ* 'wheelwright iron workshop'.

kuṭhi kaṇḍa kaṃīka 'smelting furnace supercargo account (scribe)'

 Lothal217ALothal217B

kõda 'young bull' Rebus: *kõdā* 'lathe-turner' *koḍa* 'horn' *koḍ* 'workshop'; *sangaḍa* 'lathe, portable furnace' Rebus: *jangaḍ* 'entrustment articles'.

ḍangar 'bull'; rebus: *ḍangar* 'blacksmith' (Hindi); *pātra* 'trough' in front of wild/domesticated/ composite animals. *pattar* 'trough' (dedr 4079) 4080 ta. cavity, hollow, deep hole; *pattar* (DEDR 4080) rebus: **பத்தர்**[2] *pattar , n. < t. battuḍu.* a caste title of goldsmiths.

 kolmo 'three' Rebus: kolami 'smithy/forge'; *baṭhu* 'large pot' *Rebus: baṭa* = a kind of iron (Gujarati) *bhaṭa* 'furnace' (Gujarati)

 *kāṭhī meḍ* 'stature of person, body' Rebus: *kāṭī meḍ* 'wheelwright iron'; *bhaṭu* 'large pot' *Rebus: bhaṭa* 'furnace'

 *kaṇḍa kaṃīka* 'smelting furnace supercargo account (scribe)'

 Segment 1: *dula eraka āra* 'nave of wheel, spokes' Rebus: *dul erako āra* 'cast metal,

moltencast copper, brass'.

 Segment 2: *karṇīka* 'supercargo' கண்டம்³ kaṇṭam , *n.* < *khaṇḍa.* 1. Piece, cut or broken off; fragment, slice, cutting, chop, parcel, portion, slip; துண்டம். செந்தயிர்க் கண்டம் (கம்பரா. நாட்டுப். 19). *khāṇḍā* 'tools, pots and pans, metal-ware'. Thus, together read rebus: *karṇīka khāṇḍā* 'supercargo tools, metalware'.

Lothal148A7270 *kõda* 'young bull' Rebus: *kõdā* 'lathe-turner' *koḍa* 'horn' *koḍ* 'workshop'; *sangaḍa* 'lathe, portable furnace' Rebus: *jangaḍ* 'entrustment articles'.

Text 7270: *khāṇḍā* 'moltencast copper, brass, tools'. ayo 'fish' Rebus: ayo 'alloyed metal'; *adaren* 'lid' *aduru* 'native metal'.

Lothal018 7096

kõda 'young bull' Rebus: *kõdā* 'lathe-turner' *koḍa* 'horn' *koḍ* 'workshop'; *sangaḍa* 'lathe, portable furnace' Rebus: *jangaḍ* 'entrustment articles'.

 *eraka āra* 'nave of wheel, spokes' Rebus: *erako āra* 'moltencast copper, brass'. खांडा [*khāṇḍā*] *m* a jag, notch, or indentation (as upon the edge of a tool or weapon). *khāṇḍā* 'tools, pots and pans, metal-ware'.

 *koḍa* 'one' Rebus: *koḍ* 'workshop'

 *aḍar* 'harrow' Rebus: *aduru* 'native metal'.

Banawali 17 9201

Message of Bronze Age Meluhha catalog item: Iron worker, engraver workshop (working in fortification); (worker in or repertoire of) stone, native metal, alloy metal

koḍ 'horn' Rebus: *koḍ* 'workshop'

kāḍ 'stature of person' Rebus: *kāḍ* 'stone'

kol 'tiger' Rebus: *kol* 'working in iron' 'smelter'

tān 'fibre, warp' Rebus: *tanana mleccha, tah'nai*, 'engraver' mleccha. (Appendix H: Interpretation of Māyā's dream in Bauddham which contains sets of Meluhha glosses which may explain meaning of 'engraving' and *sagaḍa* 'cardload' in the context of archaeologically attested trade and craftwork).

khaḍā 'circumscribe' (Marathi); Rebs: *khaḍā* 'nodule (ore), stone' (Marathi) ayo 'fish'; rebus: ayas 'metal, iron' (Pāṇini.Sanskrit) aḍaren, ḍaren lid, cover (Santali) Rebus: aduru 'native metal' (Kannada). Thus, the hieroglyphic composition red rebus: *aduru ayas khaḍā* 'nodule of native metal and alloy metal

Vidale's summary of the archaeological context of Meluhhan's life-activities also refers to the seal of Su-ilisu, 'Meluhha interpreter'. Here is the seal:

Akkadian. Cylinder seal Impression. Inscription records that it belongs to 'S'u-ilis'u, Meluhha interpreter', i.e., translator of the Meluhha language (EME.BAL.ME.LUH.HA.KI)

The Meluhha being introduced carries an goat on his arm. Musee du Louvre. Ao 22 310, Collection De Clercq 3rd millennium BCE. The antelope carried by the bearded Me-lah-ha on an Akkadian cylinder seal may be a phonetic determinant: mr..eka (Telugu)(melu-hha; also, melech, 'king'; plural form, 'melachim'). [cf. Melech Hamashiah: King Messiah; Akad: {Akkad} A city in Mesopotamia (now Iraq) which was part of Nimrod's kingdom, founded by Melech Sargon around 2350 BCE Genesis 10:10].

The Meluhha on Shu-ilishu cylinder seal is accompanied by a lady carrying a kamaṇḍalu.

The pattern of symbolic form deployed in art is not a flash-in-the pan but is relatable to many artifacts of Ancient Near East, all such artifacts may perhaps have been creations of 'meluhha pattern' of rebus representation of uttered sounds of Meluhha language. Here are some examples. Mleccha, mleccha-mukha 'copper' in Sanskrit is a gloss cognate with mlech 'goat'; the symbolic form of goat signified the ife-activity of the bearded merchant: copper-work.

The symbolic form of a 'goat' carried on the left arm of the Meluhha merchant represents the intended meaning: Meluhha. The Meluhha glosses which relate to this 'Meluhha' word are the Meluhha glosses: *mlekh* 'goat' (Brahui); *mṛeka* (Telugu); *mēṭam* (Tamil); *meṣam* (Sanskrit). This convergence in the image-sound network yields a cipher: the goat is imaged to signify that the identity of the person is identified as a Meluhha (person). He is *mṛeka~~ mlekh* signifying 'goat' but actually meaning rebus: meluhha, a person from Meluhha land – seafaring merchant from across the Persian Gulf, from the eastern land.

The goat conveys the message that the carrier is a Meluhha speaker. A phonetic determinant. Ka. mēke she-goat; mē the bleating of sheep or goats. Te. mē̃ka, mēka goat. Kol. me·ke id. Nk. mēke id. Pa. mēva, (S.) mēya she-goat. Ga. (Oll.) mēge, (S.) mēge goat. Go. (M) mekā, (Ko.) mēka id. ? Kur. mēxnā (mīxyas) to call, call after loudly, hail. Malt. méqe to bleat. [Te. mṛēka (so correct) is of unknown meaning. Br. mēlh̠ is without etymology; see MBE 1980a.] / Cf. Skt. (lex.) meka- goat (Monier-Williams lex.) (DEDR 5087) meluh.h.a !
The Meluhha is accompanied by a woman. kola 'woman' (Nahali). Rebus: *kol* 'pañcalōha, alloy of five metals' (Ta.) கொல் kol, n. 1. Iron; இரும்பு. மின் வெள்ளி பொன் கொல்லெனச் சொல்லும் (தக்கயாகப். 550). 2. Metal; உலோகம். (நாமதீப. 318.) *kola* 'blacksmith' (Ka.); Koḍ. *kollë* blacksmith (DEDR 2133). It is notable that a community of people In India are called Koles and this community are experts working with iron and other metal smelters. Maya, the mother of Gautama Buddha was a koliya, from this community who saw a dream of an

elephant entering her womb. Why elephant I her dream? She was a koliya, that is why. Koles deal with *ib* 'iron' hieroglyph meaning rebus: *ibha* 'elephant'. This is an interpretation of Maya's dream celebrated in Bauddham tradition; the dream presents the philosophy of symbolic forms.

It appears that the same hieroglyphs are used: antelope, woman in the following artifact produced during Jacques de Morgan's excavations at Susa (1905). He had also published the tokens. The tokens were used for categorizing property items.

'Based on cuneiform documents from Mesopotamia we know that there was at least one Meluhha village in Akkad at that time, with people called 'Son of Meluhha' living there. In Sargon I's reign (ca. 2370 BCE), a reference is made to 'holder of a Meluhha ship'. A seal in British Museum (ca. 2250 BCE) lists enemies of King Naram-Sin, among them is a 'man of Meluhha' by the name of _ibra. Meluhha was used as a personal name for some people. Urkal, Ur-dlam were called the 'son of meluhha'. A person called nin-ana is identified with the village of meluhha. Meluhha was also identified with specific products: giS-ab-ba-me-lu-hha (abba wood); giS-ha-lu-ub (Haluppu wood).

The cuneiform inscription (ca. 2020 BCE) says that the cylinder seal belonged to Shu-ilishu, who was a translator of the Meluhha language. "The presence in Akkad of a translator of the Meluhha language suggests that he may have been literate and could read the undeciphered Indus script. This in turn suggests that there may be bilingual Akkadian/Meluhha tablets somewhere in Mesopotamia. Although such documents may not exist, Shu-ilishu's cylinder seal offers a glimmer of hope for the future in unraveling the mystery of the Indus script."[112] Shu-ilishu cylinder seal with cuneiform text EME.BAL.ME.LUH.HA.KI (interpreter of Meluhha language), extended to contact regions with Meluhhan (Mleccha) settlers in Sumer and other settlements of Elam/Mesopotamia. A cuneiform text [Ur III (ca. 2100-2000 BC)] refers to Meluhha as a region.[113]

Figure, “nude goddess”, 7000 Years of Iranian Art, no. 204.[114]
On this statue, a ram is ligatured to a woman (*kola*). *meḍho* a ram, a sheep (G.)(CDIAL 10120); Rebus: *mẽṛhẽt,* ‘iron’ (Mu.Ho.) Rebus: meṛha, meḍhi ‘merchant’s clerk; (G.) Rebus: mḗdha m. ‘ sacrificial oblation ’ RV. mēdha -- m. ‘ sacrifice ’ (Pa.) (CDIAL 10327).
The ram could also be denoted by *tagara* ‘antelope’; takar, *n.* [தகர் T. *tagaru*, K. *tagar.*] 1. Sheep; ஆட்டின்பொது. (திவா.) 2. Ram; செம் மறியாட்டுக்கடா. (திவா.) பொருநகர் தாக்கற்குப் பேருந் தகைத்து (குறள், 486). Rebus: *ṭagara* ‘tin’.

Two Elamites carrying animals (bull, antelope) as phonetic determinatives -- the same way a Meluhha carried an antelope on his hands (as shown on a cylinder seal).[115]

Massimo Vidale presents the evidence of the following six steatite seals to show definitive links with Meluhha. I suggest that rebus readings of hieroglyphs on the the six steatite seals from locations in Ancient Near East (away from Sarasvati-Sindhu civilization area), relate to Meluhha language and consistent with the philosophy of symbolic forms evidenced by Meluhha writing (also called, Indus writing).

"...two seals with Indus bulls have cuneiform inscriptions. For Mesopotamia, the earliest known seal has a pre-Akkadian or early Akkadian inscription (hard to read and controversial)(Fig. 1,6). In contrast with the later round seals, it has a square cotour with rounded corners. Reportedly, it was found on the surfae of Diqdiqqah, a suburban portual settlement of Ur. Another important seal with an Indus bull and cuneiform inscription, presently at the Cabinet des Medailles of Paris, is still unpublished...Note also that some of the seals from Bahrein come from graves, and seals are distinctively absent from the few contemporary Indus graves excavated in the Subcontinent. A round seal in a private collection, reportedly from Iran, shows an Indus bull surmounded by a protoelamite inscription (Fig. 1,5). From a looted grave in Bactria comes a round chlorite seal coated with a gold foil, with a Indus bull on one side and a mythological Bactrian creature on the opposite face, without inscription (Fig. 1,4). Finally, from Bactria comes also another (and anomalous) cylinder seal in lapis lazuli, presently in the Schoyen collection and still unpublished, where a boar-hunting scene is accompanied by a well-carved Indus inscription. All of the round seals found in the west (Metopotamia, the Gulf, Bactria, Iran: Fig.2) show exclusively one animal icone, a powerful bull with lowered head and short horns, with a raised muscular mass on the shoulder often marked by series of parallel grooves...

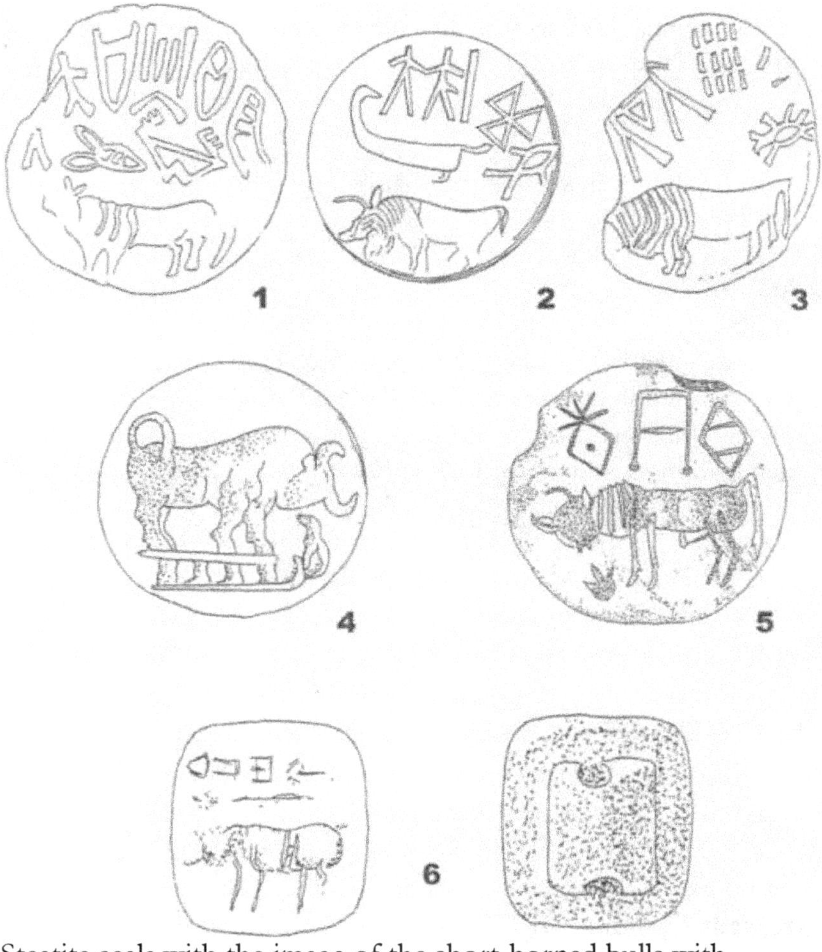

Steatite seals with the image of the short-horned bulls with lowered head from Failaka (1), Bahrein (2-3), Bactria (4), the Iranian Plateau (5). Nr. 6 comes from the surface of the site of Diqdiqqah, near Ur. Not in scale.[116]

Superset: Ox, bull hieroglyph: *kondā* , *konda* bullock, ox (Gondi) खोंड [khōṇḍa] m A young bull, a bullcalf. (Marathi) గోద [gōda] gōda. [Tel.] n. An ox. A beast. kine, cattle.(Telugu) koḍiyum 'young bull' (Gujarati) [kōḍiya] kōḍe, kōḍiya. [Telugu] n. A bullcalf. Rebus : Bengali. kōdā 'to turn in a lathe'; Oriya. kū̃nda 'lathe', kũdibā, kũd 'to turn' (→ Drav. Kuruku. kũd 'lathe') (CDIAL 3295). कोंद *kōnda* 'engraver, lapidary setting or infixing gems' (Marathi)

Subsets: Epigraphs with strings of hieroglyphs (cf. Images of seals 1 to 6).

Subset 1:

ḍhāla n. 'shield' M. *ḍhāl* f. WPah.kṭg. (kc.) *ḍhāl* f. (obl. -- *a*) 'shield' (a word used in salutation), J. *ḍhāl* f. (CDIAL 5583). Rebus: *ḍhālakī* = a metal heated and poured into a mould; a solid piece of metal; an ingot (Gujarati) Rebus: *ḍhālako* 'large ingot'.

S. *kuṇḍa* f. ' corner '; P. *kũṭ* f. ' corner, side ' (← H.).(CDIAL 3898). Rebus: kunda1 m. ' a turner's lathe '
gaṇḍa 'four' Rebus: *kāṇḍa* 'tools, pots and pans, metal-ware'.
meḍ 'body' Rebus: *meḍ* 'iron'.

kāḍ 2 काड् । पौरुषम् m. a man's length, the stature of a man (as a measure of length) (Rām. 632, zangan kaḍun kāḍ, to stretch oneself the whole length of one's body. So K. 119).(Kashmiri) *kāṭhī* = body, person; *kāṭhī* the make of the body; the stature of a man (Gujarati.) Rebus: kāḍ 'stone'. Gadba. (Oll.) kanḍ, (S.) kanḍu (pl. kanḍkil) stone (DEDR 1298).*khātī* 'wheelwright' (Hindi)
Subset 2:

ayo 'fish' (Munda); rebus: ayo 'metal' (Gujarati); ayas 'alloy' (Sanskrit)

kolmo 'three' (Mu.) Rebus: *kolami* 'smithy' (Telugu) *ḍāngā* = hill, dry upland (Bengali); *ḍā̃g* mountain-ridge (Hindi)(CDIAL 5476).ṭākuro = hill top (N.); ṭāngī = hill, stony country (Oriya.); ṭāngara = rocky hilly land (Oriya.); ḍāngā = hill, dry upland (Bengali.); ḍā̃g mountain-ridge (Hindi)(CDIAL 5476). Rebus: *dhangar* 'blacksmith'

(Maithili) *ḍangar* 'blacksmith' (Hindi) ḍānro = a term of contempt for a blacksmith (Nepali)(CDIAL 5524). ṭhākur = blacksmith (Maithili) (CDIAL 5488).

koḍa 'one' (Santali) Rebus: *koḍ* 'artisan's workshop' (Kuwi) *dula* 'pair' Rebus: *dul* 'cast (metal) *meḍ* 'body' Rebus: *meḍ* 'iron'. kāḍ 2 काड् । पौरुषम् m. a man's length, the stature of a man (as a measure of length) (Rām. 632, zangan kaḍun kāḍ, to stretch oneself the whole length of one's body. So K. 119).(Kashmiri) *kāṭhī* = body, person; *kāṭhī* the make of the body; the stature of a man (Gujarati.) Rebus: kāḍ 'stone'. Gadba. (Oll.) kanḍ, (S.) kanḍu (pl. kanḍkil) stone (DEDR 1298).*khātī* 'wheelwright' (Hindi)

Subset 3:
kolom 'three' Rebus: *kolami* 'smithy'.
gaṇḍa 'four' Rebus: *kāṇḍa* 'tools, pots and pans, metal-ware'.
meḍ 'body' Rebus: *meḍ* 'iron'. kāḍ 2 काड् । पौरुषम् m. a man's length, the stature of a man (as a measure of length) (Rām. 632, zangan kaḍun kāḍ, to stretch oneself the whole length of one's body. So K. 119).(Kashmiri) *kāṭhī* = body, person; *kāṭhī* the make of the body; the stature of a man (Gujarati.) Rebus: kāḍ 'stone'. Gadba. (Oll.) kanḍ, (S.) kanḍu (pl. kanḍkil) stone (DEDR 1298).*khātī* 'wheelwright' (Hindi)

Subset 4:
Bos indicus, zebu
adar ḍangra 'zebu or humped bull'; rebus: aduru 'native metal' (Kannada); ḍhangar 'blacksmith' (Hindi)

Subset 5

sā̃gāḍā m. ' frame of a building ' (M.)(CDIAL 12859) Rebus: jaṅgaḍ 'entrustment articles' *sā̃gaṛh* m. ' line of entrenchments, stone walls for defence ' (Lahnda).(CDIAL 12845) Allograph: *saṅgaḍa* 'lathe'. *sang* 'stone', *gaḍa* 'large stone'.

S. *kuṇḍa* f. ' corner '; P. *kū̃ṭ* f. ' corner, side ' (← H.).(CDIAL 3898). Rebus: *kunda*1 m. ' a turner's lathe '
meḍha 'polar star' (Marathi). Rebus: meḍ (Ho.); mẽṛhet 'iron' (Munda.Ho.)

Subset 6

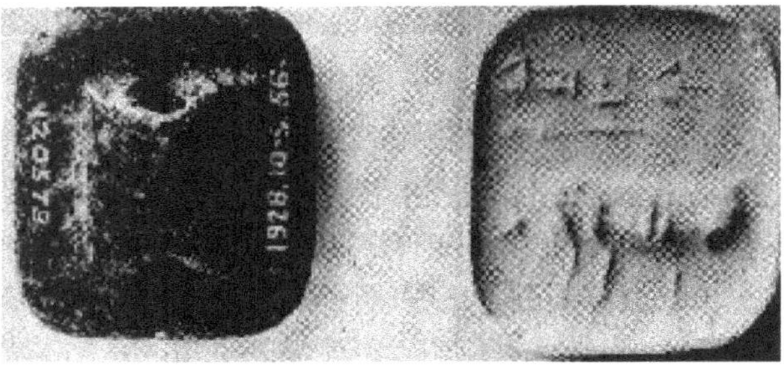

Seal impression and reverse of seal (with pierced lug handle) from Ur (U.7683; BM 120573); image of bison and cuneiform inscription; length 2.7, width 2.4, ht. 1.1 cm. cf. Gadd, PBA 18 (1932), pp. 5-6, pl. I, no.1; Mitchell 1986: 280-1 no.7 and fig. 111; Parpola, 1994, p. 131: signs may be read as
(1) *sag(k)* or *ka,* (2) *ku* or *lu* or *ma*, and (3) *zi* or *ba (4)?.*
SAG.KU(?).IGI.X or SAG.KU(?).P(AD)(?) The commonest value: *sag-ku-zi* Seal.

Rebus readings: Could this be a combined Sumerian and Meluhha words? sag in Sumerian means 'head'. ku-zi-da may refer to the Taittiriya Samhita term कुसीद *n.* any loan or thing lent to be repaid with interest , lending money upon interest, usury (TS); *mf.* a money-lender , usurer (Sanskrit) kuśī´ f. ' small wooden pin used to mark in recitation ' MaitrS., ' do. of metal ' ŚBr., ' ploughshare ' lex., °*śika*<-> m.n. lex., *kuśā* -- f. ' pin for marking in recitation ' Pāṇ., °*śikā*-- f. ' piece of wood used as a splint for a broken limb ' Car.Pk. *kusī* -- f. ' a tool made of iron ', L. *kuhī*, *kahī* f. ' mattock ', P. *kahī* f. (*a*?); H. *kusī*, °*siyā* f. ' ploughshare ', *kus*, *kussā* m. ' mattock '; G. *kaś*, *kɔś* f. ' iron instrument for digging ', *kɔs/*ũ n. ' bar of iron attached to a plough ', *kɔśiyāḷɔ* m. ' wooden wedge holding ploughshare in wooden frame of plough '; M. *kusā* m. ' hand implement for turning up clods (a pole with an iron blade or head) '.S.kcch. *khau* f. ' sharp iron bar for digging '; L. *kuhī*, *kahī* f. ' mattock ', P. *kahī* f.; WPah.kṭg. *kɔ́śṭɔ* m. ' hoe ', *kɔ́śṭi* f. ' little hoe '; J. *kaśī* f. ' mattock ' (CDIAL 3367).

Steffen Terp Laurssen[117] has reviewed 121 seals and seal impressions of 'Gulf type' dated to the end of 3rd millennium BCE, which 'come from a vast geographical area encompassing Bahrain, the Indus Valley (Mohenjo-daro and Chanhu-daro), Iran (Kerman, Luristan, Susa and the western Iranian plateau), Kuwait (Failaka), Mesopotamia (Ur, Girsu, Babylon and others unspecified) and the United Arab Emirates (Tell Abraq).'118

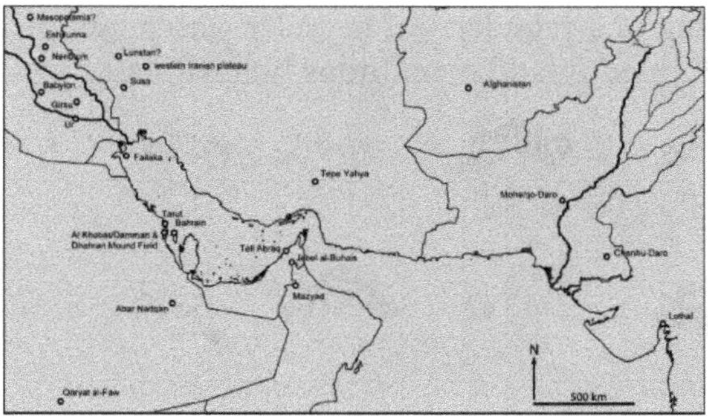

Indus Valley, and areas with which Gulf merchants traded and with whom they shared a common visual vocabulary. Distribution of Gulf and Dilmun type seals and geographical vastness of the underlying networks (After Fig. 13, Laurssen, 2010).

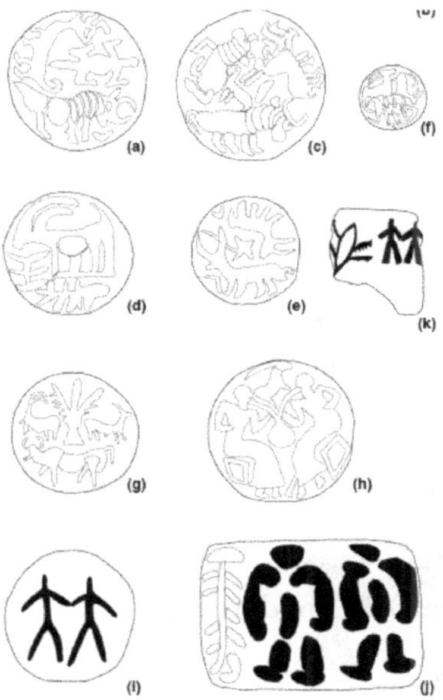

Inscribed circular seals show bison or short-horned bulls. Dominant iconographic motifs are: caprids, ibexes, scorpions, human footprints, crescents and anthropomorphic figures.119 Twelve Gulf type seals with pictorial motifs. (After Fig. 17, Laurssen, 2010). "The transformation of the Indus script into 'western' grammar as testified by the prefix 'twins' on the seals suggests that the process occurred in relative isolation from the Indus valley centres."120

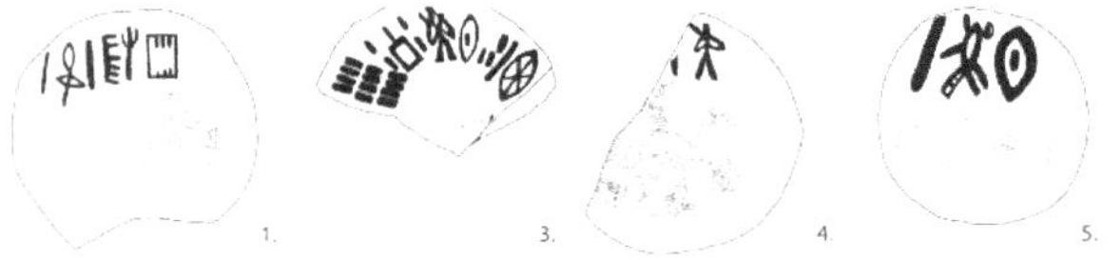

The seal impressions drawings from Mohenjo-daro and Chanhu-daro seals. (After Fig. 8, Laurssen, 2010).

(a. impression drawing of a cylinder seal from Ur with a humped bull and a 'blade of fodder' (Gadd 6); c. Indus bull without

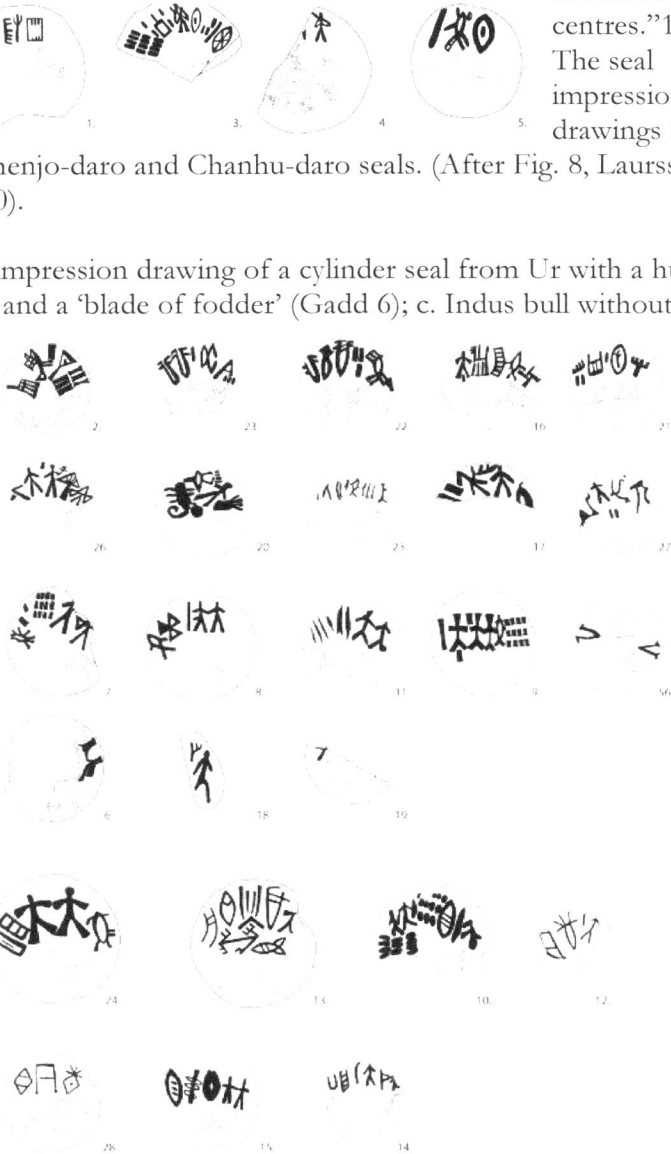

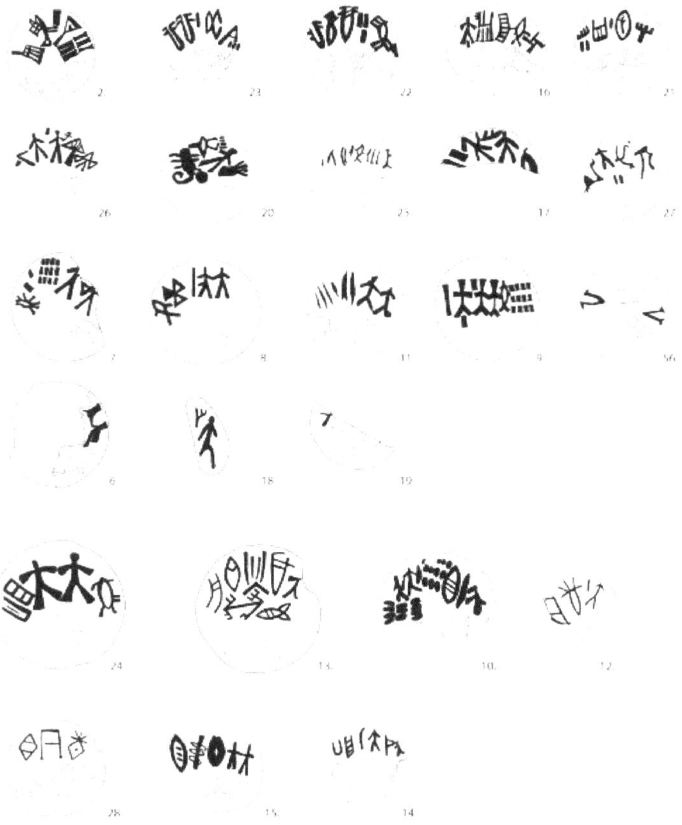

inscription; d-f Gulf type seals from Bahrain: d. two palm

branches below a quadruped; e. two quadrupeds and pair of crescents, shooting star? F. scorpion below a pair of quadrupeds; g. vulture above a bull; h. two men drinking scene; k. fragment of cylinder seal from Mohenjo-daro with twins and another undistinguishable sign. After Fig. 10, Laurssen, 2010).
Impression drawings of inscribed seals. The numbers refer to the Table of 121 seals. (After Fig. 9, Laurssen, 2010).

Laurssen argues that these seals correspond to different areas of production and that those with inscriptions have a predominant use of the glyphs of prefixed 'twins'. He also posits that 'break-away Harappans operting in the western orbit invented the Gulf Type seals but that the type from around 2050 BCE became practically synonymous with the merchant communities in Dilmun.'121 The predominant use of 'twins' glyph should not lead to an assumption that the language different from that of the Harappans was used on the seals invented by 'break-away Harappans.' It is possible to read rebus most of the inscriptions on such Gulf Type seals, including a reading of the 'twins' in the underlying Meluhha language of the Harappan scribes, artisans, merchants and seal-makers.

sangaḍa 'pair' (Marathi) Rebus: *jaṅgaḍ* 'entrustment articles'. *jangaḍiyo* 'military guard who accompanies treasure into the treasury' Glyph: kāḍ, to stretch oneself the whole length of one's body. (Kashmiri). Glyph: *kaṇṭa* bulbous root as of lotus, plantain; point where branches and bunches grow out of the stem of a palm (Malayalam) Rebus: kāḍ 'stone'. Ga. (Oll.) kanḍ, (S.) kanḍu (pl. kanḍkil) stone (DEDR 1298).

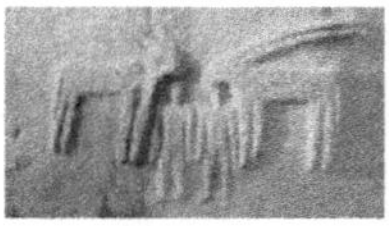

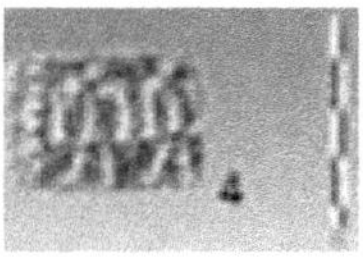

Two oryx in confrontation, with two figures and beneath them, holding hands; the Hili tomb. (After Fig. 8.12, Michael Rice, 1994).122
Possible representation of 'alliance' in late 3rd millennium BCE eastern Arabia. Ra'sal Jinz seal (with dotted circles flanking the boss of the seal on reverse).

A stamp seal with two human figures holding hands, alongside a palm branch from Building VII, room 1, Ra'sal Jinz. (After Fig. 6, Serge Cleuziou, 2003; After Fig. 5, ibid.) "Two individuals holding hands beside a vegetal motif, possibly a palm branch, are engraved on a small rectangular stamp seal found inside the northern compound at RJ-2 and dated around 2300-2200 BCE (figs. 5.4 and 6.1). This theme is displayed in two other examples: a smaller stamp seal of the same period recovered in an early second millennium context at Kalba (fig. 6.2), and the bas-relief carved on the southern door of tomb 1051 at Hili (fig. 6.4), one of the most monumental graves presently known, also dated around 2300 BCE. The latter represents two individuals very close in attitude to those of the RJ-2 seal, holding hands while standing between two oryx. The context of this seal is in itself illustrative. Recovered from the same house building (building VII) were two stamp seals with three engraved characters of writing (figs. 5.2-3), a complete incense burner (fig. 5.1) and a fragment of the upper jaw of a leopard."[123]

The presence of Indus texts on circular seals has been noted by a number of researchers. The pioneering effort was that of Gadd who communicated on eight circular seals, 'Seals of ancient Indian style found in Ur.'[124] A substantial number of seals without 'inscription' have been found[125] and not enough attention has been paid to the pictorial motifs or 'iconographic resemblances' of such seals which are an Indus writing continuum. Within these types of seals, some are categorised as 'Dilmun type' which show three grooves and four dots-in-circles on the reverse. The further assumption has been that the round form of the seals 'could very well have been a special trademark of some unexplored Harappan community.'[126]

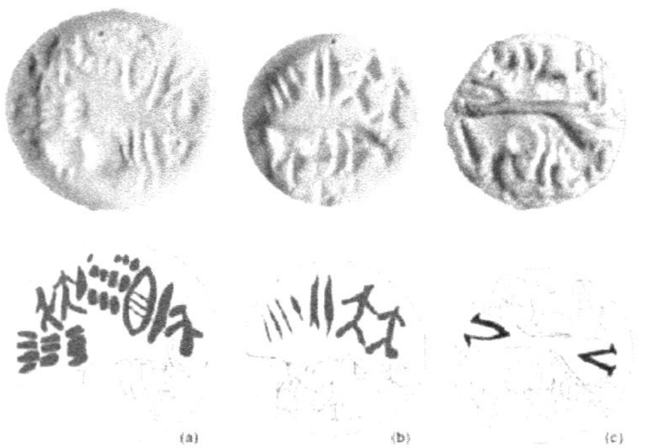

One guess that the round form was associated with the maritime trade.[127]

Impressions and drawings of Gulf type steatite seals (with a white glaze and a pierced boss), with Indus text and bull motif found in Early Dilmun burial mounds. (After Fig. 1, Laurssen, 2010).

Indus inscriptions and indus-related characters on Gulf type seal

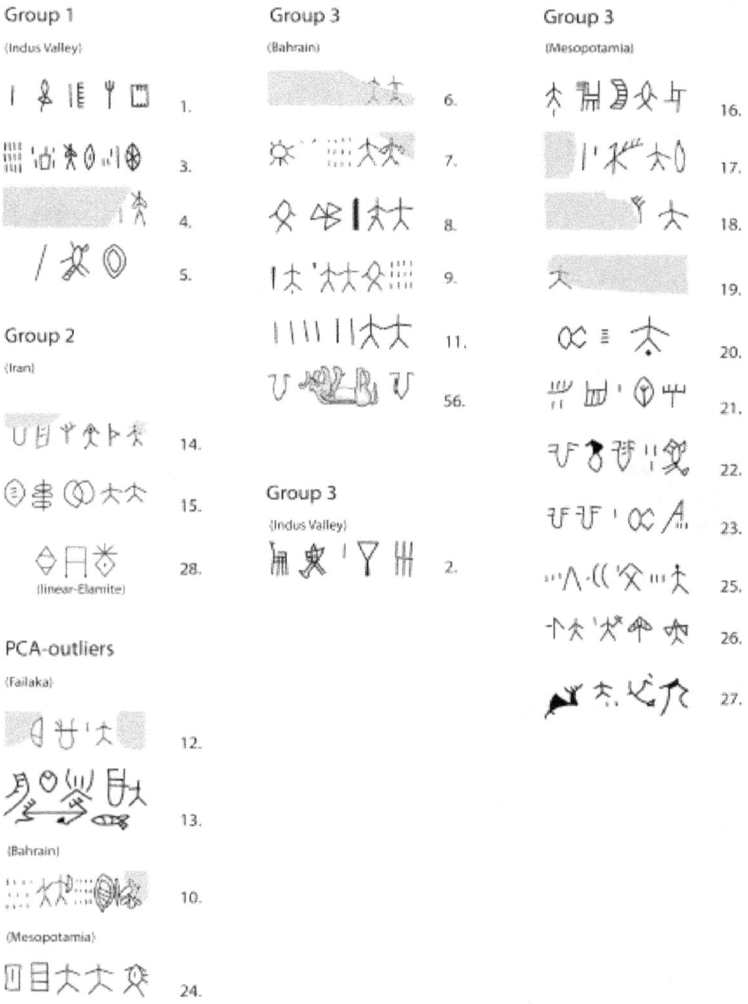

impressions. Note the general abundance of 'twin' signs, especially at the beginning of the sequences. (After Fig. 11, Laurssen, 2010).Vidale suggests: "…a correlate of my hypothesis is that the 'man' and 'twins' Indus signs, in the inscriptions from Failaka and Bahrain (and Ur?), might be interpreted as patronymic logograms, to be phonetically read in one or more (still unidentified) ancient Semitic languages…"128 Patronymic, ordered family sequences, personal or group affiliations? The answer will come from the cypher and rebus readings of Indus hieroglyphs.

The dominance of 'twin' glyphs is matched by the antithetical antelopes which become the Gulf standard of 3rd millennium

9852 Telloh

9903 Prob. West Asian find

9904 Prob. West Asian find

BCE.

9851 Telloh

[Pierre de talc. Louvre, AO 9036. P. Amiet, Bas-relliefs imaginaries de l'Orient ancien, Paris, 1973, p. 94, no. 274…ils proviendrait de Tello, l'ancienne Girsu, une des cites de l'Etat sumerien de Lagash. Musee National De Arts Asiatiques Guimet, 1988-1989, *Les cites oubliees de l'Indus Archeologie du Pakistan*.]

Texts related to West Asian inscriptions (either not illustrated or not linked):

9801Susa

9811 Djoka (Umma)

9821 Kish

9822 Kish

Tree in front. Fish in front of and above a one-horned bull. Cylinder seal impression (IM 8028), Ur, Mesopotamia. White shell. 1.7 cm. High, dia. 0.9 cm. 129

9834 Ur

9842 Ur

"No.7...A bull, unhumped, of the so-called 'unicorn' type,

raises his head towards a simplified version of a tree, and two uncertain objects, one a sort of trefoil, are shown above his back. Under his head is an unmistakable character of the Indus script, the 'fish' with cross-hatchings..." 130
Seal; BM 122187; dia. 2.55; ht. 1.55 cm. Gadd PBA 18 (1932), pp. 6-7, pl. 1, no.

9832 Shaped like a 7.
First hieroglyph from the right: मेंढा [mēṇḍhā] A crook or curved end (of a stick, horn &c.) and *attrib.* such a stick, horn, bullock. मेढी [mēḍhī] *f* (Dim. of मेढ) A small bifurcated stake: also a small stake, with or without furcation, used as a post to support a cross piece.

Rebus: One word glossed in *Deśīnāmamālā* is: *meḍho* 'helper of merchant'. (*Deśīnāmamālā* of Hemacandra).

मेढो vi. 138 वणिक्सहायः, one who helps a merchant.

Deśīnāmamālā Glossary, p. 71. *Deśīnāmamālā131* provides a remarkable resource for ancient lexemes of Indian linguistic area.
Also, meḍ 'iron' (Munda. Ho.)

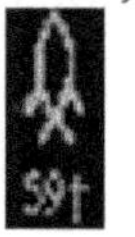

ayo, hako 'fish'; ãs = scales of fish (Santali); rebus: aya = iron (Gujarati); ayah, ayas = metal (Sanskrit)
ḍhāla n. ' shield ' M. *ḍhāl* f. WPah.kṭg. (kc.) *ḍhā`l* f. (obl. -- *a*) ' shield ' (a word used in salutation), J. *ḍhāl* f. (CDIAL 5583).Rebus: *ḍhālakī* = a metal heated and poured into a mould; a solid piece of metal; an ingot (Gujarati) Rebus: *ḍhālako* 'large ingot'.

Fig. 88; Susa, stamp seal from the Gulf, Teheran museum, MDAI, 43, no. 1717; an animal tamer wearing a skirt and grasping with one hand a goat-antelope with its head turned back and with its feet bound; with the other hand, the person holds a large object which looks like an architectural feature or shield.

 *ranku* 'antelope'; rebus: *ranku* 'tin' (Santali)

Ligatured 'body, stature of person' glyph:  काठी [kāṭhī] The frame or structure of the body: also stature. Rebus: *khāti* 'wheelwright' (Hindi); *med* 'body'(Mu.); rebus: 'iron' (Ho.); thus, together 'wheelwright iron'. ఆరకాటి [ārakāṭi] *ārakāṭi*. [Tel.] n. A boatman, a sailor. ఓడనడపువాడు, నావికుడు. (Telugu)

खांड [*khāṇḍa*] A jag, indentation, denticulation. kāṇḍā 'tools, pots and pans, metalware' (Marathi) Thus, the composition hieroglyph with ligature of 'notch' reads rebus: *kāthi meḍ kāṇḍā* 'wheelwright iron (metal) tools'. Another example can be cited for the use of kāṭhī to denote a set, set of tools: अऊतकाठी [aūtakāṭhī] *f* A comprehensive term for the implements of husbandry.

Ligatured 'body, stature of person' glyph:  (Also variants without a line drawn below the legs stretched apart): 1. *meḍ* 'body'(Mu.); rebus: 'iron' (Ho.); *kāḍ* 2 काड़ a man's length, the stature of a man (as a measure of length); rebus: *kāḍ* 'stone'; Ga. (Oll.) *kanḍ* , (S.) *kanḍu (pl. kanḍkil)* stone; 2. *aḍar* 'harrow'; rebus: *aduru* 'native metal'.

 Twin bodies shown as a hieroglyph-composite, frequently on Dilmunite seals (Persian Gulf) are symbolic forms signifying: *dula* 'pair' Rebus: *dul* 'cast (metal)' + *meḍ kāḍ* 'body, stature of person' Rebus: 'iron stone'. Thus, the hieroglyph composition reads rebus: 'cast iron stone': *dul meḍ kāḍ*. The Meluhha glosses attested are: *dul mẽṛhẽt, dul meṛeḍ, dul* 'cast metal (iron)'; as distinct from: *koṭe meṛeḍ* 'forged iron' (Santali).

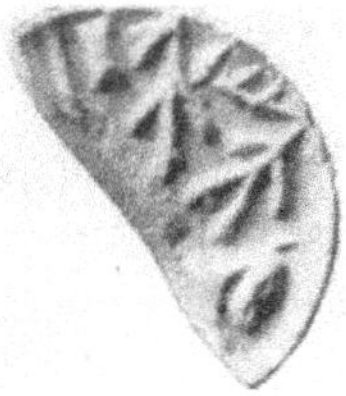

Seal; BM 122946; Dia. 2.6; ht. 1.2cm.; Gadd PBA 18 (1932), p. 7, pl. I, no.3; Legrain, *Ur Excavations*, X (1951), no. 629.

Seal; BM 118704; U. 6020; Gadd PBA 18 (1932), pp. 9-10, pl. II, no.8; two figures carry between them a vase, and one presents a goat-like animal (not an antelope) which he holds by the neck. Human figures wear early Sumerian garments of fleece.

Seal; BM 122945; U. 16181; dia. 2.25, ht. 1.05 cm; Gadd PBA 18 (1932), p. 10, pl. II, no. o; each of four quadrants terminates at the edge of the seal in a vase; each quadrant is occupied by a naked figure, sitting so that, following round the circle, the head of one is placed nearest to the feet of the preceding; two figures clasp their hands upon their breasts; the other two spread out the arms, beckoning with one hand.

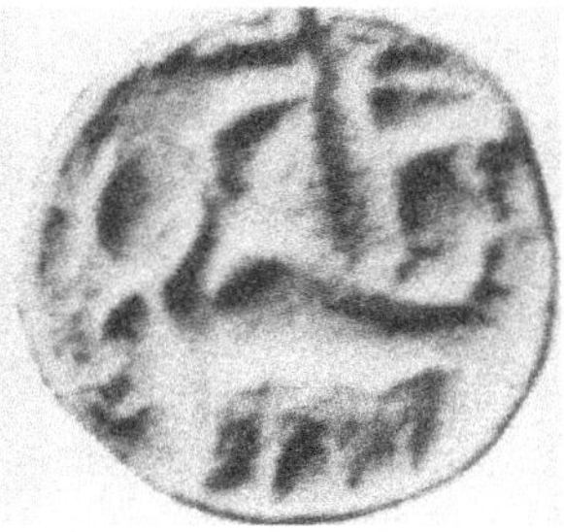

Seal; BM 120576; U. 9265; Gadd, PBA 18 (1932), p. 10, pl. II, no. 10; bull with long horns below an uncertain object, possibly a quadruped and rider, at right angles to the ox (counter clockwise)

Seal; UPenn; a scorpion and an elipse [an eye (?)]; U. 16397; Gadd, PBA 18 (1932), pp. 10-11, pl. II, no. 11 *bica* 'scorpion' Rebus *bica* 'stone ore'. *ḍhāḷako* = a large metal ingot (Gujarati)

Seal impression, Ur (Upenn; U.16747); dia. 2.6, ht. 0.9 cm.; Gadd, PBA 18 (1932), pp. 11-12, pl. II, no. 12; Porada 1971: pl.9, fig.5; Parpola, 1994, p. 183; water carrier with a skin (or pot?) hung on each end of the yoke across his shoulders and another one below the crook of his left arm; the vessel on the right end of his yoke is over a receptacle for the water; a star on either side of the head (denoting supernatural?). The whole object is enclosed by 'parenthesis' marks. The parenthesis is perhaps a way of splitting of the ellipse (Hunter, G.R., *JRAS*, 1932, 476). An unmistakable example of an 'hieroglyphic' seal.

Seal; BM 122841; dia. 2.35; ht. 1 cm.; Gadd PBA 18 (1932), p. 12, pl. II, no. 13; circle with centre-spot in each of four spaces formed by four forked branches springing from the angles of a small square. Alt. four stylised bulls' heads (bucrania) in the quadrants of an elaborate quartering device which has a cross-hatched rectangle in the centre.

Seal; UPenn; cf. Philadelphia *Museum Journal*, 1929; ithyphallic bull-men; the so-called 'Enkidu' figure common upon Babylonian cylinders of the early period; all have horned head-dresses; moon-symbols upon poles seem to represent the door-posts that the pair of 'twin' genii are commonly seen supporting on either side of a god; material and shape make it the 'Indus' type while the device is Babylonian.

Seal impression; UPenn; steatite; bull below a scorpion; dia. 2.4cm.; Gadd, PBA 18 (1932), p. 13, Pl. III, no. 15; Legrain, MJ (1929), p. 306, pl. XLI, no. 119; found at Ur in the cemetery area, in a ruined grave .9 metres from the surface, together with a pair of gold ear-rings of the double-crescent type and long beads of steatite and carnelian, two of gilt copper, and others of lapis-lazuli, carnelian, and banded sard. The first

sign to the left has the form of a flower or perhaps an animal's skin with curly tail; there is a round spot upon the bull's back.

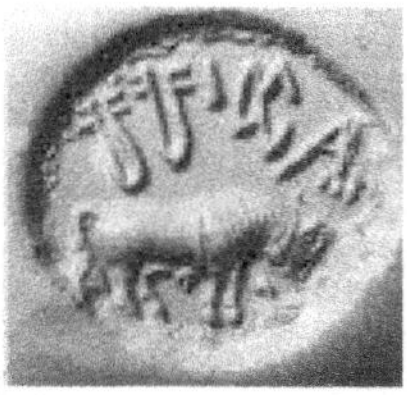

Seal impression; BM 123208; found in the filling of a tomb-shaft (Second Dynasty of Ur). Dia. 2.3; ht. 1.5 cm.; Gadd, PBA 18 (1932), pp. 13-14, pl. III, no. 16; Buchanan, *JAOS* 74 (1954), p. 149.

Seal impression, Mesopotamia (?) (BM 120228); cf. Gadd 1932: no.17; cf. Parpola, 1994, p. 132. Note the doubling of the common sign, 'jar'.

urseal189902 Seal and impression (BM 123059), from an antique dealer, Baghdad; script and motif of a bull mating with a cow; the tuft at the end of the tail of the cow is summarily shaped like an arrow-head; inscription is of five characters, most prominent among them the two 'persons' standing side by side. To the right of these is a damaged 'fish' sign.cf. Gadd 1932: no.18; Parpola, 1994, p.219.

dula 'pair' Rebus: *dul* 'cast (metal) *meḍ* 'body' Rebus: *meḍ* 'iron'.

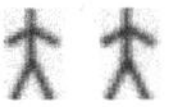 *kāṭhī* the make of the body; the stature of a man (Gujarati) *meḍ* 'body' Rebus: *khāṭī meḍ* "wheelwright iron'. Thus, the twin hieroglyph denotes *khāṭī dul meḍ* 'wheelwright cast iron' (Punjabi).

This orthographic evaluation of the extraordinary hieroglyphs shows the sexual act and gets deployed on many epigraphs,.

ṛanku, ranku 'fornication, adultery' (Telugu) Rebus: *ranku* 'tin' (Santali) Alternative/Supplementary reading: *kamḍa, khamḍa* 'copulation' (Santali) Rebus: *kampaṭṭa* 'mint, coiner'. *khāṇḍā* tool, pots and pans, metalware (Marathi) *ayo* ‘fish’ Rebus: *ayo, ayas* ‘metal’. *aḍaren* ‘lid’ Rebus: *aduru* ‘native, unsmelted metal’ (Kannada)

dula ‘pair’ Rebus: *dul* ‘cast (metal)’ + *meḍ kāḍ* ‘body, stature of person’ Rebus: ‘iron stone’. Thus, the hieroglyph composition reads rebus: ‘cast iron stone’: *dul meḍ kāḍ.*

खांडा [*khāṇḍā*] A division of a field. (Marathi) Rebus: *khāṇḍā* tool, pots and pans, metalware (Marathi) The pair of glyphs of ‘square with divisions’ connotes: cast metalware.

Failaka seal. The Yale tablet is dated to ca. the second half of the

twentieth century B.C.... Trade3 on the Persian gulf was in existence well before that time-- about 2350 B.C.-- when Sargon, the first Akkadian king referred to ships from or destined for Melukhkha, Magan and Tilmun (Dilmun) at his wharves. in the Third Dynasty of Ur (around 2000), when trade apparently was centred at Magan. It is even better documented on other tablets from Ur (from about 1900 and from about 1800), belonging to various kings of Larsa. At this time the trade was centered at Tilmun... Cuneiform inscriptions naming Inzak, the god of Tilmun, were found on Failaka and, a long time ago, one on Bahrein... Failaka can be equated with Tilmun, or at least was an important part of it. (Briggs Buchanan, A dated seal impression connecting Babylonia and ancient India, Archaeology, Vol. 20, No.2, 1967, pp. 104-107).

Yale tablet. Bull's head (bucranium) between two seated figures drinking from two vessels through straws. YBC. 5447; dia. c. 2.5 cm. Possibly from Ur. Buchanan, studies Landsberger, 1965, p. 204; A seal impression was found on an inscribed tablet (called Yale tablet) dated to the tenth year of Gungunum, King of Larsa, in

southern Babylonia--that is, 1923 B.C. according to the most commonly accepted ('middle') chronology of the period. The design in the impression closely matches that in a stamp seal found on the Failaka island in the Persian Gulf, west of the delta of the Shatt al Arab, which is formed by the confluence of the Tigris and Euphrates rivers.

Reduplication connotes dul 'likeness'; rebus: 'cast (metal)' to prefix the following lexemes which explain the semantics of each reduplicated glyph e.g., dul meṛed, cast iron (Mu.) dol = likeness, picture, form (Santali)

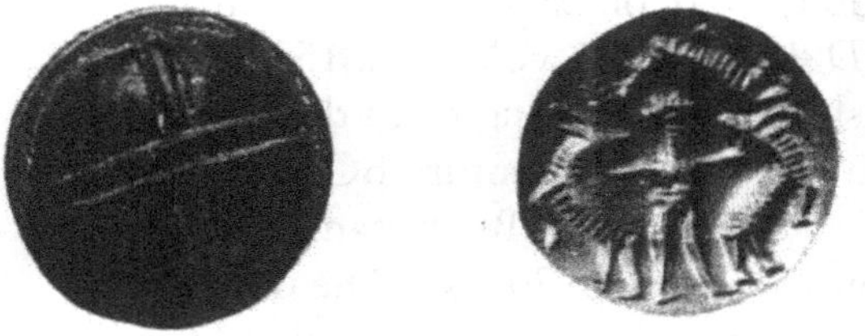

Fig. 92; Susa, stamp seal made of bitumen compound, Louvre, MDAI, 43, no. 1726; a tamer with three heavily hatched animals

Fig. 93; Susa stamp seal made of bitumen compound, Louvre, MDAI, 43, no. 1720

Fig. 94;

Susa, stamp seal from a butimen compound, Louvre, MDAI, 43, no. 1726

"Susa... profound affinity between the Elamite people who migrated to Anshan and Susa and the Dilmunite people... Elam proper corresponded to the plateau of Fars with its capital at Anshan. We think, however that it probably extended further north into the Bakhtiari Mountains... likely that the chlorite and serpentine vases reached Susa by sea... From the victory proclamations of the kings of Akkad we also learn that the city of Anshan had been re-established, as the capital of a revitalised political ally: Elam itself... the import by Ur and Eshnunna of inscribed objects typical of the Harappan culture provides the first reliable chronological evidence. [C.J. Gadd, Seals of ancient Indian style found at Ur, *Proceedings of the British Academy, XVIII*, 1932; Henry Frankfort, Tell Asmar, Khafaje and Khorsabad, *OIC*, 16, 1933, p. 50, fig. 22). It is certainly possible that writing developed in India before this time, but we have no real proof. Now Susa had received evidence of this same civilisation, admittedly not all dating from the Akkadian period, but apparently spanning all the closing years of the third millennium (L. Delaporte, *Musee du Louvre. Catalogues des Cylindres Orientaux*..., vol. I, 1920, pl. 25(15), S.29. P. Amiet, Glyptique susienne, *MDAI*, 43, 1972, vol. II, pl. 153, no. 1643)... B. Buchanan has published a tablet dating from the reign of Gungunum of Larsa, in the twentieth century BC, which carries the impression of such a stamp seal. (B.Buchanan, *Studies in honor of Benno Landsberger*, Chicago, 1965, p. 204, s.). The date so revealed has been whollyconfirmed by the impression of a stamp seal from the same group, fig. 85, found on a Susa tablet of the same period. (P. Amiet, Antiquites du Desert de Lut,*RA*, 68, 1974, p. 109, fig. 16. Maurice Lambert, *RA*, 70, 1976, p. 71-72). It is in fact, a receipt of the kind in use at the beginning of the Isin-Larsa period, and mentions a certain Milhi-El, son of Tem-Enzag, who, from the name of his god, must be a Dilmunite. In these circumstances we may wonder if this document had not been drawn up at Dilmun and sent to Susa, after sealing with a local stamp seal. This seal is decorated with six tightly-packed, crouching animals, characterised by their vague shapes, with legs tucked under their bodies, huge heads and necks sometimes striped obliquely. The impression of another seal of similar type, fig. 86, depicts in the centre a throned figure who seems to dominate the animals, continuing a tradition of which examples are known at the end of the Ubaid period in Assyria... Fig. 87 to

89 are Dilmun-type seals found at Susa. The boss is semi-spherical and decorated with a band across the centre and four incised circles. [Pierre Amiet, Susa and the Dilmun Culture, pp. 262-268].

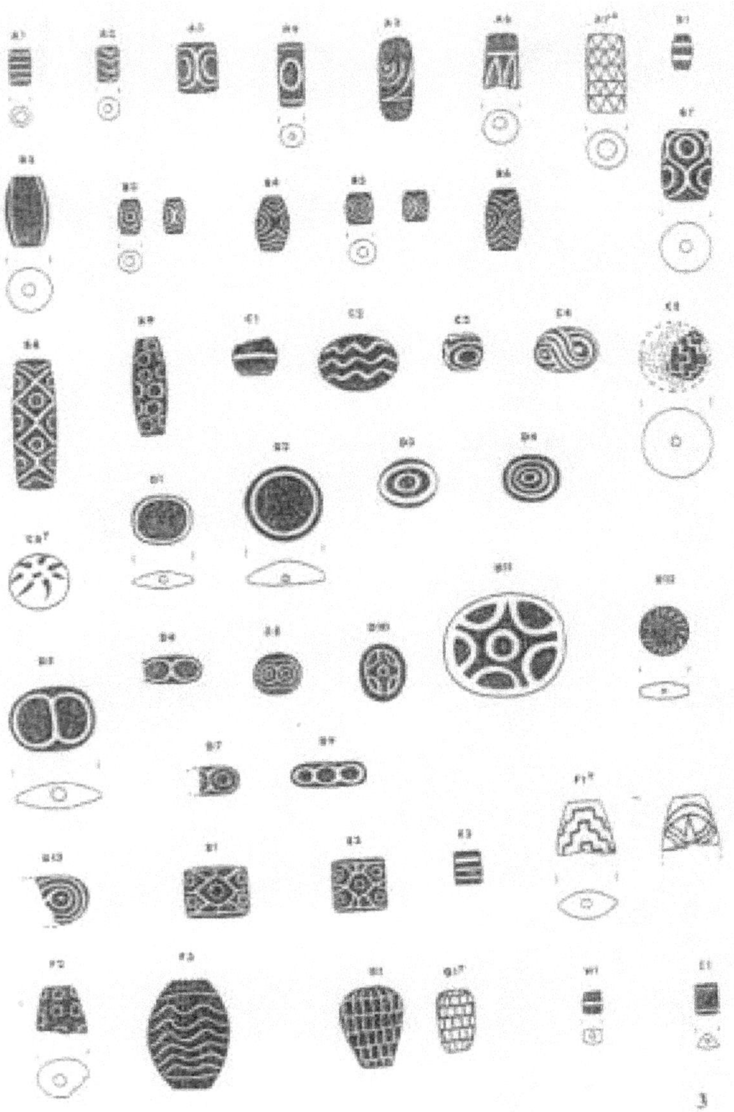

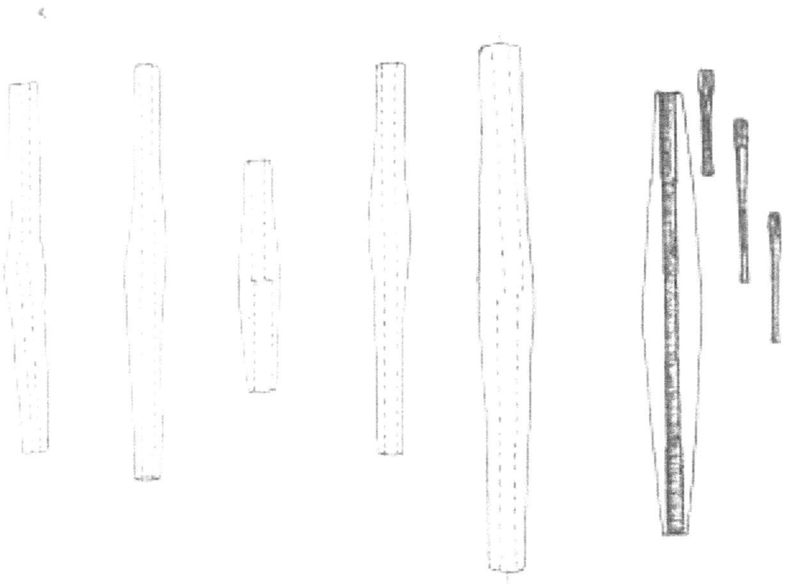

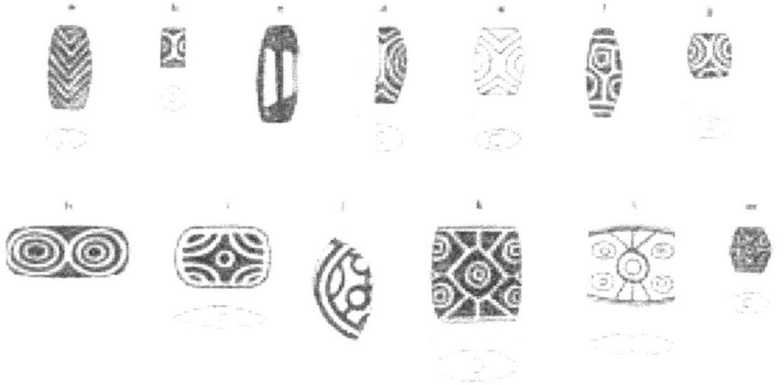

"...it is impossible to discuss the role of the Indus communities in the west without considering in detail some aspects of the international trade in semiprecious materials and beads. In contemporary Gujarat, carnelian, a form of agate that in nature has a distinctive dull olive-brown colour, is turned red artificially in special ceramic containers and kilns. The most important mines are still exploited in Gujarat, and the production of high quality carnelian remained for 5000 years a craft specialization of the Subcontinent, particularly in the north-western regions of Gujarat and Sindh."

The exposition tests this hypothesis and validates Meluhha cipher: hieroglyphs and rebus readings of *vāk* composed/recorded as epigraphical sequences or sets on a variety of media: potsherds, tokens, tablets, seals, copper plates, metal tools and weapons including bronze anvils (snarling iron or rods), stone statues or ivory carvings or monolithic board of Dholavira. *vāk* is restrictively interpreted – only as a method to arrive at plain texts distinct from cipher texts in cryptography -- 'areal language universals' of Meluhha, the ancient Indian vernacular, in Indian *sprachbund.*

The limitations of the study are 1. That no apriori assumptions are made about non-linguistic symbolic forms since no known method exists to identify such non-linguistic representations; and 2. that Meluhha is not a hypothetical language and reconstructions of glosses arrived at are quite unlike the hypothetical etyma for Indo-European. As a first step in outling arious facets of linguistic characteristics of Meluhha language, vernacular or parole glosses are clustered together, matched rebus with uambiguous, clearly identified hieroglyphs.

Action narratives as hieroglyphs

Meluhha glosses related to stone work and fortification

sangatarāśū = stone cutter; sangatarāśi = stone-cutting (Telugu) రాజు [rāzu] rāḍzu. [Tel.] v. n. To take fire, flame, begin to burn.(Telugu) రాచ (adj.) Pertaining to a stone. (Telugu) sang 2 संग् m. a stone (Rām. 199, 143, 1412; YZ. 557). L. 65 gives a list of the most common local stones used for ornaments, and other purposes. These are (in his spelling) bilor, a white crystal; sang-i-baswatri, a yellow stone used in medicine; sang-i-dálam, used by goldsmiths; sang-i-farash (p. 64), a kind of slate; sang-i-Nadid, of a dark coffee colour; sang-i-Nalchan, a kind of soap-stone, from which cups and plates are made; sang-i-Musá, of a black colour; sang-i-Ratel, of a chocolate colour; sang-i-Shalamar, of a green colour; sang-i-sumák, coloured blue or purple, with green spots; Takht-i-Sulimán, coloured black, with white streaks. (Kashmiri) *sangaḍa* 'lathe' Rebus: *jangaḍa* 'entrustment articles'.Rebus 2: samgara 'living in the same house, guild', sangar 'fortified place' (Pushto). L. *sā̃gaṛh* m. ' line of entrenchments, stone walls for defence '.(CDIAL 12845) Hence, smith guild in a fortification, which is a characteristic architectural feature of hundreds of civilization sites. The hieroglyph which denotes sangaḍa is the 'standard device' shown often in front of a one-horned young bull. Seals with field symbols and Indus texts found at Dholavira during excavations in the 1990s. Rebus 3: *sang* 'stone', *gaḍa* 'large stone'.

Meluhha artisans had blazed the trail of lost-wax metallurgy

Meluhha hieroglyphs evidence (elaborated in Meluhha -- A visible language), that the Indus script was a writing system invented to communicate information – in the language of the inventors -- on the technologies, resources, and processes involved in the production and distribution of select commodities surplus to the requirements of the inventors. Such a writing system also involved communicating information about administrative structures (such as guilds of artisans) which supported/authenticated the production processes.

Thus, the writing system was a complementary innovation, used to enhance or to substitute oral communication (or speech) related to metallurgical technologies. Almost all the epigraphs of the script (including epigraphs incised on metallic weapons/tools/ copper tablets, painted on bangles and a gold pendant, incised on a gold fillet headband and a steatite pectoral ornament) are professional guild tokens, authenticating the traded alloy/metal/ mineral products, decoding the underlying mleccha speech. The guild tokens were, thus, professional calling cards of the guilds which could also be used to create sealed impressions on packages traded in an impressive long-distance trade.

A remarkable action narrative is archaeologically attested from two locations, though simultaneous appearance of new things in different places in the world, may or may not have proved connections.: 1. At a place called Nahal Mishmar in the Fertile Crescent, nomad artisans of 5th millennium BCE had left in a cave arsenical copper artifacts cast using cire perdue (lost-wax casting method). The hoard included 432 copper, bronze, ivory and stone decorated objects; 240 mace heads, about 100 scepters, 5 crowns, powder horns, tools and weapons. At least one of the scepters (or standards) compares with the standard device shown as a Meluhha hieroglyph (Indus script corpora).

Archaeological context of Dholavira compares

Dholavira stone-polished pillars and an 8-shaped circular stone structure comparable to the Ein Gedi structure near Nahal Mishmar.

This photograph shows the two pillars in relation to the 8-shaped stone structure holding two altars.

If the two pillars had held Nahal Mishmar type of crowns, depicting hieroglyphs denoting the repertoire of metal-/stone-work of the arisan guild, the two altars with holes could have held the scepters of the Nahal Mishmar type or standards depicting hieroglyphs of the type shown by the Mohenjo-daro tablets of processions of standards.

A demonstration of how the altars close to the Dholavira pillars of the stadium could have held standards mounted through the holes of ring-stones.

Such ring stones could also have held Varna-type sepulchers with gold plates of Nahal Mishmar type hieroglyphs.

If this speculation is plausible, the stadium could have functioned as the ground for display of the procession of standards, advertising the weapons, tools, pots and pans offered from the Dholavira fortification *sangar* 'fortified place' (Pushto). L. *sā̃gaṛh* m. ' line of entrenchments, stone walls for defence '(CDIAL 12845). This suggestion is consistent with the reading of the Dholavira signboard mounted on the North Gateway as an announcement of the wares offered by Dholavira artisan workshops. This could be the herald, demonstrating the competence of the metals-minerals/stone-work guilds of the city of Kotda Timba (also called Dholavira). *sang* 'stone', *gaḍa* 'large stone'.

Close to the two standing pillars is an 8-shaped enclosure with some pillars of a shorter height, perhaps stools for placing offerings or and a rock-cut vat. Holes hae been drilled into the top surface of these polished stone 'altars' perhaps for holding scepters or flag posts. The two slightly taller polished stoe pillars nearby may denote *kunda* 'pillar, post' signifying the space used for turners' workshops.

Dholavira (Kotda).The two 'sthambs', or polished pillars, which are claimed to resemble Sivalingas, in the citadel. Were they markers of water-channels to fill the water reservoirs in the city?
Kannada. kunda a pillar of bricks, etc. Tulu. kunda pillar, post. Telugu. kunda id. Maltese. kunda block, log. (DEDR 1723). Rebus: kunda 'turner' (Gujarati) kundār turner (Assamese)

One possible explanation for the stone pillars is that they were announcement posts of a bead turner's or lapidary workshop.

The word *dhokra* is attested emphatically on two Indus seals showing a decrepit old woman with breasts hanging down indicating that this ancient word was from Indian *sprachbund* (Meluhha hieroglyph). It is in vogue in the Indian vernacular and of course, *dhokra* means also lost-wax casting. One exquisite seal is from Dholavira. Another is from Mohenjo-daro.

Dhokra as a Meluhha hieroglyph

Consistent with the philosophy of symbolic forms recognizable in Meluhha hieroglyphs of a tiger looking back or an upraised arm of a person about to deliver a blow presented in the evidences of five Harappa molded tablets h1970, h1971, h1972, h1973, h1974 a semantic expansion occurs in the denotation of a specialist blacksmith who could create lost-wax metal casts.

A seal from Mohenjo-Daro is presented in Appendix F: *dhokra kamar* 'lost-wax metal caster'.

A terracotta object was discovered in Dholavira with a narrative comparable to the hieroglyphs of Mohenjo-daro seal.This may be called *dhokra kamar* seal based on rebus readings of the Meluhha hieroglyphs on Dholavira tablet and the archaeological context presented in this section.

Mahābhārata narrates in *Jātugṛhaparva* of the Great Epic, Khanaka's explanation rendered to Yudhiṣṭira in *mleccha* (cognate *meluhha*) language of metallic and non-metallic weapons embedded in the shellac palace in the context of a conspiracy to assassinate Yudhiṣṭira and his other four *pāṇḍava* brothers, as their exile period was coming to a close. Three contexts are apparent: 1. mleccha speech which was the parole of Yudhiṣṭira, Khanaka and Vidura (uncle of pāṇḍava) could convey meaning; 2. the locus of the conspiratorial place (referred to in Marathi as *kārasthān*) was shellac framework (comparable to the gloss: *dhokra* 'lost-wax method of metal casting'); and 3. A gloss derived from mleccha speech -- Mlecchita vikalpa -- is a written cryptography to represent uttered words and taught as one of 64 arts to youth. Richard Burton translates 'mlecchita vikalpa' as one of the 64 arts mentioned in Vatsyayana's Kamasutra as follows: "the art of understanding writing in cipher, and the writing of words in a peculiar way." Writing in cypher. Vikalpa is an alternative representation of language, in this case, spoken words expressed in writing (cipher).

"In his commentary on the Kama-sutra, Yashodhara describes two kinds of mlecchita-vikalpa. One is called kautilyam in which the letter substitutions are based upon phonetic relations -- the vowels become consonants, for example. A simplification of this form is called durbodha. Another kind of secret writing is muladeviya. Its cipher alphabet consists merely of the reciprocal one with all other letters remaining unchanged. Muladeviya existed in both a spoken form -- as such it figures in Indian literature and is used by traders, with geographical variations -- and a written form, in which case it is called gudhalekhya."[132]

The use of the name, *khanaka* is also significant. It is cognate with *kaṁṇaka* (Sanskritized literary form of vernacular phonetic form) *kan-ka* 'scribe'. This is the most frequently deployed symbolic form in Mleccha (cognate Meluhha) cryptography to signified by 'rim-of-jar' (not the jar itself, which is *kaṇḍa Rebus: khāṇḍā.* 'metalware'. If read rebus together, the jar and the rim signify: *kaṇḍa kan-ka (hieroglyphs) Rebus: khāṇḍā kan-ka* 'metalware account.'

The structure of the building, *jātugṛha*, 'shellac palace' is another frequently hieroglyph: sangaḍa, 'framework of a building'. This meaning is signified by the hieroglyphs: sangaḍa 'portable furnace'; sangaḍa 'lathe, gimlet' – both combined together as a standard device generally in front of .one-horned young bull: *kõdā 'young bull' Rebus: kõdā 'turn on a lathe'; kõdār* 'turner' working on a workshop (*koḍ 'horn'*) *Rebus: koḍa 'workshop'*).

Thus, the philosophy of symbolic forms is exemplified by these frequently deployed hieroglyphs with meanings related to the life-activities of lapidaries (stone-workers) and smiths [working on smelters, furnaces, smithy, forge and with anvils, crucibles, ores, metals, alloys (such as brass, bronze, pewter), lost-wax casting method] and the documentation of trade transactions for administrative control of caravan or boat-loads conveyed by donkey-caravans or sea-faring merchants.

The objective of this work is to validate the formulations of philosophy of symbolic forms with the evidence in archaeological context of tokens, tablets, seals, epigraphs and varieties of stoneware and metalware artifacts (of the types discovered in Nahal Mishmar arsenical-copper lost-wax method castings, the dancing girl of Mohenjo-daro or inscribed stone image of a 'priest' or advertisement board of Dholavira).

A unique characteristic of Meluhha language is re-duplication. This re-duplication is consistent with the rebus readings of hieroglyphs made possible by uttered words conveying 'images' – such as ibha 'elephant', kol 'tiger' -- reading rebus the intended 'meanings or sounds of similar-sounding words' – such as *ib* 'iron', *ibbo* 'merchant', *kol* 'smelter', 'working in iron', 'working in 5 alloy metals, *pañcaloha*'.

Archaeological context has also provided evidence of Meluhha colonies or settlements and of nomads who contributed to life-activities of the Bronze Age in Ancient Near East and the Fertile Crescent. This has provided corpora of epigraphs of pictorial motifs (with or without cuneiform texts) which bear resemblance to Meluhha hieroglyph symbolic forms. This is an intimation of the possibility that

Meluhhans in such nomadic settlements had contributed to the use of the writing system conveying meanings by deploying Meluhha hieroglyphs.
Thus, two levels of validation are attempted: Meluhha speakers relating meaning using hieroglyphs 1. in non-Meluhha speech areas and 2. in Meluhha speech area which is denotated by the term Indian *sprachbund*, characterized by re-duplicatio across dialects.
Body or stature of person hieroglyph
The 'body' hieroglyph of a human being is used in a lapidary/artisan and trade context. On a three-sided prism tablet, text of 8 hieroglyphs (including 'body' hieroglyph terminating or starting the sequence) is shown on side A. A boat hieroglyph is shown on side B; a crocodile + fish hieroglyph is shown on side C.
khaḍaka ' *erect ', m. ' bolt, post ' KātyŚr. 2. *khaḍati ' stands '. 3. *khāḍayati ' makes stand '. [Cf. *khadáti* ' is firm ' Dhātup.] and *khalati2 1. K. *khoru* ' standing ', ḍoḍ. *khaṛo* ' up ', pog. *khaṛkhuṛ* ' erect '; S. *khaṛo* ' standing erect ', P. *khaṛā*, WPah. paṅ. *khaṛā*, bhad. *khaṛo*, Or. B. *khāṛā*, H. *khaṛā* (→ N. *khaṛā*), Marw.*khaṛo*, G. *khaṛũ*; M. *khaḍā* ' standing, constant '. 2. K. pog. *khaṛnu* ' to stand ', rām. *khaṛōnu*, ḍoḍ. *khaṛōnō*; WPah. bhal. caus. *khaṛēṇu* ' to fix '; -- G. *khaṛakvũ* ' to make a heap '. 3. K. *khārun* ' to make ascend, lift up '. WPah.kṭg. *khɔ́ṛɔ* ' erect, upright '; *khɔ́ṛhnõ*, kc. *khɔṛiṇo* ' to stand, rise ', J. *khaṛuwṇu.* (CDIAL 3784).

kāḍ 2 काड् । पौरुषम् m. a man's length, the stature of a man (as a measure of length) (Rām. 632, zangan kaḍun kāḍ, to stretch oneself the whole length of one's body. So K. 119). Rebus: खडा [khaḍā] *m* A small stone, a pebble (Marathi) *kāḍ* 'stone'. Ga. (Oll.) *kanḍ*, (S.) *kanḍu* (pl. kanḍkil) stone (DEDR 1298). *maypoṇḍi kanḍ* whetstone; (Ga.)(DEDR 4628).

m1429Atm1429Bt Pict-125: Boat.
m1429Ct Gharial holding a fish in its jaws.

ayo 'fish' Rebus: ayas 'metal'. kāru 'crocodile' Rebus: kāru 'artisan'. Thus, together read rebus: ayakara 'metalsmith'

Alloys and lapidary products Text 3246

The text of 8 hieroglyphs sequence can be segmented into three segments, assuming the 'body' hieroglyph is a set relatable to the other two subsets. The 'rim-of-jar' hieroglyph as the terminal sign identifies the two subsets.

Set 1Subset 1Subset 2

Cast metal, alloy account

kāḍ काड़ ', the stature of a man'

Rebus: खडा [khaḍā] *m* A small stone, a pebble (Marathi) dula 'pair' Rebus: dul 'cast (metal)' shapes objects on a lathe' (Gujarati) *kanka, karṇaka* 'rim of jar' Rebus: *karṇaka* 'account scribe'. *kārṇī(ka)* 'supercargo of a ship' (Marathi)

Alloy ingots

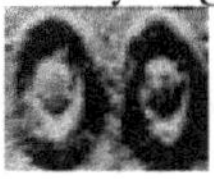 A pair of ingots with notches in-fixed as ligatures.

ḍhālako 'large ingot'. खोट [*khōṭa*] 'ingot, wedge'; A mass of metal (unwrought or of old metal melted down)(Marathi) *khoṭ* f 'alloy (Lahnda) Thus the pair of ligatured oval glyphs read: *khoṭ ḍhālako* 'alloy ingots'.

Forge: stone, minerals, gemstones

khaḍā 'circumscribe' (M.); Rebs: *khaḍā* 'nodule (ore), stone' (M.) *kolom* 'cob'; rebus: *kolmo* 'seedling, rice (paddy) plant' (Munda.) kolma hoṛo = a variety of the paddy plant (Desi)(Santali.) kolmo 'rice plant' (Mu.) Rebus: *kolami* 'furnace,smithy' (Telugu) Thus, the ligatured glyph reads: *khaḍā* 'stone-ore nodule' *kolami* 'furnace,smithy'. Alternatives: 1. *koṛuŋ* young shoot (Pa.) (DEDR 2149) Rebus: *kol* iron, working in iron, blacksmith (Tamil) kollan blacksmith, artificer (Malayalam) kolhali to forge.(DEDR 2133).2. *kaṇḍe* A head or ear of millet or maize (Telugu) Rebus: *kaṇḍa* 'stone (ore)(Gadba)' Ga. (Oll.) kanḍ, (S.) kanḍu (pl. kanḍkil) stone (DEDR 1298).
kolmo 'three' Rebus: *kolami* 'furnace,smithy'. Thus, the pair of glyphs may denote lapidary work – working with stone, mineral, gemstones.
Out of 587 signs in Bryan's sign list133, the following are at least 70 'body' glyphs with ligatures which can be identified:

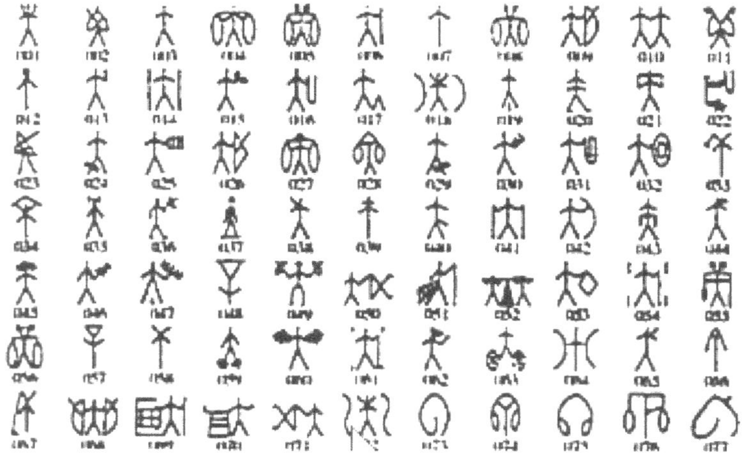

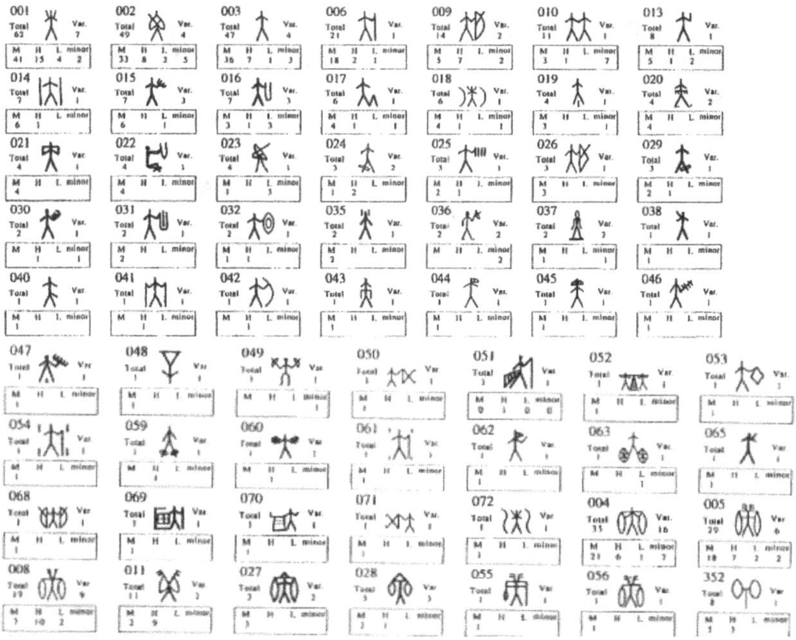

Argument for the method: The philosophical insight of *sphōṭa* will be tested and validated by the evidence drawn from Meluhha *vāk*, life-activities and hieroglyphs. Two examples of symbolic forms are: words (uttered vernacular sounds of Meluhha language and heard sounds) and images. Hypothesising that *sphōṭa,* the 'bursting forth in and of consciousness' occurs as an ordered or constructed 'image' in the human neural network, Meluhha words and images categorized as Meluhha hieroglyphs will be matched. The underlying assumption is that when the writer writes-down an epigraph or inscribes features on an image, he or she signifies his or her 'mental' images (symbolic forms of recorded sound sequences or recorded images) in two- or three-dimensional forms. Such a recorded image (in human neural networks) is likely to be a rebus representation of Meluhha words used in his or her cultural context; and this context enables the reader of the written texts or perceiver of the images to recollect related Meluhha words and 'meaningful' sentences. Because the hypothesized cipher is rebus, there should be at least two Meluhha words which should match: Meluhha word signifying an image; Meluhha language word signifying the uttered or heard sound in the cultural context of the Meluhhan environment related to Meluhhan life-activities.

Reduplication and homonyms with rebus readings as 'areal universals'

Reduplication as a characteristic feature of almost all languages of Indians *sprachbund* is well-recognized. I suggest that this feature may also explain the presence of many homonyms in Mleccha (Meluhha) which enabled symbolic forms of words to be signified by Meluhha hieroglyphs. Reduplication and homonyms can thus be identified as 'areal universals' of Indian *sprachbund*.

The credit for using the term 'linguistic area' goes to MB Emeneau, even though he used the term as a translation of '*sprachbund*' invented by HV Velton in 1943. Linguistic areas are areas in which 'languages belonging to more than one family show traits in common which do not belong to the other members of (at least) one of the families'.The methodology used to recognize a linguistic area is a bifurcate one. First, a typological feature is established as pan-Indic and at the same time not extra-Indic. Second, the historical diffusion of features throughout the languages of the linguistic area are investigated through questions of lexical lists, phonology, syntactic, morphological and semantic development and sociolinguistic questions. Emeneau recognizes (1956: 1,2) that '...it is rarely possible to demonstrate this (Indo-Aryan to Dravidian) direction (except for diffusion of lexical items).

The term *sprachbund* was used in 1931 by Nikol Trubetzkoy and Roman Jakobson when they discussed the long-recognized linguistic areas such as the languages of the Caucasus or of the Balkans. The following works have been reviewed: *Language and Linguistic Area, Essays by Murray B. Emeneau*, (selected and introduced by Anwar S. Dil), 1980, Stanford University Press, California (which includes: Emeneau, MB, 1956, India as a linguistic area, in: Language, 32.3-16 Kuiper, FBJ, 1967, The genesis of a linguistic area, *Indo-Iranian Journal* 10: 81-102 Masica, Colin P., 1976, *Defining a linguistic area, South Asia*,

Chicago, University of Chicago Press (Based on the author's thesis, 1971).

"Duplicatig a morphme or a word to coin new words and express various grammatical aspects is a common phenomenin with the languages of the Tibeto Burman (T.B.) family of South East and South Asia...Indian subcontinent. The Indian T.B. languages are surrounded by Indo Aryan languages on the one hand and are affected by a strong areal pull on the other. The combinational factors of retention and diffusion have produced structures belonging to South Asian 'areal universals' along with those which identify these languages as of T.B. stock. Among two major kinds of reduplication available to these languages: i.e. morphological and lexical it is the latter which is discussed here...Data is drawn from Meitei, Paite, Thado, Kabui, Taizang, Mizo, Lahuli, and Gangte. 'Reduplication' in general stands for repetition of all or part of a lexical item carrying a semantic modification, e.g. Gangte: sel 'boys' and sel sel 'boys boys' or ol 'slow' ad ol ol 'slow slow'. Reduplication may also refer to the iteration of syllables which constitute a single word/lexeme. For instance, kinship mama 'mother' or onomatopoeias such as tep tep 'rain pattering', Mizo olep olep 'sticky' are instances of reduplicatio in spite of the fact that part which is repeated is either a lexical item nor a part of a lexical item...Lexical Reduplication can be constructed by three different processes which are instances of either partial or complete reduplicatio. These processes are: (1) Echo formation; (2) Compounding and (3) Word reduplication...Complete Word Reduplications (CWR) refers to all those reduplicated structures which consist of two identical (bimodal) iterated words. Thus any sequence of phonological units comprising a word may be repeated once (or twice in some rare cases). Hence X may become XX...Paite: *naupan pai pai eketa* boy walking walkig fell down; 'the boy fell down while walking';...Paite: *ema tai tai la: In epau* he running running spoke 'He spoke while running'...T.B. languages show structural affiity to the Indian linguistic area as well as they keep themselves apart from this area by retaining structures pecular to these languages as reduplication of the main verbs (MVs)...Kharia and Khasi (Austroasiatic languages of India) have been noted by the author to have reduplication of the MVs. "(Abbi, Anvita, 1990, Reduplication in Tibeto Burman languages of South Asia, in *Southeast Asian Studies*, Vol. 28, No. 2, September 1990.) Since 1956 when Emeneau referred to an ancient linguistic area in India, there has been a paradigm shift in IE linguistics as applied to the area called 'India' using terms such as areal linguistics,*sprachbund*, linguistic area.

With Emeneau, I reiterate re-duplication as a feature common to all languages of the Indian *sprachbund* and as an explanation for the rebus cipher of Meluhha hieroglyphs.

Starting with verbs depicted as hieroglyphs

The method is deployed on some vivid, emphatic, unambiguous pictorial motifs in Meluhha hieroglyph (symbolic forms) corpora which signify action and hence may be interpreted rebus as, grammatical verbs.

The selected actions signified or selected expressive representations are: 1. to impede, to stop; 2. to turn back (head); 3. to lift up arm.

Meluhha sounds of speech which relate to these expressions or actions are hieroglyphs which signify: 1. *takar*, to impede, to stop; 2. *krammara*, to turn back head; 3. *e̱raka*, upraised arm.
Rebus readings of the three Meluhha hieroglyphs related to the Meluhhan life-activities are the semantics: *tagar* 'tin (ore)'; *kammara* 'artisan/smith-lapidary'; *eraka* 'moltencast copper'.
These three examples will be elaborated further by meanings traditionally attributed – by tradition and as recorded on lexicons to --Meluhha glosses.

Semantic 1: takar, tagar to impede, to stop (Meluhha glosses resulting in these sememes are provided in Appendix A: *tagar* symbolic forms).

Subsets of these symbolic forms are the representations of 1. only one eye; 2. Six-curls on hair; 3. Two tigers. (Meluhha glosses resulting in the sememes related to this imaging is in Appendix C: काण *kāṇa* 'one-eyed', *āra* 'six', 'six rings of hair' symbolic forms)
I sugest that the writer is signifying in the hieroglyphs of one-eye, six hair-curls and a woman, the compound gloss: Meluhha gloss: *kanahār* m. ' helmsman, fisherman ' (Hindi); phonemic variant: *kaṇṇahāra* -- m. 'helmsman, sailor' (Prākṛt)

Alternative: *kāṇ* 'arrow' *(Gaw.)* + *āra* 'six' (Marathi) = *kāṇ āra* 'arrow-maker' expressed in Meluhha gloss variants: *kā̃ḍerā, kanīrā* 'arrow-maker'.

The act of 'impeding, stopping' two tigers is signified by the glosses: *tagara* 'tin (ore)' and *kol* 'working in iron, five metals'; *kol, kolhe*, 'the koles, an aboriginal tribe if iron smelters speaking a language akin to that of Santals' (Santali) See: Appendix A: *tagar* symbolic forms; Appendix D: *kol* 'tiger' symbolic forms. A pair of tigers as mirror-images is signified by the gloss: dula 'pair' Rebus: dul 'cast metal'.

The 'woman' image reinforces the phoneme (symbolic form) *kol* by the meanings traditionally assigned to similar sounding Meluhha glosses: *kuṛā́* 'girl'; *kola* 'woman'. See Appendix D: *kol* 'tiger' symbolic forms.

Thus, the narrative of a woman with six hair-curls and one-eye impeding or stopping two tigers is a set of symbolic forms imaging the sounds of Meluhha language glosses connoting a helmsman transporting, on a magilum (?) Meluhha boat, alloyed metal: *kaṇṇahāra* -- m. 'helmsman, sailor'. (Appendix C: काण *kāṇa* 'one-eyed', *āra* 'six', 'rings of hair' symbolic forms).

This 'helmsman, sailor' *kaṇṇahāra* representation is shown between two hieroglyphs: 1. spoked-wheel hieroglyph on the top register; and 2. elephant (*ibha*) hieroglyph on the bottom register. These two hieroglyphs signify subsets of alloying metals: *eraka* 'moltencast copper', *arā 'brass'; ib* 'iron', *ibbo* 'merchant'. *Ibbo* is thus a merchant of iron, alloy metals and moltencast copper (ingots).

m0306 Person grappling with two tigers standing on either side of him and rearing on their hindlegs. 2086

m0307 Person grappling with two tigers standing on either side of him and rearing on their hindlegs. 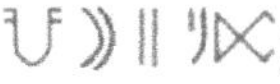2122

That the person impeding the two standing tigers is a woman one-eyed and with six curls on her hairstyle is interpreted as *kaṇṇahāra* -- m. 'helmsman, sailor'. Hieroglyphs: *kaṇ* 'one eye' *āra* 'six', 'curls'.

Semantic 2: krammara, to turn back head (Meluhha glosses resulting in this sememe are provided in Appendix B: *krəm* 'neck' symbolic forms).

An Early Dynastic II votive plaque from the Inanna temple at Nippur VIII (after Pritchard, 1969: 356, no. 646). "It has something very Harappan about it also in the lower part depicting two 'unicorn' bulls around a tree. The six dots around the head of the Harappan hero, clearly visible in one seal (Mohenjodaro, DK 11794; cf. Mackay, 1937: II, pl. 84:75) may be compared to the six locks of hair characteristic of the Mesopotamian hero from Jemdet Nasr to Akkadian times (cf. Calmeyer, 1957-71: 373). From the Early Dynastic period onwards the scene usually comprises a man fighting with one or two bulls, and a bull-man fighting with one or two lions....North-west India of the third millennium BC can be considered as an integral, if marginal, part of the West Asian cultural area."[134]

Rebus readings: *dula* 'pair' Rebus: *dul* 'cast metal' kol 'tiger' Rebus: kol 'working in iron, alloys, smelter' *kõda* 'yung bull' Rebus: *kõdār* 'turner' (Bengali) *kolmo* 'seedling' Rebus: *kolami* 'smithy, forge'.

Dark grey steatite bowl carved in relief. Zebu or brahmani bull is shown with its hump back; a male figure with long hair and wearing akilt grasps two sinuous objects, representing running water, which flows in a continuous stream. Around the bowl, another similar male figure stands between two lionesses with their head turned back towards him; he grasps a serpent in each hand. A further scene (not shown) represents a prostrate bull which is being attacked by a vulture and a lion.

The zebu is reminiscent of Sarasvati Sindhu seals. The stone used, steatite, is familiar in Baluchistan and a number of vessels at the Royal Cemetery at Ur were made out of this material.

The bowl dates from c. 2700-2500 B.C. and the motif shown on it resembles that on a fragment of a green stone vase from one of the Sin Temples at Tell Asmar of almost the same date.

Khafajeh bowl; a man sitting, with his legs bent underneath, upon two zebu bulls. This evokes the proto-Elamite bull-man; the man holds in his hands streams of water and issurrounded by ears of corn. He has a crescent beside his head. On the other side of the bowl, a man is standing upon two lionesses and grasping two serpents.

nāga 'serpent' Rebus: *nāga* 'lead' *adar ḍangra* 'zebu' Rebus: *aduru ḍhangar* 'native metal smith' *kol* 'tiger' Rebus: *kol* 'working iron, alloys, smelter'.

In corpora of Meluhha hieroglyphs, two animals are shown with their heads turned back; the animals are: tiger and antelope.

m0310AC 1355

m0271 Goat-antelope with horns turned backwards and a short tail

m0272 Goat-antelope with horns bending backwards and neck turned backwards  2554

Semantic 3 : eraka 'nave of wheel', *eraka* 'upraised arm'.

Glyph: *eṛaka* 'upraised arm' (Tamil) Rebus: *eraka* 'copper' (Kannada) Glyph: *tagara* '*tabernae montana*', 'tulip'. The sound of the

word signifying the fragrant tulip is reinforced by the pictorial motif of the person with the upraised arm about to deliver a 'blow'. This may be signifying a threatening gesture as a symbolic form. *ṭakkar* 'blow' (Hindi. Bengali. Gujarati. Marathi) Rebus: *tagara* 'tin'. Thus, the two glyphs, tulip and upraised arm about to deliver a blow signify tagara + eraka; the signified 'meanings' are:: tin + copper as the minerals alloyed to create the axe.

The following superset mold of a hieroglyphic composition deploys hieroglyph *eraka* 'nave of wheel' Rebus: *erako* 'moltencast copper'. See hieroglyph signifiers in Appendix E: *eṟaka* 'upraised arm' (Tamil)

Superset on Obverse side of 5 Harappa tablets, h1970, h1971, h1972, h1973, h1974 :

Obverse of Slide 89 and Slide 185: woman impeding/stopping tigers + elephant + spoked wheel hieroglyphs is therefore, a superset Meluhha hieroglyph composition signifying tin ore, iron ore, moltencast copper, brass by worker, *kol*, on smelters.

That Obverse of Slide 89 and Slide 185 is a superset is

archaeologically evidenced that the obverse is made from the same mold while the reverse of the two tablets is made from two different molds: "We have found two other broken tablets at Harappa that appear to have been made from the same mold that was used to create the scene of a deity battling two tigers and standing above an elephant. One was found in a room located on the southern slope of Mount ET in 1996 and another example comes from excavations on Mound F in the 1930s. However, the flat obverse of both of these broken tablets does not show the spearing of a buffalo, rather it depicts the more well-known scene showing a tiger looking back over its shoulder at a person sitting on the branch of a tree. Several other flat or twisted rectangular terracotta tablets found at Harappa combine these two narrative scenes of a figure strangling two tigers on one side of a tablet, and the tiger looking back over its shoulder at a figure in a tree on the other side."[135]

Obverse side of Harappa tablets h1970, h1971 and h1972 shows an elephant, a person strangling two tigers (jackals or foxes) and a six-spoked wheel.

The superset glyphs on Obverse side refer to : merchant (of) furnace (outputs) account (from) smithy/forge of turner, working in copper and brass.

Subset 1 on two Harappa tablets, h1973, h1974:

Harappa tablets. h1973B h1974B Two tablets. One side shows a

person seated on a tree branch, a tiger looking up, a crocodile on the top register and rhinoceros in procession, ahead of tiger, in the bottom register.

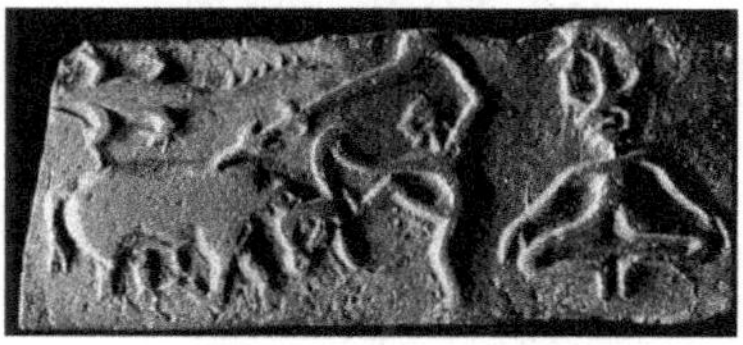

Subset 2 on three Harappa tablets, h1970, h1971, h1972: h1971B Harappa. Crocodile +

person with foot on head of animal + spearing + bison. Seated person with a ligature on head: twig between horns. Left: H95-2524; Right: H95-2487.

Subset 1 and Subset 2 are distinct subsets. A common hieroglyph on Subsets 1 and 2 is: crocodile. *karā* 'crocodile' (Telugu). Rebus: *khar* 'blacksmith' (Kashmiri). Thus, both the subsets 1 and 2 refer to the activities of blacksmiths.

Distinctive narratives on Subset 2 are of life-activities of artisans working in wood, iron and alloy metals and moltencast copper, large ingots and turner (working on forge of smithy):

1. *karā* 'crocodile' (Telugu). Rebus: *khar* 'blacksmith' (Kashmiri).
2. *badhi* 'castrated boar', 'rhinoceros' Rebus: *badhoe* 'worker in wood and iron'.
3. Hieroglyph composition of tiger looking back + leafless tree + person seated on tree branch. Hieroglyph components are read rebus: *kol kammara* 'smelter, artisan working in iron, alloy metals' *erako* 'moltencast copper' *kõdār* 'turner' working on a lathe; *ḍhālako*, 'large metal ingot'.
   kol 'tiger' Rebus: *kol* 'working in iron', 'working in alloy metals'
   krammara 'lookingback' Rebus: *kammara* 'artisan, smith'
   heraka 'spy' Rebus *erako* 'moltencast copper'
   khōṇḍa 'leafless tree' Rebus: *kõdār* 'turner'; *kõdā* ' to turn in a lathe.'
   ḍāḷ, 'branch of a tree' Rebus: *ḍhālako*, 'large metal ingot'

Notes on heraka:

Ko. er uk- (uky-) to play 'peeping tom'. *Kui* ēra (ēri-) to spy, scout; *n.* spying, scouting; *pl action* ērka (ērki). ? *Kuwi* (S.) hēnai to scout; hēri kiyali to see; (Su. P.) hēnḍ- (hēṭ-) id. *Kur.* ērnā (īryas) to see, look, look at, look after, look for, wait for, examine, try; ērta'ānā to let see, show; ērānakhrnā to look at one another. *Malt.*ére to see, behold, observe; érye to peep, spy. Kur. ēthrnā. / Cf. Skt. heraka- spy, Pkt. her- to look at or for, and many NIA verbs (DEDR 903). *hērati 'looks for or at'. 2. hēraka -- , °*rika* -- m. 'spy' lex., *hairika* -- m. 'spy' Hcar., 'thief' lex. [J. Bloch FestschrWackernagel 149 ← Drav., Kui *ēra* 'to spy', Malt. *ére* 'to see']1. Pk. *hēraï* 'looks for or at' (*vihīraï* 'watches for'); K.ḍoḍ. *hērūō* 'was seen'; WPah.bhad. bhal. *he_rnū* 'to look at' (bhal. *hirāṇū* 'to show'), pāḍ. *hēraṇ*, paṅ.*hēṇā*, cur. *hērnā*, Ku. *herṇo*, N. *hernu*, A. *heriba*, B. *herā*, Or. *heribā* (caus. *herāibā*), Mth. *herab*, OAw. *heraï*, H. *hernā*; G. *hervũ* 'to spy', M. *herṇẽ*.2. Pk. *hēria* -- m. 'spy'; Kal. (Leitner) "*hériu*" 'spy'; G. *herɔ* m. 'spy', *herũ* n. 'spying'. WPah.kṭg. (Wkc.) *hèrnõ*, kc. *erno* 'observe'; Garh. *hernu* 'to look'.(CDIAL 14165).

Distinctive narratives on Subset 2 are life-activities of: *kuṭhi* 'smelter' *koḍ* 'artisan's workshop' *kol* 'working in iron', 'working in 5 alloy metals', *ranga* 'pewter or alloy of tin.

1. *karā* 'crocodile' (Telugu). Rebus: *khar* 'blacksmith' (Kashmiri).
2. *kamaḍha* 'penance' Rebus: *kammaṭa, kampaṭṭa* 'mint, coiner'
3. *kūdī* 'twig' (on plumed headdress rising out of the horns) Rebus: *kuṭhi* 'smelter'
4. *koḍ* 'horns' Rebus: *koḍ* 'artisan's workshop'
5. *kolsa* 'kicking' Rebus: *kol* 'working in iron', 'working in 5 alloy metals'
6. *rangā* 'buffalo' Rebus: *ranga* 'pewter or alloy of tin (*ranku*) [A person spearing with a barbed spear a buffalo; he presses his foot down the buffalo's head.]
7. *kol* 'to kill' Rebus: *kol* 'working in iron, 5 alloy metals, smelter'.
8. మేడెము [mēḍemu] or మేడియము *mēḍemu*. [Tel.] n. A spear or dagger. Rebus: *meḍ* 'iron'.

Thus, while Subsets 1 and 2 record hieroglyphs with meanings connoting life-activities of blacksmiths,

Subset 1 connotes smelter work (*kol*) and forge/smithy work; Subset 2 signifies *kampaṭṭa* 'mint, coiner' alloy work.

Both blacksmiths of subsets 1 and 2 deliver the products of their life-activities to be taken into the citadel warehouse for trade by *ibbo* 'merchant' (hieroglyph: *ibha* 'elephant' Rebus: *ib* 'iron'). Two specialist guilds of workers' bronze age products are being collected together – using the two distinct subsets 1 and 2 on molded tablets (both belong to the superset of *erako* 'molten cast metalwork' of *koles*, smelters) -- from workers' platforms into warehouse to further compile the bills of lading for trade loads to be sent as consignments on boats or on donkey caravans.

Details of the tiger + spy + leafless tree glyphics are clearly seen on a Mohenjodaro seal m0309.

ayakāra 'ironsmith' (fish, *aya* + crocodile, *karā*) + era 'copper' (eraka 'spy') + ḍhālako, 'large metal ingot' (ḍāḷ, 'branch of a tree') + three animals in procession: badhoe 'worker in wood and iron' [badhi 'castrated boar'] + kol 'smith working in iron with smithy/forge' [kol + kammara 'tiger looking up'] + kolami 'smithy/forge' [kola 'tiger']

m0309  2522

Glyphs on text inscription

V284 Glyph: *kōnṭa* 'corner' (Nk.); Tu. *kōṇṭu* 'angle, corner' (Tu.). Rebus: *kōdā* 'to turn in a lathe' (B.)

Four corners marked may denote a worker guild working with 4 types of pure metal and alloyed ingots (copper + arsenic/tin/zinc).

Glyph: 'splinter' sal 'splinter'. Rebus: sal 'artisan's workshop'. खांडा [khāṇḍā] *m* A jag, notch, or indentation (as upon the edge of a tool or weapon. Rebus: *kāṇḍa* 'tools, pots and pans and metal-ware'.

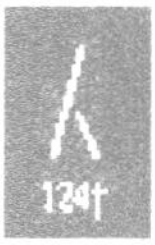

Glyph: taṭṭai 'mechanism made of split bamboo for scaring away parrots from grain fields (Ta.); taṭṭe 'a thick bamboo or an areca-palm stem, split in two'

(Ka.) (DEDR 3042) Rebus: toṭxin, toṭ.xn goldsmith (To.); taṭṭāṉ

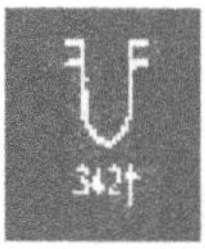

'gold- or silver-smith' (Ta.); taṭṭaravāḍu 'gold- or silver-smith' (Te.); *ṭhaṭṭakāra 'brass-worker' (Skt.)(CDIAL 5493). Thus, the glyph is decoded: taṭṭara 'worker in gold, brass'.

Hieroglyph: *kaṇḍa kan-ka* 'rim of jar'. *kan-ka, karṇaka* 'rim of jar' Rebus: *kaṇḍa karṇaka* 'furnace account scribe'. *kārṇī(ka)* 'supercargo of a ship' (Marathi)

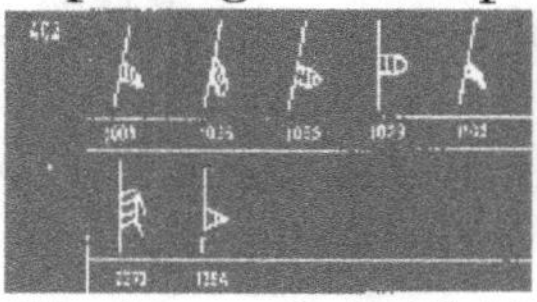

Allographs of Glyph 402 Glyph: *koḍi* 'flag' (Ta.)(DEDR 2049). Rebus: *koḍ* 'workshop' (Kuwi)

Glyph: *ayo, hako* 'fish'; a~s = scales of fish (Santali). Rebus: aya = iron (G.); ayah, ayas = metal (Skt.)

Glyph: one long linear stroke. koḍa, koṛa = in arithmetic one; 4 koṛa or koḍa = 1 gaṇḍa = 4 (Santali) Rebus: koḍ, 'artisan's workshop' (Kuwi.)

The text inscription reads rebus: Lathe-turner metal-ware workshop; brass-worker, furnace (stone ore) account (scribe); metal artisan's workshop.

kõdā 'lathe-turner'; *kāṇḍa* 'tools, pots and pans and metal-ware'. *sal* 'artisan's workshop'. taṭṭara 'worker in gold, brass'; *kan-ka, karṇaka* 'rim of jar' Rebus: *kaṇḍa karṇaka* 'furnace account scribe'. *kārṇī(ka)* 'supercargo of a ship' (Marathi)

koḍ 'workshop'; *aya* 'metal'; *koḍ* 'artisan's workshop'.

Meaning and functions of molded tablets, incised miniature tablets

Meluhha hieroglyphs on seals are mean to be impressed on clay to create seal impressions as descriptive invoices to accompany consignments of ston-ware, metal-ware.

A remarkable archaeologically attested context indicates the functions of molded tablets, incised miniature tablets as 'tokens' to be mirrored onto the seal hieroglyph sequences.

Structural characteristics of hieroglyphs

It is generally surmised that short numeral strokes ranging from one stroke to seven strokes are numerical signifiers.
In the case of Meluhha hieroglyphs, the numerical signifiers signify the sounds of associated 'numerical words or glosses'.
For example, one short linear stroke or two short linear strokes are superfixed on particular differentiated hieroglyphs to connote:
| one long linear stroke: *koḍa* 'one' (Santali) Rebus: *koḍ* 'artisan's workshop' (Kuwi)
' one short linear stroke or "two short linear strokes (generally deployed as superfixes): खांडा [khāṇḍā] *m* A jag, notch, or indentation (as upon the edge of a tool or weapon or as superfix on select hieroglyphs). Rebus: *khāṇḍā* 'tools, pots and pans and metal-ware'; खांडा [khāṇḍā] *m* A kind of sword, straight, broad-bladed, two-edged, and round-ended. (Marathi). காண்டம் kāṇṭam Weapon; ஆயுதம். (சூடா.)

Thus, when two short linear strokes " are superfixed on a 'spoked-wheel' or nave of the wheel through which the axle passes; cf. arā, spoke, hieroglyph the combined reading of the two hieroglyphs read rebus:

Two hieroglyphs read rebus together as *eraka khāṇḍā* 'moltencast copper tools, weapons, pots and pans, metalware':

खांडा [khāṇḍā] *m* A jag, notch, or indentation.

eraka, era, er-a = syn. erka, copper, weapons. Rebus: er-r-a = red; *eraka* = copper (Ka.) *erka* = *ekke* (Tbh. of arka) aka (Tbh. of *arka*) copper (metal); crystal (Kannada) *eraka, er-aka* = any metal infusion (Ka.Tu.); *erako* molten cast (Tulu) (arkasāle) with variant phonemes and pronounciations, as uttered, spoken words: agasāle, agasāli, agasālavāḍu = a goldsmith (Telugu) cf. eruvai = copper (Tamil) arká1 m. ' flash, ray, sun ' RV. [√arc] Pa. Pk. *akka* -- m. ' sun ', Mth. *āk;* Si. *aka* ' lightning ', inscr. *vid* -- *äki* ' lightning flash '.(CDIAL 624) அருக்கன் *arukkaṉ, n. < arka. Sun;* சூரியன். அருக்க னணிநிறமுங் கண்டேன் (திவ். இயற். *3, 1).*(Tamil) agasāle 'goldsmithy' (Kannada) అగసాలి [agasāli]

or అగసాలెవాడు *agasāli.* n. A goldsmith. కంసాలివాడు. (Telugu) erka

= ekke (Tbh. of arka) aka (Tbh. of arka) copper (metal); crystal (Kannada) cf. eruvai = copper (Tamil) eraka, er-aka = any metal infusion (Ka.Tu.); erako molten cast (Tulu) Rebus: eraka = copper (Ka.) eruvai = copper (Ta.); ere - a dark-red colour (Ka.)(DEDR 817). eraka, era, er-a = syn. erka, copper, weapons (Ka.) erka = ekke (Tbh. of arka) aka (Tbh. of arka) copper (metal); crystal (Kannada) akka, aka (Tadbhava of arka) metal; akka metal (Te.) arka = copper (Skt.) erako molten cast (Tulu)
Rebus:

erako 'molten cast copper'.

खांडा [*khāṇḍā*] 'tools, pots and pans and metal-ware' In Meluhha reckoning or numerical systems, one is represented by the gloss: *koḍa*

| | | | Four such long linear strokes have a set word to signify numeral four or a count of four: *gaṇḍa* 'four' (Santali) Rebus 1: *kaṇḍ* fire-altar, furnace' (Santali) Rebus 2: खांडा [*khāṇḍā*] ' tools, pots and pans and metal-ware'.

| | | |
| | | The numeral count of 'seven' is broken down into 'four' + 'three' and each component is read rebus: *gaṇḍa* 'four' Rebus: *khāṇḍā* 'metalware' (from) *kolom* 'three' Rebus: *kolami* 'smithy,forge'.

| | |

| | | Six long linear strokes: Hieroglyph: आर [*āra*] A term in the play of इटीदांडू,--the number six. (Marathi) *āṟu* six (Meluhha) Rebus: āra 'brass'. Meluhha glosses:*Ta.* āṟu six; aṟu-patu sixty; aṟu-nūṟu 600; aṟumai six; aṟuvar six persons; avv-āṟu by sixes. *Ma.* āṟu six; aṟu-patu sixty; aṟu-nnūṟu 600; aṟuvar six persons.*Ko.* a·r six; ar vat sixty; a·r nu·r 600; ar va·ṇy six pa·ṇy measures. *To.* o·ṟ six; pa·ṟ sixteen; aṟoQ sixty; o·ṟ nu·ṟ 600; aṟ xwa·w six kwa·x measures. *Ka.* āṟu six;aṟa-vattu, aṟu-vattu, ar-vattu sixty; aṟu-nūṟu, āṟu-nūṟu 600; aṟuvar, ārvaru six persons. *Koḍ.* a·rï six; a·rane sixth; aru-vadï sixty; a·r-nu·rï 600.(DEDR 2485).

| |Two long linearstrokes: sangaḍa 'a pair, two' as in sangaḍa 'two boats joined together as canoe'. Rebus 1: *sãgaṛh* m. ' line of entrenchments, stone walls for defence '. Rebus 2: sang संग् m. a stone (Kashmiri) sanghāḍo (G.) = cutting stone, gilding; sangatarāśū = stone cutter; sangatarāśi = stone-cutting; sangsāru : Rebus 3: *jangaḍ* 'entrusted articles on approval basis'. Rebus 4: *sangaḍa* 'association' (guild) – a variant meaning expanding the locus of stone walls for defence to signify an association or guild of artisans. An allograph to signify one or more of these 'meanings' is a standard device (hieroglyphically interpreted as *sangaḍa* 'lathe, gimlet' atop a *sangaḍa* 'portable furnace'). Rebus 4: *sang* 'stone', *gaḍa* 'large stone'.

Indus script "fish-eyes" traded with Ur

'Fish-eyes' mentioned in ancient cuneiform texts refer to copper work.

From rebus readings of Indus text hieroglyphs, it may be concluded that the 'fish-eye' connotes 'alloy (*ayas*) metalware, metal stone, nodule of metal'. Fish a symbolic form gloss is signified by *ayo* 'fish' Rebus: *aya* 'iron' (Gujarati); *ayas* 'metal (alloy)' (Sanskrit).

Hieroglyph: *Ta.* kaṇ eye, aperture, orifice, star of a peacock's tail. (DEDR 1159a) Rebus 'brazier, bell-metal worker': **கன்னான்** kaṉṉāṉ , *n.* < **கன்**[1]. [M. *kannān.*] Brazier, bell-metal worker, one of the divisions of the Kammāḷa caste; **செம்புகொட்டி**. (**திவா**.) *Ta.* kaṉ copper work, copper, workmanship; kaṉṉāṉ brazier. *Ma.* kannān id. (DEDR 1402).

kaṇi 'stone' (Kannada) with Tadbhava *khaḍu. khaḍu, kaṇ* 'stone/nodule (metal)'. Ga. (Oll.) *kanḍ*, (S.) *kanḍu* (pl. *kanḍkil*)

stone (DEDR 1298). **கன்**[1] *kaṉ* Copper (Tamil) **கன்**[2] kaṉ , n. < **கல்**. stone (Tamil) **खडा** (Marathi) is 'metal, nodule, stone, lump'. These could be the substratum glosses for *kāṇḍa* in *ayas kāṇḍa* 'excellent iron' (Pāṇini) h329A has a fish-shaped tablet with two signs: fish + arrow (which has been decoded as *ayaskāṇḍa* on a *bos indicus* seal). The 'fish-eye' is a reinforcement of the gloss *kāṇḍ*'stone/nodule (metal)'. The dotted circle (eye) is decoded rebus as *kaṇ* 'aperture' (Tamil); *kāṇũ* hole (Gujarati) (i.e. glyph showing dotted-circle); *kāṇa* 'one eye' and these glyphs may have been interpreted as the 'fish-eyes' or 'eye stones' (Akkadian IGI-HA, IGI-KU6) mentioned in Mesopotamian texts. The commodities denoted may be nodules of mined stones/nodules of chalcopyrite. 'Eye stones' elucidating, based on textual and archaeological contexts, that 'fish-eyes' do NOT refer to pearls. Donkin[136] surmises that they refer to agate stones. He notes that 'fish-eyes' were among a number of valuable commodities (gold, copper, lapis lazuli, stone beads) offerings made at the temple of Ningal at Ur by seafaring merchants who had returned safely from Dilmun and perhaps further afield. One text notes that they were bought in Dilmun. It is also not clear if 'fish-eyes' were differentiated from 'fish-eye stones' (NA4 IGI HA NA4 IGI-KU6). 'Fish-eye stones' are clearly markied as imports from Meluhha (NA4 IGI-Me-LUH-HA) in a text dated ca. 1816-1810 BCE.[137] This monograph argues that the glyphs of 'dotted circles' denoting 'fish-eyes' or 'antelope-eyes', refer to 'stone/nodules of mineral (perhaps, chalcopyrite)', decoded rebus as *kāṇḍ* as in *ayaskāṇḍa* 'excellent iron'.

On this seal, ayo 'fish' read rebus ayas 'metal'; ḍangar 'bull' read rebus ḍangar 'blacksmith'; koṭ 'horn; red rebus: khoṭ 'alloy'; khoṇḍ 'young bull-calf' read rebus khuṇḍ '(metal) turner'. Rebus: *kẽṛẽ kõṛẽ* an aboriginal tribe who work in brass and bell-metal (Santali)
Thus, when one-eye of a woman is used as a hieroglyph together with six knobs on her hair, as she impedes two rearing tigers/jackals, the 'eye' is a symbolic form for the gloss: *kaṇ* 'eye' *kāṇa 'one eye'*. Rebus reading: *kāṇḍa* 'tools, pots and pans, metal-ware' (Marathi).

 h337A  h337B  4417 Pict-79: shape of a leaf. Dotted circle on obverse

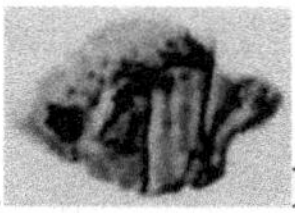 h338A 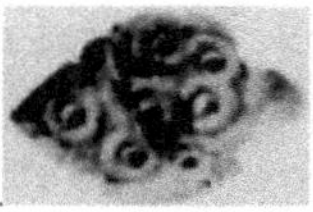 h338B 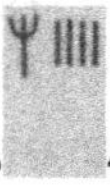 4426 Pict-39: Inscribed object in the shape of a tortoise (?) or leaf (?). Dotted circles on obverse.

 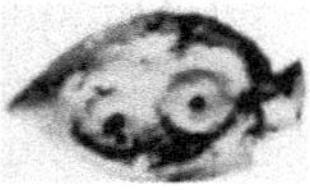

loa 'fig leaf; Rebus: loh '(copper) metal'

gaṇḍa 'four' Rebus: *kaṇḍa* 'fire-altar' కండె [kaṇḍe] *kaṇḍe* [Telugu] n. A head or ear of millet or maize. కందళము [Skt.] n. A germ or shoot, a sprout. కొత్తమొలక. కందళించు *kandaḷinṭsu.* v. n. To sprout, germinate, shoot. (Telugu) Alternative: kolmo 'seedling' Rebus: kolami 'smithy/forge'. Thus, these incised miniature tablets may relate to perforated metal beads delivered from the 'furnace' to the smithy for further polishing (lapidary) work, warehousing and dispatch through caravans or seafaring merchants.

khāṇḍā 'dotted circles' Rebus 1: *khāṇḍā* 'tools, pots and pans and metal-ware'. Rebus 2: kāḍ 'stone'. Ga. (Oll.) kanḍ, (S.) kanḍu (pl. kanḍkil) stone (DEDR 1298). *kolom* 'three' Rebus: *kolami* 'smithy/forge'. *kanḍkil* stones; Rebus: kandil 'beads'.

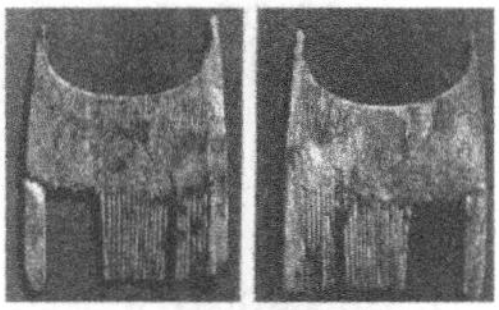

After Vats, Pl.CXIX,.No.6 An ivory comb fragment with one preserved tooth and ornamented with double incised circles (3.8 in. long).

Kalibangan, Ivory comb with three dotted circles; Kalibangan, Period II; Thapar 1979, Pl.XXVII, in: Ancient Cities of the Indus.

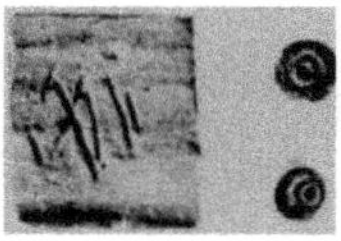 

Ivory rod, ivory plaque with dotted circles. Mohenjodaro. [Musee National De

Arts Asiatiques Guimet, 1988-1989, Les cites oubliees de l'Indus Archeologie du Pakistan.] h1017 ivorystick
Ivory comb with Mountain Tulip motif and dotted circles. TA 1649 Tell Abraq. [D.T. Potts, South and Central Asian elements at Tell Abraq (Emirate of Umm al-Qaiwain, United Arab Emirates), c. 2200 BC—AD 400, in Asko Parpola and Petteri Koskikallio, South Asian Archaeology 1993: , pp. 615-666] h337, h338 Texts 4417, 4426 (Dotted circles on leaf-shaped tablets) Tell Abraq comb and axe with epigraph After Fig. 7 Holly Pittman, 1984, Art of the Bronze Age: Southeastern Iran, Western Central Asia, and the Indus Valley, New York, The Metropolitan Museum of Art, pp. 29-30].

Wild tulip motif. A motif that occurs on southeast Iranian cylinder seals and on Persian Gulf seals. 1st row: Bactrian artifacts; 2nd row: a comb from the Gulf area and late trans-Elamite seals.[138]

The ivory comb found at Tell Abraq measures 11 X 8.2 X .4 cm. Both sides of the comb bear identical, incised decoration in the form of two long-stemmed flowers with crenate or dentate leaves, flanking three dotted circles arranged in a triangular pattern. Bone and ivory combs with dotted-circle decoration are well-known in the Harappan area (e.g. at Chanhu-daro and Mohenjo-daro), but none of the Harappan combs bear the distinctive floral motif of the Tell Abraq comb. These flowers are identified as tulips, perhaps Mountain tulip or Boeotian tulip (both of which grow in Afghanistan) which have an undulate leaf. There is a possibility that the comb is an import from Bactria, perhaps transmitted through Meluhha to the Oman Peninsula site of Tell Abraq. Orthographically, the dotted circle is also a fish-eye or eye of an antelope. The eye is *kāṇ* rebus: *kāṇḍ* 'tools, pots and pans, metal-ware' as in *ayaskāṇḍa* 'excellent iron' (Pan.). It may also be rebus for *kaṇḍ* 'fire-altar'. *kaṇḍ* also denotes 'ivory'.

The gloss related to the dotted circle is thus, decoded rebus as *kāṇ*.

- kandhi = a lump, a piece (Santali.lex.) [The dotted circle thus connotes an ingot taken out of a kaṇḍ, furnace; *kāṇḍ* 'tools, pots and pans, metal-ware']. kāndavika = a baker; kandu = an iron plate or pan for baking cakes etc. (Ka.lex.)
- kaṇḍ = altar, furnace (Santali) लोहकारकन्दुः f. a blacksmith's smelting furnace (Grierson Kashmiri lex.) payĕn-kō̃da पयन्-कौँद । परिपाककन्दुः f. a kiln (a potter's, a lime-kiln, and brick-kiln, or the like); a furnace (for smelting) This yajn~a kuṇḍam can be denoted rebus, by perforated beads (kandi) or on ivory (khaṇḍ)

- kandi (pl. -l) beads, necklace (Pa.); kanti (pl. -l) bead, (pl.) necklace; kandit. bead (Ga.)(DEDR 1215). The three stringed beads depicted on the pictograph may perhaps be treated as a phonetic determinant of the substantive, the rimmed jar, the khaṇḍa kanka. khaṇḍa, xanro, sword or large sacrificial knife. kandil, kandi_l = a globe of glass, a lantern (Ka.lex.)

- khaṇḍ 'ivory' (H.) jaṇḍ khaṇḍ = ivory (Jaṭkī) khaṇḍ ī = ivory in rough (Jaṭkī); gaṭī = piece of elephant's tusk (S.) [This semant. may explain why the dotted circle -- i.e., kandi, 'beads' -- is often depicted on ivory objects, such as ivory combs]. See also: khaṇḍiyo [cf. khaṇḍaṇī a tribute] tributary; paying a tribute to a superior king (G.lex.) [Note glyph of a kneeling adorant]. kandi (pl. -l) beads, necklace (Pa.); kanti (pl. -l) bead, (pl.) necklace; kandit. bead (Ga.)(DEDR 1215). The three stringed beads depicted on the pictograph may perhaps be treated as a phonetic determinant of the substantive, the rimmed jar, the khaṇḍa kanka. khaṇḍa, xanro, sword or large sacrificial knife. kandil, kandīl = a globe of glass, a lantern (Ka.lex.) kandhi 'a lump, a piece' (Santali) काढतें [kāḍhatēṃ] n Among gamesters. An ivory counter &c. placed to represent a sum of money. (Marathi) The dotted circles also adorn the standard device which is a drill-lathe, sangaḍa खंड [khaṇḍa] A piece, bit, fragment, portion.(Marathi) Rebus: khaṇḍaran, khaṇḍrun 'pit furnace' (Santali)

- Rebus: kaṇḍ 'tools, pots and pans, metal-ware'. kaṇḍ = altar, furnace (Santali) लोहकारकन्दुः f. a blacksmith's smelting furnace (Grierson Kashmiri lex.) payĕn-kō̆da पयन्-कौँद । परिपाककन्दुः f. a kiln (a potter's, a lime-kiln, and brick-kiln, or the like); a furnace (for smelting) This yajn~a kuṇḍam can be denoted rebus, by perforated beads (kandi) or on ivory (khaṇḍ):
- aya = iron (G.); ayah, ayas = metal (Skt.) *ayaskāṇḍa* 'excellent iron (metal) tools, pots and pans, metal-ware'. Allograph: Glyph: 'eye'.

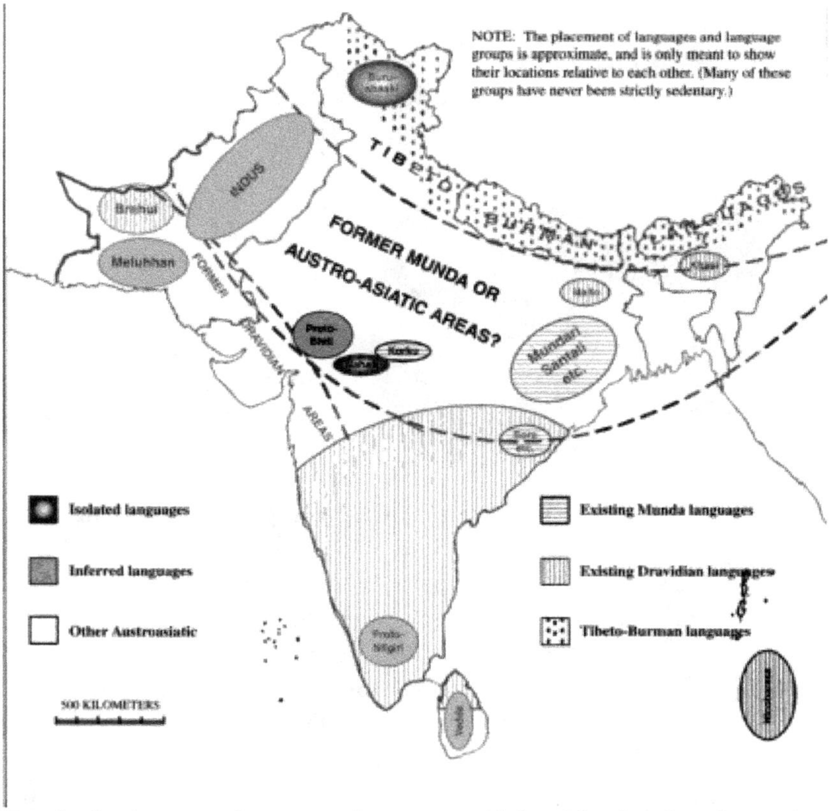

Pre-Indo-Aryan substratum languages (After Fig. 3.1 Southworth, FC, 2005, *Linguistic Archaeology of South Asia*, London: Routledge-Curzonp. 65).

The flow (diffusion) of the civilization is from Sarasvati basin to lower Sindhu areas and thereafter to upper Sindhu regions.
The continued use of hieroglyphs of Indus writing together with cuneiform texts is a characteristic feature of the evolution of writing in ancient Near East as it progressed from the use of tokens and

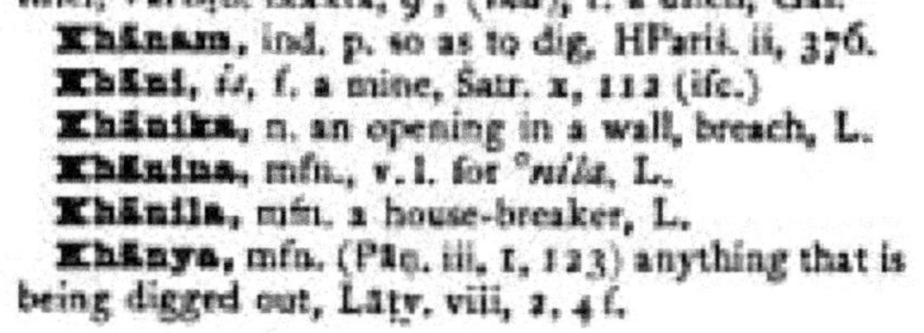
Khānaka, mfn. ifc. one who digs or digs out, Mn. viii, 260; (cf. *khāpa-*); m. a house-breaker, thief, VarBṛS. lxxxix, 9; (*ikā*), f. a ditch, Gal.
Khānam, ind. p. so as to dig, HParis. ii, 376.
Khāni, *is*, f. a mine, Śatr. x, 112 (ifc.)
Khānika, n. an opening in a wall, breach, L.
Khānina, mfn., v.l. for °*nila*, L.
Khānila, mfn. a house-breaker, L.
Khānya, mfn. (Pāṇ. iii, 1, 123) anything that is being digged out, Lāṭy. viii, 2, 4 f.

bullae to the use of glyphs to denote many metallurgical categories. A method of rebus readings evidenced for Narmer palette in Egypt applied to the Indus writing glyphs reveals Meluhha (mleccha) substrate lexemes from Indian *sprachbund.*

Tokens of Susa evolve into hieroglyphic Indus writing in ancient Near East

Shape of a token representing one ingot of metal, Susa, Iran, ca. 3300 BCE.

Complex tokens representing (from r. to l.) – (Top row) one sheep, one jar of oil, one ingot of metal, one garment; (Bottom row) one garment, ?, one honeycomb. Musee du Louvre.

The development of the power of abstraction as illustrated by the evolution of counting in the ancient Near East. Tokens indicates that counting was first done concretely in one-to-one correspondence. The claytokens, that appeared in the Near East about 7500 BC, abstracted the goods they represented. For example a cone abstracted a measure of grain. About 3300 BC, when tokens were kept in envelopes, markings on envelopes abstracted the tokens held inside. Abstract numbers are the culmination of the process, following the invention of writing. 'For example, the number of token shapes which was limited to about 12 around 7500 BC, increased to some 350 around 3500 BC, when urban workshops started contributing to the redistribution economy. Some of the new tokens stood for raw materials such as wool and metal while others represented finished products, among them textiles, garments, jewelry, bread, beer and honey.[139]

The token shape used for 'metal' continues to be used as a hieroglyph on Indus writing. Source: "Catalogue de l'exposition: LUT/xabis 'Shahdad'- Premier Symposium Annuel de la recherche Archéologique en Iran, Festival de la Culture et des arts, 1972," and published in Tehran. The text on p. 20 (French portion of the publication) identifies the bulla (No. 54 in the catalogue) as "Boule en terre cuite rouge creuse qui contient des cailloux. Décor estampé. Diam: 6 cm, Xabis "Shahdad" Kerman. 2ème moité du IV mill. av. J.-C. No. F.258/48."

The philosophical framework of analysis, updates the evidences provided in *Indus Script Cipher* and *Meluhha – A visible language* in the context of the rediscovery of a language which was called Meluhha/Mleccha in the archaeological contexts of India (Sarasvati-Sindhu civilization), Ancient Near East and Fertile Crescent. Did words of this language find expression in symbolic forms of writing? What did the symbolic forms 'mean'?

To unravel the cultural context of formation and evolution of symbolic forms, philosophical reflections on thought or consciousness provide some insights. One such reflection in the Indian tradition is: *aham brahmāsmi* 'brahman (supreme divinity) manifests in every *ātman*.' The meaning of the two symbolic forms -- *brahman, ātman* -- have to be experienced in a cultural context, transmitted from generation to generation by the ancestors.

Language is not a satisfactory medium to communicate the experience of brahman which has to be realized in one's private language. This is elaborated in Appendix H: Interpretation of Māyā's dream in Bauddham..

This is evidence of the application of the philosophy of symbolic forms pointing to the reality that cultural contexts provide 'areal universals' of hieroglyphs signifying human sounds of language (words, in this instance) due to the intervention of *sphōṭa* 'bursting forth'.

A girl in our family is pregnant. The life-form in her womb is already alive; the heart is beating, externally audible through a stethoscope.

Neuroscience tells us that the child in the womb can also register external sounds. Tomorrow is the उदक शान्ति संस्कार of Indian tradition, sprinkling water rendered sacred with अभिमन्त्रणम् squeezing in some banyan tree leaves juice in her nostrils and a porcupine quill placed in such a way as to have the tip of this touching her navel and possibly impacting cognitive/memory of life developing in the womb. What is going on here? Mirroring consciousness by mimicry of reality of water, banyan juice and porcupine quill to communicate with the unfolding life-form?

What is the reality in this unfolding event of a life-form? It is debatable if the inadequate disciplines of quantum physics or DNA studies can provide the answer to this unreality. It is like Māyā's dream which announces the descent of the elephant in mother Māyā's womb, which turns out to be the *okkanti* ('descent, appearance' – attested in an ancient epigraph) of Gautama, the Buddha. (See Appendix H: Interpretation of Māyā's dream in Bauddham). Meluhha language and Meluhha hieroglyph writing system provide the leads to unravel the philosophy of symbolic forms in 'areal universals'. [The 'areal universals' are consistent with the ongoing investigations in cognitive sciences which even suggest a paradigm change in language studies by focusing on cultural contexts of specific languages, rather than walking up the garden path of identifying 'universal grammar'. 'Areal' is a term used in the context of the reality of Indian *sprachbund* which enables the re-disovery of Meluhha language semantics.] In symbology, a symbol is an energy evoking, and directing, agent. (Campbell, Joseph (2002). *Flight of the Wild Gander - The Symbol without Meaning*. California: New World Library. p. 143.) This *bole* "a throwing, a casting, the stroke of a missile, bolt, beam" is *sphōṭa* 'bursting forth'. This is contrasted in Indian linguistic theory elaborated by Bhartṛhari, starting with *brahma-kāṇḍa* treating symbolic forms as endowed with 'meaning'. The 'meaning' may emanate from *brahman* or from life-activity contexts, memory markers of life-experiences manifested in *ātman* – of the speaker/writer and of the listener/reader.

Absolute reality (*brahman*) is believed to manifest itself in several forms; logos (*vac*) being one of the most engaging of them. The Vedic seers and Upanishadic poets "apprehended" Absolute reality through intuitive imagination and inscribed it textually/orally in Chandas for the benefit of succeeding generations.

In *Tantravarttika*, Kumarila, a Mimamsa philosopher discusses mlechas engaged in *dṛṣṭārthavyavahāra* 'empirical transactions' in the professional domains of culture, astronomy or drama. Not all *mleccha* words (many *deśī* words), in actual use, need be derived from Sanskrit roots and many mleccha words do get incorporated in *parole* or Prākṛts. Sanskrit also borrows Prākṛt forms of subject-object-verb order and uses *iti*. This usage is a borrowing from Prākṛt which allows only direct discourse. A quote is therefore followed by *iti* in Sanskrit.

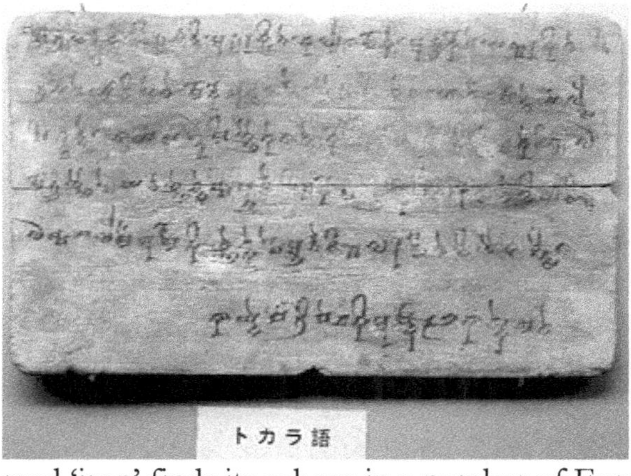

Munda word, med 'iron' finds its echoes in a number of European languages: мед [Med] *Bulgarian* медзь [medz'] *Belarusian* měď *Czech* Miedź *Polish* медь [Med'] *Russian* meď *Slovak*

мідь [mid'] *Ukrainian* – all meaning 'copper'; *midnycia* 'copper bowl'. Ṛgveda *amśu* finds its cognate in *ancu* 'iron' (Tocharian).
Tocharian languages known from the manuscripts of 6th to 8th centurie were a branch of the Indo-European family. Many Tocharians migrated to Bactria in the second century BCE and later to northwest India as Yuezhi to found the Kushan empire. The term Tocharian is derived from Old Persian tuxāri-, Khotanese ttahvāra and Sanskrit tukhāra. It also refers to Takhar province of Afghanistan.
Wooden plate with inscriptions in the Tocharian language. Kucha, China, 5th–8th century. Tokyo National Museum.

A gloss identifiable as part of mleccha repertoire occurs in Rigveda and in Tocharian. The word is ancu. Rigveda refers to cognate amśu as a synonym of Soma. Tocharian attests *ancu* as meaning, 'iron'.[140]

Lubotsky, Alexander opines[141] that *ancu*, 'soma plant' is the substratum source of Vedic amśu; Late Av. Asu 'Soma/Haoma plant'. Vedic *amśu*, 'twigs, sprigs, stalks' are units of Soma. TS I.2.11a cited in ŚB III.4.3.19): *amśur-- amśuṣ ṭe deva somāpyāyatām indrāyaikadhanavide*, 'let stalk after stalk of thine swell strong, O divine Soma, for Indra, the winner of one part of the booty!' In metonymy, the word amśu refers to the entire holy soma material. In Tocharian A we have **añcu*, 'iron'; derived *añcwāṣi*, 'made of iron'. This corresponds with Toch. B *eñcuwo*, adjective eñcuwaññe, 'made of iron'. These words and related semantics occur in Sanskrit *ayas* 'iron, metal.' In Tocharian B *yasa* (A *was*) 'gold'. Pinault notes that Vālakhilya hymn (RV VIII.53.4c: *śīṣṭeṣu cit te madirāso amśavah*) indicates that Soma processing also extended to non-Aryans with the use of śīṣṭa- with variants śīṣṭra-, śīrṣṭra-, with intrusive –r- (Kuiper, FBJ, 1991, Aryans in the Rigveda, Leiden Studies in Indo-European, I, Amsterdam/Atlanta: Rodopi.: 7, 70).

A hypothesis is postulated that the donor language for these forms of *amśu* is mleccha (meluhha).

The forms go back to CTocharian *oeñuwō which has no convincing IE etymology. Cognates are Chorasmian hncw, 'iron', 'iron tip' < Iranian *anśuwan. The reasoned conjecture is that the Tocharian words may be traceable to a common substratum language. The CTocharian word can be explained if the semantics of soma, amśu are related to electrum processing in incessant fire of about 1500 degrees centigrade continuously for 5 days and nights in *ati-rātra* of *soma yajña.*

Tushara (tukhara, tocharoi) were mleccha located in northwest India. MBh (1:85) refers to mleccha as descendants of Anu (Anavas), one of the sons of King Yayati. Yayati eldest son Yadu (of Yadavas) and youngest son Puru (of Pauravas) are part of Kurus and Panchalas. Anava migrated to Iran and settled in Bactria and were called Tushara. This could be a reference to Tocharistan/Tokharistan/Tukharistan of Tocharians/ Tokharians/Yuezhi. They are the same people who used surnames Thakurs/Tagores/Thakkars/Thackerays. Tushara (Tocharoi) are associated with Saka (Indo-Scythians), Yavana/Yona (Indo-Greeks) and Bahlika (Bactria). The phrase used is: saka yavana tushara bahlikaśca. (*AV-Par* 57.2.5). These are people of Uttarapatha, Dasyu. (MBh. 12.65.13-15). Tushara, together with Bahlika, Kirata, Pahlava, Parada, Darada, Kamboja, Saka, Kanka, Romaka, Yavana, Trigarta, Kshudraka, Malava, Anga, Vanga brought gifts to Yudhishthira. (MBh. 2.51-2.53; 3.51). Many including Tukhara also brought millions of gold. (MBh. 2:50). Rājasūya of Yudhiṣṭhira (MBh. 3:51) records the presence of Pahlava, Darada, Kirata, Yavana, Sakra, Harahuna, Tukhara, Sindhava, Jaguda, Ramatha, Tangana, Kekaya, Malava, Munda and inhabitants of Kāśmīra.

The vernacular turns out to be Meluhha of Indian *sprachbund.* The concept of *sprachbund* in the Indian context is accepted given the common language traits among all Indian language families: for e.g. the feature of 're-duplication' in utterances. This linguistic insight is matched by cognitive-science-based researches in linguistics: "The recent work (in cognitive sciences) points to linguistic diversity at every level, with family resemblances largely accounted for by common cultural descent." (Levinson, S. C. (2009). Rethinking the language sciences. Talk presented at the Symposium on 'Why aren't the social sciences Darwinian?'. Cambridge, UK. 2009-05-15.) Appendix I: *Sphōṭavāda* critiques Levinson's arguments using the 'areal' context of Indian sprachbund and Indian theory of *sphōṭa.*

The finds of seals with hieroglyphs of Indus writing in stratified contexts in some Sumerian cities led archaeologists to identify presence of individuals or groups from Sarasvati-Sindhu civilization. CJ Gadd published a paper in 1932 on 'Indian style' seals based on such finds. These examples are now seen to represent a corpus of Dilmunite epigraphs from Gulf islands of Failaka and Bahrain linking a sea-route, say from Dwaraka to Ur. Symbolic forms of animals shown on such epigraphs had vivid similarities with thousands of inscriptions unearthed in Sarasvati-Sindhu civilization 'areal' sites. These finds reinforced the Meluhha symbolic forms as belonging to the Bronze Age. The hypothesis of this book is premised on the identification of Meluhhans settled in Mesopotamia or Ancient Near East in 3rd millennium BCE.

Question of Meluhhan communities in Ancient Near East

There is universal acceptance among archaeologists that Meluhha was the coastal area in the Sarasvati-Sindhu civilization domain. There is also evidence that Meluhha was a language different from Akkadian. A cylinder, described on a cuneiform text, Su-ilisu as a 'Meluhha interpreter' signifying that the language required interpretation into Akkadian. "…the textual evidence dealing with individuals qualified as 'men' or 'sons' of Meluhha or called with the ethnonym Meluhha, living in Mesopotamia and of a 'Meluhha village' established at Lagash (and presumably at other major cities as well) unescapably points to the existence of enclaves settled by Indian immigrants (see Parpola et al. 1977; Possehl 1984: 185; for the original debate Lamberg-Karlovsky 1972)…Sargon claimed with pride that under his power Meluhhan ships docked at his capital, and at least one tablet mentions a person with an Akkadian name qualified as 'the holder of a Meluhha ship.'..according to literary sources, between the end of the 3rd and the beginning of the 2nd millennium BCE Meluhhan ships exported to Mesopotamia precious goods among which exotic animals, such as dogs, perhaps peacocks, cocks, bovids, elephants, precious wood and royal furniture, precious stones such as carnelian, agate and lapislazuli, and metls like gold, silver and tin. In his famous inscriptions, Gudea, in the second half of the 22nd century BCE, states that Meluhhans came with wood and other raw materials for the construction of the main temple in Lagash. Archaeologically, the most evident raw materials imported from India are marine shell, used for costly containers and lamps, inlay works and cylinder seals; agate, carnelian and quite possibly ivory. Hard green stones, including garnets and abrasives might also have been imported from the Subcontinent and eastern Iran. Carnelian could have been importe in form of raw nodules of large size (as implied by some texts) to be transformed into long beads, or as finished products…recent studies would better suggest that the Indus families in Mesopotaia imported raw materials rather than finished beads, and expediently adapted their production to the changing needs of Mesopotamian demand and markets. To the same period is ascribed a famous cylinder seal owned by a certain Su-ilisu, 'Meluhhan interpreter'. Another Akkadian text records that Lu-sunzida 'a man of Meluhha' paid to the servant Urur, son of Amarlu KU 10 shekels of silver as payment for a tooth broken in a clash. The name Lu-sunzida literally means 'Man of the just buffalo cow,' a name that, although rendered in Sumerian, according to the authors does not make sense in a Mesopotamian cultural sphere, and must be a translation of an Indian name…By Ur III times, this intense trade had definitely promoted the formation of local enclaves of Indus origin…Lagash settlement… the ethnic name points to a settlement originally founded as a trade enclave by foreign merchants. The texts indicate that Meluhhans were perceived as distinct ethnic group, living in a separate settlement but largely integrated in the contemporary Sumerian society, owning or renting land and accumulating and variously distributing their agricultural products…"[142]

'Fish' hieroglyph on Susa pot connotes alloy metal

A miniature, incised tablet from Harappa h329A has a fish-shaped tablet with two signs: fish + arrow (which combination was also pronounced as *ayaskāṇḍa* on a *bos indicus* seal Kalibangan032).

The dotted circle (eye) is decoded rebus as *kaṇ* 'aperture' (Tamil); kāṇū hole (Gujarati) (i.e. glyph showing dotted-circle); kāṇa 'one eye' and these glyphs may have been interpreted as the 'fish-eyes' or 'eye stones' (Akkadian IGI-HA, IGI-KU6) mentioned in Mesopotamian texts. ayo 'fish' 9Mu.); rebus: aya = iron (G.); ayah, ayas = metal (Skt.) kaṇi 'stone' (Kannada) கன்[1] kaṉ Copper (Tamil) கன்[2] kaṉ , n. < கல். stone (Tamil) खडा (Marathi) is 'metal, nodule, stone, lump'. *kaṇi* 'stone' (Kannada) with Tadbhava *khaḍu. khaḍu, kaṇ* 'stone/nodule (metal)'. . Ga. (Oll.) kanḍ, (S.) kanḍu (pl. kanḍkil) stone (DEDR 1298). These could be the substratum glosses for *kāṇḍa* in ayas *kāṇḍa* 'excellent iron' (Pan.) 'metal tools, pots and pans and metal-ware'. h329A has a fish-shaped tablet with two signs: fish + arrow (which has been decoded as *ayaskāṇḍa* on a *bos indicus* seal). The 'fish-eye' is a reinforcement of the gloss *kāṇḍ*'stone/nodule (metal)'. The dotted circle (eye) is decoded rebus as *kaṇ* 'aperture' (Tamil); kāṇū hole (Gujarati) (i.e. glyph showing dotted-circle); kāṇa 'one eye' and these glyphs may have been interpreted as the 'fish-eyes' or 'eye stones' (Akkadian IGI-HA, IGI-KU6) mentioned in Mesopotamian texts. The commodities denoted may be nodules of mined stones/nodules of chalcopyrite. See Annex. 'Eye stones' elucidating, based on textual and archaeological contexts, that 'fish-eyes' do NOT refer to pearls. While one surmises that they refer to agate stones, it can be evidenced that the glyphs of 'dotted circles' denoting 'fish-eyes' or 'antelope-eyes', refer to 'stone/nodules of mineral (perhaps, chalcopyrite)' or 'tools, pots and pans and metal-ware', decoded rebus as *kāṇḍ* as in *ayaskāṇḍa* 'excellent iron'.

Metal tools, pots and pans found in the Susa pot. Old Elamite period. ca. 2400-2300 BCE.

Picture of Susa pot (cf. Maurizio Tosi) is, in my view, a 'rosetta stone' of Indus script. The 'fish' hieroglyph painted below the rim of the pot conveys 'meaning' associating the symbolic form of 'fish' word semantics evidenced by the contents of the pot: alloyed metalware – tools, weapons, pots and pans. The scribe has conveyed, deploying the 'fish' hieroglyph that the symbolic form signifies alloyed metal.

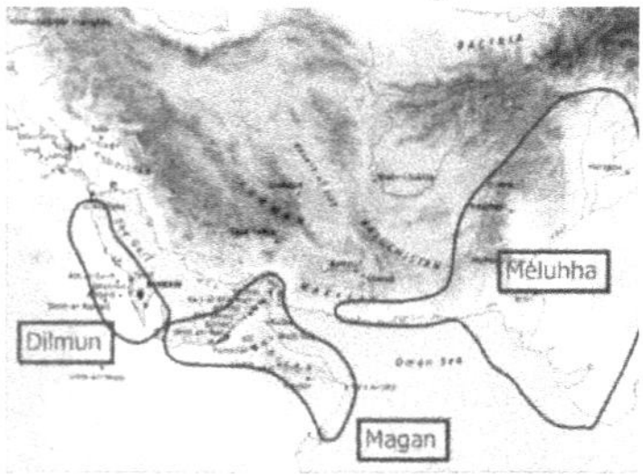

The pot and its contents had perhaps originated from Meluhha since the pot had a 'fish' glyph inscribed. I suggest that this Indus script glyph conveyed the message from Indus artisans to merchant associates of Susa, that the pot had 'metal' contents. The glyph is read rebus in *mleccha* (cognate, *meluhha*), the underlying Indus language. *ayo* 'fish'; rebus: *ayo* 'metal'. With this decoding framework of Indus script cipher, the ligatured-fish glyphs can also be read in the context of metal artifacts archaeologically attested of the bronze-age civilization.

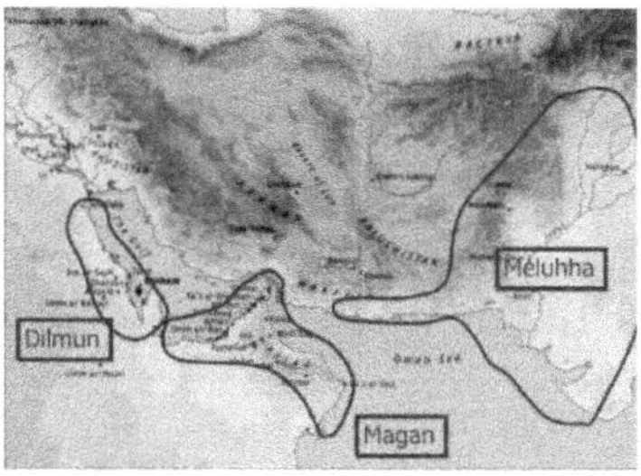

Combination of 'fish' glyph and 'four-short-linear-strokes' circumgraph also pronounced the same text *ayaskāṇḍa* on another *bos indicus* seal m1118. This seal uses circumgraph of four short linear strokes which included a morpheme which was pronounced variantly as *gaṇḍa* 'four' (Santali). Alternate rebus reading: ayas (alloy metal) (from) a furnace (fire-altar), *kaṇḍa* "furnace, fire-altar'. (Hieroglyph: *gaṇḍa* 'four' short linear strokes used as circumscript).

Alternative is to read the circumgraph of four linear strokes used on m1118 Mohenjo-daro seal as an allograph for 'arrow' glyph used on h329A Harappa tablet. *kāṇḍa* 'arrow' *khāṇḍā* 'metalware'.

Some glyphs used in the writing were combined to form words which sounded like the glyphs. For example, the glyph 'arrow' sounded like the word kāṇḍa which also expressed meaning in a similar sounding word: Pa. *khaṇḍa* -- ' broken (usu. of teeth) ', m.n. ' piece ', °*ḍikā* -- f. ' broken bit, stick '; Pk. *khaṁḍa* -- m.n., °*ḍiā* -- f. ' piece '; P. *khannā* adj. ' half ', °*nī* f. ' piece '; Ku.*dwī* -- *khan* ' two halves ', *khānuṛo* ' piece '; B. *khān*, °*nā*, °*ni* ' piece, article (as a determinative) ' ; Bhoj. *khā̃ṛā* ' piece '; K. *khaṇḍarun* ' to break in pieces '; H. *khaṇḍar* ' broken ', m. ' hole, pit ', *khā̃ṛar* ' dilapidated ', m. ' broken ground, chasm, hole ' (CDIAL 3792). *gaṇḍa*-- m. ' piece, part ' (Buddhist Hybrid Sanskrrit), which also meant 'four' to be represented by four short linear strokes. The 'arrow' glyph was combined with another 'fish' glyph which was pronounced *ayo*, 'fish' to create the text *ayaskāṇḍa* 'metal piece, part'.

The hieroglyphic use of 'fish' glyph on Indus writing resolves the transactions related 'fish-eyes' traded between Ur and Meluhha mentioned in cuneiform texts as related to ayas 'fish' and *khoṭ*f 'alloyed metal':
A 'hole' or a 'diotted-circle' glyph may denote a word which was pronounced *khoṭ*f 'alloyed metal':

खोट [khōṭa] *f* A mass of metal (unwrought or of old metal melted down); an ingot or wedge. Hence खोटसाळ [khōṭasāḷa] *a* (खोट & साळ from शाला) Alloyed--a metal. (Marathi)
Bshk. *khoṭ* 'embers', Phal. *khūṭo* 'ashes, burning coal'; L. *khoṭ*f 'alloy, impurity', °*ṭā* 'alloyed', awāṇ. *khoṭā* 'forged'; P. *khoṭ* m. 'base, alloy' M.*khoṭā* 'alloyed' (CDIAL 3931)

Kor. (O.) goḍe a rat's hole (DEDR 1660). Pk. *kōḍara* -- , *kōla*°, *kōṭa*°, *koṭṭa*° n. ' hole, hollow '; Or. *koraṛa* ' hollow in a tree, cave, hole '; H. (X *khōla -- 2) *khoḍar* m. ' pit, hollow in a tree ', *khoṛrā* m.; Si.*kovuḷa* ' rotten tree ' (< **kōḷalla* -- with H. Smith JA 1950, 197, but not < Pa. *kōḷāpa* --). (CDIAL 3496). Thus, the 'dotted circle' glyph may be distinguished from a 'wort' glyph (which is a blob or small lump). The dotted circle denotes and is an allograph hieroglyph signifying: *khoṭā* 'alloyed' (metal). Thus, when a dotted circle is infixed onto the bottom vessel or portable furnace of the standard device (which has the lathe, gimlet on top register), the intent is to denote that the artisan-turner working on alloyed metal artifacts.

[quote] The suggestion that 'fish-eyes' (IGI.HA, IGI-KU6), imported through Ur, may have been pearls has been advanced by a number of scholars. 'Fish-eyes' were among a number of valuable commodities (gold, copper, lapis lazuli, stone beads) offered in thanksgiving at the temple of the Sumerian goddess Ningal at Ur by seafaring merchants who had returned safely from Dilmun and perhaps further afield. Elsewhere they are said to have been bought in Dilmun. Whether 'fish-eyes' differed from 'fish-eye stones' (NA4 IGI.HA, NA4 IGI-KU6) and from simply 'eye-stones' is not entirely clear. The latter are included among goods imported from Meluhha (NA4 IGI-ME-LUH-HA) ca. 1816-1810 BCE and ca. 1600-1570 BCE. Any pearls from Meluhha – probably coastal Baluchistan-Sind – would have been generally inferior to those from Dilmun itself. It has been strongly argued that 'fish-eyes', 'fish-eye stones' and 'eye-stones' in Old Babylonian and Akkadian texts were not in fact pearls, but rather (a) etched cornelian beads, imported from India and/or (b) pebbles of banded agate, cut to resemble closely a black/brown pupil and white cornea. The nearest source of good agate is in northwest India, which would accord with supplies obtained from Meluhha. 'Eye-stones' of agate were undoubtedly treasured: some were inscribed and used as amulets, others have been found in votive deposits. Perhaps pearls were at times included among 'fish-eyes,' if not 'fish-eye stones'. More likely, however, the word for 'pearl' is among the 'more than 800 terms in the lexical lists of stones and gems [that] remain to be identified.[unquote][143]

Banawali 3 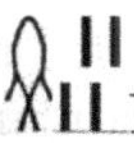 Banawali Seal Bull ID 3692
kõdā 'young bull' Rebus: kõdā 'turn on a lathe'; kõdār 'turner' working on a workshop (koḍ *'horn' Rebus:*

koḍa *'workshop')*, alloy metal (aya 'fish') + arrow (Rebus: *khāṇḍā* 'metalware'). The pair of two short linear strokes comparable to the 'circumscript' deployed on some hieroglyph compositions may signify: Hieroglyph 1: *gaṇḍa* 'four' Rebus: *kaṇḍa* "furnace, fire-altar' or Hieroglyph 2: *khaḍā* 'circumscribe' (Marathi); Rebus: *khaḍā* 'nodule (ore), stone' (Marathi). Thus the set of hieroglyphs composing the message on Banawali 3 seal: Turner workshop (for) metalware (with) a furnace (fire-altar), *kaṇḍa* "furnace, fire-altar'.

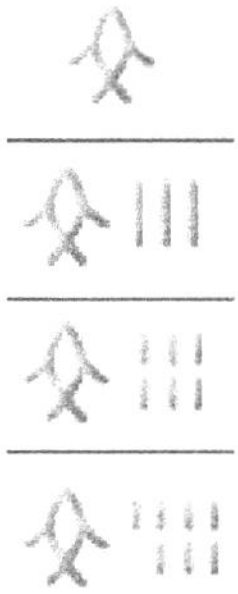

kāṇḍa 'arrow' (Skt.); rebus: *kāṇḍa* 'iron' as in *ayaskāṇḍa* 'excellent metal' (Pāṇini. Sanskrit)

A significant number of incised miniature tablets of Harappa have the following types of frequently deployed hieroglyph sequences:

1. 'Fish' hieroglyph' associated with short numeral linear strokes of 3, 6, or 7.

U |
U | |
U | | |
U | | | |

2. 'U' or 'Rimless broad-mouthed pot' hieroglyph associated with short numeral linear strokes from 1 to 7.

U-hieroglyph may connote *kọ̃ṇḍu* m. ' large cooking pot '(Kashmiri) Rebus: *kõdā* 'to turn in a lathe' (B.) कोंद *kōnda* 'engraver, lapidary setting or infixing gems' (Marathi) One, two, three or four short linear strokes may convey 'meanigns' rendered by rebus readings:

koḍa 'one' Rebus: *koḍ* 'workshop' U + 'one' = *koḍ* 'workshop' + *kõdā* 'to turn in a lathe'. The token containing such incised miniature tablets may be meant to be conveyed from workers' platforms into the smithy, forge (or, artisans' workshop).

sangaḍa 'two' Rebus: *sangaḍa* 'fortification' or jangaḍa 'entrustment article' + *kõdā* 'to turn in a lathe'.(that is, artifacts turned in a lathe to be inventoried in fortification or inscribed on seal as 'entrustment articles' for onward trade consignment). *sang* 'stone', *gaḍa 'large stone'.*

kolmo 'three' Rebus: *kolami* 'smithy, forge' + *kõdā* 'to turn in a lathe'. (that is, artifacts turned in a lathe and sent into the smithy, forge workshop for further forging or inscription activity).

ganḍa 'four' Rebus: ka*nḍa 'furnace, fire-altar'* + *kõdā* 'to turn in a lathe'. (that is, artifacts turned in a lathe to be subjected to furnace firing in a furnace).

The U-hieroglyph infixed into a structural form. The 'U' glyphic is a semantic determinant to emphasise that this is a temple with a smithy furnace and a consecrated fire-pit. The structural form within which this 'U' glyphic is enclosed may represent a temple: kole.l 'temple, smithy' (Ko.); kolme smithy' (Ka.) The structural form (*sangaḍa* 'frame of a building') within which this sign is enclosed may represent a temple: kole.l 'temple, smithy' (Ko.); kolme smithy' (Ka.) The ligatured sign may thus be read: *sangaḍa kunḍ* to mean 'entrustment articles (of) consecrated fire-altar or furnace (of) temple'. *sang* 'stone', *gaḍa 'large stone'.*

khaḍā 'circumscribe' (M.); Rebs: khaḍā 'nodule (ore), stone' (M.)

ayo 'fish'; rebus: ayas 'metal, iron' (Pan.Skt.) aḍaren, ḍaren lid, cover (Santali)

Rebus: aduru 'native metal' (Ka.) This may also signify a guild given the Meluhha glosses relatable to the ^ superscript hieroglyph: Woṭ. šen ' roof ', Bshk. šan, Phal. šān(AO xviii 251) Rebus: seṇi (f.) [Class. Sk. śreṇi in meaning "guild"; Vedic= row] Thus, the glyphic composition reads: stone-metal-guild khaḍā ayas seṇi (glyphic: circumscribe+fish+roof). An alternative reading of four short linear strokes deployed as a 'circumscript' is to read rebus: *gaṇḍa* 'four' (Santali) Rebus 1: *kaṇḍ* fire-altar, furnace' (Santali) Rebus 2: खांडा [*khāṇḍā*] ' tools, pots and pans and metal-ware'. Thus the entire hieroglyphic composition of hieroglyph components may signify the meaning: guild (or artisans making) (native) metal alloy metalware.

Fish + scales aya ãs (amśu) 'metllic stalks of stone ore. *ãs*, cognate with *añc* 'iron' (Tocharian) may be a determinative of 'iron' as the 'metal'. Hence, the ligatured glyph may connote 'iron or stony metal'.

Fish + notch: *ayo* 'fish'+ खांडा [khāṇḍā] *m* A jag, notch, or indentation (as upon the edge of a tool or weapon). Rebus: khāṇḍa 'tools, pots and pans, and metal-ware'. *ayaskāṇḍa* is a compounde word attested in Pāṇini.

Hieroglyph: *ayo, hako* 'fish'; a~s = scales of fish (Santali). Rebus: aya = iron (G.); ayah, ayas = metal (Skt.) <ayu?>(A) {N} ``^fish". #1370. <yO>\\<AyO>(L) {N} ``^fish". #3612. <kukkulEyO>,,<kukkuli-yO>(LMD) {N} ``prawn". !Serango dialect. #32612. <sArjAjyO>,,<sArjAj>(D) {N} ``prawn". #32622. <magur-yO>(ZL) {N} ``a kind of ^fish". *Or.<>. #32632. <ur+Gol-Da-yO>(LL) {N} ``a kind of ^fish". #32642.<bal.bal-yO>(DL) {N} ``smoked fish". #15163.

| | | Three long linear strokes have a word to signify numeral three or a visible count of three. This visible representation signifies the gloss: *kolom* 'three' Rebus: *kolami* 'smithy, forge'. An allograph to represent the gloss: kolom is a sapling, seedling: *kolmo* cutting, graft; to graft, engraft, prune; kolma hoṛo = a variety of the paddy plant (Desi)(Santali.) Rebus: *kolimi* 'smithy, forge' (Telugu) *kolom* = Rebus: *kolami* 'smithy, forge'.

This hieroglyph is also modified by a superfix of notch of one or two short linear strokes to signify more specific meaning:

 "खांडा [*khāṇḍā*] 'tools, pots and pans and metal-ware' (from) *kolami* 'smithy, forge'. An alternative meaning representation is also possible for the hieroglyph of two short linear strokes: "*sal* 'splinter' Rebus: *sal* 'workshop'. With this

 signification, the combined two hieroglyphs read rebus: *kolami sal* 'smithy, forge workshop'.

Functions of tablets and seals: an archeological context

Examples of 22 duplicates steatite triangular tablets h-2218 to h-2239 were excavated in an archaeological context by HARP Project144. Tablets were tallies of products from workers' platforms. Seals were consolidated data from tablets to prepre bills of lading or 'entrustment notes', *jangaḍa*, for approval. *sang* 'stone', *gaḍa 'large stone'*.

h2219A First side of three-sided tablet

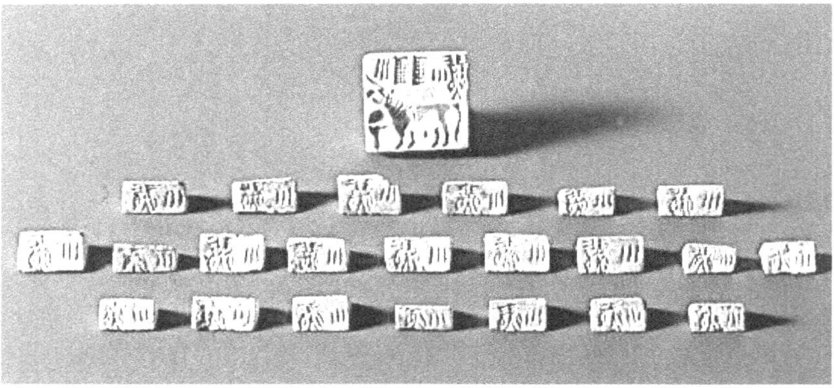

h2219B Second side of three-sided tablet

h2219C Third side of three-sided tablet

The two glyphs which appear on the h2219A example also appear on a seal. "In a street deposit of similar age just inside the wall, a seal was found with two of the same characters as seen on one side of the tablets."

h1682A. The seal which contained the two glyphs used on the 'tally' three-sided tablets. The seal showed a one-horned heifer + standard device and two segments of inscriptions: one segment showing the two glyphs shown on one side of the 'tally' tablet; the other segment showing glyphs of a pair of 'rectangle with divisions' + 'three long linear strokes'.

Treating each side of a tablet as a token information presented from the workers' platforms to the storehouse. The seal h1682

can be taken as a bulla prepared in a storehouse, consolidating information on two sides of the tablet. With the bossed reverse which has a hole, the seals can be strung together to constitute a bill of lading consolidated information for a consignment from the storehouse.

The first set of glyphs may connote furnace output (accounted smelted metal) delivered to smithy.

The second set of glyphs may connote ingots (cast metal) delivered to smithy.

These duplicated inscriptions on tablets found indicates that there was a differentiation among professions, say between workers working on working platforms and using tablets to document delivery of products for 'approval' as entrustment notes --*jangaḍ* and the scribes documenting the furnace accounts. Such tablets delivered by the artisans will be compiled into seals by scribes to describe the consolidated consignment. The seal impressions could then be used as tallies or accompaniments to bills of lading of a consignment entrusted to a courier, *jangaḍiyo.* Such seal impressions constituted enrustment notes of the package: *jangaḍ.*] *sang* 'stone', *gaḍa 'large stone'.*

Tablets (tokens) strung together as bullae

Another archaeological context demonstrating the functions of strings of tablets to constitute a bulla comes from the finds of Kanmer.

In the Elam-Susa-Mesopotamia interaction area of Ancient Near East and Meluhha, tokens designed to count goods evolved into hieroglyphs to represent words which constitution information transferred on the bronze-age goods and processes. This stage of rebus representation of sounds of words of meluhha (mleccha language) was the stage penultimate to the culminating stage which used representation of syllables graphically in kharoṣṭī and brāhmī scripts. This culmination of the process for literacy and civilization was the contribution made by artisans of the bronze-age of Indus-Sarasvati civilization (also called Harappan or Indus civilization).

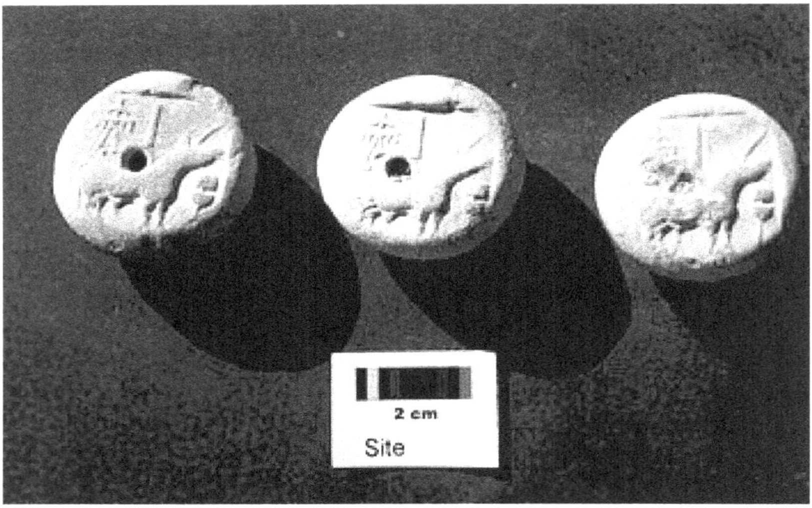

An evidence comes from Kanmer, for the use of tablets created with duplicate seal impressions. These tablets may have been used as category tallies of lapidary workshops.[145]

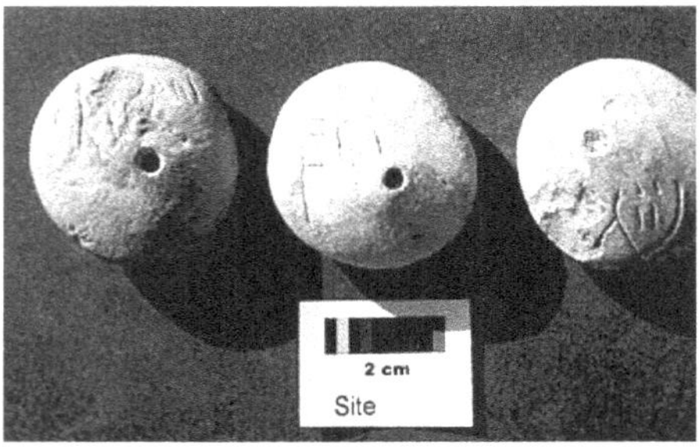

Alternative reading for the ligaturing element, if interpreted as hoe or spade: Hieroglyph: *kaṇṭhāla* 'a hoe, spade' (Sanskrit) Hieroglyph/Rebus:

†*kaṇṭhāla* कण्ठाल -- *m.* a boat , ship (Sanskrit) [kaṇṭhá --] *kā̃ṭhāḷ* 'maritime'(Gujarati) (CDIAL 2682a). Thus, an alternative reading rebus – boat-load cargo of iron stone (ore), alloy: *kā̃ṭhāḷ* 'boat' with *meḍ kāḍ* 'iron stone (ore)'. *koḍa 'one' Rebus: koḍ* 'workshop' or *khoṭ* 'alloy'.

It is a category mistake to call these as 'seals'. These are three duplicate tablets created with seal impressions (glyphs: one-horned heifer, standard device, PLUS two text inscription glyphs (or 'signs' as written characters): one long linear stroke, ligatured glyph of body + 'harrow' glyph. There are perforations in the center of these duplicate seal impressions which are tablets and which contained identical inscriptions. It appears that three duplicates of seal impressions -- as tablets -- were created using the same seal.

Obverse of these tiny 2 cm. dia. tablets show some incised markings. It is unclear from the markings if they can be compared with any glyphs of the Indus script corpora. They may be 'personal' markings like 'potter's marks' – designating a particular artisan's workshop (working platform) or considering the short numerical strokes used, the glyphs may be counters (numbers or liquid or weight measures). More precise determination may be made if more evidences of such glyphs are discovered. Excavators surmise that the three tablets with different motifs on the obverse of the three tablets suggest different users/uses. They may be from different workshops of the same guild but as the other side of the tables showed, the product taken from three workshops is the same.

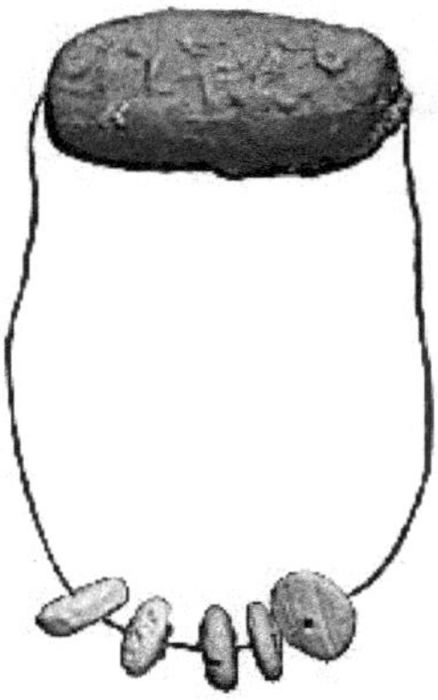

Decoding of the identical inscription on the three tablets of Kanmer.

Hieroglyph: One long linear stroke. koḍa 'one' (Santali) Rebus: koḍ 'artisan's workshop' (Kuwi) Glyph: meḍ 'body' (Mu.) Rebus: meḍ 'iron' (Ho.) Ligatured glyph : aḍar 'harrow' Rebus: aduru 'native metal' (Kannada). Thus the glyphs can be read rebus. Glyph: koḍiyum 'heifer' (G.) Rebus: koḍ 'workshop (Kuwi) Glyph: sangaḍa 'lathe' (Marathi) Rebus 1: Rebus 2: sangaḍa 'association' (guild). Rebus 2: sangatarāsu 'stone cutter' (Telugu). The output of the lapidaries is thus described by the three tablets: *aduru meḍ sangaḍa koḍ* 'iron, native metal guild workshop'.

Appendix A: *tagar* symbolic forms

Ta. takaram tin, white lead, metal sheet, coated with tin. *Ma.* takaram tin, tinned iron plate. *Ko.* tagarm (*obl.* tagart-) tin. *Ka.* tagara, tamara, tavara id. *Tu.* tamarů, tamara, tavara id. *Te.* tagaramu, tamaramu, tavaramu id. *Kuwi* (Isr.) ṭagromi tin metal, alloy. / Cf. Skt. tamara- id. (DEDR 3001).

Ta. taṅkam pure gold, that which is precious, of great worth. *Ma.* taṅkam pure gold. / ? < Skt. ṭaṅka- a stamped (gold) coin.(DEDR 3013).

ṭaṅgaṇa -- a tribe (Sanskrit)

Ta. takaram wax-flower dog-bane, *Tabernae montana*; aromatic unguent for the hair, fragrance. *Ma.* takaram *T. coronaria.* *Ka.* tagara id. / Cf. Skt. sthakara-, sthagara-, tagara, tagaraka-; Pali tagara-; Pkt. ṭagara-, tagara-. (DEDR 3002). tagara1 n. ' the shrub Tabernaemontana coronaria and a fragrant powder obtained from it ' Kauś., °*aka*<-> VarBr̥S. [Cf. *sthagara* -- , *sthakara* -- n. ' a partic. fragrant powder ' TBr.] Pa. *tagara* -- n., Dhp. *takara;* Pk. *tagara* -- , *ṭayara* -- m. ' a kind of tree, a kind of scented wood '; Si. *tuvara, tōra* ' a species of Cassia plant. ' (CDIAL 5622). tagaravallī f. ' Cassia auriculata ' Npr. [tagara -- 1, vallī --]
Si. *tuvaralā* ' an incense prepared from a species of Tabernaemontana '.(CDIAL 5624).

Ta. takar sheep, ram, goat, male of certain other animals (yāḷi, elephant, shark). *Ma.* takaran huge, powerful as a man, bear, etc. *Ka.* tagar, ṭagaru, ṭagara, ṭegaru ram. *Tu.*tagaru, ṭagarů id. *Te.* tagaramu, tagaru id. / Cf. Mar. tagar id. (DEDR 3000).

ṭagara1 ' squinting ' lex. [Cf. ṭēraka --] H. *ṭagrā* ' cross -- eyed '(CDIAL 5425). ṭēraka ' squinting ' lex. 2. *ḍēra -- 2. 3. *ḍhēra -- 3. [Cf. ṭagara -- 1, *trēḍḍa -- , kēkara --]1. Sh. *ṭēru̯* ' slanting, crooked, squinting '; P. *ṭīrā* ' squinting '; A. *ṭeruwā* ' squinting ', *ṭerā* ' crooked ' (or < *trēḍḍa --); B. *ṭera* ' squinting ', Or. *ṭerā*; Bi. *bhaũā̃ -- ṭer* ' bullock with crooked eyebrows '; H. *ṭerā* ' squinting '.2. Pk. *ḍēra --* ' squinting ', N. *ḍero*, *ḍeṛo* (X *ṭeṛo* < *trēḍḍa --), Bi. *bhaũā̃ -- ḍer*, (SMunger) °*rā* = *bhaũā̃ -- ṭer* above; Mth. *kana -- ḍēriā* ' having half -- closed eyes '; H. *ḍerā* ' squinting '.

3. WPah. bhal. *ḍher -- śiṅgo* m. ' bullock with hanging horns ', *ḍheru* m. ' bullock with one horn hanging down '; H. *ḍherā* ' squinting '; -- prob. H. *ḍherā* m. ' crosspiece of wood for threading yarn on '; P. *ḍhērā* m. ' instrument for twisting yarn ', S. *ḍhero* m. ' ball of thread '. A. *ṭerā* (phonet. *t --*) ' squint -- eyed ' (CDIAL 5474).

ṭaṅgaṇa1 m.n. ' borax ' lex., *ṭaṅkaṇa* -- 1 m. Kād., °*na-* m. lex. (*ṭaṅka* -- 7 m.n., *ṭaṅga* -- 5 m. lex.). 2. ṭagara -- 2 VarBr̥S. 1. Or. *ṭā̃gaṇā*; -- Kho. (Lor.) *danākār* ' borax, alum ' prob. ← Ir., cf. Pers. *tangār*. 2. Si. *ṭagara* ' borax ' (GS 53) ← Sk. (CDIAL 5437).

ṭaṅkaṇakṣāra m. ' borax ' Suśr. [ṭaṅkaṇa -- 1, kṣārá -- 1] M. *ṭā̃kaṇkhār* m. ' brute borax, tincal '. (CDIAL 5431) ṭaṅkaśālā -- , *ṭaṅkakaś*° f. ' mint ' lex. [ṭaṅka -- 1, śā́lā --]N. *ṭaksāl*, °*ār*, B. *ṭaksāl*, *ṭā̃k*°, *ṭek*°, Bhoj. *ṭaksār*, H. *ṭaksāl*, °*ār* f., G. *ṭā̃ksāḷ* f., M. *ṭā̃ksāl*, *ṭāk*°, *ṭā̃k*°, *ṭak*°. -- Deriv. G. *ṭaksāḷī* m. ' mint -- master ', M. *ṭāksāḷyā* m. Brj. *ṭaksāḷī*, °*sārī* m. ' mint -- master '.(CDIAL 5434)

ṭáṅkati1, *ṭaṅkáyati* ' ties ' Dhātup. 2. *ṭañcati.

1. S. *ṭākaṇu* ' to stitch ', *ṭā̃ko* m. ' a stitch '; Ku. *ṭā̃ko* ' sewing, joining, patch '; N. *ṭā̃knu* ' to join, tack, button up ', *ṭā̃ko* ' stitch, seam '; A. *ṭākiba* ' to tie loosely '; B. *ṭā̃kā* ' to stitch ', Or. *ṭāṅkibā*, *ṭāk* ' hand -- stitching '; Bhoj. *ṭā̃kal* ' to sew '; H. *ṭā̃knā* ' to stitch, join, rivet, solder ', *ṭā̃kā* m. ' stitch, join '; G. *ṭā̃kvũ* ' to stitch ', *ṭā̃kɔ* m., M. *ṭā̃kā*, *ṭākā* m.

2. G. *ṭā̃cvũ* ' to stitch ', *ṭā̃cṇī* f. ' small pin '; M. *ṭā̃cṇẽ*, *ṭāc*° ' to sew

lightly ', *ṭā̃c̣ṇī*, *ṭā̃c°* f. ' pin '. (CDIAL 5432). cf. *āṇī* 'pin, nail' (Tamil. Ṛgveda)

Ta. takai (-v-, -nt-) to stop, resist, check, deter, obstruct or forbid by oath, seize, take hold of, overpower, subdue, shut in, enclose, include, bind, fasten, yoke; (-pp-, -tt-) to check, resist, stop, deter, bind, fasten; *n.* binding, fastening, garland, obstruction, check, hindrance, armour, coat of mail; takaippu surrounding wall, fortress, palatial building, section of house, apartment, battle array of an army. *Ka.* taga, tagave, tagahu, tage delay, obstacle, hindrance, impediment; tage to stop, arrest, obstruct, impede, stun; tagar to be stopped or impeded, impede, etc. (DEDR 3006). *Ta.* takkai roll of palm leaves or plug put into a perforation of the ear to enlarge it, cork, roll of cloth or paper used as a cork, plug to stop up a crack, etc., sola pith, piece of pith attached to a fishing rod, clot, congealed mass, float,
raft; takkal plug. *Ma.* takka what is placed in the ear instead of an ornament, ivory, wood, etc. (DEDR 3012).

తాగు [tāgu] or త్రాగు *tāgu.* [Tel.] v. a. To drink. చుట్టతాగు to smoke

a cigar. తాగించు *tāginṭsu.* v. a. To cause to

drink. తాగునట్లుచేయు. తాగుబోతు *tāgu-bōtu.* n. A drunkard.

Pa. tāk- to walk; tākip- (tākit-) to make to walk. *Ga.* (Oll., S.) tāk- to walk. *Go.* (A. Y. Tr. W. Mu. Ma. S. Ko.) tāk-
id.; *caus.* (Tr.) tākstānā, (W.) tāksahtānā; (Y.) tākmaṛwalking (*Voc.* 1695). *Pe.* tāŋ(g)- (tāŋt-) to walk. *Manḍ.* tāŋ- id. *Kui* tāka (tāki-) id.; *n.* act of walking; ? (K.) tāŋgu (*pl.* tākaka)
hoof. *Kuwi* (F.) tākali, (S.) tākinai, (Isr.) tāk- (-it-) to walk. (DEDR 3151).

Ta. tākku (tākki-) to come in contact, collide, strike against as a vessel on a rock, be severe in reproof, attack, assault, strike, beat, dash, pounce upon, charge; *n.* attack, assault, dash, blow, clash; tākkam attack, assault, hit; tākkal striking, attacking, charging; tāṅku to hit against, strike. *Ma.* tākkuka to hit, touch, beat. *Ko.* ta·k- (ta·yk-) to touch with hand. *To.*to·k- (to·ky-) to touch (sacred bell in diary, of one who should not do so); shout with anger. *Ka.* tāku, tāgu, tāṅgu to come in contact with, touch, hit, strike or dash against, collide with, close with, attack; *n.* joining, touching; (PBh.) tāpu to hit, strike, attack. *Tu.* tākuni to hit, touch; tāguni id., to come in collision or contact with; tāgāvuni to cause to touch; tācuni, tāñcunito come into collision. *Te.* tāku to touch, hit, attack, encounter, oppose in battle; *n.* combat, attack; tākuḍu touch, contact; tākudala encounter, meeting, coming together, collision, impact, shock; tācu to kick; tāpu a kick (DEDR 3150). தாக்கு[2] tākku , *n.* < தாக்கு-. [K. *tāgu.*] 1. Attack, assault; எதிர்க்கை. 2. Beat, dash, blow, clash; அடி. 3. Fight; போர். (சூடா.) 4. Army, forces; படை. தாக்கர்தாக் 5. Reaction, rebound; எதிரெழுகை. (W.) 6. Impetus, force, momentum; வேகம். 7. Affecting, as one's mind; பாதிக்கை. 8. Heavy weight, heaviness; அதிபாரம். தாக்குரலடிகொள் யானை (பாரத. திரௌபதி. 14). 9. Robustness, stoutness, corpulency; புஷ்டி. தாக்கிலே அவன் தாழ்ச்சியில்லை. 10. Application; சாதனை. (W.) 11. Drum-stick; குறுந்தடி. தாக்கிற் றாக்குறும் பறையும் (கம்பரா. நாட்டு. 57). 12. (Arith.) Multiplication; பெருக்கல். 13. Plot of land; rice- field; வயற்பகுதி. 14. Place; இடம். பள்ளத்தாக்கு. 15. Vault, cellar; நிலவறை. (W.)தாக்குதல் tākku- , *5 v. intr.* 1. [T. *tāku*, K. *tāgu.*] To come in contact, collide, strike against, as a vessel on a rock; மோதுதல். . 4. To take revenge; பழிவாங்கு தல். W.) 5. To interfere; தலையிட்டுக் கொள்ளு தல். (W.) 6. To involve, as consequences; பலித் தல். (W.) 7, To increase; பெருகுதல். அருளா னந்தந் தாக்கவும் (தாயு.

ஆக்குவை. 1). 8. To fall heavily, as charges, expenses; to press heavily, as a burden, as responsibility; பாரமாதல். 9. To react, rebound; அதைத்தல். (W.) 10. To hobble, limp; நெளித்துப்போதல். (W.)--*tr.* 1. To attack, assault; எதிர்த்தல். ஒருத்தலோ டாய் பொறி யுழுவை தாக்கிய (கலித். 46). 2. To strike, beat, dash; அடித்தல். 3. To cut, cut off; வெட்டு தல். அருஞ்சமம் ததையத் தாக்கி (புறநா. 126). 4. To butt; முட்டுதல். மாடு கொம்பால் தாக்கிற்று. 5. To pounce or dart upon, attack, charge; பாய்ந்து மோதுதல். பொருதகர் தாக்கற்குப் பேருந் தகைத்து (குறள், 486). 6. To touch, strike, come in contact with, as heat; to burst on the sight, as lightning; to beat against; to penetrate, as a sting; தீண்டுதல். மருந்து தன்னைத் தாக்குதன் முன்னே (கம்பரா. வேலேற்று. 42). 7. To rest upon, depend on, lean against; பற்றியிருத்தல். 8. To adjust or settle, as accounts; to increase the profits of an article; to make up for losses; சரிக்கட்டுதல். 9. (Arith.) To multiply; பெருக்கு தல். நின்றதோ ரேழிற் றாக்கி நேர்பட வெட்டுக்கீந் தால் (சோதிடவிடுகவி: சங். அக.). 10. [T. *tāgu.*] To consume, drink; குடித்தல். கள்ளை நிறையத் தாக்கிவிட்டான்.

Glyph: K. *daka* m. ' a push, blow ', S. *dhaku* m., L. P. *dhakkā* m.; Ku. *dhakkā* ' collision ', *dhā̃kā* ' forcibly pushing '; N. *dhakkā* ' collision, push '; B. *dhā̃kkā* ' push ', Or. *dhakā*; H.*dhak* m. ' shock, sudden terror ', *dhakkā* m. ' push '; OMarw. *dhakā -- dhakī* f. '

rush '; G. *dhakkɔ* m. ' push ', M. *dhakā*, *ḍhakā* m.; -- P. *dhakkṇā* ' to push, oust '; -- S.*dhakiṛaṇu* ' to half -- clean rice by beating it in a mortar '; -- Ku. *dhakelṇo* ' to push ', N. *dhakelnu*, H. *dhakelnā*, *ḍha°*, G. *dhakelvũ*. S.kcch. *dhakko ḍeṇo* ' to push '; WPah.kṭg. *dhàkkɔ* m. ' push, dash ', J. *dhākā* m. ṭakkarā f. ' blow on the head ' Rājat. [Cf. *ṭakk -- 2] Pk. ṭakkara -- m. ' collision ', K. ṭakara m.; S. ṭakaru m. ' knocking the head against anything, butting ', ṭakiraṇu ' to knock against, encounter, be compared with '; L. ṭakkaraṇ ' to meet, agree '; P. ṭakkar f. ' pushing, knocking ', ṭakkarṇā ' to collide, meet '; Ku. ṭakkar ' shock, jerk, loss '; N. ṭakar ' obstacle, collision '; B. ṭakkar ' blow ', Or. ṭakkara, ṭākara, H. G. M. ṭakkar f. (CDIAL 5424) தகரார் takarār , n. < Arab. takrar. Colloq. 1. Altercation, objection. ṭakkarā -- : S.kcch. ṭakrāṇū ' to collide ', G. ṭakrāvũ AKŚ 37. *dhakk ' push, strike '. [dhakkayati ' annihilates ' Dhātup.]K. daka m. ' a push, blow ', S. dhaku m., L. P. dhakkā m.; Ku. dhakkā ' collision ', dhā̃kā ' forcibly pushing '; N. dhakkā ' collision, push '; B. dhā̃kkā ' push ', Or. dhakā; H. dhak m. ' shock, sudden terror ', dhakkā m. ' push '; OMarw. dhakā -- dhakī f. ' rush '; G. dhakkɔ m. ' push ', M. dhakā, ḍhakā m.; -- P. dhakkṇā ' to push, oust '; -- S. dhakiṛaṇu ' to half -- clean rice by beating it in a mortar '; -- Ku. dhakelṇo ' to push ', N. dhakelnu, H. dhakelnā, ḍha°, G. dhakelvũ. *dhakk -- : S.kcch. dhakko ḍeṇo ' to push '; WPah.kṭg. dhàkkɔ m. ' push, dash ', J. dhākā m.(CDIAL 6701). L. *ḍakkaṇ*, (Ju.) *ḍa°* ' to stop, obstruct '; P. *ḍakkṇā* ' to block up, hinder ', *ḍakk* m. ' hindrance ', *ḍakkā* m. ' plug '. (CDIAL 5518). Ka. (Jenu Kuruba, LSB 4.12) dūku, (HavS.) dūku, (Bark.) dūki, (Coorg) dūku to push (or with 3722 Ta. nūkku). Kur. tukknā to give a push to, shove. Malt. tuke to push, remove. (DEDR 3286) Ka. tagalu, tagilu, tagulu to come in contact with, touch; taguḷisu to chase, drive away; Te. tagulucu to cause to touch; taguluḍu, taguludala touching, contact, catching, addictedness; taguluvaḍu to be caught, seized, or entangled. Koṇḍa tagli (-t-) to touch, hit. (DEDR 3004) Ta. takai (-v-, -nt-) to stop, resist, check, deter, obstruct or forbid by oath, seize, take hold of, overpower, subdue, shut in, enclose, include, bind, fasten, yoke; (-pp-, -tt-) to check, resist, stop, deter, bind, fasten; n. binding, fastening, garland, obstruction, check, hindrance, armour, coat of mail; takaippu surrounding wall, fortress, palatial building, section of house, apartment, battle array of an army. Ka. taga, tagave, tagahu, tage delay, obstacle, hindrance, impediment; tage to stop, arrest, obstruct, impede, stun; tagar to be stopped or impeded, impede, etc. (DEDR 3006).

Ta. takai (-v-, -nt-) to stop, resist, check, deter, obstruct or forbid by oath, seize, take hold of, overpower, subdue, shut in, enclose, include, bind, fasten, yoke; (-pp-, -tt-) to check, resist, stop, deter, bind, fasten; *n.* binding, fastening, garland, obstruction, check, hindrance, armour, coat of mail; takaippu surrounding wall, fortress, palatial building, section of house, apartment, battle array of an army. *Ka.* taga, tagave, tagahu, tage delay, obstacle, hindrance, impediment; tage to stop, arrest, obstruct, impede, stun; tagar to be stopped or impeded, impede, etc. (DEDR 3006)

தாக்கல்² tākkal, *n.* < U. *dākhil.* 1. Registration, entry; பதிகை. (W. G.) 2. Giving of a notice; reference; தகவல். (C. G.) 3. Taking possession, occupancy; சுவாதீனப்படுத்துகை. (C. G.) 4. Information, news, intimation; செய்தி. அவன் போன விஷயமாக ஒரு தாக்கலும் கிடைக்கவில்லை. 5. Connection; சம்பந்தம். இவ னுக்கும் அவனுக்கும் தாக்கல் இல்லை. *Loc.* தாக்கலா tākkalā , *n.* < U. *dākhila.* 1. Entry in an account; கணக்கிற் பதிவு. தாக்கல்செய்-தல் tākkal-cey-, *v. tr.* < தாக் கல்² +. To file as documents, etc., in court; கோர்ட்டில் பதிவாகும்படி தஸ்தவேசுகளைத் கொடுத் தல்.

Ka. tagalu, tagilu, tagulu to come in contact with, touch, hit, have sexual intercourse with; tagalisu, tagilisu, tagulisu to cause to come in contact with, etc.; taguluviketouching; taguḷ to be joined together, come near, approach, meet, unite oneself with, commence, run after, chase, pursue, drive away, push back; taguḷisu to chase, drive away;taguḷcu to join (*tr.*), attach, put to, join oneself to, get to, come under the rule of, undertake anything, engage in, employ, set on fire, kindle, damage with fire; taguḷpa state of being joined, union. *Tu.* tagaruni to draw near. *Te.* tagulu, tavulu to touch, come in contact with, strike against, follow, pursue, be entangled, ensnared or caught, be found or met with; *n.* attachment, interest, wish, desire; tagilincu to cause to touch, catch, adhere or stick to, attach, fix, fasten, insert, hang on, apply; tagulã-baḍu to burn, be on fire; tagulã-beṭṭu to set on fire; tagulamu, tagulāṭamu attachment, tie, affection, fondness, love, passion, addictedness, connexion, relation, hindrance, obstacle, a fetter;tagulukonu to get entangled or ensnared, catch fire; tagulucu to cause to touch; taguluḍu, taguludala touching, contact, catching, addictedness; taguluvaḍu to be caught, seized, or entangled. *Konḍa* tagli (-t-) to touch, hit. *Kur.* taknā to rub or graze in passing, give a very slight knock; *refl.-pass.* takrnā to get a slight knock. *Malt.* take to touch, hurt (as a sore); takuwre to be pained or grieved. ? *Ta.* tai-vā- to touch. (DEDR 3004).

తాగల్లు [tāgallu] , తాగాడి or తాగాణి *tāgallu.*

[Tel. తాకు+కల్లు or కాడి.] n. The stone beam placed across the mouth of a well: పరుపు జిమ్మ, నూతిమీద నడ్డముగా వేసే కర్ర లేక రాయి.

தாக்கல்[1] *tākkal , n. < தாக்கு-.20). 1. Striking, attacking, charging; பாய்ந்துமோ , 486). 2. Opposing; எதிர்க்கை. (சூடா.)*

தாக்கம்[1] *tākkam, n. < தாக்கு-. 1. Attack, assault, hit;* தாக்கு. *Loc. 2. Reaction, counter- action;* எதிர்தாக்குகை. *(W.) 3. Force; strength; power, as of blow, medicine or fire; momentum;* வேகம். *(W.) 4. Onerousness, heaviness;* கனத் திருக்கை. *(யாழ். அக.)*

5. Swelling; வீக்கம். *(யாழ். அக.) 6. Preponderance;* மிக்கிருக்கை. *(W.)*

తాకు [tāku] *tāku.* [Tel.] n. A touch, contact. తాకుట. An attack. A toe-ring. కాలిటాకు. v. a. & v. n. To touch; to strike, to push, to encounter, oppose, front. To be attached to join, apply. To strike (as heat does.) తాకేముందు a potent drug. నీవు చేసినపనులు నీ తలకే తాకినవి your sin has fallen on your own head. వానికి దిష్టి తాకినది he is suffering from the effects of an evil eye. వానికి రోగము తాకినది he has caught the disease. తాకించు *tākintsu.* v. a. To cause to touch, to put in contact with, to apply. తాకజేయు. To trouble శ్రమపరుచు. తాకుడు*tākuḍu.* n. Touching. తాకుట. స్పర్శము. తాకుడువేకి *tākuḍu-vēki.* n. An intermittent fever వరుసమేరకువచ్చు జ్వరము. తాకుదల *tāku-dala.* n. A meeting, shock, encounter in a battle.యుద్ధప్రారంభము. M. XII. iii. 10.

Appendix B: *krəm* 'neck' symbolic forms

krammara 'look back' (Telugu)

క్రమ్మరు [krammaru] *krammaru.* [Tel.] v. n. To turn, return, go back. మరలు. క్రమ్మరించు or క్రమ్మరుచు *krammarintsu.* V. a. To turn, send back, recall. To revoke, annul, rescind. క్రమ్మరజేయు. క్రమ్మర *krammara.* Adv. Again. క్రమ్మరిల్లు or క్రమరబడు Same as క్రమ్మరు.

krəm back' (Kho.)(CDIAL 3145) Kho. Krəm ' back ' NTS ii 262 with (?) (CDIAL 3145)[Cf. Ir. *kamaka – or *kamraka -- ' back ' in Shgh. Čůmč ' back ', Sar. Čomǰ EVSh 26] (CDIAL 2776) cf. Sang. kamak ' back ', Shgh. Čomǰ (< *kamak G.M.) ' back of an animal ', Yghn. kama ' neck ' (CDIAL 14356). Kár, kãr 'neck' (Kashmiri) Kal. gřä ' neck '; Kho. Goḷ ' front of neck, throat '. gala m. ' throat, neck ' MBh. (CDIAL 4070)

Appendix C: काण *kāṇa* 'one-eyed', *āra* 'six', 'six rings of hair' symbolic forms

A one-eyed woman with six curls or rings of hair or six knots around her hairdo is shown impeding two rearing tigers.
Could the representation of six knots + one-eye be rebus reading: *khāṇ* 'mine' *āra* 'brass', that is, an arsenical copper mine? This could be a denotation of arsenical bronze. Sphalerite (ZnS2), for example, is not uncommon in copper sulfide deposits, and the metal smelted would be brass, which is both harder and more durable than bronze.
Rebus reading could suggest: *kanahār* 'helmsman, sailor' (Prākṛt) 2836 karṇadhāra m. ' helmsman ' Suśr. [kárṇa -- , dhāra -- 1] Pa. *kaṇṇadhāra* -- m. ' helmsman '; Pk. *kaṇṇahāra* -- m. ' helmsman, sailor '; H. *kanahār* m. ' helmsman, fisherman '.
Hieroglyph: 'one-eyed': काण *a.* [कण् निमीलने कर्तरि घञ्

Tv.] 1 One-eyed; अक्ष्णा काणः Sk; काणेन चक्षुषा किं वा H. Pr.12; Ms.3.155. -2 Perforated, broken (as a cowrie) <kaNa>(Z) {ADJ} ``^one-^eyed, ^blind''. Ju<kaNa>(DP),,<kana>(K) {ADJ} ``^blind, blind in one eye''. (Munda)
Rebus 1: Pk. khāṇī -- f. ' mine '; Gy. as. xani, eur. sp. xaní f., boh. xaníg f., gr. xaníng f. ' well '; K. khān f. ' mine '; S. khāṇi f. ' mine, quarry, water in a pit '; L. khāṇ f. 'mine' (CDIAL 3873)
Rebus 2: 'to engrave, write; lapidary': <kana-lekhe>(P) {??} Cf.

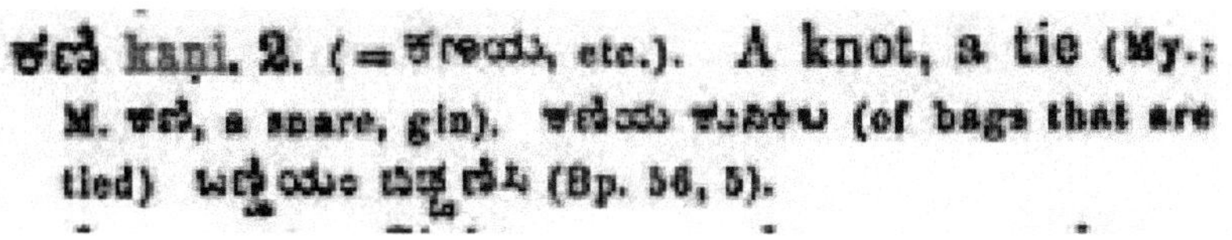
kaṇi. 2. (= ..., etc.). A knot, a tie (My.; M. ..., a snare, gin). ... (of bags that are tied) ... (Bp. 56, 5).

<kana->. %16123. #16013. <lekhe->(P),,<leke->(KM) {VTC} ``to ^write''. Cf. <kana-lekhe>. *Kh.<likhae>, H.<lIkhAna>, O.<lekhIba>, B.<lekha>; Kh.<likha>(P), Mu.<lika>. %20701. #20541. Kashmiri: khanun खनुन् । खननम् conj. 1 (1 p.p. khonu for 1, see s.v.; f. khüñü to dig (K.Pr. 155, 247; L. 459; Śiv. 59, 746,

994, 143, 1197, 1214, 1373, 1754; Rām. 343, 958, 1147, 1724; H. xii, 6); to engrave (Śiv. 414, 671, 176; Rām. 1583). khonu-motu खनुमतु; । खातः perf. part. (f. khüñümüťsü) dug (e.g. a field, or a well); engraved. mohara-khonu म्वहर-खनु; or (Gr.M.) mohar-kan । मुद्राखननकारुः m. a seal-engraver, a lapidary (El. *mohar-kand*). -wöjü । *अङ्गुलिमुद्रा f. a signet-ring. *Ta.* kaṇṭam iron style for writing on palmyra leaves. *Te.* gaṇṭamu id. (DEDR 1170).
Six knobs on fish: sailor, wheelwright

Elamite lady spinner. Musee du Louvre. Paris. An elegantly coiffed, exquisitely-dressed and well fanned Elamite woman sits

on a lion footed stool winding thread on a spindle. The stool on which the lovely Elamite lady sits has the legs of a lion or panther; the fish is also placed on a similar stool in front her.This five-inch fragment is dated 8th century BCE. It was molded and carved from a mix of bitumen, ground calcite, and quartz. The Elamites used bitumen, a naturally occurring mineral pitch, or asphalt, for vessels, sculpture, glue, caulking, and waterproofing.H. 9.3 cm; W. 13 cm. Excavations led by Jacques de Morgan; distribution after excavation.Sb 2834[146]

ఆరకాటి [ārakāṭi] *ārakāṭi.* [Tel.] n. A boatman, a sailor. ఓడనడపువాడు, నావికుడు. (Telugu) Together with ayo 'fish' Rebus: ayo 'metal alloy', the Elamite spinner composition signifies a seafaring merchant in metals, brass, alloys.

The rebus readings of the hieroglyphs : *khāṭī* 'wheelwright' (working on) *ārakūṭa aya* 'brass, alloyed metal';

आर [āra] A term in the play of इटीदांडू,--the number six.

(Marathi) आर [āra] A tuft or ring of hair on the body. (Marathi) Rebus: āra 'brass'.

aya 'fish' Rebus: aya 'iron' ayas 'metal (alloy)'
kuṭhe = leg of bedstead or chair (Santali.lex.) Rebus: *kuṭhi* 'a furnace for smelting iron ore, to smelt iron'; *koṭe* 'forged (metal)(Santali)

arye 'lion' Rebus: āra 'brass'. *āra* as in *ārakūṭa* (Skt.) *āram* 'brass' (Tamil).

Alternative: *kaṇḍō* 'a stool' (Kur.)(DEDR 1179). Rebus: *kaṇḍ* 'fire-altar' (Santali)

kāṭī 'woman who spins the thread' Rebus: *khāḍ* 'trench, fire-pit' (Gujarati.) *khattar* 'attendant' (Pali) *khāṭī* 'wheelwright' (Hindi)

Cylinder seal. British Museum. 89538. Length: 4.120 cm. Diameter: 3.650 cm. Early dynastic period ca. 2700 BCE. Depicts a person grappling with and flanked by two unicorns. The person is shown with six hair-knots projecting out of the hero's head.[147] Source:

ārakāṭi 'sailor' (Telugu): *āra* 'six curls' *kāṭhī* 'stature of person'.

शरीराची काठी The frame or structure of the body, stature; काठीवर कांबळा घेणें or घालणें (To free one's body from the embarrassment of the कांबळा; to *strip*.) To start up or stand out ready (to quarrel or for other evil work). (Marathi)

Hieroglyph: six curls on hair. Glyphs: six (numeral) + ring of hair: आर [āra] A term in the play of इटीदांडू,--the number six. (Marathi) आर [āra] A tuft or ring of hair on the body. (Marathi) Rebus: āra 'brass'. *āra* as in *ārakūṭa* (Skt.) *āram* 'brass' (Tamil). Alternative: bhaṭa 'six '; rebus: bhaṭa 'furnace'. baṭa = kiln (Santali) baṭa = a kind of iron (Gujarati) *bhaṭa* 'furnace' (Santali) *aryeh* 'lion' (Akkadian) Rebus: *arā* 'brass'.

मेढा mēḍhā A twist or tangle arising in thread or cord, a curl or snarl. (Marathi) Rebus: meḍ 'iron' (Ho.)

m0308 Mohenjodaro seal. m0308AC Pict-105: One-eyed person with six hair-culs impeding or stopping two tigers standing on either side of her and rearing on their hindlegs.

2075 [The third sign from left may be a stylized 'standard device'?] Comparable to the Mesopotamian cylinder seal (BM 89538), this Indus seal depicts a person with six hair-knots.

White and cream calcite (marble) cylinder seal

mēḍhā मेढा A twist or tangle arising in thread or cord, a curl or snarl (Marathi) कांड [*kāṇḍa*] Thrashed or trodden stalks of leguminous plants, pulse-straw. Rebus: *meḍ* 'iron' *kaṇḍa* 'tools, pots and pans, weapons'. *dula* pair' *dul* 'cast metal'. *pasaramu* 'quadrupeds' Rebus: *pasra* 'smithy'. *karaḍa* 'safflower' Rebus: *karaḍa* 'hard alloy of silver, gold etc.'

From Uruk, southern Iraq About 3200-3100 BCE **One of the tools of a Mesopotamian bureaucrat**

"The figure depicted here is often referred to as a priest-king because he undertakes activities which could be described as religious and royal (although there was no clear division of these functions in the ancient world)… The poles with loops were probably actually made from reeds bound together and are the symbol of Inana..."[148]

करडी [*karaḍī*] *f* (See करडई) Safflower: also its seed. Rebus: karaḍa 'hard alloy'. *kāḍ* reed Rebus: *kāṇḍa* 'tools, pots and pans, metal-ware'. *dhatu* 'scarf' rebus: *dhatu* 'ore'. *mr̤eka, melh* 'goat' (Telugu. Brahui) Rebus: *melukkha* '*milakkha*, copper'. *pasaramu, pasalamu* 'an animal, a beast, a brute, quadruped' (Telugu); rebus: *pasra* 'smithy' (Santali). Rings atop scarfed reed posts: *koṭiyum* [*koṭ, koṭī* neck] a wooden circle put round the neck of an animal (Gujarati) Rebus: *ācāri koṭṭya* = forge, *kammārasāle* (Tulu)

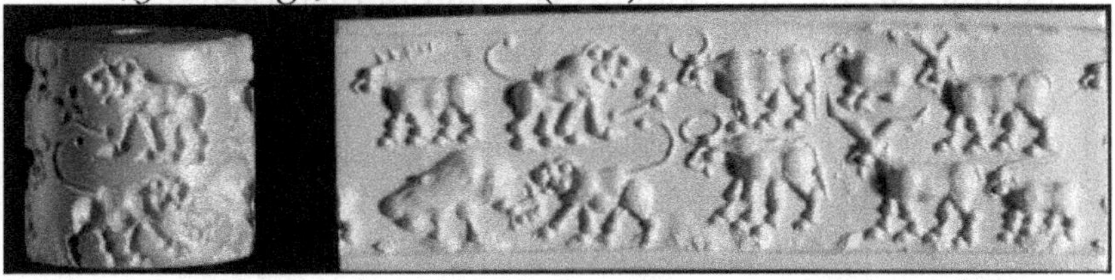

British Museum number113875 Grey-green serpentine cylinder seal; two rows of animals; upper row - stag, lion, bull, goat; lower row - eagle, lion, two bulls, goat, ibex; drill-hole technique; chipped. Jemdet Nasr. Frankfort, Henri, Cylinder Seals: a documentary essay on the art and religion of the ancient Near East, London, Macmillan, 1939, Pl. Vib. Animals: arye 'lion' Rebus: ara 'brass'. *ḍhangra* 'bull'. *Rebus: ḍhangar* 'blacksmith'. Tagara 'ram' Rebus: tagaram 'tin'. Mlech 'goat' Rebus: milakkha 'copper'. *miṇḍāl* 'markhor' (Tōrwālī) *meḍho* a ram, a sheep (Gujarati)(CDIAL 10120); rebus: *mẽṛhẽt, meḍ* 'iron' (Munda.Ho.)

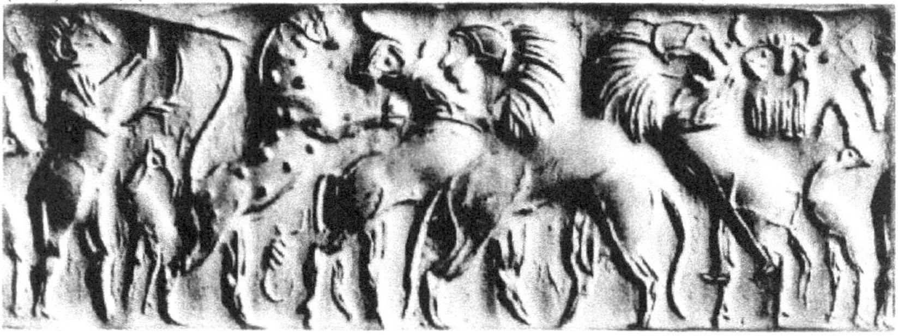

British Museum No. 120530. Cylinder seal; Early Dynastic III; Ur. Large, cream marble or shell cylinder seal with patches of yellow/ brown and grey / green; contest frieze; hero with stick and knife before leopard which attacks bull which is also being fought by lion. Another lion (crossed) fights bull-man. In field: goat, scorpion, antelope. Woolley et al 1934, p. 526, pl. 197, 58. koṭiya ' leopard ' (Sinhala)GS 42 (CDIAL 3615). kul 'tiger' (Santali); kōlu id. (Te.) kōlupuli = Bengal tiger (Te.)Pk. Kolhuya -- , kulha — m. ' jackal ' Rebus: kol 'furnace, forge' (Kuwi) kol 'alloy of five metals, pañcaloha' (Ta.) *Ta.* kol working in iron, blacksmith; kollaṉ blacksmith. *chita* 'spotted' (Hindi) bicha 'scorpion' Rebus: bica 'stone iron ore'. Mlech 'goat' Rebus: milakkha 'copper'. In Hindi *chita* means 'spotted' (Yule and Burnell 1886: 187). S. *ciṭro* m. ' panther '; L. *citrā* m. ' leopard, a spotted fish ', (awāṇ.) ' tiger '; P. *cittrā, citrā, cittā* m. ' leopard ', N. *cituwā*, B. Or. *citā*, Mth. *cittā*, H. *cītā* m. (→ S. *cīto*, P. *cītā* m.); G. *citrɔ*, *cittɔ* m. ' leopard, a kind of snake '; M. *citā, cittā* m. ' leopard '.A. *citā* (phonet. *s* --) ' leopard ' AFD 202, Ko. *ciṭṭo* (= *ciṭṭyā vāgu*).(CDIAL 4804). Rebus: P. *citrērā, cat°, citērā, cat°* m. ' engraver '; OAw. *citerā* m. ' painter ', *citeraï* ' paints ', lakh. *citērā*; H. *citerā* m. ' painter, engraver '.(CDIAL 4805). Thus, together with a one-horned young bull, the message is: *citerā* 'engraver' + *kundār* 'turner' (A.); kũdār, kũdāri (B.); kundāru (Or.); kundau to turn on a lathe, to carve, to chase; kundau dhiri = a hewn stone; kundau murhut = a graven image (Santali) kunda a turner's lathe (Skt.)(CDIAL 3295). citrakāra m. ' painter ' BrahmaP.

[Cf. citrakara -- . -- citrá -- , kāra -- 1]Pa. *cittakāra* -- m., Pk. *cittaāra* -- m.; H. *citārnā* ' to paint ', *citārī* m. ' painter ', G. *citārɔ* m., OM. *citāraṇī* f., M. *citārī* m., Si.*sitiyara, sittarā.* S.kcch. *catār ḍīṇū* ' to describe ' (= G. *citār devɔ*)(CDIAL 4807).

Gold foil feline from Tal-i Malyan, Banesh period (courtesy of WM Sumner).

It is possible that the cheetah from Meluhha was the animal given to Ibbi-Sin with the legend 'let him catch'.

British Museum No. 121547. Akkadian Cylinder seal of lapis lazuli with original gold mounting or ornamental caps; long haired bull-man in conflict with a lion. Bearded hero, wearing an outward-flaring cap decorated with fluting, and a draped skirt, grasping the neck and foreleg of a bull into which a hero with a beehive cap and a skirt, is plunging a dagger while grasping it's throat in his other hand. 2200BCE-2100BCE. Royal cemetery. arye 'lion' Rebus: ara 'brass'. *ḍhangra* 'bull'. *Rebus: ḍhangar* 'blacksmith'.

British Museum No. 122947. Dilmun period.
Excavated/Findspot: Ur, Filling of Shulgi mausoleum Fired white steatite cylinder seal originally with a cap at each end; some glaze survives now generally white with turquoise fragments; design shows a palm-tree with humped bull (zebu), serpent, scorpion and recumbent human figure at the top. Mitchell, Terence C; Al-Khalifa, Shaikha Haya Ali (ed), Indus and Gulf type seals from Ur, London, KPI, 1986, no.17, pp.282-283, fig.118.

British Museum No. 124016. 6th c. BCE. Findspot: Takht-i-Kuwad, Tajikistan. Achaemenid (Mixed II, Late). Inscription language: Aramaic? Translation: 'Rababath'. A name. Particularly translucent, dark pink-brown cornelian cylinder seal; engraved in intaglio with a scene showing seated and standing figures, and ancillary animal. A personage (deity?) seated on a high-backed chair, facing left, is possibly female as there is no evidence of a beard, but probably male as there are no sign of the breasts that are so obvious on the attendant; the nose is prominent and the hair seems to be bunched at the back of the head; the figure appears to be wearing a thigh-length, belted garment, the feet point downwards, one hand with palm outwards is stretched along the thigh, the other is raised to receive a spherical object (ball or mirror or cup?) from a slightly smaller, female figure standing before the personage. The latter has long plaited hair ending in three tassels (?) and seems to be naked; her hair, breasts and hips are indicated by drill-holes and the outline of her pubic triangle appears between her thighs; one hand, with palm facing inwards, is stretched out, the other is raised and just about to pass the ball or mirror to the seated figure. Behind the chair or throne stands a small, humped, zebu bull facing left, its curved horns shown from a three-quarter angle and its tufted tail hanging down. The engraving is crude and drill-holes are used to emphasize the various features. Above the figures, a four letter inscription is placed horizontally. Pitted on the surface and worn along the edges. Dalton, Ormonde Maddock, The treasure of the Oxus with other examples of early oriental metal-work, London, BMP, 1964, p. 32, fig. 63 or 66, cat. no. 115.

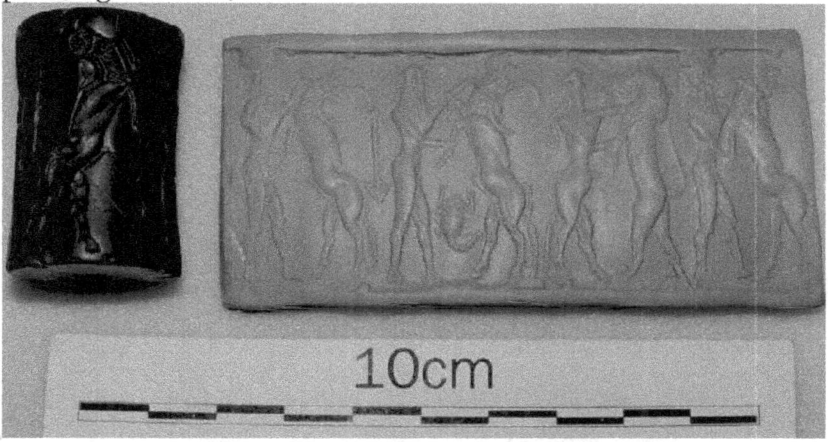

British Museum No. 134763 Akkadian. 2400-2200 BCE. Greenstone facies cylinder seal; contest scene - bearded hero (full-face) naked except for a belt, in conflict with a bull. Long-haired bull-man in conflict with a lion (head seen from above). First group repeated. In the field, a scorpion; a star-spade; very slightly chipped along the edges. Collon 1982a 33, pl.VI. Star-spade signifies an iron space: *meḍha* 'polar star' Rebus: *meḍ* 'iron'. *kaṣī̆* -- f. ' spade ' Pr. *kṣe_* ' plough -- iron ', Paš. *kaṣí* ' mattock,hoe ';

Shum. *káṣi* ' spade, pickaxe '; S. *kasī* f. ' trench, watercourse '; L. *kass* m. ' catch drain,ravine ', *kassī* f. ' small distributing channel from a canal '; G. *kā̃s* m. ' artificial canal for irrigation ' -- Dm. Phal. *khaṣī́* ' small hoe '(CDIAL 2909). Rebus: *kā̃s* 'bronze'.

British Museum No. 89322 Black hematite cylinder seal; Old Babylonian. 2000-1600 BCE. Ur. contest scene; a lion attacks a goat which looks back over its shoulder at its assailant; a lion (head seen from above) approaches a nude figure who wears a cap and belt, kneels on one knee, turns to look back at the lion and raises one arm to ward off its attack; he is about be devoured by a lion-griffin. In the field are a tortoise and a small lion (!) playing a flute. Line border round the bottom of the scene; slightly chipped. Collon 1986 pl.XLVII. Wing on lion: eraka 'wing' Rebus: erako 'moltencast copper'. కమండలువు [kamaṇḍaluvu] *kamanḍaluvu.* [Skt.] n. A bowl or cruise carried by a Hindu ascetic. సన్యాసులుంచు కొనే గిన్నె వంటి మంటిపాత్రము. కమండలి *kamanḍali.* A hermit: "he who carries a cruise." Rebus: కమటము [kamatamu] *kamaṭamu.* [Tel.] n. A portable furnace for melting the precious metals. అగసాలెవాని కుంపటి. Allograph 1: కమఠము [kamaṭhamu] *kamaṭhamu.* [Skt.] n. A tortoise. Allograph 2: कमटा or ठा [kamaṭā or ṭhā] *m* (कमठ S) A bow (esp. of bamboo or horn) (Marathi). Allograph 3: kamaḍha 'penance' (Pkt.) Rebus: kampaṭṭam 'coiner, mint' (Tamil).

British Museum No. 22962. Early Dynastic III. 2600 BCE. Lapis lazuli cylinder seal; design in two parts; above, two human-headed bulls (bison?) are lying on either side of a hill or mountain on which a triple plant is growing; they are being attacked by lion-headed eagles or vultures, which are being stabbed by a hero and a bull-man; in front of the bull-man is a scorpion (and a snake?); below, a bird hovers between two bulls behind which are a small goat and stag.Strommenger, E; Hirmer, M, Funf Jahrtausende Mesopotamien, Munich, Hirmer Verlag, 1962, pl.64, p.65.

British Museum No. 89308. Akkadian. 2250 BCE. Greenstone facies cylinder seal; contest scene; antithetical group. In the centre stands a sacred tree on a cone-shaped mountain. On either side is a rearing up bison which is being grasped by the tail and stabbed in the neck, on the left by a bull-man (full-face) and on the right by a bearded hero (full-face) who is naked except for a belt; slightly chipped. Barnett, Richard D; Wiseman, Donald J, Fifty masterpieces of Ancient Near Eastern Art, London, BMP,

1960, p.84, no. 38. Hieroglyph: डोंगरी [ḍōṅgarī] f (Dim. of डोंगर) A little hill. a Growing or produced on hills; consisting of hills; relating to hills or a hill. डोंगर [ḍōṅgara] m A hill. Rebus: *dhokra* 'cire perdue casting metalsmith'. Dhokra (Oriya: ଢୋକରା, Bengali: ডোকরা) Hieroglyph: *loa* 'ficus religiosa' Rebus: *lo* 'copper'. dangra 'bull' Rebus: *ḍhangar* 'blacksmith' *kond* 'ox, bullock' Rebus: *kond* 'turner, to turn in a lathe'.

British Museum No. 89078. Early Dynastic III. 2400 BCE. Shell cylinder seal; hero is protecting a stag which a second hero is stabbing in the back; two gods, wearing an early form of the horned head-dress of deities, protect a human-headed bull (a bison?) and a bull from the attack of a very small lioness; inscription cut above a small bull. Inscription, possibly name of the owner.

British Museum No. 89111. Akkadian. 2400-2200 BCE. Quartz var chalcedony (green jasper) cylinder seal; contest scene; bearded hero (full-face), naked except for a belt, in conflict with a bison which a bull-man (also full-face) is grasping from behind by the tail and horn (? damaged). Lion in conflict with a hero similar to the first. Terminal, erased inscription with traces of the frame remaining; below inscription a small oryx (?) lying down turned towards the left; concave; small chips around top and bottom.

> Boehmer, R M, Die Entwicklung der Glyptik wahrend der Akkad-Zeit, 4, Berlin, 1965, cat.665, pp.36, 39, 42-43, 46, 92, fig. 199.

British Museum No. 2012.6003.6. Akkadian 2400-2200 BCE. Dark grey stone cylinder seal. Engraved with design showing a double contest scene. A hero in a short tasselled kilt struggles with a rampant roaring lion. He has one leg bent over a mountain there is a linear object, possibly a plant. A nude bearded hero fights a water buffalo with horns seen from above. There is a framed (pseudo ?) inscription above the mountain. *ḍāngā* = hill, dry upland (B.); *ḍā̃g* mountain-ridge (H.)(CDIAL 5476). Rebus: *dhangar* 'blacksmith' (Maithili) *kaṭāi* ' buffalo calf '(Gaw.) *kāṭo* ' young buffalo bull ' (Kumaoni) (CDIAL 2645). *kāṛā* 'buffalo' bull (Tamil) *khaḍā* 'nodule (ore), stone' (Marathi). Arye 'lion' Rebus: ara 'brass'.

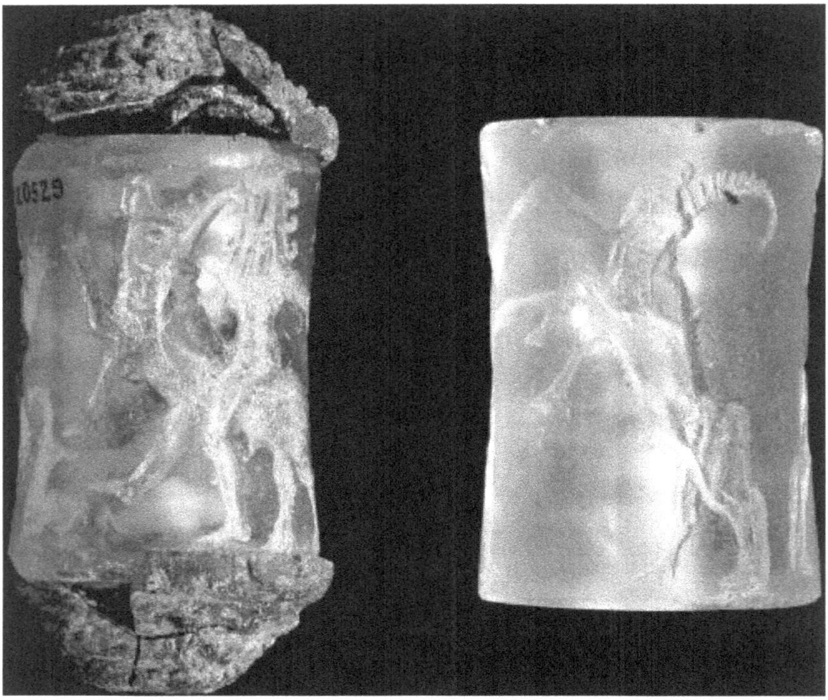

British Museum No. 134752. Akkadian 2400-2200 BCE. Umma. Quartz var crystal cylinder seal; lead tube? painted with a chevron design in red and white stripes, which are visible through the design, inserted in the perforation to add colour; seal has ornamental copper or bronze caps over a bitumen core; edges of seal are bevelled; contest scene; antithetical group consisting of two bearded, naked? heroes (full-face) each grasping the tail and one foreleg of, respectively, a water buffalo and a lion. The hero on the left is astride the water buffalo. In the field between the two pairs of contestants is an ibex lying down; two lines of inscription. Quartz var crystal cylinder seal, contest scene - lion in conflict with bull-man (full-face). Water buffalo in conflict with a bearded hero (full-face) who is naked except for a belt; inscription; the perforation is painted on the inside in red on white paint in eight horizontal stripes. Collon, Dominique, Catalogue of the Western Asiatic Seals in the British Museum: Cylinder Seals II: Akkadian, Post Akkadian, Ur III Periods, II, London, BMP, 1982. Pl. XII.

British Museum No. 89353. Akkadian. 2400-2200 BCE. Greenstone facies cylinder seal, contest scene - bull-man (full-face) in conflict with a lion. Water-buffalo in conflict with a bearded hero (full-face) who is naked except for a belt. Terminal, framed panel left blank for an inscription, but instead "Etana and the Eagle" and a dog, sitting and looking upwards have been cut, perhaps slightly later; a previous terminal had been erased; concave; chipped along the edge. Boehmer, R M, Die Entwicklung der Glyptik wahrend der Akkad-Zeit, 4, Berlin, 1965. Representation of Etana (?)

British Museum No. 134928. Middle-elamite. 13th cent. BCE. Glass cylinder seal, originally opaque blue, now weathered to translucent white colour; engraved scene divided into two panels; left panel contains a deity wearing a long gown facing right, with hair tied with fillet and bunched at the neck, holding a sickle-sword, and looking towards two figures, one placed above the other: a griffin seated to the left, a recumbent horned animal (goat?), and a frontal head of an antelope (or gazelle), placed horizontally; inscription; right panel contains an inscription in three vertical lines, below a hatched band and two lozenges, with another hatched band to the right; many small and a few elongated bubbles with pointed ends, in axial position; drilled perforation; surface dulled and weathered; small chips missing at both ends. Inscription: Sin umun gal igi-tab-a-ni arkhush tuk-a Translation: O Sin, great lord look (with favour) have mercy. Prayer to the moon god. Barag, Dan; (with contributions by Veronica Tatton-Brown, R J F Burleigh, Mavis Bimson , Catalogue of Western Asiatic glass in the British Museum, Volume I, I, London, BMP, 1985, p. 48, fig. 2, pl. 2.

British Museum No. 138115. Neo-elamite II. 750-550 BCE. Edfu. Brown, translucent glass cylinder seal; figure with animal: his torso is in three-quarter view and he strides to the left. The figure seems to be bareheaded with his hair in a bunch round the back of the head and ridged over the forehead, his beard is long, full and square-tipped, his shoulders are wide and bulky, possibly representing an upper, sleeveless garment (but there is no other indication of this), he wears a pleated thigh-length kilt, and possibly trousers as his legs appear quite thick in comparision with his thin arms. He holds a stick, rod or goad in his raised left hand and with the other guides a horned and hoofed antelope or gazelle by a rein or cord lasso tied around its neck; one horn is depicted, angled up and back from the top of the head, one long ear is visible and the long tufted tail hangs down; it has a heavily-modelled body for its spindly legs. A kudu has similar horns but it has a short tail; there are two large chips on the lower edge and surface of the seal, eliminating a small portion of the bottom section of the engraving. According to Merrillees catalogue "seals in alabaster and faience from Surkh Dum-i-Luri, Luristan show single figures standing just before or behind animals, and although not similar in style" to this seal "they indicate that such a design, which may signify some kind of hunting, was part of the provincial repertory. An impression from Susa shows a scene of animal husbandry; the figure, although long-robed, has the rounded, muscled shoulders in three-quarter view of our figure. Achaemenid ploughing scenes occur on Delaporte and Frankfort. A seal interpreted by Vollenweider as showing a ploughing scene, has a Median figure holding a spear (or goad?), walking with a bull just before him as he were marching the animal to sacrifice, similarities with" this seal "may indicated the same interpretation". Cf. L Delaporte, 'Musée du Louvre, Catalogue des cylindres orientaux II. Acquisitions', Paris 1920-1923, pl.91:21 (A.791). Frankfort, Henri, Cylinder Seals: a documentary essay on the art and religion of the ancient Near East, London, Macmillan, 1939, pl.XXXVIIg (cf:); Merrillees, Parvine H, Catalogue of the Western Asiatic seals in the British Museum: Pre-Achaemenid and Achaemenid periods, 6, London, BMP, 2005, p. 68.

British Museum No. 129479. Akkadian 2800 BCE. Royal cemetery. Green serpentine cylinder seal; a war-goddess stands full-face with weapons rising from her shoulders; she wears a flounced robe and a multiple-horned head-dress; her left leg is thrust forward and she holds a dagger in her right hand while raising her left above an altar on which lies a noosed rope or a necklace of beads. A worshipper in a fringed robe stands facing her on the other side of the altar and holds an antelope resembling an addax while raising his right hand. Behind him, also facing left, stands a goddess in a striped robe who holds a flowing vase and raises her right hand. A bearded god stands facing right with his back to her; he is wearing a cap decorated with wavy lines, sandals and a lion's pelt; he holds a club in his right hand, two objects in his left which may be a symbol of fertility such as onions or testicles or may be a sling and sling-stones, while in the crook of his left arm lies a twisted, burgeoning stick and three branches of vegetation sprout from each shoulder. Facing him stands a goddess in a flounced robe who stretches out her right hand and holds two sticks (?) in her left; she has three branches of vegetation rising from one shoulder and four from the other. Between these two figures is a small sheep leaping up before god. Inscription: i-li-esh-dar / dub-sar. Translation: Illi-Eshtar, scribe.. Collon, Dominique, Catalogue of the Western Asiatic Seals in the British Museum: Cylinder Seals II: Akkadian, Post Akkadian, Ur III Periods, II, London, BMP, 1982, cat.213, pl.XXXI.

British Museum No. 89802. Akkadian. 2400-2200 BCE. Greenstone facies cylinder seal; vegetation god scene and battle of the gods; a worshipper wearing a fringed robe, carries an antelope resembling an addax in his arms. He is preceded by two bearded gods who are holding out their hands; one wears a striped skirt while the other wears a striped robe, has branches spouting from his shoulders and holds a frond in his right hand. They approach a goddess who wears a fringed robe, holds two-fronds in her right hand and one in her left and who is seated on a wicker-work (?)

throne. Terminal, a scaly mountain before which kneels a bearded god, facing right, who is naked except for a loin-cloth. A bearded god, who wears a skirt and holds a mace in his left hand, grasps him by his horned head-dress and places his foot on his adversary's hip in a gesture of triumph. All the deities on the seal wear multiple-horned head-dresses though that of the kneeling god is not the same as the others. Above the mountain is a short inscription. This was cut positive on the seal and is obviously secondary. There are marks of erasure, the kneeling god's right arm may have been recut and there are unexplained marks in the design. Inscription: lugal-kas e / dumu shesh-shesh.Translation: Lugal-kase, son of Sheshshesh Frankfort, Henri, Gods and myths on Sargonid seals, Iraq, 1, London, British School of Archaeology in Iraq, 1934, pl. IIg..

koḍ 'horn' Rebus: *koḍ* 'workshop' *kāṇa* 'full of holes', 'perforations' Rebus: *kandil* 'beads' Rebus: *kand* 'fire-altar' (Santali) An allograph for kand: kŏṇḍ क्वंड् or kŏṇḍa क्वंड । कुण्ड m a deep still spring (El., Gr.Gr. 145); (amongst Hindūs) a hole dug in the ground for receiving consecrated fire; cf. agana-kŏṇḍ (p. 16*b*, l. 34) (Rām. 631). kọṇḍu or konḍu । कुण्डम् m. a hole dug in the ground for receiving consecrated fire kō̃da कोँद । कुलालादिकन्दुः f. a kiln; a potter's kiln (Rām. 1446; H. xi, 11); a brick-kiln (Śiv. 133); a lime-kiln. (Kashmiri)

Hieroglyph: <kana.kana>(A) {ADJ} 'perforated' #15890. <kaNa>>: *De.<kana> (GM) `a hole; perforated'. ??hole, to make a hole? #10761. <kaNa-gu-nu> {ADJ} 'perforated'. |<gu> `?perfect/past', <nu> `adjective'. *De.<kana> (GM) `a hole; perforated'. (Munda) Pk. *kāṇa* -- ' full of holes ', G. *kāṇũ* ' full of holes ', n. ' hole ' (CDIAL 3019) Rebus: *kandi* (pl. -l) beads, necklace (Pa.); kanti (pl. -l) bead, (pl.) necklace; kandit. bead (Ga.)(DEDR 1215).

kōṭu (in cmpds. *kōṭṭu-*) horn (Tamil)(DEDR 2200). Rebus 1: *koḍ* 'workshop' Rebus 2: *khōṭ* 'alloyed' (Punjabi) *koṭe* 'forged (metal) (Santali) koṭe meṛed = forged iron (Munda)

The hieroglyph of a slanted stroke in front of the animal on m1909 is: *dhāḷ* 'a slope'; 'inclination of a plane' (G.); ḍhāḷiyum = adj. sloping, inclining (G.) Rebus: *ḍhālako* = a large metal ingot (G.) ḍhālakī = a metal heated and poured into a mould; a solid piece of metal; an ingot (Gujarati) Antelope: miṇḍāl 'markhor' (Tōrwālī) meḍho a ram, a sheep (G.)(CDIAL 10120); rebus: mẽṛhẽt, meḍ 'iron' (Mu.Ho.) meṛed-bica = iron stone ore, in contrast to bali-bica, iron sand ore (Munda)

Read together rebus: *dul kānḍa kan-ka* 'cast metal tools, metalware account', *ḍhālako* 'ingot'. *kan-ka, karṇaka* 'rim of jar' Rebus: *kaṇḍa karṇaka* 'furnace account scribe'. *kārṇī(ka)* 'supercargo of a ship' (Marathi)

dula 'pair' *Rebus: dul* 'cast metal'. *kaṇḍe* A head or ear of millet or maize. కందళము [Skt.] n. A germ or shoot, a sprout.

కొత్తమొలక. కందళించు *kandaḷinṭsu.* v. n. To sprout, germinate,

shoot. (Telugu) काँड् | काण्डः m. the stalk or stem of a reed, grass, or the like, straw. In the compound with dan 5 (p. 221*a,* l. 13) the word is spelt kāḍ. The rebus reading of the pair of reeds in Sumer standard is: *khānḍa* 'tools, pots and pans and metal-ware'.

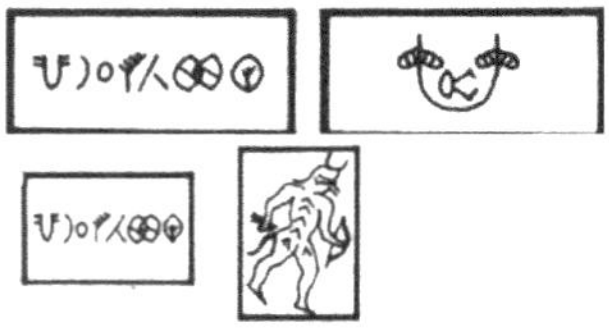

Thus, together, the rebus reading is: *khānḍ āra* 'maker of metalware'. *kaṇḍe.* [Tel.] n. Rebus: rebus: *kaṇḍa* '(mineral)stone', *kānḍā* 'metal tools, pots and pans'.

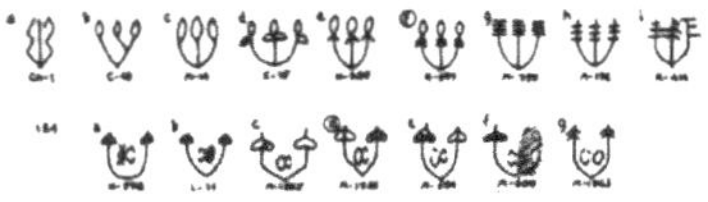

This seal has Glyph 347, 342 sequence, which is a terminal pair

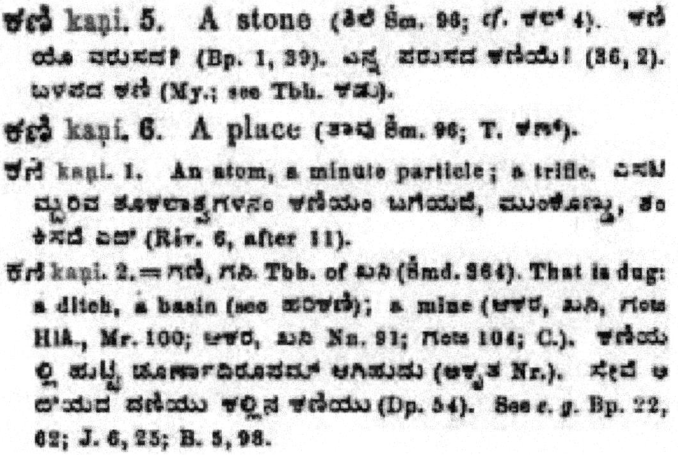
[illegible] kaṇi. 5. A stone ([illegible] Śm. 96; cf. [illegible] 4). [illegible] (Bp. 1, 39). [illegible] (36, 2). [illegible] (My.; see Tbh. [illegible]).

[illegible] kaṇi. 6. A place ([illegible] Śm. 96; T. [illegible]).

[illegible] kaṇi. 1. An atom, a minute particle; a trifle. [illegible] (Rāv. 6, after 11).

[illegible] kaṇi. 2. = [illegible], [illegible] Tbh. of [illegible] (Śmd. 364). That is dug: a ditch, a basin (see [illegible]); a mine ([illegible], [illegible], [illegible] Hlā., Mr. 100; [illegible], [illegible] Nn. 91; [illegible] 104; C.). [illegible] ([illegible] Nr.). [illegible] (Dp. 54). See e. g. Bp. 22, 62; J. 6, 25; B. 5, 98.

with 110 occurrences. An additional glyph shown in front of the animal is: a sloped/slanted stroke.

*kāṇḍakara ' worker with reeds or arrows '. [kā´ṇḍa -- , kará -- 1] L. *kanērā* m. ' mat -- maker '; H. *kā̃ḍerā* m. ' a caste of bow -- and arrow -- makers '(CDIAL 3024). kā´ṇḍīra ' armed with arrows ' Pāṇ., m. ' archer ' lex. [kā´ṇḍa -] H. *kanīrā* m. ' a caste (usu. of arrow -- makers) '. (CDIAL 3026).

Allograph: rays of the sun. Mohenjo-daro seal. M428b The 'rays of the sun' hieroglyph of this Mohenjodaro seal also recurs on early punch-marked coins of India. Rebus reading: arka 'sun'; agasāle 'goldsmithy' (Ka.) erka = ekke (Tbh. of arka) aka (Tbh. of arka) copper (metal); crystal (Ka.lex.) cf. eruvai = copper (Ta.lex.) eraka, er-aka = any metal infusion (Ka.Tu.); erako molten cast (Tulu) Rebus: eraka = copper (Ka.) eruvai = copper (Ta.); ere - a dark-red colour (Ka.)(DEDR 817). eraka, era, er-a = syn. erka, copper, weapons (Ka.)

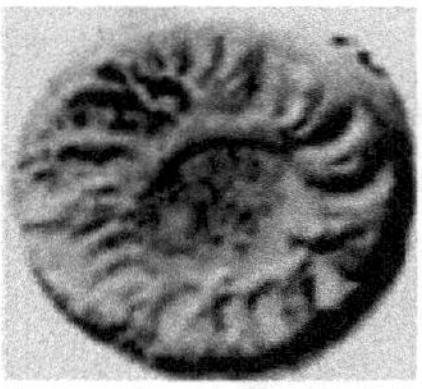

The Tablet of Shamash. Relief image on the Tablet of Shamash, British Library room 55. Found in Sippar (Tell Abu Habbah), in

Ancient Babylonia ; it dates from the 9th century BC and shows

the sun god Shamash on the throne, in front of the Babylonian king Nabu-apla-iddina (888-855 BC) between two interceding deities. The text tells how the king made a new cultic statue for the god and gave privileges to his temple.

Šamaš ';Sun' (Akkadian) (As shown in the cuneiform text on Sit Shamshi bronze).

Cognates in Meluhha --Indian *sprachbund*: शुष्णः [शुष्-नः कित् Uṇ.3.12] 1 The sun. -2 Fire. शुष्मन् *m.* 1 Fire; Śi.14.22; सार्धं तेनानुजेना प्रतिहतगतिना मारुतेनेव शुष्मा Śiva B.2.68; ऋतुशुष्ममहोष्मभिः N.17.168. 1 Strength, prowess. -2 Light, lustre. (Sanskrit) شعاعه *<u>sh</u>uœā-œa'h*, s.f. (3rd) (from شع) Light, splendor, lustre, rays of the sun, radiance, sunshine, etc. Pl. يْ *ey*.
لو شه پ *palo<u>sh</u>a'h*, s.f. (3rd) A ray of light, as of the sun, a lamp, etc. Pl. يْ *ey*. (Pashto)

A bronze plate with the ritual scene called *sit shamshi* (Soutzo et al., 1911, pp. 143-51), which the inscription attributes to Shilhak-Inshushinak (ca. 1150-20; Scheil, 1911, pp. 58-59, pl. 11.1). A further discovery was the statue of Napir-Asu, wife of Untash-Napirisha (r. ca. 1340-1300), the builder of the new city of Dur-Untash, which is better known by the modern name of Chogha Zanbil (see <u>ČOĞĀ ZANBIL</u>; Jéquier et al., 1905,pp. 245-50 and pls. XV-XVI). The two temples of the Acropolis were situated, one to the west, the other to the east of the High Terrace of the Agade Period (ca. 2335-2155) (Steve and Gasche, 1971, pp. 46, 59-62, and plan 1 at end), and what was left of them was razed to the ground by the de Morgan excavations. The High Terrace may have had an Ur III phase or, more probably, contained a first ziggurat, the remains of which were described as a "nucleus in unbaked bricks and crushed earth" (see, e.g., Soutzo et al., 1911, p. 65).

Sit Shamshi bronze plate is a model of *kole.l* 'smithy, temple' Elamitic inscription on it, mentions "*Sit Shamshi*" (= the rising of the Sun)

Model of a temple, called the Sit-shamshi, made for the ceremony of the rising sun -12th century B.C.E. is a model of a smithy, as evidenced by the meanings conveyed by Meluhha hieroglyphs read rebus as Meluhha glosses:

Four knobbed indentations or clumps flank the ziggurat. If they denotate ingots (like round-shaped bun ingots), the rebus readings are: खोट [khōṭa] *f* A mass of metal (unwrought or of old metal melted down); an ingot or wedge. Hence खोटसाळ [khōṭasāḷa] *a* (खोट & साळ from शाला) Alloyed--a metal. (Marathi)
Bshk. *khoṭ* 'embers', Phal. *khūṭo* 'ashes, burning coal'; L. *khoṭ*f. 'alloy, impurity', °*ṭā* 'alloyed', awāṇ. *khoṭā* 'forged'; Punjabi. *khoṭ* m. 'base, alloy' M.*khoṭā* 'alloyed' (CDIAL 3931)
Alternative: *ḍhāḷ* = a slope; the inclination of a plane;m ḍhāḷiyum = adj. sloping, inclining (Gujarati) Rebus: *ḍhāḷako* = a large metal ingot (Gujarati).

gaṇḍa 'four' (santali); rebus: kaṇḍ fire-altar, furnace' (santali)
खांडा [khāṇḍā] *m* A jag, notch, or indentation (as upon the edge of a tool or weapon). (Marathi) Rebus: *khāṇḍā* 'tools, pots and pans, metal-ware'.

Dotted circle glyph: context, vedi glyph, ivory artifacts
There are three distinct glyphs in this composition:
1. Round dot like a blob -- . raised large-sized dot -- (*gōṭī* 'round pebble);

2. Dotted circle *khaṇḍa* 'A piece, bit, fragment, portion'; *kandi* 'bead';

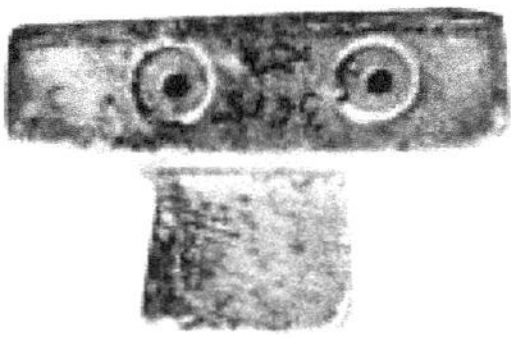

3. A + shaped structure where the glyphs 1 and 2 are infixed. The + shaped structure is *kaṇḍ* 'a fire-altar' (which is associated with glyphs 1 and 2)..

Rebus readings are: 1. *khoṭ* m. 'alloy'; 2. *khaṇḍā* 'tools, pots and pans and metal-ware'; 3. *kaṇḍ* 'furnace, fire-altar, consecrated fire'. Four 'round spot'; glyphs around the 'dotted circle' in the center of the composition: *gōṭī* 'round pebble; Rebus 1: L. *khoṭ* f 'alloy, impurity', °*ṭā* 'alloyed', awāṇ. *khoṭā* 'forged'; P. *khoṭ* m. 'base, alloy' M.*khoṭā* 'alloyed' (CDIAL 3931) Rebus 2: kōṭhī] f (कोष्ट S) A granary, garner, storehouse, warehouse, treasury, factory, bank. *khoṭā* 'alloyed' metal is produced from *kaṇḍ* 'furnace, fire-altar' yielding *khaṇḍā* 'tools, pots and pans and metal-ware'. This word *khaṇḍā* is denoted by the dotted circles.

In this hieroglyphic composition, there are three distinct rebus readings: 1. Fire-altar, *kaṇḍ* 2. Dotted circles signifying perforated beads, *kandil* 3. Raised round-shaped buns, *khoṭ* 'alloy'.

Three stalks: *kolmo* 'three'; rebus: *kolami* 'smithy'. *khūṭā* m. ' peg, stump ' (Hindi) Rebus: *kūṭa* 'workshop'. Alternative readings of symbolic form 'stalk' are: Pa. *kaṇḍa* -- m.n. joint of stalk, lump. Rebus 1: *kaṇḍa* 'fire-altar, furnace' (Santali) Rebus 2: खांडा [khāṇḍā] *m* A jag, notch, or indentation (as upon the edge of a tool or weapon). Thus, three stalks are read rebus: *kaṇḍa kolami* 'fire-altar smithy'.

kole.l 'smithy'; *kuṇḍ* 'pot used for oblation with fire' *dula kunda* 'pillars' Rebus: *kũdār* 'turn: *kh*ũṭ 'native-metal-blacksmith community (guild)(making) excellent metal'. *kūṭa* 'workshop'; *āra* 'six' Rebus: *āra* 'brass'; खांडा [*khāṇḍā*] A division of a field (into six rectangle holes). (Marathi) Rebus: *khāṇḍā* 'tool, pots and pans, metalware' (Marathi).

(w. 53 cm x h. 12 cm x d. 35 cm)

On the Sit Shamshi bronze, six rectangular holes are shown on a slab placed in front of the ziggurat. Maquette d'un lieu de culte, dite le Sit-shamshi ou "(cérémonie du) lever du soleil"XIIe siècle avant J.-C. The slab is flanked by two polished lingas (conical in shape). The slab with six rectangular holes may be read rebus: खांडा [*khāṇḍā*] A division of a field. (Marathi) Rebus: *khāṇḍā* 'tool, pots and pans, metalware' (Marathi).

Two flanking pillars; a large storage pot is shown on the model next to a pillar.

dula 'pair' Rebus: dul 'cast (metal)'

Consecrated fire, pot, pillar

Ka. *kunda* a pillar of bricks, etc. *Tu.* kunda pillar, post. *Te.* kunda id. *Malt.* kunda block, log. (DEDR 1723). Rebus 1: *kund* ' brassfounder's lathe ' (Bihari)(CDIA 3295). *kũdār 'turner'* (Bengali) कोंद *kōnda* 'engraver, lapidary setting or infixing gems' (Marathi) Rebus 2: *kuṇḍamu* 'a pit for receiving and preserving consecrated fire' (Te.) Skt. kuṇḍa-round hole in ground (for water or sacred fire), pit, well, spring (DEDR 1669).

WPah.ktg. *kʋ́ṇḍh* m. ' pit or vessel used for an oblation with fire into which barley etc. is thrown ' (CDIAL 3264). *kõda* कोँद । कुलालादिकन्दुः f. a kiln; a potter's kiln (Rām. 1446; H. xi, 11); a brick-kiln (Śiv. 133); a lime-kiln. -bal -बल् । कुलालादि कन्दुस्थानम् m. the place where a kiln is erected, a brick or potter's kiln (Gr.Gr. 165).(Kashmiri)

कुलालादिकन्दुयथावद्भावः f.inf. a kiln to arise; met. to become like such a kiln (which contains no imperfectly baked articles, but only well-made perfectly baked ones), hence, a collection of good ('pucka') articles or qualities to exist.
There are three stakes on the bronze model close to water tubs.

Ku. *khuṭī* ' peg '; N. *khuṭnu* ' to stitch ' (der. **khuṭ* ' pin ' *khilnu* from *khil* s.v. khī´la --); Mth. *khuṭā* ' peg, post '; H. *khūṭā* m. ' peg, stump '; Marw. *khuṭī* f. ' peg '; M. *khuṭā* m. ' post '.2. Pk. *khuṁṭa* -- , *khoṁṭaya* -- m. ' peg, post '; Dm. *kuṇḍa* ' peg for fastening yoke to plough -- pole '; L. *khū̃ḍī* f. ' drum -- stick '; P. *khuṇḍ*, °*ḍā* m. ' peg, stump '; WPah. rudh. *khuṇḍ* ' tethering peg or post '; A. *khũṭā* ' post ', °*ṭi* ' peg '; B. *khũṭā*, °*ṭi* ' wooden post, stake, pin, wedge '; Or. *khuṇṭa*, °*ṭā* ' pillar, post '; Bi. (with -- *ḍa* --) *khũṭrā*, °*rī* ' posts about one foot high rising from body of cart '; H. *khū̃ṭā* m. ' stump, log ', °*ṭī* f. ' small peg ' (→ P. *khū̃ṭā* m., °*ṭī* f. ' stake, peg '); G. *khū̃ṭ* f. ' landmark ', *khũṭɔ* m., °*ṭī* f. ' peg ', °*ṭũ* n. ' stump ', °*ṭiyũ* n. ' upright support in frame of wagon ', *khū̃ṭṛũ* n. ' half -- burnt piece of fuel '; M. *khũṭ* m. ' stump of tree, pile in river, grume on teat ' (semant. cf. kīla -- 1 s.v. *khila -- 2), *khũṭā* m. ' stake ', °*ṭī* f. ' wooden pin ', *khũṭaḷṇẽ* ' to dibble '.WPah.kṭg. *khv́ndɔ* ' pole for fencing or piling grass round ' (Him.I 35 *nd* poss. wrong for *ṇḍ*); J. *khuṇḍā* m. ' peg to fasten cattle to '. (CDIAL 3893). Rebus: *khũṭ* 'native-metal-blacksmith community (guild)(making) excellent metal'. *kūṭa* 'workshop', Allograph: *khũṭ* = brāhmaṇi bull (G.) *khuṇṭiyo* = an uncastrated bull (Kathiawad. Gujarat)

Bronze platform shows a religious ceremony. Multi-tiered ziggurat. Two cylindrical posts flank the ziggurat. (Compare with two polished stone pillars in Dholavira; stone śivalinga-s of

Stupendous? The domed structure at Mohenjo Daro may date to Indus times, not later.

Harappa). Temple on a terrace. Sacred wood. Large storage jar. Water tubs. Three stalks. Two persons offering libations. Mid-Elamite period (15th to 12th cent. BCE)

Evokes image of the ziggurat in Mohenjo-daro fronting Great Bath. In Mohenjo-Daro, were libations similar to Sit shamshi libations offered in front of the ziggurat, to venerate ancestors?

Statue of Queen Napirasu, wife of King Untash-Napirisha

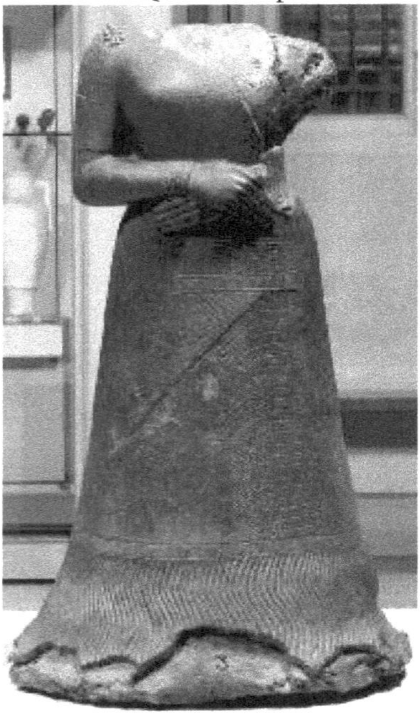

C. 1340-1300 BC. Tell of the Acropolis, Susa. J. de Morgan excavations, 1903 Sb 2731. Bronze and copper. 1,750 kg of metal used. "The work must have been cast in two successive parts: a lost-wax cast for the copper and tin shell, followed by a full cast alloy of bronze and tin for the core, rather than the more usual refractory clay. The two parts are held together with pins and splints. The sides would have originally been covered with gold or silver."149

Sculptural segments of Sit Shamshi bronze. 1. Water ablutions. 2. Ziggurat, as temple.

The ceremony involved *lo* 'pouring (water) oblation' (Munda) for the setting sun. Rebus: *loa* 'copper' (Santali) The glyphic representations connote a guild of coppersmiths in front of a ziggurat, temple and is a veneration of ancestors. It is not unlikely that the authors of the bronze Sit Shamshi model had interacted with the groups of artisans of Mohenjo-daro who had a ziggurat in front of the 'Great bath'. *kuṇḍa* ' earthen vessel ', (Oriya) **kuṇḍá**1 n. (RV. in cmpd.) ' bowl, waterpot '; *kunnu* n. ' cistern for washing clothes in '(WPah.) (CDIAL 3264). Rebus: *kv̄ṇḍh* m. ' pit or vessel used for an oblation with fire into which barley etc. is thrown '; J. *kũḍ* m. ' pool, deep hole in a stream ' (WPah.)(CDIAL 3264).

Three stakes on Sit Shamshi bronze are interpreted as hieroglyphs. *kaṇḍa* 'stake, stalk' Rebus: *kaṇḍa* 'tools, weapons, pots and pans'. kolmo 'three' Rebus: kolami 'smithy,forge'.

Three jagged sticks (stakes) on the Sit Shamshi bronze, in front of the water tank (Great Bath replica?)

Utu in Sumerian is the synonym of Akkadiam Shamash, sun divinity. Rebus: *uḍu* 'star, moon' *uḍu* f.n. ' star ' Kālid. [If isolated from uḍupa -- ' moon ', derivation from *r̥tu -- pa -- (Mayrhofer EWA i 100 with lit.) is made doubtful by the Pa. form] Pa. *uḷu* -- f. ' lunar mansion '; Pk. *uḍu* -- ; n. ' constellation '; Si. uḷu ' star '(CDIAL 1694).

In the same area, (where Sit Shamshi bronze was found), but in a particularly unclear context, a rather motley heap was found in 1904, which some described as "foundation offerings," and others as "funerary deposits." This included, notably, small lamb bearers in gold and silver, and a sharpening stone with a gold handle in the shape of a lion, as well as many intact or broken objects, jewelry, statuettes, votive arms, utensils, nails (de Morgan et al., 1905, pp. 61-136), and perhaps at this time the head of a statue (ibid., p. 125, fig. 448) which, sixty-four years later, joined its body (excavated in 1907) at the Louvre Museum (Spycket, 1968). This was the so-called "statue of the goddess Narundi," a name based on an interpretation by Walther Hinz (1962, p. 16), rather than on the inscriptions engraved on it (cf. Scheil and Legrain, 1913, pp. 17-19 and pl. 3).

H. 42 ½ in. ca. 2300 BCE. Found in Nirhursag temples. Sb6617.

She wears a flounced garment of lambswool and a headdress with horns over the hair. Rivet holes attest to gold plating of the face.

Perhaps eyes had shell and lapislazuli inlays embedded in bitumen. She holds a goblet and a palm leaf against her chest. The throne has six lions sculpted in bas-relief. Under the bare feet, two recumbent lions flank a flower. Two lions are on either side of the throne and two holding staffs stand in human posture as hero-guardians at the temple-entrance. Inscription in cuneiform Akkadian and linear Elamite. "Puzur-Inshushinak, prince (or governor) of Susa." Right edge of the throne has an Elamite inscription, read possibly as Narundi or Narunte.150

"Shilhak-Inshushinak was one of the most brilliant sovereigns of the dynasty founded by Shutruk-Nahhunte in the early 12th century BC. Numerous foundation bricks attest to his policy of construction. He built many monuments in honor of the great god of Susa, Inshushinak. The artists of Susa in the Middle-Elamite period were particularly skilled in making large bronze pieces. Other than the Sit Shamshi, which illustrates the complex technique of casting separate elements joined together with rivets, the excavations at Susa have produced one of the largest bronze statues of Antiquity: dating from the 14th century BC, the effigy of "Napirasu, wife of Untash-Napirisha," the head of which is missing, is 1.29 m high and weighs 1,750 kg. It was made using the solid-core casting method. Other bronze monuments underscore the mastery of the Susa metallurgists: for example, an altar table surrounded by snakes borne by divinities holding vases with gushing waters, and a relief depicting a procession of warriors set above a panel decorated with engravings of birds pecking under trees. These works, today mutilated, are technical feats. They prove, in their use of large quantities of metal, that the Susians had access to the principal copper mines situated in Oman and eastern Anatolia. This shows that Susa was located at the heart of a network of circulating goods and long-distance exchange."[151]

Stele representing King Untash Napirisha, "King of Anzan and Susa"
Stele of Untash Napirisha, king of Anshan and Susa. Sandstone, ca. 1340–1300 BC, brought from Chogha Zanbil to Susa in the 12th century BCE. Sb 12 A fish-tailed woman is shown holding rope-like flows of water flowing out of four vases, from one into another vase like an endless knot. Sandstone.

కాండము [kāṇḍamu] *kānḍamu*. [Sanskrit] n.

Water. నీళ్లు (Telugu) kaṇṭhá--'water -- channel'; Paš. *kaṭā´* 'irrigation channel ', Shum. *xāṭṭä*. (CDIAL 14349).
lo 'pot to overflow' Rebus: *loh* 'copper'. (A person with a vase with overflowing water; sun sign. C. 18th cent. BCE. E. Porada,1971, Remarks on seals found in the Gulf states, Artibus Asiae, 33, 31-7.)
Hieroglyph: *lokhãḍ, kāṇḍa* 'flowing water' 'overflowing pot'
Rebus: *lokhãḍ, kāṇḍā* 'metalware, tools, pots and pans'(Gujarati)
Axe inscribed with the name of King Untash-Napirisha. Wild boar figurine on the heel

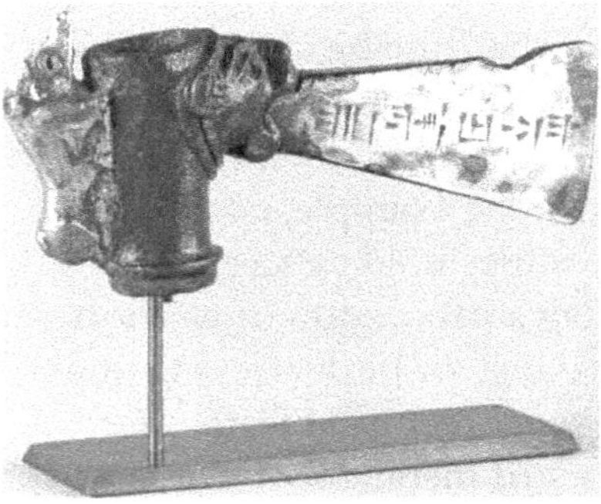

Circa 1340-1300 BCE Temple of Kiririsha in Tchoga Zanbil, Iran. Silver and electrum. Excavations by R. Ghirshman 1951-62 H. 5.9 cm; L. 12.5 cm Sb3973

Bronze fitting in the form of a seated figure.Elamite, about 1450-1200 BCE. "This bronze figure was originally fitted onto a larger object such as a piece of furniture, hence the two rivet holes for attachment through the tail-liker projection. It was obtained in south-west Iran, near the ancient town-site of Tang-e Sarvak."[152]

Appendix D: *kol* 'tiger' symbolic forms

kŕtā -- 'girl' (RV); *kuṛä´* 'girl' (Ash.); *kola* 'woman' (Nahali); 'wife'(Assamese). *kuḍa1 ' boy, son ', °*ḍī* ' girl, daughter '. [Prob. ← Mu. (Sant. Muṇḍari *koṛa* ' boy ', *kuṛi* ' girl ', Ho *koa, kui,* Kūrkū *kōn, kōnje*); or ← Drav. (Tam. *kuṟa* ' young ', Kan.*koḍa* ' youth ') T. Burrow BSOAS xii 373. Prob. separate from RV. *kŕtā* -- ' girl ' H. W. Bailey TPS 1955, 65. -- Cf. *kuḍáti* ' acts like a child ' Dhātup.] NiDoc. *kuḍ'aǵa* ' boy ', *kuḍ'i* ' girl '; Ash. *kū´ṛə* ' child, foetus ', *istrimalī* -- *kuṛä´* ' girl '; Kt. *kŕū, kuŕuk* ' young of animals '; Pr. *kyútru* ' young of animals, child ', *kyurú* ' boy ',*kurī´* ' colt, calf '; Dm. *kúŕa* ' child ', Shum. *kuṛ*; Kal. *kūŕ**l*k* ' young of animals '; Phal. *kuṛī̃* ' woman, wife '; K. *kūrü* f. ' young girl ', kash. *kōṛī*, ram. *kuṛhī*; L. *kuṛā* m. ' bridegroom ',*kuṛī* f. ' girl, virgin, bride ', awāṇ. *kuṛī* f. ' woman '; P. *kuṛī* f. ' girl, daughter ', P. bhaṭ. WPah. khaś. *kuṛi*, cur. *kuḷī*, cam. *kŏḷā* ' boy ', *kuṛī* ' girl '; -- B. *āṭ* -- *kuṛā* ' childless ' (*āṭa* ' tight ')? -- X pṓta -- 1: WPah. bhad. *kō* ' son ', *kūī* ' daughter ', bhal. *ko* m., *koi* f., pāḍ.*kuā, kōī*, paṅ. *koā, kūī.* (CDIAL 3245) kōla1 m. ' name of a degraded tribe ' Hariv. Pk. *kōla* -- m.; B. *kol* ' name of a Muṇḍā tribe '(CDIAL 3532).

M. *koḷẽ* n. ' hump on a bull '(CDIAL 3607).

Ku. *kol* ' womb '; OMarw. *kola* m. ' foetus H. *kor* f. ' womb 'M. *koḷ* m. ' lap ' (CDIAL 3607)

kola, kolum = a jackal (G.) kolhuyo (Dh.Des.); kulho, kolhuo (Hem.Des.); kroṣṭṛ (Skt.) kul seren = the tiger's son, a species of lizard (Santali) kolo, kolea_ jackal (Kon.lex.) Jackal: kuṟi-nari jackal (Kur-r-ā. Tala. Vēṭan-valam. 13)(Ta.); id. (Ma.)(Ta.lex.) kul tiger; kul dander den of tiger; an.d.kul to become tiger; hudur. to growl as tiger; maran. d.at.kap kul a big-headed tiger (Santali.lex.) kōlupuli = a big, huge tiger, royal or Bengal tiger; kōlu = big, great, huge (Te.lex.) kula tiger; syn. of maran: kula, burukula, kamsikula, the striped royal tiger; syn. of maran: kula, laṛokula, the brown royal tiger without stripes; syn. of hur.in: kula, soncita, leopard: sin:kula = the lion; kindorkula, kinduakula = the panther; tagukula (lit. the shaggy tiger), the hyena; ḍurkula, a smaller feline animal, which when attacking a man bites him in the knee, probably a tiger-cat; kula-bin: collective noun for all dangerous animals; kulabin:-o to become infested by dangerous animals; kla (Khasi.Rongao) tiger (Mundari.lex.) kroṣṭṛ. = jackal (RV.); kroṣṭu = id. (Pa_.n.); kroṣṭṛ = crying (BhP.); koṭṭhu, koṭṭhuka, kotthu, kotthuka = jackal (Pali); koṭṭhu (Pkt.); koṭa (Si.); koṭiya = leopard (Si.); kōlhuya, kulha = jackal (Pkt.); kolhā, kolā jackal; adj. crafty (H.); kohlũ, kohlū jackal (G.); kolhā, kolā (M.)(CDIAL 3615). Fr. krus' = cry, call; krōśati cries out (RV)(CDIAL 3613). *koṭho* = a call, a messenger; koṭha invitation; koṭhaṇu = to send for (S.)(CDIAL 3614). koś to abuse, curse, blame (Gypsy); kosna_ to curse (H.); kosn.a_ (P.); akos' to abuse (Gypsy); kros'ati cries out (RV)(CDIAL 3612). krośa shout (VS); kuru_ voice, word (Pas'); kosā curse (H.)(CDIAL 3611). kuḷ = the tiger, filis tigris; kul en:ga = tigress; *kul seren* 'the 'tiger's song', a species of lizard (Santali) Rebus: kol metal (Ta.) kol = pañcalōkam (five metals) (Ta.) pañcaloha = a metallic alloy containing five metals: copper, brass, tin, lead and iron (Sanskrit); an alternative list of five metals: gold, silver, copper, tin (lead), and iron (dhātu; Nānārtharatnākara. 82; Mangarāja's Nighaṇṭu. 498)(Ka.) *kol, kolhe*, 'the koles, an aboriginal tribe if iron smelters speaking a language akin to that of Santals' (Santali) kol = kolla ṉ, kammāḷan- (blacksmith or smith in general)(Ta.) kollar = those who guard the treasure (Ta.lex.) cf. golla (Telugu) khol, kholī = a metal covering; a loose covering of metal or cloth (Gujarati) [The semant. expansions to kollāpuri or kolhāpur and also to 'kollāppaṇṭi' a type of cart have to be investigated further].

kol 'working in iron, blacksmith (Ta.); *kollan-* blacksmith (Ta.); *kollan* blacksmith, artificer (Ma.)(DEDR 2133)

Appendix E: *eṟaka* 'upraised arm'

m1405 Tablet. Person standing at the center points with his right hand at a bison facing a trough, and with his left hand points to the ligatured glyph. This tablet is a clear and unambiguous example of the fundamental orthographic style of Indus Script inscriptions that: both signs and pictorial motifs are integral components of the message conveyed by the inscriptions. The inscription on the tablet juxtaposes – through the hand gestures of a person - a 'trough' gestured with the right hand; a ligatured glyph composed of 'rim-of-jar' glyph and 'water-carrier' glyph (Sign 15) gestured with the left hand.

The inscription of this tablet is composed of four glyphs: bison, trough, shoulder (person), ligatured glyph -- Glyph 15 (rim-of-jar glyph ligatured to water-carrier glyph).

Variants for Glyph 15 (Mahadevan)

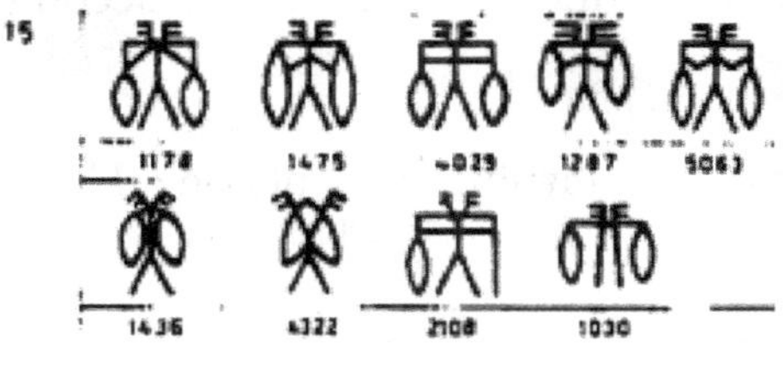

Variants (Parpola)

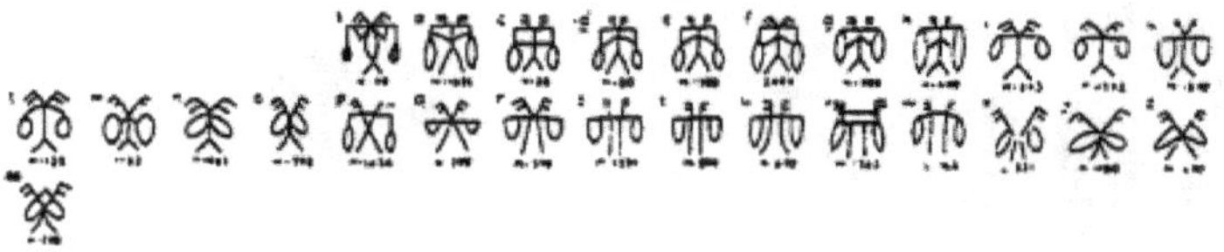

ḍangur m. 'bullock', rebus: ḍāṅro 'blacksmith' (Nepali) Alternative: *kondā* , *konda* bullock, ox (Gondi) Rebus: *kõda* 'turner, to turn in a lathe'. *pattar* 'trough' (Ta.), rebus *paṭṭar-ai* community; guild as of workmen (Ta.); pattar merchants (Ta.); perh. *vartaka* (Skt.) *pātharī* 'precious stone' (OMarw.) (CDIAL 8857)

meḍ ‘body’ (Mu.); rebus: *meḍ* ‘iron’ (Ho.); *eṛaka* 'upraised arm' (Ta.); rebus: *eraka* ‘copper‘ (Kannada)
Ligature in composite glyph: kan-ka ‘rim of jar’ (Santali), rebus karṇaka ‘scribe, accountant’ (Pa.); vikalpa: 1. kāraṇika -- m. ‘arrow-maker’ (Pa.) 2. khanaka ‘miner, digger, excavator’ (Skt.). Ligature 2 in composite glyph: *kuṭi* ‘water-carrier’ (Telugu), rebus: *kuṭhi* ‘smelter furnace’ (Santali)

Water-carrier glyph kuṭi ‘water-carrier’ (Telugu); Rebus: kuṭhi ‘smelter furnace’ (Santali) kuṛī f. ‘fireplace’ (H.); krvṛI f. ‘granary (WPah.); kuṛī, kuṛo house, building’(Ku.)(CDIAL 3232) kuṭi ‘hut made of boughs’ (Skt.) guḍi temple (Telugu) [The bull is shown in front of the trough for drinking; hence the semantics of ‘drinking’.]

The most frequently occurring glyph is thus explained as a ‘furnace scribe’ and is consistent with the readings of glyphs which occur together with this glyph. Kan-ka may denote an artisan working with copper, *kan̲* (Ta.) *kan̲n̲ār* ‘coppersmiths, blacksmiths’ (Ta.) Thus, the phrase *kaṇḍ karṇaka* may be decoded rebus as a brassworker, scribe. *karṇaka* ‘scribe, accountant’. *karṇī* ‘supercargo’.

The entire composition of glyphic elements on a Harappa tablet, h180:

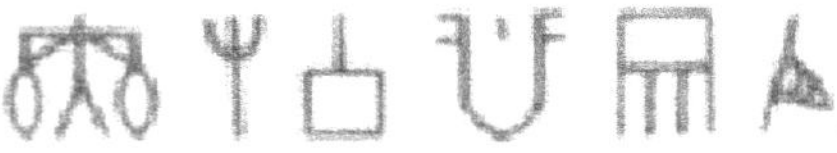
4304

Other glyphic elements of the tablet:

Text 4304

This narrative shows upraised arms of the seated woman with disheveled hair confronted by A person carrying a sickle-shaped weapon and a wheel on his hands. kuṭhāru 'armourer' (Skt.) *rabca* 'dishevelled' <rabca?>(D) {ADJ} ``with ^dishevelled ^hair''. Rebus: రాచ rāca (adj.) Pertaining to a stone.

Two tigers rearing on their hindlegs standing face to face.

Glyph: tiger: kola 'tiger'. Rebus: kol 'working in iron'
Glyph: dula 'pair'. Rebus: dul 'casting (metal).

A person carrying a sickle-shaped weapon and a wheel on his bands faces a woman with disheveled hair and upraised arm. kuṭhāru 'armourer' (Skt.) The glyptic composition is decoded as kuṭhāru sal 'armourer workshop.' eṛaka 'upraised arm' (Ta.). Rrebus: eraka = copper (Ka.) Thus, the entire composition of these glyphic elements relate to an armourer's copper workshop. The hairstyle of the woman is comparable to the wavy hair shown on the Samarra bowl (Image 2. Six women, curl in hair, six scorpions).

The glyphic elements shown on the tablet are: copulation, vagina, crocodile. h180 tablet. Gyphic: 'copulation': kamḍa, khamḍa 'copulation' (Santali) Rebus: kammaṭi a coiner (Ka.); kampaṭṭam coinage, coin, mint (Ta.) kammaṭa = mint, gold furnace (Te.) *khāṇḍā* tool, pots and pans, metalware (Marathi) Vikalpa: kaṇḍa 'stone (ore)'. Glyph: vagina: kuṭhi 'vagina'; rebus: kuṭhi 'smelting furnace'. The descriptive glyphics indicates that the smelting furnace is for stone (ore). This is distinquished from sand ore. Glyph: 'crocodile': karā 'crocodile'. Rebus: khar 'blacksmith'. kāru a wild crocodile or alligator (Te.) కారు mosale 'wild crocodile or alligator. S. ghaṛyālu m. ' long — snouted porpoise '; N. ghaṛiyāl ' crocodile' (Telugu)'; A. B. ghā̃ṛiyāl ' alligator ', Or. Ghaṛiāḷa, H. ghaṛyāl, ghariār m. (CDIAL 4422) கரவு[2] karavu, n. < கரா. Cf. grāha. Alligator; முதலை. கரவார்தடம் (திவ். திருவாய். 8, 9, 9). கரா karā, n. prob. Grāha. 1. A species of alligator; முதலை. கராவதன் காலினைக்கதுவ (திவ். பெரியதி. 2, 3, 9). 2. Male alligator; ஆண்முதலை. (பிங்.) கராம் karām Thus, the message of the glyphic composition is: kammaṭa kaṇḍa kuṭhi khar mint

(coiner) stone (ore) smelting furnace,

blacksmith. A comparable glyphic composition is a naked woman seated with her legs spread out flanked by two scorpions. Cylinder-seal impression from Ur showing a squatting female. L. Legrain, 1936, Ur excavations, Vol. 3, Archaic Seal Impressions. This glyphic composition depicts a smelting furnace for stone ore as distinguished from a smelting furnace for sand ore. meṛed-bica = iron stone ore, in contrast to bali-bica, iron sand ore (Mu.lex.)

bicha, bichā 'scorpion' (Assamese) Rebus: bica 'stone ore' (Mu.) sambr.o bica = gold ore (Mundarica) meṛed-bica = iron stone ore, in contrast to bali-bica, iron sand ore (Mu.lex.)

bhaṭa 'six '; rebus: bhaṭa 'furnace'.

satthiya 'svastika glyph'; rebus: satthiya 'zinc', jasta 'zinc' (Kashmiri), satva, 'zinc' (Pkt.)

kola 'woman'; rebus: kol 'iron'. kola 'blacksmith' (Ka.); kollë 'blacksmith' (Koḍ)

muha -- n. 'mouth, face' (Pkt.) mũh 'face'; rebus: mũh 'ingot' (Mu.)

kul 'tiger' (Santali); kōlu id. (Te.) kōlupuli = Bengal tiger (Te.) कोल्हा [kōlhā] कोल्हें [kōlhēṃ] A jackal (Marathi) rebus: kol 'furnace, forge' (Kuwi) kol 'alloy of five metals, pañcaloha' (Tamil) kol 'working in iron, blacksmith'; kollan̲ 'blacksmith' (Tamil).

ṭagara = tabernae montana (Skt.) ṭagara 'antelope'; rebus: ṭagara 'tin'. Cf. cognate: tamkāru, damgar 'merchant'(Sumerian).

ḍā̃gar 'horned cattle' (K.) rebus: ḍāṅgar 'blacksmith' (H.) damgar 'merchant, trader'(Sumerian).

A seal from Saar. 4025:06. Dia. 2.45. Ht. 0.95. Central figure with upraised arms, legs splayed and a prominent vulva. Below her is a flat-topped stand with two hoofed legs. Standing males flank her. One has a large erect penis. *eraka* 'upraised arm' Rebus: *eraka* 'copper'.

Saar. K16:29:13. Dia 0.9 ht 1.75. Schematic design. Snake as a vertical zigzag with a beak-like antelope head. To either side is a stylized human figure with upraised arms. In the right field, a hatched motif, perhaps a fish.

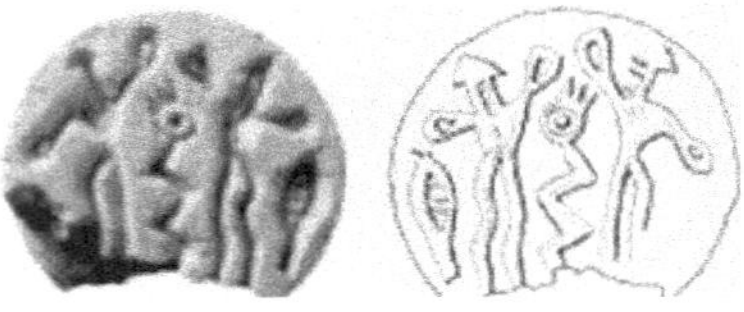

1224

m1224e

Pict-88

1227 Standing person with horns and bovine features (hoofed legs and/or tail).

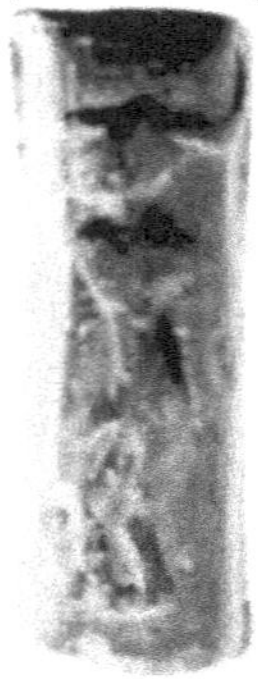

h175B Pict-87 Text 4319 Standing person with horns and bovine features (hoofed legs and/or tail).

h714A Standing person with horns and bovine features (hoofed legs and/or a tail)

Icon of a person has bull's legs and a raised club.

4305 Pict-90: Standing person with horns and bovine features holding a staff or mace on his shoulder.

Appendix F: *dhokra kamar* 'lost-wax metal caster'

Evidence obtained so far, during the last 140 years since the publication of the first seal from Harappa by Alexander Cunningham, Director General of Archaeological Survey of India, from an interaction area which also spanned the Fertile Crescent, is consistent that Meluhha artisans had blazed the trail of lost-wax metallurgy. For a Meluhhan, smithy kole.l (Kota language) was also a temple.

Cire perdue or lost-wax casting metallurgy spread from Meluhha into the Fertile Crescent (Nahal Mishmar). The lost-wax casting method was also evidenced in Sarasvati-Sindhu civilization area. A good example is that of a dancing girl metal statue, perhaps of bronze.

The rebus reading of two epigraphs: one from Mohenjo-Daro and another from Dholavira, refers to a very unique technique in metallurgy called *cire perdue* (lost wax) technique for casting metal objects like the dancing girl statue of a dancing girl in Mohenjo-daro. This technique is called dhokra.

The hieroglyph denotes this word in Meluhha semantics. Risley defines 'Dhokra' as: "A sub-caste of kamars or blacksmiths in Western Bengal, who make brass idols." (Risley, HH ,1891, The Tribes and Castes of Bengal. Government of Bengal, Calcutta Vol. 1, p. 236)

Dholavira molded terracotta tablet with Meluhha hieroglyphs written on two sides.

Hieroglyphs: karnaka 'rim of jar'. eraka 'upraised arm'. dhokra 'decrepit woman with breasts hanging down'. kara 'crocodile'. *ḍhangar* 'bull'; *ḍhagaram* 'buttock'.

adaren 'lid'. **खांडा** khāṇḍā 'notch'. kot 'curved'. sal 'splinter'. dula 'pair'. **kuṭilá** ' bent, crooked ' KātyŚr., °*aka* -- Pañcat., n. ' a partic. plant ' lex. [√kuṭ1] Pa. *kuṭila* -- ' bent ', n. ' bend '; Pk. *kuḍila* -- ' crooked ', °*illa* -- ' humpbacked ', °*illaya* -- ' bent '(CDIAL 3231) *sangaḍa* 'frame of building'; *kuṭila* = bent, crooked (Skt.Rasaratna samuccaya, 5.205) Humpbacked *kuḍilla* (Pkt.) Rebus: *ḍhangar* 'blacksmith' aduru 'native metal' khaṇḍa 'tools, vessels, or articles in general.' (Marathi); *sangaḍa* 'fortification', j*angaḍ* 'entrustment articles' *kuṭila, katthīl* = bronze (8 parts copper and 2 parts tin) [cf. āra-kūṭa, 'brass' (Sanskrit). *eraka* 'upraised arm' Rebus: *erako* 'moltencast copper'. Thus, the entire set of hieroglyphs on the tablet conveys the message of metal, alloy, moltencast copper artifacts made by cireperdue method by *dhokra* blacksmith (of fortification) and conveyed as 'entrustment articles'.

Rebus readings:
Side 1: *kole.l* 'smithy'; *koṭ-sal* 'alloy furnace'; adaren khanda 'native metal tools, pots and pans'; dul 'metal casting'; kan-ka 'scribe'. *kan-ka, karṇaka* 'rim of jar' Rebus: *kaṇḍa karṇaka* 'furnace account scribe'. *kārṇī(ka)* 'supercargo of a ship' (Marathi)
Side 2: khar 'blacksmith, artisan'; dhokra 'cire perdue' metal casting; dhangar 'smith'; eraka 'copper'

Meluhha glosses:

Ko. kole·l smithy, temple in Kota village. To. kwala·l Kota smithy. (DEDR 2133).
B. kerā ' clerk ' (kerāni ' id. ' < *kīraka-- karaṇika<-> ODBL 540)(CDIAL 3170) kāraṇika m. ' teacher ' MBh., ' judge ' Pañcat. [kā- raṇa --]Pa. usu -- kāraṇika -- m. ' arrow -- maker '; Pk. kāraṇiya -- m. ' teacher of Nyāya '; S. kāriṇī m. ' guardian, heir '; N. kārani ' abettor in crime '; M. kārṇī m. ' prime minister,

supercargo of a ship ', kul -- karṇī m. ' village accountant '.(CDIAL 3058).

kárṇaka m. ' projection on the side of a vessel, handle ' ŚBr. [kárṇa --]Pa. kaṇṇaka -- ' having ears or corners '; Wg. kaṇə ' ear -- ring ' NTS xvii 266; S. kano m. ' rim, border '; P. kannā m. ' obtuse angle of a kite ' (→ H.kannā m. ' edge, rim, handle '); N. kānu ' end of a rope for supporting a burden '; B. kāṇā ' brim of a cup ', G. kānɔ m.; M. kānā m. ' touch -- hole of a gun '.(CDIAL 2831).

sal 'splinter' Rebus: sal 'workshop', 'furnace'.

Ta. koṭu curved, bent, crooked; koṭumai crookedness, obliquity; koṭukki hooked bar for fastening doors, clasp of an ornament; koṭuṅ-kāy cucumber; koṭuṅ-kaifolded arm; koṭu-maram bow; koṭu-vāy curved or bent edge (as of billhook); koṭu-vāḷ pruning knife, billhook, sickle, battle-axe; kuṭa curved, bent; kuṭakkam bend, curve, crookedness; kuṭakki that which is crooked (DEDR 2054). Rebus: khōṭ 'alloyed ingot'.

खांडा [khāṇḍā] m a jag, notch, or indentation (as upon the edge of a tool or weapon); rebus: khāṇḍā 'metal tools, pots and pans'.

aḍaren, ḍaren lid, cover (Santali) Rebus: aduru 'native metal' (Ka.)

கராம் karām, n. prob. grāha. 1. A species of alligator; முதலைவகை. முதலையு மிடங்கருங் கராமும் (குறிஞ்சிப். 257). 2. Male alligator; ஆண் முதலை. (திவா.) కారుమొసలి a wild crocodile or alligator. (Telugu)

khār 1 खार् । लोहकारः m. (sg. abl. khāra 1 खार; the pl. dat. of this word is khāran 1 खारन्, which is to be distinguished from khāran 2, q.v., s.v.), a blacksmith, an iron worker (cf. bandūka-khār, p. 111b, l. 46; K.Pr. 46; H. xi, 17); a farrier (El.). This word is often a part of a name, and in such case comes at the end (W. 118) as in Wahab khār, Wahab the smith (H. ii, 12; vi, 17).(Kashmiri)

Hieroglyph: Ku. ḍokro, ḍokhro ' old man '; B. ḍokrā ' old, decrepit ', Or. ḍokarā; H. ḍokrā ' decrepit '; G. ḍokɔ m. ' penis ', ḍokrɔ m. ' old man ', M. ḍokrā m. -- Kho. (Lor.) duk ' hunched up, hump of camel '; K. ḍọ̄ku ' humpbacked ' perh. < *ḍōkka -- 2. Or. dhokaṛa ' decrepit, hanging down (of breasts) '.(CDIAL 5567). M. ḍhẽg n. ' groin ', ḍhẽgā m. ' buttock '. M. dhõgā m. ' buttock '. (CDIAL 5585).

Hieroglyph: N. dhokro ' large jute bag ', B. dhokaṛ; Or. dhokaṛa ' cloth bag '; Bi. dhōkrā ' jute bag '; Mth. dhokṛā ' bag, vessel, receptacle '; H. dhukṛīf. ' small bag '; G. dhokṛũ n. ' bale of cotton '; -- with -- ṭṭ -- : M. dhokṭī f. ' wallet '; -- with -- n -- : G. dhokṇũ n. ' bale of cotton '; -- with -- s -- : N. (Tarai) dhokse ' place covered with a mat to store rice in '.2. L. dhohẽ (pl. dhūhī̃) m. ' large thatched shed '.3. M. dhõgḍā m. ' coarse cloth ', dhõgṭī f. ' wallet '.4. L. ḍhok f. ' hut in the fields '; Ku. ḍhwākā m. pl. ' gates of a city or market '; N. ḍhokā (pl. of *ḍhoko) ' door '; -- OMarw. ḍhokaro m. ' basket '; -- N.ḍhokse ' place covered with a mat to store rice in, large basket '.(CDIAL 6880)

Rebus: *dhokra* 'cire perdue' casting metalsmith.

Hieroglyph: Br. kōnḍō on all fours, bent double. (DEDR 204a) Rebus: kunda 'turner' kundār turner (A.); kūdār, kūdāri (B.); kundāru (Or.); kundau to turn on a lathe, to carve, to chase; kundau dhiri = a hewn stone; kundau murhut = a graven image (Santali) kunda a turner's lathe (Skt.)(CDIAL 3295)

Tiger has head turned backwards. క్రమ్మర krammara. adv.

క్రమ్మరిల్లు or క్రమరబడు Same as క్రమ్మరు (Telugu). Rebus: krəm back'(Kho.)(CDIAL 3145) karmāra 'smith, artisan' (Skt.) kamar 'smith' (Santali)

Continuing lost-wax legacy of Dholavira, Mohenjo-daro evidenced in Meluhha hieroglyphs

dhokra kamar metalworker, *sangatarāśū* stone-cutter
Meluhhan metalsmiths knew the techniques of bead making, soldering, sheet making, riveting, coiling and cire perdue casting (lost wax metal casting process).

Lost-wax method mentioned in ancient Indian texts

The 5th-century CE Vishnusamhita, an appendix to the *Viṣṇu Purāṇa*, refers directly to the modeling of wax for making metal objects in chapter XIV: "if an image is to be made of metal, it must first be made of wax." Chapter 68 of the ancient Sanskrit text *Mānasāra Śilpa* details casting idols in wax and is entitled *maduchchhista vidhānam*, or the "lost wax method". The *Mānasollāsa* (also known as the *Abhilasitārtha chintāmani*), allegedly written by King Bhūlokamalla Somesvara of the Chalukya dynasty of Kalyāni in CE 1124-1125, also provides detail about lost-wax and other casting processes. In a 16th-century treatise, the Uttarabhaga of the Śilparatna written by Srïkumāra, verses 32 to 52 of Chapter 2 ("Linga lakshanam"), give detailed instructions on making a hollow casting.

Metalcasting examples of the Indus Valley Civilization which began around 3500 BCE, include the buffalo, bull and dog found at Mohenjodaro and Harappa, two copper figures found at the Harappan site Lothal in the district of Ahmedabad of Gujarat,and likely a covered cart with wheels missing and a complete cart with a driver found at Chanhudaro.

During the post-Harappan period, hoards of copper and bronze implements made by the lost-wax process are known from Uttar Pradesh, Bihar, Madhya Pradesh, Odisha, Andhra Pradesh and West Bengal.Gold and copper ornaments, apparentlyHellenistic in style, made by cire perdue were found at the ruins at Sirkap. One example of this Indo-Greek art dates to the 1st century BC, the juvenile figure of Harpocrates excavated at Taxila. Bronze icons were produced during the 3rd and 4th centuries, such as the Buddha image at Amaravati, and the images of Rama and Kartikeya in the Guntur district of Andhra Pradesh. A further two bronze images of Parsvanatha and a small hollow-cast bull came from Sahribahlol, Gandhara, and a standing Tirthankara (2nd, 3rd century CE) from Chausa in Bihar should be mentioned here as well. Other notable bronze figures and images have been found in Rupar, Mathura (in Uttar Pradesh) and Brahmapura, Maharashtra.

Gupta and post-Gupta period bronze figures have been recovered from the following sites: Saranath, Mirpur-Khas (in Pakistan), Sirpur (District of Raipur), Balaighat (near Mahasthan now in Bangladesh), Akota (near Vadodara, Gujurat), Vasantagadh, Chhatarhi, Barmer and Chambi (in Rajesthan). Producing images by the lost-wax process reached its peak from 750 to 1100, and still remained prevalent in south India between 1500 and 1850[153]:

Dhokra (Oriya: ଢୋକରା, Bengali: ডোকরা) (also spelt Dokra) is non–ferrous metal casting using the lost-wax casting technique. This sort of metal casting has been used in India for over 4,000 years and is still used. One of the earliest known lost wax artefacts is the dancing girl of Mohenjo-daro… Dhokra Damar tribes are the traditional metalsmiths of West Bengal. Their technique of lost wax casting is named after their tribe, hence Dhokra metal casting. The tribe extends from Jharkhand to West Bengal and Orissa; members are distant cousins of the Chattisgarh Dhokras. A few hundred years ago the Dhokras of Central and Eastern India traveled south as far as Kerala and north as far as Rajasthan and hence are now found all over India.[154]

"The basic process for lost wax casting consists of a clay core that is approximately the shape of the desired final image. The clay core is then covered by a layer of wax composed of pure bee's wax, resin from the tree Damara orientalis, and nut oil. The wax is then carved and shaped into a detailed model for the final image. The model is then covered by layers of clay, which takes the negative form of the wax on the inside thus becoming a mold for the metal that will be poured inside it. Drain ducts are left for the wax, which melts away when the clay is cooked. The wax is then replaced by the molten metal, which is poured in and hardens between the core and the inner surface of the mold. The metal fills the mold and takes the same shape as the wax. The outer layer of clay is then chipped off and the metal icon is polished and finished as desired… Dhokra Damar tribes are the traditional metalsmiths of West Bengal. Their technique of lost wax casting is named after their tribe, hence Dhokra metal casting. The tribe extends from Bihar to West Bengal and Orissa; members are distant cousins of the Madhya Pradesh Dhokras. A few hundred years ago the Dhokras of Central and Eastern India traveled south as far as Kerla and north as far as Rajasthan.

There are two main processes of lost wax casting: solid casting, which is predominant in the south of India, and hollow casting, which is more common in Central and Eastern India. As the names imply, solid casting does not use a clay core but instead a solid piece of wax to create the mold; hollow casting is the more traditional method and uses the clay core.[155]

डोंगरी [ḍōṅgarī] f (Dim. of डोंगर) A little hill. a Growing or produced on hills; consisting of hills; relating to hills or a hill.
डोंगर [ḍōṅgara] m A hill. डोंगरकणगर or डोंगरकंगर [ḍōṅgarakaṇagara or ḍōṅgarakaṅgara] m (डोंगर & कणगर form of redup.) Hill and mountain; hills comprehensively or indefinitely.
डोंगरकोळी [ḍōṅgarakōḷī] m A caste of hill people or an individual of it. (Marathi)

डोकरा [ḍōkarā] a (H) Aged or old. Used of persons abusively or contemptuously. डोकरी or डोकरीण [ḍōkarī or ḍōkarīṇa] f (डोकरा) A very aged woman, a.crone. Always implying abuse on account of decrepitude, deformity, or ugliness. (Marathi) Kuwi (P.2) ḍong- (-it-), (Isr.) ḍōṅg- (-it-) to be bent, crooked; (P.2) ḍok- (-h-), (Isr.)ḍōk- (-h-) to bend (elbow, wrist, finger)(DEDR 2054) Mar. ḍõgā curved, bent.
Re(B)F {N(F)} ``^woman, ^old_woman, ^wife''. Masc. . *Des.. `being an old woman what shall I do?'. @B23080,N113. #31841.(B)F {N(F)} ``^woman, ^old_woman, ^wife''. Masc. . *Des.. @B12770,N120. #9051. So,,(L) {NK} ``^wife, to take a wife, ^marry''. *Or.K. `you (pl.) have become old'. *Des.. (F) {N} ``^old_^woman''. @N120. #9062.(C) {ADJ} ``^old''. {N} ``^old ^man''. @S,N119. #4711. a>(F) {ADJ(M)} ``^tall (masc.)''. @N200. #8092.
(F) {ADJ(M)} ``^old (masc.)''. @N119. #9022. `if you were old your skin would have contracted'. @B19040. #5891. (B) {N} ``a ^certain man and woman (used mostly in stories)''. @B12780. #8332.(B) {N(M)} ``^male, ^old man, ^elder, ^man, ^husband''. Fem. . E.g. `male monkey (i.e. leader)'; `you (pl.) have become old'. *Des.. @B12750, B12760,N119. #9021.(Munda etyma)

Dhokra kamar as a Meluhha hieroglyph: Dholavira, Mohenjo-daro seals Rebus: lost-wax casting

Dholavira molded terracotta tablet with Meluhha hieroglyphs written on two sides. Hieroglyph: Ku. ḍokro, ḍokhro ' old man '; B. ḍokrā ' old, decrepit ', Or. ḍokarā; H. ḍokrā ' decrepit '; G. ḍokɔ m. ' penis ', ḍokrɔ m. ' old man ', M. ḍokrā m. -- Kho. (Lor.) duk ' hunched up, hump of camel '; K. ḍọ̆ku ' humpbacked ' perh. < *ḍōkka -- 2. Or. dhokaṛa ' decrepit, hanging down (of breasts) '.(CDIAL 5567). M. ḍhẽg n. ' groin ', ḍhẽgā m. ' buttock '. M. dhõgā m. ' buttock '. (CDIAL 5585). Glyph: Br. kōnḍō on all fours, bent double. (DEDR 204a) Rebus: kunda 'turner' kundār turner (A.); kūdār, kūdāri (B.); kundāru (Or.); kundau to turn on a lathe, to carve, to chase; kundau dhiri = a hewn stone; kundau murhut = a graven image (Santali) kunda a turner's lathe (Skt.)(CDIAL 3295)
The hieroglyph of an old female with breasts hanging down and ligatured to the buttock of a bovine is deployed on a Mohenjo-daro seal. The ligatured, horned woman is standing near a tree fisting a horned tiger rearing on its hindlegs and looking back.

Mohenjo-daro Seal. Pict-103 Horned (female with breasts hanging down?) person with a tail and bovine legs standing near a leaf-less tree raising her hand to fist a horned tiger looking back, rearing on its hindlegs. 1357

Dholavira. Seal. heraka 'spy' Rebus: eraka 'copper, molten cast'. *khōṇḍa* 'leafless tree' Rebus: *kõdā* ' to turn in a lathe.'

Tiger has head turned backwards. క్రమ్మర *krammara.* adv. Type 2: melh 'goat' (Br.); milakkhu 'copper' (Pali) Type 3: tagara 'ram' Rebus: tagara 'tin' damgar 'merchant' (Akkadian)

kola 'tiger' Rebus: kol 'working in iron'. kot 'horn' Rebus: khot 'alloyed metal'. Dhokra 'decrepit woman with breasts hanging down' Rebus: dhokra 'cire perdue' casting metalsmith. Eraka 'raised arm' Rebus: eraka 'copper'. kuti 'tree' Rebus: kuti 'smelter furnace'.

Tiger has head turned backwards. క్రమ్మర krammara. adv.

క్రమ్మరిల్లు or క్రమరబడు Same as క్రమ్మరు (Telugu). Rebus: krəm back'(Kho.)(CDIAL 3145) karmāra 'smith, artisan' (Skt.) kamar 'smith' (Santali)

Ta. karaṭi, karuṭi, keruṭi fencing, school or gymnasium where wrestling and fencing are taught. *Ka.* garaḍi, garuḍi fencing school. *Tu.* garaḍi, garoḍi id. *Te.* gariḍi, gariḍī id., fencing.(DEDR 1262).

1264 *Ta.* karaṭi, karaṭi-ppaṟai, karaṭikai a kind of drum(said to sound like a bear, karaṭi). *Ka.* karaḍi, karaḍe an oblong drum beaten on both sides, a sort of double drum. / Cf. Skt. karaṭa- a kind of drum.(DEDR 1264).

1265 *Ta.* karaṭu roughness, unevenness, churlish temper; karaṭṭu rugged, uneven, unpolished; karaṇ uneven surface in vegetables and fruits, scar; karu prong, barb, spike;karumai, karil severity, cruelty; karukku teeth of a saw or sickle, jagged edge of palmyra leaf-stalk, sharpness. *Ma.* karaṭu what is rough or uneven; kaṟu rough;kaṟuppu roughness; karuma sharpness of sword; karukku teeth of a saw or file, thorns of a palmyra branch, irregular surface; karukarukka to be harsh, sharp, rough, irritating; karikku edge of teeth; kari-muḷ hard thorn; projecting parts of the skin of custard-apples, jack-fruits, etc.; kari-maṭal rind of jack-fruits. *Ko.* karp keenness or harshness (of wind); ? kako·ṭ hoe with sharp, broad blade (for -ko·ṭ, see 2064). *Ka.* karaḍu that is rough, uneven, unpolished, hard, or waste, useless, or wicked; kaṟaku, karku, kakku, gaṟaku, garaku, garku, garasu a jag, notch, dent, toothed part of a file or saw, rough part of a millstone, irregular surface, sharpness. *Tu.* karaḍů, karaḍurough, coarse, worn out; wastage, loss, wear; kargōṭa hardness, hard-heartedness; hard, hard-hearted; garu rough; garime severity, strictness; gargāsů a saw. *Te.* karasharp; karagasamu a saw; karakasa roughness; karusu rough, harsh; harsh words; kaṟaku, kaṟuku harshness, roughness, sharpness; rough, harsh, sharp; gari hardness, stiffness, sharpness; (B.) karaṭi stubborn, brutish, villainous; kakku a notch or dent, toothed part of a saw, file, or sickle, roughness of a millstone. *Go.* (Ma.) karkara sharp (*Voc.* 543). *Kur.* karcnā to be tough, (Hahn) be hardened. ? Cf. 1260 Ka. garasu. / Cf. Skt. karaṭa- a low, unruly, difficult person; karkara- hard, firm; karkaśa- rough, harsh, hard; krakaca-, karapattra- saw; khara- hard, harsh, rough, sharp-edged; kharu- harsh, cruel; Pali kakaca- saw; khara- rough; saw; Pkt. karakaya- saw; Apabhraṃśa (*Jasaharacariu*) *karaḍa-* hard. Cf. esp. Turner, *CDIAL*, no. 2819. Cf. also Skt. karavāla- sword (for second element, cf. 5376 Ta. vāḷ)(DEDR 1265).

Kol. keḍiak tiger. Nk. khaṛeyak panther. Go. (A.) khaṛyal tiger; (Haig) kariyāl panther (Voc. 999). Kui kṛāḍi, krānḍi tiger, leopard, hyena. Kuwi (F.) kṛani tiger; (S.) klā'ni tiger, leopard; (Su. P. Isr.) kṛaˀni (pl. -ŋa) tiger. / Cf. Pkt. (DNM) karaḍa- id.(DEDR 1132).

Hieroglyph: N. dhokro ' large jute bag ', B. dhokaṛ; Or. dhokaṛa ' cloth bag '; Bi. dhokrā ' jute bag '; Mth. dhokṛā ' bag, vessel, receptacle '; H. dhukṛīf. ' small bag '; G. dhokṛũ n. ' bale of cotton '; -- with -- ṭṭ -- : M. dhokṭī f. ' wallet '; -- with -- n -- : G. dhokṇũ n. ' bale of cotton '; -- with -- s -- : N. (Tarai) dhokse ' place covered with a mat to store rice in '.2. L. dhohẽ (pl. dhūhīˇ) m. ' large thatched shed '.3. M. dhõgḍā m. ' coarse cloth ', dhõgṭī f. ' wallet '.4. L. ḍhok f. ' hut in the fields '; Ku. ḍhwākā m. pl. ' gates of a city or market '; N. ḍhokā (pl. of *ḍhoko) ' door '; -- OMarw. ḍhokaro m. ' basket '; -- N.ḍhokse ' place covered with a mat to store rice in, large basket '.(CDIAL 6880) Rebus: *dhokra* 'cire perdue' casting metalsmith.

Lost-wax casting. Bronze statue, Mohenjo-daro. Bronze statue of a woman holding a small bowl, Mohenjo-daro; copper alloy made using cire perdue method (DK 12728; Mackay 1938: 274, Pl. LXXIII, 9-11)

Dance-step of Mohenjodaro as a hieroglyph. Rebus: metal, 'iron'

dance-stepas hieroglyph on a potsherd, Bhirrana.

meṭ sole of foot, footstep, footprint (Ko.); meṭṭu step, stair, treading, slipper (Te.)(DEDR 1557). Rebus:*meḍ* 'iron'(Munda); मेढ meḍh'merchant's helper'(Pkt.) *meḍ* iron (Ho.) *meṛed-bica* = iron stone ore, in contrast to bali-bica, iron sand ore (Munda)

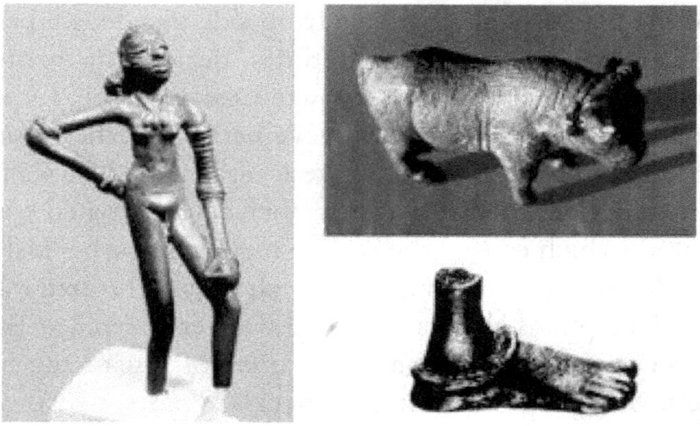

The 'Dancing Girl' (Mohenjo-daro), made by the lost-wax process; a bronze foot and anklet from Mohenjo-daro; and a bronze figurine of a bull (Kalibangan). (Courtesy: ASI)

"Archaeological excavations have shown that Harappan metal smiths obtained copper ore (either directly or through local communities) from the Aravalli hills, Baluchistan or beyond. They soon discovered that adding tin to copper produced bronze, a metal harder than copper yet easier to cast, and also more resistant to corrosion.

Whether deliberately added or already present in the ore, various 'impurities' (such as nickel, arsenic or lead) enabled the Harappans to harden bronze further, to the point where bronze chisels could be used to dress stones! The alloying ranges have been found to be 1%–12% in tin, 1%–7% in arsenic, 1%–9% in nickel and 1%–32% in lead. Shaping copper or bronze involved techniques of fabrication such as forging, sinking, raising, cold work, annealing, riveting, lapping and joining. Among the metal artefacts produced by the Harappans, let us mention spearheads, arrowheads, axes, chisels, sickles, blades (for knives as well as razors), needles, hooks, and vessels such as jars, pots and pans, besides objects of toiletry such as bronze mirrors; those were slightly oval, with their face raised, and one side was highly polished. The Harappan craftsmen also invented the true saw, with teeth and the adjoining part of the blade set alternatively from side to side, a type of saw unknown elsewhere until Roman times. Besides, many bronze figurines or humans (the well-known 'Dancing Girl', for instance) and animals (rams, deer, bulls...) have been unearthed from Harappan sites. Those figurines were cast by the lost-wax process: the initial model was made of wax, then thickly coated with clay; once fired (which caused the wax to melt away or be 'lost'), the clay hardened into a mould, into which molten bronze was later poured. Harappans also used gold and silver (as well as their joint alloy, electrum) to produce a wide variety of ornaments such as pendants, bangles, beads, rings or necklace parts, which were usually found hidden away in hoards such as ceramic or bronze pots. While gold was probably panned from the Indus waters, silver was perhaps extracted from galena, or native lead sulphide...While the Indus civilization belonged to the Bronze Age, its successor, the Ganges civilization, which emerged in the first millennium BCE, belonged to the Iron Age. But recent excavations in central parts of the Ganges valley and in the eastern Vindhya hills have shown that iron was produced there possibly as early as in 1800 BCE. Its use appears to have become widespread from about 1000 BCE, and we find in late Vedic texts mentions of a 'dark metal' (krṣnāyas), while earliest texts (such as the Rig-Veda) only spoke of ayas, which, it is now accepted, referred to copper or bronze.

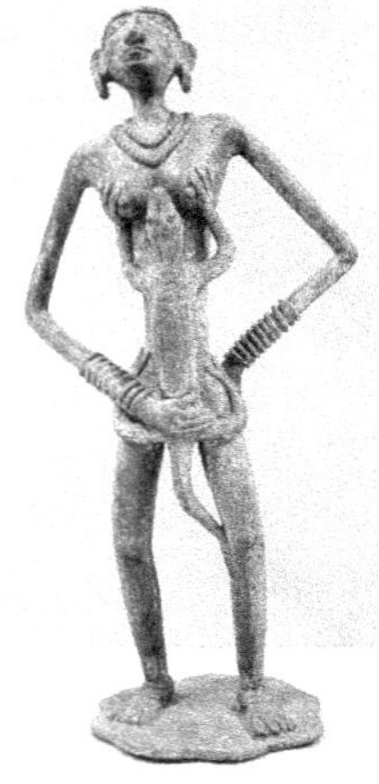

The Mother Goddess folk bronze from bastar. Plate XXIIIB includes picture of two footprints. This glyph occurs on Indus writing. *meḍ* 'body' Rebus: *meḍ* 'iron' (Ho.Mu.) ḍokka 'body' Rebus: *ḍokke* 'lizard' Rebus: *dhokra* 'lost-wax cast'.

Ka. ḍokke the body. *Tu.* (BRR) dokkè id. *Te.* ḍokka skeleton, belly. *Nk. (Ch.)* ḍokka bone; ciparta ḍokka rib. *Go.* (Ko.) ḍokka belly (*Voc.* 1596). *Pe.* nenja-ḍaki chest. *Kui* ḍaki breastbone, chest. *Kuwi* (F.) dōkkū skeleton;

(Su.) hīpa-ḍaki, (P.) sīpa-ḍaki chest (DEDR 2976).

Kol. (Kin.) ḍokke lizard. *Pa.* ḍokka id. *Ga.* (S.3) ḍokoḍe a kind of lizard. *Go.* ḍokke (A. W. Ph.) sp. lizard, (Mu. Ma.) garden lizard; (M.) ḍoke lizard; (Tr.) dokkē a small lizard (*Voc.* 1597); (Tr.) pidrī-ḍokkē the house-lizard (*Voc.* 2227); (Tr.) ḍoggāl chameleon (*Voc.* 1600). *Konḍa* ḍōki lizard. *Kui* ḍoi chameleon. *Kuwi*(Su. P.) ḍru'i sp. lizard; (S.) droi, (Mah.) ḍorgi, (Ṭ.) ḍrogi chameleon; (Isr.) ḍrōgi lizard. ? Cf. 3289 Kur. tuska.(DEDR 2977).
bal ḍok(k)e house lizard (Voc. 2160). (DEDR 3994).
Rebus: *dhokra* 'cire perdue' casting metalsmith. *Dhokra* (Oriya: ଢୋକରା, Bengali: ডোকরা) (also spelt *Dokra*) is non–ferrous metal casting using the lost-wax casting technique.
āra 'six' Rebus: *āra* 'brass' as in ārakūṭa (Sanskrit)

Dhokra guild

Six legs of a lizard are an enumeration of brass *āra* together with cast iron, *dul meḍ*. Read together with hieroglyph:
ḍokke lizard. Rebus: *dhokra* '*cire perdue* casting metalsmith'. Thus, the seal message is: cire perdue casting metalsmith working with brass, cast iron.

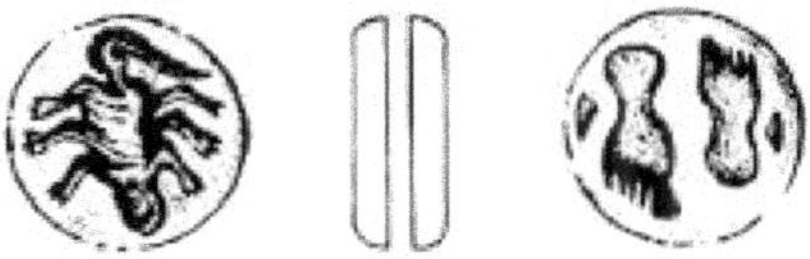

Disk seal (glyptic catalogue no. 58; 15 mm in dia. X 8 mm) Excavations at Tepe Yahya, 3rd millennium, p. 154 Double-sided steatite stamp seal with opposing foot prints and six-legged creature on opposite sides. Tepe Yahya. Seal impressions of two sides of a seal. Six-legged lizard and opposing footprints shown on opposing sides of a double-sided steatite stamp seal perforated along the lateral axis.

Rebus readings of the six-legged lizard and a pair of foot impressions: dula 'pair' Rebus: dul 'cast metal' *goṛo* 'foot' Rebus: *khōṭa* 'alloyed metal'. *ḍokke* lizard. Rebus: *dhokra* '*cire perdue* casting metalsmith'. Thus, the seal is an intimation of the *cire perdue* casting metalsmith working with casting of alloyed metal or working with brass, cast iron.

Hieroglyph: 'foot, hoof': खोँट *f* The heel (Marathi) ***gōḍḍa** 'foot, leg, knee '. [Cf. the word -- group ' heel - ankle -- knee -- wrist ' s.v. *kuṭṭha -- : → Brah. *goḍ* ' knee ']Pk. *goḍḍa* -- , *gōḍa* -- m. ' foot ', Gy. as. *gur;* K. *gŏḍ* m. ' ankle, foot of tree, beginning of anything '; S. *goḍo* m. ' knee ', *guḍa* f. ' knee bone '; L. *goḍḍā* m. ' knee ', awāṇ.*gōḍā*, P. *goḍḍā* m.; Ku. *gwāṛo* ' foot ', gng. *gōṛ*; N. *goṛo* ' foot, leg '; A. *gor* ' foot, kick, foot of tree ', *guri* ' kick, foot of tree ', *gorohani* ' stamp of the foot '; B. *goṛ* ' foot, leg ', °*ṛā* ' foot of tree, root, origin '; Or. *goṛa* ' foot, heel, leg, base '; Mth. *goṛ* ' leg '; Bhoj. *gōṛ* ' foot, leg '; Aw. lakh. *goṛ* pl. ' feet '; H. *goṛ*, °*ṛā* m. ' foot, leg '.(CDIAL 4272). Ku. *khuṭo* ' leg, foot ', °*ṭī* ' goat's leg '; N. *khuṭo* ' leg, foot '(CDIAL 3894). S. *khuṛī* f. ' heel '; WPah. paṅ. *khūṛ* ' foot '. khura m. ' hoof ' KātyŚr̥. 2. *khuḍa -- 1 (*khuḍaka* -- , *khula*° ' ankle -- bone ' Suśr.). [← Drav. T. Burrow BSOAS xii 376: it belongs to the word -- group ' heel <-> ankle -- knee -- wrist ', see *kuṭṭha --](CDIAL 3906). *Ta.* kuracu, kuraccai horse's hoof. *Ka.* gorasu, gorase, gorise, gorusu hoof. *Te.* gorija, gorise, (B. also) gorije, korije id. / Cf. Skt.khura- id. (DEDR 1770). खोटवाद [khōṭavāda] *m* The heel leash or tie of a sandal.(Marathi)

Rebus: खोट [khōṭa] *f* A mass of metal (unwrought or of old metal melted down); an ingot or wedge. खोटसाळ [khōṭasāḷa] *a* (खोट & साळ from शाला) Alloyed--a metal खोटा [khōṭā]

Debased, alloyed, bad--money. Pr. खोटा तरी गांठ- चा वेडा तरी पोटचा If the money be bad, it is yet out of one's own purse: if the child be mad, it is yet from one's own belly; "one's own is faultless." खोटानाटा [khōṭānāṭā] *a* (खोटा by redup.) Bad, false, debased--articles of merchandise, money, the precious metals. (Marathi)

Allograph: (Kathiawar) *khũṭ* m. ' Brahmani or zebu bull ' (G.) Rebus: *khũṭ* 'community, guild' (Santali)

Ia. 18

Lamberg- Karlovsky 1971: fig. 2C Shahr-i-Soktha Stamp seal shaped like a foot.

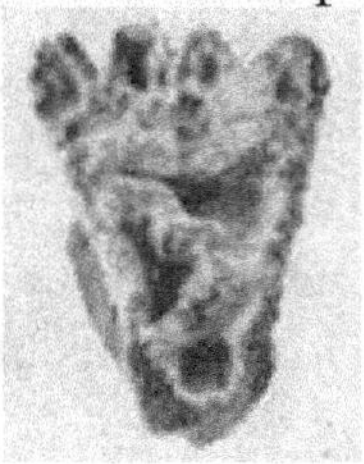

Shahdad seal (Grave 78). It is significant that a footprint is used as a seal at Shahdad. The glyph is read rebus as rebus word for 'iron':

āra 'six' Rebus: *āra* 'brass' as in ārakūṭa (Sanskrit)

Rebus readings:

Hieroglyph: meṭ sole of foot, footstep, footprint (Ko.); meṭṭu step, stair, treading, slipper (Te.)(DEDR 1557). Rebus: मेढ 'merchant's helper' (Pkt.); *meḍ* 'iron' (Munda).

Hieroglyph: *meṭṭu* 'foot'. Rebus: *meḍ* 'iron' (Ho.Mu.) dula 'pair' (Kashmiri); dul 'cast (metal)(Santali).

Alternative: Rebus: kakra. 'lizard'; kan:gra 'portable furnace'.

Alternative: Hieroglyph: araṇe 'lizard' (Tulu) Rebus: eraṇi f. ' anvil ' (Gujarati); aheraṇ, ahiraṇ, airaṇ, airṇī, haraṇ f. 'anvil'(Marathi)

Spread of lost-wax casting across Eurasia

Lost-wax casting (also called "investment casting", "precision casting", or cire perduein French) is the process by which a duplicate metal sculpture (often silver, gold, brassor bronze) is cast from an original sculpture. Dependent on the sculptor's skills, intricate works can be achieved by this method. The oldest known examples of the lost-wax technique are the objects discovered in the Cave of the Treasure (Nahal Mishmar) hoard in southern Israel, and which belong to theChalcolithic period (4500-3500 BCE). Conservative Carbon 14 estimates date the items to c.3700 BCE, making them more than 5700 years old.[156]

... In Mesopotamia, from c. 3500-2750 BCE, the lost-wax technique was used for small-scale, and then later large-scale copper and bronze statues. One of the earliest surviving lost-wax castings is a small lion pendant from Uruk IV. Sumerian metalworkers were practicing lost-wax casting from approximately c. 3500-3200 BCE. Much later examples from northeastern Mesopotamia/Anatolia include the Great Tumulus at Gordion (late 8th century BCE), as well as other types of Urartian cauldron attachments.[157]

... The inhabitants of Ban Na Di were casting bronze from c. 1200 BCE to 200 CE, using the lost-wax technique to manufacturebangles.[158]

There are technological and material parallels between northeast Thailand and Vietnam concerning the lost-wax technique. Some of the bangles from Ban Na Di revealed a dark grey substance between the central clay core and the metal, which on analysis was identified as an unrefined form of insect wax.It is likely that decorative items, like bracelets and rings, were made by *cire perdue* at Non Nok Tha andBan Chiang.[159]

The sites exhibiting artifacts made by the lost-mould process in Vietnam, such as the Dong Son drums, come from the Dong Son, and Phung Nguyen cultures,[3] such as one sickle and the figure of a seated individual from Go Mun (near Phung Nguyen, the Bac Bo Region), dating to the Go Mun phase (end of the General B period, up until the 7th century BC). Bangles made by the lost-wax process are characteristic of northeast Thailand.[160]

Two birds on Nahal Mishmar crown and two birds on Mohenjo-daro boat.

The Nahal Mishmar crown shows the following hieroglyphs: model of a building and two birds which are read rebus as Meluhha glosses.

miṇḍāl markhor (Tor.wali) meḍho a ram, a sheep (G.)(CDIAL 10120) Rebus: meḍ (Ho.); mẽṛhet 'iron' (Mu.Ho.) mẽṛh t iron; ispat m. = steel; dul m. = cast iron (Munda) Nahal mishmar hoard: ram, limestone.

"Late Harappan Period dish or lid with perforation at edge for hanging or attaching to large jar. It shows a Blackbuck antelope with trefoil design made of combined circle-and-dot motifs, possibly representing stars. It is associated with burial pottery of the Cemetery H period,dating after 1900 BC.The Late Harappan Period at Harappa is represented by the

Cemetery H culture (190-1300 BC) which is named after the discovery of a large cemetery filled with painted burial urns and some extended inhumations. The earlier burials in this cemetery were laid out much like Harappan coffin burials, but in the later burials, adults were cremated and the bones placed in large urns (164). The change in burial customs represents a major shift in religion and can also be correlated to important changes in economic and political organization. Cemetery H pottery and related ceramics have been found throughout northern Pakistan, even as far north as Swat, where they mix with distinctive local traditions. In the east, numerous sites in the Ganga-Yamuna Doab provide evidence for the gradual expansion of settlements into this heavily forested region. One impetus for this expansion may have been the increasing use of rice and other summer (kharif) crops that could be grown using monsoon stimulated rains. Until late in the Harappan Period (after 2200 BC) the agricultural foundation of the Harappan cities was largely winter (rabi) crops that included wheat and barley. Although the Cemetery H culture encompassed a relatively large area, the trade connections with thewestern highlands began to break down as did the trade with the coast. Lapis lazuli and turquoise beads are rarely found in the settlements, and marine shell for ornaments and ritual objects gradually disappeared. On the other hand the technology of faience manufacture becomes more refined, possibly in order to compensate for the lack of raw materials such as shell, faience and possibly even carnelian."[161]

Chalcolithic Levant Nahal Mishmar treasure: Model of a building. Shaped like a copper crown

Later 4th millennium BCE
Crown, copper, lost wax technique, from the Cave of the Treasure (Nahal

Mishmar) Judean Desert. The hoard was made up mainly of copper objects, 240 mace heads, 80 sceptres and 10 crowns,

probably from the sanctuary at Ein Geddi.[162] Hieroglyphs: *dula* 'pair' Rebus: *dul* 'cast metal' *karaḍa* 'aquatic bird' Rebus: *karaḍa* 'hard alloy' (Marathi) This is complemented by explaining the pair of birds perched on the edge of the crown, as Meluhha hieroglyphs. Alternative reading (assuming the identification of the birds on Nahal Mishmar crown as vultures): *eruvai* 'kite' Rebus: *eruvai* 'copper'. Thus, the pair of vultures read: *dul erako* 'molten cast copper'.

sangaḍa 'frame of building'; *koḍ* 'horn' Rebus: 'fortification' 'entrustment articles', 'workshop'.

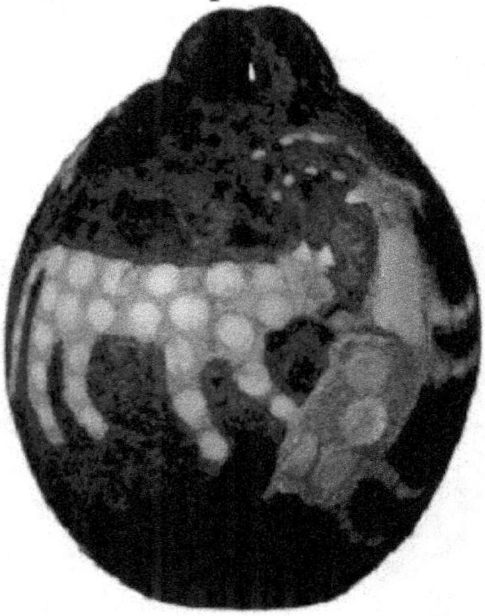

Leopard weight. Shahi-Tump (Balochistan).

Meluhha hieroglyphs; rebus readings: Leopard, *kharaḍā*; rebus:karaḍā 'hard alloy from iron, silver etc.'; ibex or markhor 'meḍh' rebus: 'iron stone ore, metal merchant.'

खरडा [kharaḍā] A leopard. खरड्या [kharaḍyā] m or खरड्यावाघ m A leopard (Marathi). Kol. keḍiak tiger. Nk. khaṛeyak panther. Go. (A.) khaṛyal tiger; (Haig) kariyāl panther Kui kṛāḍi, krānḍi tiger, leopard, hyena. Kuwi (F.) kṛani tiger; (S.) klā'ni tiger, leopard; (Su. P. Isr.) kṛaˀni (pl. -ŋa) tiger. / Cf. Pkt. (DNM) karaḍa- id. (CDIAL 1132+). Rebus 1: kharādī ' turner, a person who fashions or shapes objects on a lathe' (Gujarati) Rebus 2: करड्याची अवटी [karaḍyācī avaṭī] f An implement of the goldsmith. Rebus: करडा [karaḍā] Hard from alloy--iron, silver &c. (Marathi)

miṇḍāl 'markhor' (Tōrwālī) meḍho a ram, a sheep (G.)(CDIAL 10120); rebus: meḍ (Ho.); mẽṛhet 'iron' (Mu.Ho.)mẽṛh t iron; ispat m. = steel; dul m. = cast iron (Munda)
Lost-wax casting, Nineveh, 3rd millennium BCE

Akkadian head from Nineveh, 2300-2159 BCE (from Iraq 3 pl. 6) Lost-wax casting of large-scale statuary was well developed in Mesopotamia in the second half of the 3rd millennium BCE. The object was mjade of copper. X-radiographs confirm tha the hair lines were chased onto the object after casting. Only the last stage of 'sloshing' was yet to be developed. "At some stage during the 3rd millennium BCE, more care was taken in constructing the moulds so that the surface of the casting would not require attention. A fine slip-like material, probably mixed with cow dung, was applied repeatedly to the model until a reasonable thickness was established; a coarse refractory clay was then applied to complete the mould. This technique is demonstrated by the Tell edh-Dhiba'I mould."[163]

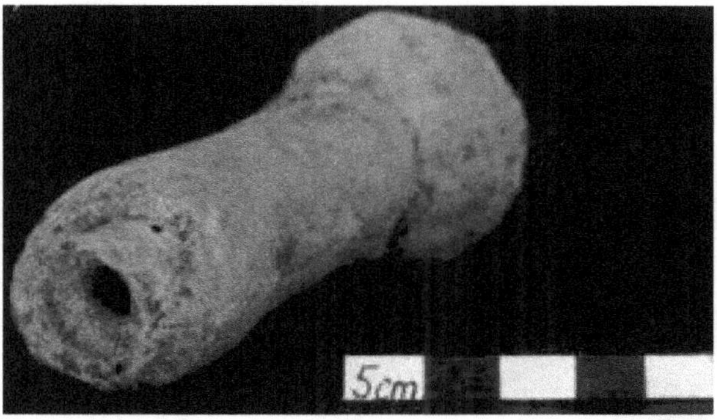

Tell edh-Dhiba'i is located in the suburbs of Baghdad dated to Isin-Larsa and Old Babylonian periods, ca. first half of the 2nd millennium BCE. A lost-wax mould was found. "The inner surface was smooth and had the shape of a short pin with a knob and probably a spherical top…Pins with round heads hav been found in Early Dynastic graves. The 'A' cemetery at Kish, for example, has a number of pins, the round heds of which were deemed by the excavators to be cast. This cemetery has been redated to Early Dynastic III (2500-2600 BCE)…This reliably attests to this process of lost-wax casting in Mesopotami at about 2500 BCE…The ease with which a round cross section can be formed using a soft wax material explains much of the attractiveness of lost-wax casting. The shape thus formed may not be complex, but it has smooth curved surfaces and it is this feature that is the hallmark of objects produced by lost-wax casting. Objects with delicate round sections such as the Mohenjo-Daro dancing girl are classical lost-wax casting shapes. The second important feature of the Telledh-Dhiba'I mould is its heterogeneous composition. The use of fine and coarse clays reveal that the practices described by the Sanskrit and medieval texts were established by 1700 BCE in Mesopotamia. The attention to the quality of the casting's surface represents an advance in the technology of lost-wax casting…A copper standard recently found at Qiryat Gat has a multilayered mould remaining inside the shaft. There is a layer of clay and grass and a layer of lime and quartz sand. This demonstrates that there was a discrimination of clay types for moulding prior to the 3rd millennium, the purpose of which is uncertain."[164]

Yuval Goren analysed ceramic mold remains that were still attached to a large number of copper implements together with those of Nahal Mishmar artifacts…supports the idea that all of these items were produced by a single workshop or workshop cluster.[165]

Appendix G: Processions of stone-/metal-ware competence

Stone-smithy guild on a Meluhha standard

Two archaeological sites, Harappa and Mohenjo-Daro of Sarasvati Civilization have deployed almost identical hieroglyphs on two tablets signifying processions of lapidary-artisan competence.

Harappa Tablet. Pict-91 (Mahadevan) m0490At m0490B Mohenjodaro Tablet showing Meluhha combined standard of three standards carried in a procession, comparable to Tablet m0491.

m0491 Tablet. Line drawing (right). This tablet showing three hieroglyphs may be called the Meluhha standard.Combined reading for the joined or ligatured glyphs

Rebus reading is: *dhatu kõdā sangaḍa* 'mineral, turner, stone-smithy guild'.

Dawn of the bronze age is best exemplified by this Mohenjo-daro tablet which shows a procession of three hieroglyphs carried on the shoulders of three persons. The hieroglyphs are: 1. Scarf carried on a pole (dhatu Rebus: mineral ore); 2. A young bull carried on a stand *kõdā* Rebus: turner; 3. Portable standard device (Top part: lathe-gimlet; Bottom part:

portable furnace *sāgāḍ Rebus: stone-cutter sangatarāśū*).
sanghāḍo (Gujarati) cutting stone, gilding (Gujarati); *sangsāru karaṇu* = to stone (Sindhi) *sanghāḍiyo*, a worker on a lathe (Gujarati)

The procession is a celebration of the graduation of a stone-cutter as a metal-turner in a smithy/forge. A sangatarāśū 'stone-cutter' or lapidary of neolithic/chalolithic age had graduated into a metal turner's workshop (*koḍ*), working with metallic minerals (*dhatu*) of the bronze age.
Three professions are described by the three hieroglyphs: scarf, young bull, standard device *dhatu kõdāsāgāḍī* Rebus words denote: ' mineral worker; metals turner-joiner (forge); worker on a lathe' – associates (guild).

On this tablet, the standard on the very front is not clear.
It is surmised that this standard carried on the procession may be comparable to the standard shown on Tikulti-Ninurta I altar discovered in the Ashur temple.
This fourth standard could be compared with this hieroglyph of the Tikulti-Ninurta altar:

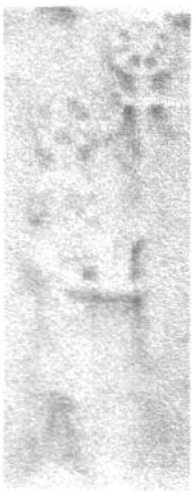

A spoked wheel is shown atop on the standard and the hieroglyph is also reinforced by depicting the hieroglyph on the top of the standard-bearer's head. This Meluhha hieroglyph is read rebus: *eraka*'knave of wheel'
Rebus: 'moltencast copper'; *āra* 'spokes'
Rebus: *āra* 'brass'.
Thus, the fourth profession is depicted as the smith working with metal alloys.
Thus, together the four professions depicted on the Mohenjodaro -standard showing four hieroglyphs in procession are read rebus:

Hieroglyph: *dhàṭṭu* m. 'woman's headgear, kerchief'; *dhaṭu* m. (also *dhaṭhu*) m. 'scarf' (WPah.); rebus: *dhātu*'mineral' (Skt.), *dhatu* id. (Santali).

Hieroglyph: *kõdā* 'young bull calf' *Rebus: kõdā* 'turner-joiner' (forge), worker on a lathe
Hieroglyph: *sā̃gāḍī* 'lathe (gimlet), portable furnace' Rebus: *sā̃gāḍī* 'metalsmith associates (guild)'
Hieroglyph *eraka āra* 'knave of wheel', 'spokes of wheel'
Rebus: *eraka āra* 'copper alloy brass'
Thus Rebus readings of the four hieroglyphs denote: ' mineral worker; metals turner-joiner (forge); worker on a lathe' – associates (guild), copper alloy brass.
dhatu kõdā sā̃gāḍī eraka āra

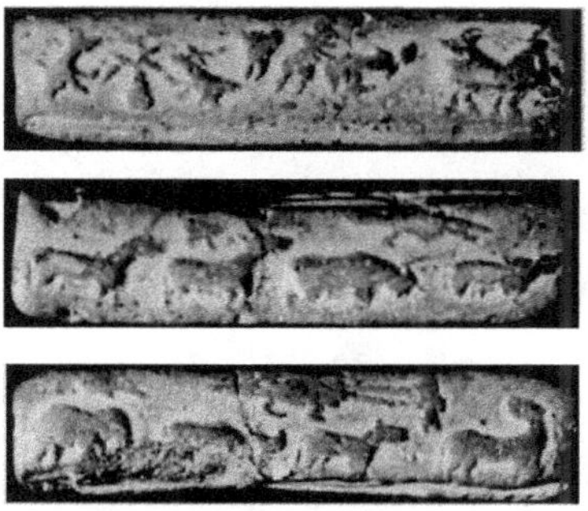

m0489A, B, C Prism Tablet. A standing human couple mating (*a tergo*); one side of a prism tablet from Mohenjo-daro (m489b). Other motifs on the inscribed object are: two goats eating leaves on a platform; a cock or hen (?) and a three-headed animal (perhaps antelope, one-horned bull and a short-horned bull).

Tell Abraq. Gold objects recovered. Joined back-to-back: pusht 'back'; rebus: pusht 'ancestor'. pus<u>h</u>t bah pus<u>h</u>t 'generation to generation.' *pr̥ṣṭhá* n. ' back, hinder part ' Rigveda; *puṭṭhā* m. ' buttock of an animal ' (Punjabi) Rebus: *puṭhā, puṭṭhā* m. 'buttock of an animal, leather cover of account book' (Marathi) tagara 'antelope' Rebus: damgar 'merchant'. This may be an artistic rendering of a 'descendant' of a ancient (metals) merchant.

r-an:ku, ran:ku = fornication, adultery (Telugu); rebus: ranku 'tin' (Santali)
Alternative/Supplementary reading: *kamḍa, khamḍa* 'copulation' (Santali) Rebus: *kampaṭṭa* 'mint, coiner'. *khāṇḍā* tool, pots and pans, metalware (Marathi) (See Appendix G for examples of hieroglyphs deployed to connote a superset of metalwork of a mint, displayed on three sides of a prism tablet – m0489).
loa 'ficus' Rebus: *loh* 'copper'. The leaf (ficus) pictorial + the goat composition connotes *loa* + *melh*; hence, the reading is of this pictorial component is: *mleccha* loha= 'copper metal'. melh 'goat' (Brahui) Rebus: milakkhu 'copper' (Pali)

Alternative: *patra* 'leaf' (Skt.) Rebus: *pattar* 'goldsmiths (guild)' (Ta.)

Hieroglyphs on m0489B:

kāruvu 'crocodile' Rebus: *khar* 'artisan, blacksmith' (Kashmiri). Signifiers: 1. Young bull, 2. Goat/antelope, 3. Bull, 4. Buffalo Meanings: 1. Turner 2. *damgar* 'Merchant' 3. *ḍhangar* 'smith' 4. Stone-worker (lapidary, mason).

Hieroglyphs: *kondā , konda* bullock, ox (Gondi) Alternative: *dāmṛa, damrā* 'young bull' (A.)(CDIAL 6184). 2. *melh,*'goat' Rebus: Meluhha, i.e. *milakkhu* 'copper-worker'; 3. *adar ḍangra* Rebus: *kundār* 'turner'; *kundā* 'turn on a lathe'; Alternative: tam(b)ra 'copper'; *damgar* 'merchant'; *aduru* 'native metal' (Kannada); *ḍhangar* 'blacksmith' (Hindi) 4. *kaṭái* ' buffalo calf '(Gaw.) *kāṭo* ' young buffalo bull ' (Kumaoni) (CDIAL 2645).*kāṛā* 'buffalo' bull (Tamil) Rebus 1: *khaḍā* 'nodule (ore), stone' (Marathi). Rebus 2: *kãṭhāḷ* 'maritime'; *kaṭalar, n.* < seamen, inhabitants of maritime tracts.
Alternative: கண்டி kaṇṭi buffalo. Rebus: *kāḍ* 'stone ore', *gaḍa* 'large stone mould'. Glyph: kuṇḍī 'crooked buffalo horns' (Lahnda.) Rebus: kuṇḍī = chief of village (Prākṛt).The artisan is kundakara— m. 'turner' (Skt.); H. kũderā m. 'one who works a lathe, one who scrapes' (CDIAL 3297). *ḍabe, ḍabea* 'large horns,

with a sweeping upward curve, applied to buffaloes' (Santali) Rebus: *ḍab*, ḍhimba, ḍhompo 'lump (ingot?)', clot, make a lump or clot, coagulate, fuse, melt together (Santali)
Glyph: *ḍaṅgara1 ' cattle '. 2. *daṅgara -- . [Same as ḍaṅ- gara -- 2 s.v. *ḍagga -- 2 as a pejorative term for cattle] 1. K. ḍangur m. ' bullock ', L. ḍaṅgur, (Ju.) ḏã̄gar m. ' horned cattle '; P. ḍaṅgar m. ' cattle ', Or. ḍaṅgara; Bi. ḍã̄gar ' old worn -- out beast, dead cattle ', dhūr ḍã̄gar ' cattle in general '; Bhoj. ḍāṅgar ' cattle '; H. ḍã̄gar, ḍã̄grā m. ' horned cattle '.2. H. dã̄gar m. = prec. (CDIAL 5526) Rebus: ḍaṅgar 'blacksmith'. ḍāṅgar 'blacksmith' (H.); ḍhā~gar., dhā~gar blacksmith; digger of wells (H.) Nepali. डाड़े ḍāṅre , or ḍã̄gre, adj. Large; lazy; working with- out thoroughness or seriousness; -- s. A partic. kind of bird, the mainā; -- a contemptuous term for a blacksmith डाड़ो ḍāṅro , or ḍã̄gro, s. A term of contempt used for a blacksmith (kāmi). [v.s.v. ḍāṅre.] ḍān:ro = a term of contempt for a blacksmith (N.)(CDIAL 5524). Thus, this side of the prism connotes metalsmithy artisans: turner, copper-worker, merchant, native-metal smith.

Hieroglyphs on m0489C:

karā 'crocodile' + aya 'fish' together read rebus: *ayakāra* 'metalsmith' (Pali)[fish = aya (Gujarati); crocodile = kāru (Telugu.)] *karā* 'crocodile' Rebus: *khar* 'blacksmith'.

Thus, crocodile is a set of which other animals in procession are subsets, specific metalsmithy-cum-lapidary/mason functions. On m0489B, crocodile is shown. On m0489C crocodile holding fish in its jaw is shown.

Group of animals in procession: *pasaramu, pasalamu* = an animal, a beast, a brute, quadruped (Telugu) Thus, the depiction of animals in epigraphs is related to reading, Rebus: *pasra* = smithy (Santali) Signifiers: 1. elephant, 2. boar/rhinoceros, 3. tiger, 4. tiger face turned. Meanings : 1. *ibbo* 'iron merchant', 2. carpenter, 3. smith, 4. artisan-alloysmith.

Hieroglyphs: 1. *ibha,* 2. *badhia,* 3. *kol,* 4. *krammara kol*
Rebus: *ib* 'iron', *ibbo* 'merchant' , *badhi* 'carpenter', *kol* 'smelter', *kol* 'pancaloha': *krammara kol* 'forge artisan'. *kole.l* = smithy (Ko.) Rebus: *kolhali* to forge (Kuwi). *kollë* blacksmith (Koḍ.). (DEDR 2133).

Thus, this side of the prism connotes: artisans working on iron, carpentry, smelting alloys and forge.

Hieroglyph: Elephant 'ibha'. Rebus: *ibbho* 'merchant' (cf.Hemacandra, *Desinamamala*, vaṇika). *ib* 'iron' (Santali) *karibha* 'elephant' (Sanskrit); rebus: *karb* 'iron' (Kannada) Alternative: కరటి [karaṭi] *karaṭi.* [Skt.] n. An elephant. ఏనుగు

(Telugu) Rebus: *kharādī* ' turner' (Gujarati)

Hieroglyph, read rebus:Rhinoceros: gaṇḍá4 m. ' rhinoceros ' lex., °*aka* -- m. lex. 2. *ga- yaṇḍa -- . [Prob. of same non -- Aryan origin as khaḍgá --1: cf. *gaṇōtsāha* -- m. lex. as a Sanskritized form ← Mu. PMWS 138]1. Pa. *gaṇḍaka* -- m., Pk. *gaṁḍaya* -- m., A. *gã̄r*, Or. *gaṇḍā*. 2. K. *gö̃ḍ* m., S. *geṇḍo* m. (lw. with *g* --), P. *gaĩḍā* m., °*ḍī* f., N. *gaĩṛo*, H. *gaĩṛā* m., G. *gẽḍɔ* m., °*ḍī* f., M. *gẽḍā* m. WPah.kṭg. *geṇḍɔ mirg* m. ' rhinoceros ', Md. *genḍā* ← H. (CDIAL 4000).காண்டாமிருகம் kāṇṭā-mirukam , *n.* [M. *kāṇṭāmṛgam.*] Rhinoceros; கல்யானை.

(Tamil) Rebus: *khāṇḍa* 'tools, pots and pans, and metal-ware'.

badhi 'castrated

boar' <*boRia*>(A) {N} `boar''.

#5620.<*badia*> {N}'boar'. *De.<*baria*>(M) `pig(G), boar(M)'. @N0749. *barae* 'blacksmith' (Mundarica) . A carpenter వడ్లవాడు.(Telugu) badhoe 'worker in wood and iron'.

Buffalo. Mohenjo-daro.

Buffalo. Daimabad bronze. Prince of Wales Museum, Mumbai.

Were the Daimabad artisan guilds carrying these bronze models as standards in processions on a festival day celebrating their work and advertising their professional metallurgical competence?

Bronze chariot. Daimabad, Maharashtra.

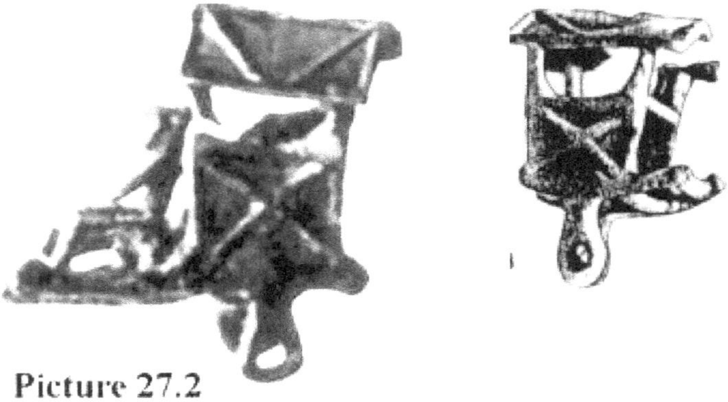

Picture 27.2
Bronze model. Chariot box. Chanhu-daro. ca. 2000 BCE.

Hieroglyph: *grālu* 'calf' *kaṭā* கடவு[3] kaṭavu , *n.* < கடா .1. Male buffalo 'buffalo' *kāṛā* young buffalo (Go.) *kaṭā, kaṭamā* 'bison' (Ta.)(DEDR 1114) Rebus: *kāṭhāḷ* 'maritime'; *kaṭalar, n.* < seamen, inhabitants of maritime tracts. *malla* 'wrestler' (Kannada); Rebus: *malla* m. pl. ' name of a people' (Sanskrit). *malah* 'sailor' (Akkadian) *māluti* 'sailor' (Tamil) A ملاح *mallāḥ*, s.m. (5th) (adj. sup. of ملح) A sailor, a boatman, a mariner, a waterman. Pl. ملاحان *mallāḥān*. See مانګي and مهانه (Pashto) *malla, mallā-malli* pugilistic encounter.

Indian tradition refers to *utsava bēra*, idol taken ou in processions. Archaeological context of Meluhha hieroglyphs provides many instances of animals and scepters held aloft in processions. Maybe, processions were trade-fairs, advertising and celebrating the artisanal competence displayed by the artifacts signified by the 'idols' or 'symbolic forms' on scepters or flagposts.
One such celebration is called *koṇḍa habba* of Lingavants, a community venerating *linga* (also attested in Sarasvati-Sindhu civilization in archaeological context).Five stone *linga* were found in Harappa and a terracotta *linga* in Kalibangan. Polished stone pillars and stone pedestals found in Dholavira – the functions which these symbolic forms related to are issues of archaeological reconstruction of the cultures of Bronze Age period.

Etyma from Meluhha (Mleccha) point to *khoṇḍ* as a square (Santali), the type of square on which two pillars are found in Dholavira. Rebus: *kõdā* 'to turn in a lathe' (Bengali). *kũdar* 'brass-worker, turner'.

Thus, *koṇḍa habba* is a celebration of the life-activity of the lapidaries/smiths of the civilization: *kõdā* meaning 'lathe-turning' for making perforated beads or for turning/forging metalware..This may explain why in the tablets showing procession as a festival ceremony, two hieroglyphs are carried as standards: both hieroglyphs relate to the one-horned young bull and the standard device (lathe). The related words reading hieroglyphs rebus from Meluhha (Mleccha) speech are: *kõdā sãgāḍī* Rebus words denote: 'metals turner-joiner (forge); worker on a lathe' – associates (guild)'.

This *khoṇḍ* 'square' could have been used to celebrate a festival which is called *koṇḍahabba.* The adorants walk on a bed of burning embers in fulfilment of their vows. Sucha bed of burning embers might have been laid on the square linking these two pillars of Dholavira shaped like sivalingas, symbolising pillars of fire. The significance attached to th word *khoṇḍ* may explain the local name for Dholavira: *Kotḍa.*

It is notable that a smithy was a temple for Meluhhans (Mlecchas). This is evidenced by the lexeme kole.l of Kota language which means 'smithy' and also 'temple'. Thus, a smithy is a temple -- kole.l Such a gestalt relatable to the lapidaries and smiths -- miners/metalworkers may explain why the *agama*s prescribe the procedures for invoking divinities in sculptures in a *sanctum* of a temple, adorned with metallic weapons on their multiple hands. It is, thus, possible to hypothesise that the religious practices of the people of the civilization at Mohenjodaro, Harappa, Kalibangan (where a terracotta Sivalinga has been found) and Dholavira are represented by the continuum of *koṇḍahabba* (lit. festival held in a *khoṇḍ* 'square') festivals celebrated by Lingavantas.

kundau, *kundhi* corner (Santali) *kuṇḍa* corner (S.): *khoṇḍ* square (Santali) *khuṇṭa2 ' corner '. 2. *kuṇṭa -- 2. [Cf. *khōñca --] 1. Phal. *khun* ' corner '; H. *khū̃ṭ* m. ' corner, direction ' (→ P. *khū̃ṭ* f. ' corner, side '); G. *khū̃ṭrī* f. ' angle '. <-> X kōṇa -- : G. *khuṇ* f., *khū̃ṇɔ* m. ' corner '. 2. S. *kuṇḍa* f. ' corner '; P. *kū̃ṭ* f. ' corner, side ' (← H.).(CDIAL 3898).

ಕೊಣ್ಡ kōṇḍa. Tbh. of ಕುಣ್ಡ (Śmd. 355; Abh. P. 10, after 183; My.). — ಕೊಣ್ಡಸ್ತ. -ಅಸ್ತ. N. among Brâhmaṇas (S. Mhr.). — ಕೊಣ್ಡಬಣ್ಡಿ. A cart used at the kōṇḍa feast (My.). — ಕೊಣ್ಡಹಬ್ಬ. A feast in honor of Vîrabhadra at which Liṅgavantas carry an idol of Vîrabhadra and dance with it on live coals in a pit (My.).

ಕುಣ್ಡ kuṇḍa. = ಕೊಣ್ಡ. A hole in the ground, a pit. 2, a pot (ಹಡೆ, ಕುಣ್ಡಿ, etc. Mr. 209; see B. 3, 80). 3, a pool,

Evidence for Sivalinga is provided in other sites (Mohenjodaro and Harappa) of the civilization:

Lingam in situ in Trench Ai (MS Vats, 1940, Excavations at Harappa, Vol. II, Calcutta) Lingam, grey sandstone in situ, Harappa, Trench Ai, Mound F, Pl. X (c) (After Vats). "In an earthenware jar, No. 12414, recovered from Mound F, Trench IV, Square I… in this jar, six lingams were found along with some tiny pieces of shell, a unicorn seal, an oblong grey sandstone block with polished surface, five stone pestles, a stone palette, and a block of chalcedony…"166

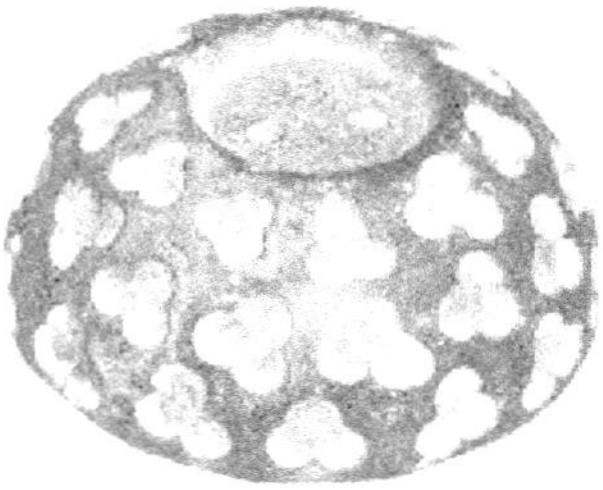

Tre-foil inlay decorated base (for linga icon?); smoothed, polished pedestal of dark red stone; National Museum of

Pakistan, Karachi; After Mackay 1938: I, 411; II, pl. 107:35; Parpola, 1994, p. 218.

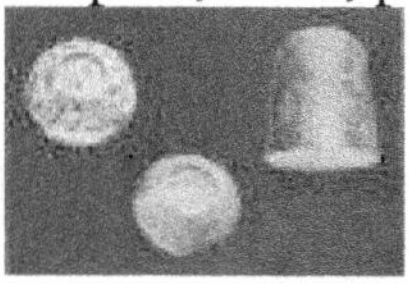

Two decorated bases and a lingam, Mohenjodaro.

Lingam, grey sandstone *in situ*, Harappa, Trench Ai, Mound F, Pl. X (c) (After Vats). "In an earthenware jar, No. 12414, recovered from Mound F, Trench IV, Square I... in this jar, six lingams were found along with some tiny pieces of shell, a unicorn seal, an oblong grey sandstone block with polished surface, five stone pestles, a stone palette, and a block of chalcedony..." (Vats,MS, *Excavations at Harappa*, p. 370)

Hieroglyph: **உற்சவபேரம்** uṟcava-pēram , *n.* < *ut-sava* + *bēra.* Idol taken out in processions; **உற்சவ விக்கிரகம்**. *Loc.* **उत्सवः** utsavaḥ **उत्सव-उदयम्** The height of the vehicle animal in comparison with that of the principal idol; **मूलबेरवशं मानमुत्सवोदयमीरितम्** (Māna- sāra.64.91-93). **उत्सव- विग्रहः** Image for procession (Kondividu Inscription of Krisṇarāya). **బేరము** [bēramu] *bēramu.* [Skt.] n. An image. **ప్రతిమ.** "**పంకములోని హైమబేరము.**" **పర.** v.

Rebus: [bērizu] *bērīḍzu.* [Hindi] n. An account. A total sum, **మొత్తము. బేరము** [bēramu] *bēramu.* [Tel.] n. Trade, dealing, a bargain, **బేరముసారము** or **బేరసారము** trade, &c. (**సారము** being a mere expletive.) **బేరకాడు** *bēra-kāḍu.* n. One who makes a bargain, a purchaser, buyer. **కొనువాడు, బేరమాడువాడు. బేరకత్తె** *bēra-katte.* n. A woman who bargains or purchases. **బేరమాడు** or **బేరముచేయు** *bēram-āḍu.* v. n. To bargain. **బేరముపోవు** to go on a trading journey. **బేరి** *bēri.* n. A man of the Beri or merchant caste.

బేరి [bēri] *bēri*. [from Skt. భేరి.] n. A kettle drum. దుందుభి, నగరా.

భేరి [bhēri] *bhēri*. [Skt.] n. A kettle drum. దుందుభి, నగారా.

జయభేరులు వాయించినాడు he sounded the drums in triumph. भेर [bhēra] *f* (भेरी S) A large kind of kettledrum. 2 Applied fig. to a potbelly, a bulging trunk of a tree, a block or huge stone &c. (Marathi)

भराड [bharāḍa] *n* A religious service or entertainment performed by a भराडी; consisting of singing the praises of some idol or god with playing on the डौर and dancing. (Marathi) بت *but*, s.m. (5th) An idol, image, statue; *but k̲h̲āna'h*, s.f. An idol temple. (Pashto. Persian)
uḍupa m. ' raft ' MBh. [Cf. *hōḍa* -- m. lex. prob. ← Drav., Tam. *ōṭam*] Pa. *uḷumpa* -- m.n. ' raft '; Pk. *uḍuva* -- m. ' boat '; Or. *uṛu* ' boatman '; G. *oṛvũ* n. ' small boat '; Si. mald. *oḍi* ' boat '; -- Si. *oruva* ' boat, canoe ' (CDIAL 1695). உடு; uṭu Oar, boatman's pole; ஓடம் இயக் குங் கோல். (பிங்.) hōḍa m. ' raft, boat ' lex. [← Drav., Kan. ōḍa., &c. DED 876] H. hoṛī f., holā m. ' canoe, raft '; G. hoṛī f. ' boat '; M. hoḍī f. ' canoe made of hollowed log '..hōḍa -- : Md. oḍi ' large kind of boat ' ← Drav.(CDIAL 14174).

Rebus: *huṇaï* ' offers oblation ' (Prākṛt)

bēḍā f. ' boat ' lex. 2. vēḍā, *vēṭī* -- f. lex. 3. bhēḍa -- 3 m., *bhēla* -- 1, °*aka* -- m.n. lex.1. Pk. *bēḍa* -- , °*aya* -- m., *bēḍā* -- , °*ḍiyā* -- f. ' boat ', Gy. eur. *bero*, S. *b̲eṛo* m., °*ṛī* ' small do. '; L. *bēṛā* (Ju. *b̲* --) m. ' large cargo boat ', *bēṛī* f. ' boat ', P. *beṛā*m., °*ṛī* f.; Ku. *beṛo* ' boat, raft ', N. *beṛā*, OAw. *beḍā*, H. *beṛā* m., G. *beṛɔ* m., *beṛi* f., M. *beḍā* m. 2. Pk. *vēḍa* -- m. ' boat '.3. Pk. *bhēḍaka* -- , *bhēlaa* -- m., *bhēlī* -- f. ' boat '; B. *bhelā* ' raft ', Or. *bheḷā*.*bēḍḍa -- , *bēṇḍa -

- ' defective ' see *biḍḍa -- . 1. S.kcch. *beṛī* f. ' boat ', *beṛo* m. ' ship '; WPah.poet. *beṛe* f. ' boat ', J. *beṛī* f. (CDIAL 9308).

In the context of veneration of ancestors, Varna gold finds of ca. 5th millennium BCE point to the possible functions served by scepters which might have been held aloft in processors to exhibit the artisans' competence. Maybe, the scepters of Nahal Mishmar also served a similar function.

A gold plate is shaped like a one-horned bull. If the bull was intended to be a representation of someone held in esteem by the community, it may have connoted a symbolic form comparable to the following Meluhha glosses: *ṭhakkura,* 'idol', *ṭhākur* ' blacksmith ', *ṭhākur* m. 'master'.

ṭhakkura m. ' idol, deity (cf. *ḍhakkārī* --), ' lex., ' title ' Rājat. [Discussion with lit. by W. Wüst RM 3, 13 ff. Prob. orig. a tribal name EWA i 459, which Wüst considers nonAryan borrowing of *śākvará* -- : very doubtful] Pk. *ṭhakkura* -- m. ' Rajput, chief man of a village '; Kho. (Lor.) *takur* ' barber ' (= *ṭ*° ← Ind.?), Sh. *ṭhăkŭr* m.; K. *ṭhôkur* m. ' idol ' (← Ind.?); S. *ṭhakuru* m. ' fakir, term of address between fathers of a husband and wife '; P. *ṭhākar* m. ' landholder ', ludh. *ṭhaukar* m. ' lord '; Ku. *ṭhākur* m. ' master, title of a Rajput '; N.*ṭhākur* ' term of address from slave to master ' (f. *ṭhakurāni*), *ṭhakuri* ' a clan of Chetris ' (f. *ṭhakurni*); A. *ṭhākur* ' a Brahman ', *ṭhākurānī* ' goddess '; B.*ṭhākurāni*, *ṭhākrān*, °*run* ' honoured lady, goddess '; Or. *ṭhākura* ' term of address to a Brahman, god, idol ', *ṭhākurāṇī* ' goddess '; Bi. *ṭhākur* ' barber '; Mth.*ṭhākur* ' blacksmith '; Bhoj. Aw.lakh. *ṭhākur* ' lord, master '; H. *ṭhākur* m. ' master, landlord, god, idol ', *ṭhākurāin*, *ṭhākurānī* f. ' mistress, goddess '; G. *ṭhākor*, °*kar* m. ' member of a clan of Rajputs ', *ṭhakrāṇī* f. ' his wife ', *ṭhākor* ' god, idol '; M. *ṭhākur* m. ' jungle tribe in North Konkan, family priest, god, idol '; Si. mald. "*tacourou*" ' title added to names of noblemen ' (HJ 915) prob. ← Ind. Garh. *ṭhākur* ' master '; A. *ṭhākur* also ' idol ' (CDIAL 5488).

A remarkable object from Varna indicates the possible function served by the 'scepters' of Nahal Mishmar. Possibly, the scepters were held aloft by standard bearers as shown on Mohenjo-daro procession of standards. "In 1972, during excavations at the Chalcolithic necropolis of a settlement dating to the end of the fifth millennium BC near the present-day city of Varna on the Black Sea coast, archaeologists revealed traces of a civilization equal to that of Egypt and Mesopotamia. During the digs many tombs were found with over 300 objects made of pure gold - scepters, axes, bracelets, other decorative pieces, bull-shaped plates. Most amazing is the sepulcher of a ruler/high priest with a gold scepter and a set of gold regalia, symbols of power and authority."[167]

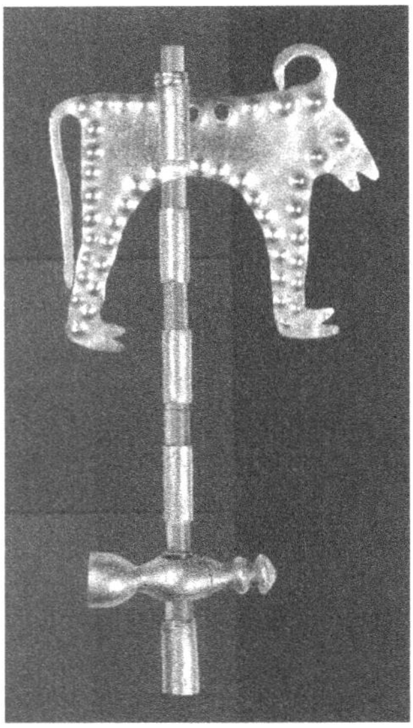

Eneolithic period (5th millennium BCE)

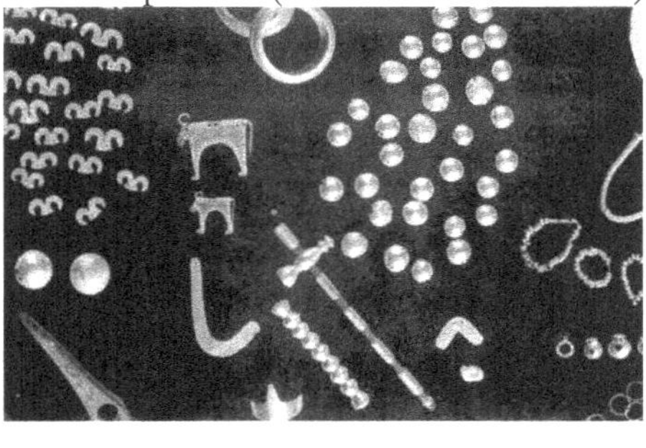

Hammered copper and gold ornaments from an early Chalcolithic (or Eneolithic) cemetery in Varna, on the Bulgarian coast of the Black Sea a bustling maritime center and the home of one of the world's earliest metal industries. The grave finds included 23.5-carat gold beads, scepters, bracelets, rings and animal- and horn-shaped plaques.

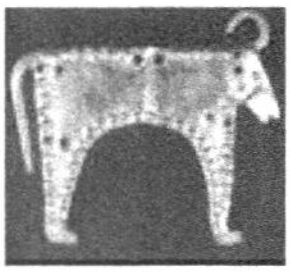

Zoomorphous applications, gold, Eneolithic necropolis – Varna, late Eneolithic Period

Necklace of gold and mineral pieces with gold amulet, Eneolithic necropolis, late Eneolithic period.

Specific feature of these tombs are the warders or scepters – symbols of high rank state or spiritual power. Three tombs contain 3D human face made of clay and on specific places on the face – front, eyes, mouth, ears – are placed as applications gold objects.

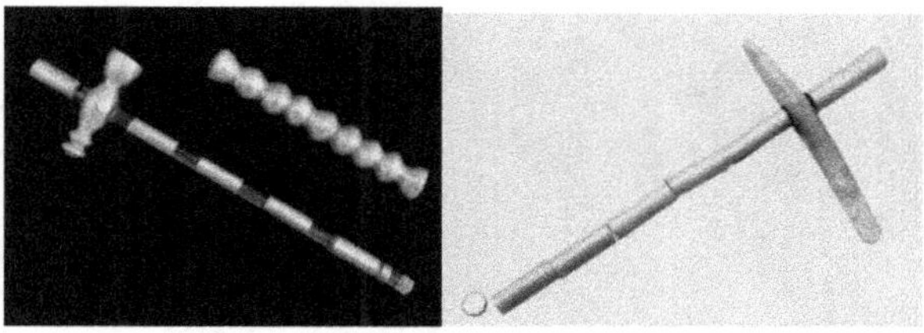

Sceptre, bone and gold, Eneolithic necropolis – Varna, tomb 4 - late Eneolithic period

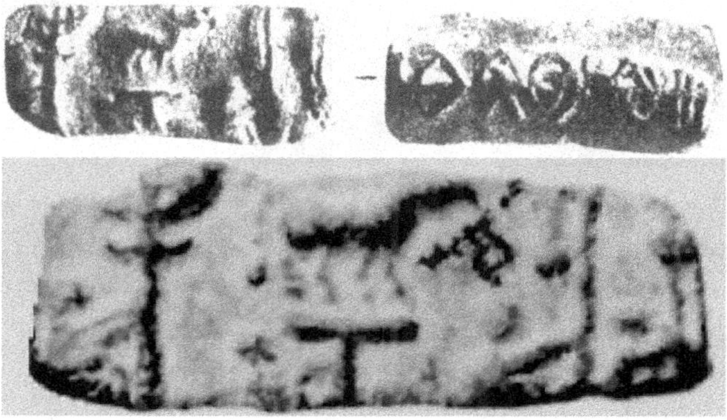

Two Mohenjo-daro tablets showing a procession of four standard bearers; the four standards are: lathe, one-horned young bull; scarf; spoked-circle (knave + spokes). All four are hieroglyphs

read rebus related to lapidary/smith turner work on metals and minerals (copper 'eraka', brass 'ara', dhatu 'ores')

Part of the arsenical copper hoard discovered in 1961 at Nahal Mishmar.

Meluhha standard compares with Nahal Mishmar standard.

Meluhha (Asur) guild processions

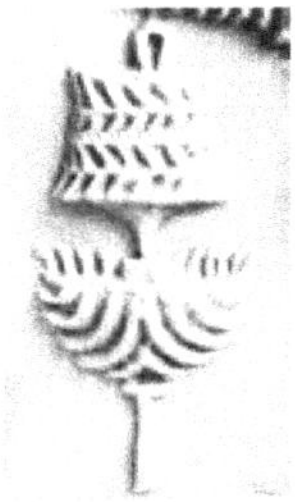

Nahal Mishmar hoard also had a copper alloy U-shaped vessel comparable in shape to the one shown on Meluhha standard as a crucible or portable furnace. The zig-zag shaped decoration on the copper vessel is comparable to the zig-zag shape shown on the 'gimlet' ligature on Meluhha standard (Mohenjo-dao seal m008). The zig-zag pattern shows the circular motion of the lathe -- *sangaḍa* --Drawing showing three components of Meluhha standard device: scepter, portable furnace, gimlet (lathe) juxtaposed to a standard in the Nahal Mishmar hoard of lost-wax castings. See, in particular, the three components of the Meluhha standard shown on Mohenjo-daro seal m008.

Mohenjo-daro seal m008 and variants of flagposts on Meluhha standard. (Note: Meluhha refers to mleccha vernacular language of the people of Indus-Sarasvati also called Harappa-Mohenjo-daro or Indus Valley Civilization Sets of Meluhha hieroglyphs refer to Indus script discussed in my book. Thus, Meluhha, mleccha vernacular of India is clearly attested in 4400 BCE at Nahal Mishmar.)

The Nahal Mishmar standard is comparable to the Meluhha standard which carried hieroglyphs in a trade-guild procession.

Meluhha: spread of lost-wax casting in the Fertile Crescent. Smithy is the temple. Veneration of ancestors.

two Meluhha seals with inscriptions from Dholavira and Mohenjo-daro demonstrating the dhokra was a Meluhha word for cire perdue (lost-wax) casting method evidenced by Nahal Mishmar copper hoard and that dhokra metal casting is practiced even today in many parts of India

The hieroglyphs carried on the Meluhha standard represented the tools-of-trade and denoted professional competence of the Meluhha lapidary-smithy artisans as the artisans transited from the chalcolithic to true bronze-age with competence in creating metal alloys and cast objects using the lost-wax casting method as demonstrated by the over 429 copper alloy objects discovered in Nahal Mishmar (ca. 4400 BCE).

The shape of this standard compares with the standard which holds the 'standard device' often shown in front of one-horned young bull on many Meluhha (Indus script) inscriptions.

The Meluhha standard holds two devices on top: 1. bowl-shaped crucible or portable furnace; 2. gimlet (lathe) There are two Mohenjo-daro tablets which show the Meluhha standared carried by a standard-bearer in a procession with three other standard-bearers bearing the standards of 'one-horned young bull', 'scarf', 'spoked nave of wheel'.

The argument in the context of Indus writing is that these are Meluhha hieroglyphs read rebus . The readings are: *sangaḍa*, 'lathe, portable furnace' rebus: 'entrustment articles of guild'; Rebus: *sang* 'stone', *gaḍa* 'large stone'. *konda* 'young bull' rebus: konda 'turner'; dhatu 'scarf' rebus: *dhatu* 'ore'; *eraka* 'nave of wheel'; *ara* 'spoke of wheel' rebus: *eraka* 'copper casting' ara 'brass (alloy)'.

The Susa panels show the standard bearers ligatured to the buttock of a bovine. This characteristic ligaturing style showing bovine features such as hindlegs of bovine, or bovine horns or tails, is also seen on Meluhha artifacts (seals and tablets).

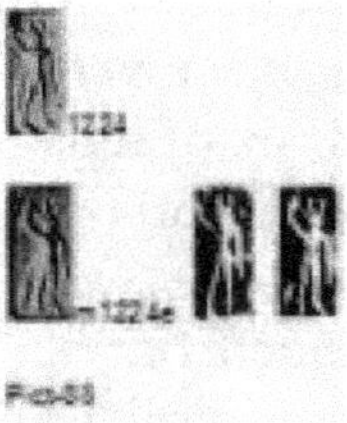

Pict-87 Standing horns and (hoofed legs and/or

Mohenjo-daro tablets. Standing person with horns and bovine features (hoofed legs and/or tail). person with bovine features tail).

Harappa tablets. Pict-85, Pict-86 Standing person with horns and bovine features (hoofed legs and/or tail).

Pict-90: Standing person with horns and bovine features holding a staff or mace on his shoulder.

Chalcolithic scepter with ibex and ram's heads.

The standard has a hole at the top of the tube.
Chalcolithic scepter.
Scepter with ibex heads.
From Nahal Mishmar, a wadi on the western side of the Dead Sea 429 object were discovered: 416 of metal, six of ivory and six hematite mace-heads and one mace-head of limestone. "A technical analysis has revealed that the objects are made from antimony-arsenic-rich copper, pure copper o nickel-arsenical copper. The source of the ores remained largely problematic, however, high nickel coppers are reported to be found in artefacts from Ur and this leads to some speculation about Iranian plateau as an origin. The ceremonial objects are reported to be cast using lost-wax techniques over cores in single castings."

Now known as the Nahal Mishmar hoard, the collection dates to the Chalcolithic period (4000–3300 B.C.E.) and is made up mostly of copper objects—240 mace heads, 80 scepters and 10 crowns—created using the "lost-wax technique." Scholars suggest that the hoard, which was found wrapped in a straw mat, may have been sacred artifacts from the treasury of the shrine at Ein Gedi, just 6 miles north of the cave. The treasure was probably hidden in the cave for safe-keeping when the shrine was mysteriously abandoned.

Processions of animals shown on Ancient Near East artifacts and Indus inscriptions

Processions depicted on Narmer palette

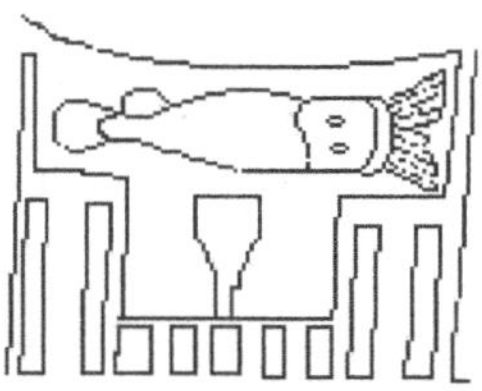

At the top of both sides of the Palette are the central serekhs bearing the rebus symbols n'r (catfish) and m'r (chisel or awl) inside, being the phonetic representation of Narmer's name.

He holds a mace and a flail, two traditional symbols of kingship. To his right are the hieroglyphic symbols for his name. Behind him is his sandal bearer, whose name may be represented by the rosette appearing adjacent to his head, and a second rectangular symbol that has no clear interpretation but which has been suggested may represent a town or citadel.[168]

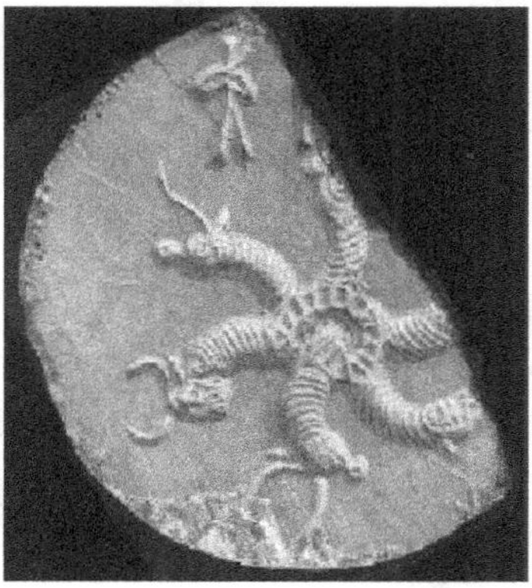

It is certain that the design known as the animal file *motif* is extremely early in Sumerian and Elamitic glyptic; in fact is among the oldest known glyptic designs.

A characteristic style in narration is the use of a procession of animals to denote a professional group. The grouping may connote a smithy-shop of a guild --*pasāramu.* Mohenjo-daro seal m417 six heads from a core.*śrēṇikā* -- f. ' tent ' lex. and mngs. ' house ~ ladder ' in *śriṣṭa -- 2, *śrīḍhi -- . -- Words for ' ladder ' see śrití -- . -- √śri]H. *sainī*, *senī* f. ' ladder '; Si. *hiṇi*, *hiṇa*, *iṇi* ' ladder, stairs ' (GS 84 < *śrēṇi* --).(CDIAL 12685). Woṭ. Šen ' roof ', Bshk. Šan, Phal. Šān(AO xviii 251) Rebus: seṇi (f.) [Class. Sk. Śreṇi in meaning "guild"; Vedic= row] 1. A guild Vin iv.226; J i.267, 314; iv.43; Dāvs ii.124; their number was eighteen J vi.22, 427; VbhA 466. ° -- pamukha the head of a guild J ii.12 (text seni --). — 2. A division of an army J vi.583; ratha -- ° J vi.81, 49; seṇimokkha the chief of an army J vi.371 (cp. Senā and seniya). (Pali)

This denotes a mason (artisan) guild -- seni -- of 1. brass-workers; 2. blacksmiths; 3. iron-workers; 4. copper-workers; 5. native metal workers; 6. workers in alloys.

The core is a glyphic 'chain' or 'ladder'. Glyph: kaḍī a chain; a hook; a link (G.); kaḍum a bracelet, a ring (G.) Rebus: kaḍiyo [Hem. Des. kaḍaio = Skt. sthapati a mason] a bricklayer; a mason; kaḍiyaṇa, kaḍiyeṇa a woman of the bricklayer caste; a wife of a bricklayer (Gujarati)

The glyphics are:

1. Glyph: 'one-horned young bull': *kondh* 'heifer'. *kũdār* 'turner, brass-worker'.
2. Glyph: 'bull': *ḍhangra* 'bull'. *Rebus: ḍhangar* 'blacksmith'.
3. Glyph: 'ram': *meḍh* 'ram'. Rebus: *meḍ* 'iron'
4. Glyph: 'antelope': *mṛeka* 'goat'. Rebus: *milakkhu* 'copper'. Vikalpa 1: *meluhha* '*mleccha*' 'copper worker'. Vikalpa 2: *meṛh* 'helper of merchant'.
5. Glyph: 'zebu': *khũṭ* 'zebu'. Rebus: *khũṭ* 'guild, community' (Semantic determinant of the 'jointed animals' glyphic composition). *kūṭa* joining, connexion, assembly, crowd, fellowship (DEDR 1882) Pa. *gotta* 'clan'; Pk. *gotta, gōya* id. (CDIAL 4279) Semantics of Pkt. lexeme *gōya* is concordant with Hebrew *'goy'* in *ha-goy-im* (lit. the-nation-s) Pa. *gotta* -- n. ' clan ', Pk. *gotta* -- , *gutta* -- , amg. *gōya* -- n.; Gau. *gū* ' house ' (in Kaf. and

Dard. several other words for ' cowpen ' > ' house ': gōṣṭhá -- , Pr. *gū´ṭu* ' cow '; S. *goṭru* m. ' parentage ', L. *got* f. ' clan ', P. *gotar*, *got* f.; Ku. N. *got* ' family '; A. *got -- nāti* ' relatives '; B. *got* ' clan '; Or. *gota* ' family, relative '; Bhoj. H. *got* m. ' family, clan ', G. *got* n.; M. *got* ' clan, relatives '; -- Si. *gota* ' clan, family ' ← Pa. (CDIAL 4279). Alternative: adar ḍangra 'zebu or humped bull'; rebus: aduru 'native metal' (Ka.); ḍhangar 'blacksmith' (H.)

6. The sixth animal can only be guessed. Perhaps, a tiger (A reasonable inference, because the glyph 'tiger' appears in a procession on some Indus script inscriptions. Glyph: 'tiger?': *kol* 'tiger'.Rebus: *kol* 'worker in iron'. Vikalpa (alternative): perhaps, rhinoceros. gaṇḍa 'rhinoceros'; rebus:khaṇḍ 'tools, pots and pans and metal-ware'. Thus, the entire glyphic composition of six animals on the Mohenjodaro seal m0417 is semantically a representation of a *śrēṇi*, 'guild', a *khũṭ* , 'community' of smiths and masons.

This guild, community of smiths and masons evolves into Harosheth Hagoyim, 'a smithy of nations'.

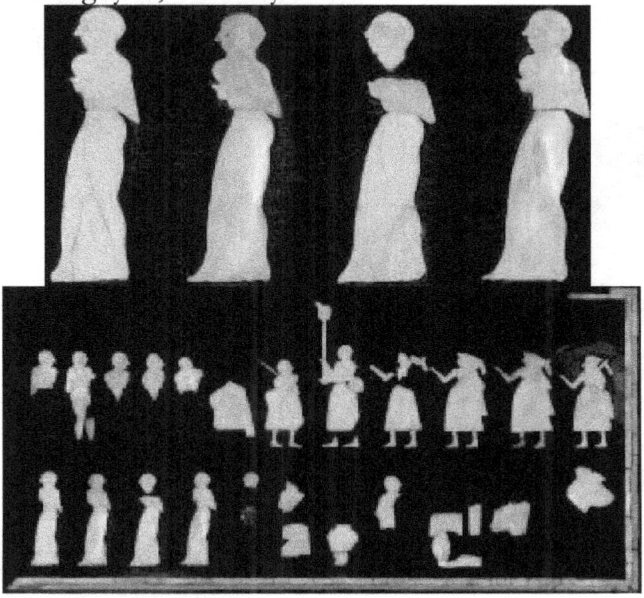

Frieze of a mosaic panel Circa 2500-2400 BCE Temple of Ishtar, Mari (Tell Hariri), Syria Shell and shale André Parrot excavations, 1934-36 AO 19820. The standard-bearer glyph bearing the one-horned young bull is replicated on this panel. This is a signature Meluhha hierogyph of Indus writing. "Reconstruction of the original panel is based on guesswork, since shell pieces are missing. The soldiers wear helmets, carry spears or adzes, and are dressed in kaunakes (fleecy skirts or kilts) and scarves. The dignitaries wear kaunakes and low fur hats, and each carries a long-handled adze on the left shoulder. Their leader appears to be a shaven-headed figure: stripped to the waist and wearing kaunakes, he carries a standard showing a bull standing on a pedestal. The lower register, on the right, features traces of a chariot drawn by onagers, a type of wild ass."[169]

These inlaid mosaics, composed of figures carved in mother-of-pearl, against a background of small blocks of lapis lazuli or pink limestone, set in bitumen, are among the most original and attractive examples of Mesopotamian art. It was at Mari that a large number of these mosaic pieces were discovered. Here they depict a victory scene: soldiers lead defeated enemy captives, naked and in chains, before four dignitaries.

A person is a standard bearer of a banner holding aloft the one-horned young bull which is the signature glyph of Indus writing. The banner is comparable to the banner shown on two Mohenjo-daro tablets.

A victory scene

The pieces that make up this shell mosaic composition were found scattered on the floor of the Temple of Ishtar, and therefore the reconstruction of the original panel is based on guesswork, all the more so in that the shell pieces are missing. The shell figures were arranged on a wooden panel covered with a layer of bitumen. The whole composition was organized in several registers, and the frame of the panel was emphasized by a double red and white line of stone and shell. The spaces between the figures were filled by small tiles of gray-black shale. The panel depicts the end of a battle, with soldiers leading their stripped and bound captives before dignitaries. The soldiers wear helmets, carry spears or adzes, and are dressed in kaunakes (fleecy skirts or kilts) and scarves. The dignitaries wear kaunakes and low fur hats, and each carries a long-handled adze on the left shoulder. Their leader appears to be a shaven-headed figure: stripped to the waist and wearing kaunakes, he carries a standard showing a bull standing on a pedestal. The lower register, on the right, features traces of a chariot drawn by onagers, a type of wild ass. *khara* 'ass' Rebus: *khar* 'blacksmith' (Kashmiri)

Mosaic art

Many fragments of mosaic panels were discovered in the temples of Mari. Used to decorate the soundboxes of musical instruments, "gaming tables," or simple rectangular wooden panels, the pieces of mosaic seen here were like scattered pieces of a jigsaw puzzle when they were found. Mosaic pictures were particularly prized in Mesopotamia. Fragments can be found in Kish, Tello, and Tell Asmar, in Mesopotamia, and in Ebla, Syria, where these extremely fragile works of art did not survive the destruction of the buildings in which they were housed. Only the Standard of Ur has been preserved, an object which offers many points of comparison with the present work, since one side of this artifact is devoted to the theme of war. We know that the fragments discovered at Mari were manufactured locally, for the workshop of an engraver using mother-of-pearl was found in the palace. By the delicacy of their carving and engraving, the mother-of-pearl figures produced in this capital of a kingdom on the Middle Euphrates distinguish it from other centers of artistic production; they sometimes even surpass works of art produced in the Mesopotamian city of Ur. One of the distinctive features of Mari is the diversity of the scenes depicted: battles and scenes of offerings made to the gods, religious scenes with priests and priestesses, and sacrifices of rams.These scenes provide us with invaluable insights into the social, political, and religious life of Mari.[170]

Pre-cuneiform tablet with seal impressions

[quote] Administrative tablet with cylinder seal impression of a male figure, hunting dogs, and boars, 3100–2900 B.C.; Jemdet Nasr period (Uruk III script) Mesopotamia ClayH. 2 in. (5.3 cm) Purchase, Raymond and Beverly Sackler Gift, 1988 (1988.433.1) ON VIEW: GALLERY 402 Last Updated April 26, 2013 In about 3300 B.C., writing was invented in Mesopotamia, perhaps in the city of Uruk, where the earliest inscribed clay tablets have been found in abundance. This was not an isolated development but occurred during a period of profound transformation in politics, the economy, and representational art. During the Uruk period of the fourth millennium B.C., the first Mesopotamian cities were settled, the first kings were crowned, and a range of goods—from ceramic vessels to textiles—were mass-produced in state workshops. Early writing was used primarily as a means of recording and storing economic information, but from the beginning a significant component of the written tradition consisted of lists of words and names that scribes needed to know in order to keep their accounts. Signs were drawn with a reed stylus on pillow-shaped tablets, most of which were only a few inches wide. The stylus left small marks in the clay which we call cuneiform, or wedge-shaped, writing. This tablet most likely documents grain distributed by a large temple,

although the absence of verbs in early texts makes them difficult to interpret with certainty. [unquote][171]

Line drawing showing the seal impression on this tablet. Illustration by Abdallah Kahil. The imagery of the cylinder seal records information. A male figure is guiding dogs (?Tigers) and herding boars in a reed marsh. Both tiger and boar are Indus writing hieroglyphs, together with the imagery of a grain stalk. All these hieroglyphs are read rebus in Meluhha (mleccha),of Indian *sprachbund* in the context of metalware catalogs of bronze age. kola 'tiger'; rebus: kol 'iron'; kāṇḍa 'rhino'; rebus: kāṇḍa 'metalware tools, pots and pans'. *Ka.* (Hav.) aḍaru twig; (Bark.) aḍïrï small and thin branch of a tree; (Gowda) aḍəri small branches. *Tu.* aḍaru twig.(DEDR 67) Rebus: aduru *gan.iyinda tegadu karagade iruva aduru* = ore taken from the mine and not subjected to melting in a furnace (Ka. Siddhānti Subrahmaṇya' Śastri's new interpretation of the AmarakoŚa, Bangalore, Vicaradarpana Press, 1872, p.330) Alternative rebus: If the imagery of stalk connoted a palm-frond, the rebus readings could have been:
Ku. N. tāmo (pl. ' young bamboo shoots '), A. tām, B. tā̃bā, tāmā, Or. tambā, Bi tā̃bā, Mth. tām, tāmā, Bhoj. tāmā, H. tām in cmpds., tā̃bā, tāmā m. (CDIAL 5779) Rebus: tāmrá ' dark red, copper -- coloured ' VS., n. ' copper ' Kauś., tāmraka -- n. Yājñ. [Cf. tamrá -- . -- √tam?] Pa. tamba -- ' red ', n. ' copper ', Pk. taṁba -- adj. and n.; Dm. trāmba -- ' red ' (in trāmba -- laçuk ' raspberry ' NTS xii 192); Bshk. lām ' copper, piece of bad pine -- wood (< ' *red wood '?); Phal. tāmba ' copper ' (→ Sh.koh. tāmbā), K. trām m. (→ Sh.gil. gur. trām m.), S. ṭrāmo m., L. trāmā, (Ju.) tarāmā̃ m., P. tāmbā m., WPah. bhad. ṭḷām n., kiũth. cāmbā, sod. cambo, jaun. tā̃bō (CDIAL 5779) tabāshīr तबाशीर् । त्वक्ॱक्षीरी f. the sugar of the bamboo, bamboo-manna (a siliceous deposit on the joints of the bamboo) (Kashmiri)

Proto-Cuneiform tablet with seal impressions. Jemdet Nasr period, ca. 3100-2900 BCE. Mesopotamia. Clay H. 5.5 cm; W.7

cm.[172]

Late Uruk and Jemdet Nasr seal; ca. 3200-3000 BC; serpentine; cat.1; boar and bull in procession; terminal: plant; heavily pitted surface beyond plant

Daimabad procession of animals

Buffalo. Mohenjo-daro.

Buffalo. Daimabad bronze. Prince of Wales Museum, Mumbai.

ran:gā 'buffalo'; ran:ga 'pewter or alloy of tin (ran:ku), lead (nāga) and antimony (*añjana*)'(Santali)

kaṭái ' buffalo calf '(Gaw.) *kāṭo* ' young buffalo bull ' (Kumaoni) (CDIAL 2645).

kāṛā 'buffalo' bull (Tamil) *khaḍā* 'nodule (ore), stone' (Marathi). Alternative: கண்டி kaṇṭi buffalo. Rebus: *kāḍ* 'stone ore'*gaḍa* 'large stone mould'. Glyph: kuṇḍī 'crooked buffalo horns' (Lahnda.) Rebus: kuṇḍī = chief of village (Prākṛt).The artisan is kundakara— m. 'turner' (Skt.); H. kũderā m. 'one who works a lathe, one who scrapes' (CDIAL 3297).*ḍabe, ḍabea* 'large horns, with a sweeping upward curve, applied to buffaloes' (Santali)

Rebus: *ḍab*, ḍhimba, ḍhompo 'lump (ingot?)', clot, make a lump or clot, coagulate, fuse, melt together (Santali)

Hieroglyphs, read rebus:Rhinoceros: gaṇḍá4 m. ' rhinoceros ' lex., °*aka* -- m. lex. 2. *ga- yaṇḍa -- . [Prob. of same non -- Aryan origin as khaḍgá --1: cf. *gaṇōtsāha* -- m. lex. as a Sanskritized form ← Mu. PMWS 138]1. Pa. *gaṇḍaka* -- m., Pk. *gaṁḍaya* -- m., A. *gãr*, Or. *gaṇḍā*. 2. K. *gõḍ* m., S. *geṇḍo* m. (lw. with *g* --), P. *gaĩḍā* m., °*ḍī* f., N. *gaĩṛo*, H. *gaĩṛā* m., G. *gẽḍɔ* m., °*ḍī* f., M. *gẽḍā* m. WPah.kṭg. *geṇḍɔ mirg* m. ' rhinoceros ', Md. *genḍā* ← H. (CDIAL 4000).காண்டாமிருகம் kāṇṭā-mirukam , *n.* [M. *kāṇṭāmṛgam.*] Rhinoceros; கல்யானை. (Tamil) Rebus: *khāṇḍa* 'tools, pots and pans, and metal-ware'.

badhi 'castrated boar' <boRia>(A) {N} ``^boar''. #5620.<badia> {N} ``^boar''. *De.<baria>(M) `pig(G), boar(M)'. @N0749. bar.ae 'blacksmith' (Mundarica) . A carpenter వడ్లవాడు.(Telugu) badhoe 'worker in wood and iron'

Elephant 'ibha'. Rebus: ibbo (merchant of ib 'iron')ibha 'elephant' (Skt.) Rebus: ibbho 'merchant' (cf.Hemacandra, *Desinamamala*, vaṇika). ib 'iron' (Santali) karibha 'elephant' (Skt.); rebus: karb 'iron' (Ka.)

కరటి [karaṭi] *karaṭi*. [Skt.] n. An elephant. ఏనుగు (Telugu) Rebus: *kharādī* ' turner' (Gujarati)

Were the Daimabad artisan guilds carrying these bronze models as standards in processions on a festival day celebrating their work and advertising their professional metallurgical competence? Asur community in India.

"The Agaria are a tribal community that have inhabited the Central Indian region and their name comes from the word aag or fire. The Agaria were less numerous in the Ranchi plateau but had become incorporated with the Asurs of the region. Lohars are a group of communities who work on iron and they may have either a tribal or a non-tribal origin…In the Santal Paraganas, they trace their origin from Birbhum, Manbhum or Burdwan, as well as from Magahi…In fact, the word Munda (as a tribe of this region is called) also means a ball of iron…In Birbhum, the iron smelters included Santals, Bonyahs and Kols. Such activity was part-time and seasonal and was combined with agriculture. 'Iron earth' was obtained either from the surface or by digging small shafts under the ground. The extraction was normally in the open, but the smelting houses were like blacksmith's workshops and run by Kol-lohars, who were a non-agricultural group. They were in contact with iron merchants and received advances from them. There wee also others who sold it to others and carried to iron markets called aurangs. (Dasgupta, PC, 1997, The excavations at Pandu Rajar Dhibi, F. Raymond Allchin and Dilip K. Chakrabarti, eds., A sourcebook of Indian archaeology, vol. II, New Delhi, Munshiram Manoharlal Publishers Pvt. Ltd., pp. 200-205). In Bihar and Jharkhand, such iron-smelting was an ancient craft in the Rajahal Hills, Palamu-Ranchi and Dhalbhum-Singhbhum regions. Many tribals participated. In the Rajmahals it was the Kols, who were migrants with hunting as a subsidiary occupation or even some agriculture. Then, there were the Agaria/Asura of Ranchi and Chotanagpur, the Cheros and Bhoktas of Palamau, Hos and Kharis of Dhalbhum, Korahs and Nyahs of Bhagalpur district, often on their way to becoming settled agriculturists. They handed over iron to the Lohars for cash. In the Rajmahal hills and Santal Paraganas there were larger forges and indications of organized, large-scale and long-term smelting of iron also, leading to fundamental specialization and blacksmith colonies. In Orissa, Patuas and Juangs creted iron of the best quality. In Bonai it was done by the Kols, probably from Singhbhum…In Darjeeling, iron was manufactured but not smelted by the Kamins. In Khasia hills it was done by the Garos, Khasis and Nagas, though this region had features different from that of the Chotanagpur…Tripathi and Mishra[173] also studied the iron-making communities in detail and found out that the Mahuli garias produced white iron which was used for preparing weapons. A high grade iron was also produced by the Parsa group of Agarias as well as the Kamis of Darjeeling…Munda mythology refers to the Asuras as being killed by their gods, the variety of Asura sites and their graveyards. Roy (Roy, Sarat Chandra, 1926. The Asurs – Ancient and modern, Journal of the Bihar and Orissa Research Society 12: 243-285) claims that the preent-day Asurs took up the name of this ancient group and its iron-smelting. These Asurs are divided into three kinds: there are the Soika Asurs, also called Agarias or Agaria Asurs (the iron-smelters), the Birjias who have also taken up plaiting bamboo baskets, etc. with iron-smelting and the Jait Asurs who live in villages, smelt iron and manufacture ploughshares and other rude iron implements…iron-smelting Agarias are also found in Uttar Pradesh and Madhya Pradesh sttes…A further division among the Birjias are those who anoint their brides and bridegrooms only with oil (Telia Birjias) and those who use vermilion as well as oil (Sinduraha Birjias). The Asurs seem to have similar practices with the Mundas and the Birjias seem to have clan as well as individual totems. They now practice only cremation of the dead and there is no urn-burial. However, such burial is seen among the Hos and Mundas..."[174]

Animals in procession: Two gazelles (antelopes?), stalks, two tigers Two eagles, sprout between

Base for a ritual offering, carved with animals Elamite period, mid-3rd millennium BC Tell of the Acropolis, Susa, Iran Bituminous rock H. 19 cm; Diam. 11 cm Jacques de Morgan excavations, 1908 Lions and gazelles passant; eagles protecting their young Sb 2725

This base for a ritual offering is made of bitumen. This material was plentiful throughout the Middle East, but only in Susa was it used in sculpture. The object is carved with big cats, gazelles, and eagles. The theme of the eagle spreading its wings to protect its young was found only in Iran and also features on painted ceramics of the same period.

Bitumen: a plentiful material used in an unusual manner

This object in the form of a truncated cone is a base for a ritual offering. It is carved from bituminous rock, found throughout the region but used in sculpture only in Susa. It was used to make vases similar to this object (Louvre, Sb2726), and later, in the early years of the 2nd millennium BC, vases carved with bas-relief decorations and an animal's head in high relief (Louvre, Sb2740). The shape of this object - a truncated cone - is similar to other pieces made of chlorite and dating from the same period. The mortise at the top of the cone and the unfinished lip suggest that the object originally had a second part that fitted on top of the cone. However, the precise purpose of the object remains a mystery.

The animal carvings

The cone is carved with two registers separated by a narrow strip. The upper register is decorated with two gazelles calmly grazing on vegetation, represented by stalks between each animal.

Alongside the two gazelles are two big cats, almost certainly lions, with their backs to each other. Their stylized manes are shown as vertical strips, reminiscent of those of the woolen Mesopotamian garments known as kaunakes. Their tails are raised horizontally over their backs, similar to depictions of lions on cylinders from Uruk or Susa. Their heads are depicted in geometrical form. All four animals are shown in profile. The artistic desire to create a scene and a landscape imbued with life is also evident in two cylinders from Uruk and Khafaje.

The lower register shows two highly stylized eagles, upright, as if resting on their tail feathers. Their wings and talons are spread to protect the chicks beneath them. These eagles differ somewhat from the usual representation of eagles as the attribute of the Sumerian god Ningirsu, where the birds are depicted with a lion's head, holding two lion cubs, which are shown face on.

Mythological creatures or carvings of local wildlife?

Eagles were a major theme in Susian and Mesopotamian art. This depiction of an eagle resting on its tail feathers is also found in ceramics, glyptics, and perforated plaques dating from the 3rd millennium BC. However, unlike Mesopotamian eagles, Susian eagles never resembled composite animals. Likewise, Mesopotamian eagles had a mythological dimension, which was absent from Susian portrayals of the bird. In Susa, eagles were simply considered ordinary birds of prey.175

Late Uruk and Jemdet Nasr seal; ca. 3200-3000 (?) BC; marble; cat.3; loop bore; an antelope with two tigerss, one with head turned. kola 'tiger' Rebus: kol 'working in iron'. tagara 'antelope' Rebus: tagara 'tin'. krammara 'head turned back' Rebus: kamar 'smith, artisan'.

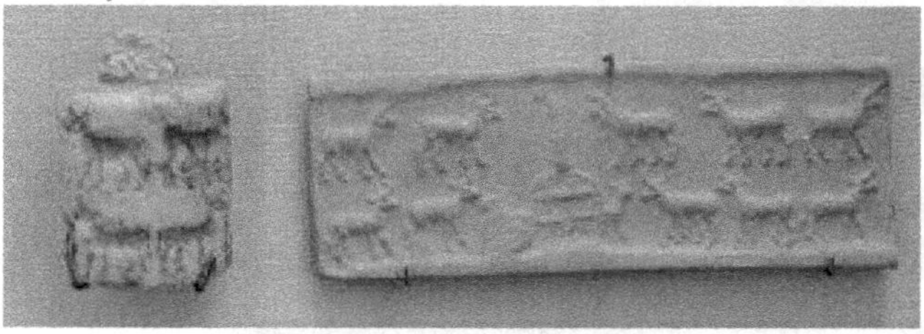

Cylinder seal and impression: cattle herd at the cowshed. White limestone, Mesopotamia, Uruk Period (4100 BC–3000 BC). Louvre Museum.

Bronze dish found by Layard at Nimrud: circular objects are decorated by consecutive chains of animals following each other round in a circle. A similar theme occurs on the famous silver vase of Entemena. In the innermost circle, a troop of gazelles (similar to the ones depicted on cylinder seals) march along in file; the middle register has a variety of animals, all marching in the same direction as the gazelles. A one-horned bull, a winged griffin, an ibex and a gazelle, are followed by two bulls who are being attacked by lions, and a griffin, a one-horned bull, and a gazelle, who are all respectively being attacked by leopards. In the outermost zone there is a stately procession of realistically conceived one-horned bulls marching in the opposite direction to the animals parading in the two inner circles. The dish has a handle. (Percy S.P.Handcock, 1912, *Mesopotamian Archaeology*, London, Macmillan and Co., p. 256).

Cylinder seal and impression: cattle herd in a wheat field. Limestone, Mesopotamia, Uruk Period (4100 BC–3000 BC).

kuṇḍa n. 'clump' (Sanskrit) A phonetic determinant of the young bull *kõḍā* खोंड [khōṇḍa] m 'A young bull, a bullcalf'. (Marathi)

read rebus: *kũderā* m. 'one who works a lathe'. Alternative: The cob is kolmo 'seeding, rice-plant'(Munda) rebus: kolami 'smithy'; (Telugu)

Hieroglyphs of Uruk trough

Two views of the trough. "Two lambs exit structure identical to the present-day mudhif on this ceremonial trough from

the site of Uruk in southern Iraq…Dating to ca. 3000 BCE, the trough documents the extraordinary length of time such arched reed buildings have been in use." Sumerian mudhif[176] facade, with uncut reed fonds and sheep entering, carved into a gypsum trough from Uruk, c. 3200 BCE (British Museum WA 120000). Maybe a sacred object in the temple of Inana (Ishtar) of Uruk.

The animals exiting the mudhif are comparable to the animals shown in procession on Warka vase.

The rebus reading of the pair of reeds in Sumer standard is: *khāṇḍa* 'tools, pots and pans and metal-ware', *khōṭ* 'alloyed

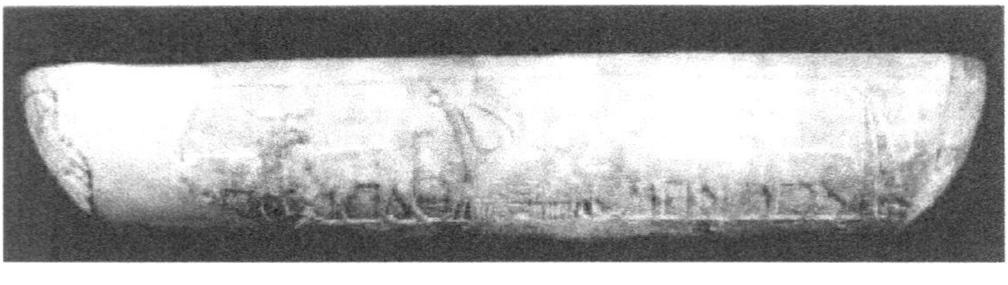

ingots', dhatu 'mineral (ore)'.

Glyph: कोंडण [kōṇḍaṇa] f A fold or pen. (Marathi) goṭ = the place where cattle are collected at mid-day (Santali); goṭh (Brj.)(CDIAL 4336). Goṣṭha (Skt.); cattle-shed (Or.) koḍ = a cow-pen; a cattlepen; a byre (G.) कोठी cattle-shed (Marathi) कोंडी [kōṇḍī] A pen or fold for cattle. गोठी [gōṭhī] f C (Dim. Of गोठा) A pen or fold for calves. (Marathi) Allograph: koṭṭhaka1 (nt.) "a kind of koṭṭha," the stronghold over a gateway, used as a store — room for various things, a chamber, treasury, granary Vin ii.153, 210; for the purpose of keeping water in it Vin ii.121=142; 220; treasury J i.230; ii.168; -- store — room J ii.246; koṭthake pāturahosi appeared at the gateway, i. e. arrived at the mansion Vin i.291. (Pali) kuṛī, kuṛo house, building'(Ku.)(CDIAL 3232) कोठी [kōṭhī] f (कोष्ट S) A granary, garner, storehouse, warehouse, treasury, factory, bank. (Marathi) कोठी The grain and provisions (as of an army); the commissariat supplies.

Rebus: कोंदण [kōndaṇa] n (कोंदणें) Setting or infixing of gems.(Marathi) *kõdā* 'to turn in a lathe'(B.)

Text 1330 (appears with Zebu glyph) showing Glyph 39.

Pictorial motif: Zebu (*Bos indicus*) This sign is comparable to the cattle byre of Southern Mesopotamia dated to c. 3000 BCE. The hut of a Toda Tribe of Nilgiris, India. Note the decoration of the front wall, and the very small door.

The architecture of Iraqi mudhif and Toda mund — of Indian linguistic area — is comparable.177

Cattle Byres c.3200-3000 B.C. Late Uruk-Jemdet Nasr period. Magnesite. Cylinder seal. In the lower field of this seal appear three reed cattle byres. Each

byre is surmounted by three reed pillars topped by rings, a motif that has been suggested as symbolizing a male god, perhaps Dumuzi. Within the huts calves or vessels appear alternately; from the sides come calves that drink out of a vessel between them. Above each pair of animals another small calf appears. A herd of enormous cattle moves in the upper field.

Cattle and cattle byres in Southern Mesopotamia, c. 3500 BCE. Drawing of an impression from a Uruk period cylinder seal. (After Moorey, PRS, 1999, Ancient materials and industries: the archaeological evidence, Eisenbrauns.) The extensive use of hieroglyphs in Indus writing is comparable to the ones used on Narmer palette which is rebus method of writing. The name of the king ca. 31st century BCE was depicted by two

glyphs (on top of the palette between two ox-heads). The same set of hieroglyphs is repeated on the second register which shows Narmer in a procession with some carrying banners. A person following Narmer is shown with a 'rosette' hieroglyph. The 'rosette' hieroglyph is also shown together with 'scorpion' hieroglyph on what has been referred to as a 'Scorpion macehead'. (Ashmolean museum). kunda m. 'Jasminum multiflorum or pubescens' MBh. (' olibanum or resin of Boswellia thurifera ' lex., see kunduru -), n. 'its flower'. Pa. *kunda* -- n. 'jasmine'; Pk. *kuṁda* -- m. 'a flowering tree', n. 'a kind of flowe '; B. *kũd* 'J.

multiflorum', M. *kũd* m. ' id. ', *kũdā* m. 'a partic. kind of flowering shrub'; Si. *koňda* 'jasmine'. (CDIAL 3296)
meṭ sole of foot, footstep, footprint (Ko.); meṭṭu step, stair, treading, slipper (Te.)(DEDR 1557). Rebus: मेढ 'merchant's helper' (Pkt.); *m.* an elephant-keeper Gal. (cf. मेठ).
Ta. mēṭṭi haughtiness, excellence, chief, head, land granted free of tax to the headman of a village; *mēṭṭimai* haughtiness; leadership, excellence. *Ka.* mēṭi loftiness, greatness, excellence, a big man, a chief, a head, head servant. *mēti.* n. Lit: a helper. A servant, a cook, a menial who cleans plates, dishes, lamps and shoes, &c. (Eng. 'mate') మేటి [mēṭi] or మేటరి *mēṭi* [Tel.] n. A chief, leader, head man, lord (Telugu) மேட்டி mēṭṭi, *n.* Assistant house-servant; waiting-boy (Tamil)

There are two types of hieroglyphic compositions on mudhif (Iraqi marsh hut) or munda (Toda hut): 1. Three reed shafts with six rings on top; 2. Reed shaft with a curved end and a dangling scarf on top.

Hieroglyph: *dhàṭṭu* m. 'woman's headgear, kerchief'; *dhaṭu* m. (also *dhaṭhu*) m. 'scarf' (WPah.) Rebus: *dhātu*'mineral' (Skt.), *dhatu* id. (Santali).

Hieroglyph: Six rings or curls: *āra* 'six' Rebus: *āra* 'brass'.
The composition of three reeds topped with six rings is flanked by two jars with overflowing water.

<lo->(B) {V} ``(pot, etc.) to ^overflow''. See <lo-> `to be left over'. @B24310. #20851. Re<lo->(B) {V} ``(pot, etc.) to ^overflow''. See <lo-> `to be left over'. (Munda) Rebus: loh 'copper' (Hindi) The hieroglyph clearly refers to the metal tools, pots and pans of copper.

కొండము [kāṇḍamu] *kāṇḍamu.* [Skt.] n. Water.

నీళ్ళు (Telugu) kaṇṭhá -- : (b) ' water -- channel ': Paš. *kaṭá´* '

irrigation channel ', Shum. *xãṭṭä* (CDIAL 14349). **காண்டம்²**

kāṇṭam, *n.* < *kāṇḍa.* 1. Water; sacred water; நீர். **துருத்திவா**

யதுக்கிய குங்குமக் காண் டமும் (கல்லா. 49,

16). Rebus: *khāṇḍā* 'metal tools, pots and pans' (Marathi)
lokhāḍ 'overflowing pot' Rebus: 'tools, iron, ironware' (Gujarati)
The following semantic cluster indicates that the early
compound: *loha* + *kāṇḍa* referred to copper articles, tools, pot and
pans. The early semantics of 'copper' got expanded to cover 'iron
and other metals'. It is suggested that the hieroglyph of an
overflowing vase refers to this compound: *lohakāṇḍā.*

खांडा [khāṇḍā] *m* A kind of sword, straight, broad-bladed, two-
edged, and round-ended (Marathi) M. *lokhãḍ* n. 'iron'(Marthi)
yields the clue to the early semantics of khāṇḍā which should
have referred to tools, pots and pans (of metal). Kumaoni has
semantics: *lokhaṛ* 'iron tools'. **लोहोलोखंड** [lōhōlōkhaṇḍa] *n* (लोह &

लोखंड) Iron tools, vessels, or articles in general (Marathi).

Thus *lohakāṇḍā* would have referred to copper tools. The
overflowing vase on the hands of Gudea would have referred to
this compound, represented by the hieroglyphs and rendered
rebus.

N. *lokhar* ' bag in which a barber keeps his tools '; H. *lokhar* m. '
iron tools, pots and pans '; -- X lauhabhāṇḍa -- : Ku. *lokhar* ' iron
tools '; H. *lokhaṇḍ* m. ' iron tools, pots and pans '; G. *lokhāḍ* n. '
tools, iron, ironware '; M. *lokhãḍ* n. ' iron ' (LM 400 < -- *khaṇḍa* -
-)(CDIAL 11171). lōhitaka ' reddish ' Āpast., n. ' calx of brass,
bell- metal ' lex. [lṓhita --]K. *lŏy* f. ' white copper, bell -- metal '.
(CDIAL 11166). lōhá ' red, copper -- coloured ' ŚrS., ' made of
copper ' ŚBr., m.n. ' copper ' VS., ' iron ' MBh. [*rudh --

] Pa. *lōha* -- m. ' metal, esp. copper or bronze '; Pk. *lōha* -- m. ' iron ', Gy. pal. *li°*, *lihi*, obl. *elhás*, as. *loa* JGLS new ser. ii 258; Wg. (Lumsden) "*loa*" ' steel '; Kho. *loh* ' copper '; S. *lohu* m. ' iron ', L. *lohā* m., awāṇ.*lō`ā*, P. *lohā* m. (→ K.rām. ḍoḍ. *lohā*), WPah.bhad. *lɔ̃u* n., bhal. *lòtilde;* n., pāḍ. jaun. *lōh*, paṅ. *luhā*, cur. cam. *lohā*, Ku. *luwā*, N. *lohu*, *°hā*, A. *lo*, B. *lo*, *no*, Or. *lohā*, *luhā*, Mth. *loh*, Bhoj. *lohā*, Aw.lakh. *lōh*, H.*loh*, *lohā* m., G. M. *loh* n.; Si. *loho*, *lō* ' metal, ore, iron '; Md. *ratu* -- *lō* ' copper '.(CDIAL 11158). lōhakāra m. ' iron -- worker ', *°rī* -- f., *°raka* -- m. lex., *lauhakāra* -- m. Hit. [lōhá -- , kāra -- 1] Pa. *lōhakāra* -- m. ' coppersmith, ironsmith '; Pk. *lōhāra* -- m. ' blacksmith ', S. *luhăru* m., L. *lohār* m., *°rī* f., awāṇ. *luhār*, P. WPah.khaś. bhal. *luhār* m., Ku. *lwār*, N. B. *lohār*, Or. *lohaḷa*, Bi.Bhoj. Aw.lakh. *lohār*, H. *lohār*, *luh°* m., G. *lavār* m., M. *lohār* m.; Si. *lōvaru* ' coppersmith '. Addenda: lōhakāra -- : WPah.kṭg. (kc.) *lhwā`r* m. ' blacksmith ', *lhwàri* f. ' his wife ', Garh. *lwār* m.(CDIAL 11159). lōhahala 11161 lōhala ' made of iron ' W. [lōhá --](CDIAL 11161). Bi. *lohrā*, *°rī* ' small iron pan '(CDIAL 11160). Bi. *lohsārī* ' smithy '(CDIAL 11162). P.ludh. *lōhṭiyā* m. 'ironmonger'(CDIAL 11163). लोहोलोखंड [lōhōlōkhaṇḍa] *n* (लोह & लोखंड) Iron tools, vessels, or articles in general.रुपेशाई लोखंड [rupēśāī lōkhaṇḍa] *n* A kind of iron. It is of inferior quality to शिक्केशाई. लोखंड [lōkhaṇḍa] *n* (लोह S) Iron. लोखंडाचे चणे खावविणें or चारणें To oppress grievously. लोखंडकाम [lōkhaṇḍakāma] *n* Iron work; that portion (of a building, machine &c.) which consists of iron. 2 The business of an ironsmith. लोखंडी [lōkhaṇḍī] *a* (लोखंड) Composed of iron; relating to iron. 2 fig. Hardy or hard--a constitution or a frame of body, one's हाड or natal bone or parental stock. 3 Close and hard;--used of kinds of wood. 4 Ardent and unyielding--a fever. 5 लोखंडी, in the sense Hard and coarse or in the sense Strong or enduring, is freely applied as a term of distinction or designation. Examples follow. लोखंडी [lōkhaṇḍī] *f* (लोखंड) An iron boiler or other vessel. लोखंडी जर [lōkhaṇḍī jara] *m* (लोखंड & जर) False brocade or lace; lace &c. made of iron.लोखंडी रस्ता [lōkhaṇḍī rastā] *m* लोखंडी सडक *f* (Iron-road.) A railroad. लोह [lōha] *n* S Iron, crude or wrought. 2 *m* Abridged from लोहभस्म. A medicinal preparation from rust of iron.लोहकार [lōhakāra] *m* (S) A smelter of iron or a worker in iron.लोहकिट्ट [lōhakiṭṭa] *n* (S) Scoriæ or rust of iron, *klinker*.लोहंगी or लोहंगी काठी [lōhaṅgī or lōhaṅgī kāṭhī] *f* (लोह & अंग) A club set round with iron clamps and rings, a sort of bludgeon.लोहार [lōhāra] *m* (H or लोहकार S) A caste or an individual of it. They are smiths or workers in iron. लोहारकाम [lōhārakāma] *n* Iron-work, work proper to the blacksmith.लोहारकी [lōhārakī] *f* (लोहार) The business of the blacksmith.लोहारडा [lōhāraḍā] *m* A contemptuous form of the word लोहार.लोहारसाळ [lōhārasāḷa] *f* A smithy.

0m 15 (Tranchée VII). — Presque à fleur de sol, vers l'extrémité Sud de la tranchée n° VII, j'ai eu la satisfaction de recueillir, au point marqué *d* sur notre Plan E, dans une terre de remblai noire et fine, un beau cylindre en marbre d'un ton blanchâtre

Grandeur naturelle

Au dieu Nin-ghish-zida, — son roi, — pour la vie — de Dounghi, — le mâle fort, — Nig-kal-la, — pasteur des moutons gras, — a voué (ceci).

au nom du roi Dounghi. C'est une pièce historique, figurant la présentation au dieu Nin-ghish-zida; nous la donnons avec sa légende, d'après la traduction de M. Thureau-Dangin (*Inscriptions de Sumer et d'Akkad*, p. 281, sceau G) :

Source: Thureau-Dangin.[178]

Seal of Gudea: Gudea, with shaven head, is accompanied by a minor female diety. He is led by his personal god, Ningishzida, into the presence of Enlil, the chief Sumerian god. Wind pours forth from of the jars held by Enlil, signifying that he is the god of the winds. The winged leopard (griffin) is a mythological creature associated with Ningishzida, The horned helmets, worn even by the griffins, indicates divine status (the more horns the higher the rank). The writing in the background translates as: "Gudea, *Ensi* [ruler], of Lagash".

The 'fox' and 'overflowing water' hieroglyphs on Gudea cylinder seal evoke cognate Meluhha gloss: *lo* 'fox'. *lo* 'overflow of pot' (Munda).

The fox has wings, as a semantic reinforcement of *loh* 'copper metal': Rebus: erako 'moltencast copper' Hieroglyph: *Te.* eṟaka, ṟekka, rekka, neṟaka, neṟi wing, feather *Ta.* ciṟai, ciṟaku, ciṟakar wing; iṟai, iṟaku, iṟakar, iṟakkai wing, feather, *Ma.* iṟaku, ciṟaku wing. *Ko.* rek wing, feather. *Ka.* eṟake, eṟaṅke, ṟakke, ṟekke wing; ṟaṭṭe, ṟeṭṭe wing, upper arm *Koḍ.* rekke wing; raṭṭe upper arm. *Tu.* ediṅke, reṅkè wing. *Kol.* reḍapa, (SR.) reppā id.; (P.) reṛapa id., feather. *Nk.* rekka, reppa wing. *Pa.* (S.) rekka

id. *Go.* (S.) rekka wing-feather; reka (M.) feather, (Ko.) wing (*Voc.* 3045). *Konḍa* ṟeka wing, upper arm. *Kuwi* (Su.) rekka wing (DEDR 2591).

lōī f., *lo* m.2. Pr. *ẓūwī* 'fox' (Western Pahari)(CDIAL 11140-2). Rebus: *loh* 'copper' (Hindi). *Te.* eṟaka, ṟekka, rekka, neṟaka, neṟi id. (DEDR 2591). Rebus: eraka, eṟaka = any metal infusion

(Ka.Tu.); urukku (Ta.); urukka melting; urukku what is melted; fused metal (Ma.); urukku (Ta.Ma.); eragu = to melt; molten state, fusion; erakaddu = any cast thng; erake hoyi = to pour meltted metal into a mould, to cast (Kannada)

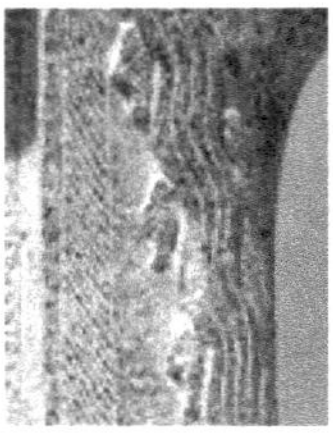

Overflowing pot. Relief fragment. Girsu (Tello).

Fish in water on viewer's right. Historical Archive: Gudea, prince of Lagash, holding an overflowing vase; Gudea "au vase jaillissant". Pedestal also shows an overflowing vase.

From Girsu (modern Tello, Iraq). Neo-Sumerian, c.2120 BCE. Dedicated to the goddess Geshtinanna.Dolerite, 62 x 25.6 cm. Louvre, Near Eastern Antiquities AO 22126
According to the inscription this statue was made by Gudea, ruler of Lagash (c. 2100 BCE) for the temple of the goddess Geshtinanna. Gudea refurbished the temples of Girsu and 11 statues of him have been found in excavations at the site. Nine others including this one were sold on the art market. It has been suggested that this statue is a forgery. Unlike the hard diorite of the excavated statues, it is made of soft calcite, and shows a ruler with a flowing vase which elsewhere in Mesopotamian art is only held by gods. It also differs stylistically from the excavated statues. On the other hand, the Sumerian inscription appears to be genuine and would be very difficult to fake. Statues of Gudea show him standing or sitting. Ine one, he

rests on his knee a plan of the temple he is building. On some statues Gudea has a shaven head, while on others like this one he wears a headdress covered with spirals, probably indicating that it was made out of fur. Height 61 cm. The overflowing water from the vase is a hieroglyph comparable to the pectoral of Mohenjo-daro showing an overflowing pot together with a one-horned young bull and standard device in front. The diorite from Magan (Oman), and timber from Dilmun (Bahrain) obtained by Gudea could have come from Meluhha. "The goddess Geshtinanna was known as "chief scribe" (Lambert 1990, 298– 299) and probably was a patron of scribes, as was Nidaba/ Nisaba (Micha-lowski 2002)."[179]

Dilmun, sea of Magan, the power of the bull

Bahrain. Seal impression. Two bull-men standing before a podium. They raised a horned altar or table, which is surmounted by a crescent and sun-disc. Alsendi 1994, No. 115.

If the crescent is a stylized glyph comparable to the bottom part of the standard device, the rebus reading could be *sangaḍa* 'portable furnace'. Rebus: *jangaḍa* 'entrustment articles'. *jangaḍiyo* 'military guard who accompanies treasure into the treasury'.

arka 'sun' Rebus: erka = ekke (Tbh. of arka) aka (Tbh. of arka) copper (metal); crystal (Kannada) eraka, er-aka = any metal infusion (Ka.Tu.); erako molten cast (Tulu) *agasāle, agasāli, agasālavāḍu* = a goldsmith (Telugu)

ḍhangar 'bull' Rebus: *dhangar* 'blacksmith' (Maithili) *ḍangar* 'blacksmith' (Hindi)

खांडा [*khāṇḍā*] A division of a field. (Marathi) Rebus: *kāṇḍā* 'metalware' (Marathi) *karaṇḍa* 'duck', 'water-pot' (Sanskrit) *karaṛa* 'a very large aquatic bird' (Sindhi) Rebus: करडा [*karaḍā*] Hard from alloy--iron, silver &c. (Marathi)

The pair of hieroglyphs flanking the 'partitioned square' glyph may compare with the Kafajeh vase fragment showing Sin temple? The Meluhha word for the temple is

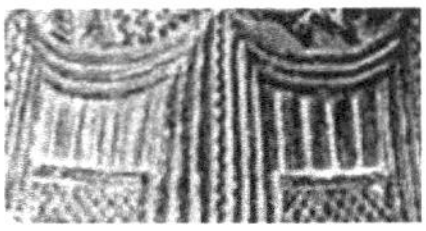

kole.l Rebus: *kolami* 'smithy'; *kol* 'working in iron.' Alternative: करडा [karaḍā] *m* The arrangement of bars or embossed lines (plain or fretted with little knobs) raised upon a तार of gold by pressing and driving it upon the अवटी or grooved stamp. Rebus: करडा [karaḍā] Hard from alloy--iron, silver &c. (Marathi)

m1656 Mohenjodro Pectoral. kāṇṭam காண்டம் kāṇṭam, *n.*

< *kāṇḍa.* 1. Water; sacred water; நீர். துருத்திவா யதுக்கிய குங்குமக் காண் டமும் (கல்லா. 49, 16). <kanda> {N} ``large earthen water ^pot kept and filled at the house''. @1507. #14261.(Munda)

Rebus: *khāṇḍā* 'metal tools, pots and pans' (Marathi)
<lo->(B) {V} ``(pot, etc.) to ^overflow''. See <lo-> `to be left over'. @B24310. #20851. Re<lo->(B) {V} ``(pot, etc.) to ^overflow''. See <lo-> `to be left over'. (Munda) Rebus: loh 'copper' (Hindi) The hieroglyph clearly refers to the metal tools, pots and pans of copper. Thus, the two words read together

Rebus: lōkhaṇḍa लोखंड Iron tools, vessels, or articles in general (Marathi).

The pot carried by the woman accompanying the Meluhha seafaring merchant (on Su-ilisu cylinder seal) could also be a hieroglyphic rebus reading of *kāṇṭam* signifying metal pots and pans and tools.

On loha in *similes* see *J.P.T.S.* 1907, 131. Cp. A iii.16=S v.92 (five alloys of gold: ayo, loha, tipu, sīsaŋ, sajjhaŋ); J v.45 (asi°); Miln 161 (suvaṇṇam pi jātivantaŋ lohena bhijjati); PvA 44, 95 (tamba°= loha), 221 (tatta -- loha -- secanaŋ pouring out of boiling metal, one of the five ordeals in Niraya). -- kaṭāha a copper (brass) receptacle Vin ii.170. -- kāra a metal worker, coppersmith, blacksmith Miln 331. -- kumbhī an iron cauldron Vin ii.170. Also N. of a purgatory J iii.22, 43; iv.493; v.268; SnA 59, 480; Sdhp 195. -- guḷa an iron (or metal) ball A iv.131; Dh 371 (mā °ŋ gilī pamatto; cp. DhA iv.109). -- jāla a copper (i. e. wire) netting PvA 153. -- thālaka a copper bowl Nd1 226. -- thāli a bronze kettle DhA i.126. -- pāsāda"copper terrace," brazen palace, N. of a famous monastery at Anurādhapura in Ceylon Vism 97; DA i.131; Mhvs passim. -- piṇḍa an iron ball SnA 225. -- bhaṇḍa copper (brass) ware Vin ii.135. -- maya made of copper, brazen Sn 670; Pv ii.64. -- māsa a copper bean Nd1 448 (suvaṇṇa -- channa). -- māsaka a small copper coin KhA 37 (jatu -- māsaka, dāru -- māsaka+); DhsA 318. -- rūpa a bronze statue Mhvs 36, 31. -- salākā a bronze gong -- stick Vism 283. Lohatā (f.) [abstr. fr. loha] being a metal, in (suvaṇṇassa) aggalohatā the fact of gold being the best metal VvA 13. (Pali)

Vase dedicated by Entemena, king of Lagash, to Ningirsu. Silver and copper, ca. 2400 BC. Found in Telloh, ancient city of Girsu. H. 35 cm (13 ¾ in.), Diam. 18 cm (7 in.) Louvre Museum.AO 2674

Hieroglyphs: Bull calves, lion, markhor, Anzu

Rebus readings: Anzu 'falcon' Rebus: *aṁśú* 'soma' (Rigveda), *ancu* 'iron'(Tocharian).

āra 'lion' Rebus: 'brass'.
Te. eṟaka, ṟekka, rekka, neṟaka, neṟi id. *Kol.* reḍapa, (SR.) reppā id.; (P.) reṛapa id., feather. *Nk.* rekka, reppa wing. *Pa.* (S.) rekka id. *Go.* (S.) rekka wing-feather; reka (M.) feather, (Ko.) wing (*Voc.* 3045). Rebus: *erako* 'moltencast copper'.

miṇḍāl 'markhor' (Tōrwālī) *meḍho* a ram, a sheep (G.)(CDIAL 10120); rebus: *mẽṛhẽt, meḍ* 'iron' (Mu.Ho.) *Te.* kōḍiya, kōḍe young bull; *adj.* male (e.g. kōḍe dūḍa bull calf), young, youthful; kōḍekā̆ḍu a young man. *Kol.* (Haig) kōḍē bull. *Nk.* khoṛe male calf. *Konḍa* kōḍi cow; kōṛe young bullock. *Pe.* kōḍi cow. *Manḍ.* kūḍi id. *Kui* kōḍi id., ox. *Kuwi* (F.) kōdi cow; (S.) kajja kōḍi bull; (Su. P.) kōḍi cow. (DEDR 2199). *Ka.* gōnde bull, ox. *Te.* gōda ox. *Kol.* (SR.) kondā bull; (Kin.) kōnda bullock. *Nk.* *(Ch.)* kōnda id. *Pa.* kōnda bison. *Ga.* (Oll.) kōnde cow; (S.) kōndē bullock. *Go.* (Tr.) *kōnḍā*, (other dialects) kōnda bullock, ox (*Voc.* 972). (DEDR 2216). खोंड [khōṇḍa] *m* A young bull, a bullcalf. 2 A variety of जोंधळा. कोंडण [kōṇḍaṇa] गोठा [gōṭhā] A fold or pen. (Marathi). Rebus: *kõdār* 'turner' (Bengali)

See: Ancient Near east Anzu, falcon-shaped fire-altar

Uttarakhand, turning *aṁśú* (Rigveda), *ancu* (Tocharian) in smithy.[180]

From Purulia, Uttarakhand, a brick altar identified as Syenachiti. The structure is in the shape of a flying eagle Garuda, head facing east with outstretched wings. In the center of the structure is the chiti is a square chamber yielded remains of pottery assignable to circa first century B.C. to second century AD. In addition copper coin of Kuninda and other material i.e. ash, bone pieces etc and a thin gold leaf impressed with a human figure tentatively identified as Agni have also been recovered from the central chamber.

A parallel in Pahlavi is senmurw, Sina-Mru (Pazand), a fabulous, mythical bird (also called simorgh). The name derives from Avestan *merəγo saeno* 'the bird Saena', originally a raptor, either eagle or falcon, etymologically identical Sanskrit *śyena*. Nicholas Kazanas has demonstrated that Avestan (OldIranian) is much later than Vedic. " 'Vedic and Avestan' by N. Kazanas In this essay the author examines independent linguistic evidence, often provided by iranianists like R. Beekes, and arrives at the conclusion that the Avesta, even its older parts (the gaθas), is much later than the Rigveda. Also, of course, that Vedic is more archaic than Avestan and that it was not the Indoaryans who moved away from the common Indo-Iranian habitat into the Region of the Seven Rivers, but the Iranians broke off and eventually settled and spread in ancientv Iran."[181]

Seventh century BCE cylinder seal found in Israel depicting the battle of Ninurta and Anzu. Nili Wazana, in a brilliant exposition on Anzu and Ziz asks and tentatively answers the question: "Were the Israelites acquainted with the Epic of Anzu?" She cites this rendering of a seventh century BCE cylinder seal portraying the battle of Ninurta and Anzu, discovered in Israel.[182]

Zu or Anzu (from An 'heaven' and Zu 'to know' in Sumerian language), as a lion-headed eagle, ca. 2550–2500 BCE, Louvre. Votive relief of Ur-Nanshe, king of Lagash, representing the bird-god Anzu (or Im-dugud) as a lion-headed eagle. Alabaster, Early Dynastic III (2550–2500 BCE). Found in Telloh, ancient city of

Girsu. H. 21.6 cm (8 ½ in.), W. 15.1 cm (5 ¾ in.), D. 3.5 cm (1 ¼ in.)

The seventh century BCE cylinder seal found in Israel, is paralleled in an Akkadian cylinder seal.
ḍāngā = hill, dry upland (B.); *ḍā̃g* mountain-ridge (H.)(CDIAL 5476). Rebus: *dhangar* 'blacksmith' (Maithili) *ḍangar* 'blacksmith' (Hindi) *kāṇḍa* 'flowing water' Rebus: *kāṇḍā* 'metalware, tools, pots and pans'.

This votive plaque with its relief decoration and central perforation is characteristic of Early Dynastic Sumer. The

narrative motif, as was customary, is organized in horizontal registers. A Sumerian inscription identifies the person portrayed as

Dudu, high priest of the god Ningirsu in the reign of Entemena, king of Lagash around 2450 BC. Occupying the height of two registers, Dudu wears the kaunakes, the fleecy skirt characteristic of the period. Around him are symbolical figures, no doubt connected with his religious functions. At the top, the god Ningirsu is evoked by his emblem, the lion-headed eagle called Imdugud, shown with wings outspread, two lions gripped in his talons. In the middle a calf, perhaps intended for sacrifice, is shown lying down, while the lower register is filled by a plait-like motif, probably representing the subterranean reserve of fresh water. The lion-headed eagle, symbolizing the storm that brings life-giving rain, the sacrificial calf, and the subterranean reserve from which comes water for the crops evoke the celestial, terrestrial, and chthonian sources of fertility which all contribute to the prosperity of human communities.

Dimensions H. 25 cm (9 ¾ in.), W. 23 cm (9 in.), D. 8 cm (3 in.)

Excavations of Ernest de Sarzec, 1881 The Louvre Museum - Paris

Eagle with lion's head. Lapis lazuli, gold, copper and bitumen pendant Early dynastic period II (2658 BCE) from the Treasure of Ur, Mari.

Shaft-hole axe head with bird-headed demon, boar, and dragon Period: Bronze Age Date: ca. late 3rd–early 2nd millennium BCE. Geography: Bactria-Margiana

A Lion-Headed Eagle Grasping Two Mountain Goats, Cylinder seal and impression. Mesopotamia, Post-Akkadian period (ca. 2154–2100 BCE.)Steatite 30 x 17 mm

Seal no. 267

Relief showing lion-headed eagle Imdugud, grasping hind-quarters of pair of stags standing back-to-back beneath its outstretched wings. This monumetal copper relief was discovered, along with numerous other objects, at the foot of a high terrace which once supported a temple dedicated to the goddess Ninhursag and built by one of the kings of Ur at the neighboring site of al 'Ubaid. (British Museum No. 114308. Early Dynastic III).

Narrative of Anzu: *ancu* 'iron' (Tocharian); cognate: *amśu* 'soma' (maybe, electrum). The association of Anzu with the stealing of the tablets and a reference to *śyena* 'falcon' in a comparable role for 'soma' may explain the hieroglyphs of eagle, tiger, hill goat, twisted rope related rebus to metals: *eruvai* 'copper'; *kol* 'working in iron'; *khaḍā* 'nodule (ore), stone'; *meḍ* 'iron'. Hieroglyph: *śyena* 'falcon' Rebus: *senaka* a carter (Pali) Hieroglyph: *khaḍḍu* -- 'ram'. [Cf. words listed under **kaḍḍa* --] P. *khāḍū* m. 'hill goat'; WPah.J. *khāḍū* m. 'ram', kṭg. (kc.) *kháḍḍu* m., poet. *khaṛu* m. (Him.I 31 all prob. conn. K. *kaṭh*, stem *kaṭ* -- , < *kaṭṭa -- 2).

(CDIAL 3790a). Rebus: *kāḍ* 'stone ore'*gaḍa* 'large stone mould'. *khaḍā* 'nodule (ore), stone' (Marathi).

Hieroglyph: 'Twisted rope' hieroglyph: S. dhāī f. ' wisp of fibres added from time to time to a rope that is being twisted ', L. dhāī̃ f.(CDIAL 6773).

Rebus: Pa. dhātu -- m. ' element, ashes of the dead, relic '; KharI. dhatu ' relic '; Pk. dhāu -- m. ' metal, red chalk '; N. dhāu ' ore (esp. of copper) '; Or. ḍhāu ' red chalk, red ochre ' (whence ḍhāuā ' reddish '; M. dhāū, dhāv m.f. ' a partic. soft red stone ' (whence dhā̆vaḍ m. ' a caste of iron -- smelters ', dhāvḍī ' composed of or relating to iron '); -- Si. dā ' relic '(CDIAL 6773). S. mī˜ḍhī f., °ḍho m. ' braid in a woman's hair ', L. mē̃ḍhī f.; मेढा [mēḍhā] A twist or tangle arising in thread or cord, a curl or snarl (Marathi). Rebus: mẽṛhẽt, meḍ 'iron' (Mu.Ho.) meṛed-bica = iron stone ore, in contrast to bali-bica, iron sand ore (Mu.lex.) Hieroglyph: *Ta.* eruvai a kind of kite whose head is white and whose body is brown; *தலைவெளுத்து உடல் சிவந்திருக்கும் பருந்து. விசும்பா டெருவை பசுந்தடி தடுப்ப (புறநா. 64, 4). Eagle; கழுகு. எருவை குருதி பிணங்க வருந் தோற்றம் (களவழி. 20).* *Ma.* eruva eagle, kite. Rebus: *எருவை eruvai 'copper' செம்பு. எருவை யுருக்கினா லன்ன குருதி (கம்பரா. கும்பக. 248* (DEDR 817).

Hieroglyph: meṛha = twisted, crumpled, as a horn (Santali) meli, melika = a turn, a twist, a loop, entanglement; meliyu, melivad.u, meligonu = to get twisted or entwined (Te.lex.) meṛhao 'twisted' M. *meḍhā* m. 'curl, snarl, twist or tangle in cord or thread' (CDIAL 10312) Glyph: mEḍi plait (Kannada). *Ta.* miṭai (-v-, -nt-) to weave as a mat, etc. *Ma.* miṭayuka to plait, braid, twist, wattle; miṭaccal plaiting, etc.; miṭappu tuft of hair; miṭala screen or wicket, ōlas plaited together. *Ka.* meḍaṟu to plait as screens, etc. (Hav.) maḍe to knit, weave (as a basket); (Gowda) mEḍi plait. *Ga.* (S.3) miṭṭe a female hair-style. *Go.* (Mu.) mihc-to plait (hair) (DEDR 4853) Rebus: meḍ 'iron' (Ho.)

Alternative: Bi. *baṭnāī* ' act of rope -- twisting '; H. *bāṭnā* ' to twist, twine '(CDIAL 11356). S. *vaṭu* m. ' twist ' (CDIAL 11346). N. *baṭernu* ' the stick on which a rope is twisted '.(CDIAL 11351). Rebus: Paš.lauṛ. *wāṛ*, kuṛ. *wō* ' stone ', Shum. *wāṛ* Ḍ. *boṭ* m. ' stone ', Ash. Wg. *wāṭ*, Kt. *woṭ*, Dm. *bɔ̄'ṭ*, Tir. *baṭ*, Niṅg. *bōṭ*, Woṭ. *baṭ* m., Gmb. *wāṭ*; Gaw. *wāṭ* ' stone, millstone '; Kal.rumb. *bat* ' stone ' (*bad -- váṣ* ' hail ') (CDIAL 11348). Or. *baṭā* ' metal pot for betel ', *bāṭi* ' cup, saucer '; Mth. *baṭṭā* ' large metal cup ', *bāṭī* ' small do. ', H. *baṭrī* f.; G. M. *vāṭī* f. ' vessel '.(CDIAL 11347).

Alabaster votive relief of Ur-Nanshe, king of Lagash, showing Anzû as a lion-headed eagle, ca. 2550–2500 BC; found at Tell Telloh the ancient city of Girsu, (Louvre). "On the mountainside Anzu and Ninurta met … Clouds of death rained down, an arrow flashed lightning. Whizzed the battle force roared between them." Anzu Epic, tablet 2, in S. Dalley, Myths from Mesopotamia (Oxford - New York, 1989), p. 21.

Anzu[183] or Zu, as a lion-headed eagle, ca. 2550–2500 BCE. Anzu(d) bird is the divine storm-bird which stole the 'Tablets of Destiny' from Enlil,inventor of the mattock (a key agricultural pick, hoe, ax or digging tool of the Sumerians) and hid the tablets on a mountain-top.

Magilum Boat (Magilum: from Sumerian ma-gi-lum, a ship of the netherworld) in Sumerian mythology was one of the valuable items seized by Ninurta, patron divinity of Lagash. This spoil was hung on an unknown part of his chariot according to the ancient source, cf. lines 40-63:

"(Ninurta) brought forth the Magilum boat from …his *abzu*… The warrior Ninurta, with his heroic strength, wreaked his vengeance (?). 52-54. On his shining chariot, which inspires terrible awe, he hung his captured wild bulls on the axle and hung his captured cows on the cross-piece of the yoke. 55-63. He hung the Six-headed wild ram on the dust-guard. He hung the Warrior dragon on the seat. He hung the Magilum boat on the .... He hung the Bison on the beam. He hung the Mermaid on the foot-board. He hung the Gypsum on the forward part of the yoke. He hung the Strong copper on the inside pole pin (?). He hung the Anzud bird on the front guard. He hung the Seven-headed serpent on the shining cross-beam."

Cylinder seal from Khafaje, Baghdad Museumca. Beginning of third millennium BCE.

Mudhif and three reed banners. A cow and a stable constructed of wickerwork with sculpted columns in the background. Fragment of a cult vase of alabaster (era of Djemet-Nasr), from Uruk, Mesopotamia (Iraq). Limestone, 16 x 22,5 cm - AO 8842 Louvre, Departement des Antiquites Orientales, Paris, France.

Six circles decorated on the reed post are semantic determinants.

Six rings atop each post may denote a forge: *koṭiyum* [*koṭ, koṭī* neck] a wooden circle put round the neck of an animal (Gujarati) Rebus: *ācāri koṭṭya* = forge, *kammārasāle* (Tulu) Together with reed post, the signifier may be: *khānḍāra koṭṭya* 'forge of an arrow-maker'. *kāṇḍakara ' worker with reeds or arrows '. [kā´ṇḍa -- , kará -- 1]L. *kanērā* m. ' mat -- maker '; H. *kãḍerā* m. ' a caste of bow -- and arrow -- makers '. 3026 kā´ṇḍīra ' armed with arrows ' Pāṇ., m. ' archer ' lex. [kā´nda --]H. *kanīrā* m. ' a caste (usu. of arrow -- makers) '.(CDIAL 3024, 3026). கோட்டம்[1] *kōṭṭam, n.* < கோடு-. *cf. kuṭ.* *1. [M. kōṭṭam.] Bowing in worship, adoration;* வணக் கம். *முன்னோன் கழற்கே கோட்டந் தருநங் குருமுடி வெற்பன் (திருக்கோ. 156)*; camp.

Allographs: கோட்டம்[1] kōṭṭam cf. *kōṭa.* Lines, figures an diagrams drawn with rice-flour on the ground, on festive occasions; மாக்கோலம். (J.) கோட்டம் kōṭṭam, n. (அக. நி.) 1. Monkey; குரங்கு.

Hieroglyph: आर [āra] A tuft or ring of hair on the body. (Marathi) Rebus 1: āra 'brass'. Hieroglyph: *bhaṭa* 'six' Rebus 2: *bhaṭa* 'furnace'. आर [āra] A term in the play of इटीदांडू,--the number six. (Marathi) Hieroglyph: आर [āra] A tuft or ring of hair on the body. (Marathi) Rebus: āra 'brass'. काँड् । काण्डः m. the stalk or stem of a reed, grass, or the like, straw. In the compound with dan 5 (p. 221*a*, l. 13) the word is spelt *kāḍ*. The rebus reading of the pair of reeds in Sumer standard is: *khānḍa* 'tools, pots and pans and metal-ware'. Thus, read a composition, each of the three posts atop the mudhif connotes: *āra khānḍa* 'brass metalware'.

Allograph: *Kur. kaṇḍō* a stool. *Malt. kanḍo* stool, seat. గడమంచె *gaḍa-manche.* n. A wooden frame like a bench to keep things on. గంపలు మొదలగువాటిని ఉంచు మంచె.(DEDR 1179).

A pot with overflowing water is shown on the field. It may signify, *lokhāṇḍ* Rebus: *loh* +*khāṇḍā* 'metalware'.

Since three such flagposts are shown, the three as a set may connote *kolom* 'three' Rebus: *kolami* 'smithy, forge' working on 'brass metalware'.

Shown as exiting the *kole.l* 'smithy, temple' are and *kũderā 'lathe-workers'*. *koli* 'tail' (atop the mudhif or mund) Rebus: *kol* 'smelters, blacksmiths'

Reading 1: goṭ = the place where cattle are collected at mid-day (Santali); goṭh (Brj.)(CDIAL 4336). Goṣṭha (Skt.); cattle-shed (Or.) koḍ = a cow-pen; a cattlepen; a byre (G.) कोठी cattle-shed (Marathi) कोंडी[kōṇḍī] A pen or fold for cattle. गोठी [gōṭhī] f C (Dim. Of गोठा) A pen or fold for calves. (Marathi) கோட்டம் kōṭṭam , *n.* < *gō-ṣṭha.* 1. Cow- shed; பசுக்கொட்டில். ஆனிரைக டுன்னு கோட்டம் (வாயுசங். பஞ்சாக். 58). 2. Herd of cows; பசுக் கூட்டம். (பிங்.) The young bulls emerging from the smithy. *kõdā* खोंड [khōṇḍa] m A young bull, a bullcalf. (Marathi) Rebus 1: kǒnḍu or konḍu । कुण्डम् m. a hole dug in the ground for receiving consecrated fire (Kashmiri)Rebus 2: A. *kundār*, B. *kũdār*, °*ri*, Or. *kundāru*; H. *kũderā* m. ' one who works a lathe, one who scrapes ', °*rī* f., *kũdernā* ' to scrape, plane, round on a lathe '.(CDIAL 3297).

Rebus: कोंदण [kōndaṇa] n (कोंदणें) Setting or infixing of gems.(Marathi) *kõdā* 'to turn in a lathe'(B.)

Text 1330 (not illustrated; appears with Zebu glyph) showing Glyph 39. Pictorial motif: Zebu (*Bos indicus*) This sign is comparable to the cattle byre of Southern Mesopotamia dated to c. 3000 BCE. The first hieroglyph is *kole.l mund* 'smithy, temple, mund hut of Toda'. This is ligatured with superscript two short linear strokes. Thus, read together as *kole.l mund khāṇḍā* 'smithy tools, metalware' खांडा [khāṇḍā] *m* A jag, notch, or indentation (as upon the edge of a tool or weapon). Rebus: khāṇḍa 'tools, pots and pans, and metal-ware'. kole.l = smithy (Ko.) Rebus: *Kuwi* (F.) kolhali to forge. *Koḍ.* kollë blacksmith. (DEDR 2133).

kuṭila 'bent'; rebus: kuṭila, katthīl = bronze (8 parts copper and 2 parts tin) [cf. āra-kūṭa, 'brass' (Skt.) (CDIAL 3230) kuṭi— in cmpd. 'curve' (Skt.)(CDIAL 3231). Rebus: *kuṭhi* 'smelter'. Alternative: *கோட்டம்*[1] *kōṭṭam, n. < கோடு-. cf. kuṭ. 1. [M. kōṭṭam.] Bend, curve, warp, as in timber; வளைவு. மரத்தின் கனக் கோட்டந் தீர்க்குநூல் (நன். 25). Rebus: koṭṭya* = forge, *kammārasāle* (Tulu) *கோட்டம்*[1] *kōṭṭam, n. < கோடு-. cf. kuṭ. 1. [M. kōṭṭam.] Bowing in worship, adoration; வணக் கம். முன்னோன் கழற்கே கோட்டந் தருநங் குருமுடி வெற்பன் (திருக்கோ. 156).* Temple; கோயில். கோழிச் சேவற் கொடியோன் கோட்டமும் (சிலப். 14, 10);

 Rebus: *kaṃika 'accountant'. kul -- kaṃī* m. 'village accountant' (Marathi); *kaṃikan* id. (Tamil) *kan-ka, kaṃaka* 'rim of jar' Rebus: *kaṇḍa kaṃaka* 'furnace account scribe'. *kāṃī(ka)* 'supercargo of a ship' (Marathi)

கணக்கு kaṇakku, n. cf. gaṇaka. [M. kaṇakku] 1. Number, account, reckoning, calculation, computation (Tamil) *kaṃī* ' supercargo' (Marathi) Rebus: 'to engrave, write; lapidary': <kana-lekhe>(P) {??} Rebus: 'to engrave, write; lapidary': <kana-lekhe>(P) {??} ``??''. |. Cf. <kana->. %16123. #16013. <lekhe->(P),,<leke->(KM) {VTC} ``to ^write''. Cf. <kana-lekhe>. *Kh.<likhae>, H.<lIkhAna>, O.<lekhIba>, B.<lekha>; Kh.<likha>(P), Mu.<lika>. %20701. #20541. (Munda etyma)

khanun खनुन् । खननम् conj. 1 (1 p.p. khonu for 1, see s.v.; f. khüñü to dig (K.Pr. 155, 247; L. 459; Śiv. 59, 746, 994, 143, 1197, 1214, 1373, 1754; Rām. 343, 958, 1147, 1724; H. xii, 6); to engrave (Śiv. 414, 671, 176; Rām. 1583). khonu-motu खनुमतु; । खातः perf. part. (f. khüñümütsü) dug (e.g. a field, or a well); engraved. mŏhara-khonu म्वहर-खनु; or (Gr.M.) mŏhar-kan । मुद्राखननकारुः m. a seal-engraver, a lapidary (El. *mohar-kand*). -wöjü । *अङ्गुलिमुद्रा f. a signet-ring.(Kashmiri)

 Text 1330. The epigraph is associated with zebu (Not illustrated): Rebus 1: *adar* 'zebu' rebus: *aduru* 'unsmelted metal or ore' (Kannada) *aduru* native metal (Ka.); *ayil* iron (Ta.) *ayir, ayiram* any ore (Ma.); *ajirda karba* very hard iron (Tu.)(DEDR 192). a*duru* =*gaṇiyinda tegadu karagade iruva aduru* = ore taken from the mine and not subjected to melting in a furnace.[184] Rebus 2: *khũṭ* m. ' Brahmani or zebu bull ' (Kathiawar. Gujarati) Rebus: *khũṭ* 'community, guild' (Santali)

 These hieroglyphs may signify a *mund* 'temple' of *koles* 'smelters' or *kole.l* 'smithy, temple'. *qoli* 'tail' Rebus: kol 'smelter' 'working in iron, 5 alloy metals'. kole.l = smithy (Ko.)

Rebus: *Kuwi* (F.) kolhali to forge. *Koḍ. kollë* blacksmith. (DEDR 2133). It is a kole.l 'smithy' where tools are forged: खांडा [*khāṇḍā*] *m* A jag, notch, or indentation (as upon the edge of a tool or weapon). Rebus: *kāṇḍā* 'tools, pots and pans, and metal-ware'.

The other three hieroglyphs are: *ayo* 'fish' Rebus: *ayo, ayas* 'alloy metal', *kaṇḍ kan-ka* 'rim-of-jar' Rebus: 'fire-altar *karṇīka* supercargo'. Thus, the entire message is: 'scribe account metalware out of *kole.l* 'temple, smithy'. Rebus: *Ta. kaṇṭam* iron style for writing on palmyra leaves. *Te. gaṇṭamu* id. (DEDR 1170).

m0702 m0702 Text 2206 Glyph 39, a glyph which compares with the Sumerian mudhif or Toda munda structure.

Temple, smithy flame for alloys

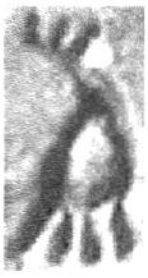

[*kōḍu* 'flag' (Kannada)] [Kannada. *kōḍu*] Tusk;
யானை பன்றிகளின் தந்தம்.
மத்த யானையின் கோடும் (தேவா. 39, 1).

Rebus: खोट [khōṭa] A lump or solid bit (as of phlegm, gore, curds, inspissated milk); any concretion or clot. (Marathi) Rebus: L. *khoṭ*f. ' alloy, impurity ', °*ṭā* ' alloyed ', awāṇ. *khoṭā* ' forged '; P. *khoṭ* m. ' base, alloy ' M.*khoṭā* ' alloyed ', (CDIAL 3931)

Hieroglyph: *Kur.* xolā tail. *Malt.* qoli id.(DEDR 2135) The 'tail' atop the reed-structure banner glyph is a phonetic determinant for kole.l 'temple, smithy'. Alternative: *pajhaṛ* = to sprout from a root (Santali); Rebus: *pasra*'smithy, forge' (Santali)
Hieroglyph: *kuṭṭuva* = big copper pot for heating water (Kod.)(DEDR 1668). gudgā to blaze; guḍva flame (Man.d); gudva, gūdūvwa, guduwa id. (Kuwi)(*Kur. xolā* tail. *Malt. qoli* id.(DEDR

2135) The 'tail' atop the reed-structure banner glyph is a phonetic determinant for *kole.l* 'temple, smithy'. The ligatured structure may be a representation of mund, mudhif, ancient Toda or ancient hut of Iraq marshes.

Reading 2: *kole.l* = smithy (Ko.) Rebus: *Kuwi* (F.) *kolhali* to forge. *Koḍ. kollë* blacksmith. (DEDR 2133).

Smithy was designated by a term which also meant 'temple'. *kole.l* 'smithy, temple' (Kota): Ta. *kol* working in iron, blacksmith; kollaṉ blacksmith. Ma. *kollan* blacksmith, artificer. Ko. *kole·l* smithy, temple in Kota village. To. *kwala·l* Kota smithy. Ka. *kolime, kolume, kulame, kulime, kulume, kulme* fire-pit, furnace; (Bell.; U.P.U.) *konimi* blacksmith; (Gowda) *kolla* id. Koḍ. *kollë* blacksmith. Te. *kolimi* furnace. Go. (SR.) *kollusānā* to mend implements; (Ph.) *kolstānā, kulsānā* to forge; (Tr.) *kōlstānā* to repair (of ploughshares); (SR.) *kolmi* smithy (Voc. 948). Kuwi (F.) *kolhali* to forge. (DEDR 2133).

The hut of a Toda Tribe of Nilgiris, India. Note the decoration of the front wall, and the very small door.

The architecture of Iraqi mudhif and Toda mund — of Indian linguistic area — is comparable.185

Cylinder seal impression, Uruk period, Uruk?, 3500-2900 BCE. Note a load of livestock (upper), overlapping greatly (weird representation), and standard 'mudhif' reed house form common to S. Iraq (lower)[186]. Cattle Byres c. 3200-3000 BCE. Late Uruk-Jemdet Nasr period. Magnesite. Cylinder seal. In the lower field of this seal appear three reed cattle byres. Each

byre is surmounted by three reed pillars topped by rings, a motif that has been suggested as symbolizing a male god, perhaps Dumuzi. Within the huts calves or vessels appear alternately; from the sides come calves that drink out of a vessel between them. Above each pair of animals another small calf appears. A herd of enormous cattle moves in the upper field. Cattle and cattle byres in Southern Mesopotamia, c. 3500 BCE. Drawing of an impression from a Uruk period cylinder seal.[187]

The young bulls emerging from the smithy.

kōḍā खोंड [khōṇḍa] m A young bull, a bullcalf. (Marathi) Rebus 1: kǒṇḍu or konḍu । कुण्डम् m. a hole dug in the ground for receiving consecrated fire (Kashmiri) Rebus 2: A. *kundār*, B. *kũdār*, °*ri*, Or. *kundāru*; H. *kũderā* m. ' one who works a lathe, one who scrapes ', °*rī* f., *kũdernā* ' to scrape, plane, round on a lathe '.(CDIAL 3297). ayo 'fish' Rebus: ayas 'metal'.

Quadrupeds exiting the mund (or mudhif) are *pasaramu, pasalamu* 'an animal, a beast, a brute, quadruped' (Telugu) పసరము [pasaramu] or పసలము *pasaramu.* [Tel.] n. A beast, an animal. గోమహిషహోతి.

Rebus: pasra = a smithy, place where a black-smith works, to work as a blacksmith; kamar pasra = a smithy; pasrao lagao akata se ban:? Has the blacksmith begun to work? pasraedae = the blacksmith is at his work (Santali.lex.) pasra meṛed, pasāra meṛed = syn. of koṭe meṛed = forged iron, in contrast to dul meṛed, cast iron (Mundari.lex.) పసారము [pasāramu] or పసారు *pasāramu.* [Tel.] n. A

shop. ಅಂಗಡಿ. Allograph: pacar = a wedge driven ino a wooden pin, wedge etc. to tighten it (Santali.lex.) Allograph: pajhar 'eagle'.

A Toda temple in Muthunadu Mund near Ooty, India. For example, on a cylinder seal from Uruk, a professional group of workers in a smithy are shown as a procession of young bull calves and other quadrupeds emerging out of the smithy.

kole.l = smithy (Ko.) Rebus: *Kuwi* (F.) kolhali to forge. *Koḍ.* kollë blacksmith. (DEDR 2133).

Reading 1: kole.l = smithy, temple in Kota village (Ko.) Rebus 1: *Ta. kol* working in iron, blacksmith *kollaṉ* blacksmith. *Ma.* kollan blacksmith, artificer. *Ka.* kolime, kolume, kulame, kulime, kulume, kulme fire-pit, furnace; (Bell.; U.P.U.) konimi blacksmith; (Gowda) kolla id. *Koḍ.* kollë blacksmith. *Te.* kolimi furnace. *Go.* (SR.) kollusānā to mend implements; (Ph.) kolstānā, kulsānā to forge; (Tr.) kōlstānā to repair (of ploughshares); (SR.) kolmi smithy (*Voc.* 948). *Kuwi* (F.) kolhali to forge. (DEDR 2133). Rebus 2: *Ko.* kole·l smithy, temple in Kota village. *To.* kwala·l Kota smithy (DEDR 2133).

Reading 2: goṭ = the place where cattle are collected at mid-day (Santali); goṭh (Brj.)(CDIAL 4336). Goṣṭha (Skt.); cattle-shed (Or.) koḍ = a cow-pen; a cattlepen; a byre (G.) कोठी cattle-shed (Marathi) कोंडी[kōṇḍī] A pen or fold for cattle. गोठी [gōṭhī] f C (Dim. Of गोठा) A pen or fold for calves. (Marathi) Cattle Byres c.3200-3000 B.C. Late Uruk-Jemdet Nasr period. Magnesite. Cylinder seal. In the lower field of this seal appear three reed cattle byres. Each byre is surmounted by three reed pillars topped by rings, a motif that has been suggested as symbolizing a male god, perhaps Dumuzi. Within the huts calves or vessels appear alternately; from the sides come calves that drink out of a vessel between them. Above each pair of animals another small calf appears. A herd of enormous cattle moves in the upper field. Cattle and cattle byres in Southern Mesopotamia, c. 3500 BCE. Drawing of an impression from a Uruk period cylinder seal. (After Moorey, PRS, 1999, Ancient materials and industries: the archaeological evidence, Eisenbrauns.)

Carved gypsum trough from Uruk. Two lambs exit a reed structure. A bundle of reeds (Inanna's symbol) can be seen projecting from the hut and at the edges of the scene.

The British Museum. WA 120000, neg. 252077 Part of the right-hand scene is cast from the original fragment now in the Vorderasiatisches Museum, Berlin. Sumerian mudhif facade, with uncut reed fonds and sheep entering, carved into a gypsum trough from Uruk, c. 3200 BCE. This trough was found at Uruk, the largest city so far known in southern Mesopotamia in the late prehistoric period (3300-3000 BC). The carving on the side shows a procession of sheep (a goat and a ram)

A cylinder seal with zebu and lion, Sibri {Jarrige)

A set of four symbolic forms shown in a procession of scepter-bearers includes the following form:

Hieroglyphs on top register of cylinder seal with kneeling nude heroes, ca. 2220–2159 b.c.; Akkadian Mesopotamia Red jasper H. 1 1/8 in. (2.8 cm), Diam. 5/8 in. (1.6 cm) Metropolitan Museum of Art - USA

The flagpost (*kāca* 'banghi-pole' -- Kuwi) carriers are *kājahāraka* (Pali) signifying that they are workers in *kā̃s* 'bronze' *āra* 'brass' -- *kā̃sār* 'worker in bronze, pewterer, brazier, coppersmith'. The conical storage jar filled with ingots shown atop the fourth flagpost carrier, together with a 'crescent' hieroglyph makes the foursome artisans working with alloy metals and *sangaḍa* 'portable furnace' (perhaps crucible) Rebus: *jangaḍ* 'entrustment articles for approval'. Rebus: *sang* 'stone', *gaḍa* 'large stone'.The other three hieroglyphs signifying special metals are: *arka* 'sun' *erako* 'moltencast copper'; *lo* 'overflowing pot' *kāṇḍa* 'water' Rebus: l*okhaṇḍā* 'metal tools, pots and pans, metalware'; *ayo* 'fish' Rebus: *ayo, ayas* 'alloyed metal'.
kāgni m. ' a small fire ' Vop. [ka -- 3 or kā -- , agní --]K. *kang* m. ' brazier', fireplace'?(CDIAL 2999).

Ta. kā pole with ropes hung on each end, used to carry loads on the shoulder; lever or beam for a well-sweep, lever of a steelyard;kāvaṭi pole used for carrying burdens; kāvu (kāvi-) to carry on the shoulder (as a palanquin, a pole with weight at each end), bear anything heavy on the arms or on the head; kāvuvōr palanquin-bearers. *Ma.* kāvu, kāvaṭi split bamboo with ropes suspended from each end for carrying burdens; kāvuka, kāvikka to carry on a pole. *Ka.* kāgaḍi, kāvaḍi bamboo lath or pole provided with slings at each end for the conveyance of pitchers, etc. *Tu.* kāvaḍi split bamboo with ropes suspended from each end for carrying burdens across the shoulders. *Te.* kāvaṭi, kāvaḍi yoke or pole with a sling attached to each end, placed upon the shoulder for carrying burdens; kā̆ḍi, (*VPK*)kāḍi, kāḍimānu, kāḍimāku, kāṇḍi, kāṇi, kāni, kāvaḍi yoke of plough, etc. *Kol.* (Kin.) kāvaṛi carrying yoke. *Pa.* kāñ- to carry with carrying yoke; kācal carrying yoke. *Ga.* (Oll.) kā̆j-, kāñ- to carry with carrying yoke; (S.) kānj- to carry on the shoulders; (Oll. S.) kāsalcarrying yoke. *Go.* (Tr. Ph. SR.) kānjānā, (G. Mu. Ma. Ko.) kānj- to carry on the shoulders (*Voc.* 624); (Y.) kāvṛi, (Ma.) kāveṛi, (G.)kāviṛ(i), (Ko.) kāveṛ, (A.) kāhaṛi carrying yoke (*Voc.* 660). *Koṇḍa* (Sova dial.) kāsa the shaft of a kāvṛi; (BB) kānj carrying yoke. *Pe.* kavṛi id. *Manḍ.* kavṛi id. *Kui* kāsa pole or stick carried on the shoulder from the ends of which loads are suspended and carried; (K., Mah. p. 77) kānju carrying yoke. *Kuwi* (Su.) kānju (*pl.* kāska) id.; (F.) kāca banghi-pole; kānjū (*pl.* kāska) a banghi. ? *Kur.* xāxō a triangular frame made by foldig a bamboo stem (used in pairs for carrying logs.) ? *Malt.* qowe to carry or lift on the shoulders. / Cf. Skt. kāca-, kāja-, Pali kāca-, kāja-, Pkt. kāa- a yoke to support burdens; Pkt. kāvaḍa- carrying yoke, kāvaḍia- one who carries burdens with yoke; H. kāwaṛ, etc. carrying yoke; Turner, *CDIAL*, nos. 3009, 3011, and (part of) 2760.(DEDR 1417).

Storage pot with ingots: *goṭ 'pebbles' Rebus: khoṭ* 'alloyed ingots' Snake occupying the field provides the semantics of the superset – the common alloying element lead or tin: Hieroglyph: *nāga* 'snake' Rebus: *nāga* 'lead'; alternative *anāku* 'cassiterite (tin)'. நாகம் nākam Black lead; காரீயம். (பிங்.) 9. Zinc; துத்த நாகம். (பிங்.) 10. A prepared arsenic; பாஷாண வகை (Tamil). The phrase *tuthunāg* as a synonym for zinc or pewter indicates that the gloss *nāg* meant 'alloying mineral' to create a hard bronze -- a substitute for arsenical bronze which was in short supply in the Ancient Near East and in Sarasvati-Sindhu civilization. And, hence, the recurring hieroglyph of a serpent on hundreds of cylinder seals and artifacts including those with Indus writing -- to denote an alloying mineral to create bronzes.

An alternative reading would present the foursome as presenting four types of brasses (that is, copper alloys in four forms: 1. ingots on approval basis, 2. moltencast copper ingots, 3. alloyed metal tools, 4. alloyed metal ingots): A serpent leads the field: *āra* 'serpent' Rebus; *āra* 'brass'.

A comparable hieroglyph composition may be seen on Warka vase.

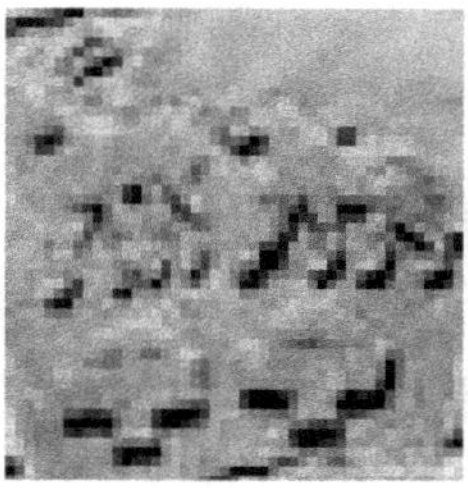

Two animals stride atop two symbolic forms of 'bun ingots' mounted on fire-altars. One ingot may connote: copper ingot. The other may connote: alloy metal ingot. This interpretation of symbolic forms is consistent with the hieroglyphs: *mlech* 'goat' Rebus: *milakkhu* 'copper'; *kola* 'tiger' Rebus: *kol* 'pañca loha, five alloyed metals' (Alternative: *karaḍa* 'panther' Rebus: *karaḍa* 'hard alloy of gold, silver etc.(i.e. any hard alloy metal). These are the types of ingots being delivered using conical storage vases or containers to Inanna symbolized by a pair of scarfed-reeds [*dhaṭu* 'scarf' (WPah.). Rebus: dhatu 'mineral' (Santali); dula 'pair' Rebus: dul 'cast metal']. The delivery may be into *kole.l* 'temple' Rebus: *kole.l* 'smithy'. The bottom register of Warka vase shows *kāṇḍa* stalks Rebus: *kāṇḍā* 'tools, pots and pans, metalware'.

kā́ṁsya ' made of bell -- metal ' KātyŚr., n. ' bell -- metal ' Yājñ., ' cup of bell -- metal ' MBh., °aka -- n. ' bell -- metal '. 2. *kāṁsiya -- . [kaṁsá -- 1]1. Pa. kaṁsa -- m. (?) ' bronze ', Pk. kaṁsa -- , kāsa -- n. ' bell -- metal, drinking vessel, cymbal '; L. (Jukes) kã̄jā adj. ' of metal ', awāṇ. kāsā ' jar ' (← E with -- s -- , not ñj); N. kã̄so ' bronze, pewter, white metal ', kas -- kuṭ ' metal alloy '; A. kã̄h ' bell -- metal ', B. kã̄sā, Or. kãsā, Bi. kã̄sā; Bhoj. kã̄s ' bell -- metal ', kã̄sā ' base metal '; H. kās, kã̄sā m. ' bell -- metal ', G. kã̄sũ n., M. kã̄sẽ n.; Ko. kã̄śẽ n. ' bronze '; Si. kasa ' bell -- metal '.2. L. kā̃ihā̃ m. ' bell -- metal ', P. kā̃ssī, kā̃sī f., H. kā̃sī f. A. kā̃h also ' gong ', or < kaṁsá -- *kāṁsyakara ' worker in bell -- metal '. [See next: kā´ṁsya -- , kará -- 1]L. awāṇ. kasērā ' metal worker ', P. kaserā m. ' worker in pewter ' (both ← E with -- s --); N. kasero ' maker of brass pots '; Bi. H. kaserā m. ' worker in pewter '. kāṁsyakāra m. ' worker in bell -- metal or brass ' Yājñ. com., kaṁsakāra -- m. BrahmavP. [kā´ṁsya -- , kāra -- 1] N. kasār ' maker of brass pots '; A. kãhār ' worker in bell -- metal '; B. kā̃sāri ' pewterer, brazier, coppersmith ', Or. kãsārī; H. kasārī m. ' maker of brass pots '; G. kãsārɔ, kas° m. ' coppersmith '; M. kā̃sār, kās° m. ' worker in white metal ', kāsārḍā m. ' contemptuous term for the same '.(CDIAL 2987-2989). *kāccakāra ' glass maker '. 2. *kāccakara -- . [*kācca- s.v. kācá -- 1, kāra -- 1, kara -- 1]1. Or. *kacarā* ' dealer in glass bangles ', M. *kā̃cār,* °*rī, kā̃cār,* °*rī* m. ' maker of glass bangles '.2. H. *kā̃cerā* m. ' glass -- worker '.(CDIAL 3012). kāñcaná ' golden ' MBh., n. ' gold ' Mn. Pa. *kañcana* -- n. ' gold ', °*aka* -- ' golden '; Pk. *kaṁcaṇa*<-> n. ' gold '; Si. *kasuna* ' gold ', *kasun* -- 'golden'.(CDIAL 3013).

An organizational superset which may denote such an organization of life in an ancient Meluhha village is provided by the symbolic form of 'one-horned young bull' frequently deployed and evidenced in Indu script corpora (of Meluhha hieroglyphs): *kōḍu* horn (Kannada. Tulu. Tamil) **खोंड** [*khōṇḍa*] m A young bull, a bullcalf. (Marathi) Rebus: **कोंड** [*kōṇḍa*] A circular hamlet; a division of a **मौजा** or village, composed generally of the huts of one caste. *kõdā* 'lathe-turner'. **खोट** [*khōṭa*] Alloyed--a metal (Marathi).

They are four Glyphs: *paṭākā* 'flag' Rebus: *pāṭaka,* four quarters of the village.
Hieroglyph 402: *koḍi* 'flag' (Ta.)(DEDR 2049). Rebus: Bshk. *kōr* 'large stone' (CDIAL 3018). Rebus2: *koḍ* 'workshop'.

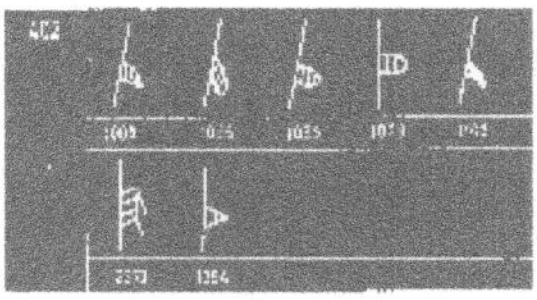

The flagpost carriers are in a salutation form: *erugu* 'to bow, to salute or make obeisance' *erãguḍu* bowing, salutation (Telugu) *iṟai* (-v-,-nt) to bow before (as in salutation), worship (Tamil)(DEDR 516). Rebus: *eraka, eṟaka* any metal infusion (Kannada.Tulu) *eruvai* 'copper' (Tamil); *ere* dark red (Kannada)(DEDR 446). Alternative, supplementary symbolic forms: *saman* = to offer an offering, to place in front of; front, to front or face (Santali) Rebus: *samṛobica*, stones containing gold (Mundari) samanom = an obsolete name for gold (Santali) [*bica* 'stone ore' (Munda): *meṛed-bica* = iron stone ore, in contrast to *bali-bica*, iron sand ore (Munda]

They have six curls on thei hairstyle: : आर [āra] A term in the play of इटीदांडू,--the number six. (Marathi) आर [āra] A tuft or ring of hair on the body. (Marathi) Rebus: āra 'brass' (that is, eraka 'moltencast copper' alloyed with *jasta* 'zinc': hieroglyph: svastika symbolic phonetic variant form, *sattiya*). This symbolic form of six hair curls is a hieroglyphic determinative signifying the flagpost carrier as 'copper-brass smithy artisan/trader' Alternative, reinforcement rebus readings: मेढा *mēḍhā* A twist or tangle arising in thread or cord, a curl or snarl. (Marathi) Rebus: *meḍ* 'iron' (Ho.) *bhaṭa* 'six (hair-curls)' Rebus: *bhaṭa* 'furnace'.

1. *ayo* 'metal, alloy' (Gujarati. Sanskrit)

Glyph: *ayo, hako* 'fish'; *ãs* = scales of fish (Santali). Rebus: aya = iron (G.); ayah, ayas = metal (Skt.) cf. *ancu* 'iron' (Tocharian)

2.*lo* 'pouring (water) oblation' (Munda) Rebus: *loa* 'copper' (Santali) *kāṇḍa 'water'* (Tamil. Sanskrit) *lokhãḍ* 'metalware, tools, pots and pans'(Gujarati)

3.Utu in Sumerian is the synonym of Akkadiam Shamash 'sun' Rebus: *uṛu* ' boatman ' (Oriya) Allograph: *huṛeāl, huṛeār* m. ' the wild hill sheep or oorial ' (Lahnda) huḍa 'ram'. Rebus: Or. uṛa ' vow '; (oṭṭu ' wager ' ← Tam. oṭṭu).(CDIAL 14175)

4. *ḍhāla* n. 'shield' Rebus: *ḍhālako* = a large metal ingot (Gujarati) The 'crescent' symbolic form may be a crucible or portable furnace: *kammaṭa* (a portable furnace for melting precious metals) Rebus: 'coiner, mint'.

காண்டம் kāṇṭam , *n.* < *kāṇḍa.* 1. Water; sacred water; நீர். துருத்திவா யதுக்கிய குங்குமக் காண் டமும் (கல்லா. 49, 16). 2. Staff, rod; கோல். (சூடா.) 3. Stem, stalk; அடித்தண்டு. (யாழ். அக.) 4. Arrow; அம்பு. (சூடா.) 5. Weapon; ஆயுதம். (சூடா.) Collection, multitude, assemblage; திரள். (அக. நி.) கண்டானுமுண்டானும் kaṇṭāṉumuṇṭ-āṉum, *n.* Redupl. of கண்டானும். Household utensils, great and small, useful and useless; வீட்டுத் தட்டுமுட்டுகள். கண்டானு முண்டானும் இத் தனை எதற்கு? *Loc.*

ढाल [ḍhāla] *f* (S through H) The grand flag of an army directing its march and encampments: also the standard or banner of a chieftain: also a flag flying on forts &c.

ढालकाठी [ḍhālakāṭhī] *f* ढालखांब *m* A flagstaff; esp.the pole for a grand flag or standard. 2 fig. The leading and sustaining member of a household or other commonwealth. 5583 ḍhāla n. ' shield ' lex. 2. *ḍhāllā -- . 1. Tir. (Leech) "*dàl*" ' shield ', Bshk. *ḍāl*, Ku. *ḍhāl*, gng. *ḍhāw*, N. A. B. *ḍhāl*, Or. *ḍhāḷa*, Mth. H. *ḍhāl* m.2. Sh. *ḍal* (pl. °*lẹ̄*) f., K. *ḍāl* f., S. *ḍhāla*, L. *ḍhāl* (pl. °*lā̃*) f., P. *ḍhāl* f., G. M. *ḍhāl* f. WPah.kṭg. (kc.) *ḍhā`l* f. (obl. -- *a*) ' shield ' (a word used in salutation), J. *ḍhāl* f. (CDIAL 5583).

The flagposts held by the kneeling persons have rings on top: *pheṭ*, *phẽṭ* 'snake's hood' (Assamese); पेंढें 'rings' Rebus: पेढी 'shop' (Gujarati). Alternative 1: *paṭam* , *n.* < *phaṭa.* 'cobra's hood' phaṭa n. ' expanded hood of snake ' MBh. 2. *phēṭṭa -- 2. [Cf. *phuṭa* --

m., °*ṭā* -- f., *sphuṭa* -- m. lex., °*ṭā* -- f. Pañcat. (Pk. *phuḍā* -- f.), *sphaṭa* -- m., °*ṭā*-- f., *sphōṭā* -- f. lex. and phaṇa -- 1. Conn. words in Drav. T. Burrow BSOAS xii 386]1. Pk. *phaḍa* -- m.n. ' snake's hood ', °*ḍā* -- f., M. *phaḍā* m., °*ḍī* f.2. A. *pheṭ*, *phẽṭ*. (CDIAL 9040). Rebus: 'sharpness of iron': *padm* (obl.*padt-*) temper of iron (Kota)(DEDR 3907); *patam* 'sharpness, as of the edge of a knife' (Tamil) Alternative 2: kāca m. 'loop, string fastened to both ends of a pole, carrying yoke'. Thus, *kācahāra* 'bearer of a carrying – pole'. Rebus: kāṁsyakara 'worker in bell -- metal'. [See next: kā'ṁsya -- , kará -- 1] *kasērā* ' metal worker ' (Lahnda), *kaserā* m. ' worker in pewter '(Punjabi. Bihari. Hindi) Alternative 3: <naG bubuD>(Z) {N} ``^cobra". |<naG> `?'. ^snake. *IA<naG>. ??is IA form <naG> or <nag>? #23502. nāgá1 m. ' snake ' ŚBr. 2. ' elephant ' BhP. [As ' elephant ' shortened form of **nāga -- hasta* -- EWA ii 150 with lit. or extracted from *nāga -- danta* -- ' elephant tusk, ivory ' < ' snake -- shaped tusk '].

Pa. *nāga* -- m. ' snake ', NiDoc. *nāǵa* F. W. Thomas AO xii 40, Pk. *ṇāya* -- m., Gy. as. *nâ* JGLS new ser. ii 259; Or. *naa* ' euphem. term for snake '; Si. *nay*, *nā*,*nayā* ' snake '. -- With early nasalization **nāṅga* -- : Bshk. *nāṅg* ' snake '. -- Kt. Pr. *noṅ*, Kal. *nhoṅ* ' name of a god < *nā'ga* -- or ← Pers. *nahang* NTS xv 283. 2. Pa. *nāga* -- m. ' elephant ', Pk. *ṇāya* -- m., Si. *nā*. śiśunāka -- . (CDIAL 7039)

Rebus: nāga2 n. ' lead ' Bhpr. [Cf. raṅga -- 3] Sh. *naṅ* m. ' lead ' (< **nāṅga* -- ?), K. *nāg* m. (< **nāgga* -- ?).(CDIAL 7040) cf. annaku, anakku 'tin' (Akkadian) A type of produced metal is mentioned in Pali which distinguishes between jātilohaŋ, vijātilohaŋ 'natural metal, produced metal'. Vijātilohaŋ = nāga – nāsikalohaŋ 'produced metal' (Pali) Thus, it is inferred that *nāgalohaŋ* was a mixed ore containing lead and tin (?), together with copper, comparable to *morakkhaka loha* as a sediment-held lead-zinc-copper carbonate. There is a possibility that the 'snake' hieroglyph was intended to convey the message of an alloying metal like lead or tin or zinc which had revolutionised the bronze age with tin-bronzes, zinc-copper brass and other alloys to substitute for arsenical copper to make hard weapons and tools.

kamaṭha m. ' bamboo ' lex. *kārmuka* -- 2 n. ' bow ' Mn., ' bamboo ' lex. which may therefore belong here rather than to kr̥múka -- . Certainly ← Austro -- as. PMWS 33 with lit. -- See kāca -- 3]1. Pk. *kamaḍha* -- , °*aya* -- m. ' bamboo '; Bhoj. *kōro* ' bamboo poles '.2. N. *kāmro* ' bamboo, lath, piece of wood ', OAw. *kām̐vari* ' bamboo pole with slings at each end for carrying things ', H. *kā̃waṛ*, °*ar*, *kāwaṛ*, °*ar* f., G. *kāvaṛ* f., M. *kāvaḍ* f.; -- deriv. Pk. *kāvaḍia* -- , *kavvāḍia* -- m. ' one who carries a yoke ', H. *kā̃waṛī*, °*ṛiyā* m., G. *kāvaṛiyɔ* m. 3. S. *kāvāṭhī* f. ' carrying pole ', *kāvāṭhyo* m. ' the man who carries it '.4. Or. *kāmaṛā*, °*muṛā* ' rafters of a thatched house '; G. *kāmṛ*ũ n., °*ṛī* f. ' chip of bamboo ', *kāmaṛ* -- *koṭiy*ũ n. ' bamboo hut '.5. B. *kāmṭhā* 'bow ', G. *kāmṭh*ũ n., °*ṭhī* f. ' bow '; M. *kamṭhā*, °*ṭā* m. ' bow of bamboo or horn '; -- deriv. G. *kāmṭhiyɔ* m. ' archer '.6. A. *kabāri* ' flat piece of bamboo used in smoothing an earthen image '.7. M. *kā̃bīṭ*, °*baṭ*, °*bṭī*, *kāmīṭ*, °*maṭ*, °*mṭī*, *kāmṭhī*, *kāmāṭhī* f. 'split piece of bamboo &c., lath '.(CDIAL 2760).

kāca3 m. ' loop, string fastened to both ends of a pole, carrying yoke ' lex. [← Drav. Kui *kāsa*, Kuvi *kāñju*, Kan. *kāgaḍi*, *kāvaḍi* T. Burrow BSOAS xii 372, EWA i 195. See kamaṭha --]Pa. *kāca* -- , *kāja* -- m. ' carrying -- pole ', Pk. *kāya* -- , *kāva* -- , m. (deriv. *kāvōya* -- m. ' one who carries a yoke '); S. *kāo*, *kāyo* m. ' rafter '; Si. *kada* ' carrying -- pole '; -- Pk. *kāvaḍa*<-> m., H. *kā̃waṛ*, *kāwaṛ*, °*war* f., G. *kāvaṛ* f., M. *kāvaḍ* f. (CDIAL 3009).

*kācahāra ' bearer of a carrying -- pole '. [kāca -- 3, hāra --] Pa. *kājahāraka* -- m.; Pk. *kāhāra* -- m. ' carrier of water or other burdens ', n. ' carrying -- pole '; K. *kahar* m. ' palanquin -- bearer ', S. *kahāru* m.; P. *kahār* m. ' palanquin -- bearer, water -- carrier '; N. *kahār* ' a class of cultivators who also act as bearers '; B. *kāhār* ' a low caste of palanquin -- bearers and water -- carriers '; Or. *kāhāḷa*, °*āra*, *kāā̃ḷa*, °*ā̃ra* ' a low caste of bearers ', Bhoj. *kahār*, Aw. lakh. *kahār*, *kaharawā*; H. *kahār* m. ' palanquinbearer, water --

drawer '; M. *kahār* m. ' palanquin -- bearer '._ G. *kahār* m. ' litter -- bearer '. (CDIAL 3011).
*kāṁsyakara ' worker in bell -- metal '. [See next: kā´ṁsya -- , kará -- 1] L. awāṇ. *kasērā* ' metal worker ', P. *kaserā* m. ' worker in pewter ' (both ← E with -- *s* --); N. *kasero* ' maker of brass pots '; Bi. H. *kaserā* m. ' worker in pewter '.

kāṁsyakāra m. ' worker in bell -- metal or brass ' Yājñ. com., *kaṁsakāra* -- m. BrahmavP. [kā´ṁsya -- , kāra -- 1] N. *kasār* ' maker of brass pots '; A. *kãhār* ' worker in bell -- metal '; B. *kā̃sāri* ' pewterer, brazier, coppersmith ', Or. *kãsārī*; H. *kasārī* m. ' maker of brass pots '; G. *kãsārɔ*, *kas°* m. ' coppersmith '; M. *kā̃sār*, *kās°* m. ' worker in white metal ', *kāsārḍā* m. ' contemptuous term for the same '.(CDIAL 2988, 2989).

These rebus readings of hieroglyphs carried on flagposts as trade announcements, are consistent with the reading of the hieroglyphs on Tukulti Ninurta altar: prayers to fire-god *karandi* (Hieroglyph: करडी [*karaḍī*]'safflower'); and *arka* 'copper metal' (Hieroglyph: *eraka*, 'nave of wheel'). *arā* 'spokes of wheel' Rebus: *arā* 'brass'.

This consistency in semantics between sacredness and smithywork is exemplified by the Kota language (Meluhha) gloss: *kole.l* with two meanings: smithy, temple.

So, I suggest Tukulti Ninurta I was offering prayers to the fire-god *karandi* and announcing the technological contributions made to the bronze-age evolution by using the 'nave of wheel' hieroglyph to denote *eraka* 'nave of wheel' Rebus: *arka*, *eraka* 'moltencast copper' traded across the Tin Road from Assur to Kanesh.

Irit Ziffeer presents motifs comparable to the architectural model of Naham Mishmar crown.[188]

kharādī ' turner' (Gujarati) *karaḍo –kār* : an artisan-turner who works on a lathe – on hard alloys (Gujarati)

Meluhha examples of processions of hieroglyphs as artisan repertoire lists.

m0488At

m0488Bt

m0488Ct

2802 Prism: Tablet in bas-relief. Side b: Text +One-horned bull + standard. Side a: From R.: a composite animal; a person seated on a tree with a tiger below looking up at the person; a svastika within a square border; an elephant (Composite animal has the body of a ram, horns of a zebu, trunk of an elephant, hindlegs of a tiger and an upraised serpent-like tail). Side c: From R.: a horned person standing between two branches of a pipal tree; a ram; a horned person kneeling in adoration; a low pedestal with some offerings.

h1966A h1966B 1. Glyph: 'bull': *ḍhangra* 'bull'. *Rebus: ḍhangar*

'blacksmith'. *pattar* 'trough' Rebus: *pattar* 'guild'. *dula* 'pair, likenes' Rebus: *dul* 'cast metal. *pasara* 'quadrupeds' Rebus: *pasra* 'smithy' (Santali) Thus the hieroglyphs denote *pattar* 'guild' of blacksmiths, casters of metal.

h1973B h1974B Two tablets. One side shows a person seated on a tree branch, a tiger looking up, a crocodile on the top register and other animals in procession in the bottom register. Obverse side (comparable to h1970, h1971 and h1972) shows an elephant, a person strangling two tigers (jackals or foxes) and a six-spoked wheel.

The glyphic which is common to both set 1 (h1970B, h1971B and h1972B) and set 2: (h1973B and h1974B) is: crocodile on the top register. *kāru* 'crocodile' Rebus: *khar* 'blacksmith' (Kashmiri)

Set 1: crocodile + person with foot on head of animal + spearing + bison + horned (with twig) seated person in penance

Set 2: crocodile + person seated on branch of tree + tiger looking back and up + rhinoceros + tiger in procession.

h1971B Harappa. Three tablets with identical glyphic compositions on both sides: h1970, h1971 and h1972. Seated figure or deity with reed house or shrine at one side. Left: H95-2524; Right: H95-2487.

Harappa. Planoconvex molded tablet found on Mound ET. A. Reverse. a female deity battling two tigers and standing above an elephant and below a six-spoked wheel; b. Obverse. A person spearing with a barbed spear a buffalo in front of a seated horned deity wearing bangles and with a plumed headdress. The person presses his foot down the buffalo's head. An alligator with a narrow snout is on the top register. "We have found two other broken tablets at Harappa that appear to have been made from the same mold that was used to create the scene of a deity battling two tigers and standing above an elephant. One was found in a room located on the southern slope of Mount ET in 1996 and another example comes from excavations on Mound F in the 1930s. However, the flat obverse of both of these broken tablets does not show the spearing of a buffalo, rather it depicts the more well-known scene showing a tiger looking back over its shoulder at a person sitting on the branch of a tree. Several other flat or twisted rectangular terracotta tablets found at Harappa combine these two narrative scenes of a figure strangling two tigers on one side of a tablet, and the tiger looking back over its shoulder at a figure in a tree on the other side."[189]

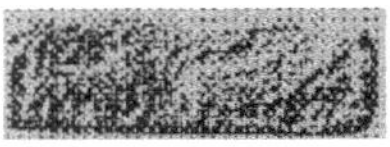

Pict-47 Row of uncertain animals in file.

m1405At Pict-97: Person standing at the center pointing with his right hand at a bison facing a trough, and with his left hand pointing to the sign 

Obverse: A tiger and a rhinoceros in file. m1405Bt Pict-48 A tiger and a rhinoceros in file 2841 

Animals in procession: खांडा [*khāṇḍā*] A flock (of sheep or goats) (Marathi) கண்டி[1] kaṇṭi Flock, herd (Tamil) Rebus: *khāṇḍā* 'tools, pots and pans, and metal-ware'.

Zebu on m1431C is a superse: *adar ḍangra* 'zebu or humped bull' Rebus: *aduru* 'native metal' (Kannada); ḍhangar 'blacksmith' (Hindi)

m1431B Crocodile+ three animal glyphs: rhinoceros, elephant, tiger (with fishes on top?).

m1431C

m1431E

m1431A 

m1431E. From R.—a person holding a vessel; a woman with a platter (?); a kneeling person with a staff in his hands facing the woman; a goat with its forelegs on a platform under a tree. [Or, two antelopes flanking a tree on a platform, with one antelope looking backwards?]

Line drawing of Indus script seal impression on one side of a prism tablet M1431E. Mohenjodaro. Symmetrically flanking goats with feet on central tree and mountain (ASI).

The turner on a lathe is depicted on this glyphic narrative. kõdā 'to turn in a lathe' (Bengali)

Glyph: 'broken tree branch': khōṇḍa A tree of which the head and branches are broken off, a stock or stump: also the lower portion of the trunk—that below the branches. (Marathi) Rebus 1: koḍ 'workshop' (G.)

Allograph glyph: खोंड [khōṇḍa] m A young bull, a bullcalf. (Marathi) గోద [gōda] gōda. [Tel.] n. An ox. A beast. kine,

cattle.(Telugu) koḍiyum 'heifer' (G.) [kōḍiya] kōḍe, kōḍiya. [Tel.] n. A bullcalf. . k* దూడA young bull. Plumpness, prime.

తరుణము. జోడుకోడయలు a pair of bullocks. kōḍe adj. Young.

kōḍe-kāḍu. n. A young man.పడుచువాడు. [kārukōḍe] kāru-kōḍe.

[Tel.] n. A bull in its prime. koḍiyum (G.) Rebus : B. kõdā 'to turn in a lathe'; Or. kũnda 'lathe', kũdibā, kũd 'to turn' (→ Drav. Kur. kũd 'lathe') (CDIAL 3295).M1431E shows a turner at work, assisted by a person bending on all fours. kunda 'turner' kundār turner (A.); kũdār, kũdāri (B.); kundāru (Or.); kundau to turn on a lathe, to carve, to chase; kundau dhiri = a hewn stone; kundau murhut = a graven image (Santali) kunda a turner's lathe (Skt.)(CDIAL 3295) Glyph: Br. Kōṇḍō on all fours, bent double. (DEDR 204a) The seated person is shown wearing knot of hair at back. Sūnd gaṭ (Go.) cundī the hairtail as worn by men (Kur.)(DEDR 2670). Rebus: cundakāra a turner J vi.339 (Pali) cundakāra cognate kundār.

m1431E 2805 Row of animals in file (a one-horned bull, an elephant and a rhinoceros from right); a gharial with a fish held in its jaw above the animals; a bird (?) at right. Pict-116: From R.—a person holding a vessel; a woman with a platter (?); a kneeling person with a staff in his hands facing the woman; a goat with its forelegs on a platform under a tree. [Or, two antelopes flanking a tree on a platform, with one antelope looking backwards?]
koḍe 'young bull' (Telugu) खोंड [khōṇḍa] m A young bull, a bullcalf. Rebus: kõdā 'to turn in a lathe' (B.) कोंद *kōnda* 'engraver, lapidary setting or infixing gems' (Marathi) कोंडण [kōṇḍaṇa] f A fold or pen. (Marathi) ayakāra 'ironsmith' (Pali)[fish = aya (G.); crocodile = kāru (Te.)] baṭṭai quail (N.Santali) Rebus: bhaṭa = an oven, kiln, furnace (Santali)
ayo 'fish' Rebus: ayas 'metal'. *kaṇḍa* 'arrow' Rebus: *khāṇḍa* 'tools, pots and pans, and metal-ware'. *ayaskāṇḍa* is a compounde word attested in Panini. The compound or glyphs of fish + arrow may denote metalware tools, pots and pans.kola 'tiger' Rebus: kol 'working in iron, alloy of 5 metals - pancaloha'. ibha 'elephant' Rebus ibbo 'merchant'; ib 'iron'. Alternative: కరటి [karaṭi] *karaṭi*.

[Skt.] n. An elephant. ఏనుగు (Telugu) Rebus: *kharādī* ' turner'

(Gujarati) *kāṇḍa* 'rhimpceros' Rebus: *khāṇḍa* 'tools, pots and pans, and metal-ware'. The text on m0489 tablet: loa 'ficus religiosa' Rebus: loh 'copper'. kolmo 'rice plant' Rebus: kolami 'smithy, forge'. dula 'pair' Rebus: dul 'cast metal'. Thus the display of the metalware catalog includes the technological competence to work with minerals, metals and alloys and produce tools, pots and pans. The persons involved are krammara 'turn back' Rebus: kamar 'smiths, artisans'. kola 'tiger' Rebus: kol 'working in iron, working in pancaloha alloys'. పంచలోహము *pancha-lōnamu.* n. A mixed metal, composed of five ingredients, viz., copper, zinc, tin, lead, and iron (Telugu). Thus, when five svastika hieroglyphs are depicted, the depiction is of satthiya 'svastika' Rebus: satthiya 'zinc' and the totality of 5 alloying metals of copper, zinc, tin, lead and iron.

Procession of animals. Bronze dish found by Layard at Nimrud: circular objects are decorated by consecutive chains of animals following each other round in a circle. A similar theme occurs on the famous silver vase of Entemena. In the innermost circle, a troop of gazelles (similar to the ones depicted on cylinder seals) march along in file; the middle register has a variety of animals, all marching in the same direction as the gazelles. A one-horned bull, a winged griffin, an ibex and a gazelle, are followed by two bulls who are being attacked by lions, and a griffin, a one-horned bull, and a gazelle, who are all respectively being attacked by leopards. In the outermost zone there is a stately procession of realistically conceived one-horned bulls marching in the opposite direction to the animals parading in the two inner circles. The dish has a handle. (Percy S.P.Handcock, 1912, *Mesopotamian Archaeology*, London, Macmillan and Co., p. 256). Cf. pasaramu, pasalamu = quadrupeds (Telugu); rebus: pasra = smithy ! (Santali) Smithy for varieties of minerals and metals, indeed.

"Of lasting significance were attempts to lighten the disk wheels, as first seen on a third-millennium seal from Hissar IIIB (fig.2). On it, the central plank, through which the axle passes, is narrowed to a diametral bar; the flanking planks of the Hissar. Depiction of a wheel on a seal from Hissar IIIB. 3rd millennium BCE (After Figure 2, Littauer and Crouwel, 979). tripartite wheel are eliminated, and the former bonding slats are turned into sturdy transverse bars between the diametral bar and the felloe. This crossbar wheel is also clearly illustrated in the second millennium BCE, fixed on a revolving axle; it has remained in use with simple carts in various parts of the world.

Warka stone (alabaster) vase dated to c. 3000 BCE, has relief decoration in four registers.190 On top register are glyphs of a goat and a tiger/jackal above two glyphs (which may denote bun-ingots out of a furnace). On bottom register are shown *tabernae montana* sprouts. The second and third registers of the vase seem to show a procession of metal workers and animals bringing alloyed metal ingots in pots.

A soft-stone flask, 6 cm. tall, from Bactria (northern Afghanistan) showing a winged female deity (?) flanked by two flowers similar to those shown on the comb from Tell Abraq.(After Pottier, M.H., 1984, *Materiel funeraire e la Bactriane meridionale de l'Age du Bronze*, Paris, Editions Recherche sur les Civilisations: plate 20.150) Possibly, the flask held the essence of the fragrant flowers, *tagaraka*, hair-fragrance.

h1973B h1974B Two tablets. One side shows a person seated on a tree branch, a tiger looking up, a crocodile on the top register and other animals in procession in the bottom register.

Glyph: seven: eae ‘seven’ (Santali); rebus: eh-ku ’steel’ (Ta.)

खांडा [khāṇḍā] *m* A jag, notch, or indentation (as upon the edge of a tool or weapon). Rebus: khāṇḍa 'tools, pots and pans, and metal-ware'. Alternative: *aṭar* 'a splinter' (Ma.) *aṭaruka* 'to burst, crack, sli off,fly open; *aṭarcca* ' splitting, a crack'; *aṭarttuka* 'to split, tear off, open (an oyster) (Ma.); *aḍaruni* 'to crack' (Tu.) (DEDR 66) Rebus: *aduru* 'native, unsmelted metal' (Kannada) Alternative: *sal* 'splinter' Rebus: *sal* 'artisan's workshop'.
ayo 'fish' Rebus: ayas 'metal'. *kaṇḍa* 'arrow' Rebus: *khāṇḍa* 'tools, pots and pans, and metal-ware'. *ayaskāṇḍa* is a compounde word attested in Panini. The compound or glyphs of fish + arrow may denote metalware tools, pots and pans.
G. khuṇ f., khū˘ṇɔ m. ' corner '.2. S. kuṇḍa f. ' corner '; P. kū̃ṭ f. ' corner, side ' (← H.). (CDIAL 3898) Phal. Khun ' corner ';
H. khū̃ṭ m. ' corner, direction ' (→ P. khũṭ f. ' corner, side ');
G. khū̃ṭṛī f. ' angle '. Rebus: khū̃ṭ 'guild, community'.
Kolhes; iron produced by the Kolhes and formed like a four-cornered piece a little pointed at each end; mūhā me~r.he~t = iron smelted by the Kolhes and formed into an equilateral lump a little pointed at each end; kolhe tehen me~r.he~tko mūhā akata = the Kolhes have to-day produced pig iron (Santali.lex.)
Thus the message conveyed by the text is that the metalware -- a*yaskāṇḍa* -- is of guild, community workshop -- *khū̃ṭ sal.*
h1966A h1966B 1. Glyph: 'bull': *ḍhangra* 'bull'. *Rebus: ḍhangar* 'blacksmith'.pattar 'trough' Rebus: pattar 'guild'. dula 'pair, likenes' Rebus: dul 'cast metal. Thus the hieroglyphs denote pattar 'guild' of blacksmiths, casters of metal.

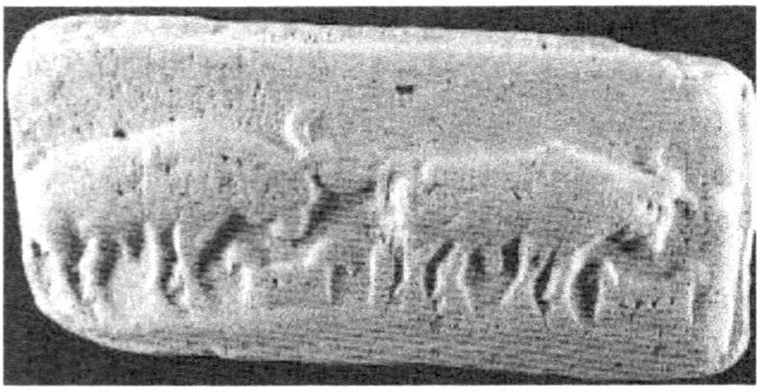

pasara 'quadrupeds' Rebus: pasra 'smithy' (Santali)

642

kāru 'crocodile' Rebus: *kāru* 'artisan'; khar 'blacksmith' (Kashmiri).*ibha* 'elephant' Rbus: *ibb o*'merchant', *ib* 'iron'

காண்டாமிருகம் kāṇṭā-mirukam , *n.* [M. *kāṇṭāmṛgam.*] Rhinoceros; கல்யானை. Rebus: *kāṇḍā*'metalware, tools, pots and pans'. Alternative: Hieroglyph: *baḍhia* 'castrated boar' Rebus: vardhaki m. ' carpenter ' MBh. Pa. *vaḍḍhaki* -- m. ' carpenter, building mason mason '; Pk. *vaḍḍhaï* -- m. ' carpenter ', °*aïa* -- m. ' shoemaker '; WPah. jaun. *bāḍhōī* ' carpenter ', (Joshi) *bāḍhi* m., N. *baṛhaï*, *baṛahi*, A. *bārai*, B. *bāṛaï*, °*ṛui*, Or. *baṛhaï*, °*ṛhāi*, (Gaṛjād) *bāṛhoi*, Bi. *baṛahī*, Bhoj. H. *baṛhaī* m., M. *vāḍhāyā* m., Si. *vaḍu* -- *vā.*WPah.kṭg. *báḍḍhi* m. ' carpenter '; kṭg. *bəṛh*e\i, *báṛhi*, kc. *baṛhe* ← H. beside genuine *báḍḍhi* Him.I 135), J. *bāḍhi*, Garh. *baṛhai*, A. also *bāṛhai* AFD 94; Md. *vaḍīn*, *vaḍin* pl.Md. *vaḍām* ' carpentry '.(CDIAL 11375). A group of animal hieroglyphs (including tiger/jackal, rhinoceros/boar) are show on many tablets with Indus writing

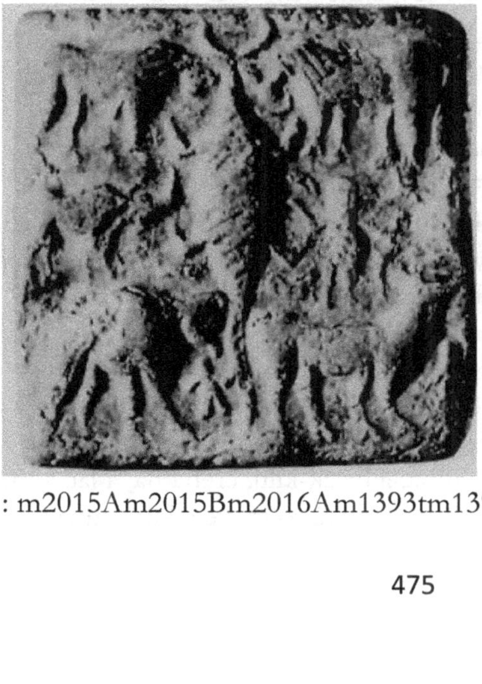

: m2015Am2015Bm2016Am1393tm1394tm 1395Atm1395Bt

m1431B

m1431A, B, C, E and Text 2805 Row of animals in file (a one-horned bull, an elephant and a rhinoceros from right); a gharial with a fish held in its jaw above the animals; a bird (?) at right. Pict-116: From R.—a person holding a vessel; a woman with a platter (?); a kneeling person with a staff in his hands facing the woman; a goat with its forelegs on a platform under a tree. [Or, two antelopes flanking a tree on a platform, with one antelope looking backwards?]

koḍe 'young bull' (Telugu) खोंड [khōṇḍa] m A young bull, a bullcalf. Rebus: kõdā 'to turn in a lathe' (B.) कोंडण [kōṇḍaṇa] f A fold or pen. (Marathi) ayakāra 'ironsmith' (Pali)[fish = aya (G.); crocodile = kāru (Te.)]baṭṭai quail (N.Santali) Rebus: bhaṭa = an oven, kiln, furnace (Santali) baṭhi furnace for smelting ore (the same as kuṭhi) (Santali) bhaṭa = an oven, kiln, furnace; make an oven, a furnace; iṭa bhaṭa = a brick kiln; kun:kal bhaṭa a potter's kiln; cun bhaṭa = a lime kiln; cun tehen dobon bhaṭaea = we shall prepare the lime kiln today (Santali); bhaṭṭhā (H.) bhart = a mixed metal of copper and lead; bhartīyā= a barzier, worker in metal; bhaṭ, bhrāṣṭra = oven, furnace (Skt.) mẽṛhẽt baṭi = iron (Ore) furnaces. [Synonyms are: mẽt = the eye, rebus for: the dotted circle (Santali.lex) baṭha [H. baṭṭhī (Sad.)] any kiln, except a potter's kiln, which is called coa; there are four kinds of kiln: cunabat.ha, a lime-kin, it.abat.ha, a brick-kiln, ērēbaṭha, a lac kiln, kuilabaṭha, a charcoal kiln; trs. Or intrs., to make a kiln; cuna rapamente ciminaupe baṭhakeda? How many limekilns did you make? Baṭha-sen:gel = the fire of a kiln; baṭi [H. Sad. baṭṭhi, a furnace for distilling) used alone or in the cmpds. arkibuṭi and baṭiora, all meaning a grog-shop; occurs also in ilibaṭi, a (licensed) rice-beer shop (Mundari.lex.) bhaṭi = liquor from mohwa flowers (Santali)

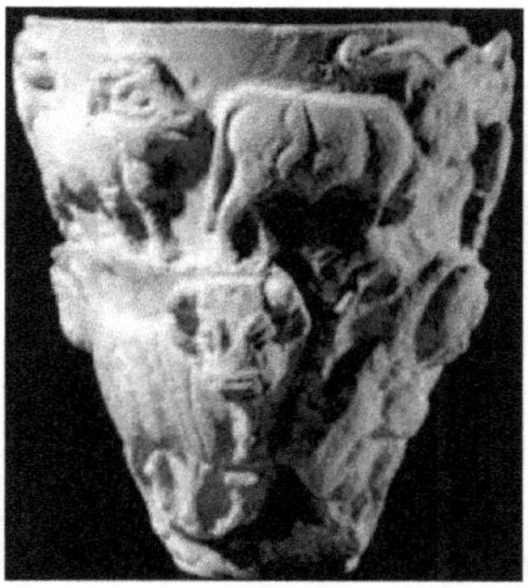

Stone vase from Mesopotamia.Late Uruk period, about 3400-3200 BCE. Ht. 1.2 cm. It shows a bull, goat and ram.

adar ḍangra 'zebu or humped bull'; rebus: aduru 'native metal' (Ka.); ḍhangar 'blacksmith' (H.) aduru = *gaṇiyinda tegadu karagade iruva aduru* = ore taken from the mine and not subjected to melting in a furnace (Ka. Siddhānti Subrahmaṇya' Śastri's new interpretation of the Amarakośa, Bangalore, Vicaradarpana Press, 1872, p.330); adar = fine sand (Ta.); ayir – iron dust, any ore (Ma.) Kur. adar the waste of pounded rice, broken grains, etc. Malt. adru broken grain (DEDR 134). *Ta.* ayil iron. *Ma.* ayir, ayiram any ore. *Ka.* aduru native metal. *Tu.* ajirda karba very hard iron. (DEDR 192).

ranku 'antelope'Rebus: ranku = tin (santali)

tagara 'ram' Rebus: tagaram 'tin'.

A neo-Babylonian cylinder seal shows the Sumerian hero Gilgamesh circa 900-700 BCE. Glyphs of bull-men with horns and eagle in the field. aryeh 'lion' Rebus: arā 'brass'. *kõdā* खोंड [khōṇḍa] m A young bull, a bullcalf. (Marathi) Rebus 1: kọnḍu or konḍu । कुण्डम् m. a hole dug in the ground for receiving consecrated fire (Kashmiri) Rebus 2: A. *kundār*, B. *kũdār*, °*ri*, Or. *kundāru*; H. *kũderā* m. 'one who works a lathe, one who scrapes ', °*rī* f., *kũdernā* ' to scrape, plane, round on a lathe '.(CDIAL 3297). The crossed animals thus denote: brass-turner.

Pict-97: Person standing at the center pointing with his right hand at a bison facing a trough, and with his left hand pointing to the sign

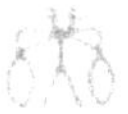

2841 Obverse: A tiger and a rhinoceros in file. Pict-48 A tiger and a rhinoceros in file

kola 'tiger' Rebus: kol 'working in iron, alloy of 5 metals - pancaloha'. ibha 'elephant' Rebus ibbo 'merchant'; ib 'iron'. *kāṇḍa* 'rhimpceros' Rebus:*khāṇḍa* 'tools, pots and pans, and metal-ware'. The text on m0489 tablet: loa 'ficus religiosa' Rebus: loh 'copper'. kolmo 'rice plant' Rebus: kolami 'smithy, forge'. dula 'pair' Rebus: dul 'cast metal'. Thus the display of the metalware catalog includes the technological competence to work with minerals, metals and alloys and produce tools, pots and pans. The persons involved are krammara 'turn back' Rebus: kamar 'smiths, artisans'. kola 'tiger' Rebus: kol 'working in iron, working in pancaloha alloys'. పంచలోహము *pancha-lōnamu.* n. A mixed metal, composed of five ingredients, viz., copper, zinc, tin, lead, and iron (Telugu). Thus, when five svastika hieroglyphs are depicted, the depiction is of satthiya 'svastika' Rebus: satthiya 'zinc' and the totality of 5 alloying metals of copper, zinc, tin, lead and iron.

Akkadian cylinder seal, showing kneeling heroes. Around 2200 BCE. While this seal shows 'safflower' as a hieroglyph, another seal shows 'sun' as a hieroglyph (sometimes interpreted as Shamash, sun divinity).

Cylinder seal with kneeling nude heroes, ca. 2220–2159 b.c.; Akkadian Mesopotamia Red jasper H. 1 1/8 in. (2.8 cm), Diam. 5/8 in. (1.6 cm) Metropolitan Museum of Art - USA

Four flag-posts(reeds) with rings on top held by the kneeling persons define the four components of the iron smithy/ forge. This is an announcement of four shops, पेढी (Gujarati.

Marathi). पेंढें 'rings' Rebus: पेढी 'shop'. Alternative: *koṭiyum* [*koṭ, koṭī* neck] a wooden circle put round the neck of an animal (Gujarati) Rebus: *ācāri koṭṭya* = forge, *kammārasāle* (Tulu) āra 'serpent' Rebus; āra 'brass'. *karaḍa* 'double-drum' *Rebus: karaḍa* 'hard alloy'. The 'offering' posture connotes āsana mudrā of an 'archer': *kāmṭhiyɔ* m. 'archer'(Gujarati) Rebus: *kammaṭa* 'coiner, mint'.

Specific materials offered for sale/exchange in the shop are: hard alloy brass metal (*ayo*, fish); *lokhaṇḍ* (overflowing pot) 'metal tools, pots and pans, metalware'; *arka/erka* 'copper'; *kammaṭa* (a portable furnace for melting precious metals) 'coiner, mint' Thus, the four shops are: 1. brass alloys, 2. metalware, 3. copper and 4. mint (services).
erãguḍu bowing, salutation (Telugu) *iṟai* (-v-, -nt-) to bow before (as in salutation), worship (Tamil)(DEDR 516). Rebus: *eraka, eṟaka* any metal infusion (Kannada.Tulu) *eruvai* 'copper' (Tamil); *ere* dark red (Kannada)(DEDR 446).
puṭa Anything folded or doubled so as to form a cup or concavity; crucible. Alternative: *ḍhālako* = a large metal ingot (G.) *ḍhālakī* = a metal heated and poured into a mould; a solid piece of metal; an ingot (Gujarati)

Allograph: ढाल [ḍhāla] *f* (S through H) The grand flag of an army directing its march and encampments: also the standard or banner of a chieftain: also a flag flying on forts &c. ढालकाठी [ḍhālakāṭhī] *f* ढालखांब *m* A flagstaff; esp.the pole for a grand flag or standard. 2 fig. The leading and sustaining member of a household or other commonwealth. 5583 ḍhāla n. ' shield ' lex. 2. *ḍhāllā -- . 1. Tir. (Leech) "*dàl*" ' shield ', Bshk. *ḍāl*, Ku. *ḍhāl*, gng. *ḍhāw*, N. A. B. *ḍhāl*, Or. *ḍhāḷa*, Mth. H. *ḍhāl* m.2. Sh. *ḍal* (pl. °*lẹ*) f., K. *ḍāl* f., S. *ḍhāla*, L. *ḍhāl* (pl. °*lā̃*) f., P. *ḍhāl* f., G. M. *ḍhāl* f. WPah.kṭg. (kc.) *ḍhā`l* f. (obl. -- *a*) ' shield ' (a word used in salutation), J. *ḍhāl* f. (CDIAL 5583).
They are four Glyphs: *paṭākā* 'flag' Rebus: *pāṭaka,* four quarters of the village.
kā̃ḍ reed Rebus: *kāṇḍa* 'tools, pots and pans, metal-ware'.
1. Pk. *kamaḍha* -- , °*aya* -- m. ' bamboo '; Bhoj. *kōro* ' bamboo poles '. 2. N. *kāmro* ' bamboo, lath, piece of wood ', OAw. *kāṁvari* ' bamboo pole with slings at each end for carrying things ', H. *kā̃waṛ*, °*ar*, *kāwaṛ*, °*ar* f., G. *kāvaṛ*f., M. *kāvaḍ* f.; -- deriv. Pk. *kāvaḍia* -- , *kavvāḍia* -- m. ' one who carries a yoke ', H. *kā̃waṛī*, °*ṛiyā* m., G. *kāvaṛiyɔ* m. 3. S. *kāvāṭhī* f. ' carrying pole ', *kāvāṭhyo* m. ' the man who carries it '. 4. Or. *kāmaṛā*, °*muṛā* ' rafters of a thatched house '; G. *kāmṛũ* n., °*ṛī* f. ' chip of bamboo ', *kāmaṛ -- koṭiyũ* n. ' bamboo hut '. 5. B. *kāmṭhā* ' bow ', G. *kāmṭhũ* n., °*ṭhī* f. ' bow '; M. *kamṭhā*, °*ṭā* m. ' bow of bamboo or horn '; -- deriv. G. *kāmṭhiyɔ* m. ' archer '. 6. A. *kabāri* ' flat piece of bamboo used in smoothing an earthen image '.
7. *kā̃bīṭ*, °*baṭ*, °*bṭī*, *kāmīṭ*, °*maṭ*, °*mṭī*, *kāmṭhī*, *kāmāṭhī* f. ' split piece of bamboo &c., lath '.(CDIAL 2760). kambi f. ' branch or shoot of bamboo ' lex. Pk. *kaṁbi* -- , °*bī* -- , °*bā* -- f. ' stick, twig ', OG. *kāṁba*; M. *kā̃b* f. ' longitudinal division of a bamboo &c., bar of iron or other metal '. (CDIAL 2774). कंबडी [kambaḍī] *f* A slip or split piece (of a bamboo &c.)(Marathi)

The rings atop the reed standard: पेंढें [pēṇḍhēṃ] पेंडकें [pēṇḍakēṃ] n Weaver's term. A cord-loop or metal ring (as attached to the गुलडा of the बैली and to certain other fixtures). पेंडें [pēṇḍēṃ] n (पेड) A necklace composed of strings of pearls. 2 A loop or ring. Rebus: पेढी (Gujaráthí word.) A shop (Marathi) Alternative: *koṭiyum* [*koṭ, koṭī* neck] a wooden circle put round the neck of an animal
(Gujarati) Rebus: *ācāri koṭṭya* = forge, *kammārasāle* (Tulu)

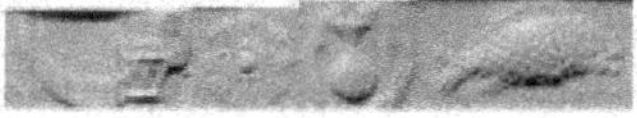

The four hieroglyphs define the four quarters of the village smithy/forge: alloy, metalware, turner's lathe-work, cruble (or, ingot).
ayo 'fish' Rebus: *ayo* 'metal, alloy'
కాండము [kāṇḍamu] *kāṇḍamu.* [Skt.] n.

Water. నీళ్లు (Telugu) kaṇṭhá -- : (b) ' water -- channel ':

Paš. *kaṭā´* ' irrigation channel ', Shum. *xãṭṭä.* (CDIAL 14349).
lokhãḍ 'overflowing pot' Rebus: 'tools, iron, ironware' (Gujarati)
arká1 m. ' flash, ray, sun ' RV. [√arc] Pa. Pk. *akka* -- m. ' sun ', Mth. *āk;* Si. *aka* ' lightning ', inscr. *vid* -- *äki* ' lightning flash '.(CDIAL 624) *அருக்கன் arukkaṉ, n. < arka. Sun; சூரி யன். அருக்க னணிநிறமுங் கண்டேன் (திவ். இயற். 3, 1).*(Tamil) agasāle 'goldsmithy' (Kannada) అగసాలి [agasāli] or అగసాలెవాడు *agasāli.* n. A goldsmith. కంసాలివాడు. (Telugu) erka = ekke (Tbh. of arka) aka (Tbh. of arka) copper (metal); crystal (Kannada) cf. eruvai = copper (Tamil) eraka, er-aka = any metal infusion (Ka.Tu.); erako molten cast (Tulu) Rebus: eraka = copper (Ka.) eruvai = copper (Ta.); ere - a dark-red colour (Ka.)(DEDR 817). eraka, era, er-a = syn. erka, copper, weapons (Ka.) erka = ekke (Tbh. of arka) aka (Tbh. of arka) copper (metal); crystal

(Kannada) akka, aka (Tadbhava of arka) metal; akka metal (Te.) arka = copper (Skt.) erako molten cast (Tulu) Alternative: *kunda* 'jasmine flower' Rebus: kunda 'a turner's lathe'. kundaṇa pure gold.

The image could denote a crucible or a portable furnace: *kammaṭa* 'coiner, mint, a portable furnace for melting precious metals (Telugu) On some cylinder seals, this image is shown held aloft on a stick, comparable to the bottom register of the 'standard device' normally shown in front of a one-horned young bull. Alternatives: *puṭa* Anything folded or doubled so as to form a cup or concavity; crucible. *Ta.* kuvai, kukai crucible. *Ma.* kuva id. *Ka.* kōve id. *Tu.* kōvè id., mould. (DEDR 1816). Alternative: Shape of ingot:

దళము [daḷamu] *daḷamu.* [Skt.] n. A leaf. ఆకు. A petal. A

part, భాగము. dala n. ' leaf, petal ' MBh. Pa. Pk. *dala* -- n. '

leaf, petal ', G. M. *daḷ* n.(CDIAL 6214). <DaLO>(MP) {N} ``^branch, ^twig''. *Kh.<DaoRa>(D) `dry leaves when fallen', ~<daura>, ~<dauRa> `twig', Sa.<DAr>, Mu.<Dar>, ~<Dara> `big branch of a tree', ~<DauRa> `a twig or small branch with fresh leaves on it', So.<kOn-da:ra:-n> `branch', H.<DalA>, B.<DalO>, O.<DaLO>, Pk.<DAlA>. %7811. #7741.(Munda etyma) Rebus: *ḍhālako* = a large metal ingot (G.) *ḍhālakī* = a metal heated and poured into a mould; a solid piece of metal; an ingot (Gujarati).

Appendix H: Interpretation of Māyā's dream in Bauddham

The historical narrative is a continuum in use of Meluhha hieroglyphs of Sarasvati-Sindhu civilization of the bronze age Ancient Near East.

Māyā's dream is a sacred, hallowed tradition in Bauddham and the narrative is revered in ancient sculptures and ancient texts. This tradition is further elaborated by the use of Meluhha hieroglyphs which are read rebus, validating the Meluhha hieroglyph cipher for the ancient, unambiguous vernacular of Indian *sprachbund.*

Argument

Māyā had a dream in which she saw an elephant (*ibha* 'elephant' dream rebus: *ib* 'iron'). King Śuddhodana and his soothsayers interpreted the she would bear a son who with detached passion would satisfy the world with sweetness of his ambrosia. Can this dream be reinterpreted in the context of philosophy of symbolic forms?

The central thesis is: many hieroglyphs rendered on the 'Māyā's dream sculptures' are a continuum of the Meluhha hieroglyphs (aka Indus writing).

From Nagarjunakonda, 2nd Century CE Courtesy: National Museum, New Delhi.

The engraver, scribe is shown

holding a wedge on the Nagarjunakonda sculptural frieze: The phrase, *tanana mleccha* may be related to: (i) tah'nai, 'engraver' mleccha; or (ii) tana, 'of (mleccha) lineage'. 1. See Kuwi. *tah'nai* 'to engrave' in DEDR and Bsh. *then, thon*, 'small axe' in CDIAL: DEDR 3146 *Go.* (Tr.) *tarcana* (Mu.) *tarc-* to scrape; (Ma.) *tarsk-* id., plane; (D.) *task-*, (Mu.) *tarsk-/tarisk-* to level, scrape (*Voc.*1670). Alternative: *kõda* 'young bull-calf'. koḍe 'young bull' (Telugu) खोंड [khōṇḍa] m A young bull, a bullcalf. Rebus: kõdā 'to turn in a lathe' (B.) कोंद *kōnda* 'engraver, lapidary setting or infixing gems' (Marathi)

Segments of the sculpture showing: 1. scribe; 2. stacks of straw asociated with epigraphs (incribed ovals -- cartouches -- atop the stacks) and the row of seated artisans. There are two hieroglyphs on these segments: 1. scribe; 2. straw-stacks. Both can be read as Meluhha hieroglyphs.

The scribe shown on Nagarjunakonda sculpture is *kaṇḍa kan-ka* 'stone scribe'. The gloss is reinforced by the hieroglyph: stack of straw: *kaṇḍa* (See Meluhha glosses from Indian *sprachbund* appended).

From Nagarjunakonda, 2nd Century CE Courtesy: National Museum, New Delhi.

Māyā is a Koliya, i.e. she is a kole, a community working in iron. *kol* 'working in iron' (Tamil).

Koles are the outstanding smelters of iron.

There is an article [191] by Suniti Kumar Chatterjee explaining that the word 'kol' meant 'man' in general.

An old Munda word, kol means 'man'. S. K. Chatterjee called the Munda family of languages as Kol, as the word, according to him, is (in the Sanskrit-Prākṛt form Kolia) an early Aryan modification of an old Munda word meaning 'man'. Przyluski accepts this explanation.[192]

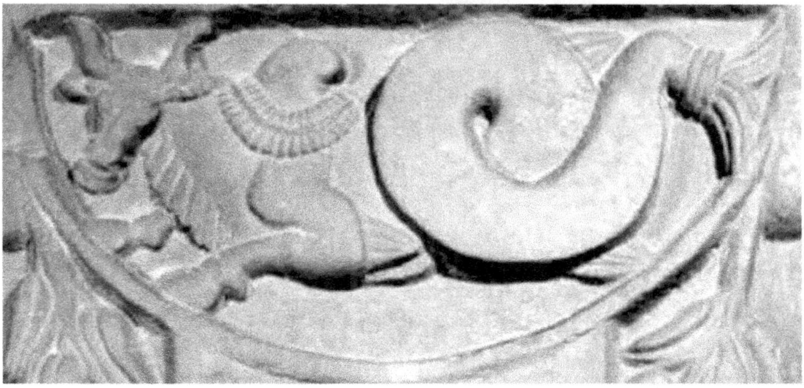

The crocodile ligatured to the bull is: *kāru* 'crocodile' Rebus: *khar* 'blacksmith' (Kashmiri) *ayakara* 'fish+crocodile' rebus: 'metal-smith'. *adar* 'zebu' rebus: *aduru* 'unsmelted metal or ore' (Kannada) aduru native metal (Ka.); ayil iron (Ta.) ayir, ayiram any ore (Ma.); ajirda karba very hard iron (Tu.)(DEDR 192). aduru =*gaṇiyinda tegadu karagade iruva aduru* = ore taken from the mine and not subjected to melting in a furnace. Kannada. Siddhānti Subrahmaṇya śāstri's new interpretation of the Amarakośa, Bangalore,Vicaradarpana Press, 1872, p. 330.

Note: In this remarkable ligature, the crocodile+fish hieroglyphs are NOT ligatured to the trunk of an elephant because the scribe wants to precisely communicate the nature of the profession of the artisan guild involved with the prayer to the Buddha narrating his birth. If the elephant was intended, the rebus readings would have included: *ibha* 'elephant' (Samskrtam) Rebus: *ibbo* 'merchant' (Hemacandra Desināmamāla - Gujarati) *ib* 'iron' (Santali). Vikalpa: the bull is: *ḍangar* 'bull'

Rebus: *dhangar* 'blacksmith' (Maithili) *ḍangar* 'blacksmith' (Hindi).

The two antelopes joined back-to-back: pusht 'back'; rebus: pusht 'ancestor'. pus<u>h</u>t bah pus<u>h</u>t 'generation to generation.' The ram could also be denoted by *tagara* 'antelope'; takar, *n*. [தகர் T. *tagaru*, K. *tagar*.] 1. Sheep; ஆட்டின்பொது. (திவா.) 2. Ram; செம் மறியாட்டுக்கடா. (திவா.) பொருநகர் தாக்கற்குப் பேருந் தகைத்து (குறள், 486).

Rebus: *ṭagara* 'tin'. dula 'pair' (Kashmiri); rebus: dul 'cast metal' (Munda). Rebus: damgar 'merchant'. Thus the pair of antelopes on the top register denotes: tin smith artisan, *dul ṭagara* 'cast tin'. The associated hieroglyphs, in the context of depicting the narratives of Māyā's dream, in particular (and their rebus readings) which are elaborated further in this monograph pointing to a continuum of writing systems from the days of Meluhha hieroglyphs (aka Indus writing) are:

- stack of straw
- scribe

- bull ligatured to makara (crocodile,fish tail)
- antelopes ligatured back-to-back

Amaravati. Portion of narrative frieze

depicting Māyā's Dream. ca. second century CE, 101 CE - 200 CE H - ca. 12.50 in Madras Government Museum, Madras, Tamil Nadu, India.

Peshawar sculptural fragment depicting Māyā's Dream. Kusana. a. mid-first to mid-third century CE, 50 CE - 250 CE grey stone H - ca. 5.00 in Indian Museum, Calcutta, West Bengal, India

North West Frontier relief sculpture fragment Māyā's Dream Kusana ca. 1st c.-2nd c. CE, 100 BCE - 300 CE grey schist H - ca. 5.50 in National Museum, Karachi, Pakistan

Sarnath. Buddha life scenes. ca. fifth century CE, 401 CE - 500 CE buff sandstoneH - ca. 35.13 in W - ca. 19.50 inNational Museum, New Delhi, India. The bottom register to the left, interpretsMāyā's dream. Descent of the elephant.

Bharhut stupa. Inscription in Brahmi. brown sandstone Sunga ca. 100-80 BCE, 100 BCE - 80 BCE Indian Museum, Calcutta, West

Bengal, India. Bottom register shows descent of elephant in Māyā's dream.

Māyā's Dream at Bharhut. from the collection of Dr David Efurd, Wofford College.

"Dreams (*supina*) are mental images that occur during sleep. There is widespread belief that dreams have some significance. Some people believe they foretell the future, others that the dead can communicate with the living through them. Modern psychoanalysts say that when interpreted correctly, dreams can offer an insight into suppressed desires and drives and thus can lead to a deeper self-understanding. Buddhist psychology recognizes several types of dreams. According to the *Milindapanha* these are (1) dreams caused by physical stress, (2) by psychological irritability, (3) by spirits, (4) because of mental clarity and (5) prophetic dreams (Mil.II,298). It also says that dreams mainly occur in the interval either between falling asleep or waking up (*okkante middhe*) and deep sleep (*asampatte bhavnge*, Mil.II,299), a fact confirmed by science. Before the Buddha was enlightened, he had seven dreams full of strange symbolism which did in fact foretell his enlightenment (A.III,240). However, he was sceptical of those who claimed that they could interpret other people's dreams and he forbade monks and nuns from doing so (D.I,8). He said that a person who does loving kindness meditation (metta bhavana) will not be disturbed by nightmares (A.V,342) and also that a monk who falls to sleep mindfully will not have a wet dream (A.III,251). The Buddha also said that dreaming of doing something, i.e. killing someone or stealing something, is not ethically significant and therefore has no kammic effect (Vin.III,111). Thus he understood that dreams are beyond the power of the will. Legend says Maha Māyā, Prince Siddhattha's mother, had a dream dreamed of a white elephant soon after he was conceived and that this was a portent of his future greatness. The story is not in the Tipitaka and the earliest version of it is found in the *Jatakanidana* 50."

This quote refers to *okkanti* in the context of dreams and I suggest that Rhys Davids' reading of the inscription on Bharhut stupa is the correct one. ("According to the *Milindapanha* these are (1) dreams caused by physical stress, (2) by psychological irritability, (3) by spirits, (4) because of mental clarity and (5) prophetic dreams (Mil.II,298). It also says that dreams mainly occur in the interval either between falling asleep or waking up (*okkante middhe*) and deep sleep (*asampatte bhavnge*, Mil.II,299), a fact confirmed by science.")

Sage Asita explaining Māyā's dream, Kushan, Gandhara, India, 2nd-3rd C. Indian Sculpture-The Asian Arts Museum of Sanfrancisco, California, ACSAA

Government Museum, Chennai. "Māyā's Dream and Interpretation (Period III) On the left panel, *Māyā* is shown reclining. Below the couch four women attendents are shown half asleep. Four turbaned men of rank stand as guards at the four corners of the couch. In the right panel *Māyā* is seen seated on a small wicker seat in front of the King while a *Brahmana* is seated to the left of the king. The *Brahmana* holds up his two fingers suggesting two possibilities regarding the future of the child to be born. The two possibilities are that either he would be a monarch, if he adopted the life of a house-holder or he would become the Buddha, if he renounced the world."

Detail of the top of the sandstone Vedica pillar, half-roundel at top of vedika pillar with composite creatures in relief:

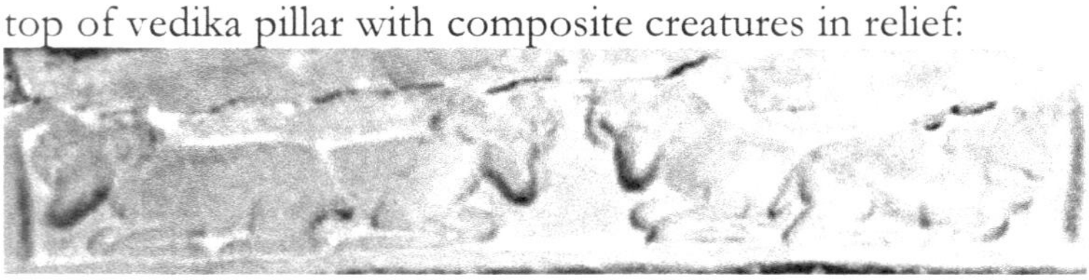

The top register o this relief shows ligatured antelopes back-to-back; the next register from the top shows a bull ligatured to a makara (crocodile with curved fish tail).

Detail of the roundel:

Borobodur Indonesia 3rd level (gallery); volcanic rock; wall east side, south end Māyā's dream bove: Queen Māyā dreams (from *Lalitavistara*); below: Sudhana learns about Manohara from his mother (from Jataka). Saildendra Dynasty (778- 926) ca. late 8th century CE, 750 CE - 799 CE.

A makara and merchant Ship Scene, Borobudur

Sarasvati -- divinity of knowledge -- holding a veena on her left hand. Sarasvati sculpture from Uttar Pradesh. 6th century. Sandstone. H 84.2 cm. Museum of Fine Arts,

Houston. *Sarasvati* 33 1/8 x 24 1/2 x 7 3/4 inches "Sarasvati is the Hindu goddess of learning and the arts. She is the consort of Brahma, the god of creation and source of all knowledge. Because Brahma created Sarasvati from his own flesh and blood, she is often regarded as the embodiment of knowledge and creativity. This sandstone representation draws attention to Sarasvati's importance as the divine patron of the arts. As in many depictions, she is seen here seated upon a sacred lotus blossom, the symbol of supreme knowledge and spiritual truth. An avid musician, Sarasvati is shown playing a musical instrument called a *veena.* The neck and base of the veena can still be seen on this figure, though the body of the instrument is no longer intact. Sarasvati is depicted with a serene smile as she sways gently to the music. Her attendants dance around her, one accompanying Sarasvati on a flute and another on a small drum. Because of Sarasvati's importance in all things intellectual and artistic, many students, scholars, poets, musicians, painters, and sculptors look to her for guidance and support."

Interpretation of Māyā's dream by a Brahman.
Borobodur Indonesia Above: a brahman interprets QueenMāyā's dream (from *Lalitavistara*); below: Sudhana visits King Druma

(from Jataka)

Buddha annunciates in the form of Mahā Māyā's dream in which Māyā sees a white elephant descending from the skies to enter her womb. The would-be son was to be a Universal Emperor or a Buddha. Dream turned into reality, she goes to her parents in Devahrada, the child Gautama is born as she supports herself by the branch of a tree in Lumbini park and the Buddha was turning the wheel to be Lord.

Queen Maha Māyā was the daughter of King Anjana of the Koliyas. The Koliyan princess was named Mahā Māyā. Māyā and Suddhodana ruled over the Sakyas, a warrior tribe living next to the Koliya tribe, in the north of India, in what is now known as Nepal.

Interpreting the dream, Bauddham literature has this narrative:

"(Queen Māyā)...had a vivid dream. She felt herself being carried away by four devas (spirits) to Lake Anotatta in the Himalayas. After bathing her in the lake, the devas clothed her in heavenly cloths, anointed her with perfumes, and bedecked her with divine flowers. Soon after a white elephant, holding a white lotus flower in its trunk, appeared and went round her three times, entering her womb through her right side. Finally the elephant disappeared and the queen awoke, knowing she had been delivered an important message, as the elephant is a symbol of greatness in Nepal. The next day, early in the morning, the queen told the king about the dream. The king was puzzled and sent for some wise men to discover the meaning of the dream.The wise men said, "Your Majesty, you are very lucky. The devas have chosen our queen as the mother of the Purest-One and the child will become a very great being." The king and queen were very happy when they heard this. They were so pleased that they invited many of the noblemen in the country to the palace to a feast to tell them the good news. Even the needy were not forgotten. Food and clothes were given to the poor people in celebration. The whole kingdom waited eagerly for the birth of the new prince, and Queen Māyā enjoyed a happy and healthy pregnancy, living a pure life for herself and her unborn child."[193]

The dream is rendered as a metaphor in texts and in sculptures. One sculptural representation comes with every book from Sahitya Akademi, India with a note:

The sculpture reproduced on the end-paper depicts a scene where three soothsayers are interpreting to King Suddhodana the dream of Queen Māyā, mother of Lord Buddha. Below them is seated a scribe recording the interpretation. This is perhaps the earliest available pictorial record of the art of writing in India.

"The Dream of Queen Māyā" Sanchi Stupa torana, 1st c. Dream of elephant entering by her side.

Musée des Arts Asiatiques de San Francisco Asie du Sud jusqu'en

600 Asie du Sud (Inde - Pakistan - Bangladesh - Sri Lanka) Troisième étage - Section 1 Sept scènes de la vie de Bouddha Elément 7 sur 28 Arts d'Extrême-Orient Sculpture (Bas-relief) 28 cm X 25 cm X 5 cm Object ID: B64S5 Avery Brundage Collection.

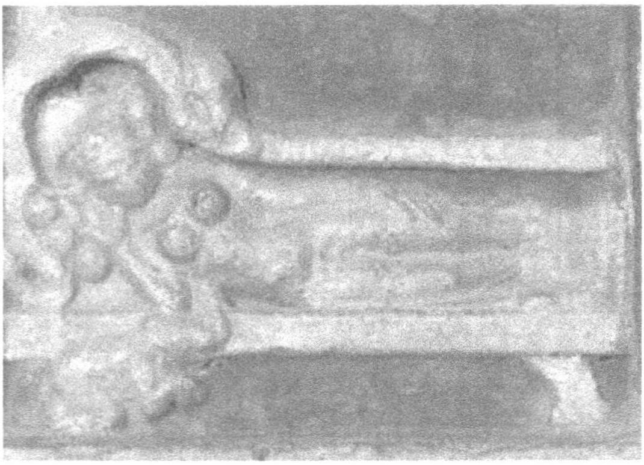

Gandhara.Designation: The Conception of the Buddha-to-be in Queen Māyā's dream. "And lying down on the royal couch, Queen Māyā fell asleep and dreamed the following dream: Four guardian angels came and lifted her up, together with her couch, and took her away to the Himalaya Mountains. . . Now the Buddha-to-be had become a superb white elephant and was wandering about at no great distance. . . . And three times he walked round his mother's couch, with his right side towards it, and striking her on her right side, he seemed to enter her womb. Thus the conception took place in the Midsummer Festival." (Adapted from Henry Clark Warren's 1896 translation of an ancient Buddhist text)

Queen Māyā's white elephant dream, and the conception of the Buddha. Gandhara, 2-3rd century CE.

Ananda temple revering the Buddha's life. Stone sculpture. Southeast of Tharabar gate. 1105 CE. Region: Old Bagan, Myanmar. (King Kyanzittha).

The descent of Buddha, Bharhut. British Library. Beglar, Joseph David, 1875

Buddha's birth (Bharhut) Brahmi text: bhagavato rukdanta. Gen. Cunningham reads the letters as Bhagavato *okkanti* (?ukkanti); thus, the text simply says: 'descent of the blessed one'. Association with the elephant in Māyā's dream may be a figure of speech to explain the incarnation, avatāra. General Cunning-ham says of the description placed above this sculpture : ' Above it in large characters is inscribed Bhagavato rukdanta, which may perhaps be translated, "Buddha as the sounding elephant," from ru, to sound, to make a particular sort of sound.' Now the first word of the inscription is in the genitive case, so that if the second word could mean an elephant, the whole would signify, ' The Buddha's elephant.' But the characters which General Cunningham reads rukdanta are, I venture to suggest, *okkanti* (^ ukkanti); and the inscription simply says, ' The descent of the blessed One.' As I have pointed out in 'Buddhism'.[194]

This interpretation of the Brahmi text is rejected by Rhys Davids. **Brāhmī inscription says *okkanti*, NOT *rukdanti* (falsely claimed by Cunningham)**

"Plate xxviii has a scene entitled *Bhagavato Okkanti* (The descent of the blessed one), in illustration of Māyā Devi's dream...Footnote 7: General Cunningham's reading of this inscription as Bhagavato *rukdanta* seems to me to be incorrect, and his translation of it ('Buddha as the sounding elephant') to be grammatically impossible."[195]

Gloss: *okkanti* explained in Pali:

Avakkanti (f.) [fr. avakkamati] entry, appearance, coming down into, opportunity for rebirth S ii.66 (nāmarūpassa); iii.46 (pañcannaŋ indriyānaŋ); Pug 13 (= okkantinibbatti pātubhāvo PugA 184); Kvu 142 (nāmarūpassa); Miln 123 (gabbhassa). *okkanta* [pp. of okkamati] coming on, approaching, taking place D ii.12; Miln 299 (middhe okkante).

Cognates: ā´kramatē ' approaches ' RV., ' ascends ' AV., ' seizes ' MBh.[√kram] Pa. *akkamati* 'approaches, treads on, attacks '; Pk. *akkamaï* ' presses, attacks '; N. *ā̃knu* ' to venture, dare ' (?); Si. *äkmenavā* ' to be crushed, be seized ' der. tr. (CDIAL 1017).

okkanti (f.) [fr. okkamati] entry (lit. descent), appearance, coming to be. Usually in stock phrase jāṭi sañjāti o. nibbatti M iii.249; S ii.3; iii.225; Nd2 257; Pug A 184. Also in gabbh° entry into the womb DA i.130. okkantika (adj.) [fr. okkanti] coming into existence again and again, recurring. Only as epithet of pīti, joy. The opposite is khaṇika, momentary Vism 143 = DhsA 115 (*Expositor*153 trsls. "flooding"). Okkanta [pp. of okkamati] coming on,approaching, taking place D ii.12; Miln 299 (middhe okkante).

The author of the translation of Lalita-vistara, Rajendralal Mitra comments about the references to Buddha as 'Bhagavato':

"*Bhagavan*, nominative singular of the crude form Bhagavat -- Bhagava, Pali, Btchcom Idandasa, Tibetan. The technology of the Buddhists is to a great extent borrowed from the literature of the Brahmans. The *Vija-mantra* of Buddha begins with *Om*, their metaphysical terms are exclusively Hindu, and the names of most of their divinities are taken from the Hindu pantheon.
The word Bhagavan, which, according to the *Abhidharma-kosha-vyakhya*, a Bauddha work of great repute, "is not an arbitrary or superflous, but the most appropriate title of Buddha," has been, by the Vedas, used to designate the Deity's self. It is said in the *Vishnu Purana*, in accordance with the interpretation of Yaksa, that, "the essence of the Supreme is defined by the term *Bhagavan*: the word *Bhagavan* is the denomination of the primeval and eternal god: and he who fully understands the meaning of that expression is possessed of holy wisdom, the sum and substance of the three Vedas. The word Bhagavan is a convenient form to be used in the

adoration of that Supreme Being, to whom no terms is applicable, and therefore Bhagavan expresses that supreme spirit, which is individual, almighty, and the cause of all things."

"The dissyllable *Bhaga* indicates the six properties, dominion, might, glory, splendour, wisdom, and dispassion. The purport of that *va* is that elemental spirit in which all beings exist, and which exists in all beings." (The usual itymon of the word, however, is *Bhaga* with the possessive affix.) "This word, therefore, which is the general denomination of an adorable object, is not used in reference to the Supreme in a general, but a special signification. When applied to any other (person) it is used in its customary or general import. In the latter case, it may purport one who knows the origin and end and revolutions of beings, and what is wisdom, what ignorance. In the former it denotes wisdom, energy, dominion, might, glory, without end, and without defect. All the Sutras invest S'akya Sinha with this title, and, next to Tathagata, it is perhaps the most common appellation of Buddha."

Lalitavistara (trans. "The Play in Full" or "Extensive Play"): Chapter 6 The Bodhisattva enters into the human world via the womb of Queen Māyā, where he resides for the duration of the pregnancy within a beautiful temple, enjoying the happiness of absorption. On Lalitavistara: http://www.ibiblio.org/radha/rpub007.htm

The birth of the Buddha is described in Chapter 6 ६ गर्भावक्रान्तिपरिवर्तः षष्ठः *6 garbhāvakrāntiparivartaḥ ṣaṣṭhaḥ | That is, the incarnation in birth.*

Māyā's dream is part of many narratives. One such narrative is: The Illustrated Jataka & Other Stories of the Buddha by C.B. Varma excerpted:

"The day when the Buddha was to be conceived she kept fast; and at night she had a dream. In her dream she saw that the four *devas,* called the Chatumaharajas, took her to the Himava and placed her on a bed under a Sal tree. Then the wives of the *devas* came and bathed her in the Lake Anottata and dressed her in divine robes. They then took her to a golden palace and laid her in a magnificent couch, where the Bodhisatta in the form of a white elephant holding a white lotus in his resplendent trunk entered her womb through her right side. That was a full-moon day of Uttara Asalha to mark the beginning of a seven-day festival. She, too, had participated in the festival. Furthermore, on that day she did not sleep with her husband.

Mahā Māyā musing at her dream

"Next day, she told the dream to the king, who in turn consulted the court astrologers, and from them heard the prophecy that the child would either be universal monarch or a Buddha."

King Suddhodana and Mahā Māyā analysing the dream

Jatakanidana 50 also has an account of Māyā's dream.

A red sandstone head of the Buddha from Mathura, 2nd Century CE.

Encyclopaedia Britannica reproduces the following images titled Dream of Māyā"

Dream of Mahā Māyā presaging the Buddha's birth, marble relief from Nagarjunakonda, Andhra Pradesh state, India, Amaravati style, *c.* 3rd century *ce*; in the Indian Museum, Calcutta (Kolkata).

Mahā Māyā dreaming of the white elephant, Gandhara relief, 2nd century CE; in the British Museum.

Another version of the birth in sculpture:

A version in text:

६ गर्भावक्रान्तिपरिवर्तः षष्ठः

6 garbhāvakrāntiparivartaḥ ṣaṣṭhaḥ |

iti hi bhikṣavaḥ śiśirakālavinirgate vaiśākhamāse viśākhānakṣatrānugate ṛtupravare vasantakālasamaye taruvarapatrākīrṇe varapravarapuṣpasaṁkusumite śītoṣṇatamorajovigate mṛduśādvale susaṁsthite tribhuvanajyeṣṭho lokamahito vyavalokya ṛtukālasamaye pañcadaśyāṁ pūrṇamāsyāṁ poṣadhagṛhītāyā mātuḥ puṣyanakṣatrayogena bodhisattvastuṣitavarabhavanāccyutvā smṛtaḥ saṁprajānan pāṇḍuro gajapoto bhūtvā ṣaḍdanta indragopakaśirāḥ suvarṇarājīdantaḥ sarvāṅgapratyaṅgo'hīnendriyo jananyā dakṣiṇāyāṁ kukṣāvavakrāmat | avakrāntaśca sa dakṣiṇāvacaro'bhūnna jātu vāmāvacaraḥ | māyādevī sukhaśayanaprasuptā imaṁ svapnamapaśyat—

himarajatanibhaśca ṣaḍviṣāṇaḥ
sucaraṇa cārubhujaḥ suraktaśīrṣaḥ |
udaramupagato gajapradhāno
lalitagatirdṛḍhavajragātrasaṁdhiḥ | | 1 | |

na ca mama sukha jātu evarūpaṁ
dṛṣṭamapi śrutaṁ nāpi cānubhūtam |
kāyasukhacittasaukhyabhāvā
yathariva dhyānasamāhitā abhūvam | |2| |
atha khalu māyādevī ābharaṇavigalitavasanā prahlāditakāyacittā prītiprāmodyaprasādapratilabdhā śayanavaratalādutthāya nārīgaṇaparivṛtā puraskṛtā prāsādavaraśikharādavatīrya yenāśokavanikā tenopajagāma | sā aśokavanikāyāṁ sukhopaviṣṭā rājñaḥ śuddhodanasya dūtaṁ preṣayati sma- āgacchatu devo devī te draṣṭukāmeti | |
atha sa rājā śuddhodanastadvacanaṁ śrutvā praharṣitamanā ākampitaśarīro bhadrāsanādutthāya amātyanaigamapārṣadyabandhujanaparivṛto yenāśokavanikā tenopasaṁkrāmat, upasaṁkrāntaśca na śaknoti sma aśokavanikāṁ praveṣṭum | gurutaramivātmānaṁ manyate sma | aśokavanikādvāre sthito muhūrtaṁ saṁcintya tasyāṁ velāyāmimāṁ gāthāmabhāṣata—
na smari raṇaśauṇḍi mūrdhasaṁsthasya mahyam
eva guru śarīraṁ manyamī yādṛśo'dya |
svakulagṛhamadya na prabhomi praveṣṭuṁ
kimiha mama bhave'ṅgo kānva pṛccheya cāham | |3| | iti | |
atha khalu śuddhāvāsakāyikā devaputrā gaganatalagatā ardhakāyamabhinirmāya rājānaṁ gāthayādhyabhāṣanta—
vratatapaguṇayuktastisralokeṣu pūjyo
maitrakaruṇalābhī puṇyajñānābhiṣiktaḥ |
tuṣitapuri cyavitvā bodhisattvo mahātmā
nṛpati tava sutatvaṁ māyakukṣaupapannaḥ | |4| |
daśanakha tada kṛtvā svaṁ śiraṁ kampayanto
nṛpatiranupraviṣṭaścitrikārānuyuktaḥ |
māya tada nirīkṣya mānadarpopanītāṁ
vadahi kurumi kiṁ te kiṁ prayogo bhaṇāhi | |5| |
devyāha—
himarajatanikāśaścandrasūryātirekaḥ
sucaraṇa suvibhaktaḥ ṣaḍviṣāṇo mahātmā |
gajavaru dṛḍhasaṁdhirvajrakalpaḥ surūpaḥ
udari mama praviṣṭastasya hetuṁ śruṇuṣva | |6| |
vitimira trisahasrāṁ paśyamī bhrājamānāṁ

devanayuta devā ye stuvantī sayānā |
na ca mama khiladoṣo naiva roṣo na moho
dhyānasukhasamaṅgī jānamī śāntacittā | | 7 | |
sādhu nṛpati śīghraṁ brāhmaṇānānayāsmin
vedasupinapāṭhā ye gṛheṣū vidhijñāḥ |
supinu mama hi yemaṁ vyākarī tattvayuktaṁ
kimida mama bhaveyā śreyu pāpaṁ kulasya | | 8 | |
vacanamimu śruṇitvā pārthivastatkṣaṇena
brāhmaṇa kṛtavedānānayacchāstrapāṭhān |
māya purata sthitvā brāhmaṇānāmavocat
supina mayi ha dṛṣṭastasya hetuṁ śṛṇotha | | 9 | |
brāhmaṇā āhuḥ-brūhi devi tvayā kīdṛśaṁ svapnaṁ dṛṣṭam | śrutvā jñāsyāmaḥ |
devyāha—
himarajatanikāśaścandrasūryātirekaḥ
sucaraṇa suvibhaktaḥ ṣaḍviṣāṇo mahātmā |
gajavaru dṛḍhasaṁdhirvajrakalpaḥ surūpaḥ
udari mama praviṣṭastasya hetuṁ śṛṇotha | | 10 | |
vacanamimu śruṇitvā brāhmaṇā evamāhuḥ
prīti vipula cintyā nāsti pāpaṁ kulasya |
putra tava janesī lakṣaṇairbhūṣitāṅgaṁ
rājakulakulīnaṁ cakravarti mahātmaṁ | | 11 | |
sa ca pura vijahitvā kāmarājyaṁ ca gehaṁ
pravrajita nirapekṣaḥ sarvalokānukampī |
buddho bhavati eṣo dakṣiṇīyastriloke
amṛtarasavareṇā tarpayet sarvalokam | | 12 | |
vyākaritva giraṁ saumyāṁ bhuktvā pārthivabhojanam |
ācchādanāni codgṛhya prakrāntā brāhmaṇāstataḥ | | 13 | |
iti hi bhikṣavo rājā śuddhodano brāhmaṇebhyo lakṣaṇanaimittikavaipañcakebhyaḥ svapnādhyāyīpāṭhakebhyaḥ pratiśrutya hṛṣṭastuṣṭa udagra āttamanāḥ pramuditaḥ prītisaumanasyajātastān brāhmaṇān prabhūtena khādanīyabhojanīyāsvādanīyena saṁtarpya saṁpravāryācchādanāni ca datvā visarjayati sma | tasyāṁ velāyāṁ kapilavastuni mahānagare caturṣu nagaradvāreṣu sarvanagaracatvaraśṛṅgāṭakeṣu ca dānaṁ dāpayati sma

annamannārthikebhyaḥ, pānaṁ pānārthikebhyaḥ, vastrāṇi vastrārthikebhyaḥ, yānāni yānārthikebhyaḥ | evaṁ gandhamālyavilepanaśayyopāśrayaṁ prājīvikaṁ prājīvikārthibhyo yāvadeva bodhisattvasya pūjākarmaṇe ||

atha khalu bhikṣavo rājñaḥ śuddhodanasyaitadabhavat- katamasmin gṛhe māyādevī sukhamanupakliṣṭā viharediti | atha tatkṣaṇameva catvāro mahārājāno rājānaṁ śuddhodanamupasaṁkramyaivamāhuḥ—

alpotsuko deva bhava sukhaṁ tiṣṭha upekṣako |

vayaṁ hi bodhisattvasya veśma vai māpayāmahe || 14 ||

atha khalu śakro devānāmindro rājānaṁ śuddhodanamupasaṁkramyaivamāha—

hīnā vimānā pālānāṁ trayatriṁśānamuttamāḥ |

vaijayantasamaṁ veśma bodhisattvasya dāmyaham || 15 ||

atha khalu suyāmo devaputro rājānaṁ śuddhodanamusaṁkramyaivamāha—

madīyaṁ bhavanaṁ dṛṣṭvā vismitāḥ śakrakoṭayaḥ |

suyāmabhavanaṁ śrīmadbodhisattvasya dāmyaham || 16 ||

atha khalu saṁtuṣito devaputro rājānaṁ śuddhodanamupasaṁkramyaivamāha—

yatraiva uṣitaḥ pūrvaṁ tuṣiteṣu mahāyaśāḥ |

tadeva bhavanaṁ ramyaṁ bodhisattvasya dāmyaham || 17 ||

atha khalu sunirmito devaputro rājānaṁ śuddhodanamupasaṁkramyaivamāha—

manomayamahaṁ śrīmadvaśma tadratanāmayam |

bodhisattvasya pūjārthamupaneṣyāmi pārthiva || 18 ||

atha khalu paranirmitavaśavartī devaputro rājānaṁ śuddhodanamupasaṁkramyaivamāha—

yāvantaḥ kāmadhātusthā vimānāḥ śobhanāḥ kvacit |

bhābhiste madvimānasya bhavantyabhihataprabhāḥ || 19 ||

tat prayacchāmyahaṁ śrīmadveśma ratnamayaṁ śubham |

bodhisattvasya pūjārthamānayiṣyāmi pārthiva || 20 ||

divyaiḥ puṣpaiḥ samākīrṇaṁ divyagandhopavāsitam |

upanāmayiṣye vipulaṁ yatra devī vasiṣyati || 21 ||

iti hi bhikṣavaḥ sarvaiḥ kāmāvacarraidaiveśvarairbodhisattvasya pūjārthaṁ kapilāhvaye mahāpuravare svakasvakāni gṛhāṇi māpitānyabhūvan | rājñā

capi śuddhodanena manuṣyātikrāntaṁ divyāsaṁprāptaṁ gṛhataraṁ pratisaṁskāritamabhūt| tatra bodhisattvo mahāsattvo mahāvyūhasya samādheranubhāvena sarveṣu teṣu gṛheṣu māyādevīmupadarśayati sma| abhyantaragataśca bodhisattvo māyādevyāḥ kukṣau dakṣiṇe pārśve paryaṅkamābhujya niṣaṇṇo'bhūt| sarve ca te deveśvarā ekaikamevaṁ saṁjānīte sma-mamaiva gṛhe bodhisattvamātā prativasati nānyatreti||
tatredamucyate—

mahāvyūhāya sthitaḥ samādhiye
acintiyā nirmita nirmiṇitvā|
sarveṣa devānabhiprāya pūritā
nṛpasya pūrṇaśca tadā manorathaḥ||22||

atha khalu tasyāṁ devaparṣadi keṣāṁciddevaputrāṇāmetadabhavat-ye'pi tāvaccāturmahārājakāyikā devāste'pi tāvanmanuṣyāśrayagatatvena nirvidyāpakramanti| kaḥ punarvādo ye tadanye udāratamā devāḥ trāyatriṁśā vā yāmā vā tuṣitā vā| tatkathaṁ hi nāma sarvalokābhyudgato bodhisattvaḥ śucirnirāmagandhaḥ sattvaratnaḥ saṁtuṣitāddevanikāyāccyutvā durgandhe manuṣyāśraye daśamāsān mātuḥ kukṣau sthita iti||

atha khalvāyuṣmānānando buddhānubhāvena bhagavantametadavocat-āścaryaṁ bhagavan yāvajjugupsanīyaśca mātṛgrāmastathāgatenokto yāvadrāgacaritaśca| idaṁ tu bhagavan āścaryataram| kathaṁ hi nāma sarvalokābhyudgato bhagavān pūrvaṁ bodhisattvabhūta eva tuṣitāddevanikāyāccyavitvā manuṣyāśraye (durgandhe) māturdakṣiṇe (pārśve) kukṣāvupapanna iti| nāhaṁ bhagavan idamutsahe evaṁ vaktaṁ yathaiva pūrve bhagavatā vyākṛtamiti| bhagavānāha-icchasi tvamānanda ratnavyūhaṁ bodhisattvaparibhogaṁ draṣṭuṁ yo mātuḥ kukṣigatasya bodhisattvasya paribhogo'bhūt| ānanda āha-ayamasya bhagavan kālaḥ, ayaṁ sugata samayaḥ, yattathāgatastaṁ bodhisattvaparibhogamupadarśayed yaṁ dṛṣṭvā prītiṁ vetsyāmaḥ||

atha khalu bhagavāṁstathārūpanimittamakarot, yad brahmā sahāpatiḥ sārdhamaṣṭaṣaṣṭibrahmaśatasahasrairbrahmaloke'ntarhito bhagavataḥ purataḥ pratyasthāt| sa bhagavataḥ pādau śirasābhivandya bhagavantaṁ tripradakṣiṇīkṛtyaikānte'sthāt prāñjalībhūto bhagavantaṁ namasyan| tatra khalu bhagavān jānanneva brahmāṇaṁ sahāpatimāmantrayate sma-gṛhītastvayā brahman sa bodhisattvaparibhogo daśamāsiko yo mama pūrvaṁ bodhisattvabhūtasya mātuḥ kukṣigatasyābhūt | brahmā āha-evametadbhagavan, evametat sugata | bhagavānāha-kva sa idānīṁ brahman? upadarśaya tam | brahmā cāha-brahmaloke sa bhagavan | bhagavānāha-tena hi tvaṁ brahman upadarśaya taṁ daśamāsikaṁ bodhisattvaparibhogam, jñāsyanti kiyatsaṁskṛtamiti | |

atha khalu brahmā sahāpatistān brāhmaṇānetadavocat-tiṣṭhatu tāvadbhavanto yāvadvayaṁ ratnavyūhaṁ bodhisattvaparibhogamānayiṣyāmaḥ | |

atha khalu brahmā sahāpatirbhagavataḥ pādau śirasābhivanditvā bhagavataḥ purato'ntarhitastatkṣaṇameva brahmaloke pratyasthāt | |

atha khalu brahmā sahāpatiḥ subrahmāṇaṁ devaputrametadavocat-gaccha tvaṁ mārṣā ito brahmalokamupādāya yāvattrāyatriṁśadbhavanam-śabdamudīraya, ghoṣamanuśrāvaya | ratnavyūhaṁ bodhisattvaparibhogaṁ vayaṁ tathāgatasyāntikamupanāmayiṣyāmaḥ | yo yuṣmākaṁ draṣṭukāmaḥ sa śīghramāgacchatviti | |

atha khalu brahmā sahāpatiścaturaśītyā devakoṭyā nayutaśatasahasraḥ sārdhaṁ taṁ ratnavyūhaṁ bodhisattvaparibhogaṁ parigṛhya mahati brāhme vimāne triyojanaśatike pratiṣṭhāpyānekairdaivakoṭīnayutaśatasahasraiḥ samantato'nuparivārya jambūdvīpamavatārayati sma | |

tena khalu punaḥ samayena kāmāvacarāṇāṁ devānāṁ mahāsaṁnipāto'bhūt bhagavatsakāśe gantum | sa khalu puna ratnavyūho bodhisattvaparibhogo divyairvastrairdivyairmālyairdivyairgandhairdivyaiḥ puṣpairdivyairvādyairdivyaiśca paribhaugairabhisaṁskṛto'bhūt | tāvanmaheśākhyaiśca devaiḥ parivṛto'bhūd yacchakro devānāmindraḥ sumerau(samudre) sthitvā dūrata eva mukhe tālacchatrakaṁ dattvā śīrṣavyavalokanenānuvilokayati sma unmeṣadhyāyikayā vā | na ca śaknoti sma draṣṭum | tatkasmāt? maheśākhyā hi devā brāhmaṇāḥ | itarāstrāyatriṁśā yāmāstuṣitā nirmāṇaratayaḥ paranirmitavaśavartinaḥ | kaḥ punarvādaḥ śakro devānāmindraḥ | mohaṁ te vai yānti sma | |

atha khalu bhagavāṁstaṁ divyaṁ vādyanirghoṣamantardhāpayati sma | tatkasmāt? yatsahaśravaṇādeva jāmbudvīpakā manuṣyā unmādamāpatsyanta iti | |

atha khalu catvāro mahārājānaḥ śakraṁ devānāmindramupasaṁkramyaivamāhuḥ-kathaṁ devānāmindra kariṣyāmo na labhāmahe ratnavyūhaṁ bodhisattvaparibhogaṁ draṣṭum| sa tānavocat-kimahaṁ mārṣāḥ kariṣyāmi? ahamapi na labhe draṣṭum| api tu khalu punarmārṣā bhagavatsamīpamupanītaṁ drakṣyāmaḥ| te tadā āhuḥ-tena hi devānāmindra tathā kuru yathāsya kṣipraṁ darśanaṁ bhavet| śakra āha-āgamayata mārṣā muhūrtaṁ yāvadatikrāntātikrāntatamā devaputrā bhagavantaṁ pratisaṁmodayante sma| tadekānte sthitvā śīrṣonmiñjitakayā bhagavantamanuvilokayanti sma||

atha khalu brahmā sahāpatiḥ sārdhaṁ taiścaturaśītyā devakoṭīnayutaśatasahasraistaṁ ratnavyūhaṁ bodhisattvaparibhogaṁ gṛhītvā yena bhagavāṁstenopasaṁkrāmayati sma| sa khalu puna ratnavyūho bodhisattvaparibhogo'bhirūpaḥ prāsādiko darśanīyaścaturasraścatuṣṭhūṇaḥ| upariṣṭācca kūṭāgārasamalaṁkṛtaḥ| evaṁpramāṇaḥ tadyathāpi nāma ṣaṇmāsajāto dāraka uccaistvena| tasya khalu punaḥ kūṭāgārasya madhye paryaṅkaḥ prajñaptaḥ tadyathāpi nāma ṣaṇmāsajātasya dārakasya bhittīphalakaḥ| sa khalu puna ratnavyūho bodhisattvaparibhoga evaṁ varṇasaṁsthāno yasya na kaścit sadevake loke samārake sabrahmake sadṛśo'sti ākṛtyā vā varṇena vā| devāḥ khalvapi taṁ dṛṣṭvā āścaryaprāptā abhuvan| cakṣūṁṣi teṣāṁ vibhramanti sma| sa ca tathāgatasyāntika upanīto'tīva bhāsate tapati virocate sma| tadyathāpi nāma dvinirdhāntaṁ suvarṇaṁ kuśalena karmakāreṇa supariniṣṭhitamapagatakācadoṣam, evaṁ (tasmin samaye) sa kūṭāgāro virājate sma| tasmin khalu punarbodhisattvaparibhoge paryaṅkaḥ prajñapto yasya sadevake loke nāsti kaścit sadṛśo varṇena vā saṁsthānena vā anyatra kambugrīvāyā bodhisattvasya| yat khalu mahābrahmaṇā cīvaraṁ prāvṛtamabhūt, tattasya bodhisattvaparyaṅkasyāgrato na bhāsate sma tadyathāpi nāma vātavṛṣṭyābhihataḥ kṛṣṇakambalaḥ| sa khalu punaḥ kūṭāgāra uragasāracandanamayo yasyaikasuvarṇadharaṇī sāhasraṁ lokadhātuṁ mūlyaṁ kṣamate, tathāvidhenoragasāracandanena sa kūṭāgāraḥ samantādanupaliptaḥ| tādṛśa eva dvitīyaḥ kūṭāgāraḥ kṛto yastasmin prathame kūṭāgāre'bhyantarataḥ asakto'baddhasthitaḥ| tādṛśa eva tṛtīyo'pi kūṭāgāro yastasmin dvitīye kūṭāgāre'bhyantare'sakto'baddhasthitaḥ| sa ca paryaṅkastasmin gandhamaye tṛtīye kūṭāgāre vyavasthitaḥ saṁpraticchannaḥ| tasya khalu punaruragasāracandanasyaivaṁrūpo varṇaḥ tadyathāpi nāma abhijātasya nīlaivaḍūryasya| tasya khalu punargandhakūṭāgārasyopari samantādyāvanti kāniciddivyātikrāntāni puṣpāṇi santi, tāni sarvāṇi tasmin kūṭāgāre bodhisattvasya pūrvakuśalamūlavipākenānuprāptānyeva jāyante sma| sa khalu puna ratnavyūho bodhisattvaparibhogo dṛḍhasāro'bhedyo vajropamaḥ sparśena ca kācilindikasukhasaṁsparśaḥ| tasmin khalu puna ratnavyūhe bodhisattvaparibhoge ye kecit kāmāvacarāṇāṁ devānāṁ bhavanavyūhāste sarve tasmin saṁdṛśyante sma||

yāmeva ca rātriṁ bodhisattvo mātuḥ kukṣimavakrāntastāmeva rātrimadha āpaskandhamupādāya aṣṭaṣaṣṭiyojanaśatasahasrāṇi mahāpṛthivīṁ bhittvā yāvad brahmalokaṁ padmabhyudgatamabhūt| na ca kaścittaṁ padmaṁ paśyati sma anyatra sārathinarottamāddaśaśatasāhasrikācca mahābrahmaṇaḥ| yacceha trisāhasramahāsāhasralokadhātāvojo vā maṇḍo va raso vā, tatsarvaṁ tasmin mahāpadme madhubinduḥ saṁtiṣṭhate sma|| tamenaṁ mahābrahmā śubhe vaiḍūryabhājane prakṣipya bodhisattvasyopanāmayati sma| taṁ bodhisattvaḥ parigṛhya bhuṅkte sma mahābrahmaṇo'nukampāmupādāya| nāsti sa kaścit sattvaḥ sattvanikāye yasya sa ojobinduḥ paribhuktaḥ samyak sukhena pariṇāmedanyatra caramabhavikādbodhisattvāt sarvabodhisattvabhūmiparipūrṇāt| kasya ca karmaṇo vipākena sa ojobindurbodhisattvasyopatiṣṭhate sma? dīrgharātraṁ khalvapi bodhisattvena pūrvaṁ bodhisattvacaryāṁ caratā glānebhyaḥ sattvebhyo bhaiṣajyaṁ dattamāśatparāṇāṁ sattvānāmāśāḥ paripūritāḥ, śaraṇāgatāśca na parityaktāḥ, nityaṁ cāgrapuṣpamagraphalamagrarasaṁ tathāgatebhyastathāgatacaityebhyastathāgataśrāvakasaṁghebhyo mātāpitṛbhyaśca dattvā paścādātmanā paribhuktam| tasya karmaṇo vipākena mahābrahmā bodhisattvasya taṁ madhubindumupanāmayati sma||

tasmin khalu punaḥ kūṭāgāre yāni kānicit santyatikrāntātikrāntāni māyāguṇaratikrīḍāsamavasṛtasthānāni, tāni sarvāṇi tasmin prādurbhāvāni saṁdṛśyante sma bodhisattvasya pūrvakarmavipākena||

tasmin khalu puna ratnavyūhe bodhisattvaparibhoge śatasahasravyūhaṁ nāma vāsoyugaṁ prādurbhūtam| na sa kaścitsattvaḥ sattvanikāye saṁvidyate yasya tatprādurbhavedanyatra caramabhavikād bodhisattvāt| na ca te kecana udārodārā rūpaśabdagandharasasparśā ye tasmin kūṭāgāre na saṁdṛśyante sma| sacetkūṭāgāraparibhoga evaṁ suparibhoga evaṁ supariniṣpannaḥ sāntarabahirevaṁ supariniṣṭhita evaṁ mṛdukaśca| tadyathāpi nāma kācilindikasukhasaṁsparśo nidarśanamātreṇa, na tu tasyopamā saṁvidyate | dharmatā khalveṣā bodhisattvasya pūrvakeṇa ca praṇidhānena iyaṁ cetanā ṛddhāvavaśyaṁ bodhisattvena mahāsattvena manuṣyaloka upapattavyamabhiniṣkramya cānuttarāṁ samyaksaṁbodhimabhisaṁbudhya dharmacakraṁ pravartayitavyam | yasyā mātuḥ kukṣāvupapattirbhavati, tasyā dakṣiṇe kukṣāvādita eva ratnavyūhakūṭāgāro'bhinirvartate | paścādbodhisattvastuṣitebhyaścyuttvā tasmin kūṭāgāre paryaṅkaniṣaṇṇaḥ saṁbhavati | na hi caramabhavikasya bodhisattvasya kalalārbudaghanapeśībhāvaṁ kāyaḥ saṁtiṣṭhate sma | atha tarhi sarvāṅgapratyaṅgalakṣaṇasaṁpannaḥ saṁniṣaṇṇa eva prādurbhavati | svapnāntaragatā ca bodhisattvamātā māyādevī mahānāgakuñjaramavakrāntaṁ saṁjānīte sma | |

tasya khalu punastathā niṣaṇṇasya śakro devānāmindraścatvāraśca mahārājāno'ṣṭāviṁśatiśca mahāyakṣasenāpatayo guhyakādhipatiśca nāma yakṣakulaṁ yato vajrapāṇerutpattiste bodhisattvaṁ mātuḥ kukṣigataṁ viditvā satataṁ samitamanubaddhā bhavanti sma | santi khalu punaścatasro bodhisattvaparicārakā devatāḥ-utkhalī ca nāma samutkhalī ca nāma dhvajavatī ca nāma prabhāvatī ca nāma | tā api bodhisattvaṁ mātuḥ kukṣigataṁ viditvā satataṁ samitaṁ rakṣanti sma | śakro'pi devānāmindraḥ sārdhaṁ pañcamātrairdevaputraśatairbodhisattvaṁ mātuḥ kukṣigataṁ jñātvā satataṁ samitamanubadhnāti sma | |

bodhisattvasya khalu punarmātuḥ kukṣigatasya kāyastathāvidho'bhūt, tadyathāpi nāma parvatamūrdhani rātrāvandhakāratamisrāyāṁ mahānagniskandho yojanādapi dṛśyate sma, yāvat pañcabhyā yojanebhyo dṛśyate sma | evameva bodhisattvasya mātuḥ kukṣigatasyātmabhāvo'bhinirvṛtto'bhūt prabhāsvaro'bhirūpaḥ prāsādiko darśanīyaḥ | sa tasmin kūṭāgāre paryaṅkaniṣaṇṇo'tīva śobhate sma | vaiḍūryapratyuptamivābhijātaṁ jātarūpam | bodhisattvasya mātā ca nidhyāya sthitā paśyati sma kukṣigataṁ bodhisattvam | tadyathāpi nāma mahato'bhrakūṭādvidyuto niḥsṛtya mahāntamavabhāsaṁ saṁjanayanti, evameva bodhisattvo mātuḥ kukṣigataḥ śriyā tejasā varṇena ca taṁ prathamaṁ ratnakūṭāgāramavabhāsayati sma | avabhāsya dvitīyaṁ gandhakūṭāgāramavabhāsayati sma | dvitīyaṁ gandhakūṭāgāramavabhāsya tṛtīyaṁ ratnakūṭāgāramavabhāsayati sma | tṛtīyaṁ ratnakūṭāgāramavabhāsya sarvāvantaṁ māturātmabhāvamavabhāsayati sma | tamavabhāsya yatra cāsane niṣaṇṇo bhavati sma tadavabhāsayati sma| tadavabhāsya sarvaṁ gṛhamavabhāsayati sma| sarvaṁ gṛhamavabhāsya gṛhasyopariṣṭānniḥsṛtya pūrvāṁ diśamavabhāsayati sma| evaṁ dakṣiṇāṁ paścimāṁ uttarāmadha ūrdhvaṁ samantāddaśadiśaḥ krośamātramekaikasyāṁ diśi mātuḥ kukṣigato bodhisattvaḥ śriyā tejasā varṇena cāvabhāsayati sma||

āgacchanti sma khalu punarbhikṣavaścatvāro mahārājāno'ṣṭāviṁśacca mahāyakṣasenāpatayaḥ sārdhaṁ pañcamātrayakṣaśataiḥ pūrvāhṇakālasamaye bodhisattvasya darśanāya vandanāya paryupāsanāya dharmaśravaṇāya ca| tadā bodhisattvastānāgatān viditvā dakṣiṇaṁ pāṇimabhyutkṣipya ekāṅgulikayā āsanānyupadarśayati sma| niṣīdanti sma te lokapālādayo yathāprajñapteṣvāsaneṣu| paśyanti sma bodhisattvaṁ mātuḥ kukṣigataṁ jātarūpamiva vigrahaṁ hastaṁ cālayantaṁ vicālayantam utkṣipantaṁ pratiṣṭhāpayantam| te prītiprāmodyaprasādapratilabdhā bodhisattvaṁ namaskurvanti sma| niṣaṇṇāṁśca tān viditvā bodhisattvo dharmyayā kathayā saṁdarśayati sma samādāpayati sma samuttejayati sma saṁpraharṣayati sma| yadā ca prakramitukāmā bhavanti tadā bodhisattvasteṣāṁ cetasaiva vicintitaṁ vijñāya dakṣiṇaṁ pāṇimutkṣipya saṁcārayati sma| saṁcārya vicārayati sma| mātaraṁ ca na bādhate sma| tadā teṣāṁ caturṇāṁ mahārājānāmevaṁ bhavati sma-visarjitāḥ sma vayaṁ bodhisattveneti| te bodhisattvaṁ bodhisattvamātaraṁ ca tripradakṣiṇīkṛtya prakrāmanti sma| ayaṁ heturayaṁ pratyayo yadbodhisattvo rātryāṁ praśāntāyāṁ dakṣiṇaṁ pāṇiṁ saṁcārya vicārayati sma| vicārya punarapi smṛtaḥ saṁprajānaṁstaṁ pāṇiṁ pratiṣṭhāpayati sma| punaraparaṁ yadā bodhisattvasya keciddarśanāyāgacchanti sma striyo vā puruṣo vā dārako vā dārikā vā, tān bodhisattvaḥ pūrvatarameva pratisaṁmodayate sma, paścādbodhisattvasya mātā||

iti hi bhikṣavo bodhisattvo mātuḥ kukṣigataḥ san sattvān pratisaṁmodanakuśalo bhavati smeti| na ca kaściddevo vā nāgo vā yakṣo vā manuṣyo vā amanuṣyo vā yaḥ śaknoti sma bodhisattvaṁ pūrvataraṁ pratisaṁmoditum| atha tarhi bodhisattva eva tāvat pūrvataraṁ pratisaṁmodate sma, paścādbodhisattvamātā||

nirgate khalu punaḥ pūrvāhṇakālasamaye madhyāhnakālasamaye pratyupasthite atha khalu śakro devānāmindro niṣkrāntaḥ| abhiniṣkrāntāśca trāyatriṁśaddevaputrā bodhisattvasya darśanāya vandanāya paryupāsanāya| dharmaśravaṇāya cāgacchanti sma| tāṁśca bodhisattvo dūrata evāgacchato dṛṣṭvā dakṣiṇaṁ suvarṇavarṇaṁ bāhuṁ prasārya śakraṁ devānāmindraṁ devāṁśca trāyatriṁśān pratisaṁmodate sma| ekāṅgulikayā cāsanānyupadarśayati sma| na ca śaknoti sma bhikṣavaḥ śakro devānāmindro bodhisattvasyājñāṁ pratiroddhum| niṣīdati sma śakro devānāmindrastadanye ca devaputrā yathāprajñapteṣvāsaneṣu| tān bodhisattvo niṣaṇṇān viditvā dharmyayā kathayā saṁdarśayati sma samādāpayati sma samuttejayati sma saṁpraharṣayati sma| yena ca bodhisattvaḥ pāṇiṁ saṁcārayati sma, tanmukhā bodhisattvamātā bhavati sma| tatasteṣāmevaṁ bhavati sma-asmābhiḥ sārdhaṁ bodhisattvaḥ saṁmodate sma| ekaikaścaivaṁ saṁjānīte sma-mayaiva sārdhaṁ bodhisattvaḥ saṁlapati, māmeva pratisaṁmodate sma iti||

tasmin khalu punaḥ kūṭāgāre śakrasya devānāmindrasya trāyatriṁśānāṁ devānāṁ ca pratibhāsaḥ saṁdṛśyate sma| na khalu punaranyatraivaṁ pariśuddho bodhisattvaparibhogo bhavati yathā mātuḥ kukṣigatasya bodhisattvasya| yadā ca bhikṣavaḥ śakro devānāmindrastadanye ca devaputrāḥ prakramitukāmā bhavanti sma, tadā bodhisattvasteṣāṁ cetasaiva cetaḥparivitarkamājñāya dakṣiṇaṁ pāṇimutkṣipya saṁcārayanti sma| saṁcārya vicārya punarapi smṛtaḥ saṁprajānan pratiṣṭhāpayati sma| mātaraṁ ca na bādhate sma| tadā śakrasya devānāmindrasyānyeṣāṁ ca trāyatriṁśānāṁ devānāmevaṁ bhavati sma-visarjitā vayaṁ bodhisattveneti| te bodhisattvaṁ bodhisattvamātaraṁ ca tripradakṣiṇīkṛtya prakrāmanti sma||

nirgate ca khalu punarbhikṣavo madhyāhnakālasamaye sāyāhnakālasamaye pratyupasthite atha khalu brahmā sahāpatiranekairbrahmakāyikairdevaputraśatasahasraiḥ parivṛtaḥ puraskṛtastaṁ divyamojobindumādāya yena bodhisattvastenopasaṁkrāmati sma bodhisattvaṁ draṣṭuṁ vandituṁ paryupāsituṁ dharmaṁ ca śrotum| samanvāharati sma bhikṣavaḥ bodhisattvo brahmāṇaṁ sahāpatimāgacchantaṁ saparivāram| punareva ca bodhisattvo dakṣiṇaṁ suvarṇavarṇapāṇimutkṣipya brahmāṇaṁ sahāpatiṁ brahmakāyikāṁśca devaputrān pratisaṁmodate sma| ekāṅgulikayā cāsanānyupadarśayati sma| na ca śaktirasti bhikṣavo brahmaṇaḥ sahāpaterbodhisattvasyājñāṁ pratiroddhum| niṣīdati sma bhikṣavo brahmā sahāpatistadanye ca brahmakāyikā devaputrā yathāprajñapteṣvāsaneṣu| tān bodhisattvo niṣaṇṇān viditvā dharmyayā kathayā saṁdarśayati sma samādāpayati sma samuttejayati sma saṁpraharṣayati sma | yena ca bodhisattvaḥ pāṇiṁ saṁcārayati sma, tanmukhaiva māyādevī bhavati sma | tatasteṣāmekaikasyaivaṁ bhavati sma-mayā sārdhaṁ bodhisattvaḥ saṁlapati, māmeva pratisaṁmodate sma iti | yadā ca brahmā sahāpatistadanye ca brahmakāyikā devaputrā gantukāmā bhavanti sma, tadā bodhisattvasteṣāṁ cetasaiva cetaḥparivitarkamājñāya dakṣiṇaṁ suvarṇavarṇaṁ bāhumutkṣipya saṁcārayati sma | saṁcārya vicārayati sma | saṁcārya vicārya avasādatākāreṇa pāṇiṁ saṁcārayati sma | mātaraṁ ca na bādhate sma | tato brahmaṇaḥ sahāpatestadanyeṣāṁ ca brahmakāyikānāṁ devaputrāṇāmevaṁ bhavati sma-visarjitā vayaṁ bodhisattveneti | te bodhisattvaṁ bodhisattvamātaraṁ ca tripradakṣiṇīkṛtya punareva prakrāmanti sma | bodhisattvaśca smṛtaḥ saṁprajānan pāṇiṁ pratiṣṭhāpayati sma ||

āgacchanti sma khalu punarbhikṣavaḥ pūrvadakṣiṇapaścimottarābhyo digbhyo'dhastāduparīṣṭāt santāddaśabhyo digbhyo bahūni bodhisattvaśatasahasrāṇi bodhisattvasya darśanāya vandanāya paryupāsanāya dharmaśravaṇāya ca dharmasaṁgītisaṁgāyanāya ca | teṣāmāgatāgatānāṁ bodhisattvaḥ kāyāt prabhāmutsṛjya prabhāvyūhāni siṁhāsanānyabhinirmimīte sma | abhinirmāya tān bodhisattvāṁsteṣvāsaneṣu niṣīdayati sma | niṣaṇṇāṁścainān viditvā paripṛcchati sma paripraśnayati sma yadutāsyaiva bodhisattvasya mahāyānasya vistaravibhāgatāmupādāya | na ca tān kaścidanyaḥ paśyati sma anyatra sabhāgebhyo devaputrebhyaḥ | ayaṁ bhikṣavo heturayaṁ pratyayo yena bodhisattvaḥ praśāntāyāṁ rātryāṁ kāyāt prabhāmutsṛjati sma ||

na khalu punarbhikṣavo māyādevī bodhisattvakukṣigate gurukāyatāṁ saṁjānīte sma anyatra laghutāmeva mṛdutāmeva saukhyatāmeva | na codaragatāni duḥkhāni pratyanubhavati sma | na ca rāgaparidāhena vā dveṣaparidāhena vā mohaparidāhena vā paridahyate sma | na ca kāmavitarkaṁ vā vyāpādavitarkaṁ vā vihiṁsāvitarkaṁ vā vitarkayati sma | na ca śītaṁ na coṣṇaṁ vā jighatsāṁ vā pipāsāṁ vā tamo vā rajo vā kleśaṁ vā saṁjānīte sma paśyati vā | na cāsyā amanāpā rūpaśabdagandharasasparśā vā ābhāsamāgacchanti sma | na ca pāpakān svapnān paśyati sma | na cāsyāḥ strīmāyā na śāṭhyaṁ nerṣyā na strīkleśā bādhante sma | pañcaśikṣāpadasamādattā khalu punaḥ śīlavatī daśakuśalakarmapathe pratiṣṭhitā tasmin samaye bodhisattvamātā bhavati sma | na ca bodhisattvamātuḥ kvacit puruṣe rāgacittamutpadyate sma, nāpi kasyacitpuruṣasya bodhisattvasya māturantike | ye ca kecitkapilāhvaye mahāpuravare anyeṣu vā janapadeṣu devanāgayakṣagandharvāsuragaruḍabhūtāviṣṭāḥ strīpuruṣadārakadārikā vā, te sarve bodhisattvamātuḥ sahadarśanādeva svasthāḥ smṛtipratilabdhā bhavanti sma | te cāmanuṣyāḥ kṣiprameva prakrāmanti sma | ye ca kecinnānārogaspṛṣṭāḥ sattvā bhavanti sma, vātapittaśleṣmasaṁnipātajai rogaiḥ pīḍyante sma, cakṣurogeṇa vā śrotrarogeṇa vā ghrāṇarogeṇa vā jihvārogeṇa vā oṣṭharogeṇa vā dantarogeṇa kaṇṭharogeṇa vā galagaṇḍarogeṇa vā uragaṇḍakuṣṭhakilāsaśoṣonmādāpasmārajvaragalagaṇḍapiṭakavisarpavicarcikādyai rogaiḥ saṁpīḍyante sma, teṣāṁ bodhisattvamātā dakṣiṇapāṇiṁ mūrdhni pratiṣṭhāpayati sma | te sahapratiṣṭhāpite pāṇau vigatavyādhayo bhūtvā svakasvakāni gṛhāṇi gacchanti sma | antato māyādevī tṛṇagulmakamapi dharaṇitalādabhyutkṣipya glānebhyaḥ sattvebhyo'nuprayacchati sma | te sahapratilambhādaroganirvikārā bhavanti sma | yadā ca māyādevī svaṁ dakṣiṇaṁ pārśvaṁ pratyavekṣate sma, tadā paśyati sma bodhisattvaṁ kukṣigatam, tadyathāpi nāma supariśuddha ādarśamaṇḍale mukhamaṇḍalaṁ dṛśyate | dṛṣṭvā ca punastuṣṭā udagrā āttamanā pramuditā prītisaumanasyajātā bhavati sma | |

bodhisattvasya khalu punarbhikṣavo mātuḥ kukṣigatasyādhiṣṭhitaṁ satataṁ samitaṁ rātriṁdivaṁ divyāni tūryāṇi abhi(nirmāya) pranadanti sma | divyāni ca puṣpāṇi abhipravarṣanti sma | kālena devā varṣanti sma | kālena vāyavo vānti sma | kālena ṛtavo nakṣatrāṇi ca parivartante sma | kṣemaṁ ca rājyaṁ subhikṣaṁ ca sumanākulamanubhavati sma | sarve ca kapilāhvaye mahāpuravare śākyā anye ca sattvāḥ khādanti sma, pibanti sma, (ramante sma,) krīḍanti sma, pravicārayanti sma, dānāni ca dadanti sma, puṇyāni ca kurvanti sma, kaumodyāmiva cāturmāsyāmekāntare krīḍāsukhavihārairviharanti sma | rājāpi śuddhodanaḥ saṁprāptabrahmacaryoparatarāṣṭrakāryo'pi supariśuddhastapovanagata iva dharmamevānuvartate sma | |

evaṁrūpeṇa bhikṣava ṛddhiprātihāryeṇa samanvāgato bodhisattvo mātuḥ kukṣigato'sthāt | tatra khalu bhagavānāyuṣmantamānandamāmantrayate sma-drakṣyasi tvamānanda ratnavyūhaṁ bodhisattvaparibhogaṁ yatra bodhisattvo mātuḥ kukṣigato vyāhārṣīt| āha-paśyeyaṁ bhagavan paśyeyaṁ sugata| darśayati sma tathāgata āyuṣmata ānandasya śakrasya devānāmindrasya caturṇāṁ ca lokapālānāṁ tadanyeṣāṁ ca devamanuṣyāṇām| dṛṣṭvā ca te tuṣṭā abhūvan udagrā āttamanasaḥ pramuditāḥ prītisaumanasyajātāḥ| sa ca brahmā sahāpatiḥ punareva brahmaloke samāropya pratiṣṭhāpayati sma caityārtham||

tatra khalu bhagavān punarapi bhikṣūnāmantrayate sma-iti hi bhikṣavo daśamāsakukṣigatena bodhisattvena ṣaṭtriṁśannayutāni devamanuṣyāṇāṁ triṣu yāneṣu paripācitānyabhūvan| yatredamucyate yat—

bodhisattva agrasattva mātukukṣisaṁsthitaḥ
prakampitā ca ṣaḍvikāra medinī sakānanā|
suvarṇavarṇa ābha mukta sarvāpāya śodhitā
praharṣitāśca devasaṁgha dharmagañju bheṣyate||23||
suṁsaṁsthito mahāvimānu naikaratnacitrito
yatra vīru āruhitva tiṣṭhate vināyakaḥ|
gandhottamena candanena pūrito virocate
yasyaikakarṣu trisahasramūlyaratnapūrito||24||
mahāsahasralokadhātu heṣvi bhindiyitvanā
udāgato guṇākarasya padmaojabinduko|
so saptarātra puṇyateja brahmaloki udgato
gṛhītva brahma ojabindu bodhisattva nāmayī||25||
na asti sarvasattvakāyi bhuktu yo jareya taṁ
anyatra bhūri bodhisattva brahmakalpasaṁnibhe|
anekakalpa puṇyateja ojabindu saṁsthito
bhujitva sattva kāyacitta jñānaśuddha gacchiṣu||26||
śakra brahma lokapāla pūjanāya nāyakaṁ
trīṇi kāla āgamitva bodhisattvamantikam|
vandayitva pūjayitva dharma śṛṇute varaṁ
pradakṣiṇaṁ karitva sarva gacchiṣū yathāgatā||27||
bodhisattva dharmakāma enti lokadhātuṣu
prabhāviyūha āsaneṣu te niṣaṇṇa dṛśyiṣu|
parasparaṁ ca śrutva dharma yānaśreṣṭhamuttamaṁ
prayānti sarvi hṛṣṭacitta varṇamāla bhāṣato||28||
ye ca iṣṭidārakāsu duḥkhitā tadā abhūt

bhūtaspṛṣṭa kṣiptacitta nagna pāṁśumrakṣitā|
te ca sarva dṛṣṭva māya bhonti labdhacetanā
smṛtīmatīgatīupeta gehi gehi gacchiṣu||29||
vātato va pittato va śleṣmasaṁnipātakaiḥ
ye ca cakṣuroga śrotraroga kāyacittapīḍitā|
naikarūpa naikajāti vyādhibhiśca ye hatā
sthāpite sma māya mūrdhni pāṇi bhonti nirjarā||30||
athāpi vā tṛṇasya tūli bhūmito gṛhītvanā
dadāti māya āturāṇa sarvi bhonti nirjarā|
saukhyaprāpti nirvikāra gehi gehi gacchiṣu
bhaiṣajyabhūti vaidyarāji kukṣisaṁpratiṣṭhite||31||
yasmi kāli māyadevi svātanuṁ nirīkṣate
adṛśāti bodhisattva kukṣiye pratiṣṭhitam|
yathaiva candra antarīkṣa tārakai parīvṛtaṁ
tathaiva nāthu bodhisattvalakṣaṇairalaṁkṛtam||32||
no ca tasya rāga doṣa naiva moha bādhate
kāmachandu naiva tasya īrṣi naiva hiṁsitā|
tuṣṭacitta hṛṣṭacitta prīti saumanasthitā
kṣudhāpipāsa śīta uṣṇa naiva tasya bādhate||33||
aghaṭṭitāśca nityakāla divyatūrya vādiṣu
pravarṣayanti divyapuṣpa gandhaśreṣṭha śobhanā|
deva paśyi mānuṣāśca mānuṣā amānuṣāṁ
no viheṭhi no vihiṁsi tatra te parasyaram||34||
ramanti sattva krīḍayanti annapānudenti ca
ānandaśabda ghoṣayanti hṛṣṭatuṣṭamānasāḥ||
kṣamā rajoanākulā ca kāli deva varṣate
tṛṇāśca puṣpa oṣadhīya tasmi kāli rohiṣu||35||
rājagehi saptarātra ratnavarṣa varṣito
yato daridrasattva gṛhya dāna denti bhuñjate|
nāsti sattva yo daridra yo ca āsi duḥkhito
bherumūrdhni nandaneva eva sattva nandiṣu||36||
so ca rāju śākiyāna poṣadhī upoṣito
rājyakāryu no karoti dharmameva gocarī|
tapovanaṁ ca so praviṣṭa māyādevī pṛcchate
kīdṛśenti kāyi saukhya agrasattva dhārati||37||

iti śrīlalitavistare garbhāvakrāntiparivarto nāma ṣaṣṭhamo'dhyāyaḥ | |

Meluhha glosses:
<karaD>(Z),,<kanaD>(Z) {N} ``^sheaf of ^straw''. #16160.(Munda)

kaṇḍa -- m.n. ' joint of stalk, stalk (Pali); *kāḍ* m. ' stalk of a reed, straw ' (Kashmiri); *kāḍ* n. ' trunk, stem '(Marathi); Or.*kāṇḍa*, *kāṛ* ' stalk (Oriya); *kāṛā* 'stem of muñja grass (used for thatching) (Bihari); *kānā* m. ' stalk of the reed Sara ' (Lahnda)(CDIAL 3023).

काड [kāḍa] n f Thrashed or trodden stalks of leguminous plants, pulse-straw. 2 f Straw (of wheat, नाचणी,उडीद, वरी and others). 3 C The chaff and bits that fall from rice-straw on beating or shaking it. 4 C Plants of rice left over from a transplantation. 5 Peeled stalks of अंबाडी or ताग. 6 n Legumes gen. (Marathi)
कांडें [kāṇḍēṃ] n (कांड S) Stalks and heads of corn once trodden or thrashed (as thrown or reserved for a second treading or thrashing).कंडारणें [kaṇḍāraṇēṃ] n An instrument of goldsmiths,--the iron spike which is hammered upon plates in reducing them to shape. 2 The handle of a ploughman's whip. 3 The central and thick part of a दावें. 4 A little indented instrument, used to cut flowers and figures out of paper. 5 A cudgel or club. 6 A large and coarse ornamental ring. Esp. used
with सरीचें, गोट्याचें, कड्यांचें &c. as सरीचें क0 7 A barber's nail-parer. (Marathi)

kā´ṇḍa (*kāṇḍá* -- TS.) m.n. ' single joint of a plant ' AV., ' arrow ' MBh., ' cluster, heap ' (in *tr̥ṇa -- kāṇḍa* -- Pāṇ. Kāś.). [Poss. connexion with gaṇḍa -- 2makes prob. non -- Aryan origin (not with P. Tedesco Language 22, 190 < *kr̥ntáti*). Prob. ← Drav., cf. Tam. *kaṇ* ' joint of bamboo or sugarcane ' EWA i 197]

Pa. *kaṇḍa* -- m.n. ' joint of stalk, stalk, arrow, lump '; Pk. *kaṁḍa* -- , °*aya* -- m.n. ' knot of bough, bough, stick '; Ash. *kaṇ* ' arrow ', Kt. *kåṇ*, Wg. *kāṇ*, *kŕãdotdot;*, Pr. *kə̃*, Dm. *kān;* Paš. lauṛ. *kāṇḍ*, *kāṇ*, ar. *kōṇ*, kuṛ. *kō̃*, dar. *kā̃ṛ* ' arrow ', *kā̃ṛī* ' torch '; Shum. *kō̃ṛ*, *kō̃* ' arrow ', Gaw. *kāṇḍ*, *kāṇ*; Kho. *kan* ' tree, large bush '; Bshk. *kā`n* ' arrow ', Tor. *kan* m., Sv. *kā̃ṛa*, Phal. *kōṇ*, Sh. gil. *kōn* f. (→ Ḍ. *kōn*, pl. *kāna* f.), pales. *kōṇ*; K. *kā̃ḍ* m. ' stalk of a reed, straw ' (*kān* m. ' arrow ' ← Sh.?); S. *kānu* m. ' arrow ',°*no* m. ' reed ', °*nī* f. ' topmost joint of the reed Sara, reed pen, stalk, straw, porcupine's quill '; L. *kānā̃* m. ' stalk of the reed Sara ', °*nī˜* f. ' pen, small spear '; P. *kānnā* m. ' the reed Saccharum munja, reed in a weaver's warp ', *kānī* f. ' arrow '; WPah. bhal. *kān* n. ' arrow ', jaun. *kā̃ḍ*; N. *kā̃ṛ* ' arrow ', °*ṛo* ' rafter '; A. *kā̃r* ' arrow '; B. *kā̃ṛ* ' arrow ', °*ṛā* ' oil vessel made of bamboo joint, needle of bamboo for netting ', *kẽṛiyā* ' wooden or earthen vessel for oil &c. '; Or. *kāṇḍa*, *kā̃ṛ* ' stalk, arrow '; Bi. *kā̃ṛā* ' stem of muñja grass (used for thatching) '; Mth. *kā̃ṛ* ' stack of stalks of large millet ', *kā̃ṛī* ' wooden milkpail '; Bhoj. *kaṇḍā* ' reeds '; H. *kā̃ṛī* f. ' rafter, yoke ', *kaṇḍā* m. ' reed, bush ' (← EP.?); G. *kā̃ḍ* m. ' joint, bough, arrow ', °*ḍũ* n. ' wrist ', °*ḍī* f. ' joint, bough, arrow, lucifer match '; M. *kā̃ḍ* n. ' trunk, stem ', °*ḍẽ* n. ' joint, knot, stem, straw ', °*ḍī* f. ' joint of sugarcane, shoot of root (of ginger, &c.) '; Si. *kaḍaya* ' arrow '. -- Deriv. A. *kāriyāiba* ' to shoot with an arrow '.kā´ṇḍīra -- ; *kāṇḍakara -- , *kāṇḍārā -- ; *dēhīkāṇḍa -- [< IE. **kondo* -- , Gk. kondu/los ' knuckle ', ko/ndos ' ankle ' T. Burrow BSOAS xxxviii 55] S.kcch. *kāṇḍī* f. ' lucifer match '? (CDIAL 3023)

*kāṇḍakara ' worker with reeds or arrows '. [kā´ṇḍa -- , kará -- 1] L. *kanērā* m. ' mat -- maker '; H. *kā̃ḍerā* m. ' a caste of bow -- and arrow -- makers '.*kāṇḍārā ' bamboo -- goad '. [kā´ṇḍa -- , ā´rā --]Mth. (ETirhut) *kanār* ' bamboo -- goad for young elephants.(CDIAL 3024,3025) kā´ṇḍīra ' armed with arrows ' Pāṇ., m. ' archer ' lex. [kā´ṇḍa --] H. *kanīrā* m. ' a caste (usu. of arrow -- makers) '.(CDIAL 3026)

*kaṇḍa ' pounding ', *kaṇḍīkarōti* ' pounds, brays ' Car. [√kaṇḍ1]Pk. *kaṁḍa* -- m. ' piece, fragment '; Or. *kaṇḍā* ' husked grain '. -- Deriv. Pk. *kaṁḍārēi* ' scrapes, engraves '; M. *kā̆ḍāṇẽ*, *karā̆ḍṇẽ* ' to gnaw', *kā̆ḍāṇẽ* n. ' jeweller's hammer, barber's nail -- parer '. (CDIAL 2683)

kaṇḍáyati, *káṇḍati*1 ' separates chaff from grain ' Dhātup. [√kaṇḍ1]Pk. *kaṁḍaï*, pres. part. °*ḍiṁta* -- ' threshes rice &c. '; P. *kaṇḍnā* ' to beat mercilessly '; A. *kā̃riba* ' to clean (grain) '; B. *kā̃ṛā* ' to clean finely (as rice) '; Or. *kāṇḍibā*, *kā̃ṛibā*' to husk grain, beat ', H. *kā̃ḍnā*, *kā̃ṛnā* ' to trample, tread on, crush '; M. *kā̃ḍṇẽ* ' to husk rice by pounding in a mortar '. A. *kā̃riba* also ' to husk paddy ' (CDIAL 2686).

kaṇḍita ' dislocated ' Apte. [√kaṇḍ1] Pk. *kaṁḍia* -- ' threshed '; A. *kā̃ri* ' cleaned (of grain) '.(CDIAL 2687)

Tu. kandůka, kandaka ditch, trench. *Te.* kandakamu id. *Koṇḍa* kanda trench made as a fireplace during weddings. *Pe.* kanda fire trench. *Kui* kanda small trench for fireplace. *Malt.* kandri a pit. (DEDR 1214)

Pa. kandi (*pl.* -l) necklace, beads. *Ga.* (P.) kandi (pl. -l) bead, (pl.1215 Pa. kandi (pl. -l) necklace, beads. Ga. (P.) kandi (pl. -l) bead, (pl.) necklace; (S.2) kandiṭ bead. (DEDR 1215)

kaṇḍa 'stone (ore)(Gadba)'. . Ga. (Oll.) kanḍ, (S.) kanḍu (pl. kanḍkil) stone (DEDR 1298).

Allographs:
kaṇḍa 'arrow' (Skt.) H. kā̃ḍerā m. ' a caste of bow -- and arrow -- makers (CDIAL 3024). Or. kāṇḍa, kā̃ṛ 'stalk, arrow '(CDIAL 3023).

खांडा [khāṇḍā] *m* A jag, notch, or indentation (as upon the edge of a tool or weapon). (Marathi)

kāṇḍa 'water'.

కండె [*kaṇḍe*] *kaṇḍe*. [Telugu] n. A head or ear of millet or maize. జొన్నకంకి.

kaṇḍ 'backbone' (Lahnda); *kaṇṭa ' backbone, podex, penis '. 2. *kaṇḍa -- . 3. *karaṇḍa -- 4. (Cf. *kāṭa -- 2, *ḍākka -- 2: poss. same as káṇṭa -- 1] 1. Pa. *piṭṭhi -- kaṇṭaka* -- m. ' bone of the spine '; Gy. eur. *kanro* m. ' penis ' (or < káṇṭaka --); Tir. *mar -- kaṇḍḗ* ' back (of the body) '; S.*kaṇḍo* m. ' back ', L. *kaṇḍ* f., *kaṇḍā* m. 'backbone', awāṇ. *kaṇḍ*, °*ḍī* ' back '; P. *kaṇḍ* f. ' back, pubes '; WPah. bhal. *kaṇṭ* f. ' syphilis '; N. *kaṇḍo* ' buttock, rump, anus ',*kaṇḍeulo* ' small of the back '; B. *kā̃ṭ* ' clitoris '; Or. *kaṇṭi* ' handle of a plough '; H. *kā̃ṭā* m. ' spine ', G. *kā̃ṭɔ* m., M. *kā̃ṭā* m.; Si. *äṭa -- kaṭuva* ' bone ', *piṭa -- k°* ' backbone '. 2. Pk. *kaṁḍa* -- m. ' backbone '. 3. Pk. *karaṁḍa* -- m.n. ' bone shaped like a bamboo ', *karaṁḍuya* -- n. ' backbone '. (CDIAL 2670).

Si. *kaṭa* ' throat, mouth ' (X skandhá -- in SigGr. *kaṇḍa* ' neck ') (CDIAL 2680).

A hieroglyph on m0304 insription: A खांडा *khāṇḍā* 'jag' infixed inside *kanka* 'rim of jar' glyph is read as the phrase: *kaṇḍa kan-ka*, 'furnace account, scribe'. *kan-ka, karṇaka* 'rim of jar' Rebus: *kaṇḍa karṇaka* 'furnace account scribe'. *kārṇī(ka)* 'supercargo of a ship' (Marathi)

The rim-of-jar is the most frequently occurring hieroglyph in the corpora of Meluhha hieroglyphs (aka Indus writing). This hieroglyph is read rebus: Glyph: *kaṇḍa kanka*, 'rim of jar' Rebus:

furnace account, scribe. cf. *kul -- karṇī* m. 'village accountant' (Marathi); *karṇikan* id. (Tamil) கணக்கு kaṇakku, n. cf. gaṇaka. [M. kaṇakku] 1. Number, account, reckoning, calculation, computation (Tamil) kaṇḍ 'fire-altar' (Santali) *kaṇḍa*, furnace (fire-altar, consecrated pit). *khondu* id. (Kashmiri) *kan-ka, karṇaka* 'rim of jar' Rebus: *kaṇḍa karṇaka* 'furnace account scribe'. *kārṇī(ka)* 'supercargo of a ship' (Marathi)

m1656 Mohenjodro Pectoral.

kāṇṭam காண்டம் kāṇṭam, *n.* < *kāṇḍa.* 1. Water; sacred water; நீர். துருத்திவா யதுக்கிய குங்குமக் காண் டமும் (கல்லா. 49, 16). <kanda> {N} ``large earthen water ^pot kept and filled at the house''. @1507. #14261.(Munda) Rebus: *khāṇḍā* 'metal tools, pots and pans' (Marathi)

<lo->(B) {V} ``(pot, etc.) to ^overflow''. See <lo-> `to be left over'. @B24310. #20851. Re<lo->(B) {V} ``(pot, etc.) to ^overflow''. See <lo-> `to be left over'. (Munda) Rebus: loh 'copper' (Hindi) The hieroglyph clearly refers to the metal tools, pots and pans of copper. Thus, the two words read together Rebus: lōkhaṇḍa लोखंड Iron tools, vessels, or articles in general (Marathi).

khaṇṭi 'buffalo bull' (Tamil) Rebus: *khā̃ḍ* '(metal) tools, pots and pans' (Gujarati) கண்டி kaṇṭi buffalo bull (Tamil) kaṇḍ 'buffalo'; rebus: kaṇḍ 'stone (ore)'. Alternative: கடவு[3] kaṭavu , *n.* < கடா .1. Male buffalo 'buffalo' *kāṛā* young buffalo (Go.) *kaṭā, kaṭamā* 'bison' (Ta.)(DEDR 1114) Rebus: *kā̃ṭhāḷ* 'maritime'; *kaṭalar, n.* < seamen, inhabitants of maritime tracts.

lokhãḍ 'overflowing pot' Rebus: 'tools, iron, ironware' (Gujarati) *ayaskāṇḍa* is a compound attested in Pāṇini; the word may be semantically explained as 'metal tools, pots and pans' or as alloyed metal.

kāru 'crocodile' (Telugu). Rebus:
artisan (Marathi) Rebus: *khar* 'blacksmith' (Kashmiri) *kola* 'tiger' Rebus:*kol* 'working in iron' (Tamil).

Mohenjo-daro seal m0304. The platform is atop two stacks of hay (straw).

Kur. kaṇḍō a stool. Malt. kanḍo stool, seat. (DEDR 1179) Rebus: kaṇḍ = a furnace, altar (Santali) H. *lokhaṇḍ* m. 'iron tools, pots and pans'; G. *lokhãḍ* n. 'tools, iron, ironware', the word *khaṇḍ* denotes 'tools, pots and pans and metal-ware'.

Ta. takar sheep, ram, goat, male of certain other animals (yāḷi, elephant, shark). பொருநகர் தாக்கற்குப் பேருந்

தகைத்து (குறள், 486).Ma. takaran huge, powerful as a man, bear, etc. Ka. tagar, ṭagaru, ṭagara, ṭegaru ram. Tu. tagaru, ṭagarů id. Te. tagaramu, tagaru id. / Cf. Mar. tagar id. (DEDR 3000). Rebus 1: tagromi 'tin, metal alloy' (Kuwi) takaram tin, white lead, metal sheet, coated with tin (Ta.); tin, tinned iron plate (Ma.); tagarm tin (Ko.); tagara, tamara, tavara id. (Ka.) tamaru, tamara, tavara id. (Ta.): tagaramu, tamaramu, tavaramu id. (Te.); ṭagromi tin metal, alloy (Kuwi); tamara id. (Skt.)(DEDR 3001). trapu tin (AV.); tipu (Pali); tau, taua lead (Pkt.); *tũ̄* tin (P.); ṭau zinc, pewter (Or.); tarūaum lead (OG.); *tarvũ* (G.); tumba lead (Si.)(CDIAL 5992).Rebus 2: damgar 'merchant'.

Known ancient sources, major deposits of tin.

Map of tin and gold deposits and occurrences in Afghanistan.

[quote] This first flurry of metallurgical activity is attested on the Iranian plateau earlier than in Mesopotamia. Nevertheless, the first indications of bronze appear simultaneously on the plateau and in the lowlands in the 4th millennium. A bronze flat axe was excavated from the necropolis at Susa I(A) (Berthoud, p. 13 no. 974) and a bronze needle from

Sialk III-5 (Ghirshman, 1938, p. 206). From Godin unpublished analyses indicate that bronze is present in period V, which dates to the second half of the 4th millennium into the early 3rd millennium B.C. (Godin Project Archives). These random initial occurrences of bronze may have resulted from trade with the east. Afghanistan, where abundant copper and tin deposits are juxtaposed, is a likely locus for the technological innovation of bronze...Only at Susa is there evidence of bronze technology from the mid-3rd millennium: the "vase à la cachette" containing four bronzes, sixteen arsenical coppers, and three artifacts containing both tin and arsenic (Amiet et al.; Berthoud, p. 14). Analyses suggest that tin was being alloyed with arsenical copper (Stech and Pigott, p. 43). In the final centuries of the 3rd millennium, a period during which Susa had strong cultural ties with Mesopotamia (Amiet, p. 197), bronze was found with some frequency there; by that time many plateau settlements, including those at Tepe Sialk, Tall-i Malyan (Tall-e Malīān), and Tepe Yahya had been abandoned...The Sumerians were active in trade and the acquisition of exotic luxury materials. The rarity of tin may have enhanced its status in Mesopotamia, whereas the peoples of the Iranian plateau remained uninfluenced by such pressures (Stech and Pigott, p. 48). At any rate, tin "bypassed" the plateau en route to Mesopotamia (Beale, p. 144; Moorey, 1982, p. 88). Iranian metallurgical traditions can thus be characterized as technologically conservative, for, though copper artifacts were manufactured in quantity and in a variety of forms, simple smelted or melted arsenical copper was the main material used. At Tepe Hissar, for example, the quantities of slag, fragments of furnace lining, and molds suggest large-scale production of arsenical copper: tools, weapons, and elaborate ornaments (Schmidt, 1937; Pigott et al.). There is also evidence of lead and silver production. Bronze, however, was found only very rarely in the analysis of metal artifacts from the site (Pigott et al., p. 230; Berthoud et al., 1982, p. 50 n. 66; Reisch and Horton apud Schmidt, 1937, p. 359). Assemblages from Shahr-i Sokhta to the southeast, Tepe Yahya to the south (Heskel and Lamberg-Karlovsky, 1980; 1986; Heskel, 1982, pp. 73-97; Tylecote and McKerrell, 1971; 1986), and probably Shahdad, also to the south (Vatandoost-Haghighi; Moorey, 1982, pp. 83, 90-91; Salvatori; Salvatori and Vidale), consist primarily of arsenical copper artifacts, with rare bronzes (Heskel 1982, pp. 97-120; Hauptmann; see also Tosi, 1993). An arsenical-copper shaft-hole axe from a burial at Khurab (Ḵᵛorāb; Stein, 1937, p. 121) in Baluchistan has been the subject of several studies (Maxwell-Hyslop; Zeuner; During Caspers), including a detailed metallurgical analysis of its composition and manufacture (Lamberg-Karlovsky, 1969; Lechtman). Farther west at Tall-i Malyan in Fārs province artifacts from the late 4th- and early 3rd-millennium Banesh (Baneš) phase (Nicholas, 1980; forthcoming) are exclusively of arsenical copper, but preliminary analyses of finds from the subsequent Kaftari phase (early 2nd millennium) indicate that several are of bronze (Pigott, 1980, pp. 107; unpublished analyses of the Museum of Applied Science, Center for Archaeology/MASCA). Slags with entrapped metal prills from Malyan have been shown by analysis to be derived from copper/bronze production (Carriveau, pp. 63-66). Unpublished analyses from the site of Godin indicate that a number of bronze artifacts occur in period III contexts, about early 3rd to early 2nd millennium B.C. (Godin Project Archives). Thus the Godin III and Kaftari Malyan contexts may be the earliest on the plateau to contain bronze with some frequency, probably reflecting the geographical and cultural proximity of these sites to the lowlands of Mesopotamia and Ḵūzestān.

The suggestion of Afghanistan as an early locus of bronze metallurgy, though attractive, cannot yet be fully substantiated archeologically. The only well-documented artifacts in bronze from the region were excavated at Mundigak (Mondīgak), in levels dating from the mid-4th through the 3rd millennium (Shaffer, p. 144; Jarrige, p. 291; see also Lamberg-Karlovsky, 1967, pp. 146-48). A few were of bronze, principally axes and a single adze, and their occurrence over a long span of time may indicate regular use of the alloy (Stech and Pigott, p. 47). Unfortunately, the bronze artifacts from Ghar-i Mar (Ḡār-e Mār "snake cave") in northern Afghanistan cannot be firmly dated (Caley, 1971, 1972, 1980;

Shaffer, p. 89; cf. Moorey, 1982, p. 99 n. 62)...The most comprehensive typological studies of a large corpus of Iranian copper-base artifacts from the region between the Indus and the Danube have been published by Deshayes (1958; 1960; 1963; 1965; Deshayes and Christophe). They include extensive discussions of techniques of fabrication and evolution of forms, as well as of the general development of metallurgy in various culture areas of southwestern Asia and adjacent regions.[unquote][196]

Trapu is tin in the Atharva Veda (11, 8.7-8: *śyāmamayah asya māmsāni lohitamasya lohitam; trapu bhasma haritam varṇah puṣkaramasya gandhah*) and vanga is also tin with the possible association of chalcolithic cultures in Bengal (2nd millennium B.C.) with possible links with the culture of Thailand of the same period (Solheim, W.C., Science, Vol. 157, p. 896). Hegde suggests the possibility that water-concentrated placer deposits referred to as 'stream tin' (alluvial cassiterite or mineral tin) in the proximity of Aravalli and Chota Nagpur Hills might have also been the sources of tin. A survey197 covered six ancient copper ore mining and smelting sites in the Aravalli (Arbuda) hills extending over a thousand kms.: Khetri and Kho Dariba in NE, Kankaria and Piplawas in the Central part and Ambaji in SW.. A large majority of mine-pits measure 7-8 metres in dia. and 3-4 metres deep showing evidence of fire-treating of the host rocks on the mine walls to widen rock joints. The evidene indicated probable mining in the chalcolithic period. Timber supports recovered from a gallery at a depth of 120 metres at Rajpura-Dariba mines in Udaipur District were radio-carbon dated to 3120+_ 160 years before the present (1987). This correlates with the zinc-containing copper artefacts of Atrañjikhera. Finely crushed ore was concentrated by gravity separation at the smelting sites which were invariably close to the banks of hill streams. This helped separate gangue from the ore. Smelting charge was by crushed quartz equal to the weight of the ore, crushed charcoal twice the weight of the ore. Furnace walls showed evidence of residues of small, hand-made, fistfuls of spherical lumps. The smelter furnace was a small, crucible-shaped, clay-walled, slag-tapping device worked on forced draught from bellows; 'this simple furnace appears to have been continuously used in India over the millennia without little innovation.' It would appear that the facilities in the metropolis of the civilization on the banks of Sarasvati and Sindhu were only purification and fabrication facilities with limited or no smelting operations. Bun-shaped copper ingots from Ganeshwar taken through the riverine routes were perhaps carried by itinerant metal-smiths of the copper-hoard culture and fabricated in cities like Mohenjodaro and Harappa to meet the specifications of the consumers of this doab or the Tigris-Euphrates doab.[198]

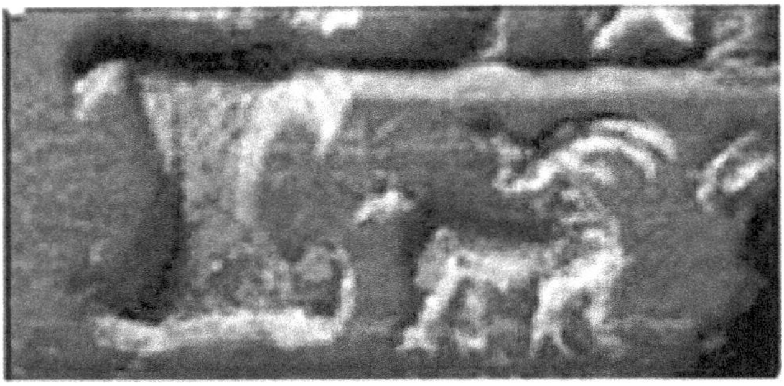

The pair of antelopes have their heads turned backwards. క్రమ్మర *krammara.* adv.

Again. క్రమ్మరిల్లు or క్రమరబడు Same as క్రమ్మరు. krəm

back'(Kho.) (CDIAL 3145) Rebus: karmāra 'smith, artisan' (Skt.) kamar 'smith' (Santali) The two antithetical antelopes thus denote: *tagar kamar*'tin artisan, tin smith, tin merchant.'

Thus, the scribe on the Nagarjunakonda sculpture can now be named: *kaṇḍa kanka* -- 1.*kanka, karṇaka* 'engraver, scribe' -- a remarkable continuum of the legacy of writing systems which originated in Sarasvati-Sindhu civilization ca. 3500 BCE.

kaṇḍa kan-ka is lit. a stone scribe account, an engraver of a writing system with representations of messages using Meluhha hieroglyphs. *kan-ka, kaṛṇaka* 'rim of jar' Rebus: *kaṇḍa kaṛṇaka* 'furnace account scribe'. *kāṛṇī(ka)* 'supercargo of a ship' (Marathi)

The cartouches shown atop haystacks (stack of straw), on the Nagarjunakonda sculptural

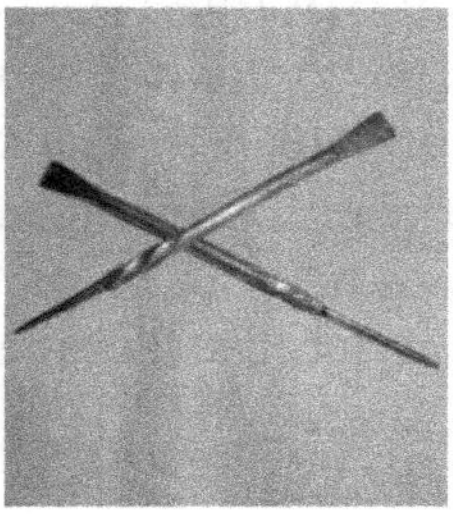

fragment depicting the 'scribe' are relatable to the same rebus readings as Meluhha hieroglyphs.

The images is only used as an example to show the nature of the stylus (possibly Roman). These are NOT an archaeologically attested, provenanced artifacts. Scribe uses a metal -- bronze stylus -- pointed needle (Pen, nib aha, as in ib, 'iron') to engrave writing on palm-leaves

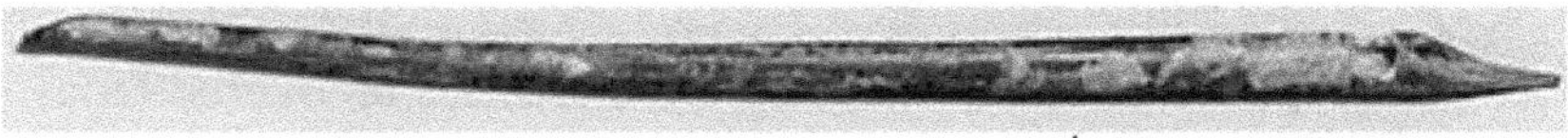

Bronze stylus Period: Imperial Roman. 1st -2nd cent. CE Bronze. 2 15/16 in. (7.5 cm.)

Paleolithic Burin

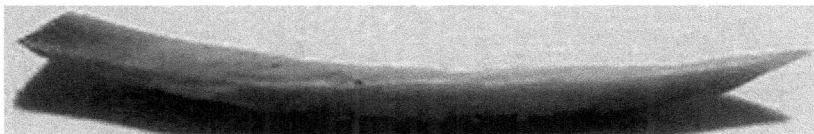

This small flint tool comes from the area of Amiens, France. It dates from the Magdalenian period of the Upper Paleolithic, or late Old Stone Age, about seventeen to eleven thousand years

ago. The tool, called a "burin" was used for engraving on bone, antler, and stone. It shows how finely the people of the Upper Paleolithic could shape and retouch their stone tools.

The people of the European Upper Paleolithic, often called Cro-Magnons, were anatomically modern humans, Homo sapiens.

Dr. Wilson adopted the accepted classificaitons of their culture at the time, which was a scheme of three stages. Each stage is defined by a characteristic technological complex and named for a French archaeological site in which that complex was found: The Aurignacian first, the Solutrean following, and finally the Magdalenian. This sequence takes in the period of 40,000 to 11,000 years ago, and we now know that it applies only to Europe.

To know more about the peoples or tools related to this treasure, follow the link to a longer article in the Wilson Museum Bulletin, Vol. 4, No. 28.

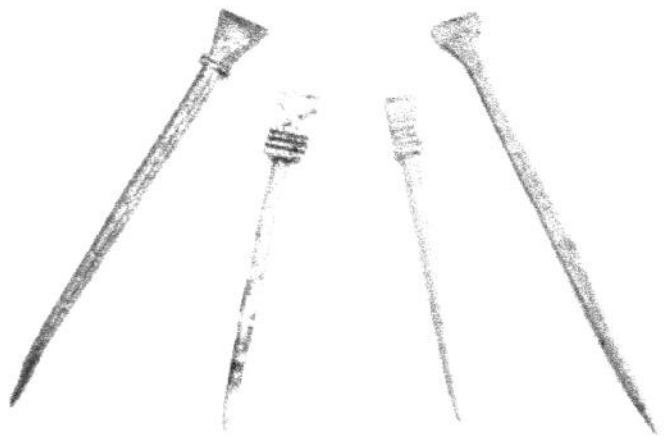

Examples of 4 Medieval styluses for writing on wax tablets. Two are made of iron, one brass and one bone stylus.

Metal styluses recovered from the urban mound, unstratified (Plate 6.20 courtesy of Mr. A. Rathnayake of Katargama). Sri Lanka.

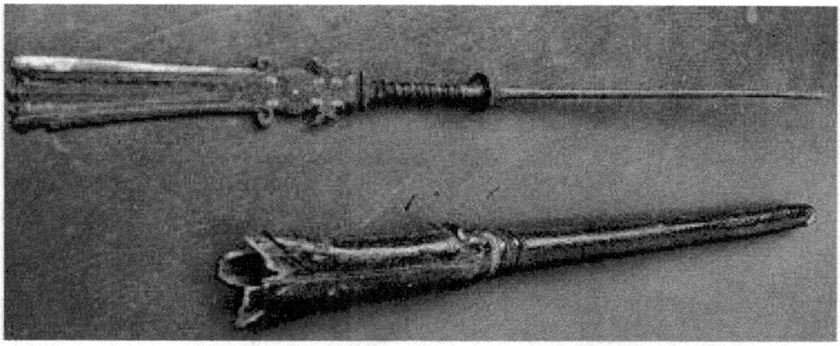

An old stylus with the steel tip to scribe on palm-leaves and its sheath

Stylus with steel tip & sheath (Sri Lanka).

Borobudur temple frieze. Narrative of the Siddhartha Gautama becoming an ascetic. At the bottom write is a scribe holding a stylus.

Palmyra leaves were used as paper to write books in ancient India. The letters were written with an iron stylus.

Halebid. Sculpture. Ganesa holds one of his broken tusks on his right hand, depicting him as a scribe (engraver). This is an abiding metaphor in Hindu civilization tradition. (*ibha* 'elephant' Rebus: *ib* 'iron' (Santali)

Depiction at Angkor Wat of Vyasa narrating the Mahabharata to Ganesha, his scribe.

Ludvik, Catherine, 2007, *Sarasvati, riverine godess of knowledge: From the manuscript-carrying Vina-player to the weapon-wielding defender of the Dharma*, Leiden, Boston, Brill. This remarkable work is referenced

because the Chinese translation (by Yijing in 703 CE) of The Sutra of Golden Light does not exist in its original Sanskrit version and is dealt with by Catherine Ludvik to demonstrate the significance of Sarasvati in Hindu-Bauddham traditions in a continuum which starts from the Rigveda for the protection of Dharma-Dhamma.

Sarasvati is a divinity of eloquence, connected with inspired thought -- *dhī* closely linked with *Vāk* as speech and knowledge -- and exemplifies the Meluhha traditions of vernacular and writing systems unraveled by the Bronze-Age Meluhha hieroglyph cipher evidenced by about 7000 epigraphs found in the Ancient Near East.

Vāk is called the language of Bharatas, *Bhāratī*. It is the voice, it is the vernacular and music. *brahma vai vāk,* mantra or chandas is speech. (ABr. 4.21.1) Hence, Sarasvati or *Brāhmī* can be related to both the literary and vernacular versions: Sanskrit and Mleccha

(Meluhha). *Vāk* is the power behind all actions (RV 10.125.4-6). This power makes her to claim in a monologue: I am the *Rāṣṭrī* (that is, feminine form of *Rāṣṭram*-- the stable, lighted path bountiful in waters).

tákṣati (3 pl. *tákṣati* RV.) ' forms by cutting, chisels ' MBh. [√takṣ] Pa. *tacchati* ' builds ', *tacchēti* ' does woodwork, chips '; Pk. *takkhaï*, *tacchaï*, *cacchaï*, *caṁchaï* ' cuts, scrapes, peels '; Gy. pers. *tetchkani* ' knife ', wel. *tax* -- ' to paint ' (?); Dm. *tac* -- ' to cut ' (*c* < IE. *k̂s* NTS xii 128), Kal. *tāč* -- ; Kho. *točhik* ' to cut with an axe '; Phal. *tạc*<-> ' to cut, chop, whittle '; Sh. (Lor.) *thačoiki* ' to fashion (wood) '; K. *tachun* ' to shave, pare, scratch ', S. *tachaṇu*; L. *tachaṇ* ' to scrape ', (Ju.) ' to rough hew ', P. *tacchṇā*, ludh. *tacchanā* ' to hew '; Ku. *tāchṇo* ' to square out '; N. *tāchnu* ' to scrape, peel, chip off ' (whence *tachuwā* ' chopped square ', *tachārnu* ' to lop, chop '); B. *cāchā* ' to scrape '; Or. *tāchibā*, *cāchibā*, *chācibā* ' to scrape off, clip, peel '; Bhoj. *cāchal* ' to smoothe with an adze '; H. *cāchnā* ' to scrape up '; G. *tāchvũ* ' to scrape, carve, peel ', M. *tāsṇẽ*; Si. *sahinavā*, *ha*° ' to cut with an adze '. <-> Kho. *trọcik* ' to hew ' with "intrusive" *r*.Kmd. *tac* -- ' to cut, pare, clip ' GM 22.6.71; A. *cāciba* (phonet. *sāsibɔ*) ' to scrape ' AFD 216, 217, ' to smoothe with an adze ' 331. (CDIAL 5620).

tákṣan (acc. *tákṣaṇam* RV., *takṣāṇam* Pāṇ.) m. ' carpenter '. [√takṣ] Pk. *takkhāṇa* -- m., Paš. ar. *tạcan* -- *kōr*, weg. *taṣā´n*, Kal. *kaṭ* -- *tačon*, Kho. (Lor.) *tačon*, Sh. *kaṭ* -- *th*°, K. *chān* m., *chöñü* f., P. *takhāṇ* m., °*ṇī* f., H. *takhān* m.; Si. *sasa* ' carpenter, wheelwright ' < nom. *tákṣā*. -- With "intrusive" *r*: Kho. (Lor.) *tračon* ' carpenter ', P. *tarkhāṇ* m. (→ H. *tarkhān* m.), WPah. jaun. *tarkhāṇ*. -- With unexpl. *d* -- or *dh* -- (X dā´ru -- ?): S. *ḍrakhaṇu* m. ' carpenter '; L. *drakhāṇ*, (Ju.) *darkhāṇ* m. ' carpenter ' (*darkhāṇ pakkhī* m. ' woodpecker '), mult. *dhrikkhāṇ* m., *dhrikkhaṇī* f., awāṇ. *dhirkhāṇ* m.(CDIAL 5621).

Hieroglyph: <sagaR>(P) {N} ``^cart''. *Mu.<sagaR>, ~<sagRi>, Ho<sagRi> `id.', Sa.<sagaR> `wheel, cart', H.<sAggARA> `cart', O.<sOgORO>. %28221. #28021.<sogoR>(B) {N} ``^cab, ^cart''. *Des. @B27380. #36351. <sAgARa>(L) {N} ``bullock cart''. #57340.Ju<sagaR>(P) {N} ``^cart''. *Mu.<sagaR>, ~<sagRi>, Ho<sagRi> `id.', Sa.<sagaR> `wheel, cart', H.<sAggARA> `cart', O.<sOgORO>. śákaṭa n. (m. R.) ' cart ' 1. Pk. *sagaḍa* -- , *sayaḍa* -- n., *saaḍha* -- m.n., *sagaḍī* -- , °*ḍiyā* -- f.; Pa. *sakaṭa* -- m.n. ' cart, waggon, cartload ', OSi. (Brāhmī) *hakaṭa*, *hakaḍa*, *yahaḍa* ' a measure of capacity ',ŚāṅkhŚr., *śakaṭī́* -- f. RV., *śakaṭiká* -- adj. Pāṇ.gaṇa, °*kā* -- f. ' small cart ' Mr̥cch. Si. *yāḷa* ' cart '.2. K. *hagoru* m. ' cart '; B. *sagṛā* ' bullock -- cart ', Or. *sagaṛa* (*sagaṛiā* ' driver of a cart '); Bi. *sāgaṛ*, *saggaṛā* ' smaller cart ', Mth. *sagaṛ*; H. *saggaṛ*, *sagaṛ* m. ' cart ', *sagṛī* f. ' small cart '.3. S. *chakiṛo* m. ' cart '; P.*chakṛā*, *chikṛā* m. ' large two -- wheeled bullock -- cart '; B. *chakṛā*, *śakṛā* ' cart '; Or. *chakaṛa* ' hackney carriage '; Bi. *chakaṛā* ' large cart ', Mth.*chakkaṛ*, *chakṛī*; H. *chakṛā* m. ' twowheeled bullock -- cart '; G. *chakṛũ* n., °*ṛɔ* m. ' cart '; M. *sākḍā* m. ' the box of a load -- cart '. †śakaṭin -- m. ' owner of a cart ' Kathās. [śákata --]S.kcch. *chaṛyo* m. ' passenger '?(CDIAL 12236) சகடக்கால் cakaṭa-k-kāl, *n.* < சகடம்[1] +. Cart-wheel, carriage-wheel; வண்டிச் சக்கரம். சகடக்கால் போல வரும் (நாலடி, 2).சகடம்[1] cakaṭam, *n.* < *śakaṭa*. 1. Cart, wheeled conveyance drawn by cattle, carriage, chariot; வண்டி. பல்கதிர் முத்தார் சகடம் (சீவக. 363). 2. Car; தேர். சகட சக்கரத் தாமரைநாயகன் (கந்தபு. காப்பு. 1). 3. See சகடயூகம். சகடமாம் வெய்ய யூகமும் (பாரத. எட்டாம். 3). 4. The 4th *nakṣatra*. See உரோகிணி. (பிங்.) 5. Wheel; சக்கரம். (சங். அக.)*சகடு cakaṭu, n. < śakaṭa. 1. [M. cakaṭu.] Cart;* வண்டி. பெருஞ்சகடு தேர்காட்ட

*(பெரியபு. திருநா. 6).***சகடை**[1] *cakaṭa, n. See* **சகடு**, *1.*
*(**புறநா.** 60, 8, **உரை.**)*(Tamil) *Pa. cakur-tol cattleshed.*
Ga. (S.2) sakkī (pl. -l) bull; (P.) sakkil (pl.) bullocks.(DEDR 2267)

Appendix I: *Sphōṭavāda*

Karl Menninger cites a remarkable instance. In the Indian tradition, finger signals were used to settle the price for a trade transaction. (Karl Menninger, 1969, *Number words and number symbols: a cultural history of numbers*, MIT Press, p.212.) Finger gestures were a numeric cipher!

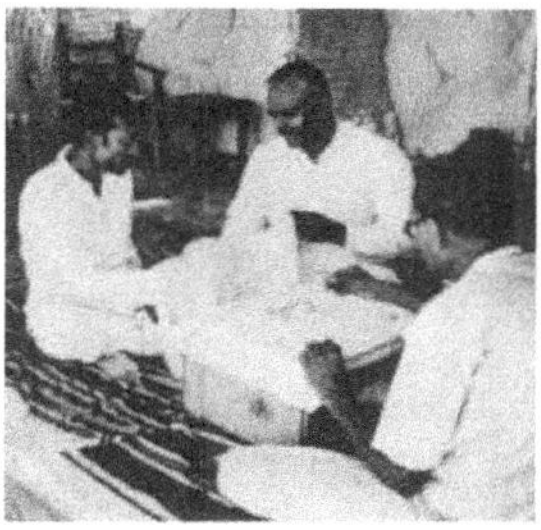

A pearl merchant of South India settling price for a pearl using finger gestures under a handkerchief.

A good beginning is with the following image (with typographical error for the word, 'system', in the legend) pointing to non-linguistic means of communication.

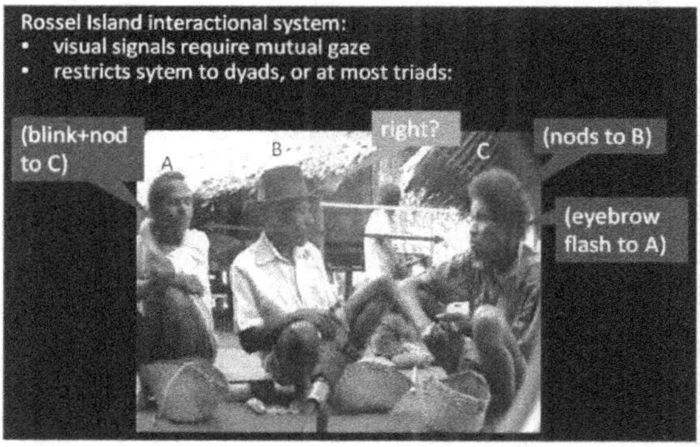
Rossel Island interactional system:
• visual signals require mutual gaze
• restricts sytem to dyads, or at most triads:
(blink+nod to C)
right?
(nods to B)
(eyebrow flash to A)
A
B
C

This image[199] is presented to make the point that non-linguistic symbolic forms can also have 'meaning' in a socio-cultural context and in a tradition which is culture-specific.

sīmánta kũkũ̄ ṭikkɔ

A good example of culture-specific form ofdecoration is provided by the following images of two terracotta toys discovered in Nausharo. The toys are shown decorated with red verimilion marks on the parting of their hair, a tradition which is followed even today in the cultural sphere of Indian *sprachbund.*

Two terracotta figurines. Nausharo. With sindhur (saffron? Vermilion mark) at the parting of the hair.

Tradition of sindhur adornment. Sindhur worn in the parting of the hair. Nausharo: female figurine. Period IB, 280-2600 BCE. 11.6X30.9 cm. (The eyes are puctated and theornaments and hair are all appliqué. This figurines come from Nausharo, Period IB, but is identical to many figurines from Mehergarh Period VII, datin between 2800 and 2600 BCE. Material: terracotta;11.6 cm. high, 30.9 cm. wide.[200] Hair is painted black and parted in the middle of the forehead, with traces of red pigment in the parting. This form of ornamentation may be the origin of the later Hindu tradition where a married woman wears a streak of vermilion or powdered cinnabar (sindhur) in the part of her hair. Choker and pentant necklace are also painted with red pigment, possibly to represent carnelian beads.

Women wearing Sindhur

(kumkum). A lady from Shillong, India wearing Sindhur at the parting of the hair.[201]

We have little documentation of the times explaining the 'meaning' of this sindhur symbolic form on the forehead, close to the parting of the hair. The tradition provides the 'meaning'. It signifies marital status. A married lady wears this symbolic form in the Hindu tradition. It is amazing that tradition has continued at least from 2800-2600 BCE evidenced by the Nausharo terracotta toys.

When the compatriots of Nausharo women represented on the Nausharo terracotta toys conversed with the women, wouldn't their conversation have referred to the symbolic form? If so, what words signified the symbolic form?

The philosophical concept of *sphōṭa,* the 'bursting forth in and of consciousness' may provide a clue to the spatial consciousness expressed in Meluhha language. There are many Meluhha glosses which precisely signify this symbolic form.

Wouldn't *sphōṭa*, the bursting forth in consciousness have linked the imagery of the symbolic form of red mark on the forehead, at the hair-parting, any one or more of these glosses? Unfortunately, we do not have the treatises of the type being worked on in human cognitive neuroscience researches with special reference to explaining or elaborating or theorizing on the significance of the Meluhha glosses which signify the symbolic form shown on the Nausharo toys, providing the meaning of 'married status of the women represented on the toys': *sī̃thi, sī̃ti, sīmánta* ' forehead where hair is parted '; *kū̃kū̃* 'saffron'; *ṭikkɔ* m. ' caste -- mark (round mark applied to forehead of women esp. when married).

We cannot assume that the artisan(s) who made the terracotta representations were lying about the meaning sought to be conveyed by these exquisite, colorful symbol forms of the two

Nausharo terracotta toys. These are not non-liguistic symbolic forms.

These are linguistic symbolic forms, in the socio-cultural, abiding, contexts of Meluhha language and cultural traditions.

Premised on the philosophical framework of symbolic forms, it can be posited that Meluhha linguistic categories -- sememes, in particular -- played a role in cognitive processes of perception, reasoning and memory even if it is assumed that the streak of red color to signify the uniqueness of the two faces is non-verbal communication to signify married status of the women.

It can be hypothesized that the sounds which signified by the image of the symbolic form are premised on Meluhha language and the sounds of the time, when the terracotta toys were used to communicate meaning, are close to the phonetic forms: *sĩti ṭikkɔ* with related 'meanings': parting-in-hair mark signifying married status'.

This hypothesis is consistent with the current statel-of-the-art, empirical inquiries into language diversity, which "is looking … more and more a matter of cultural evolution…Talk of linguistic universals has given cognitive scientists the impression that languages are all built to a common pattern. In fact, there are vanishingly few universals of language in the direct sence that all languages exhibit them. Instead, diversity can be found at almost every level of linguistic organization. This fundamentally changes the object of enquiry from a cognitive science perspective...we illustrate the ways languages vary radically in sound, meaning and syntactic organization, and then we examine in more detail the core grammatical machinery of recursion, constituency, and grammatical relations... Linguistic diversity then becomes the crucial datum for cognitive science: we are the only species with a communication syste that is fundamentally variable at all levels...confronting us with the extraordinary plasticity of the highest human skills."[202]

sīmánta m. ' parting in hair ' AV., ' boundary ', °*aka*<-> m. MBh. [Cf. *sīmantinī* -- f. ' woman ' MBh. -- sīmán --] Pa. *sīmanta* -- m. ' boundary ' (*sīmantinī* -- f. ' woman '); Pk. *sīmaṁta* -- , °*aya* -- m. ' parting in hair, outskirt of village '; Ku. *syũ̄dī*, *syūnī* f. ' forehead where hair is parted, frontal braiding of a woman's hair '; A. *xeuntā*, *xeõtā* ' parting in hair '; Or. *siuntā* ' mode of dressing ringlets of hair on brow ', *siuntiā* ' mode of parting combed hair '; M. *śītā* m., *śītẽ* n. ' parting in a woman's hair '; -- with unexpl. aspirate: S. *sīndhi* f. ' parting in a woman's hair ', L. *sīndh*, (Ju.) *sī˜dh* f., P. *sõdhā* m., N. *siũdho*, *siũdo*; B. *sīthā*, *sītā* ' parting in a woman's hair '; B. Or. *sīthi*, *sīti* 'forehead where hair is parted'; Mth. *siũ̄thi* ' parting of a woman's hair ', OG. *saïthaü* m., G. *se_thɔ*m., *se_thī*, *se_tī* f. Garh. *syũ̄d* ' hair -- parting '. (CDIAL 13436).

tila2 m. ' mole on skin ' Kālid. 2. tílaka -- 2 m. ' sectarial mark on the forehead ' Yājñ., ' freckle ' VarBr̥S. 3. *tillaka -- . 4. *ṭillaka -- . 1. S. *tiru* m. ' mole, freckle '; P. *til* m. ' mole '; H. *til* m. ' black spot, mole '; M. *tīḷ* m. ' mole, freckle '. -- Deriv. H. *tilkā* ' freckled '.2. Pa. *tilaka* -- m. ' stain, mole, freckle '; Pk. *tilaya* -- m. ' caste -- mark '; Ku. *tilo* ' mole '; N. *tili* ' small mole '; B. *tilā* ' freckled '; Or. *tiḷā* ' bits of metal put on ornaments '; Si. *talā* -- *ṭik* ' caste -- mark '. -- Deriv.: Or. *tiḷiā*, °*ḷuā* ' freckled, having moles '; H. *tilaihā* m. ' turtle -- dove '.3. P. *tilln̥ī* f. ' partic. kind of ornament '; N. *tilahari* ' gold ornament on a woman's breast '.4. N. *ṭilo* ' piece of iron presented as a coin to the departed spirit '; G. *ṭīlɔ* m., °*lũ* n. ' caste -- mark ', M. *ṭilā* m. -- Paš.lauṛ. *ṭílī*, weg. *ṭélī* f. ' forehead ' (IIFL iii 3, 181)? WPah.kṭg. *tilli* f. ' nose -- ornament for women '. (CDIAL 5828).

*ṭikka1 ' mark, spot '. [*ṭikkikā* -- f. ' white mark on fore- head of a horse ' VarBr̥S. -- Connexion, if any, with tílaka -- and *ṭillaka -- is obscure] Pk. *ṭikka* -- n. ' caste -- mark ', *ṭikkida* -- ' marked with one '; Ḍ. *ṭīke* m. pl. ' spot ', Sh. *ṭīku̯* m.; K. *ṭyoku* m. ' caste --

mark '; S. *ṭiko* m. ' mark, stain, caste -- mark ', *ṭika* f. ' stone in a ring ', L. *ṭikk* f.; L. P. *ṭikkā* m. ' mark '; WPah. bhad. *ṭikku* n. ' caste -- mark ', Ku. *ṭīko* m., N. *ṭikā*; B. Or. *ṭikā* ' mark ', Bi. *ṭīk*, Mth. *ṭīkā*, *ṭikulī*; H. *ṭīkā* m. ' caste -- mark ', Marw. *ṭīko* m.; G. *ṭīkɔ* m. ' mark '; M. *ṭikā* m. ' spot ', *ṭikẽ*, *ṭhikẽ* n. ' mole, freckle '; OSi. *ṭik* ' mark ', Si. *tik* ' spot, mark, freckle '. S.kcch. *ṭiko* m. ' mark on forehead '; WPah.kṭg. *ṭikkɔ* m. ' caste -- mark (round mark applied to forehead of women esp. when married), eldest son of a rājā ', J. *ṭikā* m. ' heir apparent of a chief ', P. *ṭikkā* m. ' caste -- mark, oldest son of a king '. (CDIAL 5458).

*agriyapāṭa ' front expanse '. [agriyá -- , pāṭa --]S. *agyāṛī* f. ' front part of the head above the forehead, forepart of any interval '.(CDIAL 93).

kuṅkuma n. ' saffron, Crocus sativus ' Suśr.Pa. *kuṅkuma* -- n., Pk. *kuṁkuma* -- , K. *köṅg* m.; S. L. *kuṅgū* m. ' a bright red dye used for marking forehead '; P. *kuṅgū* m. ' red paste for the forehead, saffron '; G.*kũkũ* n. ' turmeric '; M. *kũkū̃* n. ' saffron ', Si. *kokum*, °*kuṅ*; -- G. *kā̃kũ* n. if *a* is old may be origin of Gk. and Lat. loans: ka/gkamon Hesychius, *cancanum* Pliny: see EWA i 219 with lit. *kuṅkumapattrikā ' saffron letter '. [kuṅkuma -- , páttra --] (CDIAL 3214). G. *kā̃kotrī* f. ' invitation to a marriage party (conveyed in a letter dyed red) '.(CDIAL 3215)

*ṭikka1 ' mark, spot '. [*ṭikkikā* -- f. ' white mark on fore- head of a horse ' VarBr̥S. -- Connexion, if any, with tílaka -- and *ṭillaka -- is obscure] Pk. *ṭikka* -- n. ' caste -- mark ', *ṭikkida* -- ' marked with one '; Ḍ. *ṭīke* m. pl. ' spot ', Sh. *ṭīkụ* m.; K. *ṭyoku* m. ' caste -- mark '; S. *ṭiko* m. ' mark, stain, caste -- mark ', *ṭika* f. ' stone in a ring ', L. *ṭikk* f.; L. P. *ṭikkā* m. ' mark '; WPah. bhad. *ṭikku* n. ' caste -- mark ', Ku. *ṭīko* m., N. *ṭikā*; B. Or. *ṭikā* ' mark ', Bi. *ṭīk*, Mth. *ṭīkā*, *ṭikulī*; H. *ṭīkā* m. ' caste -- mark ', Marw. *ṭīko* m.; G. *ṭīkɔ* m. ' mark '; M. *ṭikā* m. ' spot ', *ṭikẽ*, *ṭhikẽ* n. ' mole, freckle '; OSi. *ṭik* ' mark ', Si. *tik* ' spot, mark, freckle '.

S.kcch. *ṭiko* m. ' mark on forehead '; WPah.kṭg. *ṭikkɔ* m. ' caste -- mark (round mark applied to forehead of women esp. when married), eldest son of a rājā ', J. *ṭīkā* m. ' heir apparent of a chief ', P. *ṭikkā* m. ' caste -- mark, oldest son of a king '.(CDIAL 5458).

The issue dealt with in this book relates to a dominant cognitive system of defining 'meaning' in the context of Bronze Age life-activities narrated on about 7000 epigraphs of Meluhha hieroglyphs. To my knowledge, there is no falsifiable method for identifying non-linguistic symbols in these epigraphs which contain sequences deploying – recursively -- over 600 hieroglyphs. These 600+ hieroglyphs are what are categorized in Indus script/Meluhha hieroglyphs corpora as 'signs' and 'pictorial motifs (also called field symbols)' for ease of statistical analyses. It will be an error to focus on 'signs', ignoring 'pictorial motifs' to arrive at the cipher for the writing system. It is also an error to assume that the entire set of corpora deploy only non-linguistic symbolic forms since no known method exists to identify non-linguistic from linguistic symbolic forms in written-down two-dimensional or carved three-dimensional artifacts such as steatite seals or images of 'priest' decorated with hieroglyphs of trefoils or ivory artifact of 'standard device' which frequently occurs in front of a one-horned young bull on seals.

Indus Priest/King Statue. The statue is 17.5 cm high and carved from steatite a.k.a. soapstone. It was found in Mohenjo-daro in 1927. It is on display in the National Museum, Karachi, Pakistan.

Any number of arbitrary assumptions can be made about the 'meaning' of these symbolic forms – that the bull is a 'unicorn', that the 'unicorn' is *ekaśṛnga* of vedic tradition narratives, that the 'standard device' is a 'cult symbol' (whateer it means) and so on. Such assumptions to be meaningful will have to be applied with consistently across the entire corpora. To my knowledge, no proponent of non-linguistic nature of Indus writing has proven the validity of such a consistent application of the non-linguistic symbolic form method. Vague statements about solar worship or heraldry or agricultural divination are not contributions to the advancing understanding the meanings of the symbolic forms.

Method

That the ancient languages of India, constituted a *sprachbund* (or language union) is now recognized in many language studies. The *sprachbund* area is proximate to or coterminu with the area where most of the Indus script inscriptions with Meluhha hieroglyphs were discovered, as documented in the corpora.

That hundreds of the very same hieroglyphs continued to be used in metallurgy is evidenced by their use on early punch-marked coins. This explains the combined use of syllabic scripts such as *kharoṣṭī* and *brāhmī* together with the hieroglyphs on Rampurva copper bolt, and Sohgaura copper plate from about 6th century BCE. Meluhha hieroglyphs constitute a writing system for Meluhha language and are rebus representations of stone-work and archaeo-metallurgy lexemes.

The rebus principle was employed by the early scripts and can legitimately be used to decipher the Meluhha hieroglyphs, after secure pictorial identification.

Philosophical inquiry, the argument and cipher

Language faculty is formed as an integral component of a human being. Thus, origin of language is related to origin of human consciousness.

Consciousness is an inheritance, a spark from the *brahman*, which is innate and manifests in every *ātman*. This manifestation is *sphōṭa,* the 'bursting forth in and of consciousness'.

Consciousness, as an innate, inherent reality, manifests through language and interacts with sensory impacts from the external reality of the world.

It is significant that the phoneme *cit-* signifies both consciousness and funeral pyre. This is a foundation for tracing the origin of human consciousness, *cit-*, as received wisdom from ancestors (perhaps as integral fragments of DNA sequences), passed on from generation to generation. Hence, the celebration of the memory of ancestors and the heritage they have handed down by creating a shrine and calling it *cētiya* (Pali).

Mirroring and imaging or networking of *cit-* occurs in an unceasing continuum of interaction, dialogue, between the inner reality of consciousness -- *ātman* and the external reality of the phenomena of the world.

This process of mirroring occurs in neural networks by formulating images or sensory neural vibrations which manifest as hieroglyphs or as utterances or gestures (signs). This is the philosophy of symbolic forms, presented in the thesis *Vākyapadīyam* वाक्यपदीयम्, a work attributed to Bhartṛhari (भर्तृहरि) (ca. 425-450 CE) and in the philosophical excursus of Saussure (1857-1913 CE) and Wittgenstein (1889-1951 CE). Thus, writing as a manifestation of consciousness (together with uttered or heard sound or other perceived sensory phenomena) is an integral component in the formation and origin of language. To be capable of language is to be literate – to be capable of creating the text. This is consonant with the statement of Jacques Derrida[203] 'there is nothing outside the text.' This statement is in direct contrast to Saussure's view that meaning in words is outside the text.

It will be an error to look for proto-literate stages of evolution in human civilization. Similarly, it will be a restrictive view of origin of language to assume that literacy simply means an ability to signify phonemes using syllables or alphabets. Literacy also includes an ability to draw pictures which convey words and their meanings (*logos*). Heraclitus (ca. 535–475 BCE) – dates which make Heraclitus a contemporary of Bhartr̥hari -- who used the term -- *logos* (/ˈloʊɡɒs/, /ˈlɒɡɒs/, or /ˈloʊɡoʊs/; Greek: λόγος, from λέγω *lego* "I say"). -- for a principle of order and knowledge. The cryptographic challenge of a writing system of *vāk* – the Meluhha text -- is to identify the cipher to represent meanings of utterances, *logos* represented as hieroglyphic *logographs*, or more precisely, *sememe-graphs* to represent the smallest units of meaning in language – mostly, words or glosses in a lexicon. This should be contrasted with *phonographs*, which represent phonemes (speech sounds) or combinations of *phonemes*, and determinatives, which mark semantic categories. *Phonographs* is a term applicable to syllables (such as *abjads*, *abugidas*, syllabaries) or alphabets and to diacritical marks to signify phonetic variations. The first historical civilizations of India, Near East, Africa, China, and Central America used some form of *logographic* or *sememe-graphic* writing. As writing systems evolved, phonetic elements were also fused into *sememe-graphs* as evidenced by Egyptian hieroglyphs or hieratic or demotic as *logoconsonantal* scripts; cuneiform or Maya glyphs or Han characters as *logosyllabic* scripts.

The cipher (or cypher) of Meluhha *vāk* is an ordered set of rebus *sememe-graphs*, using Meluhha glosses from Indian *sprachbund*, an algorithm for performing encryption or decryption—a series of well-defined steps that can be followed as a procedure, constituting a writing system – to read aloud and understand the 'meanig' or knowledge system of the Meluhha text.
The *vāk* embedded in Bhartr̥hari's philosophical work is traced to R̥gveda which names deified, personified *vāk* as Rāṣṭrī, community steadfastness manifested as a community, a well-watered, well-endowed grouping of nations and matching

resources with talents of people. The divinity *vāk as* Vāk devī starts her monologue: *aham rāṣṭrī samgamanī vasūnām* (Ṛgveda 10.125).Trans. I am *Rāṣṭram* taking pilgrims on a lighted, steadfast progress with wealth. The symbolic forms of *vāk* thus gain an expanded dimension related to life-activities and acquisition, accumulation of wealth, *artha.* Indian tradition also uses Vāk devī as a metaphor or synonym of *Sarasvatī,* the divinity of knowledge, also the mighty, forceful (*āsurī*) Himalayan river which nurtured and sustained a civilization on her banks. The semantics of the sememe *artha* are: in addition to wealth, 'meaning'. Thus *vāk* and *artha* are intertwined, integrating both language and meaning, while perceiving languge itself as a life-expression.

Vājasneyi Samhitā (10.4) explains the form, structure and function of Rāṣṭram:

This refrain is repeated several times, describing the attributes of Rāṣṭram.

Āpah parivahiṇī stha Rāṣṭradā Rāṣṭram me datta svāhā
Āpah parivahiṇī stha Rāṣṭradā Rāṣṭramamuṣmai datta svāhā

parivahiṇī stha -- Place with (ocean) waves
apām patirasi – Place adjoining the ocean (apām pati)
apām garśnosi – Place moistened (endowed) with water
sūryatvacas stha – Place covered by sunshine
māndā stha – Place with gladdening (potable) waters
vrajākṣita stha – Place with marked roads, cattle-sheds, enclosures or herdsmen stations
vāśā stha -- Place with plants (arable land)
śāviṣṭhā stha – Place with resolute, mightiest (craftsmen)(cf. RV 5.29.15)
śakvarī stha – Endowed with artificers
janaśnṛta stha – Place with agriculturists (anṛta)
viśvaśnṛta stha – Place with culture (cultivator tradition) of *pitṛ-s.*
vṛṣṇa ūrmirasi stha -- powerful wave (cutting like a sword)
vṛṣa senosi stha -- powerful battle-array (cutting like a spear)

artheta stha -- place with work opportunities to create wealth
ojasvatī stha -- place filled with water, vigour, lustre
viśva bhṛtam -- place bearing, nourished by the dharma of pitr-s
āpah svarāja stha -- place with self-luminous, resplendent rays of the sun and water (springs)

These are the endowments of a Rāṣṭram.

Rāṣṭradā Rāṣṭramamuṣmai means 'Rāṣṭram (in exchange for this prayer), for this (generation) and for generations'.

Rāṣṭrī is genitrix, the mother nourishing and sustaining her children.

Rāṣṭrī feminine form of *Rāṣṭram* can be summarized as a path, traveled on by a community of people, a grouping of nations, washed by the waves of oceans and endowed with people working together on a pilgrimage, *yātrā* of generations. This is the path of *abhyudayam* and *niḥśreyas* (social welfare and union of every *ātman* with *paramātman*).

A shrine is an external memory marker. *ceīya*, *ceī* m. 'shrine' (Old Gujarati); *cētiya* -- n. 'sepulchral monument'(Pali). This *cētiya* is a shrine venerating cḗtana 'visible' RV., 'sentient ' KaṭhUp., n. 'intelligence ' signifyingy *vāk*, the divinity of language. The word in Indian *sprachbund* which signifies consciousness is: cḗtas n. 'intelligence' RV., 'mind' VS., 'will' AV. [√cit] Pa. *cētas* -- n. ' intelligence ', Pk. *cēas* -- n.; OB. *cie* ' in the mind '; Si. *sey* ' mind, state '; Md. *hei*, *hē* ' mind, life, consciousness '. (CDIAL 4907). cḗtana ' visible ' RV., ' sentient ' KaṭhUp., n. ' intelli- gence ' Yājñ. [√cit] Pa. *cētanā* -- f. ' thinking '; Pk. *cēyaṇa* -- ' sentient ', n. ' intelligence '; MB. *ceana* ' sense '.(CDIAL 4905). cítti1 f. ' thought ' RV. [√cit] Pa. *citti* -- f. ' thought for, honour '; Sh. (Lor.) *čit* f. ' authority, will '; B. *citi* ' intellect ', OG. *cīti* f., M. *cit* f.; -- with *vārttā* -- : N. *bāt* -- *cit* ' conversation ', H. *bāt* -- *cīt* f., G. *vāt* --

cit f. -- In view of Sh. *čit* f. the forms of Kho. Kal. Pr. Kt. Wg. s.v. cittá -- 1 are perh. < *cítti* -- 1.(CDIAL 4801).

citā f. ' funeral pyre ' MBh. [√ci1] Pa. *citakā* -- f., Pk. *ciā* -- , *ciyayā* -- f., G. *ce* f. S.kcch. *cai* f. ' funeral pyre '. (CDIAL 4796). cíti f. ' layer, pile, stack of wood ' TS. [√ci1] Pa. *citi* -- f. ' heap (of bricks) '; Pk. *cii* -- f. ' layer, collecting together, building (a wall &c.) ', *ciigā* -- , *cīyā* -- f., °*ya* -- n. ' funeral pyre '; Ash. *čī* ' bark of tree ', Wg. *čī* (< cī´ra -- NTS ii 250), Kt. *čīk*, Paš. *čīk*, Gaw. *čīk*.(CDIAL 4798). *caitya* -- ' relating to a funeral pyre ', m.n. ' funeral monument, sacred tree ' ĀśvGr̥. [citā --] Pa. *cētiya* -- n. ' sepulchral monument ', Pk. *cēia* -- m.n.; OG. *ceīya*, *ceī* m. ' shrine '; OSi. (Brāhmī inscr.) *ceta*, *ceya*, Si. *sạya* ' heap of wood, funeral pyre ' H. Smith JA 1950, 207.(CDIAL 4914).

vā´c -- f. ' speech ' RV. vākya n. ' speech, words ' MBh. [√vac] Pa. *vākya* -- n. ' speech ', Pk. *vakka* -- n.; K. *wākh*, dat. °*kas* m. ' speech, voice ', adj. at end of cmpds. -- *wôku*; S. *vāko* m. ' outcry '; P. *vāk*, *bāk* m. ' word, speech '; Ku. *bākā*, *ākā* -- *bākā* ' abusive language '; Or. OAw. *bāka* ' word, speech '; H. *bāk* m. ' word, proverb '.(CDIAL 11468). vā´cā f. ' speech, word ' Pañcat., *Vākika* -- n. ' verbal message ' Naiṣ. [*vā´c* -- f. RV. -- √vac] Pa. *Vākā* -- f. ' speech ', Pk. *vāyā* -- , *vāā* -- f.; -- Si. *vada* ' speech ' or < *vā´dya* -- , but more prob. with H. Smith JA 1950, 187 < vácas -- ; -- Aś.shah. man. kāl. *vaca*<-> (in *vacaguti*) prob. < vácas -- .(CDIAL 11472). Vākyá ' relating to speech ' VS., *vā´cya* -- ' to be spoken ' Up., n. ' blame ' MBh. [√vac]Pk. *vacca* -- n. ' words, speech '; K. *wāc* m. ' speech, promise '; P. *Vākā* m. ' promise, agreement '; Garh. *bāc* ' speech '; Si. *vasa*, *vā* -- ' word, speech '. -- Deriv. K. *wācal* m. ' reviler '. -- Si. *vas* ' vice, depravity ' prob. < aVākya -- . Garh. *bāc* ' speech '; Md. *vāhaka* ' speech, story '.(CDIAL 11476).

Vac वच् I. 2 P. (Ā. also in non-conjugational tenses; in conjugational tenses it is said to be defective in the third person plural by some authorities, or in the whole plural by others; वक्ति, उवाच, अवोचत्, वक्ष्यति, वक्तुम्, उक्त) 1 To say, speak; वैराग्यादिव वक्षि K. P.1; (oft. with two. acc.); तामूचतुस्ते प्रियमप्यमिथ्या R.14.6; sometimes with accusative of words meaning 'speech'; उवाच धात्र्या प्रथमोदितं वचः R.3.25;2.59; क एवं वक्ष्यते वाक्यम् Rām. -2 To relate, describe; रघूणामन्वयं वक्ष्ये R.1.9. -3 To tell, communicate, announce, declare; उच्यतां मद्वचनात्सारथिः Ś.2; Me.1. -4 To name, call; तदेकसप्ततिगुणं मन्वन्तरमिहोच्यते Ms.1.79. -5 To signify, denote (as sense). -6 To recite, repeat. -7 To cen- sure; reproach; वृत्तिविज्ञानवान् धीरः कस्तं वा वक्तुमर्हति Mb. 12.132.6. -II. 1 P. To inform, to tell; L. D. B. -*Caus.* (वाचयति-ते) 1 To cause to speak. -2 To go over, read, peruse; वाचयति नान्यलिखितं लिखितमनेन वाचयति नान्यः । अयमपरोऽस्य विशेषः स्वयमपि लिखितं स्वयं न वाचयति ॥ Subhāṣ. -3 To say, tell, declare. -4 To promise. -*Desid.* (विवक्षति) To wish to speak, intend to say (something); विवक्षता दोषमपि च्युतात्मना त्वयैकमीशं प्रति साधु भाषितम् Ku.5.81. वचम् vacḥam Speaking, talk vacas वचस् *n.* 1 A speech, word, sentence; उवाच धात्र्या प्रथमोदितं वचः R.3.25,47; इत्यव्यभिचारि तद्वचः Ku.5. 36; वचस्तत्र प्रयोक्तव्यं यत्रोक्तं लभते फलम् Subhāṣ. -2 A command, order, precept, injunction. -3 Advice, counsel. -4 A hymn

Vākā वाचा 1 Speech. -2 A sacred text, a text or apho- rism. -3 An oath. Vākya वाच्य *a.* [वच्-कर्मणि ण्यत्] 1 To be spoken, told or said, to be spoken to or addressed; vāṅmaya वाङ्मय *a.* (-यी *f.*) 1 Consisting of words; लिपेर्यथावद्- ग्रहणेन वाङ्मयं

नदीमुखेनेव समुद्रमाविशत् R.3.28; इत्येषा वाङ्मयी पूजा श्रीमच्छंकरपादयोः Śiva-mahimna 4. -2 Relating to speech or words; Ms.12.6; स्वाध्यायाभ्यसनं चैव वाङ्मयं तप उच्यते Bg.17.15. -3 Endowed with speech; अयमात्मा वाङ्मयो मनोमयः प्राणमयः Bṛi. Up.1.5.3. -4 Eloquent, rhetorical, oratorical. -यम् 1 Speech, language; म्यरस्तजभ्नगैर्लान्तैरेभिर्दशभिरक्षरैः । समस्तं वाङ्मयं व्याप्तं त्रैलोक्यमिव विष्णुना Chand. M.1.7; द्विधाप्रयुक्तेन च वाङ्मयेन सरस्वती तन्मि- थुनं नुनाव Ku.7.9; Śi.2.72. -2 Eloquence. -3 Rhe- toric. -यी The goddess Sarasvatī.
वाचनम् [वच्-णिच् स्वार्थे वा णिच् ल्युट्] 1 Reading, reci- ting. -2 Declaration, proclamation, utterance; as in स्वस्तिवाचनम्, पुण्याहवाचनम्

वाच् *f.* [वच्-क्विप् दीर्घो$संप्रसारणं च Uṇ.2.67] 1 A word, sound, an expression (opp. अर्थ); वागर्थाविव संपृक्तौ वागर्थप्रतिपत्तये R.1.1. -2 Words, talk, language, speech; वाचि पुण्यापुण्यहेतवः Māl.4; लौकिकानां हि साधूनामर्थं वागनुवर्तते । ऋषीणां पुनराद्यानां वाचमर्थो$नुधावति U.1.1; विनिश्चितार्थामिति वाचमाददे Ki.1.3 'spoke these words', 'spoke as fol- lows'; R.1.49; Śi.2.13,23; Ku.2.3. -3 A voice, sound; अशरीरिणी वागुदचरत् U.2; मनुष्यवाचा R.2.33. *a.* (वाक्पति) eloquent; oratorical.

Vāgmin वाग्मिन् *a.* [वाच् अस्त्यर्थे ग्मिनिः चस्य कः तस्य लोपः; cf. P. V.2.124] 1 Eloquent, oratorical. -2 Talkative. -3 Verbose, wordy. *-m.* 1 An orator, an eloquent man; अनिर्लोडितकार्यस्य वाग्जालं वाग्मिनो वृथा Śi.2.27,19; Ki. 14.6; Pt.3.87. -2 N. of

Bṛihaspatī. -3 N. of Viṣṇu. vāgya वाग्य *a.* [वाचं यच्छति, यम्-ड] 1 Speaking little, speaking cautiously. -2 Speaking truly. -ग्यः 1 Modesty, humility. वाग्यतस् *ind.* Silently.

वाक्य विलेखः An officer in वाक्यविलेखाख्यैर्दत्तोपन्तैः स्वशक्तितः Parṇāl.4.55.

वाक्यार्थः 1 the meaning of a sentence. -2 (in Mīmāṁsā) the sense of a sente- nce derived on the strength of वाक्यप्रमाण as distinguished from श्रुति, लिङ्ग and other प्रमाणs. This is weaker than and hence sublated by the श्रुत्यर्थ or श्रुति; यत्र श्रुत्यर्थो न संभवति तत्र वाक्यार्थो गृह्यते ŚB. on MS. 6.2.14. वाक्यार्थः श्रुत्या बाध्यते ŚB. on MS.6.2.14. According to Mīmāṁsā view the अर्थs of पदs are सामान्य and when these form a sentence to yield the वाक्यार्थ, they get restricted or modified. Hence वाक्यार्थ means the पदार्थs modified or restricted; सामान्येनाभिप्रवृत्तानां पदार्थानां यद्विशेषे$वस्थानं स वाक्यार्थः ŚB. on MS.3.1.12. वाक्यम् [वच्-ण्यत् चस्य कः] 1 Speech, words, a sentence, saying, what is spoken; शृणु मे वाक्यम् 'hear my words', 'hear me'; वाक्ये न संतिष्ठते 'does not obey'; संक्षिप्तस्याप्यतो$स्यैव वाक्यस्यार्थगरीयसः Śi.1.2.24. -2 A sen- tence, period (complete utterance of a thought); वाक्यंस्याद्योग्यताकाङ्क्षासत्तियुक्तः पदोच्चयः S. D.6; पदसमूहो वाक्यम् Tarka K.; श्रौत्यार्थी च भवेद्वाक्ये समासे तद्धिते तथा K. P.1. -3 An argument or syllogism (in logic). वाकः [वच्-घञ्] 1 Speech- uttering; as in नमोवाकं प्रशास्महे U.1.1; Voice (वाणी); सर्व- मिदमभ्यात्तो$वाक्यनादरः Ch. Up.3.14.2. -3 Text

(संहिता); a Vedic portion containing mantras; यं वाकेष्वनुवाकेषु निष- त्सूपनिषत्सु च (गुणन्ति) Mb.12.49.26. -Comp. - उपवाकम् speech and reply, dialogue.

How is sense formulated in consciousness?

Either it can burst forth spontaneously -- स्फोट -- or be impelled by conscious desire.

स्फोट (in phil.) sound (conceived as eternal , indivisible , and creative); the eternal and imperceptible element of sounds and words and the real vehicle of the idea which bursts or flashes on the mind when a sound is uttered; bursting , opening , expansion , disclosure. स्फोटा shaking or waving the arms. स्फोटा for स्फटा the expanded hood of a snake. नर्म—स्फोट (dram.) the first symptoms of love.

ākāṅkṣā आकाङ्क्षा Desire, wish; (In gram.) The presence of a word necessary to complete the sense, one of the three elements necessary to convey a complete sense or thought (the other two being योग्यता 'appropriateness' and आसत्ति 'uninterrupted sequence (of words = सं-निधि'); आकाङ्क्ष *a.* 1 Desiring, wishing. - 2 (In gram.) Requiring some words to complete the sense; अङ्गयुक्तं तिडाकाङ्क्षम्. This process of completing the sentence by adding words is अध्याहारः A mode of interpreting a sentence. Ac- cording to this mode, an incomplete sentence is made to yield complete sense by supplying some extra word or words therein. अध्याहार should be clearly distinguished from अनुषङ्ग which also is a mode of interpreting an incomplete sentence; परिपूर्णमेवेदं वाक्यं नाध्याहारमर्हति विप्रलम्भ- कर्तृकम् ŚB. on MS.4.3.1 (see

अनुषङ्ग). cf. also अपरि- पूर्णं यद् वाक्यं तदध्याहारेण वा पूर्येत व्यवहितकल्पनया वा । तत्राध्या- हाराद् व्यवहितकल्पना ज्यायसी । अध्याहारे हि अश्रुतः कल्प्येत । ईत- रत्र श्रुतेन सम्बन्धः । ŚB. on MS.7.4.1.

Four cognitive stages of language production are recognized: intention, conceptualization, formulation, articulation. Articulated language is also heard in a neural feed-back loop.

Intention is a conscious selection of the mental concepts to be expressed and constitutes a preverbal stage in formulation of language.[204]

Language can be produced by sound (phonetics) and also manually by signs (body – e.g. smile, grimace; or hand-finger-wrist gestures). Signs can also be written down as hieroglyphs.

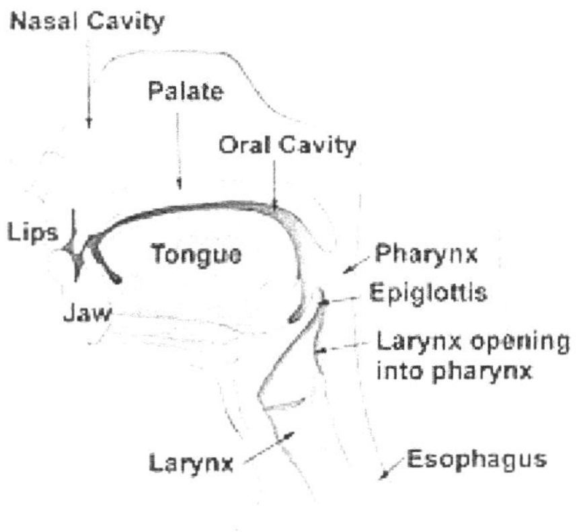

From an inventory of pre-existing, heard, or seen or sensorily-perceived phenomena recorded as repertoire in memory networks, words to be spoken or gestures (signs) to be deployed are selected in the mind, have their phonetics formulated and then finally articulated by the motor system in the vocal and body muscular-nervous system apparatus.

The vocal production of speech can be associated with the production of synchronized by signs (e.g. hand gestures) that act to enhance the comprehensibility of what is being said.

Words which are easily imaged or imagined are quicker to say.
Human vocal apparatus used to produce speech

वि-कल्प (in gram.) admission of an option or alternative , the allowing a rule to be observed or not at pleasure (वे*ति विकल्पः Pāṇini 1-1) different; a collateral form; alternation , alternative , option; contrivance; distinction; mental occupation , thinking वि-कल्पेन optionally

पश्यन्ती is linked to पश्यत् 'seeing , beholding'

वैखरी is It is speech in the fourth of its four stages from the first stirring of the air or breath , articulate utterance , that utterance of sounds or words which is complete as consisting of full and intelligible sentences.

vaikharī वैखरी शब्दनिष्पत्तिर्मध्यमा श्रुतिगोचरा । द्योतितार्था च पश्यन्ती सूक्ष्मा वागनपायिनी ॥ Malli. on Ku.2.17 Articulate utterance, production of sound; the faculty of speech or the divinity presiding over it.

sphōṭa 'bursting forth in consciousness' explained by Bhartr̥hari (भर्तृहरि) and philosophilosophical inquiries of Saussure and Wittgenstein on language and thought provide the framework for Meluhha cipher which has identified an ancient language: Meluhha *vāk* or Mleccha speech. The purpose of Meluhha hieroglyphs written and read by Meluhha speakers is integration, organization and written representation of their life-activities and hence, defined as a writing system. The writing system is related to Meluhha *vāk*.

Vāk is comparable to *parole* 'speech'.

This monograph has become possible thanks to Ashok Aklujkar and Richard Sproat. Ashok Aklujkar has commented on the works attributed to Bhartr̥hari (dated not later than 425-450 CE) --

Trikāṇḍī Vṛtti and *Vākyapadīyam* which are, by any standards of inquiry, expositions on the philosophy of speech (language), though there could be disputations on the need for reworking the available ancient texts as critical editions. Richard Sproat led me on to the current state of researches in cognitive studies with particular reference to language diversity.

The philosophical foundations are related to the evidence provided by Vātsyāyana in Kāmasūtra denoting an art of cipher-decoding called *mlecchita vikalpa.*

The purpose of this monograph is to validate insights related to philosophy of language enunciated in the context of the Indian *sprachbund.* (The word can be derived from Wittgenstein's *Sprache* variously rendered as 'language' or 'the language' or 'linguistic structure' or 'linguistic systel' and the suffix *-bund* as 'union' or 'area').

The validation is done using clearly identifiable Meluhha hieroglyphs on about 7000 epigraphs. The continuation of the tradition of writing deploying Meluhha hieroglyphs is noticed in the historical periods by the evidence of Sohgaura copper plate, and punch-marked coin symbols. In addition to the 7,000 epigraphs, there are also hundreds of cylinder seals of the ancient Near East which deploy comparable hieroglyphs: for example, Tukulti-Ninurta altar, cylinder seals with or without cuneiform texts depicting scenes such as the following.

The cipher is rebus; the language is mleccha/meluhha of Indian *sprachbund.*

In *Philosophische Grammatik*, Wittgenstein holds that 'When I think in language, there aren't meanings going through my mind in addition to the verbal expressions; the language is itself the vehicle of thought.'[205]

The sequence of 'thought' and then 'language' is articulated by Aristotle: "Words spoken are symbols or signs of affections or impressions of the soul; written words are the signs of words spoken. As writing, so also is speech not the same for all races of men. But the mental affections themselves, of which these words are primarily signs, are the same for the whole of mankind, as are also the objects of which those affectios are representations or likenesses, images, copies." (*De Interpretatione*, I). 'Objects' of the real world create 'representations' of them; Aristotle calls these 'mental affections'. Only suh a mental affection can create a 'meaningful' word or sememe. Identification of the mental affection explains what the word 'means'.

Some examples by comparative philologists of Germany and France demonstrated that homonymy is evidence that linguistic expression follows an autonomous development, unrelated to the operations of the mind. "…the reason why the English word *race* means on the one hand 'competition' and on the other hand 'people, nation' has nothing to do with any connection between the two ideas, but is the chance result of a phonetic convergence between the Old Norse word *ras* and the quite different Old French word *race*."[206]

This demonstration does not negate the fact that languages of Indian sprachbund have homonyms which might have developed autonomously but which were deployed in the system of writing called *mlecchita vikalpa*, using pictures to convey objects being traded. "…in order to understand what a knight 'means' in chess one needs to know its role in th game. To be sure, one can still distinguish between the wooden or ivory knight and a corresponding concept (the concept of a 'chess knight')."[207]

This is the crux of the argument providing the cipher for Meluhha hieroglyphs. The concept of a 'Meluhha hieroglyph 'elephant' connects in the writer's and reader's mind the known language gloss: *ibha* 'elephant' with the homonyms *ibbo* 'merchant'; *ib* 'iron'. Thus there is a mental operation, a thought process in the mind which links the image 'elephant' with the similar sounding words (homonyms) *meaning* iron merchant. Thus, thought and language are intertwined in the Meluhha artisan trade transactions recorded in writing. To ask what the 'elephant' means on a Meluhha epigraph is to ask for an elucidation of the life-activity of the Meluhha writer and reader trading in iron. It is this indivisibility which is consistent with the Saussurean doctrine identifying the signal (*significant*) and signification (*signifie*). "The association between sound pattern and concept which constitutes the linguistic sign is not an association of independently given items."[208] Saussure's chapter on 'Linguistic value' makes this clear. "Just as it is impossible to take a pair of scissors and cut one side of paper without at the same time cutting the other, so it is impossible in a language to separate sound from thought, or thought from sound. To separate the two for theoretical purposes takes us into either pure psychology or pure phonetics, not linguistics."[209] Thus, it is impossible to separe the sound *ib* 'iron' or *ibbo* 'merchant' from the thought *ibha* 'elephant' which flashes in the brain of both the writer and reader Meluhhan as *sphōṭa.*

The cipher rebus readigs of Meluhha hieroglyphs demonstrates the possibility of describing what is on the phonetic *recto* separately from describing what is on the conceptual *verso.* Meluhha hieroglyph elephant makes it possible to describe the shape of the animal – phonetic *ibha* -- evoking description of the *sphōṭa* which links the conceptual verso – truth of *ib* 'iron' *ibbo* 'merchant'. Thus, the image of written-down value of sound and thought of trade get intertwined in the neural network. One who has been taught which words mean what can perceive the recto as verso – sound with sense. One word represented as a picture is contrasted with other words of the Meluhha language system. This is premised on the doctrine that thought is language-related and that thought finds expression in signs of sound and picture(s). "Thinking is no longer an autonomous, self-sustaining activity of the human ming, and speech merely its externalization. On the contrary, speech and thought are interdependent, neither occurring without the other, and both made possible by language.

This emphasis on the interdependent relationship between thinking and speaking emerges with different nuances in the work of both thinkers (Saussure and Wittgenstein). Saussure roundly denies the possibility of pre-linguistic thought:'Pschologically, setting aside its expression in words, our thought is simply a vague, shapeless mass…No ideas are established in advance, and nothing is distinct, before the introduction of linguistic structure.'[210]

Such a Meluhhan who writes down the picture of an elephant to describe the thought of 'iron, merchant' is a literate person, versed in Meluhha language. The sound of a word *ibha* is perceptible both as sound as written-down 'elephant', whereas its meaning is not perceptible; but all three facets-- sound, picture and meaning – have intertwined linguistic experience in Meluhha language to signify *ib, ibbo* 'iron, merchant'.

Roy Harris summarises the question of literacy from a philosophical perspective in the context of the function served by writing. Viewing written communication as "a process of transferring thoughts or messages from one individual mind to another..." and, "consisting in the contextualized integration of human activities by means of signs."[211] As a non-kinetic form, writing can "in principle be processed and reprocessed as often as may be, and by as many people as have access to it, within the temporal limits determined by its own duration…the underlying formal substratum of writing is not visual but spatial."[212]

Language provides a structural complexity for entwining thought with language – both interacting with each other in neural networks. Wittgenstein distinguishes this complexity with simple forms of thought with a question and answer session: 'A dog believes his master is at the door. But can he also believe his master will come the day after tomorrow?...Can only those hope who can talk? Only those who have mastered the use of a language. That is to say, the phenomena of hope are modes of this complicated form of life.'[213]

When a Meluhhan artisan works with 'objects' of the world which are stones, ores, metals and creates new transformed artifacts, his or her mental affections determine the Meluhha words and the associated 'meaning'. The sounds associated with the words and the meanings associated with the words are entirely related to his socio-cultural context, exemplified by Meluhha as language – an agreed social convention and standard for naing objects. An inquiry as to why a Meluhhan chose to use the same sounds to denote a young bull or a turner's lathe need not detain us here. We will just take the evidence of glosses as recorded in the lexicons of languages of Indian *sprachbund.*

The surprise is that Meluhha glosses provide for homonyms which explain almost all the 600+ hieroglyphs (both 'signs' and 'pictorial motifs') deployed on Meluhha epigraphs. The surprise becomes a philosophical revelation, a thrill when the application of the rebus cipher finds the representations signifying one category of life-activities of Meluhha speakers: lapidary-artisan work with stones, metals, alloys, lathes, smelters, furnaces, crucibles, fire. One deduction is possible that the documentation achieved through the representations of Meluhha hieroglyphs was necessitated by the fact hat the Meluhha speakers had produced artifacts which had exchange-value and could be traded across the Tin Road with regions of ancient Near East and Fertile Crescent. Bronze-age revolution exemplified by Chanhu-daro which had the dimensions of Sheffied of the ancient East, in Meluhha land, had necessitated the invention of a writing system deploying Meluhha hieroglyphs.

The narrative of history of discovery of a previously unknown language of the world: Mleccha/Meluhha is a documentation of the historical role played by Mleccha/Meluhha language in human affairs. This language is central to grasping the world as it has evolved – recording social transactions and the way groups of ancient people articulated their life-activities.

The use of the gloss *mlecchita* by Vātsyāyana is evidence that the writing system was deployed by *mleccha* speakers as alternative representation (*vikalpa*) of spoken words. An inventory of written forms exists in about 7000 epigraphs identified with Meluhha hieroglyphs. The underlying assumption of the cipher is that the epigraphs were meant as communications between the writer and the reader – and not arbitrary, 'meaningless' doodles. There is evidence that these epigraphs followed a convention and standard for representation of meaning.

The compound gloss *mleccha-mukha* lit. 'ingot of copper' points to the life-activity of the *mleccha* speakers, working with fire on smelters/furnaces as an evolution of early pyrotechnics of Paleolithic era and turning/forging stones, ores, metals and alloys during the Bronze Age which evolved from the chalcolithic era. A gloss cognate with *mleccha* is *meluhha* attested in cuneiform texts of ancient Near East, the Tin Road and the Fertile Crescent.

Doctrine of signs

John Locke in his 1690 *Essay concerning Humane Understanding*, introduced the term *semiotics* as a synonym for 'doctrine of signs' (Latin. *Doctrina signorum*). He assumes, wrongly, that the mind at birth is a blank slate, filled later through experience. Semiotics as a discipline has become restrictive to study non-linguistic sign systems, ignoring the fact that semiotics is the study of meaning-making and hencel closely allied to semantics related to the discipline of language studies – that is, studies of structure and meaning in language. Signs can be logograms, syllabaries, alphabets. Signs can also be hand or finger gestures, dance, paintings, astronomical occurrences. While coceding that knowledge in some form was possible without language and existed even before spoken language came ito existence, writing systems to record spoken utterances may provide leads into the workings of the mind or cognitive faculties.

In 1952, Ignace J. Gelb coined a term, *grammatology* to signify the scientific study of history and theory of writing systems or scripts.[214]

In 1985, Gregory Ulmer, coining the term 'electracy' extended the historical trajectory of grammatology to philosophical grammatology.[215] 'Electracy' called attention to the digital technologies elaborated in the apparatus of new media forms. Marc Wilhelm Kuster extends grammatology to religion, science and other aspects of organization of society, thus extending writing systems as interactions with the world-views of the writer and the reader of the written signs.[216]

For Saussure, writing existed to represent language which is also a system of signs just as writing is a system of signs. Pierce was, with Saussure, a founder of the modern study of signs. Opting for a surrogational model of signification, Pierce noted: "A sign, or *representamen*, is something which stands to somebody for something in some respect or capacity. It addresses somebody, that is, creates in the mind of that person an equivalent sign, or perhaps a more developed sign. That sign which it creates I call the *interpretant* of the first sign. The sign stands for something, its *object*."[217]

Contrasting this theory of signs as surrogates of something, structuralist theory of signs seeks to explain signification solely in terms of signs themselves. The foundation for this theory is that signs form systems with constituent units which are conferred significance. One example cited is that a ten-dollar currency note is structurallyor internally connected to the value of a one-dollar note and hence, both signs of one-dollar and ten-dollar notes are dependent on each other.

For the surrogate theorist, different significations for different signs are substantially unconnected. Significance of each sign is determined by what it 'stands for'.

It is possible to reconcile both the structural and surrogate theorists' views of signs.

A natural process of language change is the application of pre-existing words to new situations. This results in polysemes, homonyms and rebus hieroglyphs.

In the neo-lithic era, when the discovery of alloy characteristics of arsenical copper was recognized as a revolutionary possibility to create hardened and sharp metallic tools and artefacts like exquisite bronze standards or flagposts, the Bronze Age is heralded. This is evidenced by the Nahal Mishmar artifacts of ca. 5th millennium BCE.

This created a new situation necessitating the naming of the artefacts, the alloyed metals, the ores used to create alloys and the processes involved. For such naming, pre-existing words were used resulting in polysemes, homonyms and rebus hieroglyphs. A polyseme is a word or phrase with different, but related senses. A large semantic field is created when a sign (word or phrase or sentence) or signs have multiple meanings (sememes).

Rebus representation occurs when a word with multiple meanings creates two or more mental representations of the sound connected with the word.

As a sound flashes, a related image(s) flash.

"Some apparently unrelated words share a common historical origin, however, so etymology is not an infallible test for polysemy, and dictionary writers also often defer to speakers' intuitions to judge polysemy in cases where it contradicts etymology. English has many words which are polysemous. For example the verb "to get" can mean "procure" (*I'll get the drinks*), "become" (*she got scared*), "have" (*I've got three dollars*), "understand" (*I get it*) etc."[218]

"Polysemy…is usually regarded as distinct from homonymy, in which the multiple meanings of a word may be unconnected or unrelated. Charles Fillmore and Beryl Atkins' definition stipulates three elements: (i) the various senses of a polysemous word have a central origin, (ii) the links between these senses form a network, and (iii) understanding the 'inner' one contributes to understanding of the 'outer' one."[219]

Roots of language

The ultimate reality, the Absolute, Brahman finds expression in language: *śabda-brahman, eternal verbum.*

What is the origin of Speech, vāk? *Sphōṭa* is the root, the intention. This intention finds expression through sound as utterance or speech. In psycholinguistic theories of speech production, this may be comparable to lemma. Unlike lemma, *Sphōṭa* is NOT restricted to the speaker but also includes the mental state of *Sphōṭa* in the listener. This echo in the listener – the same mental state as that of the speaker -- is induced by *nāda.*

The utterance and the heard sound comes through in a flash, as a whole recognition or intuition. This cognitive phenomenon is *pratibhā*, 'shining forth'. What started as a bursting forth by a speaker finds an echo in the listener and both together, as a whole, constitute the shining forth. This is the language capability, *pratibhā.* This *pratibhā* spontaneous cognitive utterance and cognitive resonance occurs at the level NOT of the word but of the sentence, *vākya.* This is *vākya sphōṭa*, sentence-vibration. When thought (emanating from a speaker) and grasping (heard or seen by a listener) occur together, simultaneously, *vāk* is accomplished through *sphōṭa* which is a unity, an integral, non-divisible whole.

The process of sentence-vibration, *vākya sphōṭa*, has both sound-like properties and cognitive intimations related to thought (which is internal to the brains of speaker and listener). Thought operates through *śabdana* 'uttered sound' or 'heard sound' premised on thought or intuition. This *śabdana* (cognition and resonance) constitutes language. *sphōṭa*, is the carrier of thought, the primordial vibration, mediated by language.

This formulation is comparable to a principle of linguistic relativity – the structure of language affecting the way a speaker and a listener together conceptualize – in their cognitive processes -- their world-view. The principle of linguistic relativity holds that language determines thought and that linguistic categories limit and determine cognitive categories. Non-linguistic categories may also be involved in media such as *akṣara muṣṭika kathanam*, gestures of wrists and fingers to constitute a narrative.

The principle of linguistic relativity holds that language influence cognitive processes in non-trivial ways. Language, a product of thought, also influences thought, in a continuous feed-back loop. Language and thought are intertwined and mutually determine each other.

A language a person speaks or hears influences his or her cognitive processes.[220]

An unresolved debate is whether human language competence has universal characteristics or is space and time specific, influenced by cultural-social processes of different places and different times and whether the competence results from learning through such processes.

Humans share the same set of basic faculties but cultural-social processes result in constructed and learned categories such as the repertoire of glosses, unique to a particular clime and time.
It is possible to reconcile the two diametrically opposed contentions: deterministic or universal approach and constructive

or learned approach to postulate a unified theory of language formation. Groups or individuals experience and conceptualize the world using their innate faculties and also their external environment. Language expression occurs not only at the level of consciousness recognizable at the stage of a child in the womb, but also about two years after the child is brought forth into the world surrounded by sound vibrations -- *vākya sphōṭa*, sentence-vibrations. This is primordial and also conditioned by the socio-cultural milieu where sentence-vibrations find expression. Different cultural groups have different conceptual schemes in accord with the external reality.[221] This is what makes for the impossibility of dialogue between a group which starts with an abstract notion of the Absolute (Brahman) finding expression or manifests in aatman – speakers and listeners alike and another group which starts with the definite identification of one God with a set of deterministic rules of behavior.

The challenge posed by the concept of truth, is to understand the categories of cognition: knowledge-thought-language-external world. Some philosophers like Putnam, Fodor, Davidson, Dennett see language as an expression of the pre-existing categories of cognition. Others like Wittgenstein, Quine, Searle, Foucault see language as a learned category while other categories are capable of being categorized differently in time and space, thus categorized in multiple ways.

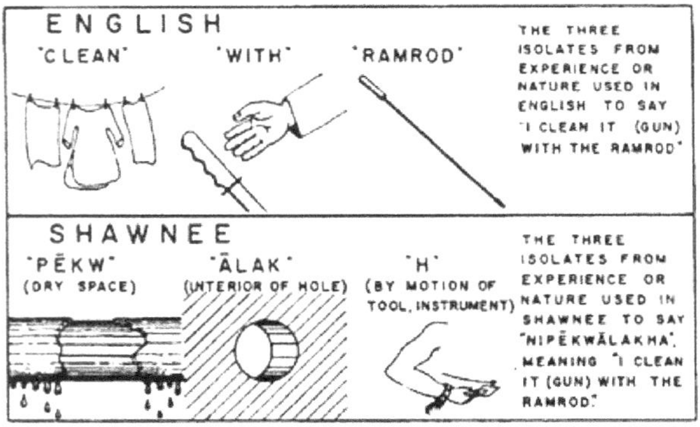
ENGLISH
"CLEAN"
"WITH"
"RAMROD"
THE THREE ISOLATES FROM EXPERIENCE OR NATURE USED IN ENGLISH TO SAY "I CLEAN IT (GUN) WITH THE RAMROD"
SHAWNEE
"PĒKW" (DRY SPACE)
"ĀLAK" (INTERIOR OF HOLE)
"H" (BY MOTION OF TOOL, INSTRUMENT)
THE THREE ISOLATES FROM EXPERIENCE OR NATURE USED IN SHAWNEE TO SAY "NIPĒKWĀLAKHA", MEANING "I CLEAN IT (GUN) WITH THE RAMROD."

Language and thought

Whorf's illustration of the difference between the English and Shawnee gestalt construction of cleaning a gun with a ramrod. From the article "Language and Science", originally published in the *MIT Technology Review*, 1940. Image copyright of MIT Press.

This is a demonstration of untranslatability of languages. As examples of polysemy, Whorf refers to a large number of words for 'snow' in the Inuit language. Hopi language has different words for 'water', one indicating drinking water in a container and another indicating natural body of water. Speakers of different languages would perceive reality differently. Direct translation between two languages, even of seemingly basic concepts like snow or water, is not always possible.

Is language a tool to represent and refer to objects in the world? Does language construct mental representations of the world that can be shared and circulated between people?

Thought is a form of internal speech. Thought is cognition and reason. Thought is independent of and before speech or language. *Sphōṭa* is the universal capability of a human being for language, which finds expression ultimately as Vāk, language. Speech is an audible -- *nāda* --expression of language. Language finds audible expression through sentence-types (vākya), elaborates into words (śabda), tokens of sounds (*varṇa,* syllables,phonemes). *Nāda* is sequences and hence, divisible.

Sphōṭa is a flash, an insight or revelation.The Absolute reveals through this flash, this bursting forth. It is already in the womb as the child is getting formed; the child can hear sounds and has consciousness. The structures of production or abstraction of speech – the larynx, the mouth, the tongue, the vocal cord, the muscles of the lips and the tongue, of the lip to provide nasal variants of *varṇa-sphōṭa*, at the syllable level or phonemes as units of sound or sound tokens -- are yet to get differentiated and evolve with precision, even after the child is brought out of the womb. It is common to find a child of about two years of age bursting forth with sounds slowly evolving, refined into words.

Bhartṛhari breaks down the levels of *Sphōṭa:*

1. *varṇa-sphōṭa*, at the syllable level,
2. *pada-sphōṭa*, at the word level, and
3. *vākya-sphōṭa*, at the sentence level.

*Sphōṭa.*is the language capability of a human being and reveals his or her consciousness.[222]

How are linguistic units of sphōṭa and dhvani ordered? The invariant, indivisible *Sphōṭa* operates at several levels or stages, starting with *dhvani.*

How are sphōṭa and dhvani organized into coherent sentences and meaning?

The formation of speech starts with cognition. It may also be called *śabda-advaita* a monistic theory which unites cognition and language.

Sphōṭavāda is detailed by Bhartṛhari of ca. 5th century in his work, *Vākyapadīya* ("[treatise] on words and sentences"). The work is in three parts:

Brahma-kāṇḍa, (or Āgama-samuccaya "aggregation of traditions")
Vākya-kāṇḍa, and
Pada-kāṇḍa (or Prakīrṇaka "miscellaneous").

It can be traced to a date earlier than Pāṇini who refers (6.1.123) to a grammarian named *Sphoṭāyana* as among his predecessors.

Yāska points the eternal qualities of language and mentions a predecessor or contemporary, Audumbarayaṇa.[223] Vyāḍi, author of the lost text *Saṃgraha*, made references to dhvani and pointed to a connection between a word and its meaning (*śabdārthasaṃbandha*).[224]

The root for the word *sphōṭa* is_*sphuṭ* 'to burst'. Patañjali (2nd century BCE), refers to the invariant quality of speech, as the idea on the mind as symbolic form of language is uttered. The acoustic element of *sphōṭa* is *dhvani*, the audible part which can be long or short, loud or soft depending upon the distance of the bheri naada (drumbeat) traveled in time and distance. Individual speakers may utter it differently, but the *sphōṭa* 'the bursting forth' remains unaffected, remains invariant. This is the sememe.

A single letter or sound ('varṇa') such as /k/, /p/ or /a/ is an abstraction, distinct from variants produced in actual enunciation.[225]

Chinese traveler Yijing (also spelt as I Tsing) **義淨** simplified义净 (635-713 CE) mentions Bhartṛhari in 670 CE had the Bauddham title Tripitaka Dharma Master Yijing (**三藏法師義淨**). He came to Srivijaya (today's Palembang of Sumatra) and traveled to the East coast of India and stayed with a senior monki studying Sanskrit.He went to Nālandā and stayed for 11 years. Returning to Srivijaya, he translated original Sanskrit scriptures into Chinese and the travel diaries.[226]

Some of the texts translated by Yijing into Chinese are:

- *Mūlasarvāstivāda Vinaya* (**一切有部毗奈耶**)
- *Suvarṇaprabhāsa Sūtra* (**金光明最勝王經**) in 703 CE.
- *Vajracchedikā Prajñāpāramitā Sūtra* (**能斷金剛般若波羅蜜多經**) (T. 239) in 703 CE.
- *Sūtra of the Original Vows of the Medicine Buddha of Lapis Lazuli Radiance and the Seven Past Buddhas* (**藥師琉璃光七佛本願功德經**) (T. 451), in 707 CE.

- *Avadana*, or *Stories of Great Deeds* (譬喻經) in 710 CE.

He returned to Luoyang of Tang China in 695. Talking of Bauddham Sanskrit scholars in Srivijaya he says: "In the fortified city of Bhoga, Buddhist priests number more than 1,000, whose minds are bent on learning and good practice. They investigate and study all the subjects that exist just as in India; the rules and ceremonies are not at all different. If a Chinese priest wishes to go to the West in order to hear and read the original scriptures, he had better stay here one or two years and practice the proper rules...." East of Bhoga city, at a distance of four or five days' journey by sea , was the Javanese kingdom of Ho-ling.

De Saussure provides two facets of linguistic signs:

1. The signifiant (that which means) s'abda
2. The signified (that which is meant) artha

In Indian tradition, the two facets are: s'abda and artha. The artha facet is a psychical entity: s'abdo'pi buddhisthah s'rutiinaam karaNam pRthak (Vākyapadīya 1.46).

This is comparable to the following explanation: 'As words exist in the possession of every individual (of a linguistic community), they are psychical entities, comprising on the one hand an area of meaning, and on the other hand the image of a particular sound susceptible of being physically reproduced whenever wanted.'[227]

Sphōṭa is a meaning unit. It is comparable to a sememe. Sphōṭa is that from which the meaning bursts forth and is expressed. (*avan sphōṭaayanasya*: *Aṣṭādhyāyī* VI, 1, 123).

What bears the meaing of a word? It is *sphōṭa* and not the phonemes strung together as a word.[228]

Sphōṭa has a corollary component attribute in *dhvani* (echo). Metaphorically, *sphōṭa* is the flame of fire; *dhvani* is the light of the flame. (*dūrat prabhavet dīpasya dhvanimātram tu lakṣyate*: Vākyapadīya, 1.105). If sphōṭa is the *jāti* (class), *dhvani* is a member (*vyakti*). (*anekavyaktyabhivyangyā jātih sphōṭa iti smrtā kaiścid vyaktaya evāsyā dhvanitvena prakalpitāh*: Vākyapadīya, 1.94).

Study of a sentence covers two aspects: 1. Sound (external facet) 2. Meaning bearing symbol, *sphōṭa* (as internal, consciousness facet).

The twin aspects are explained by an analogy:

Ātmarūpam yathā jñāne jñeyarūpam ca dṛśyate artharūpam tathā śabde svarūpam ca prakāśate (Vākyapadīya 1.50) Trans. 'As knowledge expresses its own form and also the things denoted by it, so is the case of word which reveals its own form as well as meaning.'
Grāhyatvam grāhakatvam ca dve śakti tejaso yathā tathaiva sarvaśabdānām ete pṛthagiva sthite (Vākyapadīya 1.55) Trans.. 'As light reveals its own existence and other things also, similar is the case of words."
Dhāvupādāna śabdeshu śabdau śabdavido viduh eko nimittam śabdānām aparo 'rthe prayujyate: (Vākyapadīya 1.44).
Parā vān mūlacakrasthā paśyantī nābhisamsthitā hṛdisthā madhyamā jñeyā vaikharī kaṇṭhadeśagā (*Manjūṣa*, p. 70).

Formation of speech occurs in three stages:

1. Conceptualization by the speaker (*paśyantī* 'idea')
2. Performance of speaking (*madhyamā* 'medium')
3. Comprehension by the interpreter (*vaikharī* 'complete utterance').

Vaikharyā madhyamāyāśca paśyantiyās'caitad adbhutam anekatīrtha bhedāyās trayyā Vākah param padam (Vākyapadīya 1.143) Trans 'In grammatical analysis these three only are relevant. *Vaikaharī*, the individual instance of the utterance in purely phonetic terms. *Madhyamā*, the phonological structure, the sound pattern of the norm. It is in this form *sphōṭa* 'bursting forth', the meaning-bearing linguistic symbol is expressed (sounded). *Paśyantī* is a written-down version of what is 'seen' or 'imaged' in consciousness.

Vaikharyā hi kṛto nādaḥ paraśravaṇagocaraḥ madhyamayā kṛto nādaḥ sphōṭavyañjaka ucyate. Vaikharī and *madhyamā* sounds of speech are produced almost simultaneously. The *vaikharī* sound indicates the *madhyamā* and the *madhyamā* sound expresses *sphōṭa* which is integral and meaning-bearing spect of the language. This form of speech is *śabdabrahma*:

Anādinidhanam brahma
śabdatattvam yadakṣaram
Vivartate 'rthabhāvena
Prakriyā jagato yataḥ (Vākyapadīya 1.1)

Sphōṭa's function is that of a pair of 'bursting forth' – *arthabhāvena,* 'rendering meaning' of two simultaneous linguistic symbolic forms: utterered sound, perceived image – one form is 'heard sound'; the other form is 'seen image'. A synonym of *paśyantī* is 'symbol' or 'hieroglyph' (the perceived representation of the 'idea').

This is close to the Greek concept of *logos* which conveys closely, the meaning of *sphōṭa.* Thus, logographs as hieroglyphs constitute *sphōṭa* – expressed representations.

Man is a being who has language (*logos*).

"The fact that *logos* stands for an idea as well as a word wonderfully approximates to the concept of *sphōṭa.*"[229]

What is the philosophical import of 'standing for' or 'substitution'? Is the substitution literal or metaphorical? Doesn't a substitution occur when a designer or an architect draws a diagram to denote the parts of a machine assuming that different parts of the machine are indicated by different symbols or shape drawn on the diagram?

"…follow the major concepts of the ancient and medieval Indian tradition…*brahman* (*śabda-tattva-brahman, śabda-brahman*), *vākya, pada, āgama, jāti* (*ākṛti, sāmānya*), *dravya, sambandha, guṇa, diś, sādhana or kāraka, kriyā, kāla, puruṣa* or grammatical person, *samkhyā, upagraha* or the *'parasmai-pada: ātmane-pada'* kind of verbal aspect, *vṛtti* or the grammatical phenomenon of composition or compounding, Veda, *śābda-pūrva-yoga*, forms or levels or phases of *Vāk* such as *vaikharī, sphōṭa, dhvani* and *nāda* with their *prākṛta* and *vaikṛta* divisions, *pratibhā, śābda-bodha, śabda* (*anvākhyeya* and *pratipādaka*), *artha* with its divisions, such as *apoddhāra-padārtha* and *sthita-lakṣaṇārtha* or as *bāhyārtha* (*vastvartha*) and *śabdārtha, avidyā, vivarta, pariṇāma, vikāra, prakṛti*, etc. (Note:As can be seen from this listing, the concepts indicated by the division of Bhartṛhari's magnum opus, the *Trikāṇḍī* or the *Vākyapadīya*, and by those technical expressions in his *Mahābhāṣya-dīpikā* which are not found in the earlier grammatical or philosophical works, such as Patañjali's *Mahābhāṣya*, form a subset of the set of concepts I have in mind.)"[230]

Aklujkar focuses on making a presentation of the texts of Bhartṛhari, *Trikāṇḍī* and *Vākyapadīya* as texts approaching philosophy linguistically, while making a passing mention of KA Subramania Iyer's papers structured on a broader historical framework of tracing Indian philosophical traditions, beginning in 1935/37 with *'Who are the anitya- sphōṭa-vādinah'* and 1969 monograph, *'Bhartṛhari: a study of the Vākyapadīya in the light of ancient commentaries.'* Aklujkar notes that *Trikāṇḍī* (TK) was 1. in the context of Pāṇinian grammar and larger Vedic notions of *praṇava* or *Vāk* and with 2. theoretical reflections on: *jñāna, śabda* and *artha* (cognition, language, meaning or entities). *śabdādi-bhedah* (TK 1.123); *jñāna-śabdārtha-viṣayāh* (TK 3.1.203); *evam arthasya jñānasyaca* (TK 3.3.59).

The cipher key here is *artha* translated as composite of entities and also 'meaning'. In the Indian tradition, the word *artha* is a gloss which signifies both 'meaning' and also 'wealth' as seem in the compound: *Arthaśāstra* used as a title for Kautilya's treatise on wealth-creation and polity. This meaning is consistent with the

word used for a polity: *Rāṣṭram* (lit. 'the firm, lighted path'). The feminine form of this word is *Rāṣṭrī*, a word used in the Ṛgveda in the stunning monologue of *vāk* or *Vāk*, the philosophical representation of speech or language, the metaphorical personification of the feminine divinity of knowledge, education, *vidyā*. The magical, mystical, metaphorical, metaphysical *vāk* has survived as Indian tradition in its very existence in all forms of life-activities and veneration of *vāk* as a feminine manifestation of the Absolute, *brahman*. The grammatological works by *Vaiyākaraṇa-s* and philosophical treatises of darśanas provide glimpses into the past in a continuum called philosophy of symbolic forms.
Aklujkar rightly points to the technical terms: *bāhyārtha* (*vastvartha*) and *śabdārtha* as remarkable elucidatory contributions to the philosophy of meaning and reference – a track comparable to that followed by Gottlob Frege.[231]

Reference is a relation between objects in which one object designates, or acts as a means by which to connect to or link to, another object. The first object in this relation is said to *refer to* the second object. The second object – the one to which the first object refers – is called the referent of the first object. Frege argued that reference cannot be treated as identical with meaning.[232] This can be explained in the context of two Meluhha words: tagara and ranku, both denoting 'tin (ore)'. It can be surmised that tagara denoted cassiterite (the oxide mineral of tin SnO2) while ranku denoted pure tin.

पश्यन्ती N. of a partic. Sound; वैखरी शब्दनिष्पत्तिर्मध्यमा श्रुतिगोचरा । द्योतितार्था च पश्यन्ती सूक्ष्मा वागनपायिनी ॥ Malli. on Ku.2.17; अविभागा तु पश्यन्ती सर्वतः संहृतक्रमा Mañjūṣā.
पश्य paśya पश्य *a.* What sees or looks on; पश्याः पुरन्ध्रीः प्रति...... चित्राणि चक्रे N.6.39; ददर्श पश्यामिव पुरम् N.16.122. पश्यत् *n.* Seeing, perceiving, beholding, looking at, observing; अर्थ

विरागाःपश्यन्ति Rāmāyaṇa. 2.1.58. Given these semantic forms, the root dhātu पश्‌ √ दृश्‌ and Pa1n2. 7-3 , 78 to see behold , look at , observe , perceive , notice (RV), and traditional meanings of पश्य paśya, it can be postulated that पश्यन्ती as a symbolic form of स्फोटः Symbolic forms of *sphōṭaḥ* manifest in two simultaneous expressions: one is heard or uttered sound and the other is image 'perceived' and networked into consciousness. In the context of areal studies of Indian *sprachbund*, Meluhha as speech is recognized in two symbolic forms: 1. Glosses of Meluhha; 2. Image-able glosses of Meluhha. Thus, when *sphōṭa* 'bursts forth' in consciousness, a young bull is imaged as *kondh* 'young bull', kōnda bullock (Kol.)(DEDR 2216).

Simultaneously, the gloss कोंद kōnda 'engraver, lapidary setting or infixing gems' (Marathi) *kũdār* 'turner, brass-worker'.*kõdār* 'turner' (Bengali) flashes forth as sound utterance related to a life-activity of the artisan guild, *kol*, 'smelters'. Writing is born when this 'image' is represented in a two- or three-dimensional frame of a seal or a tablet or a statue in the round or a 3-D frieze on a wall, say, on Ishtar gate.

The idea which bursts out or flashes on the mind when a sound is uttered, the impression produ- ced on the mind at hearing a sound; बुधैर्वैयाकरणैः प्रधान- भूतस्फोटरूपव्यङ्ग्यव्यञ्जकस्य शब्दस्य ध्वनिरिति व्यवहारः कृतः Kāvyaprakāśa.1; The eternal sound recognised by the Mīmāṁsakas; दिशां त्वमवकाशोऽसि दिशः खं स्फोट आश्रयः Bhāgavata 1.85.9; शृणोति य इमं स्फोटं सुपश्रोत्रे च शून्यदृक् 12.6.4.

Appendix J: Meluhha glosses related to symbolic form: helmsman, cargo *kārṇī* account

bagalā, bagala = an Arab boat of a particular description (Marathi, Kannada); bagarige, bagarage = a kind of vessel (Kannada) *bagalo* 'an Arabian merchant vessel' (Gujarati) Rebus: bangala = kumpaṭi = angāra śakaṭī = a chafing dish a portable stove a goldsmith's portable furnace (Telugu) cf. bangaru bangaramu 'gold' (Telugu) *Ta.* Kalam vessel, plate, utensil, earthenware, ship; kalavar navigators. *Ma.* kalam pot, vessel, ship. *Ko.* kalm (*obl.* kalt-) clay pot in the making; k/gal, in: ap gal (s.v. 155 Ta. appam). *Ka.* kala pot, vessel. *Koḍ.* kala big pot. *Tu.* kara an earthen vessel. *Te.* Kalamu ship; kalamari sailor. ? *Br.* kalanḍ broken earthen pot, any old pot. ? Cf. 1301 Ta. kallai. / Cf. Skt. kalā- boat; ? kalaśa- pot (DEDR 1305). **கலம்**[1] kalam , *n.* 1. [K. *kala*, M. *kalam*, Tu. *kara*.] Vessel; hollow utensil, as a cup; plate. [T. *kalamu*, M. *kalam*.] Ship, boat; **மரக்கலம். கலங்கவிழ் மாக்களை** (**மணி.** 16, 120)
Cognate Akkadian:

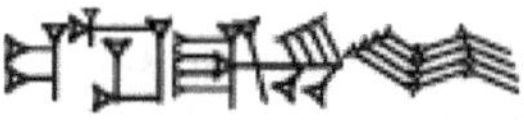
^{ĝeš}ma$_2$-gi$_4$-lum

~ ELA/Ur III/Umma ma$_2$-lah$_5$ ma$_2$-gi-lum-ma-še$_3$ AUCT 3, 501 2.

Hieroglyph: malla, mallā-malli pugilistic encounter. Rebus: Akk. *magillu* "type of boat, barge". *malah* 'sailor' (Akkadian) Cognate: malla2 m. pl. ' name of a people' MBh., °*aka* -- m. MārkP. [See bhalla -- 4]'name of a people in NE of India '. [See instead madrá -- ; like the Madras of the Panjab, the Mallas belonged to ' republican ' gaṇas and competed in wrestling at tribal meetings, hence malla -- 1: connected with a root *mad* -- ' to meet ' Burrow Tau vii 159] (CDIAL 9908). *malladvīpa ' island of the Mallas '. Si. *maldiva* 'the Maldive Islands'.(CDIAL 9911).

See ETCSL: ma$_2$-gi$_4$-lum=type of boat.

Ta. mal, mallam wrestling, boxing; mall-āṭṭam, mall-āṭal wrestling, quarrelling, fighting; mallaṉ wrestler, pugilist; great, famous man; mallu-kkaṭṭu to wrestle, scuffle, quarrel. *Ma.* mallu wrestling; mallan wrestler, boxer; strong, athletic. *Ka.* mallāḍu to strive and struggle for the retention or obtainment of things;mallāṭa mutual strife or struggle for; malla wrestler, boxer by profession, very strong man, athlete (one of the tatsamas); mallā-malli pugilistic encounter. ? *Koḍ.*mallë, mallaŋ go·ḷi cock. *Tu.* malle boxer, wrestler. *Te.* mallaḍi, mallāṭa, mallu wrestling; mallaḍincu, mallaḍi-gonu, mallāḍu to wrestle; mallūḍu wrestler, boxer. Cf. Skt. malla- wrestler, boxer by profession, athlete, very strong man; Turner, *CDIAL*, no. 9907. (DEDR 4730).

Ta. malai (-v-, -nt-) to oppose, fight against, wrangle, dispute; (-pp-, -tt-) to fight, go to war, become unfriendly; *n.* occupation of war; malaippu fighting, war, enmity, opposition; malaivu opposition, contention. *Ka.* male to oppose, fight against, contend with, be refractory; (K.2) *n.* overbearing conduct; (K.2)malepu pride, arrogance. *Te.* malayu to rage, (K. also) wrestle, fight. (DEDR 4741).

Hieroglyph: *kan-ka* 'rim of jar' (Santali), *kaṛṇa* 'ear or handle of vessel' Rebus *kaṛṇaka* 'scribe, accountant' (Pali) 2. *kāraṇika* -- m. 'arrow-maker' (Pa.) 3. *khanaka* 'miner, digger, excavator' (Skt.). 4. *kaṛṇika* कर्णिक having a helm, *m.* a steersman 5. *kāṛṇi* 'refers to a gaṇa: *sutam gamādi* (Sanskrit)
कर्णिक karṇika A knot, round protuberance; The tip of an elephant's trunk. (Sanskrit) *kaṛṇadhāra* m. 'helmsman' Suśr.; *kaṇṇadhāra* -- m. 'helmsman' (Pali); *kaṇṇahāra* -- m. 'helmsman, sailor' (Prākṛt); *kanahār* m. 'helmsman,fisherman' (Hindi)(CDIAL 2836). कारणी or कारणीक [kāraṇī or kāraṇīka] *a* (कारण S) That causes, conducts, carries on, manages. Applied to the prime minister of a state, the supercargo of a ship &c (Marathi) *kāṛṇī* m. 'prime minister, supercargo of a ship', *kul -- kaṛṇī* m. 'village

accountant'. (Marathi) kāraṇika m. 'teacher' MBh., ' judge ' Pañcat. Pa. *usu -- kāraṇika* -- m. 'arrow -- maker'; Pk. *kāraṇiya* -- m. 'teacher of Nyāya'; S. *kārinī* m. 'guardian, heir'; N. *kārani* 'abettor in crime' (CDIAL 3058). కర్ణము [karṇamu] *karṇamu.* [Skt.] n. The ear. The helm of a ship చుక్కాని. కర్ణధారుడు *karṇa-dhāruḍu.* A helmsman or steersman. ఓడనడుపువాడు. (Telugu) कर्ण [karṇa] Rudder or helm (Marathi) The helm or rudder of a ship; सेना भ्रमति संख्येषु हत-कर्णेव नौर्जले Rām.6.48.26 (Sanskrit.Apte) काणा [kāṇā] *a* (S) Of which the vision is destroyed--one of the two eyes: and *attrib.* blind of one eye, monoculous. कारकुन [kārakuna] *m* (P A factor, agent, or business-man.) A clerk, scribe, writer. (Marathi) कारण kāraṇa a number of scribes or कायस्थs *n.* 'pronunciation , articulation' (<u>Atharvaveda Prātiśākhya</u>). करण karaṇa करण *a.* [कृ-ल्युट्] writer , scribe जज्ञे धीमांस्ततस्तस्यां युयुत्सुः करणो नृप Mb.1.115. 43; Ms.1.22. Business, trade; (In law) A document, a bond, documentary proof; Ms.8.15,52,154. The usage of the writer caste.

కరణికము or కరణీకము *karaṇikamu.* Clerkship: the office of a *Karaṇam* or clerk. కరణము [karaṇamu] *karaṇamu.* [Skt.] n. A village clerk, a writer, an accountant. వాడు కూత కరణముగాని వ్రాతకరణముకాడు he has talents for speaking but not for writing. காரணிக்கன் kāraṇikkaṉ , *n.* < id. Accountant; கணக்கன். (Insc.) காரணிக்கஜோடி kāraṇikka-jōṭi , *n.* < id. +. Quit-rent paid by the accountant; கணக் கன் செலுத்தும் வரி. (I.M.P. Tj. 1302.) காரணிகன் kāraṇikaṉ , *n.* < id. Judge; arbitrator, umpire; நியாயமத்தியஸ்தன்.

நமக்கோர் காரணிகனைத் தரல்வேண்டும் (இறை. 1, உரை). கரணிகம் karaṇikam [Telugu. *karaṇikamu.*] Office of accountant. See கருணீகம். கரணிக்க சோடி karaṇikka-cōṭi, *n.* < கர ணிகம் +. Karanam's quit-rent; கணக்கர்வரி. (S.I.I. ii, 119.) கரணன் karaṇaṉ, *n.* < *karaṇa.* Accountant; கணக்கன். கரணர்கள் வந்தனர் கழல் வணங்கினார் (கந்தபு. மார்க்கண். 210).கரணம் karaṇam, *n.* < *karaṇa. Accountant, karnam;* ***கணக்கன்.*** *(S.I.I. i, 65.)* கரணம்பலம் karaṇampalam, *n.* < id. + அம் பலம். Ancient name for the office of village headman; வரிதண்டும் உத்தியோகம். *Rd.*கரணத்தான் karaṇattāṉ , *n.* < id. Accountant; கணக்கன். இந்நகரக் கரணத்தான் (S.I.I. iii, 23). கரணத்தியலவர் karaṇattiyalavar, *n.* < id. + இயலவர். Account officers working under a king, one of *eṇperu-n-tuṇaivar*, q.v.; அரசர்க்குரிய எண்பெருந்துணைவருள் ஒருவராகிய கணக்கர். (திவா.)

Brazier, bell-metal worker Copper work; கன்னார் தொழில். கன்[1] kaṉ , *n.* perh. கன்மம்.1 Workmanship; வேலைப்பாடு. கன்னார் மதில்சூழ் குடந்தை (திவ். திருவாய். 5, 8, 3). 2. Copper work; கன்னார் தொழில். (W.) 3. Copper; செம்பு. (ஈடு, 5, 8, 3.) 4. See கன்னத்தட்டு. (நன். 217, விருத்.) கன்[2] kaṉ, *n.* < கல். 1. Stone; கல். (சூடா.) 2. Firmness; உறுதிப்பாடு. (ஈடு, 5, 8, 3.) கன்னான் kaṉṉāṉ , *n.* < கன்[1]. [M. *kannān.*] Brazier, bell-metal worker, one of the divisions of the Kammāḷa caste; செம்புகொட்டி. (திவா.) கன்னுவர் kaṉṉuvar , *n.* < கன்[1]. Braziers, bell-metal workers; கன்னார். (திவா.) கொட்டுக் கன்னார் koṭṭu-k-kaṉṉār , *n.* < கொட்டு[2] +. Braziers who work by beating plates into shape and not by casting; செம் படிக்குங் கன்னார். (W.) கன்னத்தட்டு kaṉṉa-t-taṭṭu , *n.* < கன்[1] +. Scale-pan, pan of a small balance; சிறு தராசுத் தட்டு. (நன். 217, விருத்.)

கன்னி kaṉṉi , *n.* < *kanyā.* [T. K. *kanne*, M. *kanni.*] 1. Virgin, maiden, young unmarried woman; குமரி. கன்னிதன்னைப் புணர்ந்தாலும் (சிலப். 7, மன்னுமாலை.). kanyā` f. ' maiden ' RV., °*yakā* -- f. MBh. [kanya -- , *kana -- ]Pa. *kaññā* -- f., Pk. *kaṇṇā* -- , °*ṇagā* -- , ś. *kajjaā* -- , paiś. *kaṁcā* -- f., S. *kañā* f., L. *kanj* f. -- A. *kanāi* ' bundle of seven figs, rice and dūrvā grass placed in a girl's lap at puberty ceremony ' < kanyā` -- + ? -- P. ludh. *kanneā* f. ' girl ' (B. D. Jain PhonPj 116) ← Sk. (CDIAL 2737).

Glyph: 'one-eyed': काण *a.* [कण् निमीलने कर्तरि घञ् Tv.] 1 One-eyed; अक्ष्णा काणः Sanskrit; काणेन चक्षुषा किं वा H. Pr.12; Ms.3.155. -2 Perforated, broken (as a cowrie) <kaNa>(Z) {ADJ} ``^one-^eyed, ^blind''. Ju<kaNa>(DP), <kana>(K) {ADJ} ``^blind, blind in one eye''. (Munda) Go. (Ma.) kanḍ reppa eyebrow (Voc. 3047(a))(DEDR 5169). *Ka.* kāṇ (kaṇḍ-) to see; *Ko.* kaṇ-/ka·ṇ- (kaḍ-) to see; *Koḍ.* ka·ṇ- (ka·mb-, kaṇḍ-) to see; *Ta.* kāṇ (kāṇp-, kaṇṭ-) to see; *Kol.*kanḍt, kanḍakt seen, visible. (DEDR 1443). *Ta. kaṇ* eye, aperture, orifice, star of a peacock's tail. (DEDR 1159a)

Rebus 'brazier, bell-metal worker': கன்னான் kaṉṉāṉ , *n.* < கன்[1]. [M. *kannān.*] Brazier, bell-metal worker, one of the divisions of the Kammāḷa caste; செம்புகொட்டி. (திவா.) *Ta.* kan copper work, copper, workmanship; kaṉṉāṉ brazier. *Ma.* kannān id. (DEDR 1402). கன்[1] kaṉ , *n.* perh. கன்மம். 1. Workmanship; வேலைப்பாடு. கன்னார் மதில்சூழ் குடந்தை (திவ். திருவாய். 5, 8, 3). 2. Copper work; கன்னார் தொழில். (W.) 3. Copper; செம்பு. (ஈடு, 5, 8, 3.) 4. See கன்னத்தட்டு. (நன். 217, விருத்.) கன்[2] kaṉ , *n.* < கல். 1. Stone; கல். (சூடா.) 2. Firmness; உறுதிப்பாடு. (ஈடு, 5, 8, 3.)

Ta. kaṉṉam hole made by burglars in a house-wall, theft, burglary. *Ma.* kannam perforation of a wall by thieves. *Ka.* kanna hole made by burglars in a housewall, chink. *Tu.* kanna hole. *Te.* kannamu hole, bore, orifice, hole made by a burglar in a wall. *Kuwi* (S.) kannomi a hole. /Prob. < IA; cf. Pkt. khaṇṇa- dug, excavated (Turner, *CDIAL*, no. 3874).(DEDR 1412).

Ta. kaṇ eye, aperture, orifice, star of a peacock's tail. *Ma.* kaṇ, kaṇṇu eye, nipple, star in peacock's tail, bud. *Ko.* kaṇ eye. *To.* koṇ eye, loop in string. *Ka.* kaṇeye, small hole, orifice. *Koḍ.* kaṇṇï id. *Tu.* kaṇṇů eye, nipple, star in peacock's feather, rent, tear. *Te.* kanu, kannu eye, small hole, orifice, mesh of net, eye in peacock's feather. *Kol.* kan (*pl.* kanḍl) eye, small hole in ground, cave. *Nk.* kan (*pl.* kanḍḷ) eye, spot in peacock's tail. *Nk. (Ch.)* kan (*pl.* -l) eye. *Pa.* (S. only) kan (*pl.* kanul) eye.*Ga.* (Oll.) kaṇ (*pl.* kaṇkul) id.; kaṇul maṭṭa eyebrow; kaṇa (*pl.* kaṇul) hole; (S.) kanu (*pl.* kankul) eye. *Go.* (Tr.) kan (*pl.* kank) id.; (A.) kaṛ (*pl.* kaṛk) id. *Konḍa* kaṇ id. *Pe.* kaṇga (*pl.* -ŋ, kaṇku) id. *Manḍ.* kan (*pl.* -ke) id. *Kui* kanu (*pl.* kan-ga), (K.) kanu (*pl.* kaṛka) id. *Kuwi* (F.) kannū (S.) kannu (*pl.*kanka), (Su. P. Isr.) kanu (*pl.* kaṇka) id. *Kur.* xann eye, eye of tuber; xannērnā (of newly born babies or animals) to begin to see, have the use of one's eyesight (forērnā, see 903). *Malt.* qanu eye. *Br.* xan id., bud.(DEDR 1159).

Ta. kāṇ (kāṇp-, kaṇṭ-) to see, consider, investigate, appear, become visible; n. sight, beauty; kāṇkai knowledge; kāṇpu seeing, sight; kāṭci sight, vision of a deity, view, appearance; kāṇikkai voluntary offering, gift to a temple, church, guru or other great person; kāṭṭu (kāṭṭi-) to show; n. showing; kaṇṇu (kaṇṇi-) to purpose, think, consider; kaṇ-kāṭci gratifying spectacle, exhibition, object of curiosity. Ma. kāṇuka to see, observe, consider, seem; kāṇi visitor, spectator; kāṇikka to show, point out; n. offering, present; kāṭṭuka to show, exhibit; kāṟca, kāṟma eyesight, offering, show, spectacle. Ko. kaṇ-/ka·ṇ- (kaḍ-)to see; ka·ṭ- (ka·c-) to show; kaḍ aṯ- (ac-), kaḍ ayr- (arc-) to find out; ka·ṇky payment of vow to god; kaŋga·c wonderful sight such as never seen before. To.ko·ṇ- (koḍ-) to see; ko·ṭ- (ko·ṭy-) to show; ko·ṇky offering to Hindu temple or to Kurumba; koṇy act of foretelling or of telling the past. Ka. kāṇ (kaṇḍ-) to see, appear; n. seeing, appearing; kāṇike, kāṇke sight, vision, present, gift; kāṇuvike seeing, appearing; kāṇisu to show, show oneself, appear; kaṇi sight, spectacle, ominous sight, divination. Koḍ. ka·ṇ- (ka·mb-, kaṇḍ-) to see; seem, look (so-and-so); ka·ṭ- (ka·ṭi-) to show. Tu. kāṇůsāvuni, kāṇisāvuni to show, represent, mention; kāṇikè, kāṇigè present to a superior. Te. kanu (allomorph kān-), kāncu to see; kānupu seeing, sight; kānipincu to appear, seem; show; kānuka gift offered to a superior, present, tribute; kaṇṭãbaḍu to appear, be seen, come in view; kanukali seeing, sight. Kol. kanḍt, kanḍakt seen, visible. Nk. kank er- to appear (< *kanḍk or the like). Pa. kanḍp- (kanḍt-) to look for, seek. Ga. (Oll.) kanḍp- (kanḍt-) to search. Kur. xannā to be pleasant to the eye, be of good effect, suit well. Br. xaning to see (DEDR 1443).

Appendix K: Metals trade catalog on a seal

The glyphic composition denotes a *sodagor*, trader of mineral ores, metal-ware, ingots of bronze, brass, tin and iron. Broken seal m0304 Mohenjo-daro. Reconstructed as a seal impression using seal m0304 creating a pair of antelopes and a pair of hayricks below the platform (stool) base (After J. Huntington).

The platform glyphs read rebus: *kāṛ* 'stack of stalks of large millet'(Maithili) Rebus: *kaṇḍ* 'furnace, fire-altar, consecrated fire'. *khaṇḍ* 'tools, pots and pans and metal-ware' (Gujarati) *tagar kamar* 'tin artisan'. The artisan is *kũderā* m. 'one who works a lathe, one who scrapes' (CDIAL 3297).His horns denote that he is a brass worker, brass turner: *ṭhaṭera* 'buffalo horns'. *ṭhaṭerā* 'brass worker' (Punjabi) with *kuṇḍa* n. ' clump ' e.g. *darbha-kuṇḍa* — Pāṇ.(CDIAL 3236).

The first set of three glyphs are read rebus: *dhatu kuṭi* 'mineral

(ore) smelter furnace' (Santali) kuṭila, katthīl = bronze (8 parts copper and 2 parts tin).

Ta. koṭiṟu pincers. Ma. koṭil tongs. Ko. koṛ hook of tongs. / Cf. Skt. (P. 4.4.18) kuṭilikā- smith's tongs.(DEDR 2052). Rebus: kuṭi 'smelter furnace' (Santali) kuṭila, katthīl = bronze (8 parts copper and 2 parts tin)(CDIAL 3230).

'Body' glyph ligatured to 'pincers' glyph is a phonetic determinant of the nature of ore - *kanḍ* 'stone': dhaṛu 'body' (Sindhi), ḍato 'claws or pincers of crab' (Santali) rebus: dhatu 'ore' (Santali) kāḍ 2 काड् । पौरुषम् m. a man's length, the stature of a man (as a measure of length) (Rām. 632, zangan kaḍun kāḍ, to stretch oneself the whole length of one's body. So K. 119). Rebus: kāḍ 'stone'.

Ga. (Oll.) kanḍ, (S.) kanḍu (pl. kanḍkil) stone (DEDR 1298). ḍato 'claws or pincers (chelae) of crabs'; ḍaṭom, ḍiṭom to seize with the claws or pincers, as crabs, scorpions; ḍaṭkop = to pinch, nip (only of crabs) (Santali) Vikalpa: erā 'claws'; Rebus: era 'copper'.

 A खांडा *khāṇḍā* 'jag' infixed inside *kan-ka* 'rim of jar' glyph is read as the phrase: *kaṇḍa kanka*, 'fire-altar account': *kul -- karṇī* m. 'village accountant' (Marathi); *karṇikan* id. (Tamil) கணக்கு kaṇakku, n. cf. gaṇaka. [M. *kaṇakku*] 1. Number, account, reckoning, calculation, computation (Tamil) kaṇḍ 'fire-altar' (Santali) *kan-ka, karṇaka* 'rim of jar' Rebus: *kaṇḍa karṇaka* 'furnace account scribe'. *kārṇī(ka)* 'supercargo of a ship' (Marathi)

 aya 'fish' (Mu.); rebus: aya 'metal' (G.) ayo kanka 'fish rim-of-jar' rebus: metal (alloy) account (*kaṇakku*) scribe. *kan-ka, karṇaka* 'rim of jar' Rebus: *kaṇḍa karṇaka* 'furnace account scribe'. *kārṇī(ka)* 'supercargo of a ship' (Marathi)

The five hieroglyphs on either side of the seated person read rebus:

- ib, 'elephant', dhaṛu 'body', kol 'tiger', gaṇḍá 'rhinoceros'. kāṛā 'buffalo' கண்டி kaṇṭi buffalo bull (Tamil) Alternative: Hieroglyph: *ran:gā* 'buffalo' Rebus: *ran:ga* 'pewter or alloy of tin (ran:ku), lead (nāga) and antimony (*añjana*)' (Santali)
- ib 'iron' dhatu 'ore'; kol 'iron'; kaṇḍ 'fire-altar, furnace' *khaṇḍ* 'tools, pots and pans and metal-ware'; khar 'smith' *gaḍa* 'large stone mould'.
- Elephant: ibha (glyph). Rebus: ibbo (merchant of ib 'iron')
- Tiger: kola (glyph). Rebus: kol (working in iron, kolami 'smithy/forge')
- Rhinoceros: gaṇḍá4 m. ' rhinoceros ' lex., °*aka* -- m. lex. 2. *ga- yaṇḍa -- . [Prob. of same non -- Aryan

origin as khaḍgá --1: cf. *gaṇōtsāha* -- m. lex. as a Sanskritized form ← Mu. PMWS 138]1. Pa. *gaṇḍaka* -- m., Pk. *gaṁḍaya* -- m., A. *gãr*, Or. *gaṇḍā*. 2. K. *gö̃ḍ* m., S. *geṇḍo* m. (lw. with *g* --), P. *gaĩḍā* m., °*ḍī* f., N. *gaĩṛo*, H. *gaĩṛā* m., G. *gẽḍɔ* m., °*ḍī* f., M. *gẽḍā* m. WPah.kṭg. *geṇḍɔ mirg* m. ' rhinoceros ', Md. *genḍā* ← H. (CDIAL 4000). காண்டாமிருகம் kāṇṭā-mirukam , *n*. [M. *kāṇṭāmṛgam*.] Rhinoceros; கல்யானை. (Tamil)

- Buffalo: கண்டி kaṇṭi , *n*. 1. Buffalo bull; எருமைக் கடா. (தொல். பொ. 623.) *kāṛā* young buffalo (Go.) *kaṭā, kaṭamā* 'bison' (Ta.)(DEDR 1114) (glyph). Rebus 1: Hieroglyph: *gṛālu* 'calf' *kaṭā* கடவு[3] kaṭavu , *n*. < கடா .1. Male buffalo 'buffalo' kāṛā young buffalo (Go.) kaṭā, kaṭamā 'bison' (Ta.)(DEDR 1114) Rebus: *kãṭhāḷ* 'maritime'; *kaṭalar, n*. < seamen, inhabitants of maritime tracts. Rebus 2: *kaṇḍ* 'furnace, fire-altar, consecrated fire'. kaḍiyo [Hem. Des. kaḍa-i-o = (Skt. Sthapati, a mason) a bricklayer, mason (G.)] Pk. *gaḍa* -- n. 'large stone'? (CDIAL 3969) K. *garun*, vill. *gaḍun* ' to hammer into shape, forge, put together '. (CDIAL 3966). khār 1 खार् । लोहकारः m. (sg. abl. khāra 1 खार; the pl. dat. of this word is khāran 1 खारन्, which is to be distinguished from khāran 2, q.v., s.v.), a blacksmith, an iron worker. Or. *gaṛhibā* 'to mould, build', *gaṛhaṇa* 'building'; ghaṭ 'mould, form' (CDIAL 4407).Pk. *khaḍḍā* -- f. 'hole, mine, cave'(CDIAL 3970).
- Thus, *gaṇḍá* 'rhinoceros', *kaṇṭi* 'buffalo' read rebus: *kāṇḍa* 'tools, pots and pans and metal-ware'; *kaṇḍ* 'furnace, fire-altar, consecrated fire'.

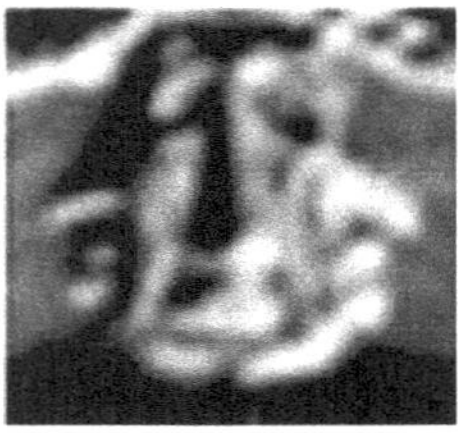

Glyphs constituting the seated person composition: Villa+ge chief brass-worker, metals turner (*kundār*).

Shoggy hair; face. *Sodo bodo, sodro bodro* adj. adv. Rough, hairy, shoggy, hirsute, uneven; *sodo* [Persian. *Sodā*, dealing] trade; traffic; merchandise; marketing; a bargain; the purchase or sale of goods; buying and selling; mercantile dealings (G.lex.) sodagor = a merchant, trader; *sodāgor* (P.B.) (Santali.lex.) The face is depicted with bristles of hair, representing a tiger's mane. *mũh* 'face; *mũhe* 'ingot' (Santali) So, this seal is an ingot trade catalog: *mũhe sodo* 'ingot trade'.
G.*karā̃* n. pl. 'wristlets, bangles'; S. *karāī* f. 'wrist' (CDIAL 2779).
Rebus: khār खार् 'blacksmith' (Kashmiri)

ṭhaṭera 'buffalo horns'. *ṭhaṭerā* 'brass worker' (Punjabi)(CDIAL 5493). *Ta.* tuttāri a kind of bugle-horn. *Ma.* tuttāri horn, trumpet. *Ka.* tutūri, tuttāri, tuttūri a long trumpet. *Tu.* tuttāri, tuttūri trumpet, horn, pipe. *Te.* tutārā a kind of trumpet. / Cf. Mar. tutārī a wind instrument, a sort of horn. (DEDR 3316). *ḍabe, ḍabea* 'large horns, with a sweeping upward curve, applied to buffaloes' (Santali) Rebus: *ḍab*, ḍhimba, ḍhompo 'lump (ingot?)', clot, make a lump or clot, coagulate, fuse, melt together (Santali) Glyph: clump between the two horns: kuṇḍa n. ' clump ' e.g. darbha—kuṇḍa—Pāṇ.(CDIAL 3236). kundār turner (A.)(CDIAL 3295). *kuṇḍī* 'crooked buffalo horns' (Lahnda.) Rebus: *kuṇḍī* = chief of village (Prākṛt). The artisan is *kundakara*— m. 'turner' (Skt.); H. *kũderā* m. 'one who works a lathe, one who scrapes' (CDIAL 3297).

Glyphs in composition of the platform: stool of a pair of hayricks flanking a pair of antelopes: kanḍo 'seat'; rebus: kaṇḍ 'furnace, fire-altar' *khaṇḍ* 'tools, pots and pans and metal-ware' (Gujarati); *kā̃ṛ* 'stack of stalks of large millet'(Maithili) Rebus: *kaṇḍ* 'furnace, fire-altar, consecrated fire'. mēṭa 'stack of hay '; rebus: meḍ 'iron'; takar 'sheep, ram'; rebus: tagara 'tin'. Thus, the platform denotes furnaces, tools, pots and pans and metal-ware of tin and iron.

Kur. kaṇḍō a stool. Malt. kanḍo stool, seat. (DEDR 1179) Rebus: kaṇḍ, 'a furnace, fire-altar' (Santali.lex.) mēṭu, mēṭa, mēṭi stack of

hay (Te.)(DEDR 5058). Rebus: meḍ 'iron' (Ho.) Vikalpa: kuntam 'haystack' (Te.)(DEDR 1236) Rebus: kuṇḍamu 'a pit for receiving and preserving consecrated fire' (Te.) *khaṇḍ* 'tools, pots and pans and metal-ware' (Gujarati).
In the following lexemes related to product derivatives of copper, H. *lokhaṇḍ* m. 'iron tools, pots and pans'; G. *lokhãḍ* n. 'tools, iron, ironware', the word *khaṇḍ* denotes 'tools, pots and pans and metal-ware'.
Ta. takar sheep, ram, goat, male of certain other animals (yāḷi, elephant, shark). பொருநகர் தாக்கற்குப் பேருந் தகைத்து (குறள், 486).Ma. takaran huge, powerful as a man, bear, etc. Ka. tagar, ṭagaru, ṭagara, ṭegaru ram. Tu. tagaru, ṭagarů id. Te. tagaramu, tagaru id. / Cf. Mar. tagar id. (DEDR 3000). Rebus: tagromi 'tin, metal alloy' (Kuwi) ran:ga, ran: pewter is an alloy of tin lead and antimony (*añjana*) (Santali). takaram tin, white lead, metal sheet, coated with tin (Ta.); tin, tinned iron plate (Ma.); tagarm tin (Ko.); tagara, tamara, tavara id. (Ka.) tamaru, tamara, tavara id. (Ta.): tagaramu, tamaramu, tavaramu id. (Te.); ṭagromi tin metal, alloy (Kuwi); tamara id. (Skt.)(DEDR 3001). trapu tin (AV.); tipu (Pali); tau, taua lead (Pkt.); tū̃_ tin (P.); ṭau zinc, pewter (Or.); tarūaum lead (OG.); tarvū̃ (G.); tumba lead (Si.)(CDIAL 5992).

The pair of antelopes have their heads turned backwards.
క్రమ్మర *krammara.* adv. Again. క్రమ్మరిల్లు or క్రమరబడు Same as క్రమ్మరు. krəm back'(Kho.) karmāra 'smith, artisan' (Skt.) kamar 'smith' (Santali) The two antithetical antelopes thus denote: *tagar kamar* 'tin artisan'; *meḍ kamar* 'iron artisan'.
kamaḍha 'penance' (Pkt.) Rebus: kampaṭṭam 'coiner, mint' (Tamil) daṭṭi 'waistband' (Kannada)(DED 2465) Ku. dhaṛo 'piece of cloth', N. dharo, B. dhaṛā; Or. dhaṛā 'rag, loincloth', dhaṛi ' rag '; Mth. dhariā 'child's narrow loincloth'.(CDIAL 6707). Rebus: dhatu '(ore) mineral' (Skt.)
Three molded tablets for boatloads of Bronze-age trade items

m0478A m0478B The same hieroglyphs are repeated on two other molded tablets: m0479 and m0480.
Side A hieroglyphs read rebus: *kōla* 'boat, raft' *kāṁsī* 'bronze' *khātī meḍ koḍ* 'wheelwright iron workshop' *kanḍa kōdā* 'furnaced, to turn in a lathe' *erako bhaṭa* 'moltencast copper furnace' *kōdār* 'turner, to turn in a lathe.'
Side B hieroglyphs read rebus: *kol kammara* 'iron smith, alloy-smith' 'smelter artisan' [*kola* 'tiger' (Telugu); *krammaru* 'head turned back' (Telugu)]; *erako* 'moltencast copper' [*heraka* 'spy']; *kōdār* 'turner' (Bengali) [*khōṇḍa* 'leafless tree' (Marathi).]

Thus, the three Mohenjo-daro tablets convey the identical message of boatload of *aduru kaṇīka* 'native metal supercargo for a boat' and consignments from wheelwright iron workshop, moltencast copper artifacts turned in a lathe, by smelter alloy-metal artisans and turners (i.e., workers in a smithy/forge).

Side A
கோலம்[1] kōlam , *n*. [T. *kōlamu*, K. *kōla*, M. *kōlam*.] 1. Beauty, gracefulness, hand- someness;

அழகு. கோலத் தனிக்கொம்பர் (திருக் கோ. 45). Ornamental figures drawn on floor, wall or sacrificial pots with rice-flour, white stone-powder, etc.; மா, கற்பொடி முதலியவற்றாலிடுங் கோலம். தரை மெழுகிக் கோலமிட்டு (குமர. மீனாட். குறம். 25). Rebus: *Ta. kōl, kōlam* raft, float. *Ma. kōlam* raft. *Ka.* kōl raft, float. *Te.* (B.) *kōlamu* id. / Cf. Skt., BHS *kola-* boat, raft, Pali *kulla-* id. (DEDR 2238). कोलकर [kōlakara] *m* (About सोळापूर) A functionary corresponding to the तराळ elsewhere. तराळ [tarāḷa] *m* A man whose employment it is to convey burdens onwards, to attend to travelers &c. तराळकी [tarāḷakī] *f* The business of तराळ.

 *kāgsī* f. ' comb ' (Gujarati), Rebus: *kāsī* 'bronze' (Punjabi).

 *kāṭhī* the make of the body; the stature of a man (Gujarati) *meḍ* 'body' Rebus: *khātī meḍ* "wheelwright iron'.

 *koḍa* 'one' Rebus: *koḍ* 'workshop'. *khātī meḍ koḍ* 'wheelwright iron workshop'.

U | | | | Meaning: *kaṇḍa kõdā* 'metal-turner furnace' *gaṇḍa* 'four' Rebus: *kaṇḍa* 'furnace, fire-altar' + *kõdā* 'to turn in a lathe'. (that is, artifacts turned in a lathe to be subjected to furnace firing in a furnace). Alternative: *kaṇḍa baṭa* 'fire-altar, furnace'.

 *eragu* 'bowing' Rebus: *erako* 'moltencast copper' *baṭṭā* ' large metal cup '(Maithili) Rebus: *bhaṭa* 'furnace'. Thus, the hieroglyphic composition reads rebus: *erako bhaṭa* 'moltencast copper furnace'.

khõṇḍa 'leafless tree' (Marathi) Rebus: *kõdār* 'turner' (Bengali) m0478A Rebus: bhrāṣṭra = furnace (Skt.) baṭa = a kind of iron (G.) bhaṭa 'furnace' (G.) baṭa = kiln (Santali). bhaṭṭha -- m.n. ' gridiron (Pkt.) *baṭhu* large cooking fire' baṭhī f. 'distilling furnace'; L. bhaṭṭh m. 'grain—parcher's oven', bhaṭṭhī f. 'kiln, distillery', awāṇ. bhaṭh; P. bhaṭṭh m., ṭhī f. 'furnace', bhaṭṭhā m. 'kiln'; S. bhaṭṭhī keṇī 'distil (spirits)'. (CDIAL 9656) 11347 *varta2 ' circular object ' or more prob. ' something made of metal ', cf. *vartaka* -- 2 n. ' bell -- metal, brass ' lex. and vartalōha -- . [√vr̥t?] Pk. *vaṭṭa* -- m.n., °*aya* -- m. ' cup '; Ash. *waṭā'k* ' cup, plate '; K. *waṭukh*, dat. °*ṭakas* m. ' cup, bowl '; S. *vaṭo* m. ' metal drinking cup '; N. *bāṭā*, ' round copper or brass vessel '; A. *bāṭi* ' cup '; B. *bāṭā* ' box for betel '; Or. *baṭā* ' metal pot for betel ', *bāṭi* ' cup, saucer '; Mth. *baṭṭā* ' large metal cup ', *bāṭī* ' small do. ', H. *baṭrī* f.; G. M. *vāṭī* f. ' vessel '.(CDIAL 11347).

 Glyph: S. baṭhu m. 'large pot in which grain is parched, Rebus; bhaṭṭhā m. 'kiln' (P.) baṭa = a kind of iron (G.)

Vikalpa: *meṛgo* = rimless vessels (Santali) Rebus: *meḍ* iron (Ho.)

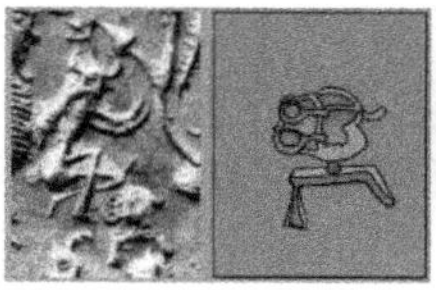  saman: = to offer an offering, to place in front of; front, to front or face (Santali) Rebus: *samṛobica*, stones containing gold (Mundari.lex.) cf. soma (ṛgveda) *samanom* = an obsolete name for gold (Santali). *barada, barda, birada* = a vow (Gujarati) Rebus: *baran, bharat* (5 copper, 4 zinc and 1 tin)(Punjabi.Bengali.) In the Punjab, bharata = a factitious metal compounded of copper, pewter, tin (M.) In Bengal, an alloy called bharan or toul was created by adding some brass or zinc into pure bronze.

Obeisance, kneeling person

erugu = to bow, to salute or make obeisance (Telugu.) eṟagu = obeisance (Ka.), iṟai (Ta.) eṟagisu = to bow, to be bent; to make obeisance to; to crouch; to come down; to alight (Ka.lex.) cf. arghas = respectful reception of a guest (by the offering of rice, dūrva grass, flowers or often only of water)(S'Br.14)(Sanskrit)

Side B

  Hieroglyph 'jar with lid' has *kan-ka* 'rim-of-jar', Rebus: *karṇī* 'supercargo (for a boat); *aḍaren* 'lid' Rebus: *aduru* 'native metal'.Thus, the ligatured hieroglyph is read rebus as: *aduru karṇīka* 'native metal supercargo for a boat'. The boatload is: *kol krammara kõdā* 'smelter-turned', 'alloy-smith artisan' (worked) *erako* 'moltencast copper'.

m0478B erga = act of clearing jungle (Kui) [Note image showing two men carrying uprooted trees].

The rebus meaning conveyed by the erga 'act of clearing jungle' is erako 'moltencast copper'. A homonym is represented as a spy seated on a leafless tree, thus making the narrative of a person seated on a branch of a leafless tree, a homonym of *erga.*

Ko. er uk- (uky-) to play 'peeping tom'. *Kui* ēra (ēri-) to spy, scout; *n.* spying, scouting; *pl action* ērka (ērki). ? *Kuwi* (S.) hēnai to scout; hēri kiyali to see; (Su. P.) hēnḍ- (hēṭ) id. *Kur.* ērnā (īryas) to see, look, look at, look after, look for, wait for, examine, try; ērta'ānā to let see, show; ērānakhrnā to look at one another. *Malt.*ére to see, behold, observe; érye to peep, spy. Kur. ēthrnā. / Cf. Skt. heraka- spy, Pkt. her- to look at or for, and many NIA verbs (DEDR 903). *hērati 'looks for or at'. 2. hēraka -- , °*rika* -- m. 'spy' lex., *hairika* -- m. 'spy' Hcar., 'thief' lex. [J. Bloch FestschrWackernagel 149 ← Drav., Kui *ēra* 'to spy', Malt. *ére* 'to see']1. Pk. *hērai* 'looks for or at' (*vihīrai* 'watches for'); K.ḍoḍ. *hērūō* 'was seen'; WPah.bhad. bhal. *he_rnū* 'to look at' (bhal. *hirāṇū* 'to show'), pāḍ. *hēraṇ*, paṅ.*hēṇā*, cur. *hērnā*, Ku. *herṇo*, N. *hernu*, A. *heriba*, B. *herā*, Or. *heribā* (caus. *herāibā*), Mth. *herab*, OAw. *herai*, H. *hernā*; G. *hervũ* 'to spy', M. *herṇẽ*.2. Pk. *hēria* -- m. 'spy'; Kal. (Leitner) "*hériu*" 'spy'; G. *herɔ* m. 'spy', *herũ* n. 'spying'. WPah.kṭg. (Wkc.) *hèrnõ*, kc. *erno* 'observe'; Garh. *hernu* 'to look'.(CDIAL 14165).

Hieroglyphs on a Mohenjodaro seal m0309 are a precise, unambiguous narrative uttered in Meluhha speech. Related sememes are: tiger (*kol*) + looking up (*krammara*); spy (*heraka*); leafless tree (*khōṇḍa*)
Meanings rendered by rebus reading: *kol* 'working in five metals'; *kammara* 'artisan'; *erako* 'moltencast copper'; *kõdār* 'turner'.
Rebus: eraka, er-aka any metal infusion (Ka.Tu.) eruvai 'copper' (Ta.); ere dark red (Ka.)(DEDR 446). erka = ekke (Tbh. of arka) aka (Tbh. of arka) copper (metal); crystal (Ka.lex.) Metal: akka, aka (Tadbhava of arka) metal; akka metal (Te.) arka = copper (Skt.) erka = ekke (Tbh. of arka) aka (Tbh. of arka) copper (metal); crystal (Ka.lex.) erako molten cast (Tu.lex.) agasāle, agasāli, agasālavāḍu = a goldsmith (Te.lex.) erakaddu = any cast thng; erake hoyi = to pour meltted metal into a mould, to cast (Ka.); cf. arika = rice beer (Santali.lex.) eṟe = to pour any liquids; to pour (Ka.); iṟu (Ta.Ma.); ira-ii (Ta.); e ṟ e = to cast, as metal; to overflow, to cover with water, to bathe (Ka.); eṟe, ele = pouring; fitness for being poured(Ka.lex.) erako molten cast (Tu.lex.) eh-kam any weapon made of steel (Cūṭā.); eh-ku steel; eh-ku-paṭutal to melt, to soften (Cilap. 15, 210, Urai.)(Ta.lex.) eraka, era, era =

syn. erka, copper, weapons (Ka.) erakōlu = the iron axle of a carriage (Kannada.Malayalam); cf. irasu (Ka.lex.) erako molten cast (Tulu)

Rebus readings of Meluhha Indus writing on the exquisite socketed seal of Bagasra (Gola Dhoro)

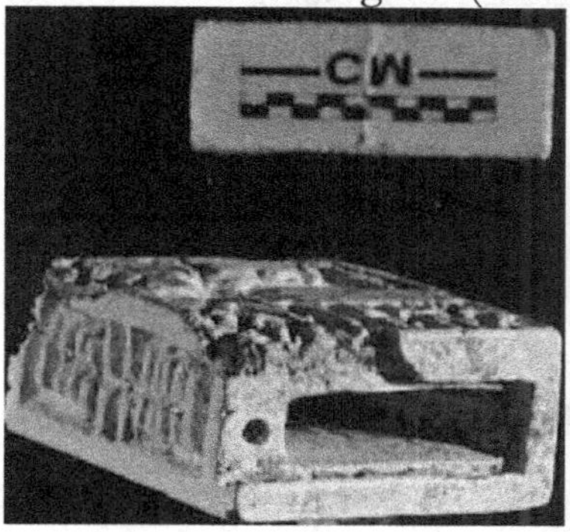

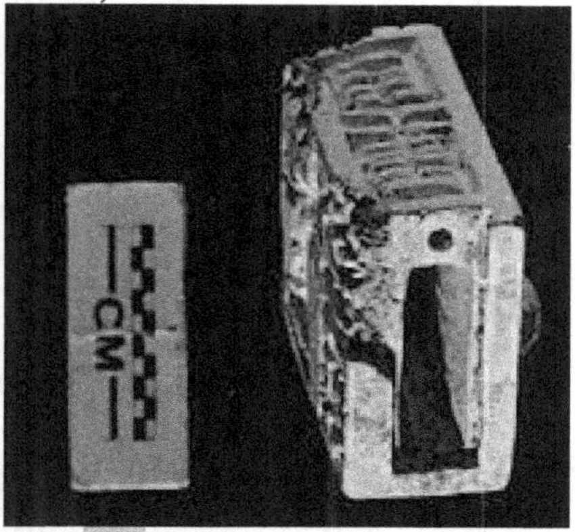

This seal (GD1) was discovered in the gateway of the city wall at Gola Dhoro (Bagasra). The socket might have held a lid to enclose a tablet containing some other message(s) to complete the metalware catalog created by the inscriptions on three sides of the uniquely fashioned seal.

Pictorial motif of a one-horned young bull in front of standard device is common to all the five seals of Gola Dhoro (Bagasra) and a sealing of Gola Dhoro: *kõdā 'young bull' Rebus: kõdā 'turn on a lathe'; kõdār* 'turner' working on a workshop (*koḍ 'horn') Rebus: koḍa 'workshop'*). *sangaḍa* 'lathe, furnace'. Rebus: *jangaḍ* 'entrustment note' (Gujarati) Rebus: *sang* 'stone', *gaḍa* 'large stone'.

ayo 'fish' Rebus: ayo 'iron'; ayas 'metal'^ glyph as a pictorial (lid) Lexemes: aḍaren, ḍaren lid, cover (Santali) Rebus: aduru 'native metal' (Ka.) The word for a 'set of four'

is: gaṇḍa (Santali); Thus, the complex glyph is read: *aduru ayo kaṇḍ* 'native metal furnace'.

seniya 'soldier' Reading 1 Rebus: *seṇi* 'a guild' Reading 2: bhaṭa 'warrior' (Gujarati) Rebus: baṭa = kiln (Santali); baṭa = a kind of iron (Gujarati)

dula 'pair' Rebus: dul 'cast metal' kāmaṭhum = a bow; kāmaḍī, kāmaḍum = a chip of bamboo (G.) Rebus: kampaṭṭam cast coinage, coin (Ta.); kammaṭṭam, kammiṭṭam id. (Ma.); kammatia coiner (Ka.)(DEDR 1236) kammaṭa = coinage, mint (Ka.M.) kampaṭṭa-k-kūṭam mint; kampaṭṭa-k-kāran- coiner; kampaṭṭa- muḷai die, coining stamp (Ta.lex.)

Rebus: dul meṛeḍ cast iron (Mundari. Santali) *dul* 'to cast metal in a mould' (Santali)

Forge -- Metal Turner Workshop

sal "stake, spike, splinter, thorn, difficulty" (H.); Rebus: sal 'workshop' (Santali); śāla_la id. (Skt.) *kuṇḍa* corner Rebus: *kũdā, kõdā* ' to turn in a lathe. Thus, together the hieroglyphs read rebus: *kũdā sal* 'turner workshop'.

Turner

kundau, *kundhi* corner (Santali) *kuṇḍa* corner (S.): *khoṇḍ* square (Santali) *khuṇṭa2 ' corner '. 2. *kuṇṭa -- 2. [Cf. *khōñca --] 1. Phal. *khun* ' corner '; H. *khū̃ṭ* m. ' corner, direction ' (→ P. *khū̃ṭ* f. ' corner, side '); G. *khū̃ṭrī* f. ' angle '. <-> X kōṇa -- : G. *khuṇ* f., *khū̆ṇɔ* m. ' corner '. 2. S. *kuṇḍa* f. ' corner '; P. *kū̃ṭ* f. ' corner, side ' (← H.).(CDIAL 3898).

Rebus: kunda1 m. ' a turner's lathe ' lex. [Cf. *cunda -- 1] N. *kũdnu* ' to shape smoothly, smoothe, carve, hew ', *kũduwā* ' smoothly shaped '; A. *kund* ' lathe ', *kundiba* ' to turn and smooth in a lathe ', *kundowā* ' smoothed and rounded '; B. *kũd* ' lathe ', *kũdā, kõdā* ' to turn in a lathe '; Or. *kū̆nda* ' lathe ', *kũdibā, kū̃d°* ' to turn ' (→ Drav. Kur. *kū̃d* ' lathe '); Bi.*kund* ' brassfounder's lathe '; H. *kunnā* ' to shape on a lathe ', *kuniyā* m. ' turner ', *kunwā* m. (CDIAL 3295). kundakara m. ' turner ' W. [Cf. *cundakāra -- : kunda -- 1, kará -- 1] A. *kundār*, B. *kũdār*, *°ri*, Or. *kundāru*; H. *kũderā* m. ' one who works a lathe, one who scrapes ', *°rī* f., *kũdernā* ' to scrape, plane, round on a lathe '.(CDIAL 3297). *Ta.* kuntaṉam interspace for setting gems in a jewel; fine gold (< Te.). *Ka.* kundaṇa setting a precious stone in fine gold; fine gold; kundana fine gold.*Tu.* kundaṇa pure gold. *Te.* kundanamu fine gold used in very thin foils in setting precious stones; setting precious stones with fine gold. (DEDR 1725).

Seafaring with metals and stones on Persian Gulf, Bronze Age trade on Tin Road.

Tin road starts from Sarasvati River basin with placer-mining for cassiterite and routes through three routes across Ancient Near East and Fertile Crescent: 1. Sea-route through Persian Gulf and 2. Land-route from Gāndhāra through Susa, Ashur to Kanesh; 3. Sea-route/land-route from Kanesh to Haifa across the Fertile Crescent.

The Tin road/Silk Route

[quote]Archaeologists now present evidence that dates the earliest international trade convoys to 2700 B.C. This trade of 5,000 years ago involved cargos of tin, brought from the mountains of Afghanistan overland across Iran to the city of Eshnunna (Tel Asmar in current-day Iraq) on the Tigris river in Mesopotamia. From there the cargos were transported overland, via the city of Mari on the Euphrates, to the port of Ugarit (current-day Ras Shamra) in northern Syria, and finally from there shipped to various destinations in the Middle East. Tin was an important commodity, as it was vital ingredient in the production of bronze. The bronze alloy formulated in the eastern Mediterranean in the 3rd Millennium BC brought about a revolution in economics, civilization and warfare. At that time, there were only two known sources of tin in the world: Afghanistan and Anatolia. Anatolian tin was used locally and the surplus was exported. The increased demand for tin for bronze production opened up trade with Afghanistan, and thus the first known trade route, the Tin Road, was born. This route was the predecessor of the much later, and more famous Silk Road, over which merchants traveled to and from China.

...Anatolia's connection with the Tin and Silk roads was not overland, but through its Mediterranean ports. The harbors on the Mediterranean coast were important junction points on this trade route. A route from the Syrian port of Ugarit passed through modern-day Antakya to Adana in Turkey. Tin mined in the Taurus mountains of southern Turkey was brought here for sale as well. In time, this route extended inland to Konya, by way of Niğde, eventually reaching as far as the Asian shore of the Bosphorus.

The Assyrian Trade Road

In the 2nd Millennium BC, a well-developed trade route between Anatolia and Mesopotamia was used by Assyrian merchants. About 500 years after the establishment of the Tin Road, a second trade route developed, still in use today. It originated in upper Mesopotamia and reached Kayseri via Mardin, Diyarbakir and Malatya. Created by Assyrian merchants who were the first to initiate trade between Anatolia and the Middle East, the route later was extended from Kayseri south to Niğde and north to Sivas. It eventually connected to Persia and was responsible for making Kayseri a leading trading center of the age.

In Seljuk times, there was a vast commercial fair called the "Yabanlu Pazari" (Bazaar of the Foreigners) that was held forty days a year at a place still called Pazarören near Kayseri. It is referred to by Mevlana in his Mesnevi. All the caravan routes converged at this point, not far from the site of a Bronze-age trading post. This fair's origins are thought to go back as far as the 2nd Millennium BC, when Kultepe, known in ancient times as Kanesh-Karum, was an important early Hittite commercial cities. Dating from 2000 BC, Kultepe near Kayseri was also one of the world's first cities to be open to free trade. Kültepe became an important Assyrian merchant stop, carrying goods up from Mesopotamia.[unquote][233]
Tin-copper alloy called tin-bronze or zinc-copper alloy called brass, were innovations that allowed for the much more complex shapes cast in closed moulds of the Bronze Age. Arsenical bronze objects appear first in the Near East where arsenic is commonly found in association with copper ore, but the health risks were quickly realized and the quest for sources of the much less hazardous tin ores began early in the Bronze Age.[234]

Thus was created the demand for tin metal. This demand led to a trade network which linked distant sources of tin to the markets of Bronze Age.

Zinc added to copper produces a bright gold-like appearance to the alloy called brass. Brass has been used from prehistoric times. (Thornton, C. P. (2007) "Of brass and bronze in prehistoric southwest Asia" in La Niece, S. Hook, D. and Craddock, P.T. (eds.) Metals and mines: Studies in archaeometallurgy London:

Archetype Publications) The earliest brasses may have been natural alloys made by smelting zinc-rich copper ores.[235]

Zinc is a metallic chemical element; the most common zinc ore is sphalerite (zinc blende), a zinc sulfide mineral. Brass, which is an alloy of copper and zinc has been used for vessels. The mines of Rajasthan have given definite evidence of zinc production going back to 6th Century BCE.[236]

Ornaments made of alloys that contain 80–90% zinc with lead, iron, antimony, and other metals making up the remainder, have been found that are 2500 years old.[237] An estimated million tonnes of metallic zinc and zinc oxide from the 12th to 16th centuries were produced from Zawar mines.[238]

The addition of a second metal to copper increases its hardness, lowers the melting temperature, and improves the casting process by producing a more fluid melt that cools to a denser, less spongy metal. (Penhallurick, R.D. (1986). Tin in Antiquity: its Mining and Trade Throughout the Ancient World with Particular Reference to Cornwall. London: The Institute of Metals.)

Tin extraction and use can be dated to the beginnings of the Bronze Age around 3000 BC, when it was observed that copper objects formed of polymetallic ores with different metal contents had different physical properties.[239]

Tin is obtained chiefly from the mineral cassiterite, where it occurs as tin dioxide, SnO_2.The first alloy, used in large scale since 3000 BC, was bronze, an alloy of tin and copper. Cassiterite often accumulates in alluvial channels as placer deposits due to the fact that it is harder, heavier, and more chemically resistant than the granite in which it typically forms. Early Bronze Age prospectors could easily identify the purple or dark stones of cassiterite from alluvial sources and could be obtained the same way gold was obtained by panning in placer deposits.

Pewter, which is an alloy of 85–90% tin with the remainder commonly consisting of copper, antimony and lead, was used for flatware.

Here is a pictorial gallery:

Panning for cassiterite using bamboo pans in a pond in Orissa. The ore is carried to the water pond or stream for washing in bamboo baskets.

People panning for cassiterite mineral in the remote jungles of central India.

The ore is washed to concentrate the cassiterite mineral using bamboo pans. Base of small brick and mud furnace for smelting tin.

The tin is refined by remelting the pieces recovered from the furnace in an iron pan. The molten tin is poured into stone-carved moulds to make square- or rectangular-ingots.

As the pictorial gallery demonstrates, the entire tin processing industry is a family-based or extended-family-based industry. The historical traditions point to the formation of artisan guilds to exchange surplus cassiterite in trade transactions of the type evidenced by the seals and tablets, tokens and bullae found in the civilization-interaction area of the Bronze Age.

Haifa: find-spot of the first two 'rosetta stones'.

At the port of Dor, south of Haifa, fisherfolk had raised about 7 tonnes of copper and tin ingots in the 1970's. In 1976 two ingots of tin were found in a shipwreck in the sea near this Phoenician port. Ingot 1 and Ingot 2; Museum of Ancient Art, Municipal Corporation of Haifa.

The modifying element | ligatured (subscripted) to X on the tin ingot inscriptions, may be read rebus: खांडा [khāṇḍā] 'notch':Marathi: खांडा [khāṇḍā] *m* A jag, notch, or indentation (as upon the edge of a tool or weapon). Rebus: *kāṇḍa* 'tools, pots and pans and metal-ware'.

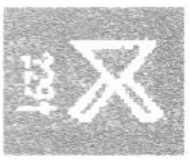

kuṭilikā- smith's tongs.(DEDR 2052). Rebus: kuṭila, katthīl = bronze (8 parts copper and 2 parts tin)(CDIAL 3230). If Sign 229 'pincers' glyph is rotated right 90-degrees, the glyph will be comparable to the variant X glyph shown on the tin ingots.

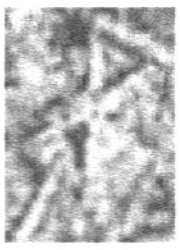

This X glyph is also ligatured (subscripted) with a short numeral stroke. *dāṭu* 'cross'(Telugu) Rebus: *dhatu* 'mineral' (Santali).

The epigraphs on the tin ingots have been decoded as related to ranku "antelope", ranku "liquid measure"; dhātu 'ore'; the two epigraphs on the two ingots are read rebus: ranku dhātu "tin unalloyed (i.e. pure metal)".

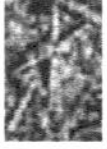 

ranku 'liquid measure, antelope' Rebus: *ranku* 'tin'.

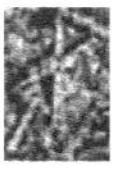 

This glyph is annotated by the variang X glyph that the tin mineral is for (alloying to) bronze tools. Thus, the composite hieroglyphic composition on the tin-ingots may be read rebus as: *dhatu kuṭila khāṇḍā* 'mineral (for) bronze tools'.

"Meluhha was certainly the most distant of the countries beyond the sea the list of its products which were embarked there is among the richest and most varied and comprises precious stones, (chalcedony, cornelian and lapis luzuli) copper, gold and other prized metals, ebony, the wood of sissoo, the gis-ab-be 'sea

wood' (maybe mangrove) cane, peacocks and roosters. The texts also speak of ships, skilled sailors and sophisticated inlaid furniture...seafaring merchants from the distant lands of Dilmun, Meluhha and Maakan tied up at Akkads quay during Sargon's reign 2334-2279 BC. Copper was shipped directly from Maakan. During the reign of Gudea of Lagas, copper diorite and wood were delivered from Maakan and Meluhha delivered rare woods, gold *Tin* lapis Lazuli and carnelian to Lagas.There are no records indicating that ships from Meluhha docked in Sumeror that Sumerian seamen were themselves in Meluhha.""Tukulti-Ninurta refers to himself as 'King of the Upper and Lower Seas and ruler over Dilmun and Meluhha."[240]

"The reference to 'the Caphtorite' and the clear implication that tin was sent from Mari to Crete are bound to arouse heated controversy. It should come as no surprise here, as this study has repeatedly emphasized the eastern connections of Minoan metallurgy. Strange as it may seem to those rooted in the insularity of the Aegean world, we must now seriously consider the possibility that the tin used by Minoan metal-workers came to Crete from Mari. The 'itinerary' (published by G. Dossin) also implies that the representatives of Crete and Caria, together with a translator (Akkadian targamannum), received their tin at Ugarit... "J. Bottero and M. Birot have assumed that the tin came from Iran and was brought to Mari by Elamites...The text TLC X 125 refers to 1 1/3 minas, 9 2/3 shekels of pure silver...This text may indicate that silver was brought to Larsa in order to purchase tin and that this tin was purchased in Susa. That is, Larsa did not

purchase tin in the north. On the contrary, it supplied tin to the north...Old Assyrian and Old Babylonian period ca. 2000 BC to 1600 BC...The tin was sent from Sippar to Mari, and from there was re-exported to Syria and Palestine. The tin came to Sippar from Susa, either by way of Dēr and Eśnunna or by way of Larsa, coming up from the south. The beginning of the trade, the determination of the ultimate origin of the tin, still remains to be established...A text from the reign of Gudea of Lagash (ca. 2143-2124 BC) provides a possible clue in this direction. In his elaborate cylinder and statue inscriptions Gudea provides considerable information concerning the origin of the various materials used in his extensive building program. Gudea says that the tin he used came from the land of Meluhha:
(urud)u AN>NA lagab-za-gin na(k)u NE gug-gi rin me luh ha da (copper and tin, blocks of lapis lazuli...bright carnelian from (the land of) Meluhha).

"The land of Meluhha is well known as a source of lapis lazui and carnelian. This is the only direct reference to tin from Meluhha, but the Gudea passage suggests that tin may be associated with the Meluhha trade, a trade also involving copper, lapis lazuli and carnelian. Of all the items involved here, the one which is most securely localized is lapis lazulip. The lapis lazuli used in Mesopotamia came from northern Afghanistan, from the Sar-i-Sang mine in Badahshan. No one has ever proposed that Meluhha be identified with Afthanistan. The current tendency is to identify Meluhha with Sind and the coastal region of western Pakistan. This would mean that the expression 'lapis lazuli from Meluhha' refers not to the actual source of the material, but rather to the entrepot from which it was sent to Mesopotamia. Lapis lazuli from Meluhha would then be an expression parallel to copper from Tilmun.

"It is now assumed that the references to the land of Meluhha in texts relating to the latter part of the third and early part of the second millennium BC are to be associated with the now established relations between Mesopotamia and the Harappn civilization of the Indus Valley during the Sargonic and Isin-Larsa periods. This was a sea-borne trade going down the Persian Gulf and across the Arabian Sea, such as existed in the Hellenistic, Roman, and Byzantine periods. The best known example of such a voyage is that undertaken by Nearchus, the admiral of Alexander the Great, in the year 325 BC. Nearchus set out from the newly built harbor at Pattala, near the mouth of the Indus river, with 1800 transports and galleys and 5000 sailors and marines, in September 325 BC. The entire voyage to the mouth of the Euphrates, with many wanderings and delays, took 130 days. As Nearchus first sailed down the Indus river to pattala, his voyage represents a rpecise example of how the lapis lazuli of Afghanistan could have reached Mesopotamia.

"The voyage of Nearchus was not the first recorded example of a voyage from India. According to Herodotus, the Persian king Darius (522-486 BC) ordered the Ionian admiral Scylax of Caryanda to make a voyage from India to Egypt, a journey said to have lasted three months. Scylax set sail from 'the city of Caspatyrus in the Paktyan country,' a site which cannot be securely identified but which, according to another passage in Herodotus, is to be placed in northern India near Bactria. According to R. Carpenter, the description in Herodotus '...best suits the borderland between modern Pakistan and Afghanistan.' Here, then, is another voyage down the Indus river and then west across the Arabian Sea. Such voyages, from Egypt to India, became very common by the early years of the Roman Empire. Strabo says that, in the reign of Augustus, as many as 120 ships a year sailed from the Red Sea ports of Myos Hormos and Berenice for northeast Africa and India. By the time of the emperor Tiberius, when the Greek explorer Hippalos discovered the monsoons and direct voyages to Bombay became possible, the traffic to India became so extensive that Tiberius began to worry about Rome's balance of payments. Roman hard currency was leaving the country to pay for the gems and silks of India. The so-called *Periplus of the Erythraean Sea* describes this trade in detail. At the time this text was written (late first century AD) India was

importing copper, tin, and lead. Her exports included such items as ivory, agate, carnelian, pearls and tortoise shell, many of which are familiar as items associated with the Meluhha trade...
"The archaeological evidence...suggests that such contacts (between Mesopotamia and the Indus Valley) began already in the Early Dynastic period and came to an end with the close of the Isin-Larsa period. In general terms, the dates 2500-1900 BC give the approximate time range for the contacts between the two areas. The period of Mesopotamian contact seems to coincide with the period of Harappan civilization itself. That such contacts were by sea is suggested not only by the geographical setting and the known historical background, but also by references in the Mesopotamian texts to ships from Meluhha. The first such reference comes from *Sammeltafel* text, in abilingual passage relating to the reign of Sargon of Akkad. It refers to the ships of Meluhha, Magan and Tilmun which are docked at the quay of harbor of the city of Agade. The ships of Meluhha are mentioned in other Mesopotamian texts, including one which actually comes from the Old Akkadian period and is not a later copy. Another Old Akkadian text seems to refer to a sailor of a Meluhhan ship. The presence of 'an official interpreter of the Meluhhan language' in Mesopotamia helps to confirm this impression…
"These are the principal products associated with the Meluhha trade. They represent exports from Meluhha, brought to Mesopotamia by traders from Meluhha in Meluhha ships...The same articles mentioned in the literary and historical texts appear as imports in the mundane economic texts of the Third Dynasty of Ur. All of the products said to be from Meluhha can be localized in Afghanistan or in the Indus Valley. This is in agreement with the generally accepted identification of Meluhha with the area of Sind and western Pakistan...The termination of this trade now seems to coincide with the collapse of Harappan civilization itself. This collapse may even be in some way responsible for the general economic decline in Mesopotamia and the absence of international trade after the Isin-Larsa period, i.e. after ca. 1900-1850 BC...The lapis lazuli of Badahshan and the other stones and metals of Afghanistan must have been brought

down the Indus river to some port on the mouth of the Indus. From Afghanistan the trade route must have gone south, over the Hindu Kush by means of the Khyber Pass to Peshawar. The Peshawar plain was known to the Persians as the satrapy of Gan-dh-a_ra and, from at least the sixth century BCE, on, there existed a major trade route across Peshawar down to southern India. The cities of Chārsaddā and Taxila testify to the importance of this route. Somewhere near the mouth of the Indus there must have been a port similar to that which Alexander the Great had built at Pattala, and from here the goods were shipped west eventually to reach southern Mesopotamia.

"It is generally assumed that such a port has been found and that it is located not on the Indus but at Lothal in the Gulf of Cambay...The radiocarbon determinations from Lothal suggest that the site was in use aproximatey in the period during which the trade with Meluhha was in existence.

"Although no actual remains of boats were found, the excavations at Lothal did uncover terracotta boat models and a number of +so-called anchors of stone. It seems that industry was located right at the harbor site, for at Lothal were excavated not only factories for making agate and carnelian beads, but also the workshops of coppersmiths together with ingots of almost pure copper...

"The quay (Sumerian kar, Akkadian kārum) is mentioned frequently in cuneiform literature and was a major factor in the economic organization of ancient Mesopotamia...The quest for metals was the factor which stimulated the trowth of an organized foreign trade. The trade with Tilmun, Magan and Meluhha must, then, be seen as part of the international age of metallurgy which developed in the second half of the third millennium BC.
"The tin of Meluhha may even have something to do with the Harappan settlement at Lothal. The use of tin-bronze in the Harappan period has been outlined above. Of particular interest is the extensive use of tin-bronze at Rangpur in Gujarat. The

bronzes here have a tin content of four to eleven percent. The absence of arsenic in the Rangpur bronzes and its presence in the bronzes from Harappa and Mohenjodaro indicates taht different sources of copper were used in each area. That used at Rangpur must have come from Rajasthan and this is the ore also worked at Lothal, because arsenic is also absent from the copper ingots found there. This indicates that the Harappans did not come to Lothal to obtain copper. They might have come in order to obtain tin...it should be pointed out that Gujarat has even been proposed as possible location for Meluhha."[241]

A good example of contact between Kish and Meluhha (Indus script corpora area) is provided by two seals with identical texts from (a) Kish (IM 1822); cf. Mackay 1925 and (b) Mohenjodaro (M-228); cf. Parpola, 1994, p. 132.

"A copper blade (Marshall 1931: pl. 136, f.3) found in one of the upper levels, though termed a spear-blade, may conceivably have been a knife (Plate IX, no.1). An exactly similar blade, but with a slightly longer tang, was found in the A mound at Kish (Mackay 1929a: pl. 39, gp. 3, f.4)... attention should be called to a steatite seal from Kish, now in Baghdad Museum, which bears the svastika symbol. This seal, both in shape and design upon it, exactly resembles the little square seals of steatite and glazed paste that are so frequently found at Mohenjodaro (Marshall 1931: pl. 144, f. 507-15). I do not think that I err in regarding the Kish example, which was found by Watelin, as either of Indian workmanship or made locally for an Indian resident in Sumer... The curious perforated vessels shown (Marshall 1931: pl. 84, f. 3-18) are very closely allied to perforated vessels found at Kish

(Mackay 1929a: pl. 54, f. 36), especially in the fact that besides the numerous holes in the sides there is also a large hole in the base, which suggests that by this means they were supported on a rod or something similar... I have suggested, from evidence obtained by Sir Aurel Stein in southern Baluchistan, that these perforated vessels were used as heaters...(E.J.H.Mackay, Further links between ancient Sind, Sumer and elsewhere, *Antiquity*, Vol. 5, 1931, pp. 459-473).

Mesopotamian carnelian, lapis lazuli, and gold beads, restored as a necklace, l. 14.3 cm, mid-third millennium BCE from Iraq, Kish, Mound A, Burial A51. Chicago, the Field Museum of Natural History, inv. no. 228533. Examples of long-barrel carnelian cylinder beads from Chanhu-daro (after Mackay 1943: Pl. LXXXI) were discovered in Tello in contexts datable to the time of Gudea or the Ur III period. Amongst the earliest evidence of Harappan carnelian in Mesopotamia15 are four 14-15-cm-long barrel-cylinder beads (Fig. XII. 7) from the Royal Cemetery at Ur (Tosi 1980:450).

The Sumerian literary composition dealing with Ninurta and the turtle has been published by CJ Gadd in UET 6/1 2. This text shows Anzu bird carrying the tablets of fate away from Enki (not Enlil). After Ninurta (divinity of storm, wind and rain, comparable to Rgveda Indra) successfully defeated the Anzu bird, he, the hero, is caught by a turtle.[242]

A synonym of anzu bird is *śyena* 'hawk, falcon, kite' of Ṛgveda.

The exclamation in the Sumerian myth: 'Let the magilum-boats of Melukkha transport gold and silver for exchange!' Enki and Ninkhursag (lines 1-9, Tr. by B. Alster) has references to the products of Melukkha: 'The land Tukrish shall transport gold from Kharali, lapis lazuli, and bright...to you. The land Melukkha shall bring carnelian, desirable and precious, sissoo-wood from

Magan, excellent mangroves, on big-ships! The land Markhashi will (bring) precious stones, *duṣia*-stones, (to hand) on the breast, mighty, diorite-stones, u-stones, *ṣumin*-stones to you!'. 'Melukkha' is cognate with Pali 'milakkha'.

See: Ancient Near east Anzu, falcon-shaped fire-altar Uttarakhand, turning *aṁśú* (Rigveda), *ancu* (Tocharian) in smithy.243 From Purulia, Uttarakhand, a brick altar identified as Syenachiti. The structure is in the shape of a flying eagle Garuda, head facing east with outstretched wings. In the center of the structure is the chiti is a square chamber yielded remains of pottery assignable to circa first century B.C. to second century AD. In addition copper coin of Kuninda and other material i.e. ash, bone pieces etc and a thin gold leaf impressed with a human figure tentatively identified as Agni have also been recovered from the central chamber.

A parallel in Pahlavi is senmurw, Sina-Mru (Pazand), a fabulous, mythical bird (also called simorgh). The name derives from Avestan merayo saeno 'the bird Saena', originally a raptor, either eagle or falcon, etymologically identical Sanskrit syena.

From 'Gods, Goddesses and Images of God in Ancient Israel' by Othmar Keel and Christoph Uchlinger, English translation by TH Trapp, 1998, Fortress Press from the German *Gottinnen, Gotter and Gottessymbole*, 1992, Herder Verlag, Fribourg. Seventh century BCE cylinder seal found in Israel depicting the battle of Ninurta and Anzu. Nili Wazana, in a brilliant exposition on Anzu and Ziz asks and tentatively answers the question: "Were the Israelites acquainted with the Epic of Anzu?" She cites this rendering of a seventh century BCE cylinder seal portraying the battle of Ninurta and Anzu, discovered in Israel.[244]

This narrative is paralleled and elaborated on an Akkadian cylinder seal.

ḍāngā = hill, dry upland (B.); *ḍā̃g* mountain-ridge (H.)(CDIAL 5476). Rebus: *dhangar* 'blacksmith' (Maithili) *ḍangar* 'blacksmith' (Hindi) *kāṇḍa* 'flowing water' Rebus: *kāṇḍā* 'metalware, tools, pots and pans'.

"On the mountainside Anzu and Ninurta met … Clouds of death rained down, an arrow flashed lightning. Whizzed the battle force roared between them." Anzu Epic, tablet 2,in S. Dalley, Myths from Mesopotamia (Oxford - New York, 1989), p. 21.
Anzu or Zu, as a lion-headed eagle, ca. 2550–2500 BCE. Anzu(d) bird is the divine storm-bird which stole the 'Tablets of Destiny' from Enlil,inventor of the mattock (a key agricultural pick, hoe, ax or digging tool of the Sumerians) and hid the tablets on a mountain-top.

Magilum Boat (Magilum: from Sumerian ma-gi-lum, a ship of the netherworld) in Sumerian mythology was one of the valuable items seized by Ninurta, patron divinity of Lagash. This spoil was hung on an unknown part of his chariot according to the ancient source, cf. lines 40-63: "(Ninurta) brought forth the Magilum boat from …… his *abzu*. …The warrior Ninurta, with his heroic strength, wreaked his vengeance (?). 52-54. On his shining chariot, which inspires terrible awe, he hung his captured wild bulls on the axle and hung his captured cows on the cross-piece of the yoke. 55-63. He hung the Six-headed wild ram on the dust-guard. He hung the Warrior dragon on the seat. He hung the Magilum boat on the ……. He hung the Bison on the beam. He hung the Mermaid on the foot-board. He hung the Gypsum on the forward part of the yoke. He hung the Strong copper on the inside pole pin (?). He hung the Anzud bird on the front guard. He hung the Seven-headed serpent on the shining cross-beam."

Shamash, the sun god, rising in the morning from the eastern mountains between (left) Ishtar (Sumerian: Inanna), the goddess of the morning star, and (far left) Ninurta, the god of thunderstorms, with his bow and lion, and (right) Ea (Sumerian: Enki), the god of fresh water, with (far right) his vizier, the two-faced Usmu. *Courtesy of the trustees of the British Museum*

Zu or Anzu (from An 'heaven' and Zu 'to know' in Sumerian language), as a lion-headed eagle, ca. 2550–2500 BCE, Louvre.

Votive relief of Ur-Nanshe, king of Lagash, representing the bird-god Anzu (or Im-dugud) as a lion-headed eagle. Alabaster, Early Dynastic III (2550–2500 BCE). Found in Telloh, ancient city of Girsu. H. 21.6 cm (8 ½ in.), W. 15.1 cm (5 ¾ in.), D. 3.5 cm (1 ¼ in.)

"…the language of Marhasi [Bampur area, just west of Iranian Baluchistan] is different from that of the Simaskians [Tepe Yahya in southern Central Iran], and only very partially Elamite-related."245 This Marhasi language could have been Meluhha. Many 'Indian' words of

Mesopotamia[246] -- gisabba-meluhha (abba wood, thorn tree) and mesu, wood of the plains of Magan; si-in-da-a, si-in-du, Sindh wood, zaza cattle (zebu?), gis'immar (śimbala, śalmali, śalmalia malabarica'), ili 'sesame' (Akkad. ellu 'sesame oil' [cf. eḷḷu 'sesamum indicum' (DravidianO] -- might have been transmitted by Dilmun (Bahrain) traders.

Pierre Amiet summarises Hakemi's report with a brilliant exposition: "The discovery, long after that of the great Mesopotamian civilization, just after World War I, of an urban civilization which emulated that of Sumer in the Indus Valley, followed even more recently by the equally impressive civilization of Turkmenia, immediately raised the question of what presumably happened in the immense territory between th two, represented by the Iranian plateau…(Aurel Stein) had crossed Baluchistan and Kerman, ultimately reaching, on the westward side, the only historical entity of Iran predating the Persians – the ancient country of Elam – to all intents and purposes part of Mesopotamia, although essentially a country of mountaineers. In its geographic duality in which the mountain valleys of Fars were associated with the lowlying plains of Susiana, Elam, which was also an ethnic duality, was presumably linked with a hinterland that had remained in the wings of history and comprised the Kerman mountains dominating the salt pans of the Lut Desert. The province which was traditionally rich in stones and metals, and scantly explored by the pioneers, must have been a home to the major witnesses of what Gordon Childe as early as 1934 called the 'mechanism of the spread' of the conquests of civilization…in eastern Bactria, bounded the wide loop of Amu Darya, the site of Shortughai corresponds to a settlement of 'colonists' from Harappan India, with their characteristic pottery, who saw to the transit of copper and doubtless also of lapis lazuli. These observations seem to be indicative of what probably happened in western Bactria where fortresses housing stores, as at Dashly Tepe, may have been built by a merchant-colonist elite to guarantee trade with the workshops set up either at Shah-I Sokhta or at Shahda and Tepe Yahya and, through them, with Elam, as

well as by sea, with Mesopotamia. Unlike Anatolia, where the intense metalworking activity does not seem to have produced any art specific to a given civilization or else highly customized before the 2nd millennium, Iran thus appears to hav been a huge community enlivened by a network of very long routes spreading out from the towns and villages of craftsmen who were creating a different art and using a wide range of techniques, perhaps simulated by Elam. These craftsmen worked copper and soft, colored stones, such as chlorite and alabaster, found locally, together with imported hard stones such as carnelian and lapis lazuli. They must have come into close contact with the transporters, presumably nomadic, according to the tradition of the bearers of the intercultural style. Shahdad lay at the crossroads of these routes, the one running north-south from Gorgan and Tepe Hissar and passing through Tepe Yahya on its way to the Persian Gulf, and those crossing the Lut desert or skirting it through Bampur, towards the north and south of the Hindu Kush and from there into India." (Introduction, pp.8 - 10)
Inter-Iranian trade community from Harappa settled on the crossroads at Shahdad?
Plate 1. The upper section of the Shahdad Standard, grave No. 114, Object No. 1049 (p.24)

Steppe eagle *Aquila nipalensis*
Shahdad standard.

Two possible rebus readings: *1. pajhaṛ* 'kite'. *Rebus: pasra* 'smithy, forge' (Santali)
2. śyēná m. 'hawk, falcon, eagle' RV.Pa. sēna -- , °aka -- m. 'hawk ', Pk. sēṇa -- m.; WPah.bhad. śeṇ 'kite'; A. xen ' falcon, hawk ', Or. seṇā, H. sen, sẽ m., M. śen m., śenī f. (< MIA. *senna --); Si. sen 'falcon, eagle, kite'. (CDIAL 12674) Rebus 1: senaka a carter ThA 271 (=sākaṭika of Th 2, 443)

(Pali) sēnāpati m. ' leader of an army ' AitBr. [sḗnā -- , páti --

Abb.3: Die Standarte von Shahdad (a: Aufnahme des Verfassers, b: nach Hakemi, A. [1997])

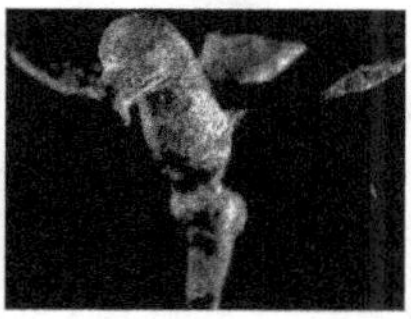

] Pa. *sēnāpati* -- , °*ika* -- m. 'general', Pk. *sēṇāvaï* -- m.; M. *śeṇvaī*, °*vī*, *śeṇai* m. 'a class of Brahmans', Ko. *śeṇvi*; Si. *senevi* 'general' (CDIAL 13589).
Rebus 2: seṇi (f.) [Class. Sk. Śreṇi in meaning "guild"; Vedic= row] 1. A guild Vin iv.226; J i.267, 314; iv.43; Dāvs ii.124; their number was eighteen J vi.22, 427; VbhA 466. ° -- pamukha the head of a guild J ii.12 (text seni --).
Kur. kaṇḍō a stool. Malt. kanḍo stool, seat. (DEDR 1179) Rebus: kaṇḍ = a furnace, altar (Santali.)
kola 'woman' (Nahali). Rebus: kol 'working in iron'; pañcaloha, alloy of five metals (Tamil)

Tukulti-Ninurta I's dream is rebus

erako 'moltencast copper' *karaḍa* 'hard alloys', *āra* 'brass' are the stock-in-trade. The scepter carriers *kaṇṇahāra* 'helmsman, sailor' (Prākṛt). The divinity venerated in *kole.l* 'smithy, temple' is: *karaṇḍi* 'fire divinity'. Since this divinity is attested in Remo, Munda language, the Asur (*koles* 'iron smelters') of India are the the ancestral Assur, the ancestors venerated by Tukulti-Ninurta I at *kaṇḍa* 'fire-altar'.

The altar is for divinity Nuska who, in Sumerian tradition is a vizier of Divinity Enlil. Nuska is not only a scribe but also a boatman who took Enlil to his future wife, Ninlil. Nuska has a shrine in Ekur ('mountain house).[247] Enlil was the Divinity of Storms. Enlil's son is Ninurta.

Mountain house ruins at Nippur, the city of Enlil. Ekur had shrines and warehouses where traders brought in offerings. This may have led to the design of ziggurats.

A drawing of a seal representing Divinity Enlil and his wife, Ninlil shows him holding a quiver of arrows; Enlil is shown ligatured to a bull signifying his function as a 'smith', ḍhangar 'bull' Rebus: ḍhangar 'blacksmith'.

The center-piece of the dream altar venerated by Tukulti-Ninurta I is hieroglyph: *kōl* 'big wooden pestle, stick'. Rebus: *kōla* 'boat'. Hence, the flag-carriers tall flagposts surmounted by spoked-wheel hieroglyphs, are sailors. The spoked-wheel is hieroglyph read rebus for their stock-in-trade: *eraka āra* 'moltencast copper, brass'.

Ta. kōl stick, staff, branch, arrow. *Ma.* kōl staff, rod, stick, arrow. *Ko.* ko·l stick, story of funeral car. *Ka.* kōl, kōlu stick, staff, arrow. *Koḍ.* ko·lï stick. *Tu.* kōlů, kōlu stick, staff. *Te.* kōla id., arrow; long, oblong; kōlana elongatedness, elongation; kōlani elongated. *Kol.* (SR.) kolā, (Kin.) kōla stick. *Nk. (Ch.)* kōl pestle. *Pa.*kōl shaft of arrow. *Go.* (A.) kōla id.; kōlā (Tr.) a thin twig or stick, esp. for kindling a fire, (W. Ph.) stick, rod, a blade of grass, straw; (G. Mu. Ma. Ko.) kōla handle of plough, sickle, knife, etc. (*Voc.* 988); (ASu.) kōlā stick, arrow, slate-pencil; (LuS.) kola the handle of an implement. *Konḍa* kōl big wooden pestle. *Pe.* kōl pestle. *Manḍ.* kūl id. *Kui* kōḍu (*pl.* kōṭka) id. *Kuwi* (F.) kōlū (*pl.* kōlka), (S. Su.)kōlu (*pl.* kōlka) id. Cf. 2240 Ta. kōlam (Tu. Te. Go.). / Cf. OMar. (Master) kōla stick. (DEDR 2237). कोलंगी [kōlaṅgī] *f* A flake of fire (Marathi)

Rebus, allograph: कोल [kōla] *n* An income, or goods and chattels, or produce of fields &c. seized and sequestered (in payment of a debt).

Allographs: कोला [kōlā] *m* (Commonly कोल्हा) A jackal कोल्हा [kōlhā] *m* A jackal, Canis aureus. Linn. कोल [kōla] *f* The hole dug at the game of विटीदांडू, at marbles &c. कोली [kōlī] *f* The hole dug at the game of विटीदांडू or at marbles. कोलणें [kōlaṇēṃ] *v c* To strike the विटी in the hole कोली with the bat or दांडू. (In the game of विटीदांडू) 2 To cast off from one's self upon another (a work). Ex. पैका मागावयास लागलों म्हणजे बाप लेंकावर कोल- तो लेंक बापावर कोलतो. 3 To cast aside, reject, disallow, flout, scout. कोलून मारणें To kick up the heels of; to trip up: also to turn over (from one side to the other). (Marathi)

Rebus: *Ta.* kōl, kōlam raft, float. *Ma.* kōlam raft. *Ka.* kōl raft, float. *Te.* (B.) kōlamu id. / Cf. Skt., BHS kola- boat, raft, Pali kulla- id. (DEDR 2238).

Altar of Tukulti-Ninurta I, Assur.

Comparable to the six spoked wheel hieroglyphs deployed on one side of the altar of Tukulti-NinurtaI, are the four spoked wheel hieroglyphs on a monumental Dholavira advertisement board mounted on a gateway to citadel. I suggest that 'spoked wheel' hieroglyph on both contexts convey the same meaning because both were made by artisans celebrated in Asur (India)/Assur (Ancient Near East) traditions.

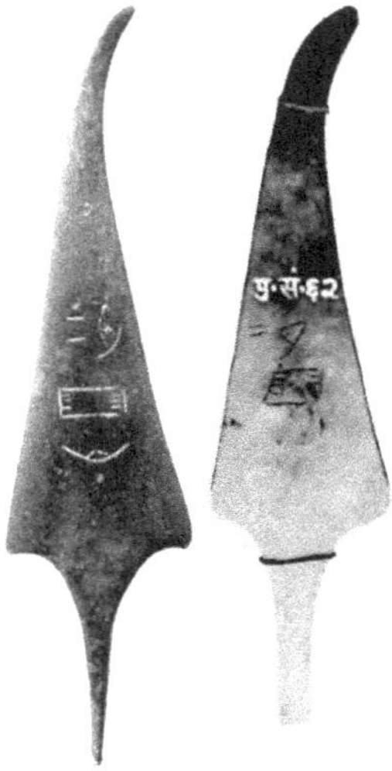

h380  4902 h381  4901 The two bronze daggers showing the hieroglyphs oriented top to bottom. The *mudhif*-shape is *mund* 'hut' in Toda language. Rebus: *mund* 'iron' (Sanskrit) *āra* 'spokes of wheel' *eraka* 'nave of wheel' *āra* 'brass' *erako* 'moltencast copper'. *sā̃gāḍā* m. ' frame of a building ' (M.)(CDIAL 12859) जांगड *jāṅgaḍa* *f* (Hindi) Goods taken from a shop on approval basis -- to be retained or returned. *mẽt* 'the eye' Rebus: *meḍ* 'iron'. The catalog provides characteristics of the metals used in the alloyed weapons. *jāṅgaḍa mund meḍ eraka āra* 'on approval basis: (made of) molten cast brass, iron'.

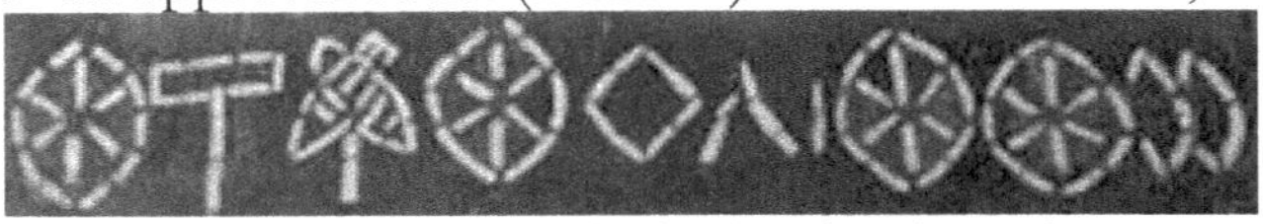

Ten Meluhha hieroglyphs on Dholavira sign board.

"The Citadel fortification walls on east, north and west had entry gates. Just near the door, chambers were built at a height with roofs supported on pillars, parts of which can be seen even today. The main through-way in the citadel was segregated in three sections, marked by means of 2 polished pillars. In one of the two north gate chambers, archaeologists found a huge name board written with 10 Indus script glyphs or symbols. Each of this was made from Gypsum and was 15 inches high. Total length of this board was about 3 meters and the gypsum symbols were embedded in wood, which had rotted away later, leaving only the symbols intact."[248]

Three artefacts with Indus writing are remarkable for their definitive intent to broadcast the metallurgical message: 1. Dholavira signboard on a gateway; 2. Shahdad standard; and 3. Tablets showing processions of three standards: scarf hieroglyph, one-horned young bull hieroglyph and standard-device hieroglyph.

Rebus readings of the inscriptions relate to and document the metallurgical competence of Meluhhan lapidaries-artisans. Some other select set of inscriptions from the wide, expansive area stretching from Haifa to Rakhigarhi, from Altyn Depe (Caucus) to Daimabad (Maharashtra) are presented to show the area which had evidenced the use of Meluhha (Mleccha) language of Indian *sprachbund.*

Hieroglyphs deployed on Indus inscriptions have had a lasting effect on the glyptic motifs used on hundreds of cylinder seals of the Meluhha contact regions. The glyptic motifs continued to be used as a logo-semantic writing system, together with cuneiform texts which used a logo-syllabic writing system, even after the use of complex tokens and bullae were discontinued to account for commodities. The Indus writing system of hieroglyphs read rebus matched the Bronze Age revolutionary imperative of minerals, metals and alloys produced as surplus to the requirements of the artisan communities and as available for the creation and sustenance of trade-networks to meet the demand for alloyed metal tools, weapons, pots and pans, apart from the supply of copper, tin metal ingots for use in the smithy of nations,*harosheth hagoyim* mentioned in the Old Testament (Judges). This term also explains the continuum of Aramaic script into the cognate *kharoṣṭī* 'blacksmith-lip' *goya* 'communities'.

Indus-Sarasvatī Signboard Text. Read rebus as Meluhha (Mleccha) announcement of metals repertoire of a smithy complex in the citadel. The 'spoked wheel' is the semantic divider of three segments of the broadcast message. Details of readings, from r. to l.:

Segment 1: Working in ore, molten cast copper, lathe (work)

ḍato 'claws or pincers of crab' (Santali) rebus: *dhatu* 'ore' (Santali)

eraka 'knave of wheel' Rebus: *eraka* 'copper' (Kannada) *eraka* 'molten cast (metal)(Tulu). *sangaḍa* 'pair' Rebus: *sangaḍa*'lathe' (Gujarati)

Segment 2: Native metal tools, pots and pans, metalware, engraving (molten cast copper)

खांडा [khāṇḍā] *m* A jag, notch, or indentation (as upon the edge of a tool or weapon). (Marathi) Rebus: *khāṇḍā* 'tools, pots and pans, metal-ware'.

aḍaren, ḍaren lid, cover (Santali) Rebus: *aduru* 'native metal' (Ka.) *aduru* = gan.iyinda tegadu karagade iruva aduru = ore taken from the mine and not subjected to melting in a furnace (Kannada) (Siddhānti *Subrahmaṇya' śāstri's new interpretation of the Amarakośa*, Bangalore, Vicaradarpana Press, 1872, p. 330)

koṇḍa bend (Ko.); Tu. Kōḍi corner; kōṇṭu angle, corner, crook. Nk. kōnṭa corner (DEDR 2054b) G. khū̃ṭṛī f. 'angle' Rebus: *kõdā*'to turn in a lathe'(B.) कोंद kōnda 'engraver, lapidary setting or infixing gems' (Marathi) koḍ 'artisan's workshop' (Kuwi) koḍ = place where artisans work (G.) ācāri koṭṭya 'smithy' (Tu.) कोंडण [kōṇḍaṇa] f A fold or pen. (Marathi) B. kõdā 'to turn in a lathe'; Or.kū̃nda 'lathe', kũdibā, kū̃d 'to turn' (→ Drav. Kur. Kū̃d ' lathe') (CDIAL 3295) A. kundār, B. kũdār, ri, Or.Kundāru; H. kũderā m. 'one who works a lathe, one who scrapes', rī f., kũdernā 'to scrape, plane, round on a lathe'; kundakara—m. 'turner' (Skt.)(CDIAL 3297). कोंदण [kōndaṇa] n (कोंदणें) Setting or infixing of gems.(Marathi)

খোদকার [khōdakāra] n an engraver; a carver. খোদকারি n. engraving; carving; interference in other's work. খোদাই [khōdāi] n engraving; carving. খোদাই করা v. to engrave; to carve. খোদানো v. & n. en graving; carving. খোদিত [khōdita] a engraved. (Bengali) खोदकाम [khōdakāma] n Sculpture; carved work or work for the carver. खोदगिरी [khōdagirī] f Sculpture, carving, engraving: also sculptured or carved work. खोदणावळ [khōdaṇāvaḷa] f (खोदणें) The price or cost of sculpture or carving. खोदणी [khōdaṇī] f (Verbal of खोदणें) Digging, engraving &c. 2 fig. An exacting of money by importunity. V लाव, मांड. 3 An instrument to scoop out and cut flowers and figures from paper. 4 A goldsmith's die. खोदणें [khōdaṇēṃ] v c & i (H) To dig. 2 To engrave. खोद खोदून विचारणें or –पुसणें To question minutely and searchingly, to probe. खोदाई [khōdāī] f (H.) Price or cost of digging or of sculpture or carving. खोदींव [khōdīṃva] p of खोदणें Dug. 2 Engraved, carved, sculptured. (Marathi)

eraka 'knave of wheel' Rebus: *eraka* 'copper' (Kannada) *eraka* 'molten cast (metal)(Tulu).

Segment 3: Coppersmith mint, furnace, workshop (molten cast copper)

loa 'fig leaf; Rebus: loh '(copper) metal' *kamaḍha* 'ficus religiosa' (Skt.); *kamaṭa* = portable furnace for melting precious metals (Te.); *kampaṭṭam* = mint (Ta.) The unique ligatures on the 'leaf' hieroglyph may be explained as a professional designation: *loha-kāra* 'metalsmith'; *kāruvu* [Skt.] n. 'An artist, artificer. An agent'.(Telugu).

khuṇṭa 'peg'; khũṭi = pin (M.) rebus: kuṭi= furnace (Santali) kūṭa 'workshop' kuṇḍamu 'a pit for receiving and preserving consecrated fire' (Te.) kundār turner (A.); kũdār, kũdāri (B.)

eraka 'knave of wheel' Rebus: *eraka* 'copper' (Kannada) *eraka* 'molten cast (metal)(Tulu).

Size matters. Archaeological context matters. How could one interpret the utility for the people of Dholavira, of 10 large glyphs (35 to 37 cm. high and 25 to 27 cm.wide) carefully laid out, in sequence, using gypsum pieces on an inscription which was a Signboard mounted on a gateway? Maybe, the Signboard text was visible from a distance for seafaring merchants and artisans from Dilmun or Magan or Elam. How can one assume it to be oral literature, for the guidance of tourists or merchants entering the citadel or even for the people of Dholavira (Kotda)? Why should any pundit conceive of the text, arbitrarily, to be non-linguistic? The glyphs are not randomly drawn but are repetitions from several tablets and seals which carry one or more of nearly 500 such distinct glyphs on nearly 7000 inscriptions of Indus writing. Why can't the glyphs be read rebus as hieroglyphs as a cypher code for the underlying sounds & semantics of words in Meluhha (Mleccha) language -- comparable to the rebus reading of N'r-M'r palette which used N'r 'cuttle-fish' and M'r 'awl' hieroglyphs to be read together as Narmer, the name of an Egyptian emperor?

RV 10.124 speaks of Agni, Varuṇa and Soma moving from Asura to Indra.

10.124.01a imáṃ no agna úpa yajñám éhi páñcayāmaṃ trivṛ́taṃ saptátantum |
10.124.01c áso havyavā́ḷ utá naḥ purogā́ jyóg evá dīrgháṃ táma ā́śayiṣṭhāḥ ||
10.124.02a ádevād deváḥ pracátā gúhā yán prapáśyamāno amṛtatvám emi |
10.124.02c śiváṃ yát sántam áśivo jáhāmi svā́t sakhyā́d áraṇīṃ nā́bhim emi ||
10.124.03a páśyann anyásyā átithiṃ vayā́yā ṛtásya dhā́ma ví mime purū́ṇi |
10.124.03c śáṃsāmi pitré ásurāya śévam ayajñiyā́d yajñíyam bhāgám emi ||
10.124.04a bahvī́ḥ sámā akaram antár asminn índraṃ vṛṇānáḥ pitáraṃ jahāmi |
10.124.04c agníḥ sómo váruṇas té cyavante paryā́vard rāṣṭráṃ tád avāmy āyán ||
10.124.05a nírmāyā u tyé ásurā abhūvan tváṃ ca mā varuṇa kāmáyāse |
10.124.05c ṛténa rājann ánṛtaṃ viviñcán máma rāṣṭrásyā́dhipatyam éhi ||
10.124.06a idáṃ svàr idám íd āsa vāmám ayám prakāśá urv àntárikṣam |
10.124.06c hánāva vṛtráṃ niréhi soma havíṣ ṭvā sántaṃ havíṣā yajāma ||
10.124.07a kavíḥ kavitvā́ diví rūpám ā́sajad áprabhūtī váruṇo nír apáḥ sṛjat |
10.124.07c kṣémaṃ kṛṇvānā́ jánayo ná síndhavas tā́ asya várṇaṃ śúcayo bharibhrati ||
10.124.08a tā́ asya jyéṣṭham indriyáṃ sacante tā́ īm ā́ kṣeti svadháyā mádantīḥ |
10.124.08c tā́ īṃ víśo ná rā́jānaṃ vṛṇānā́ bībhatsúvo ápa vṛtrā́d atiṣṭhan ||
10.124.09a bībhatsū́nāṃ sayújaṃ haṃsám āhur apā́ṃ divyā́nāṃ sakhyé cárantam |
10.124.09c anuṣṭúbham ánu carcūryámāṇam índraṃ ní cikyuḥ kaváyo manīṣā́ ||

This hymn is seen as a dialogue including Agni's acceptance of an invitation from Indra to Agni to leave the Asuras and serve at the yajña-s of Devas.

Translation by Wash Edward Hale[249]:

RV 10.124.1 (Indra): O Agni, approach this our sacrifice which has five paths, three layers, and seven threads. May you be our oblation-bearer and leader. For a long time you have lain in the long darkness. (Hymn to various deities)
RV 10.124.2 (Agni): I the god go from the ungodly on, going secretly (and) in hiding seeing immortality. When unfriendly I abandon the friendly being, I go from my own friendship to the strange clan.
10.124.3 (Agni): Seeing the guest of the other branch, I measure widely the many forms of *ṛta*. I say a kind word to the father asura. I go from exclusion from the sacrifice to a share in the sacrifice.
RV 10.124.4 (Agni): Many years I worked in this one. Choosing Indra I abandon the father. Agni, Soma, Varuṇa – they go (forth). The rulership has changed. Coming, I aid this (rulership).

RV 10.124.5 (Indra): Even these asuras have become without magic. If you love me, O Varuṇa, O king, separating *anṛta* from *ṛta*, come to rulership of my kingdom.
RV 10.124.6 (Indra): Here is the sun, here indeed is the good, here is the light, the wide atmosphere. Let us two kill Vṛtra. Come forth, O Soma. We offer with an oblation to you who are the oblation.
RV 10.124.7 The seer with his seer's ability gives shape to heaven. Because of lack of power Varuṇa sends the water forth. Making comfort like wives, the rivers the shining ones carry around his color.
RV 10.124.8 They follow his greatest Indric power. He lives with those very ones who are delighting according to their nature. These choosing him as clans their went away from Vṛtra feeling revulsion.
RV 10.124.9 They call the companion of those who feel revulsion a wild goose wandering in the friendship of the divine waters. The poets with their wisdom perceive Indra ever wandering about according to the *anuṣṭubh*.

In this narrative, RV 10.124.7 yields a clue by the phrase: *kaviḥ kavitvā divi rūpam asajad*. Interpreting *kavi* as a reference to an artisan/smith working with metals (consistent with the historical contexts of *kayanides*[250]), the translation can be: The artisan with his artisan's ability gives shape to heaven. This is contrasted with Varuṇa's lack of power (aprabhūti nir). Father Asura should be someone who is venerated by the *kavi*, the artisans/smiths who became rulers. Such a veneration is attested by Remo speakers (Asura-Munda 'iron, metal' tradition) as *karaṇḍi*, 'fire-divinity'. Rebus hieroglyph: *karaḍi* 'safflower'. The use of the 'stick' hieroglyph is noteworthy; it is signified by the gloss: kōla 'stick' Rebus: kōl 'smelters'; kola 'boat'. Allograph: kōla 'ornamental diagram'. Tukulti-Ninurta I's fire-altar evidence is consistent with these rebus readings, reinforcing the possibility that both Asur (Indian) and Assur (Ancient Near East) had Father Asur as the common divinity of their ancestors.

It is possible that Father Asura (as yet unidentified) or an ancestral symbolic form is *karaṇḍi* 'fire divinity' in Remo, Munda tradition (this symbolic form can be related to the tradition of Asurs who are metal-workers of India).

Taittiriya Samhita 2.5.1 and 2 have a narrative on how Tvaṣṭṛ created Vṛtra by throwing soma into the fire. Soma and Agni called out to Indra from within Vṛtra. Vṛtra allowed Soma and Agni to come out ad then, Indra slays Vṛtra. One speculation is that Vṛtra wrapped himself around a stone enclosure in heaven which contained the cosmic ocean which was the domain of Varuṇa. Held within this domain were Soma and Agni. This leads to an explanation that Indra's attempt was to persuade all three -- Agni, Varuṇa and Soma – to his side to slay Vṛtra.

I am thankful to RN Iyengar for the following notes: Deva is derived from div to shine, these were the celestial luminaries mainly the nakshatras (deva grihaavai nakshatraaNi Taittiriya.Br.). Quite intriguingly in many places shining objects are also qualified as Asura. For example in 3.3.4; 4.2.5 Agni is called asura. As is well known Varuṇa is also asura. In some places Indra is asura. Hence asura was not a pejorative word till something special happened. The clue is with Maruts who are also asura. Sayaṇa in most of the places accepts the derivation of the word from asu kshepaṇe = to throw, to put, to keep. The action of the Maruts was to throw stones at earth. They in fact killed Prajapati's creation once. In RV the eclipse shadow Svarbhānu is called āsura (one belonging to asura). This is so because the original Viśvarūpa Tvāṣṭra could once cover up Sun. The word asuryā has been rendered in several translations as divine, but the connection with maruts indicates the epithet to be a physical description of the flowing river affected by maruts who were always called asurāh: throwers (of stones). Significantly, in the tenth book (10.17.8-9) goddess Sarasvatī is invoked seated in the same chariot as the ancestor deities. She is आसुरी सरस्वती This in vaidika parlance means the river had dried, which, in the language

of RV should have been after frequent sightings of maruts in the visible sky above the River Sarasvatī. Asur, Assur as Meluhha were workers in stone, ores, shell and metals.
Both Deva and Asura were mleccha/meluhha speakers, according to Manu:

मुखबाहूरुपज्जानां या लोके जातयो बहिः।

म्लेच्छवाचश्चार्यवाचः सर्वे ते दस्यवः स्मृताः॥ Manu 10.45

१०अध्या.४५ तमश्लो.॥

> > व्याख्यानम् -> > ब्राह्मण-क्षत्रिय-वैश्य-शूद्राणां क्रियालोपदिना या जातयो बह्याः जाताः मेल्च्छभाषायुक्ताः आर्यभाषोपेता वा ते दस्यवः सर्वे स्मृताः।

कनीयस्विन इव वै तर्हि देवा आसन् भूयस्विनोऽसुराः ।

ता>१२/१३/३१॥ कानीयसा एव देवा ज्यायसा असुराः श.१४.४.१.१.॥

(Tāṇḍya Brāhmaṇa)

Devas or Suras were born from the Mukha or Face of Prajapati and the Asuras were from his Jaghana part : असुराणां देवानां च उत्पत्ति विषये।

सः (प्रजापतिः).....अकामयत प्रजायेयेति। स तपोऽतप्यत> सोऽन्तर्वानभूत्। स जघनादसुरान् असृजत......स मुखाद्देवानसृजत..तै.२.२.९.५-८)

१. तेनासुनासुरानसृजत। तदसुराणामसुरत्वम्। (तै.२।३।२।१॥)

"सोर्देवान् असृजत तत् सुराणां सुरत्वम्। असोरसुरानसृजत तदसुराणामसुरत्वम्।"(तै.ब्रा.२.३.८.२,४)

२. दिवादेवान्सृजत नक्तमसुरान् अद्दिवा देवनसृजत तद्देवानं देवत्वम्; यदसूर्य्यं तदसुराणामसुरत्वम्॥(षद्विंशब्राह्मणम्४.१.)

३. देवाश्च वाऽअसुराश्च। उभये प्राजापत्याः प्रजपतेः पितुर्दायत्वमुपेयुरेतावेवार्धमासौ (शुक्लकृष्णपक्षौ)॥ (श.ब्रा.१.७.२.२२)

३. देवाश्च व असुराश्च प्रजपतेर्द्वया: पुत्रा आसन्। (तां.ब्रा.१८.१.२)
४.कानीयसा एव देवा ज्यायसा असुरा:. (श.१४.४.१.१.)
५. अहर्वै देवा आश्रयन्त रात्रीमसुरा: (ऐ.४.५)
६.अर्वाग्वसुर्ह देवानां ब्रह्मा पराग्वसुरसुराणाम्. (गोपथ - उत्तरभागे १.१)

1. तदद्यवाच: परमं मंसीय येअनासुरान् अभिभवेम देवा:। असुरा: असुरता:। स्थनेष्वस्ता: स्थानेभ्य इति वा. अपि वासुरिति प्राणनाम। अस्त: शरीरे भवति। तेन तद्वन्त:। (निरुक्ते ३.८)
2. "देवाश्च वा असुराश्चास्पर्धन्त नेमे देवा आसन्नेमेऽसुरा:।" (निरुक्ते ३.२०)

An Old Iranian noun (Av. *daēuua-*, OPers. *daiva-*) corresponds to *deva* in Indian tradition. This reflects the Indo-European heritage: **deiu̯ó-*. Iranian religious tradition[251] drops out, gradually, the association of divinity with this sememe. Gathas cited *daēuua*s as divine (*daxíiu-*; *Y.* 32.3, 46.1)—as part of the Mazdean social and religious system.

10.124.03c uses the phrase 'pitre asurāya' that is, father asura. Who was this father asura? He is not named in Ṛgveda, leading many scholars to speculate on identification of Father Asura, suggesting: Rudra, Varuṇa, Vṛtra, Dyaus, or old Indo-Iranian Asura who became Ahura Mazdā in Iran using rhetoric expressions common with the Vedic tradition: *daēuua-/mašiia-*: *devá-/mártya-*, *vīspa-daēuua-* : *víśva- devá-*, and *daēuuo.zušta-:devájuṣṭa-*. There is no specification as to who the *daēuua*s were. The *daēuuaiiasna*s who offered nocturnal libations to Anāhitā (see anāhīd; *Yt.* 5.94).

In the *Vidēvdād* (10.9,19.43) Iṇdra (Ved. Índra), Sauruua (Ved. Śarvá), and Nåŋhaiθiia (Ved. Nā´satya) are mentioned at the head

of a list of *daēuua*s, immediately after reference to Aŋra Mainiiu; in the Pahlavi books the same three were recognized as the enemies of Aša, Xšaθra, and Ārmaiti respectively.
Agni calls Father Asura as fire; in Iran fire is called the son of Ahura Mazdā.

This representation of an altar on one side of Ninurta's altar is rebus of a dream, that is, a rebus of his ancestors' tradition of worship at an altar. This representation of worship on one side of the altar has two 'safflower' hieroglyphs flanking the narrative which shos a slate and a stalk rising up like a shaft in the middle of the altar. It is this 'stalk' and 'slate' image that is venerated. Hieroglyph: *kaṇḍ* 'fire-altar'.

kāṇḍá काण्डः m. the stalk or stem of a reed, grass, or the like, straw. In a compound with dan 5 (p. 221*a,* l. 13) the word is spelt *kāḍ*. Rebus: *khāṇḍa* 'tools, pots and pans and metal-ware'.

kaṇḍa '(mineral)stone, meal tools, pots and pans'.
Hieroglyph: *karaḍi*, 'safflower' Rebus 1: *karaḍa* 'hard alloy' Rebus 2: *karaṇḍi* 'fire divinity' (Remo. Munda language). The phrase *takṣat vāk* used in the Ṛgveda as a reference to 'incised speech' (RV 9.97.22). In Indian tradition, takhtī is a writing tablet. The gloss takhtī is cognate with *takṣat 'incised'*. Mohenjo-Daro. Writing tablets represented in terracotta. Mature Harappan. (After Fig. 4.70 in Verma, TP, 2013, Writing in Vedic Age, Itihas darpan, XVIII(1), 2013, Research Journal of Akhila Bhāratiya Itihāsa Sankalana Yojanā, New Delhi, pp. 40-59.)

The writing instrument was called, *kāṇḍa* 'arrow, reed, stylus'. It is suggested that the Tukulti-Ninurta I altar for Divinity Nuska had the centerpiece rerpresentation of a writing tablet and a reed pen; Meluhha glosses for these artifacts were: *takhtī* 'writing tablet' and *kāṇḍa* 'stylus pen'.

This symbolic form signifies Divinity Nuska. *kā̃ḍ* (Kashmiri) *kānā̃* m. ' stalk of the reed Sara ', °*nī̃* f. 'pen, small spear' (Lahnda) Rebus: *kāṇḍā* 'tools, pots and pans, metalware'. Cognate gloss of *takṣaṇa*: *tah'nai*, *tanana mleccha*, lit. incising mleccha or scribe mleccha. *தச்சு taccu, n. < takṣa. 1. Carpenter's work; தச்சன்றொழில். தச்சு விடுத்தலும் (திருவாச. 14, 3).* (Tamil) तक्षण [takṣaṇa] *n* S Chipping, planing, paring, shaving or slicing off. 2 Carpentry gen.(Marathi) takṣ ' hew ': takṣa in cmpd. ' cutting ', m. ' carpenter ' VarBr̥S., *vr̥kṣa -- takṣaka* -- m. ' tree -- feller ' R. [√takṣ] Pa. *tacchaka* -- m. ' carpenter ', *taccha – sūkara* -- m. ' boar '; Pk. *takkha* -- , °*aya* -- m. 'carpenter,artisan'; Bshk. *sum -- tạch* ' hoe ' (< ' *earth -- scratcher '), *tẹch* ' adze ' (< **takṣī* -- ?); Sh. *tạci* f. ' adze '; -- Phal. *tēṛchi* ' adze ' (with "intrusive" *r*). takṣaṇa n. ' cutting, paring ' KātyŚr. [√takṣ] Pa. *tacchanī* -- f. ' hatchet '; Pk. *tacchaṇa* -- n., °*ṇā* -- f. ' act of cutting or scraping '; Kal. *tĕčin* ' chip ' (< **takṣaṇī* -- ?); K. *tačhyunu* (dat. *tačhinis*) m. ' wood -- shavings '; Ku. gng. *tačhaṇ* ' cutting (of wood) '; M. *tāsṇī* f. ' act of chipping &c., adze '.Pk. *tacchaṇa* -- n. ' cutting '; Kmd.barg. *tač̣ə̃ṅ* ' chips (on roof) ' GM 22.6.71. tákṣati (3 pl. *tákṣati* RV.) ' forms by cutting, chisels ' MBh. [√takṣ] Pa. *tacchati* ' builds ', *tacchēti* ' does woodwork, chips '; Pk. *takkhaï*, *tacchaï*, *cacchaï*, *caṁchaï* ' cuts, scrapes, peels '; Gy. pers.*tetchkani* ' knife ', wel. *tax* -- ' to paint ' (?); Dm. *tač* -- ' to cut ' (*č* < IE. *kŝ* NTS xii 128), Kal. *tāč̃* -- ; Kho. *točhik* ' to cut with an axe '; Phal. *tạc*<-> ' to cut, chop, whittle '; Sh. (Lor.) *thačoiki* ' to fashion (wood) '; K. *tachun* ' to shave, pare, scratch ', S. *tachaṇu*; L. *tachaṇ* ' to scrape ', (Ju.) ' to rough hew ', P. *tacchṇā*, ludh. *tacchanā* ' to hew '; Ku. *tāchṇo* ' to square out '; N. *tāchnu* ' to scrape, peel, chip off ' (whence *tachuwā* ' chopped square

', *tachārnu* ' to lop, chop '); B. *cā̃chā* ' to scrape '; Or. *tā̃chibā*, *cā̃chibā*, *chā̃cibā* ' to scrape off, clip, peel '; Bhoj. *cā̃chal* ' to smoothe with an adze '; H. *cā̃chnā* ' to scrape up '; G. *tāchvũ* ' to scrape, carve, peel ', M. *tāsṇẽ*; Si.*sahinavā*, *ha*° ' to cut with an adze '. <-> Kho. *troçik* ' to hew ' with "intrusive" *r*.Kmd. *tac* -- ' to cut, pare, clip ' GM 22.6.71; A. *cā̃ciba* (phonet. *sā̃sibɔ*) ' to scrape ' AFD 216, 217, ' to smoothe with an adze ' 331. tákṣan (acc. *tákṣaṇam* RV., *takṣā́ṇam* Pāṇ.) m. ' carpenter '. [√takṣ] Pk. *takkhāṇa* -- m., Paš. ar. *taçan* -- *kṓr*, weg. *taṣā´n*, Kal. *kaṭ* -- *tačon*, Kho. (Lor.) *tačon*, Sh. *kaṭ* -- *th*°, K.*chān* m., *chöñü* f., P. *takhāṇ* m., °*ṇī* f., H. *takhān* m.; Si. *sasa* ' carpenter, wheelwright ' < nom. *tákṣā*. -- With "intrusive" *r*. Kho. (Lor.)*tračon* ' carpenter ', P. *tarkhāṇ* m. (→ H. *tarkhān* m.), WPah. jaun. *tarkhāṇ*. -- With unexpl. *d* -- or *dh* -- (X dā´ru -- ?): S. *ḍrakhaṇu*m. ' carpenter '; L. *drakhāṇ*, (Ju.) *darkhāṇ* m. ' carpenter ' (*darkhāṇ pakkhī* m. ' woodpecker '), mult. *dhrikkhāṇ* m., *dhrikkhaṇī* f., awāṇ. *dhirkhāṇ* m. (CDIAL 5618 to 5621)

kā̃ḍ m. ' stalk of a reed, straw ' (Kashmiri) kā´ṇḍa (*kāṇḍá* -- TS.) m.n. ' single joint of a plant ' AV., ' arrow ' MBh., ' cluster, heap ' (in *tṛṇa* -- *kāṇḍa* -- Pāṇ. Kāś.). [Poss. connexion with gaṇḍa -- 2 makes prob. non -- Aryan origin (not with P. Tedesco Language 22, 190 < *kṛntáti*). Prob. ← Drav., cf. Tam. *kaṇ* ' joint of bamboo or sugarcane ' EWA i 197] Pa. *kaṇḍa* -- m.n. ' joint of stalk, stalk, arrow, lump '; Pk. *kaṁḍa* -- , °*aya* -- m.n. ' knot of bough, bough, stick '; Ash. *kaṇ* ' arrow ', Kt. *kåṇ*, Wg. *kāṇ*, Pr. *kɔ̃*, Dm.*kā̃n;* Paš. lauṛ. *kāṇḍ*, *kāṇ*, ar. *kōṇ*, kuṛ. *kō̃*, dar. *kā̃ṛ* ' arrow ', *kā̃ṛī* ' torch '; Shum. *kō̃ṛ*, *kō̃* ' arrow ', Gaw. *kāṇḍ*, *kāṇ*; Kho. *kan* ' tree, large bush '; Bshk. *kā`'n* ' arrow ', Tor.*kan* m., Sv. *kā̃ṛa*, Phal. *kōṇ*, Sh. gil. *kōn* f. (→ Ḍ. *kōn*, pl. *kāna* f.), pales. *kōṇ*; K. *kā̃ḍ* m. ' stalk of a reed, straw ' (*kān* m. ' arrow ' ← Sh.?); S. *kānu* m. ' arrow ', °*no* m. ' reed ',°*nī* f. ' topmost joint of the reed Sara, reed pen, stalk, straw, porcupine's quill '; L. *kānā̃* m. ' stalk of the reed Sara ', °*nī*˜ f. ' pen, small spear '; P. *kānnā* m. ' the reed Saccharum munja, reed in a weaver's warp ', *kānī* f. ' arrow '; WPah. bhal. *kān* n. ' arrow ', jaun. *kā̃ḍ*; N. *kā̃ṛ* ' arrow ', °*ṛo* ' rafter ';

A. *kā̃r* ' arrow '; B. *kā̃ṛ* ' arrow ', °*ṛā* ' oil vessel made of bamboo joint, needle of bamboo for netting ', *kẽṛiyā* ' wooden or earthen vessel for oil &c. '; Or. *kāṇḍa, kā̃ṛ* ' stalk, arrow '; Bi. *kā̃ṛā* ' stem of muñja grass (used for thatching) '; Mth. *kā̃ṛ* ' stack of stalks of large millet ', *kā̃ṛī* ' wooden milkpail '; Bhoj. *kaṇḍā* ' reeds '; H. *kā̃ṛī* f. ' rafter, yoke ', *kaṇḍā* m. ' reed, bush ' (← EP.?); G. *kā̃ḍ* m. ' joint, bough, arrow ', °*ḍũ* n. ' wrist ', °*ḍī* f. ' joint, bough, arrow, lucifer match '; M. *kā̃ḍ* n. ' trunk, stem ', °*ḍẽ* n. ' joint, knot, stem, straw ', °*ḍī* f. ' joint of sugarcane, shoot of root (of ginger, &c.) '; Si. *kaḍaya* ' arrow '. -- Deriv. A. *kāriyāiba* ' to shoot with an arrow '.
kā´ṇḍīra -- ; *kāṇḍakara -- , *kāṇḍārā -- ; *dēhīkāṇḍa --[< IE. **kondo* -- , Gk. kondu/los ' knuckle ', ko/ndos ' ankle ' T. Burrow BSOAS xxxviii 55 (CDIAL 3023).
The other side of the altar has two spoked wheels hoisted on scepters or flagposts.

The two flagposts are carried by two flag-carriers who are themselves identified by two spoked wheels (perhaps as rebus representations of their functions). *kā̃ṛo* 'rafter' (Sindhi)+ *āra* 'spokes of wheel' Rebus: *kaṇṇahāra* 'helmsman, sailor' (Prākṛt) *āra* 'brass'. *eraka* 'nave of wheel' Rebus: *erako* 'moltencast copper'. The flag-carriers flank a person depicted with a sword carried on his left hand. The field of this side of the altar also has two spoked-wheels on either side of the top register. Thus, a total count of six spoked wheels are deployed on one side of Tukulti-NinurtaI fire-altar.

P.L. Bhargava says, "The word, Asura, including its variants, asurya and asura, occurs 88 times in the Rigveda, 71 times in the singular number, four times in the dual, 10 times in the plural, and three times as the first member of a compound. In this, the feminine form, asuryaa, is included twice. The word, asurya, has been used 19 times as an abstract noun, while the abstract form asuratva occurs 24 times, 22 times in each of the 22 times of one hymn and twice in the other two hymns." (Bhargava, PL, 1994, *Vedic Religion and Culture*, South Asia Books, Delhi).

Thomas Burrow argued that the **daivas* were gods of the Indian people who lived in the same territory as the Iranians. In the tradition of the Veda Asura were divinities. "Bhargava believes that, in most of the ancient hymns, the word, asura, is always used as an adjective meaning "powerful" or "mighty". In the Rigveda, two generous kings, as well as some priests, have been described as asuras. One hymn requests a son who is an asura. In nine hymns, Indra is described as asura. Five times, he is said to possess asurya, and once he is said to possess asuratva. Agni has total of 12 asura descriptions, Varuna has 10, Mitra has eight, and Rudra has six. Bhargava gives a count of the word usage for every Vedic deity. Moreover, Bhargava states that the word slowly assumed a negative connotation toward the end of the Rigvedic period. The Avesta, the book of the Zoroastrians, describes their supreme God as Ahura Mazda (compare Vedic Asura Medhira)—Mighty and Wise. For them, the word Deva (daeuua) is negative. Asura is therefore regarded as an epithet. Rāvaṇa asura means mighty Rāvaṇa. Rāvaṇa was a Brāhmaṇa —Rākṣasa (powerful flesh-eating demon). There was no "Asura Jati" in the way that there were classes of people titled Rākṣasa, Daityas, Devas, and Brāhmaṇa." http://en.wikipedia.org/wiki/Asura
Tin Road narrative

Meluhha hieroglyphs resolves the dialectic arguments to identify Father Asura. They are evidence of the deployment of Meluhhan language to describe the accomplishment of the mission of Samudra Manthanam – working with resources to create wealth. Seafaring merchants, trade on Tin Road had Meluhha Assur (who wrote using Meluhha hieroglyphs) contributing to the copper-tin-bronzes, copper-zinc brasses and lost-wax casting methods. The active Tin Road from Assur to Kanesh and beyond, revolutionized the Bronze Age of India, Ancient Near East and Fertile Crescent, for millenia starting from ca. mid-3rd millenium BCE.

The first ruler of Assur Puzur Aššur I ca 2025 BCE founded a dynasty of Assur. The 20000 tablets of Kultepe (Kanesh/Nesh) attest to the Tin Road between Assur and Kultepe rivaling or complementing the Silk Road. Images on many cylinder seals of ancient Near East were Meluhha hieroglyphs.[252] Rebus readings provide new light on the ancient Tin Road between Ashur and Kultepe, Turkey which has yielded over 20,000 cuneiform tablets of merchants' letters.

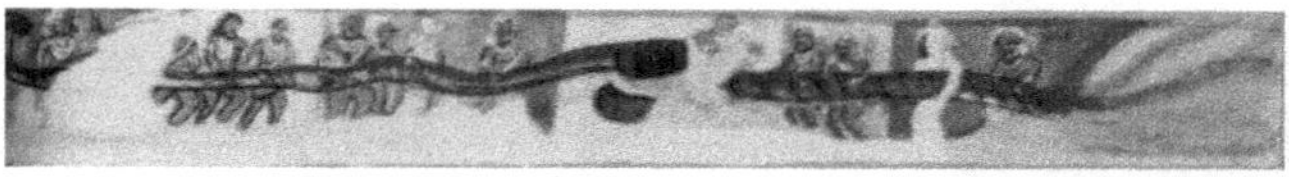

Samudra manthanam or 'Churning of Ocean of Milk' Deva and Da_nava churn the ocean, using Va_suki, the serpent as the rope and Mandara, the mountain as the churning rod. Ganesh Lena, Ellora, ca. 11th cent. CE.

The churning of the ocean of milk, Cambodia, Prasat Phnom Da, Angkor vat style, first half of the 12th century, sandstone. Musée Guimet, Paris

Angkor Thom. Part of Samudra Manthan narrative.

Four faces top Mount Meru and adorn the 5 gates of

Angkor Thom. In the Samudra Manthan narrative, Meru is the churning stick and Vishnu's avatara is Kurma, tortoise. The churning stick is flanked by Deva and Asura pulling the 7-headed snake rope Vasuki. Angkor Wat relief of Samudra Manthan shows Vishnu standing above the tortoise Kurma, the churning stick.

Krishna attacks Kamsa, Angkor Wat

The use of the name kamsa is significant in the context of Meluhha hieroglyphs and rebus representations to signify the gloss: *kā̃si* 'bronze'.

Frieze of a sculpture in Kanchi Kailasanatha temple. Dhanvantari carrying the pot from the churned ocean. This accomplishment of Asura-Deva joint mission to gather the resources across the oceans is exemplified by the sculpture of Dhanvantari carrying the jar which can be signified by rim-of-jar hieroglyph: *karṇī* 'supercargo'.

The underlying sounds of *daḷ* 'petal' and rebus reading: *ḍhālako* 'large ingot' explain the hieroglyphs, accompanying the two antelope hieroglyphs, on the following Two sides of Chanhudaro seal: The oval sign of this Jhukar culture seal is comparable to other inscriptions. Fig. 1 and 1a of Plate L. After Mackay, 1943. The hieroglyphs of the seal relate representations of bun ingots to two orthographic representations of 'antelopes': one is shown walking, the other is shown with head turned backwards. A flower is shown, perhaps, a representation of petals of tulip, *tagaraka 'tabernae montana'* Rebus: 'tin' Rebus: *damgar* 'merchant'; *krammara* 'turn back' Rebus: *kammara* 'artisan'.

The reverse of the seal shows a round numerativ particle. *goṭā* m. 'roundish stone' (Marathi) Rebus 1: *khoṭā* 'forged'; Punjabi. *khoṭ* m. 'base, alloy' M.*khoṭā* 'alloyed' Rebus 2: *kōṭhī* f (कोष्ट S) A granary, garner, storehouse, warehouse, treasury, factory, bank (Marathi)

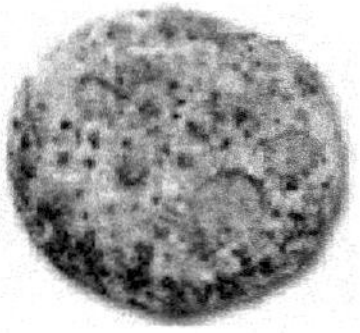

Tin bun ingot. Late Bronze Age, 10th-9th century B.C.E. Salcombe shipwreck, 300 yards off the South Devon coast, England, 2009.

Stamp seal from Susa , at Louvre Museum. "Susa is one of the oldest known settlements of the world, possibly founded about 4200 BC, although the first traces of an inhabited village have been dated to ca. 7000 BCE. The seal depicts two goat-antelopes head to tail, outside an oval." *mlech* 'antelope' Rebus: *milakkhu* 'copper' Alternative: ranku 'antelope' Rebus: ranku 'tin'; *dula* 'pair' Rebus: *dul* 'cast metal'.

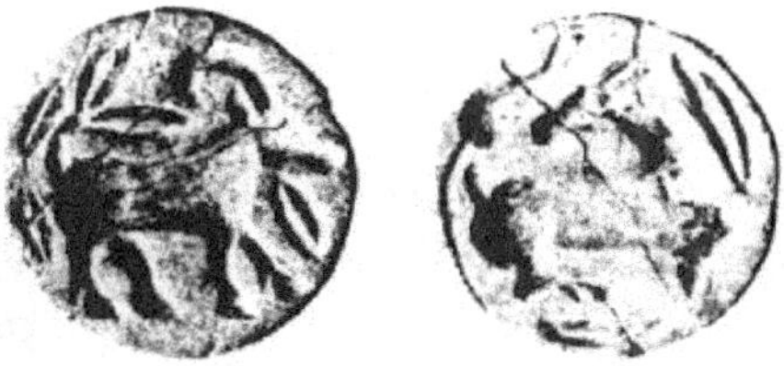

Chanhu-daro Seal obverse and reverse. The oval sign of this Jhukar culture seal is comparable to other inscriptions. Fig. 1 and 1a of Plate L. After Mackay, 1943. The hieroglyphs of the seal relate representations of bun ingots to two orthographic representations of 'antelopes': one is shown walking, the other is shown with head turned backwards. A flower is shown.

Ingot: *ḍhālako* = a large metal ingot (G.) *ḍhālakī* = a metal heated and poured into a mould; a solid piece of metal; an ingot (Gujarati)

Chanhu-daro seal hieroglyph of a small ball (Hieroglyph: *gōṭī* 'round pebble') with emerging laces, may signify *goṭṭā* 'gold or silver lace' (Punjabi), together with a bun ingot. Antelope looking back signifies the artisan: Hieroglyph: *mlech krammara* 'goat looking back' Rebus: *milakkhu* or *mleccha kamar* 'copper artisan'. Obverse of the seal shows an antelope *mlech* Rebus: milakkhu 'copper' (Alternative: ranku 'antelope' Rebus: ranku 'tin'), together with Hieroglyph: *karaḍa* 'safflower' Rebus: *karaḍa* 'hard alloy of metal (silver, gold etc.)' (Marathi)

Tam. koṭṭai ' nut, kernel ', Kan. goṟaṭe; gōṭī 'round pebble; Ko. gōṭu ' silver or gold braid '.K. goṭh f., dat. °ṭi f. ' chequer or chess or dice board '; S. g̠oṭu m. ' large ball of tobacco ready for hookah ', °ṭī f. ' small do. '; P. goṭ f. ' spool on which gold or silver wire is wound, piece on a chequer board '; N. goṭo ' piece ', goṭi ' chess piece '; A. goṭ ' a fruit, whole piece ', °ṭā ' globular, solid ', guṭi ' small ball, seed, kernel '; B. goṭā ' seed, bean, whole '; Or. goṭā ' whole, undivided ', goṭi ' small ball, cocoon ', goṭāli ' small round piece of chalk '; Bi. goṭā ' seed '; Mth. goṭa ' numerative particle '; H. goṭ f. ' piece (at chess &c.) '; G. goṭ m. ' cloud of smoke ', °ṭɔ m. ' kernel of coconut, nosegay ', °ṭī f. ' lump of silver, clot of blood ', °ṭilɔ m. ' hard ball of cloth '; M. goṭā m. ' roundish stone ', °ṭī f. ' a marble ', goṭuḷā ' spherical '; Si. guṭiya ' lump, ball '; -- prob. also P. goṭṭā ' gold or silver lace ', H. goṭā m. ' edging of such ' (→ K. goṭa m. ' edging of gold braid ', S. goṭo m. ' gold or silver lace '); M. goṭ ' hem of a garment, metal wristlet '.(CDIAL 4271).

*gōḍḍa ' foot, leg, knee '. [Cf. the word -- group ' heel - ankle -- knee -- wrist ' s.v. *kuṭṭha -- : → Brah. goḍ ' knee ']Pk. goḍḍa -- , gōḍa -- m. ' foot ', Gy. as. gur; K. gŏḍ m. ' ankle, foot of tree, beginning of anything '; S. goḏo m. ' knee ', guḏa f. ' knee bone '; L. goḏḏā m. ' knee ', awāṇ. gōḍā, P. goḍḍā m.; Ku. gwāṛo ' foot ', gng. gōṛ; N. goṛo ' foot, leg '; A. gor ' foot, kick, foot of tree ', guri ' kick, foot of tree ', gorohani ' stamp of the foot '; B. goṛ ' foot, leg ', °ṛā ' foot of tree, root, origin '; Or. goṛa ' foot, heel, leg, base '; Mth. goṛ ' leg '; Bhoj. gōṛ ' foot, leg '; Aw. lakh. goṛ pl. ' feet '; H. goṛ, °ṛā m. ' foot, leg '.S.kcch. gūḍo m. ' knee ', gauḍo in gauḍe vajṇū ' to kick ' (see vrájati Add2).(CDIAL 4272).

Kt. guṭ ' wrist ', Pr. goṭ (or < gā´tra --); L. guṭṭh f. ' corner ', guṭṭ m., °ṭī f. ' joint ', guṭṭhī f. ' wrist ', (Shahpur) g̠uṭṭhī f., awāṇ. guṭṭī f.(CDIAL 4158)

Rebus 1: *khoṭā* 'forged'; Punjabi. *khoṭ* m. 'base, alloy' M.*khoṭā* 'alloyed' (CDIAL 3931)

Rebus 2: *kōṭhī* f (कोष्ट S) A granary, garner, storehouse, warehouse, treasury, factory, bank (Marathi)

Appendix L: Seal number 198 from Legrain 1921

This representation of a seal has been debated on Cuneiform Digital Library Notes[253].

In 1921 Leon Legrain presented 339 proto-Elamite seal impressions on about 1000 objects recovered from Susa. Let us assume, with Dahl, that 'three humanoid' figures may in fact be storage containers, thus, making a total of vases and a basket followed by a lion on the top register. The bottom register shows three animals: a calf and two bulls. (See Appendix L: Seal number 198 from Legrain 1921). Dahl reiterates his 2012 view: "Remembering how high ranking members of the proto-Elamite society were represented by either lions or bulls (see in particular the so-called ruler's seal found on Sb 02801[254]), and ridding the scene of humans we may be able to read it as a simple representation of offerings of produce (represented by the different vases and baskets in the top register next to the lion) to or by the ruler (represented by the lion), either from a specific institution represented by the bovine family in the lower register (note that the small animal drawn between the bulls is not a goat, but rather a calf), or simply produce obtained from the animals… symbols, such as standards or the like, could enter into the writing system as signs for offices or households (Dahl, Jacob L., 2012, "The marks of writing." *Iran* 50, 1-11.)."

I agree with Dahl's reading of the symbolic forms and also a reasoned hypothesis that vases and basket may denote 'produce' of the offices. What were the produce and what offices? I suggest

that Meluhha hieroglyph cipher offers a possible explanation to the symbolic forms as hieroglyphs deployed on the proto-Elamite seal. Two bulls: dula 'pair' Rebus: dul 'cast metal'. Calf: खोंड [*khōṇḍa*] m 'a young bull, calf' Rebus: কোঁদন [*kōṅdana*], 'turning on a lathe'. Bag: dhokṛā 'bag' (Maithili) Rebus: *dhokra* 'cire perdue lost-wax caster'; *dhokra kamar* id.
Over a 'hand-bag' (Plate IIg) two-horned scorpion-men are in confrontation; on a small cylindrical vase, a lion-man brings down a scorpion-man…(Figure 12f).
Man seems to be playing with a cheetah (Figure 11f, Figure 12).
Zebu gores a lion (Figure 7f).
Two eagles with deployed wings hold two snakes in their claws (Figure 9a).

Lionesses stand up against one another (Figure 7).
…human figures whose lower body may be that of a bovid (Figure 11f).

Man is included (Figure 6, 11, 12), adorned with bracelets, a necklace supporting a turquoise pendent and wears a headband studded with many colored stones.

Cylindrical boxes (Figure 3b: Plate If-h), cups (Plate Ie, Plate IV m-n), high open-rim vases (Figure 3d; Plate II a-3), globular jars (Plate IVh-k), 'handbags' (Plate IIf-k) which are certainly not weights…

Jiroft has been occupied without interruption to the end of the 3rd millennium.

"In the first half of the 3rd millennium, Fars appears as the development center of the first writing, called 'proto-Elamite'…In its southern part of Kerman, tablets have been identified 75 km. away to the west of Jiroft at the small site of Tepe Yahya, located at about 130 km north of the Strait of Hormuz and the Persian Gulf."

"The interpretation of images is a risky enterprise. Decorative themes are transmitted, but they sometimes end up expressing an ideology that is different from the one that was initially symbolized...Whatever the case, the iconography of the Iranian plateau should not be viewed through the prism of the Mesopotamian civilization...the idea of a dualistic mode of thinking geared to human pursuits. This particular orientation bears the mark of the strongly contrasted natural environment of the Iranian-Indian plateau...The landscapes may have left their mark on the life of the population, its language, writing, culture, and religion since the dawn of history. " [255]

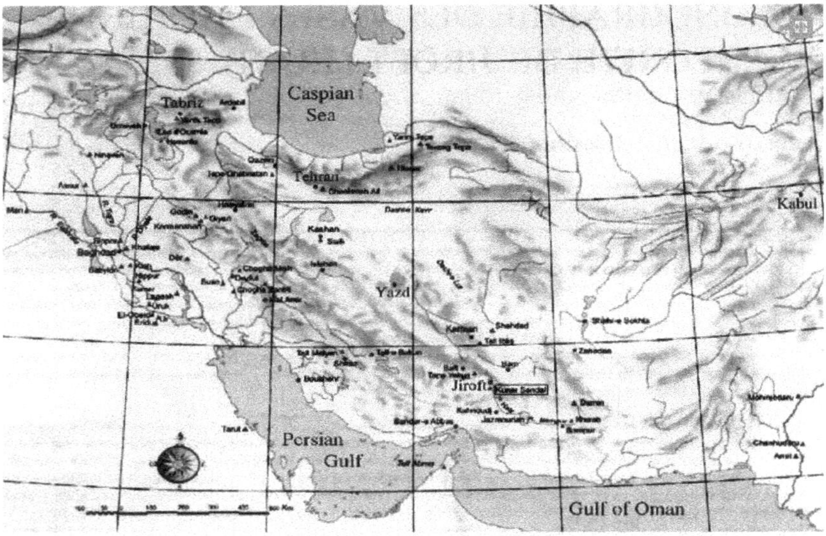

Figure 1. Map of Iran, with Jiroft, Konār Ṣandal, and sites of the 3rd millenium BCE with chlorite vessels. Courtesy of the author.

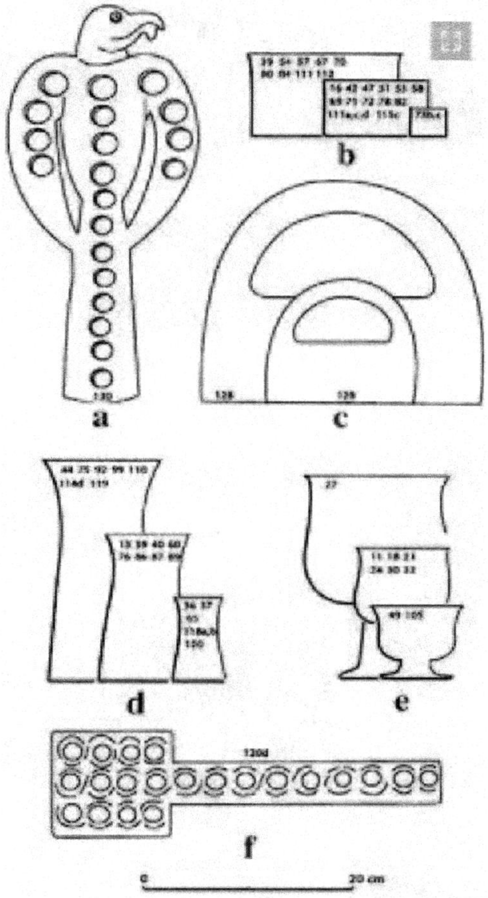

Relative scale of the types of vessels and artifacts. a and f: "gameboards"; b: small cylindrical vessels; c: "handbags"; d: high tronconical vessels; e: cups.

c

d

Figure 5 a–d ibexes and bushes

a

a

b

c

d

a
b

c
d
e
f

Figure 11. a: mountains landscape and waters: (upper part) a man under an arch with sun and crescent moon symbols. (lower part) man seated on his heels holding zebus. b: man holding a snake. c: two men (drinking) and zebus, on a small cylindrical vassel; d: head of woman protruding from a jar, and snakes; e: man falling from a tree to the trunk of which a zebu is tied; f: man with claws and bull-man playing with cheetahs, and a scorpion in the center (on a cylindrical vessel)

Plate II. High tronconical vessels: a (h 14.6 cm); b (h 16 cm); c (h 27.8 cm); d (h 17.5 cm); e (h 19.7 cm). "Handbags": f–g (w 24 cm, thks 4.8 cm); h (w 19.5 cm; h 19.4 cm, thks 4 cm), j (w 28 cm ; h 25 cm, thks 3 cm); k (w 18.5, h 18.3 cm, thks 3.2).

a

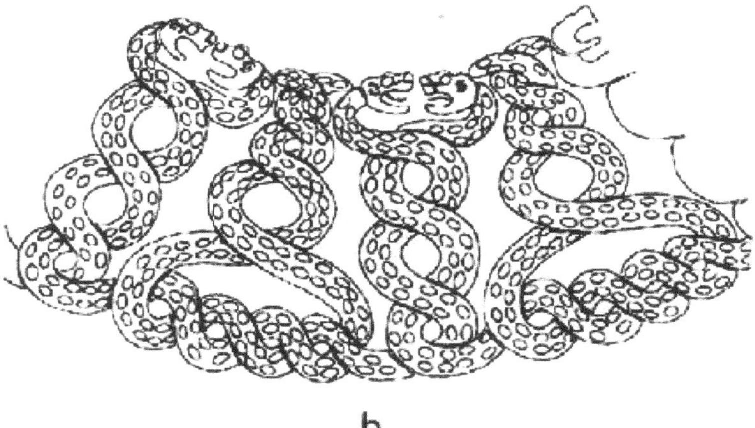

b

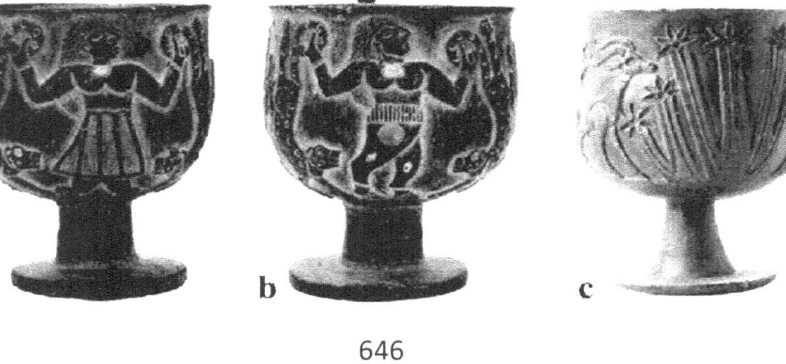

a b c

Plate I. Cups: a–b (h 14.5 cm, diam 11.5 cm); c (h 17.5 cm, diam 12.2 cm); d (h 14.7 cm, diam 10.7 cm); e (h 16 cm, diam 12.3 cm). *Cylindrical boxes*: f (h 6.5 cm); g (h 10.3 cm, diam 10.5 cm); h (h 7.4 cm, diam 11 cm).

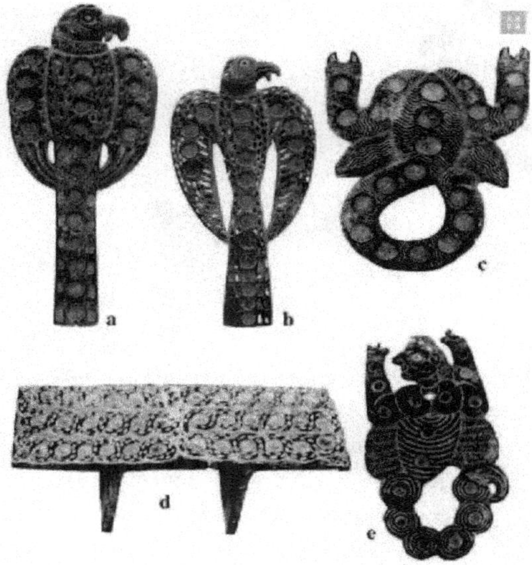

Plate III. "Gameboards": a : eagle (l 41 cm); b: eagle (l 35 cm); c: scorpion (l 28 cm); d: table on legs (l 35 cm); e: scorpion-man (27 cm).

Plate IV Various miniature vessels a–b: tronconical vessels, single-horned zebu (h 8.2 cm); c buckles (h 9.3 cm); d: scorpions (h 7 cm); e: bricks and chevrons (h 5.7 cm); f cylindrical boxes zebus (h 5.2 cm); g: small gobular jar (h 9.4 cm); h globular jar with buckles (h 9.4 cm); j small globular jar with serpents (h 6.9 cm); k. globular jar with rosettes (h 7.5 cm); l round boxes, buckles (h 6 cm); m: with mat (h 8 cm); n small cylindrical vessel with scorpion (h 7.5 cm).

f
g
h
j

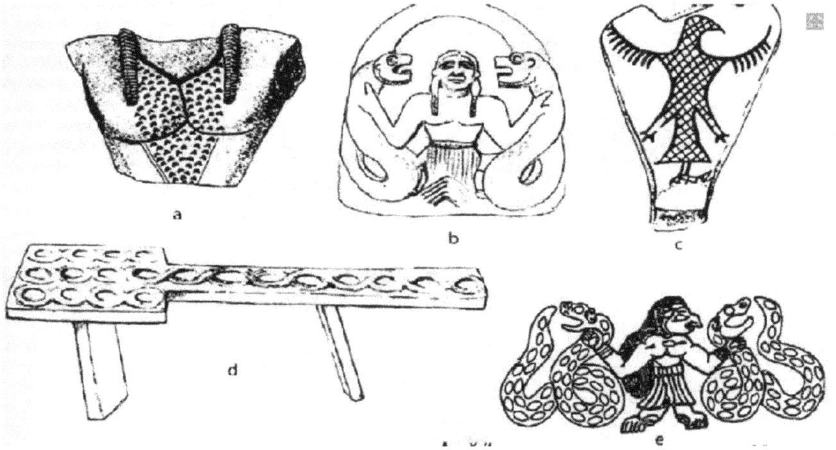
a
b
c
d
e

c
b
a

Figure 6 [illegible] typical landscape of the [illegible] area and ornamentation of a chlorite vessel [illegible] candelabrum tree; d: bush; e-f: bushes and [illegible]

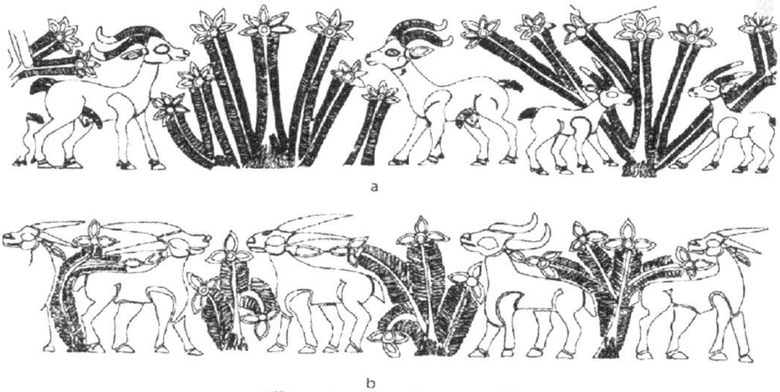

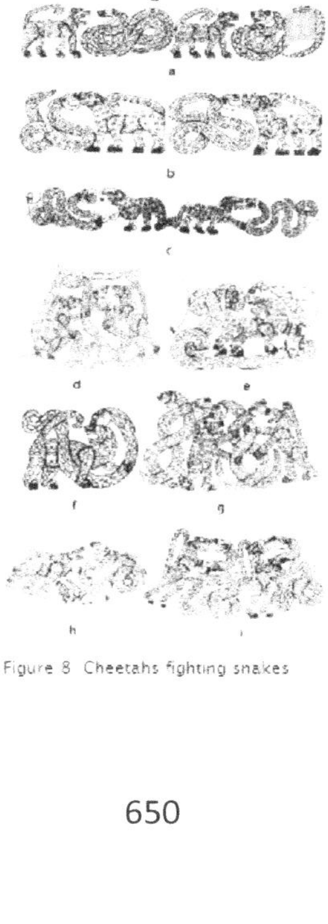

Figure 8 Cheetahs fighting snakes

Meluhha glosses:

káraṇḍa1 m.n. ' basket ' BhP., °*ḍaka* -- m., °*ḍī* -- f. lex.Pa. *karaṇḍa* -- m.n., °*aka* -- m. ' wickerwork box ', Pk. *karaṁḍa* -- , °*aya* -- m. ' basket ', °*ḍī* -- , °*ḍiyā* -- f. ' small do. '; K. *kranḍa* m. ' large covered trunk ', *kronḍum*. ' basket of withies for grain ', *krünḍü* f. ' large basket of withies '; Ku. *kaṇḍo* ' basket '; N. *kaṇḍi* ' basket -- like conveyance '; A. *kaṇi* ' open clothes basket '; H.*kaṇḍī* f. ' long deep basket '; G. *karā̃ḍɔ* m. ' wicker or metal box ', *kā̃ḍiyɔ* m. ' cane or bamboo box '; M. *karā̃ḍ* m. ' bamboo basket ', °*ḍā* m. ' covered bamboo basket, metal box ', °*ḍī* f. ' small do. '; Si. *karan̆ḍuva* ' small box or casket '. -- Deriv. G. *kā̃ḍī* m. ' snake -- charmer who carries his snakes in a wicker basket '. (CDIAL 2792)

5567 *ḍōkka2 ' defective '. 2. *dhōkka -- 2. [~ *ṭugga -- . See lists s.vv. *ḍagga -- and *ṭuṇṭa -- 2]

1. Ku. *ḍokro*, *ḍokhro* ' old man '; B. *ḍokrā* ' old, decrepit ', Or. *ḍokarā*; H. *ḍokrā* ' decrepit '; G. *ḍokɔ* m. ' penis ', *ḍokrɔ* m. ' old man ', M. *ḍokrā* m. -- Kho. (Lor.) *duk*' hunched up, hump of camel '; K. *ḍoku* ' humpbacked ' perh. < *ḍōkka -- 1.

2. Or. *dhokaṛa* ' decrepit, hanging down (of breasts) '.(CDIAL 5567).

kuṇḍá 3264 kuṇḍá1 n. (RV. in cmpd.) ' bowl, waterpot ' KātyŚr., ' basin of water, pit ' MBh. (semant. cf. kumbhá -- 1), °*ḍaka* -- m.n. ' pot ' Kathās., °*ḍī* -- f. Pāṇ.,°*ḍikā* -- f. Up. 2. *gōṇḍa -- . [← Drav., e.g. Tam. *kuṭam*, Kan. *guṇḍi*, EWA i 226 with other ' pot ' words s.v. kuṭa -- 1]

1. Pa. *kuṇḍi* -- , °*ḍikā* -- f. ' pot '; Pk. *kuṁḍa* -- , *koṁ*° n. ' pot, pool ', *kuṁḍī* -- , °*ḍiyā* -- f. ' pot '; Kt. *kuṇi* ' pot ', Wg. *kuṇḍä'i*; Pr. *künǰúdotdot;* ' water jar '; Paš. weg. *kuṛā̃*' clay pot ' < **kũṛā* IIFL iii 3, 98 (or poss. < kuṭa -- 1), lauṛ. *kuṇḍalī'* ' bucket '; Gaw. *kuṇḍuṛī'* ' milk bowl, bucket '; Kal. *kuṇḍṓk* ' wooden milk bowl '; Kho.*kúṇḍuk*, °*ug* ' milk bowl ', (Lor.) ' a kind of platter '; Bshk. *kūnḗc* ' jar ' (+?); K. *kōn̆ḍ* m. ' metal or earthenware vessel, deep still spring ', *kọn̆ḍu* m. ' large cooking pot ',*kunāla* m. '

earthenware vessel with wide top and narrow base '; S. *kunu* m. ' whirlpool ', °*no* m. ' earthen churning pot ', °*nī* f. ' earthen cooking pot ', °*niṛo* m.; L. *kunnā̃*m. ' tub, well ', °*nī* f. ' wide -- mouthed earthen cooking pot ', *kunāl* m. ' large shallow earthen vessel '; P. *kũḍā* m. ' cooking pot ' (← H.), *kunāl*, °*lā* m., °*lī* f., *kuṇḍālā* m. ' dish '; WPah. cam. *kuṇḍ* ' pool ', bhal. *kunnu* n. ' cistern for washing clothes in '; Ku. *kuno* ' cooking pot ', *kuni*, °*nelo* ' copper vessel '; B. *kũṛ* ' small morass, low plot of riceland ', *kũṛi* ' earthen pot, pipe -- bowl '; Or. *kuṇḍa* ' earthen vessel ', °*ḍā* ' large do. ', °*ḍi* ' stone pot '; Bi. *kũ̄ṛ* ' iron or earthen vessel, cavity in sugar mill ', *kũ̄ṛā* ' earthen vessel for grain '; Mth. *kũṛ* ' pot ', *kũ̄ṛā* ' churn '; Bhoj. *kũṛī* ' vessel to draw water in '; H. *kũ̄d* f. ' tub ', *kũ̄ṛā* m. ' small tub ', *kũ̄ḍā* m. ' earthen vessel to knead bread in ', *kũ̄ṛī* f. ' stone cup '; G. *kũḍ* m. ' basin ', *kũḍī* f. ' water jar '; M. *kũḍ* n. ' pool, well ', *kũḍā* m. ' large openmouthed jar ', °*ḍī* f. ' small do. '; Si. *kenḍiya*, *keḍ*° ' pot, drinking vessel '.2. N. *gũṛ* ' nest ' (or ← Drav. Kan. *gūḍu* ' nest ', &c.: see kulā´ya --); H. *gõṛā* m. 'reservoir used in irrigation '.*gōkuṇḍikā -- , taílakuṇḍa -- , *madhukuṇḍikā -- , *rakṣākuṇḍaka -- ; -- kuṇḍa -- 2?

1: S.kcch. *kũṇḍho* m. 'flower -- pot ', *kūnnī* f. ' small earthen pot '; WPah.ktg. *kv́ṇḍh* m. ' pit or vessel used for an oblation with fire into which barley etc. is thrown '; J. *kũd* m. ' pool, deep hole in a stream '; Brj. *kũ̄ṛo* m., °*ṛī* f. ' pot '.

*kaṇṭa3 ' backbone, podex, penis '. 2. *kaṇḍa -- . 3. *karaṇḍa -- 4. (Cf. *kāṭa -- 2, *ḍākka -- 2: poss. same as káṇṭa -- 1]

1. Pa. *piṭṭhi -- kaṇṭaka* -- m. ' bone of the spine '; Gy. eur. *kanro* m. ' penis ' (or < káṇṭaka --); Tir. *mar -- kaṇḍḗ* ' back (of the body) '; S. *kaṇḍo* m. ' back ', L. *kaṇḍ* f.,*kaṇḍā* m. 'backbone ', awāṇ. *kaṇḍ*, °*ḍī* ' back '; P. *kaṇḍ* f. ' back, pubes '; WPah. bhal. *kaṇṭ* f. ' syphilis '; N. *kaṇḍo* ' buttock, rump, anus ', *kaṇḍeulo* ' small of the back '; B. *kā̃ṭ* ' clitoris '; Or. *kaṇṭi* ' handle of a plough '; H. *kā̃ṭā* m. ' spine ', G. *kā̃ṭɔ* m., M. *kā̃ṭā* m.; Si. *äṭa -- kaṭuva* ' bone ', *piṭa -- k*° ' backbone '.

2. Pk. *kaṁḍa* -- m. ' backbone '.

3. Pk. *karaṁḍa* -- m.n. ' bone shaped like a bamboo ', *karaṁḍuya* -- n. ' backbone '.(CDIAL 2670).
*pōttī ' glass bead '.Pk. *pottī* -- f. ' glass '; S. *pūti* f. ' glass bead ', P. *pot* f.; N. *pote* ' long straight bar of jewelry '; B. *pot* ' glass bead ', *puti*, *pũti* ' small bead '; Or. *puti* ' necklace of small glass beads '; H. *pot* m. ' glass bead ', G. M. *pot* f.; -- Bi. *pot* ' jeweller's polishing stone ' rather than < pōtrá – (CDIAL 8403).
pṓta -- 1, °*aka* -- m. ' young of animal or plant ' MBh. a. *pōta* --, °*aka* -- m. ' young of an animal ', Aś. *potake* nom. sg. m.; NiDoc. *potaǵa* ' young (of camel) 'Pk. *pōāla* -- m. ' child, bull '; A. *powāli* ' young of animal or bird '.H. *poṭā* m. ' young of animal, unfledged bird '. Ku. *potho* ' any young animal ' (CDIAL 8399).
*dhōkka1 ' sacking, matting '. 1. Ext. -- ḍ -- : N. dhokro ' large jute bag ', B. dhokaṛ; Or. dhokaṛa ' cloth bag '; Bi. dhok̆rā ' jute bag '; Mth. dhokṛā ' bag, vessel, receptacle '; H. dhukṛī f. ' small bag '; G. dhokṛũ n. ' bale of cotton '; -- with -- ṭṭ -- : M. dhokṭī f. ' wallet '; -- with -- n -- : G. dhokṇũ n. ' bale of cotton '; -- with -- s -- : N. (Tarai) dhokse ' place covered with a mat to store rice in '.2. L. dhohẽ (pl. dhūhĩ) m. ' large thatched shed '.3. M. dhõgḍā m. ' coarse cloth ', dhõgṭī f. ' wallet '.4. L. ḍhok f. ' hut in the fields '; Ku. ḍhwākā m. pl. ' gates of a city or market '; N. ḍhokā (pl. of *ḍhoko) ' door '; -- OMarw. ḍhokaro m. ' basket '; -- N. ḍhokse ' place covered with a mat to store rice in, large basket '.(CDIAL 6880). धोकटी or धोंगटी [dhōkaṭī or dhōṅgaṭī] *f* A barber's razor-case. 2 (H) A sort of bag or wallet having two pockets. धोंगड [dhōṅgaḍa] *a* Coarse--as cloth, matting, rataning. 2 Rough, rude, coarsely executed--work.
धोंगडा [dhōṅgaḍā] *m* धोंगडें *n* Coarse mean clothes: also a coarse mean garment or cloth. Pr. गांडीं घोंगडा पोटाला तुकडा. धोक [dhōka] *a unc* (H) Large, lusty, sturdy. 2 Strong--cloth. धाकड [dhākaḍa] *a* P Coarse--cloth: rudely large--man or beast.
धाकडधोकड [dhākaḍadhōkaḍa] *a* Coarse--cloth: coarsely large--man or beast. (Marathi)

Appendix M: Rebus as dream, as literacy

Meluhha hieroglyph is a rebus

In the examples of about 7000 epigraphs using Meluhha hieroglyphs, the entire set of hieroglyphs signify representations related to a superset of stone- and metal-work. Thus, all the hieroglyphs of Meluhha vernacular are relatable to the Bronze-age trasactions for exchanges of goods or artifacts produced using processes such as turning, inscribing, alloying, casting, smelting, and transformed by the fire, crucible, forge and anvil with the lapidary's or artisan's intervention. The hieroglyphs represented a metaphysical world-view of the new inventions and technologies which had created value in exchange and also a representation of the insights into properties of ores, metals or alloys or characteristics of produced artifacts in terms of their hardness or sharpess for value in use for trade or for use in metallurgy or agricultural or architectural or artistic enterprises such as production of alloys combining two or more ores, ploughing or building or creation of *cire perdue*, lost-wax method cast figurines or drilled beads of agate, carnelian, lapis lazuli and other stones.

Thus, in the Meluhha hieroglyphic system of writing, representations categorized by corpora builders as 'signs' or 'pictorial motifs or field symbols' are all related to the same system of rebus readings of Meluhha language which is the lingua franca of the Indian *sprachbund.* The function of both 'signs' and 'pictorial motifs or field-symbols' is the same. Their representation is only constrained by the space provided by the seals or tablets which tend to be very small objects limiting the number of hieroglyphs to an average of six.

The salutary feature of Meluhha language hieroglyphs (a feature which compares with the Sumerian language cuneiform) is that a number of homonyms exist to signify both the 'hieroglyphs' and the underlying 'words' of Meluhha language.

Communication situation of the Bronze-age gave rise to the Meluhha hieroglyphs. The hieroglyphs are created in the dynamic process of Bronze0-age communication necessitated by the revolutionary nature of the technological advances such as cire perdue lost-wax casting of arsenical copper, creation of alloys of bronze combining copper and tin, creation of alloys of brass combining copper and zinc, special alloys such as pewter combing copper with lead and other mineral ores or drilling through even linear beads of carnelian and adding colored designs on the beads. The advances in stone- and metal-ware technologies involving turning, forging, using crucibles, furnaces, smelters and anvils were matched by the delineation of the Tin Road for trade mechanisms, say from Ashur to Kanesh (Kultepe, Anatolia) ad perhaps also to 1. Haifa in the Fertile Crescent where two pure tin ingots inscribed with Meluhha hieroglyphs were found in a shipwreck; and 2. Nahal Mishmar where arsenical copper artifacts were found with standards or flagposts comparable to the flagposts used as hieroglyphs on cylinder seals of Mesopotamia or steatite tablets of Mohenjo-daro.

The key point to note that the use of the Meluhha hieroglyphs was a writing system in a particular communicational context of the Bronze Age. The hieroglyphs do not cease to be a writing when there are no readers around. The hieroglyphs were a writing system *used* for the purpose of trade related to the space and time – Tin Road of the transition from Neolithic phase to Bronze Age phase of civilizational advance.

We have 'lost' Meluhha hieroglyphs because we call them 'undeciphered', i.e. the significance of the hieroglyphs is no longer understood. Champollion recovered Egyptian hieroglyphs by reading them as *texts*. He has also created a new set of readers. The Meluhha hieroglyphs will be recognized again as a writing system, once the cipher is *known*.
The hieroglyphs exist within a particular system related to space and time and constitute a contribution to knowledge systems.

If a young bull with one horn (i.e. one horn less), as a hieroglyph signified Meluhha glosses of Indian *sprachbund*; read rebus it notes a metal-alloy forge, a lapidary-turner's workshop:
Three allographs as hieroglyphs combined into a picture-puzzle: horn, curved end, one, hornless, pannier on shoulder:

'Pannier' glyph: खोंडी [*khōṇḍī*] *f* An outspread shovelform sack (as formed temporarily out of a कांबळा, to hold or fend off grain, chaff &c.) (Marathi)
kōṭu 'horn' (Tamil) *kōḍ* (pl. *kōḍul*) horn (Parji); *kōḍu* horn, tusk, branch of a tree *kōṛ* horn (Kannada); *kōḍů, kōḍu* horn (Tulu) Ko. *ko·ṛ* (obl. *ko·ṭ*) *horns* (DEDR 2200) *kōṇḍa* ' hornless '(Kalash)(CDIAL 3508). *khonḍu* ' broken, maimed '(Kashmiri); *khōṇḍ* a' half' (Kalash)(CDIAL 3792). *koḍa* 'in arithmetic, one' (Santali); मेंढा [*mēṇḍhā*] A crook or curved end (of a stick, horn &c.) and attrib. such a stick, horn, bullock. मेढा [*mēḍhā*] m A stake, esp. as forked. meḍ(h), meḍhī f., meḍhā m. 'post, forked stake'. (Marathi) (CDIAL 10317) खोंड [*khōṇḍa*] *m* A young bull, a bullcalf (Marathi), *kōnda* bullock (Kolami)(DEDR 2216)
Rebus: *koḍ* 'artisan's workshop' (Kuwi) *mẽṛhẽt, meḍ* 'iron' (Mu.Ho.) *koḍiyum* 'young bull' (Gujarati) *koḍe* 'young bull' (Telugu) *koḍ* 'workshop' (Gujarati) *koṭe* 'forged (metal) (Santali) *koṭe* meṛed = forged iron (Munda) *khoṭ* m. 'base, alloy' (Punjabi) *kõdā* 'lathe-turner'; कोंद *kōnda* 'engraver, lapidary setting or infixing gems' (Marathi) *kõdār* 'turner' (Bengali). *kũdār* 'turner, brass-worker'. (Marathi) খোদাই [khōdāi] n engraving; carving. খোদাই করা v. to engrave; to carve. খোদানো v. & n. engraving; carving. খোদিত [*khōdita*] a engraved. (Bengali) खोदकाम [*khōdakāma*] n Sculpture; carved work or work for the carver. खोदगिरी [*khōdagirī*] f Sculpture, carving, engraving: also sculptured or carved work. खोदणावळ [*khōdaṇāvaḷa*] f (खोदणें) The price or cost of sculpture

or carving. खोदणी [*khōdaṇī*] f (Verbal of खोदणें) Digging, engraving &c. (Marathi) goldsmith's die. खोदणें [*khōdaṇēṃ*] v c & i (Hindi) To dig. 2 To engrave. (Marathi)

The hieroglyph composition is a signification derived from the context and not from any invariant set of hieroglyphs stipulated in anticipation, in advance.

The Meluhha hieroglyph of a young bull is associated with an inventory of written forms used in written communication between the writer and the reader of the seals and tablets with the set of Meluhha hieroglyphs, conventionalized and standardized for bronze-age trade.
Roy Harris provides an example of the possibility of extending Saussure's structural model from languages to non-linguistic signs as well: "For example, whether an irregular, unbroken black line on a map represents a river, a road, a railway or a national boundary is not something which is determined independently of the other cartographic conventions employed for the map in question. On the contrary, a cartographer who wishes to distinguish rivers from roads, roads from railways, and railways from national boundaries must necessarily choose different types of line in each case. If the cartographer fails to do so, then whatever his or her intentions may have been, the lines drawn on the map will be ambiguous. Thus, in terms of their signification, the conventions a cartographer uses form a structural complex in which the individual elements do not have meaning independently of the whole."[256]

What we witness in these research approaches is that we have traversed a full circle back to about two thousand years Before Present, a U-turn of gaze to ancient texts and traditions, starting with the insights of origin of language, *Vāk*, in the Rigveda, to Bhartṛhari's *Vākyapadīya*, and Vātsyāyana's classification of three of sixty-four arts to be studied by youth: 1. *akṣara muṣṭika kathanam*, 'narrative using fingers and wrists or *mudrā*-s'; 2. *deśa bhāṣā jñānam* 'knowledge of the vernaculars/spoken idiom'; 3. *mlecchita vikalpa* 'cipher or alternative representations of language'. *mlecchita vikalpa* thus means 'cryptography used by mleccha' [cf. *mleccha-mukha* 'copper' (Skt.); the suffix –mukha is a reflex of mũh 'ingot' (Munda)]. This classification is in *vidyāsamuddeśa śloka* (verse detailing the objective of learning the arts) in Vātsyāyana's *Kāmasūtra.*

It is not a mere coincidence that early writing attested during historical periods was on metal punch-marked coins, copper plates, two-feet long copper bolt used on an Aśokan pillar at Rampurva, Sohoura copper plate, two pure tingots found in a shipwreck in Haifa, and even on the Delhi iron pillar clearly pointing to the smiths as those artisans who had the competence to use a writing system. In reference to Rampurva copper-bolt: "Here then these signs occur upon an object which must have been made by craftsmen working for Asoka or one of his predecessors." The Indus script inscriptions using hieroglyphs on two pure tin-ingots found in Haifa were read rebus using Meluhha glosses.[257]

Vāk 'speech' or 'utterance (sound)' can be represented (*vikalpa*) in a form so that it can be retrieved almost exactly without the intervention of the utterer or the listener. In such representation (vikalpa), the visual form using mostly two-dimensional shapes or pictures which can be recognized easily and with little ambiguity. Rebus principle means using pictograms, purely for their sounds regardless of their meaning, to represent new words.

One view is that Chinese developed their writing system using the rebus principle.[258]

Stephen D. Houston[259] endorses the views of Cooper and notes: "Reversing earlier trends toward greater phonography, in the late second and first millennia BCE the use of logograms in Babylonian cuniform expanded to over 85 percent of words in divinatory, astronomical, and other technical records. In the seenth and sixth centuries BCE the Babylonian language and its cuneiform script were superseded as a lingua franca in the Middle East by the Aramaic language and consonantary – although conservative priests and scholars continued to use Babylonian cuneiform into the first century AD. It is also not true that logophonic scripts develop into syllabic ones and syllabic scripts in turn into consonantaries and alphabets. There is no confirmed example of a logophonic script giving rise to a mainly syllabic one. There are also no examples of syllabaries developing into alphabets, consonantaries, or alphasyllabaries, supporting Sethe's (1939) conclusion that syllabic scripts represent an evolutionary dead end. In China an informal syllabary was constituted to transcribe foreign words and in Japan syllabaries were invented to help write Japanese more clearly, but I these cases also logographic writing did not disappear. In the Middle East the earliest purely phonemic scripts were the consonantaries that appear to have been inspired by the consonantal method of representing sounds in ancient Egyptian. This development, however, did not occur in Egypt and there is no evidence that Egyptians played any active part in it. Since most purely phonemic forms of writing are derived from West Semitic consonantaries, this raises the question of whether this form of writing would eventually have supplanted logophonic scripts in Egypt and the Middle East had the Egyptian logoconsonantary not existed. The Aramaic, Hebrew, and Arabic consonantaries have been adapted to write numerous languages in the Middle East, Central Asia, South Asia, and Southeast Asia."[260]

"Sumerian has a large number of homonyms and near homonyms – so many, in fact, that scholars have assumed that Sumerian must have been a tone language. It was thus particularly well suited for rebus substitution. Curiously, the principle of rebus writing was understood in the archaic period but hardly used. Examples include 𒁀 BA, probably a pictogram of a tool called *ba* in Sumerian, used to mean 'to distribute', also *ba*, and 𒄀 GI, a a pictogram of a reed (Sum. *gi*), used to represent *gi* 'to render' and in the archaic period probably also used for *sigi* 'yellow'. Massive exploitation of rebus writing quickly developed in subsequent periods. A very few examples (giving the Sumerian word, the meaning represented originally by the sign, and the homonym represented by rebus extension): *su* 'bodhy' and 'to 'replace', *si* 'horn' and 'to fill', *e* 'dike' and 'to speak', *sar* 'plant' and 'to write'. Rebus *phoneticism* – that is, the use of a sign to represent not a homonym of the word represented by the sign, but only the sound of that word in order to write phonetically – also seems to have been understood in the archaic period, but again is very rare…in each case, the semantic values of the individual signs have nothing to do with the meanings of the words. The mixture of semantic association and rebus writing resulted in an inconsistent system of representation. Whereas SU represents the homonyms 'body' and 'to replace', to represent *su(d)* 'distant' the sign for semantically associated *gid* 'long' was altered with additional strokes and the resulting sign SUD was used as well for *su(g)* 'empty, naked', based on both semantic association and rebus, and for *su* 'to sprinkle', based on rebus alone…Although rebus writing was employed with increasing frequency after about 2900, the majority of compound and complex signs and sign clusters are semantically based, without any phonetic reading clue…Sumerian homonymy and the primacy of semantic association in the mapping of the lexicon onto the sign system are responsible for the notorious homophony and polyphony of cuneiform signs, features that complicated the initial decipherment and were the source of considerable resistane to the decipherment once it was accomplished. Over twenty different signs can be read /*du*/…"[261] Jerrold Cooper[262] also notes that writers of cuneiform script augmented iconic script by the rebus principle because of the restrictive nature of pictographs. Jerrold Cooper further adds: when Sumerian cuneiform came to express adequately "natural language in a broad range of contexts – letters, commemorative inscriptions, legal documents, literary texts, technical literature – [it was facilitated by] the increasing use of rebus phoneticism to write grammatical affixes." (1996, Sumerian and Akkadian, in: *The world's writing systems*, p.43). Geoffry Sampson[263] noted that, in Sumerian, the glyph for /ti/ 'arrow' was extended to signify the near-homophone /til/ 'life'.

"...rebus glyphs (i.e. one term used to represent a homonym with different meaning, e.g. writing *soldado* as a picture of the sun (sol) with a die (dado) beside it) in pictorial manuscripts...The existence of rebus glyphs in Maya writing is well established, but little attention has been paid to rebus pictures, which, for want of a better name I shall call pictorial homonyms, and still less to pictorial synonyms. By the latter term I mean scenes in codices which express a term, often a stock phrase, which is a synonym of the word expressed graphically. It must be understood that in Maya codices the pictures supplement the hieroglyphic text; the text does not explain the pictures."[264] In Mayan logograph for 'one' was pronounced /huun/. This was substitutable for 'paper' also pronounced /huun/.

As Sigmund Freud noted, the dream is a rebus.

A rebus is an allusional device that uses pictures to represent words or parts of words.

So, too a Meluhha hieroglyph is a rebus, a writing system across Meluhha-Magan-Dilmun and on Tin Road of Bronze Age extending from Ashur on Tigris river to Kanesh (Kultepe, Anatolia) and beyond into Fertile Crescent to Haifa.
It is an irony of a scholarship genre that such a rebus writing system is labeled, *apriori* and in haste, as 'illiterate' or 'proto-literate'. It is a travesty of definition of 'literacy', because the rebus method as a cipher, is made up of at least two vocables: one vocable denoting the picture and the other similar sounding vocable denoting the solution to the puzzle that is, the cipher. A cultural context which created a cipher of logographs read rebus in Meluhha language should be deemed as literate just as the present-day cryptographers are 'literate' engaged in securing digital representations electronically.

Works of art with picture-puzzles make Meluhha, a Visible language. Rebus, a code of literacy, yields meanings of Meluhha hieroglyphs. Such a cipher is attested by Vātsyāyana (ca. 6th century BCE work) as mlecchita vikalpa(that is, alternative rendering of Meluhha/Mleccha speech or vocables -- and listed as one of the 64 arts to be learnt by youth as vidyāsamuddeśa, 'chief branches of knowledge').

Vocable is a sememe or a word that is capable of being spoken and recognized meaningfully.

Connections between glyphs and intended meanings are provided by the rebus method. If two similar sounding words have different meanings in a cultural context as, for example, in 'areal' languages of a *sprachbund* -- one, pictorial meaning and the other metallurgical meaning -- and if this happens consistently for hundreds of word-pairs, the application of the rebus method for writing is a reasonable deduction.

A vivid representation of the rebus principle of literacy is provided by Narmer Palette. (Egyptian hieroglyphs: N'r 'cuttle-fish' + m'r 'awl' Rebus: Nar-mer, name of king.)
Egyptian hieroglyphs sometimes use the rebus principle.s three

hieroglyphs are from Egyptian language to form form a "rebus" of Ramesses II's name, in a rare category of statuary: *Ra-mes-su*. Horus (as Ra), for *Ra*; the child, *mes*; and the sedge plant (stalk held in left hand), *su*.

Statue of Ramses II as a child and the god Hwrwn (god of Canaan); *ḥr* "Horus" and *su* 'stalk' hieroglyphs. Source:
http://www.egyptarchive.co.uk/html/cairo_museum_59.html

A dream is a rebus. History of Civilizations of ancient times has a record of two remarkable dreams: the first is the dream in the Epic of Tukulti-Ninurta and the second is the dream of Māyā, mother of Gautama Buddha.

There are thousands of picture-puzzles which occur on cylinder seals of Ancient Near East which are explained on many Museum catalogs as banquet scenes or animal hunts or war scenes. Many of these picture-puzzles are indeed rebus or comparable to the interpretation of dreams and attempts have not been made to identify the possible language groups who might have deployed such picture-puzzles, principally during the Bronze Age.
Rebus signifiers and the signified relate to innovations of the Bronze Age such as: bronze/brass alloys to substitute for arsenical copper, casting methods (such as cire perdue casting), alloying ores such as tin, zinc, lead and exchanges along the Tin Road set up by Meluhha artisans/traders also called Assur as metal smelters par excellence.

It will be a leap of faith to assume that the picture-puzzles are nonsensical or belong to pro-literate cultures because a contemporary observer is unable to decipher the cipher.
While early tokens and bullae (token envelopes) were recognized as ancient accounting methods and categorisation of products, the Proto-Elamite script yet remains undeciphered.
Robert K. Englund provides a succinct state of the art report on Proto-Elamite: "(Tokens) These clay objects consist on the one hand of simple geometrical forms, for instance cones, spheres, etc. and on the other, of complex shapes or of simpler, but incised, forms. Simple, geometrically formed tokens were found encased within clay balls (usually called 'bullae') dating to the period immediately preceding that characterized by the development of the earliest proto-cuneiform texts; these tokens most certainly assumed numerical functions in emerging urban centers of the late fourth millennium BCE...a strong argument from silence can be made that Sumerian is not present in the earliest literate

communities, particularly given the large numbers of sign sequences which, with high likelihood, represent personal names and thus should be amenable to grammatical and lexical analyses comparable to those made of later Sumerian onomastics...large numbers of inscribed tablets...which for purposes of graphotactical analysis and context-related semantic categorization of signs and sign combinations represents a text massof high promise...we can utilize language decipherments from texts of later periods in working hypotheses dealing with the linguistic affiliation of archaic scribes...There may, however, have been much more population movement in the area than we imagine, including early Hurrian elements and, if Whittaker, Ivanov, and others are correct, even Indo-Europeans. Fn 44. Rubio (1999: 1-16 has reviewed recent publications, and the pioneering initial work by Landsberger on possible substrate lexemes in Sumerian, and concludes that the fairly extensive list of non-Sumerian words attested in Sumerian texts did not represent a single early Mesopotamian language, but rather reflected a long history of Wanderworter from a myriad of languages, possibly including some loans from Indo-European, and many from early Semitic."

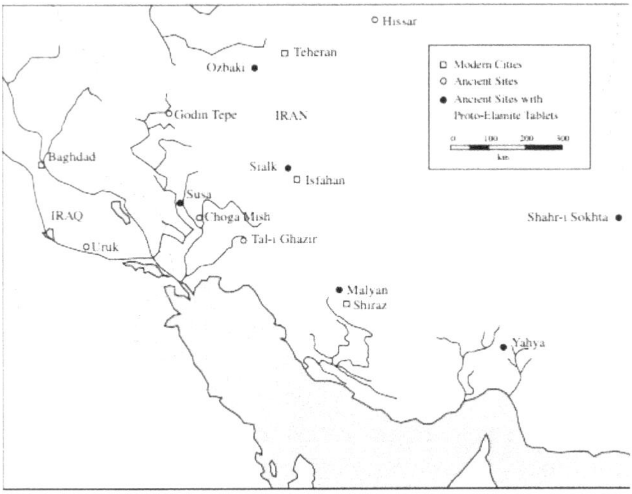

Major sites of Late Uruk and proto-Elamite inscriptions in Persia

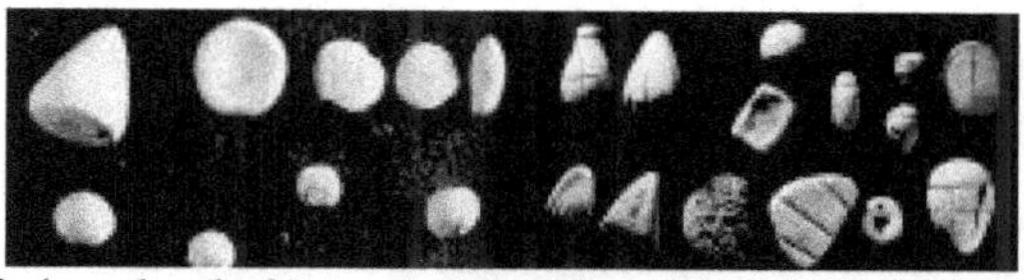

Examples of simple (left) and complex (right) 'tokens' from Uruk (digital images courtesy of CDLI).

Examples of sealed (top), sealed and impressed (middle) bullae, and a 'numerical' tablet (all from Susa--top: Sb 1932; middle: Sb 1940; bottom: Sb 2313; digital images courtesy of CDLI).

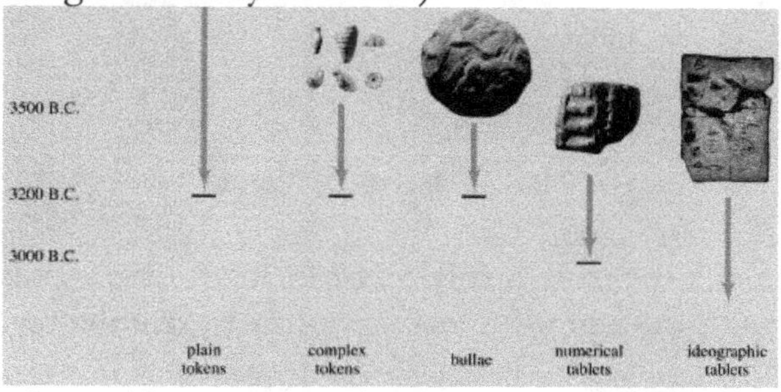

Development of cuneiform, after Schmandt-Besserat (1992).

At the same site of Susa a pot was discovered unambiguously defining the meaning of the hieroglyph which adorned the mouth of the pot since the pot contained metal artifacts (reported by Maurizio Tosi):

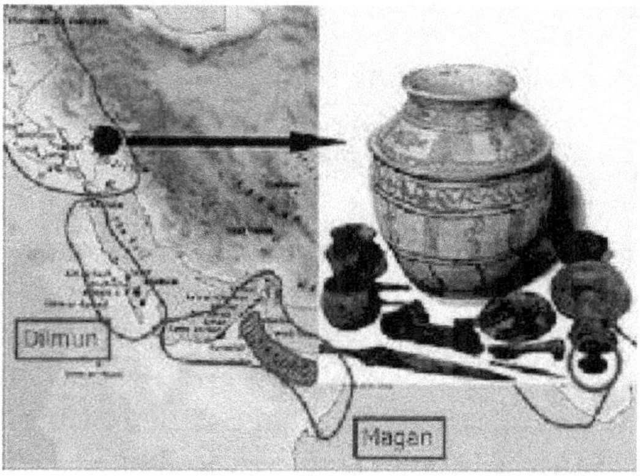

The 'fish' hieroglyph shown on this pot is a Meluhha hieroglyph ayo 'fish' (Munda)

Rebus ayo 'alloy metal' (Gujarati; ayas, Sanskrit).

In this evolutionary scheme of 'writing systems' shown on the chart after Schmandt-Besserat-- call them proto-literate or illiterate -- depending upon the definitions assumed for the term 'literate' --

a parallel development ca 3500 BCE is left out: the formation and evolution of Meluhha hieroglyphs (aka Indus writing). The date of ca 3500 BCE is related to the first evidence of writing identified in Harappa excavations by HARP with the following potsherd with a dominant hieroglyph, signifying tabernae montana fragrant wild tulip read rebus: tagaraka (hieroglyph) rebus: tagara 'tin (ore)' in Meluhha (Indian sprachbund or proto-Indian).

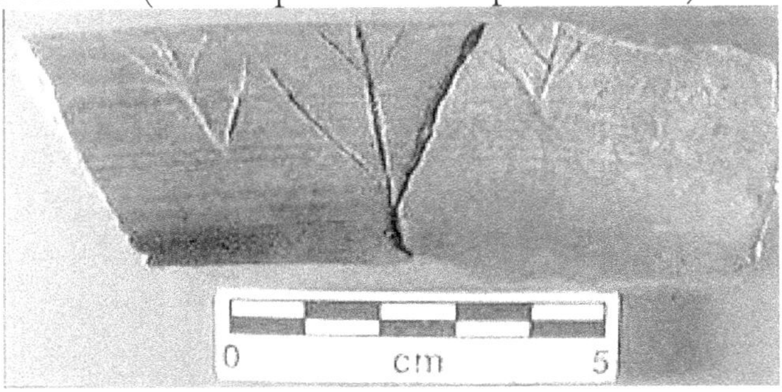

Bronze Age innovations created by *wanderworter* --seafaring and land caravans of Meluhha artisans and merchants speaking a version of Proto-Indian --result in the messaging system using hieroglyphs of Meluhha read rebus. Forcefully refuting claims (characterised as a hoax) of 'illiteracy', Massimo Vidale argues that it is a cop-out to avoid researches into meanings of picture-puzzles by assuming that 'signs' as distinct from 'pictorial motifs' have to be either alphabets or syllables resulting in inscriptions longer than 5 signs and assuming that such glyphs cannot be read as logographs. This is shoot-and-scoot scholarship because the claimants have not so far responded to the refutation by Massimo Vidale indicating the use of the writing system in the context of trade in an extensive contact area from the Fertile Crescent to the Ganga-Yamuna river basin. Allegedly scholarly, but disdainful, claims of 'illiteracy' do NOT cnnstitute an advance in knowledge to promote the study of now nearly 7000 artifacts with what I have called Meluhha hieroglyphs (aka Indus script) in Ancient Near East (not counting the Tin Road related documents). Witzel et al have erred on a simple assumption that the 'signs' of the script have to be syllabic or alphabetic. They ignored the possibility that they could be logographs including the crocodile, tiger, buffalo etc.which could have been read rebus as Meluhha hieroglyphs. I have shown that almost all the so-called 'signs' and 'pictorial motis' of Indus writing are Meluhha hieroglyphs.

The average number of hieroglyphs, about 5 or 6 are adequate to represent the vocables as pictures (hieroglyphs) to support a trading system complementing the innovations of the Bronze Age stone and metalcrafts. Most of the Meluhha hieroglyphs signify metalware and stoneware together with brief accounts of methods used to smelt or forge or cast artifacts. One most frequently deployed hieroglyph is a 'standard device' shown mostly in front of a one-horned young bull. This sangaḍa hieroglyph had rebus readings:sā̃gāḍā m. ' frame of a building
'; sangara 'fortification'; jangaḍ accounting for mercatile transactions 'goods entrusted on approval basis'.

Such rebus readings are consistent with Robert K. Englund's summing up pointing to the possibility of non-Sumerian participants in the Bronze Age stoneware, metalware repertoire which constituted a veritable multi-national, industrial revolution of those times.

Tukulti Ninurta's altar with hieroglyphs happened in a domain where cuneiform was used -- say between Assur and Kanesh on Tin Road. Do the hieroglyphs on the altar mean Tukulti was illiterate? Tukulti altar displays on one side: safflower, rod on altar and on another side 2. spoked wheel. These are hieroglyphs related to bronze age alloys and fire-god karandi in Remo language (Munda family). The identification of Meluhha hieroglyphs proceeded from DT Potts' brilliant ingisht identifying tabernae montana wild tulip glyph on Tell Abraq axe, also on a vase and on a comb. TA 1649 Tell Abraq.(D.T. Potts, South and Central Asian elements at Tell Abraq (Emirate of Umm al-Qaiwain, United Arab Emirates), c. 2200 BC—CE 400. Potts' insight is complemented by the view of an archaeometallurgist who sees a link between the evolution of Bronze Age from a chalcolithic phase and the emergence of writing systems: "The Early Bronze Age of the 3rd millennium BCE saw the first development of a truly international age of metallurgy… The question is, of course, why all this took place in the 3rd millennium BCE… It seems to me that any attempt to explain why things suddenly took off about 3000 BCE has to explain the most important development, the birth of the art of writing… As for the concept of a Bronze Age one of the most significant events in the 3rd millennium was the development of true tin-bronze alongside an arsenical alloy of copper…" (J.D. Muhly, 1973, Copper and Tin, Conn.: Archon., Hamden; Transactions of Connecticut Academy of Arts and Sciences, vol. 43, p. 221f.) In this context, it is apposite to underscore the use of Meluhha hieroglyphs on two pure tin ingots which were discovered in a shipwreck at Haifa.[265]

Potts has explained further that nomadism was a remarkable phenomenon in ancient Iran. "Although evidence of 'proto-Median' agriculture and settled life may be difficult to find outside of Iran -- particularly as their 'homeland' remains vague and ill-defined -- linguistic studies suggest that some of the earliest Iranian speakers to reach the Iranian plateau did have an agricultural background and were familiar with both ploughing ad irrigation." Potts cites J. Puhvel, 'The Indo-European and Indo-Aryan plough: A linguistic study of technological diffusion,' Technology and Culture 5/2. 1964: 184-186, the posited Indo-Iraia verb stem *karś- meaning 'to plough', may have been a loanword.'[266]

An event more profound than the Aryan nomadic movements into or out of India--was the advent of the Bronze Age which had a decisive impact on the realities of material life, culture and language – and representation of symbolic forms in writing. The Bronze Age created an adventure of ideas and experiments in metallurgy in relating artisans and traders to the material world as they travelled far and wide. Nomadic movements are complemented by the cultural advance of a writing system using Meluhha hieroglyphs.

A succinct summary of the nature of interactions between Meluhhans and the expansive region of Eurasia is provided by Massimo Vidale[267]: [quote] As well remarked by M. Tosi "...the lack of Mesopotamian imports in the Indus Valley reveals the lesser significance of these connections for the eastern pole. Very much like the Roman trade with India and Arabia, as described in the Periplus of the Erythrean Sea in the 1st century AD, the flow of goods towards the head of the Gulf in the later 3rd millennium BC was determined more by the Mesopotamian demand than by economic integration with the distant lands that supplied these goods from the shores of the Indian Ocean." (Tosi M. (1991) "The Indus Civilization beyond the Indian Subcontinent." In M. Jansen., M. Mulloy & G. Urban (eds.) Forgotten cities on the Indus. Mainz, p. 119). Sumerians and Akkadian interacted more with Dilmun sailors and traders, Indian immigrants and largely acculturated social groups than with the remote "Black Country" of Meluhha. In Mesopotamia and in the Gulf, the immigrant Indus families maintained and trasmitted their language, the writing system and system of weights of the motherland (known in Mesopotamia as the "Dilmunite" standard) as strategic tools of trade. Their official symbol of the gaur might have stressed, together with the condition of living in a foreign world, an ideal connection with the motherland. Nonetheless, they gradually adopted the use of foreign languages and introduced minor changes in the writing system for tackling with new, rapidy evolving linguistic needs. The Indus communities in Mesopotamia developed thanks to an intimate understanding of Mesopotamian culture and markets, and to a very opportunistic behaviour. They promptly adapted their products and trade to the fast-changing political and ideological environments of the local social and cultural evolution. Their success in Mesopotamia is easily measured by their efficient adaptation, in order of time, to the frantic politics and fights of the ED III city-states, to the Akkadian centralized bureaucracy and to the even more centralized empire established by Ur-nammu. By 2000 BCE, their integration with Mesopotamian social and economic reality seems to be total. The acculturation process involved collaboration with local religious institutions, worship of foreign divinities, production of ornaments with foreign religious symbols, adoption of "impure" foreign rituals in life and death and (it would be easy to imagine) at the eyes of their compatriots at home "eating impure food." The price of the success might have been their apparent "contamination" with Mesopotamian habits, creeds and ritual practices, a circumstance that – we may be sure – did not escape the attention of the traditional élites in the Indus valley. [unquote]

Even in physics or chemistry, a theory alters the facts to be observed and use of observation terms. This is demonstrated by shifts from Aristotlean to Newtonian to Einsteinian physics and from Darwinian biology to Genetic chemistry. Similarly, in the IE linguistic doctrine of Aryan Invasion Theory, the term 'invasion' was modified by using terms such as 'migration' or 'trickle-in' to explain the reality of features of Indo-Aryan languages which were found to be in common with other Indo-European languages. This theory soon ran into rough weather by questions raised by archaeological realities and by the presence of a large number of agricultural terms in many Indo-Aryan languages which had no cognates in other Indo-European languages. This led to the amendment of the doctrine of Aryan Invasion Theory to posit an Indian *sprachbund*, a linguistic area where different language families absorbed core language features from one another to create a linguistic union called the *sprachbund*. This doctrinal capitulation is merely an attempt to still retain the framework of a linguistic theory positing an essential unity of Indo-European (IE) languages including the Indo-Aryan languages. This capitulation runs into further rough weather when linguists began to see the presence of Munda words in Sanskrit and affinities between Munda and Dravidian languages. (Appendix N: Bronze Age Linguistic Doctrine)

The *tagaraka 'tabernae montana'* hieroglyph is central to the entire corpora; it is the rosetta stone; it is a signifier *tagaraka*, wild fragrant tulip and the signified word is: *tagara*, 'TIN (cassiterite ore)'.

Massimo's arguments are convincing in the context of Wanderworter evidence from an extensive area deploying Meluhha hieroglyphs.

Massimo Vidale provided an effective rebuttal of the claim made by Steve Farmer, Richard Sproat & Michael Witzel that Harappan civilization was illiterate.[268] (See Appendix Q: Archaeological context is a cultural context for symbolic forms of 'meanings')

Excerpts: "My purpose is to reply to 'The collapse of the Indus script thesis: the myth of a literate Harappan civilization', by Steve Farmer, Richard Sproat & Michael Witzel, in Electronic Journal of Vedic Studies (EJVS), 11, 2, 2004, pp. 19-57. I actually think that the Indus script was probably a protohistoric script, somehow conveying the sounds and words of one or more still unidentified languages. Although proofs are obviously lacking (the only demonstration would be a successful translation), this is the most reasonable assumption: and I must confess that I have lived so far rather content with such uncertainty…In order to decipher a lost writing system, you have to guess the language, guess the content, and you need relevant contexts on which independently and reasonably test your ideas…Farmer, Sproat & Witzel loudly stated that they have solved the mystery, that the Indus script is not writing, and that they can read or interpret part of the signs, I disagree with their arguments and, perhaps more, with the tone and language adopted by the authors…The authors would like to throw the ball to their opponents, asking them to refute their views by providing a sound decipherment in linguistic terms. But they have raised the problem, proposing a different interpretation and the first readings, and they have to provide a demonstration of their thesis by interpreting and explaining to us the symbolic sequences following the equivalent of their condition 4 (as stated at p. 48)…(but for the moment even Farmer & others will admit that their deities on vessels and seals and the solar cult advertised at Dholavira did not cost them such an impressive outburst of imagination)."

The epigraphs or artifacts so rendered as signifiers, as hieroglyphs are read rebus as Bronze Age metalware, stoneware repertoire. Cire perdue casting gets a name: dhokra (Meluhha) and the specialist artisans are called dhokra kamar (Meluhha). Zinc is sattiya, jasta and the signifier is the svastika (sattiya). Pewter is tuthnag, the signifier includes a snake. Sharpness of alloyed metal derived from alloying is padm, the signifier is the snake-hood, paṭam.

Meluhha artisans and traders operating along the Tin Road had carried with them the signifiers and signifieds and deployed them as epigraphs or artifacts to convey what they were specialists in. They had also produced 1. the flagposts found in Nahar Mishmar arsenical copper artifacts and 2. the leopard weights of Shahi Tump (Baluchistan).

Both the dreams are narrated in ancient texts and also on sculptures and epigraphs. The ancient texts describe the life-activities which the dreams signified. The hieroglyphs used on sculptures ad epigraphs provide for rebus representations of the dreams.

Rebus readings of the images (signifiers) yield the glosses related to life-activities (signifieds).

Both the dreams are presented in visible language of Meluhha using hieroglyphs, read rebus.

Dream of Tukulti-Ninurta and Māyā's dream are signified by visible language.

"The dream is a rebus." (Freud, Sigmund, 1959, Interpretation of Dreams, p. 1).

One method of derivings meanings of the symbolism in dreams (or unconscious thought) is rebus.

Defining rebus as a picture-puzzle, Sigmund Frued elaborates the concept of displacement of emphasis and affect: "A correct judgment of the picture-puzzle results only if I make no such objections to the whole and its parts, but if, on the contrary, I take pains to replace each picture by the syllable or word which it is capable of representing by means of any sort of reference, the words which are thus brought together are no longer meaningless, but may constitute a most beautiful and sensible expression. Now the dream is a picture-puzzle of this sort, and our predecessors in the field of dream interpretation have made the mistake of judging the rebus as an artistic composition. As such it appears nonsensical and worthless."[269]

The meanings of the visible images are signified by rebus readings of Meluhha language of Assur (Ancient Near East and Ancient India).

The signifier of Māyā's dream is an elephant. The word which signifies an elephant is ibha (Meluhha~Sanskrit). Rebus reading provides the signified: ib 'iron'. This is a condensation of the life activities of Māyā's clan, koliya, Koliya are koles, who are iron workers of yore from several generations. Her unconscious thought conditioned by the life of iron workers and smelters who were associated with her lineage identifies them by the product of their labour, ib 'iron'. The signifier for this life-activity of working in iron is ibha, 'elephant'.

The inscription on the Tukulti Ninurta altar says: god Nusku.

The image is that of an ancestor of Tukulti Ninurta -- ancestor remembered in his dream?-- kneeling before the empty throne of the fire-god Nusku, occupied by what appears to be a flame.

Interpretation of the dream as rebus yields the meaning, the prayer is to fire-god Karandi. So, what is depicted is a flame while signifying the fire-god Karandi. In Meluhha language, the rebus reading of a clump of wood is करंडा [karaṇḍā].

Tukulti Ninurta's ancestor is an Assur, yes, the Assur whose lineage continues to be called Assur in some parts of India: Chattisgarh, Bastar, Santal paraganas, speaking an Asuri language (Meluhha dialect in the Munda language traditions of Indian sprachbund). This is good evidence that Assur of India had travelled far and wide into on the banks of Tigris river establishing the Tin Road between Assur and Kanesh (Kultepe, Anatolia). So, unconscious thought relates to the life-activities of the Assur people on this Tin Road trading in bronze-age artifacts. Hence, the presence of the following hieroglyphs on the Tukulti Ninurta altar: 1. करडी [karaḍī] f करडई) 'Safflower':, 2. nave of spoked wheel eraka, arā (nave, spokes) carried aloft on flagposts as trade announcements. Two flagposts are shown signifying dula 'pair' rebus: dul 'cast (metal)'.

The trade announcements are comparable to the flagposts shown on Mohenjo-daro tablets (which show hieroglyphs of spoked wheel, scarf, one-horned young bull, lathe-portable furnace -- eraka 'copper', dul 'cast (metal), arā 'brass', dhatu 'ore', konda 'turner's lathe', sangada 'citadel,guild'.)

Signifier is hieroglyph: safflower करडी [karaḍī].

Signified is rebus: करडा [karaḍā] Hard from alloy--iron, silver &c. A color of horses, iron grey.

The signifier of Tukulti-Ninurta's dream is a fire-altar. The narrative of the dream is associated with the messages of the dream signifiers of the signifieds, signifiers of spoked wheels, safflowers signified as hard metal alloys of copper of the Bronze

age. The word which signifies a fire-altar
is kaṇḍa (Meluhha~Santali) The narrative is a prayer to fire-god. How to represent this prayer in a visible language detailing the life-activities which have imbued the images and related meanings into the unconscious mind? kāṇḍa is a stem or stick of the sugarcane; such a stem or stick is shown in visible language as the center-piece of the nuska-Ninurta fire altar image before which he kneels down and prays in adoration. He prays to karandi, the fire-god, the signified for which the visible language uses the signified: the stick. karandi 'fire-god' (Munda, Remo). Signifier: करंडा [karaṇḍā] 'A clump, chump, or block of wood.' 'The stock or fixed portion of the staff of the large leaf-covered summerhead or umbrella.' करांडा [karāṇḍā] m C 'A cylindrical piece as sawn or chopped off the trunk or a bough of a tree; a clump, chump, or block'. (Marathi)

The apparent, underlying assumption in the two rebus readings is that the language which provides the glosses is Meluhha and that Tukulti-Ninurta's fire-altar and sculptors who narrated Māyā's elephant are rebus representations of the life activities of Tukulti-Ninurta's clan of Assur and Māyā's clan of Koliyas.

Visible images in works of art are signifiers. Associated words of the spoken language become the signifieds. This is the rebus code. "In the Assyro-Babylonian tradition, visual representation was considered to be part of an extreme semantic constellation. Like the ideogram in the script, the visual sign had the potential of referring to a chain of referents, linked to it and to one another by a logic that may escape the contemporary viewer but that could be deciphered in antiquity through hermeneutic readings. Such readings were obviously not accessible to a general public, most of whom were most likely nonliterate; however, the potential of signs referring to other signs in a continuous chain of meanings was a knowledge not limited to the literate. The ominous nature of things was a subject of concern fo all in Babylonian and Assyrian society. It seems clear from numerous texts that signs in the environment could be read and deciphered by people other than the scholarly elite or the priesthood. For omens related to the destiny of king or country, court diviners and the priesthood studied the signs, using their scholarly knowledge of astronomy and hermeneutics. But the reading of omina in the environment was also a part of the daily lives of people in general, as we know from textual references to egirru (omens of chance utterances) or to dreams and dream interpretation. Like other signs in the world, visual images could never be seen as the relationship between one signified and one signifier. An image was a pluridimensional sign that carried latent meanings beyond the one manifest on the surface. Since many works of art were made without any intent of presentation to mortal viewers, the polyvalence inherent in their imagery was not always a code intended for a particular audience, whether literate or nonliterate, although one can imagine that the system was at times deliberately manipulated for the purposes of generating a required meaing...polyvalence was considered to be in the very nature of the image-sign. The audience or intended viewer was not of the greatest import in many cases because the work of art was put a position where it was only to be viewed by the king, his courtiers, or temple officials. In these cases whatever meanings were generated through the imagery had much less to do with the good opinion of the chance viewer than they did with the power of the image as a eans of creating an incessant presence. In attempting to catalog ancient Near Eastern images by means of an iconography of one-to-one relationships of signifiers and signifieds, of symbols and gods, for example, we have perhaps limited our readings unnecessarily in a way that the Babylonians and Assyrians would not have done."[270]

Sigmund Freud refers to a syntax of dreams noting that the pictorial language of the dream uses what Freud explains as 'condensation and displacement' (Freud 1959).

Dream depicted on Tukulti-Ninurta altar

'I have revealed to Atrahasis a dream, and it is thus that he has learned the secret of the gods.' (Epic of Gilgamesh, Ninevite version, XI, 187.)

The Pedestal of Tukulti-Ninurta I

Artifact: Stone monument
Provenience: Assur
Period: Middle Assyrian period (ca. 1400-1000 BC)
Current location: Vorderasiatisches Museum, Berlin
Text genre, language: Royal inscription; Akkadian
CDLI page *Description*: Although the cult pedestal of the Middle Assyrian king Tukulti-Ninurta mentions in its short inscription that it is dedicated to the god Nuska, the relief on the front that depicts the king in a rare kind of narrative, standing and kneeling in front of the very same pedestal was frequently discussed by art-historians. More strikingly on top of the depicted pedestal there is not the lamp, the usual divine symbol for the god Nuska, but most likely the representation of a tablet and a stylus, symbols for the god Nabû. (Klaus Wagensonner, University of Oxford) *Editions*: Grayson, A.K. 1987. *The Royal Inscriptions of Mesopotamia. Assyrian Period, I: Assyrian Rulers of the Third and Second Millennia B.C. (to 1115 B.C.)*, Toronto, p. 279ff.

An inscription of Gudea of Lagash (2143-2124 BCE) narrates that he had a dream. He describes the dream to goddess Nina: "In the dream a man, whose stature reached up to heaven (and) reached down to earth, who according to the tiara around his head was a god...at whose feet was a storm, to whose right and left a lion ws at rest, commanded me to built his house (i.e., temple)...a second (man), like a warrior...held in his hand a tablet of lapus-lazuli, (and) outlined the pattern of a temple." (Thureau-Dangin, Die

Sumerischen und Akkadischen Konigsinschriften, 94-95 Cylinder A, 4, 14--5,4).
A similar dream is explained on the Tukulti-Ninurta altar. The kneeling adorant prays in front of the altar. The visible image of this prayer is presented on one of the altar. The image on the altar is a rebus.

Tukulti-Ninurta I (1244-1208 BCE) of Assur, narrates the dreams which led to his conquests of Babylon in his epic, a lengthy poem of about 750 to 800 lines. (Lambert, WG, 1957, Three unpublished fragments of the Tukulti-Ninurta Epic, *Archiv fur Orientforschung* 18, Bd, 1957-1958, pp. 38-51).

Narratives from the dream are visible on the hieroglyphs presented on the altar.

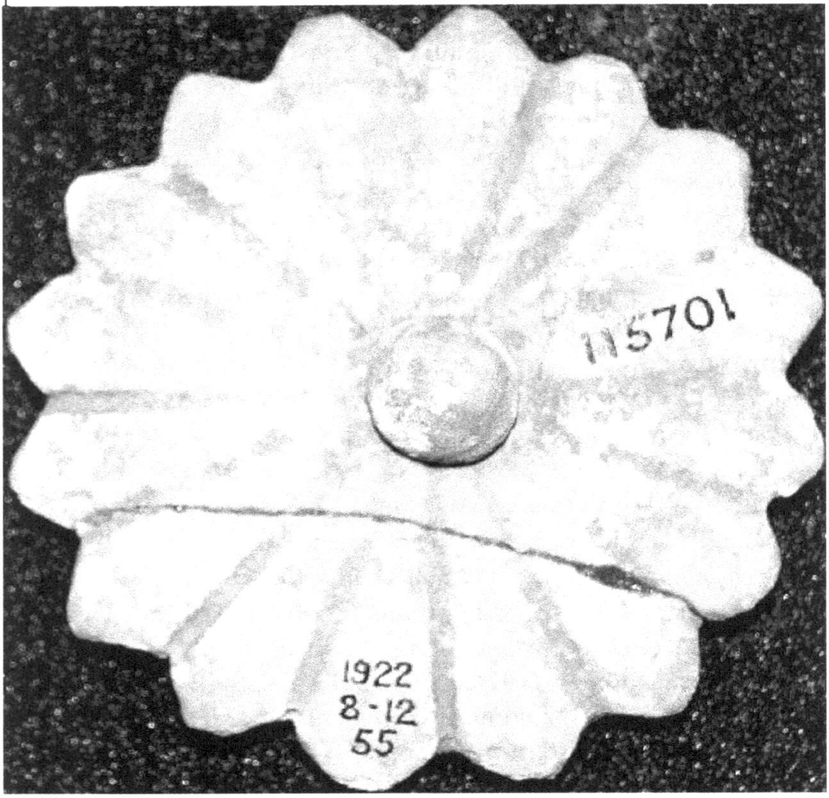

British Museum No. 115701. Terracotta ornament. Flower. Findspot: Kar-Tukulti-Ninurta. Excavated by Walter Andrae, excavator of the sites of Babylon (1899-1903) and Assur (1904-1918) in Iraq.

Palace of Tikulti Ninurta
A number of similar ornaments were found importance of the the trade transaction Kar-Tukulti-Ninurta.

Middle Assyrian, Ashur, Glass Mosaic Fragment.

Middle Assyrian, Ashur, wall painting fragments of flower indicating the hieroglyph in center of They are all glazed composition models of safflower with raised central boss; yellow and green petals; repaired.

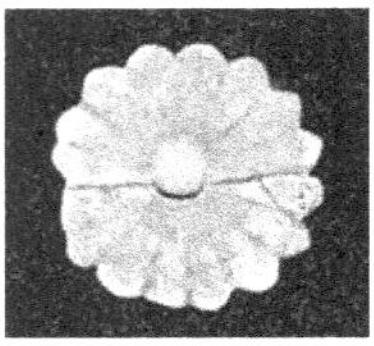

ornament; Kar-Tukulti-Ninurta

ornament; Kar-Tukulti-Ninurta

ornament; Kar-Tukulti-Ninurta

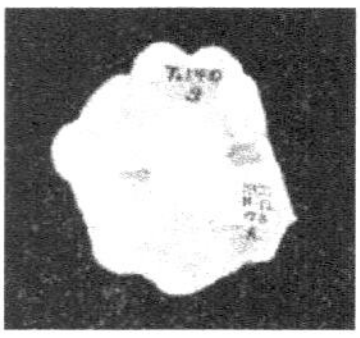

ornament; Kar-Tukulti-Ninurta

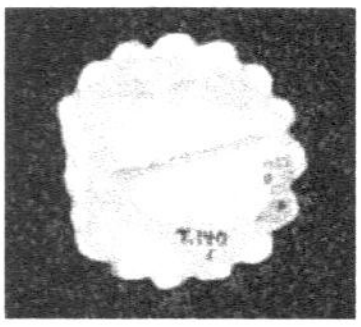

ornament; Kar-Tukulti-Ninurta

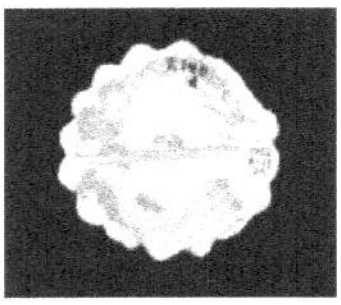

ornament; Kar-Tukulti-Ninurta

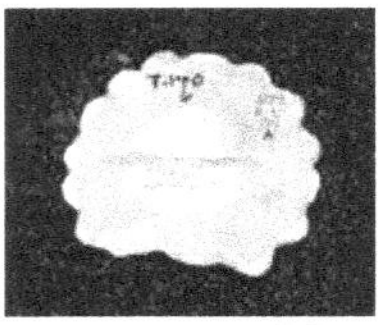

ornament; Kar-Tukulti-Ninurta

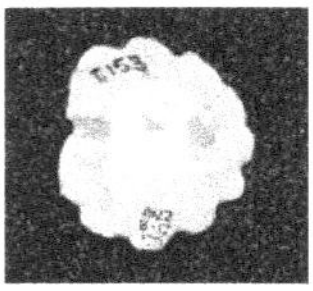

ornament; Kar-Tukulti-Ninurta

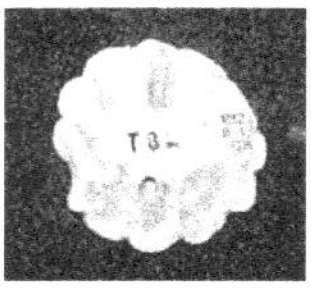

ornament; Kar-Tukulti-Ninurta

ornament; Kar-Tukulti-Ninurta

ornament; Kar-Tukulti-Ninurta

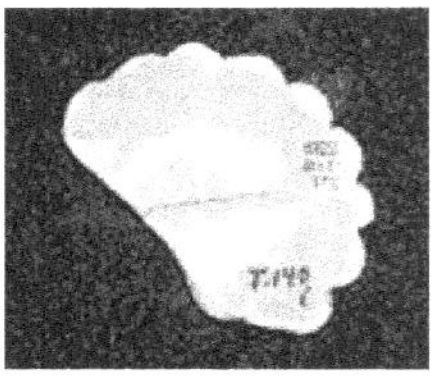

ornament; Kar-Tukulti-Ninurta

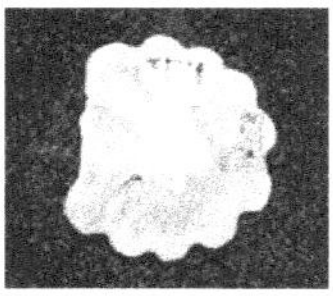

ornament; Kar-Tukulti-Ninurta

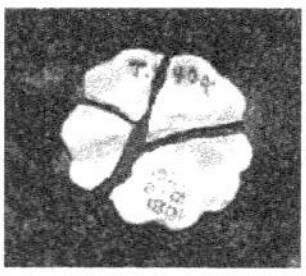

ornament; Kar-Tukulti-Ninurta

British Museum No. 116388. Statue of a seated ape; carved from basalt with polished surfaces.; Middle Assyrian; 1250BC-1200BC; Kar-Tukulti-Ninurta. Barnett, Richard D; Wiseman, Donald J, Fifty masterpieces of Ancient Near Eastern Art, London,

BMP, 1960, p. 54-55. Hieroglyph: kuṭhāru = a monkey (Sanskrit) Rebus: kuṭhāru 'armourer or weapons maker'(metal-worker), also an inscriber or writer.

Hieroglyph: करडी [*karaḍī*] *f* (See करडई) Safflower Rebus: करडा [karaḍā]Hard from alloy--iron, silver &c. (Marathi)

From the stone reliefs of Ashurnasirpal II. Wrist with a safflower bracelet. Hieroglyph: करडी [*karaḍī*] *f* (See करडई) Safflower: also its seed. Rebus: fire-god: @B27990. #16671. Remo <karandi>E155 {N} ``^fire-^god".(Munda).Rebus: करडा [karaḍā]Hard from alloy--iron, silver &c. (Marathi)

Two eagles, sprout – top register; lion, antelope, three stalks – bottom register

"This object in the form of a truncated cone is a base for a ritual offering, carved with animals. Elamite period, mid-3rd millennium BC Tell of the Acropolis, Susa, Iran Bituminous rock H. 19 cm; Diam. 11 cm Jacques de Morgan excavations, 1908 Lions and gazelles passant; eagles protecting their young Sb 2725 The lower register shows two highly stylized eagles, upright, as if resting on their tail feathers. Their wings and talons are spread to protect the chicks beneath them."[271]

miṇḍāl 'markhor' (Tōrwālī) *meḍho* a ram, a sheep (Gujarati)(CDIAL 10120); rebus: *mẽṛhẽt, meḍ* 'iron' (Munda.Ho.) *mṛeka, melh* 'goat' (Telugu. Brahui) Rebus: *melukkha* '*milakkha*, copper'.

arye 'lion' Rebus: *āra* 'brass'.

कांडें [kāṇḍēṃ] n (कांड S) Stalks and heads of corn once trodden or thrashed (as thrown or reserved for a second treading or thrashing). Rebus: Pk. *kaṁḍārēi* ' scrapes, engraves ';*kāṇḍā* 'tools, pots and pans, metalware'. Thus, the top register denotes iron, tin, brass tools and metalware. The numeral count of 'three' stalks may relate semantically to: *kolmo* 'three' Rebus: *kolami* 'smithy,forge'.

Close to the centerpiece of 'sprout' hieroglyph and below the left and right wing of the 'eagle' hieroglyph are (possibly) aquatic birds. *karaṇḍa* 'duck' (Sanskrit) *karaṛa* 'a very large aquatic bird' (Sindhi) Rebus: करडा [karaḍā] Hard from alloy--iron, silver &c. (Marathi) *kāṃī* m. 'super cargo of a ship '(Marathi)

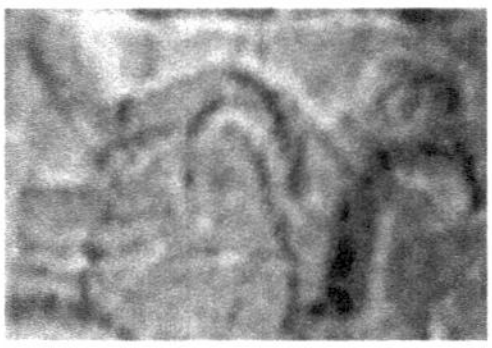

pajhaṛ 'eagle' Rebus: *pasra* 'smithy'. Thus, the bottom register denotes smithy for *karaḍā* '(artifacts) of hard alloys'. Both registers together are a catalog: *erako karaḍā kāṇḍā kolami pasra* 'smithy/forge (for) moltencast copper, hard alloy tools, pots and pans, metalware'.

tagara 'ram' Rebus: tagaram 'tin'
aryeh 'lion' Rebus: āra 'brass'
kuṇḍa n. ' clump '
e.g. *darbha -- kuṇḍa --*

Pāṇ. (CDIAL 3236).
Rebus: Skt. kuṇḍa- round hole in ground (for water or sacred fire), pit, well, spring (DEDR 1669).
kolom'sprout'; *kolom* = cutting, graft; to graft, engraft, prune; kolma hoṛo = a variety of the paddy plant (Desi)(Santali.) kolmo 'rice plant' (Mu.)
Rebus: *kolami* 'furnace,smithy' (Te.)
eraka 'wing' (Telugu) Rebus: *erako* 'moltencast copper'.
pajhar 'eagle'; rebus: *pasra* 'smithy'.

Dream of Māyā, mother of Gautama Buddha details ancient texts and sculptural representations providing signifiers of the dream: in particular, the descent of an elephant which is a hieroglyph read rebus, consistent with the dream as a rebus. The narrative is accompanied by Meluhha hieroglyphs which include a scribe of the guild of metal-/stone-work artisans who might have been involved in the construction of the monuments in Bharhut and Nagarjunakonda -- commemorative pilgrimages of Bauddham. Māyā's dream is a sacred, hallowed tradition in Bauddham and the narrative is revered in ancient sculptures and ancient texts. This tradition is further elaborated by the use of Meluhha hieroglyphs which are read rebus, validating the Meluhha hieroglyph cipher for the ancient, unambiguous vernacular of Indian *sprachbund.*

Detail of the top of the sandstone Vedica pillar, half-roundel at top of vedika pillar with composite creatures in relief:

The top register o this relief shows ligatured antelopes back-to-back; the next register from the top shows a bull ligatured to a makara (crocodile with curved fish tail).

Detail of the roundel:

Segments of the sculpture showing: 1. scribe; 2. stacks of straw asociated with epigraphs (incribed ovals -- cartouches -- atop the stacks) and the row of seated artisans. There are two hieroglyphs on these segments: 1. scribe; 2. straw-stacks. Both can be read as Meluhha hieroglyphs.

The scribe shown on Nagarjunakonda sculpture is *kaṇḍa kanka* 'stone scribe'.

The gloss is reinforced by the hieroglyph: stack of

straw: *kaṇḍa* (See Meluhha glosses from Indian *sprachbund* appended).

Māyā is a Koliya, i.e. she is a kole, a community working in iron. *kol* 'working in iron' (Tamil).
Koles are the outstanding smelters of iron.

There is an article by Suniti Kumar Chatterjee explaining that the word 'kol' meant 'man' in general. An old Munda word, *kol* means 'man'. S. K. Chatterjee called the Munda family of languages as Kol, as the word, according to him, is (in the Sanskrit-Prākṛt form Kolia) an early Aryan modification of an old Munda word meaning 'man'.[272] Przyluski accepts this explanation.[273]

Przyluski notes the principal forms of the words signifying 'man' and 'woman' in the Munda languages:
Man: hor, hōrol, harr, hõr, haṛa, hoṛ, koro
Woman: kūṛĩ, ērā, koṛi, kol
Comparing 'son' and 'daughter' in Santali:
Son = kora hapan; daughter = kuri hapan

"...a root kur, kor is differentiated in the Munda languages for signifying: man, woman, girl and boy. That in some cases this root has taken a relatively abstract sense is proved by Santali koḍa, koṛa, which signify 'one' as in the expression 'koḍa ke koḍa' 'each single one'. Thus one can easily understand that the same root has served the purpose of designating the individual not as an indivisible unity but as a numerical whole...Thus we can explain the analogy between the root kur, kor 'man' the number 20 in Munda kūṛī kūṛī , koḍī and the number 10 in Austro-Asiatic family ko, se-kūr, skall, gal." (ibid., pp. 28-30).
Homonym: कोल [kōla] *n* An income, or goods and chattels, or produce of fields &c. seized and sequestered (in payment of a debt). *V* धरून ठेव, सोड. 2 *f* The hole dug at the game of विटीदांडू, at marbles &c. कोलणें [kōlaṇēṃ] *v c* To strike the विटी in the

hole कोली with the bat or दांडू. (In the game of विटीदांडू) 2 To cast off from one's self upon another (a work). Ex. पैका मागावयास लागलों म्हणजे बाप लेंकावर कोल-तो लेंकबापावर कोलतो. 3 To cast aside, reject, disallow, flout, scout. कोलून मारणें To kick up the heels of; to trip up: also to turn over (from one side to the other). किरकोळी [kirakōḷī] *f* (किरकोळ) A heap of miscellaneous articles.

The crocodile ligatured to the bull is: *kāru* 'crocodile' Rebus: *khar* 'blacksmith' (Kashmiri) *ayakara* 'fish+crocodile' rebus: 'metal-smith'. *adar* 'zebu' rebus: *aduru* 'unsmelted metal or ore' (Kannada) aduru native metal (Ka.); ayil iron (Ta.) ayir, ayiram any ore (Ma.); ajirda karba very hard iron (Tu.)(DEDR 192). aduru =*gaṇiyinda tegadu karagade iruva aduru* = ore taken from the mine and not subjected to melting in a furnace.[274]

Note: In this remarkable ligature, the crocodile+fish hieroglyphs are NOT ligatured to the trunk of an elephant because the scribe wants to precisely communicate the nature of the profession of the artisan guild involved with the prayer to the Buddha narrating his birth. If the elephant was intended, the rebus readings would have included: *ibha* 'elephant' (Samskrtam) *ibbo* 'merchant' (Hemacandra Desināmamāla -Gujarati) *ib* 'iron' (Santali).

Vikalpa: the bull is: *ḍangar* 'bull' Rebus: *dhangar* 'blacksmith' (Maithili) *ḍangar* 'blacksmith' (Hindi).

The two antelopes joined back-to-back: pusht 'back'; rebus: pusht 'ancestor'. pus<u>h</u>t bah pus<u>h</u>t 'generation to generation.' The ram could also be denoted by *tagara* 'antelope'; takar, *n.* [தகர் T. *tagaru*, K. *tagar.*] 1. Sheep; ஆட்டின்பொது. (திவா.)

2. Ram; செம் மறியாட்டுக்கடா. (திவா.) பொருநகர் தாக்கற்குப் பேருந் தகைத்து (குறள், 486).
Rebus: *ṭagara* 'tin'. dula 'pair' (Kashmiri); rebus: dul 'cast metal' (Munda). Thus the pair of antelopes on the top register denotes: tin smith artisan, dul *ṭagara* 'cast tin'.

The associated hieroglyphs, in the context of depicting the narratives of Māyā's dream, in particular (and their rebus readings) which are elaborated further in this monograph pointing to a continuum of writing systems from the days of Meluhha hieroglyphs (aka Indus writing) are:

- stack of straw
- scribe
- bull ligatured to makara (crocodile + fish tail)
- antelopes ligatured back-to-back

Māyā had a dream in which she saw an elephant (*ibha* 'elephant' rebus: *ib* 'iron'). King Śuddhodana and his soothsayers interpreted the dream that she would bear a son who with detached passion would satisfy the world with sweetness of his ambrosia.

Appendix N: Bronze Age Linguistic Doctrine

Executive summary

How did the Meluhh (Mleccha) language, Munda, Dravidian and Indo-Aryan language families constitute themselves into an Indian *sprachbund*? Bronze Age imperative!

Bronze Age intensified the prospecting for key alloying minerals to create metal tools, pots and pans. This led to movements of lapidaries, miners and metalsmiths to move, in search of mineral resources, to places far-off from their homes.

The new revolutionary products created from precious stones, minerals of tin and zinc alloyed with copper to create bronze and brass ingots, metal tools, sharp and heavy, non-brittle metal weapons, metal pots and metal pans, by lapidaries, miners and metalsmiths resulted in a demand for the stoneware and metalware across a wide area extending from Rakhigarhi (Delhi, India) to Haifa (Israel). This demand necessitated long-distance trade by sea-faring artisans and merchants. This trade also necessitated the invention of writing systems to document the nature of products traded and identify the parties involved in the trade contracts. One such writing system was Indus Writing which provided rebuses using Meluhha (Mleccha) words to describe and incise (*takṣat vāk*, incised speech) words as Indus inscription texts and pictorial motifs which are verily stoneware and metalware catalogs. These catalogs were complemented by cuneiform texts to specify contracting parties and contract terms for the trade. The Bronze Age imperative which impacted languages is briefly delineated by the phrase, Bronze Age Linguistic Doctrine. An outline of this doctrine need not be detained by polemics of Aryan Invasion or Migration Theories or Out of India Theories since direction of borrowings is not required to be specified to delineate the Indian *sprachbund*, a linguistic area which included many cognate semantic clusters with terms necessitated by the inventions of the Bronze Age.

Nature of doctrine

A doctrine is postulated as an informative proposition or truth claim of objective reality. A doctrine gains the attributes of an authoritative dogma. Doctrines are common in theological domain but it is surprising to find a doctrine in the domain of language studies.

One such doctrine postulated by linguists to explain cognate glosses among Indo-European languages was the Aryan Invasion Theory (with variants such as Aryan Migration or Trickle-in Theories). This doctrine sought to explain many glosses in a category called Indo-Aryan languages. The doctrine was, simply that Aryan-speakers invaded India and forced their Indo-European language on the natives' and forced modifications in the natives' tongue or speech, creating Indo-Aryan. Counter-arguments have been advanced that an Out of India Theory is also consistent with the evidence of glosses in Indo-Aryan languages cognate with Indo-European and polemical views point to many areas as possible *urheimat*, original homeland of IE speakers.

Bronze Age Linguistic Doctrine as alternative for Aryan Invasion Linguistic Doctrine

An alternative to the Aryan Invasion Linguistic Doctrine is proposed to explain the essential semantic unity of many ancient Indian languages of the Bronze Age. Many cognate metallurgical terms invented during the Bronze Age were adopted within the speech area — cutting across Munda, Dravidian and Indo-Aryan language families. Bronze Age Linguistic Doctrine explains the *raison d'etre* for the formation of Indian *sprachbund*, a language union because tin-bronzes resulted in a revolution in ways of living of the people living and identified with the *sprachbund*. Earlier arsenical bronzes from the Anatolian peninsula of Turkey produced brittle weapons that shattered on impact. Widespread and large-scale use of bronze for tools such as ploughshare, hammer, sickle changed the nature and scale of daily activities and use of bronze for sharp swords, spear or arrow tips and other weapons changed the nature of warfare and areal contacts and relationships. With bronze and later iron tools, stone cutting, dressing, and sculpting were possible. The revolutionary nature of cultural change brought about by the use of bronze is comparable to the revolution witnessed in the use of modern computers and mobile phones or in the wake of industrial revolution, the use of railway trains for long-distance or commuter travel. Such technological inventions profoundly alter the speech forms in vogue all over the world with the common use of lexical terms such as train, ticket, cell-phone, call – in almost all languages of the globe.

The ruling IE linguistic doctrine is now on its last legs of decay: the fate of doctrines is that If once true, is always true and if once false, is always false.

The situation calls for a new doctrine to replace the terms of the decayed linguistic doctrine of Aryan Invasion because mere trickle-in by tourists cannot explain displacement of entire sets of languages or speech of 'natives' and there is no archaeological evidence for any Aryan invasion.

Doctrinal reconciliation, without calling for capitulation, is possible by postulating a replacement doctrine which explains the realities in three dimensions to reconstruct the living of life over millennia: anthropology/archaeology, culture (value systems) and language.

A presentation on the nature of doctrine by George Lindbeck[275] occurs in the context of his effort to seek unity in the church, reconciling varying church doctrines. Lindbeck notes that religion refers to "a kind of cultural and/or linguistic framework or medium that shapes the entirety of life and thought ... it is similar to an idiom that makes possible the description of realities, the formulation of beliefs, and the experiencing of inner attitudes, feelings, and sentiments." [Lindbeck, *The Nature of Doctrine*,

33] Lindbeck mentions that Wittgenstein conceives of private languages as "logically impossible."_[Lindbeck, *The Nature of Doctrine*, 38] However, on a closer reading, one finds that 'logical impossibility' is not a category in which Wittgenstein is working as much as the category of 'sense' [*Sinn*] and 'non-sense' [*Unsinn*].[276]

Appendix O: Eagle and snake hieroglyphs

The addition of lead ore *nāga* may be signified by the 'snake' hieroglyph vividly seen on many Jiroft artifacts in combat or intertwined with 'eagle' hieroglyph. Rebus: நாகம்² *nākam* , *n.* < *nāga.* A prepared arsenic; பாஷாண வகை; Black lead; காரீயம். (Tamil) nāga2 n. ' lead ' Bhpr. [Cf. raṅga -- 3] Sh. *naṅ* m. ' lead ' (< **nāṅga* -- ?), K. *nāg* m. (< **nāgga* -- ?).(CDIAL 7040). నాగసింధూరము [nāgasindhūramu] *nāga-sindhūramu.* [Skt.] n. A red calx of lead. (Telugu) cf. *anakku* 'tin' (Akkadian), an alloying ore to create tin-bronzes or arsenical bronzes.

At Ahed excavation site statues of the Gods of both Hindu and Jain religion are found. Of particular importance is the statue of Parvati a deity of importance to Dravidians. Also the Nag- Nagini statue indicates the presence of Naga people around Ahed those days.

Noticeable is the image of fish on the top of the figure which probably is the symbol of Bhil Meena tribe. It signifies *ayo, ayas* 'alloyed metal'.

Thanks to DMR Sekhar from whose blogpost I have obtained this image.

I suggest that the fish hieroglyph on the top register of the Nag-Nagini statue is *ayo* 'fish' (Munda) Rebus: aya = iron (G.); ayah, ayas = metal (Skt.)

Nāga and *Nāgini* are also hieroglyphs.

Hieroglyph: *nāgá*1 m. ' snake ' ŚBr. 2. ' elephant ' BhP. [As ' elephant ' shortened form of **nāga -- hasta* -- EWA ii 150 with lit. or extracted from *nāga -- danta* -- ' elephant tusk, ivory ' < ' snake -- shaped tusk ']. 1. Pa. *nāga* -- m. ' snake ', NiDoc. *nāǵa* F. W. Thomas AO xii 40, Pk. *ṇāya* -- m., Gy. as. *nâ* JGLS new ser. ii 259; Or. *naa* ' euphem. term for snake '; Si. *nay*, *nā*, *nayā* ' snake '. -- With early nasalization **nāṅga* -- : Bshk. *nāṅg* ' snake '. -- Kt. Pr. *noṅ*, Kal. *nhoṅ* ' name of a god < *nā'ga* -- or ← Pers. *nahang* NTS xv 283. 2. Pa. *nāga* -- m. ' elephant ', Pk. *ṇāya* -- m., Si. *nā*. śiśunāka -- .(CDIAL 7039). నాగము [nāgamu] *nāgamu*.

[Skt. from నగ a hill.] n. Lit: That which pertains to a mountain. A serpent, పాము. Particularly, a cobra. An elephant, ఏనుగు. నాకిని a female supernatural being, a goddess, దేవతాస్త్రీ. నాకులు *nākulu*. n. The celestials, the gods. R. v. 35. 176. నాకేశుడు *nāk-ēsuḍu*. n. A name of Indra. *நாகர்¹ nākar, n. < nāka.* Celestials; தேவர். வழுத்த வரங்கொடுப்பர் நாகர் (நான்மணி. 62). (Tamil) నాగు, నాగులు, నాగువు or నాగుబాము *nāgu*. n. A cobra. నాగము.(Telugu) *நாகம்² nākam, n. < nāga. 1. Cobra. See நல்லபாம்பு. நன்மணியிழந்த நாகம் போன்று (மணி. 25, 195). 2. Serpent;* பாம்பு. *(பிங்.)* ஆடுநாக மோட *(கம்பரா. கலன்காண். 37).*

The semantics of nāga as 'arsenic' or 'lead' are instructive in the context of the Ayad river image of Naga-Nagini and fish hieroglyphs. Arsenic or lead are alloying ores with copper to create *ayas* 'alloy metal'. Thus, *ayas* may have denoted arsenical copper or tin-bronze or zin-brass. A hypothesis can be posited that *nāga* or *anakku* connoted such an alloying metal (tin or zinc or even lead or nickel -- until the distinctive nature of the alloying mineral was recognised) to take the bronze age with the revolution of alloys to harden copper in minerals such as the copper sulfides, chalcopyrite and chalcocite, copper carbonates, azurite and malachite and the copper oxide mineral cuprite.

pajhaṛ 'eagle'; allograph: *pajhaṛ* = to sprout from a root. Rebus: *pasra* 'smithy' (Santali)
One motif that is remarkably unique in Mesopotamian seals is the LION. Only a tiger motif appears on the seals of the Sarasvati Sindhu civilization. The closest to a lion motif is the bristled-hair

(like a lion's mane) on the face of the three-faced, fully adorned, horned, seated person surrounded by animals and an inscription. *aryeh* 'lion'. Rebus: *āra* 'brass, alloy of zinc and copper' as in *ārakūṭa* (Skt.) *ayir* 'iron dust, any ore' (Malayalam). The semantics of ayir as a reference to 'any ore (perhaps an alloying mineral to harden copper)' is significant and may explain the dominance of the lion hieroglyph on hundreds of Mesopotamian inscriptions, cylinder seals and artifacts and often in juxtaposition to the bull hieroglyph.
Cylinder seal: lion and sphinx over an antelope277 Period: Late Cypriot II Date: ca. 14th century B.C.E. Geography: Cyprus Culture: Cypriot Medium: Black-grey steatite Dimensions: 0.83 in. (2.11 cm) Classification: Stone-Cylinder Seal Credit Line: The Cesnola Collection, Purchased by subscription, 1874-76 Accession Number: 74.51.4313

ṭagara 'antelope'; ḍā̄gar 'horned cattle' (K.) rebus: ḍāṅgar 'blacksmith' (H.) damgar, tamkāru 'merchant, trader'(Sumerian). Three bun ingots in relief are shown circumscribing the head of the lion. A curve with a dot is above the head of the 'composite eagle-lion'. Both animals are in combat pose flanking the antelope/ram looking back. This tagara 'ram' is the set between *arye* 'lion' and 'composite eagle-lion'. This rebus tagara 'tin' is the set between *āra* 'brass' and the alloy signified by the 'composite eagle-lion'. *eṟaka* 'wing' (Telugu) Rebus: *erako* 'moltencast copper'. Thus, an alloy of copper and brass – maybe, pewter?

The crescent above this animal's head may denote a crucible or *sangaḍa* 'a portable furnace' and the dot a crucible metal alloy. At the back of the lion are depicted: three dots. *gōṭī* 'round pebble; kōḍ कोड् m. a kernel (Kashmiri) Rebus 1: L. *khoṭ* f 'alloy, impurity', °*ṭā* 'alloyed', awāṇ. *khoṭā* 'forged'; P. *khoṭ* m. 'base, alloy' (CDIAL 3931) खोट [khōṭa] alloyed ingot (Marathi). खोट [khōṭa] alloyed ingot (Marathi). kolmo 'three' Rebus: kolami 'smithy, forge'. Thus the three 'kernel or pebble' hieroglyphs signify: *khōṭa kolami* 'alloyed ingot smithy/forge'. The entire message is a symbolic form attesting the life-activity of producing three types of metal ingots: 1. Brass 'copper + zinc; 2. Bronze 'copper + tin'; 3. Pewter *ran:ga* 'pewter or alloy of tin (*ran:ku*), lead (*nāga*) and antimony (*añjana*)'—or, a prepared arsenical copper.

The face of ox or bull is on the bottom register. *aryeh* 'lion'. Rebus: *āra* 'brass' as in ārakūṭa (Skt.) ayir = iron dust, any ore (Ma.) The 'dot' glyph is an allograph for *mũhe* 'face'; rebus: mũh 'ingot' (Santali) Thus, the lion ligatured with three dots behind its head on a Cypriot seal denotes: *āra* 'brass *khoṭ* 'alloyed ingots'. The depiction of a bull's head together with an antelope is significant and recalls the association of bull's head with oxhide ingots. The antelope looking backwards is flanked by a lion (with three dots at the back of the head) and a winged animal woman's face with talons on feet of tiger?) kola 'woman'; kol 'tiger'; rebus: kol 'smithy'.

Th eagle is ligatured to a lion identified by the curved tail, clawed feet and back. *pajhaṛ* 'eagle'; allograph: *pajhaṛ* = to sprout from a root. Rebus: *pasra* 'smithy' (Santali). The ligature is a reinforcement of the semantics of *pasra* 'smithy' working with copper, zinc alloys to produce brass.

Thus, the ligatured glyph together with a 'human face' on the Cypriot seal denotes: copper smithy. The information transferred by the hieroglyphs on the cylinder seal impression: *tagar* 'antelope'; rebus: *damgar* 'merchant' *arye* 'lion' Rebus: *āra* 'brass' (Hindi) is thus semantic determinant for an alloyed ingot (from) copper smithy. *mũh* 'face'; *muha* -- n. 'mouth,face ' (Pkt.) rebus: *mũh* 'ingot' (Munda)

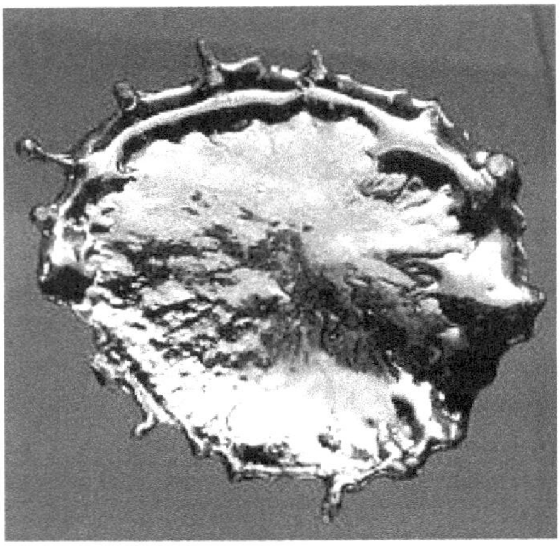

Droplet of solidified molten tin. Commercial grades of tin (99.8%) resist transformation because of the inhibiting effect of the

small amounts of bismuth, antimony, lead and silver present as impurities. Alloying elements such as copper, antimony, bismuth, cadmium and silver increase its hardness.

Sample of cassiterite, the main source of tin. Cassiterite with muscovite, from Xuebaoding, Huya, Pingwu, Mianyang, Sichuan, China (size: 100 x 95 mm, 1128 g) Cassiterite (SnO_2), the tin oxide form of tin, was most likely the original source of tin in ancient times. Cassiterite often accumulates in alluvial channels as placer deposits due to the fact that it is harder, heavier, and more chemically resistant than the granite in which it typically forms. These deposits can be easily seen in river banks as cassiterite is usually black, purple or otherwise dark in color, a feature exploited by early Bronze Age prospectors. It is likely that the earliest deposits were alluvial in nature, and perhaps exploited by the same methods used for panning gold in placer deposits.[278]

Pewter plate. Pewter is 85–99% tin. with the remainder consisting of copper, antimony, bismuth and sometimes, less commonly today, lead. Silver is also sometimes used. Copper and antimony act as hardeners while lead is common in the lower grades of pewter, which have a bluish tint. Pewter is a malleable metal alloy.

The arrival of the bronze age was maked by the invention of alloying copper with arsenic, zinc or tin to produce arsenic-alloys, and other alloys such as brass, bronze, pewter. These archaeo-metallurgial inventions enabled the production of goods surplus to the requirements of the artisan guilds. These inventions also created the imperative of and necessity for a writing system which could represent about over 500 specific categories of activities related to the artisanal repertoire of a smith. Such a large number of categories could not be handled by the limited number of geometric shapes used in the token system of accounting and documenting – goods, standard measures of grains, liquids and surface areas.[279]

Sumerian *aṇṇa*, Akkadian *anāku,* both words now translated 'tin.' Also, if the reference is to the black tinstone, cassiterite, of alluvial deposits, the name is quite appropriate.

The combat between eagle and serpent hieroglyphs may be a process of deploying cassiterite (tin) in *pasra* 'smithy': *pajhaṛ* 'eagle'

Rebus: *pasra* 'smithy'; *nāga* 'snake' Rebus: *nāga* 'lead'; alternative *anāku* 'cassiterite (tin)'.

Tin from 'Meluhha'

Aurel Stein collected a few bronzes from Shahi Tump, Mehi, Siah Damb and Segak Mound, all of which have a high tin percentage... tin was a precious commodity as is evident from the findings of bronze scraps, stored along with other valuables in copper vessels at both Harappa and Mohenjodaro.[280]

DK Chakrabarti opines281 that during the pre-Harappan and Harappan periods, the main supply of tin was from the western regions: Khorasan and the area between Bukhara and Samarkand, through sites like Shortugai. The ancient tin mines in the Kara Dagh District in NW Iran and in the modern Afghan-Iranian Seistan could have been possible sources. Harappan metal-smiths used to conserve tin by storing and re-using scrap pieces of bronze, making low-tin alloys and substituting tin by arsenic. It is possible that some of the imported tin (like lapis lazuli) was exported to Mesopotamia.

"...According to the Larsa texts, merchants were there (in Mari and Larsa) to purchase copper and tin: the copper came from Magan in Oman, via Tilmun (Bahrain), but the origin of the tin is left in question. Tin mines in north-west Iran or the Transcaucasus are highly unlikely. Fortunately, there is evidence for another tin source in texts from Lagash. Lagash, about 50 km east of Larsa, was of minor importance except under the governorship of Gudea (ca. 2143-2124 BC). His inscriptions indicate extensive trade: gold from Cilicia in Anatolia, marble from Amurra in Syria, and cedar wood from the Amanus Mountains between these two countries, while up through the Persian Gulf or 'Southern Sea' came more timber, porphyry (strictly a purplish rock), lapis lazuli and tin.282 There is evidence from a cylinder seal of Gudea, the king of Lagash (2143 – 2124 BCE) that tin came from Melukkha.[283]

One inscription has been translated: Copper and tin, blocks of lapis lazuli and ku ne (meaning unknown), bright carnelian from Meluhha.

"This is the only reference to tin from Meluhha...either Meluhha was a name vague enough to embrace Badakhshan (the northernmost province of Afghanistan) as well as some portion of the Indian subcontinent including the Indus valley, or 'tin from Meluhha' means that the metal came from some port in Meluhha -- just as 'copper from Tilmun' means copper from elsewhere shipped through the island of Bahrain. Whichever interpretation is correct, the result is the same. Tin must have come from somewhere in India, or from elsewhere along a trade route down the Indus valley. India is not without its tin locations, rare though they are...The largest deposits in India proper are in the Hazaribagh district of Bihar. 'Old workings' are said to exist... (Wheeler, R.E.M., 1953, The Indus Civilization, CUP, 58)...Tin bronzes from Gujarat are at the southernmost limit of Indus influence. The copper could have come from Rajasthan, though copper ingots at the port of Lothal, at the head of the Gulf of Cambay, suggest imports from Oman or some other Near Eastern copper mining district. Tin supplying Harappa and Mohenjo-daro, most famous of the Indus cities, may have been sent overland to Lothal for export, though the scarcity of tin in the Indus cities makes this idea unconvincing.

Homeric times refer to tin along with ivory coming from India (V. Ball, 1880, A geologist's contribution to the History of Ancient India, in: *Journal of Royal Geological Society of Ireland*, Vol. 5, Part 3, 1879-89, Edinburgh, pp. 215-63). Ball reiterates Lassen's comment that the Greek word *kassiteros* was derived from *kastira* whereas Bevan feels (E.J. Rapson ed., 1921, *The Cambridge History of India*, Vol. I, Delhi, Indian Edn., S. Chand and Co., p. 351) that *kastira* was derived from *kassiteros*. Such a controversy also existed about ā*rakūṭa* in Sanskrit and *oreichalkos* in Greek ('mountain copper') which refer to brass. Pliny called this *aurichalcum* or golden copper (since brass is yellow).[284]

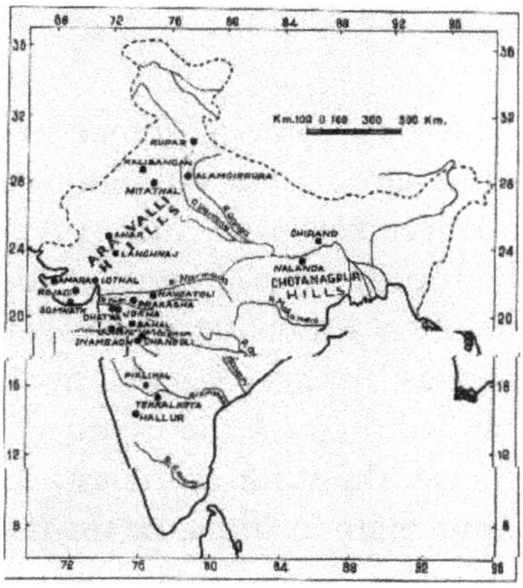

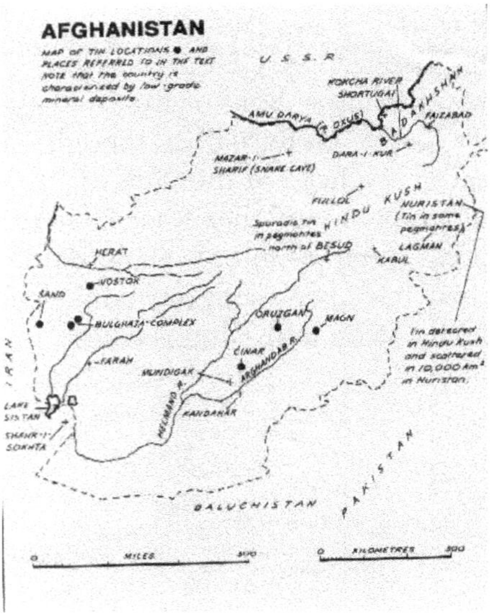

Sources of tin in India and Afghanistan (After Pennhallurick, 1986, maps 3 and 5).

Sources of Tin for the Bronze Age in the areas close to Aravalli and Chota Nagpur Hills, India

Sites of ancient Indian excavated and copper and bronze objects (Hegde, opcit.)

"I have analyzed 38 representative metal objects, selected from among 76 objects, excavated from six post-Harappan sites: Mitathal, Ahar, Somnath, Navdatoli, Jokha, and Chandoli; distributed in Central and western India and in the Deccan plateau. These objects were recovered from the strata that are

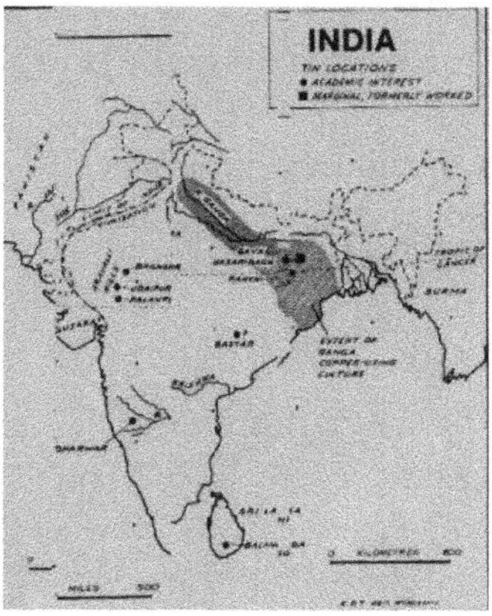

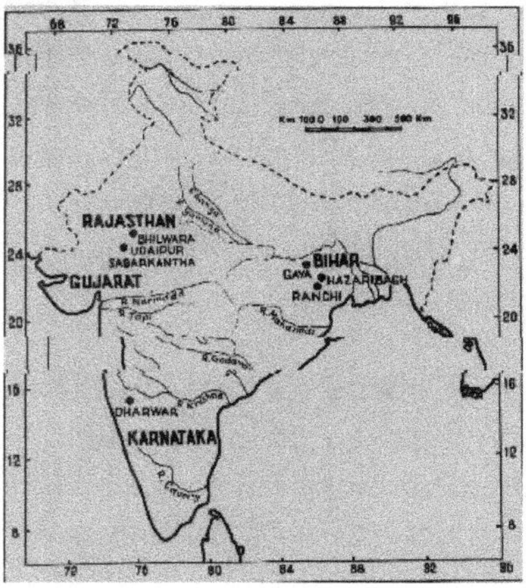

dated to ca. 1500-1000 BC. The objects included axes, chisels, knives, daggers, bracelets, and bangles. Among the 38 objects analyzed, 7 were found to be made of bronze. Their tin content varied from 3.12 to 12.82 percent. The other objects were made of copper...At Nalanda in Bihar, excavations have brought to light over five hundred metal images. These images are dated AD 800 to 1200. From among them, BB Lal selected 18 images for chemical analysis. The study revealed that 9 of the images were made of bronze. In their composition, the percentage of tin varied from 7.88 to 23.68 (Lal, 1956, p. 56)...from the foregoing, it is possible to observe that tin was used in India to produce bronze tools and ornaments during the protohistoric Bronze Age and again during historic times to produce statuary...

Out of 13 artefacts analysed from Mohenjo-daro, 6 were found to contain between 4.51% to 13.21% tin; the artefacts were: bronze rod, bronze button, bronze chisel, bronze slab, bronze chisel and bronze lump.[285]

Sites of Indian tin ore deposits (Hegde, opcit.)
Kumbharia (2 kms. east of Ambaji) is a pilgrimage centre for the Jains, which has a temple with metal images of Tīrthānkara, dated ca. 11th cent. AD. Kumbharia is located near a mountain known as Arasur which has many mines of non-ferrous metals. (cf. ancient texts: *Purātan Prabhanda San:graha*, 1030 AD and *Upades'a Saptati*, 1477 AD; the texts also refer to Ambāji in Banaskantha district of North Gujarat as sources of copper and other metals). (Swarna Kamal Bhowmik and Mudrika Jani, Literary references on metals, metallic objects of art and metal technology, in: Vibha Tripathi (ed.), 1998, *Archaeometallurgy* in India, Delhi, Sharada Publishing House).

"Tin ore deposits are known to occur in India at a number of places in Rajasthan, Gujarat, Bihar, and Karnataka. In Rajasthan, they are found in the Aravalli Hills, about 27 km north of Shahapura, near Paroli in Bhilwara district and at Soniana in Udaipur district. In Gujarat, the deposits occur within the Aravalli Hills, near Hussainpur and Palanpur, in Banaskantha district.In Bihar, tin ore deposits are reported from the Chota Nagpur Hills, in Hazaribagh, Ranchi, and Gaya districts. In Hazaribagh district, they are found at Simritari, Pihra, Chappatand, and at Nurungo. In Ranchi district, the deposits are foundat Jonha Silli and Paharsingh. In Gaya district, they are found at Dhakanahwa and Dhanras. In Karnataka, small cassiterite deposits are reported to be present in the alluvia of the streams flowing from the northern part of the Kapatgod Hills, near Dambal in Dharwar district....Cassiterite is often found in the form of water-concentrated deposits, referred to as 'stream tin'. R.F. Tylecote (1962, *Metallurgy in Archaeology*, London, Edward Arnold, p. 63), observes more likely that it was stream tin that the ancient metallurgists exploited rather than vein deposits. Vein deposits are hard to mine. Proper prospecting of the alluvial deposits of the streams that flow from the cassiterite-bearing hills in the Aravalli and Chota Nagpur ranges, is yet to be done...tin ore deposits within the proximity of the Aravalli and Chota Nagpur Hills and whether they did not form a source of ancient tin India. Our study on the source of ancient Indian copper seems to indicate this possibility. Through a spectrometric analysis and comparison of impurity patterns, we have been able to demonstrate the possibility of linking the copper in the post-Harappan copper and bronze objects with the chalcopyrite deposits in the Aravalli Hills. The chalcopyrite deposits in the Aravalli Hills form a discontinuous belt, extending over 150 km. And within the belt, there are a number of 7 to 8 m deep shafts and large slag heaps -- possible marks of ancient mining and metal-smelting activities. Among the excavated material remains, dated to ca. 1500 BC from Ahar, a site within the Aravalli Hills, there were a number of chunks of semi-fused glass-like material. This we have chemically analyzed and identified as copper metallurgical slag, a waste product of the copper smelting industry. We have therefore observed that Ahar was an ancient Indian copper smelting center. The metalworkers there appear to have exploited the locally available ores. Similarly, in Bihar chalcopyrite deposits occur at a number of places, in Hazaribagh and Singhbhum districts in the Chota Nagpur Hills. These deposits are also marked with ancient metalworking activities. In the Aravalli and Chota Nagpur Hills copper and tin ore deposits occur in proximity. There are clear indications to show that the ancient Indian metallurgists exploited the copper ore deposits occurring in the Aravalli Hills. It is likely that they took advantage of the copper ore deposits in the Chota Nagpur Hills, as well...The geographic distribution of sites, where ancient Indian bronze objects were found, supports this observation. However, this does not rule out the possibility of import of tin into India. India has had long cultural and trade contacts with Burma, Malaya and other Southeast Asian countries known for their rich deposits of tin ore. These contacts increased during the historic period...C.J.Brown and A.K. Dey (1955, *India's Mineral Wealth*, Bombay, Oxford University Press, p. 167) refer to the fact that in 1849 tin ore was being smelted in village iron furnaces at Purgo, near Parasnath in Bihar. It is therefore likely that the locally smelted tin and imported tin were both used in the production of ancient Indian bronze objects."[286]

"At Harappa, three copper alloys were used in the period 2500-2000 BC: copper and up to 2% nickel; copper and up to 5% nickel; copper with ca. 10% tin and a trace of arsenic. Ingots of tin as well as of copper were found at Harappa. (Lamberg-Karlovsky, C.C., 1967, Archaeology and metallurgy in prehistoric Afghanistan, India and Pakistan, American Anthropologist, 1967, 69, 145-62). The rarity of the metal is seen at Mohenjo-daro where, of 64 artifacts examined, only nine were of tin bronze.[287] Ingots of tin bronze have also been found at Chanhu-daro. Yet in spite of its scarcity, tin bronze was widely used. Its occasional abundance and, in the case of the bronzes from Luristan in southern Iran, the high quality of the tin bronzes produced, equally underline the fact that rich source of tin existed somewhere...

"The archaeological evidence from Afghanistan is not unequivocal...What is surprising is the discovery in 1962 of corroded pieces of sheet metal bearing traces of an embossed design and made of a low tin content bronze (5.15%)...The uncorroded metal is thought to have contained nearer 7% tin. (Caley, E.R., 1972, Results of an examination of fragments of corroded metal from the 1962 excavation at Snake Cave, Afghanistan, Trans. American Phil. Soc., New Ser. , 62, 43-84). These fragments came from the deepest level in the Snake Cave, contemporary with the earliest occupation dated by 14C to around 5487 and 5291 BC. (Shaffer, J.G., in Allchin F.R. and N. Hammond (eds.), 1979, The Archaeology of Afghanistan, Academic Press, 91, 141-4)...If this dating is acceptable, not only is this metal the earliest tin bronze known from anywhere, but it is also an isolated occurrence of far older than its nearest rival and quite unrelated to the main development of bronze age metallurgy...

"Even more exciting is the evidence from Shortugai… In 1975, French archaeologists discovered on the surface at Shortugai, sherds of Indus pottery extending over more than a millennium - the whole span of the Indus civilization. (Lyonnet, B., 1977,

Decouverte des sites de l'age du bronze dans le N.E. de l'Afghanistan: leurs rapports avec la civilisation de l'Indus, Annali Instituto Orientali di Napoli, 37, 19-35)... Particularly important is a Harappan seal bearing an engraved rhinoceros and an inscription which reinforces the belief that the site was a trading post. Shortugai is only 800 km from Harappa, as the crow flies, though the journey involves hundreds of kilometres of mountainous terrain through the Hindu Kush...Lyonnet's conclusion was that the most likely explanation for their existence was an interest in 'the mineral resources of the Iranian Plateau and of Central Asia', to which can now be added those of Afghanistan itself. Indus contacts extended well into Turkmenia where the principal bronze age settlements, such as Altin-depe and Namasga-depe, lie close to the Iranian border...

"A fine copper axe-adze from Harappa, and similar bronze examples from Chanhu-daro and, in Baluchistan, at Shahi-tump, are rare imports of the superior shaft-hole implements developed initially in Mesopotamia before 3000 BC. In northern Iran examples have been found at Shah Tepe, Tureng Tepe, and Tepe Hissar in level IIIc (2000-1500 BC)...Tin was more commonly used in eastern Iran, an area only now emerging from obscurity through the excavation of key sites such as Tepe Yahya and Shahdad. In level IVb (ca. 3000 BCE)at Tepe yahya was found a dagger of 3% tin bronze. (Lamberg-Karlovsky, C.C. and M., 1971, An early city in Iran, Scientific American, 1971, 224, No. 6, 102-11; Muhly, 1973, Appendix 11, 347); perhaps the result of using a tin-rich copper ore. However, in later levels tin bronze became a 'significant element in its material culture' comparatble with other evidence from south-east Iran where at Shadad bronze shaft-hole axes and bronze vessels were found in graves dated to ca. 2500 BC. (Burney, C., 1975, From village to empire: an introduction to Near Eastern Archaeology, 1977, Phaidon). The richness of Tepe Yahha, Shahr-i-Sokhta, and Shadad, are all indicative of trade and 'an accumulation of wealth unsuspected from the area'. (Lamberg-Karlovsky, 1973, reviewing Masson and Sarianidi (1972) in Antiquity, 43-6)....Namazga-depe and neighbouring sites are a long

way from the important tin reserves of Fergana...The origin of Near Eastern tin remains unproven; the geological evidence would favour the deposits of Fergana and the Tien Shan range..."[288]
Euphrates the copper river or URUDU and Tin from Meluhha "A copper trade down the Euphrates is extremely ancient; the river's original name was Urudu or 'copper river'. (Hawkes, J. (ed.), 1977, *The First Civilizations*, London, Pelican: 159, 167-8)...The whole purpose of sending Assyrian merchants to Anatolia was to ensure a steady supply of Anatolian silver and some gold. In exchange they gave cloth and tin, 'transported by caravans of black donkeys bred in Assyria'. They made a profit on the cloth of 100% and on the tin of 75-100%. The quantities traded could be considerable; a cargo of 410 talents of tin (more than 12 t) is once mentioned, though for some curious reason tin prices are never recorded. Trade with Kanesh continued until ca. 1757 BC when Hammurabi of Babylon destroyed Mari (900 km. up the Euphrates) and a period of wars followed which reduced 'central Anatolia, once rich, to a land of ruins'. The Kanesh tablets give no indicatin of where Assyrian tin came from...The texts from Mari show a way out of the difficulty by also recording tin being shipped up the Euphrates, presumably from the Persian Gulf, pointing to a distant origin involving maritime trade...The Arab geographer Muqadasi stated that tin occurred at Hamadan, 560 km south-west of Tehran. As Muhly wrote, 'a mineral zone running roughly from Hamadan to Tabriz seems to fit all the evidence for the Near Eastern tin trade'.[289]

Sea-faring merchants of Melukkha (Meluhha) and trade route of tin ingots

Mleccha trade was first mentioned by Sargon of Akkad (Mesopotamia 2370 B.C.) who stated that boats from Dilmun, Magan and Meluhha came to the quay of Akkad.290 The Mesopotamian imports from Meluhha were: woods, copper (ayas), gold, silver, carnelina, cotton, ivory, uśu wood (ebony), and another wood which is translated as 'sea wood' – perhaps mangrove wood on the coasts of Sind ad Baluchistan.[291] Gudea sent expeditions in 2200 B.C. to Makkan and Meluhha in search of hard wood.

Seal impression with the cotton cloth from Umma[292] and cotton cloth piece stuck to the base of a silver vase from Mohenjodaro[293] are indicative evidence.

"...an imprint of (Indus (Sarasvati-Sindhu)) seal upon the fragment of a clay label from a bale of cloth had also been published by Father Scheil[294] and this was said to come from the site of Umma, the neighbor city of Lagash...(Gadd, 1932, pp.3-32.)

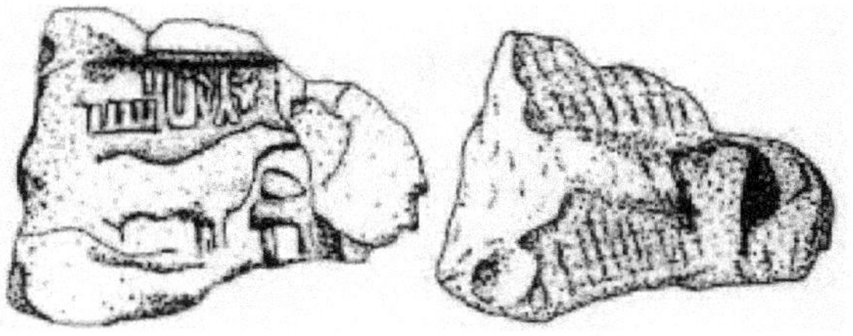

Sealing. Umma. Text 9811 Impression of a seal from Umma. One-hornd young bull. Scheil 1925. Indicative of the receipt of goods from the Sarasvati-Sindhu and of the possible presence of Indus traders in Mesopotamia. Tell Asmar seals, together with ceramics, knobbed ware, etched beads and kidney shaped inlay of bone provide supporting evidence for this possibility.

Babylonian and Greek names for cotton were: sind, sindon. This is an apparent reference to the cotton produced in the black cotton soils of Sind and Gujarat. Ca. 2150-2000 BC, ivory from Meluhha is mentioned in connection with ivory bird figurines.[295] About 2000 BCE at Ur, ivory is attributed to Dilmun (Bahrein), perhaps shipped up the Gulf from the Indus where tusks and ivory objects were plentiful. Isin-Larsa period (ca. 2000-1800 BCE) texts refer to rods, combs, inlays, boxes, spoons, and 'breastplates' of ivory donated to temples by merchants returning from Dilmun.[296]

Gudea notes that from Magan comes bronze and from the land Meluhha are derived ushu-wood, gold, precious stones and copper. "In the power of Nina and in the power of Ningirsu for Gudea, to whom a scepter was given by Ningirsu, have Magan, Meluhha, Gubin, and the land Tilmun, each of which possesses every kind o tree, brought to Shirpurla ships (laden) with wood for his buildings" (Statue D, iv.2-12). Copper of Dilmun, Magan and Meluhha is mentioned in a text.[297]

The Ur texts specifically refer to 'seafaring country of Meluhha" and hence, Leemans' thesis that Meluhha was the west coast (modern state of Gujarat) of Bhārata. The Lothal dockyard had fallen into disuse by c.1800 BCE, a date when the trade between Mesopotamia and Meluhha also ended. [WF Leemans, 'Old Babylonian Letters and Economic History', Journal of Economic and Social History of the Orient, vol. XI, 1968, pp. 215-26. P. Aalto, 1971, 'Marginal Notes on the Meluhha Problem,' Professor KA Nilakanta Sastri Felicitation Volume, Madras, pp. 222-23.] In Leemans' view, Gujarat was the last bulwark of the (Indus or Sarasvati) Civilization. Records refer to Meluhhan ships docking at Sumer. There were Meluhhans in various Sumerian cities; there was also a Meluhhan town or district at one city. The Sumerian records indicate a large volume of trade; according to a Sumerian tablet, one shipment from Meluhha contained 5,900 kg of copper (13,000 lbs, or 6 ½ tons)! The bulk of this trade was done through Dilmun, not directly with Meluhha. In our view, the formative stages of the Civilization also had their locus in the coastal areas – in particular, the Gulf of Khambat, Gulf of Kutch and Makran coast, as evidenced by the wide shell-bangle, dated to c. 6500 BCE, made of turbinella pyrum or śankha, found in Mehergarh, 300 miles north of the Makran coast.

'Melukkha' is cognate with Pali 'milakkha' or Sanskrit 'mleccha'. In Pali, 'milakkha' also means, 'copper'. In Sanskrit, 'mleccha-mukha' means 'copper'.

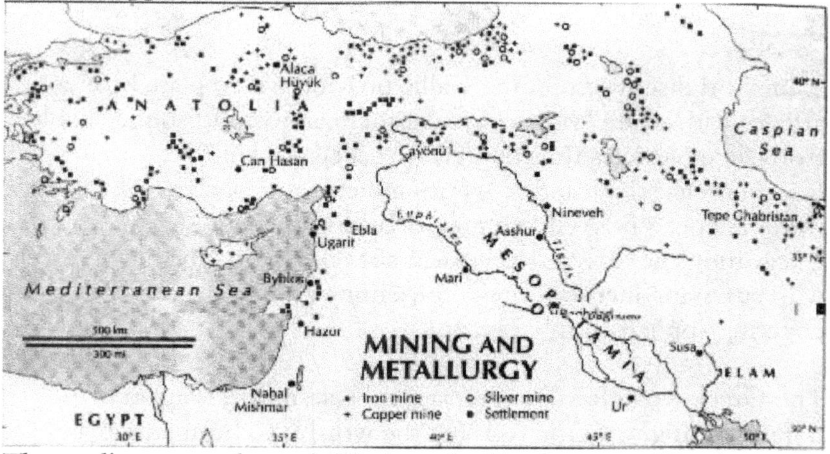

The trading route through Mari on the Euphrates to Ugarit (Mediterranean Sea) and on to Minoan Crete.[298]
This routing may explain the presence of Harappan script inscription on tin ingots found at Haifa, Israel!

The body of water called the Red Sea, Gulf of Aden, Arabian Gulf, Gulf of Oman and the Arabian Sea were referred to by Herodotus as the Erythraean Sea. Dilmun is identified with Bahrain, Magan with Oman and Melukkha with the Indian Civilization. Sargon of Akkad boasts that ships from Dilmun, Magan and Melukkha docked at the quay of his capital Akkad. This inscription affirms that Melukkha was accessible by the sea-route, through the Arabian gulf.There is significant evidence for the presence of people and goods from and frequent interaction with the Indian Civilization in the Mesopotamian and Gulf areas. There is, however, little evidence of a Sumerian, Akkadian or Babylonian presence in India.

"Latin *stagnum-stannum* only comes to mean 'tin' in Late Latin. The word originally designates 'a mixture of lead and silver'. Again, it si not clear why the word came to mean 'tin'. The original Latin designation for tin is not a distinct word at all, but the expression *plumbum album,* sometimes *plumbum candidum,* literally 'white lead'...Pliny refers to a practice of plating objects with tin to give them the appearance of silver:

A method discovered in the Gallic provinces is to plate bronze articles with white lead as to make them almost indistinguishable from silver; articles thus treated are called 'inoctilia'.
Recent archaeological discoveries indicate that such deceptions were practiced not only on metal objects, but also in clay. Excavations at several Mycenaean sites have produced clay vessels with surviving incrustations representing an original tinfoil covering applied with beeswax...

The Greek word for tin, Κασσίτερος/Kassiteros, is again of unknown origin...Some feel that the word is to be analyzed as *kassi-ti-ra,* 'from the land of the Kassites'. This derivation is of considerable interest in the light of the suggested connection of the Kassites with the Zagros mountains and the indications...that this area might have been an important source of tin. Yet this etymology is quite improbable and cannot be substantiated...there is no indication that the Greeks played any role in (Celtic) trade before the founding of the Massalia (modern Marseilles) around 600 BC. Since the Greeks did not come into contact with the Celtic peoples of Gaul much before the end of the seventh century BC, it would be strange to find a Celtic word already in Homer...this factor...rules out a Celtic origin for *kassiteros*...there is no common Indo-European word for tin. Of course the various Romance languages have a common word borrowed from Latin, and the various Germanic languages (with the exception of Gothic) seem to have a common word which may ultimately derive from the same source. This is all the result of a late development. The fact that Latin uses an expression like *plumbum album* to mean 'tin', indicates that the language lacked a real word for the metal...In fact, the earliest Indo-European texts, such as the Mycenaean Linear B tablets and the earliest Sanskrit texts, seem to lack a word for tin. What of Hittite? Unfortunately, here the situation is once again problematic. A word has been suggested, namely **dankui-*. However, even if correct, it says nothing significant about the source of tin in the Hittite empire. The word is clearly a manufactured one, derived from the adjective *dankui*, 'dark', very common in Hittite texts, especially in reference to the dark earth...a lexical text from Ras Shamra seems to equate the Hittite **dankui-* with Sumerian An.NA, Akkadian *ana_ku,* both words now translated 'tin.' Also, if the reference is to the black tinstone of alluvial deposits, the name is quite appropriate.

"The basic Hebrew word for tin is *bedi_l.* The principal reference is from the book of Ezekiel:

Tarshish traded with you because of your abundant wealth of every kind; she bartered with you silver, iron, tin, and lead.
This passage suggests that tin came to Israel from Tarshish, sometimes identified with the south coast of Iberia. The tin trade with Tarshish is thought to have been in the hands of the Phoenicians...this Hebrew word for tin has been compared with Sanskrit *pa_t.i_rah,* 'tin'...a late lexical word in Sanskrit, and seems to belong to that group of words which includes French *peautre,* Italian *peltro* and English *pewter.* These words all go back to an original **peltirum* or **peltrum,* often said to be of Ligurian origin...these words may all be based on the stem **pel-,* meaning 'gray, blackish'...the Old Testament has another word which may represent tin. *Ana_k* is traditionally translated 'plumb line' or 'plummet'. The most important reference is in the book of Amos: Thus he showed me, and lo, the Lord was standing upon a wall, with a plumb line in his hand.

"...if Hebrew *anāk* is to be compared with Akkadian *anāku*, then the *Homat. anāk* should be 'a wall made of tin'. ..The Sumerian An.NA is sometimes transcribed *nagga*, but there are objections to this reading and it is best to retain the reading AN.NA, in capitals. The meaning 'tin' is established by the fact that the cuneiform texts contain recipes involving the mixture of copper [Sum. *urudu*,

Akk. *eru*) with AN.NA in order to produce what can only be bronze (Sum. *zabar*, Akk. *siparru*). The first of these texts dates from the pre-Sargonic period: *1 ma.na 1/3 urudu luh ha AN.NA bi gin 13 igi 3 gal* (That is, 80 shekels of pure copper and 13 1/3 shekels of tin are mixed together, producing a bronze with a copper-tin ratio of 6:1. The Sumerian texts from the Third Dynasty of Ur uses the expression *zabar-7-la*, indicating a bronze with a copper-tin ratio of 6:1. A ratio of 7:1 is also known from this period as the following text indicates: *5 gin AN.NA 1/2 ma.na 5 gin urudu luh-ha* (Here 5 shekels of tin are mixed with 35 shekels of copper giving a copper-tin ratio of 7:1). In the Old Babylonian period, the ratio is again 6:1: *3 ma.na zabar s'a 6 ba-al.lu* (three minas of bronze mixed (in the ratio) of six (to one)

"...Such a ratio means a bronze with about 17% tin...This connection between the texts mentioning the mixture of URUDU and AN.NA and the copper-tin ratio established through the analysis of ancient Mesopotamian bronzes is one of the most convincing arguments for the translation of AN.NA as 'tin'...A bilingual literary text refers to the fire-god: urudu AN>NA III.III bi za e-me-en *s'a e-ri i u a-na-ki mu-bal-lil-s'u-nu at-ta*□ (you (fire) are the one who makes an alloy of copper and tin.)...The Akkadian word seems to have cognates in Hebrew *ana_k*, Arabic *a_nuk*, Syriac *a_neka_*, Ethiopic *na_'ek*, and perhaps even Armenian *anag*...already in the Old Akkadian period, there are references to ingots of tin called *s'uqlu* and weighing about 25 kg. The Old Babylonian letters from Mari refer to tin in a form designated by the word *le_'um*. This word, usually translated 'tablet,' is also used to designate the Neo-Assyrian hinged wax-covered ivory writing board foundat Nimrud in 1953. The Mari references must be to an ingot of tin shaped something like a tablet. The Cape Gelidonya ship-wreck has now produced a Late Bronze Age example of a tin ingot. The excavator of the wreck, G.F. Bass, says of this find:

At Gelidonya, therefore, we may have the shape of the end of a tin ingot which was six centimeters on a side; the length of the bar is unknown. Such a shape would correspond to the larger ingot which we have identified in the tomb of Nebamu_n and Ipuky... "...In addition to these ingots there also tin, as well as copper, ingots from the site of Harappa. (C.C. Lamberg Karlovsky, *American Anthropologist*, 69 (1967) 145-162, p. 149).The existence of tin ingots is well attested for all periods and all areas of the ancient world, from ca. 2000 BC. to 400 AD. Such an ingot the Egyptians called a *nms'.t dh* and *dh* must then be the Egyptian word for tin... "The myth of Inanna and Mount Ebih also mentions 'the high mountain land, the mountain land of carnelian and of lapis lazuli' (kur.BAD-na kur-na gug-na za-gin-na) which is of interest as there seems to be, as will be shown below, some connection between the source of tin and the sources of carnelian and lapis lazuli...since one of the exemplars of this myth mentions Enheduanna, the daughter of Sargon of Akkad, it would seem that the work may go back to the Agade period.

Tin used in Indus Valley civilization is well attested. (Muhly 1985: 283; Stech and Pigott 1986: 43-4). Gudea ca. 2100 BCE, identified Meluhha as the source of his tin (Falkenstein 1966: i.48: Cylinder B: XIV). "...tin may well often have travelled by sea up the Gulf from distribution centres in the Indus Valley. In the Old Babylonian period tin was shipped through Dilmun (Leemans 1960: 35)... It is now known that Afghanistan has two zones of tin mineralization. One embraces much of eastern Afghanistan from south of Kandahar to Badakshan in the north-east corner of the country; the other lies to the west and extends from Seistan north towards Herat (Cleuziou and Berthoud 1982), the valley of the Sarkar river, where the hills are granitic. Here tin appears commonly as cassiterite, frequently associated with copper, gold, and lead, and in quantities sufficient to attract attention in antiquity. Bronzes at Mundigak, and the controversial Snake Cave artefacts, indicate local use of bronze by at least the third millennium BCE (Shaffer 1978: 89, 115, 144). A number of scholars have pointed out the possibility that tin arrived with gold and lapis lazuli in Sumer through the same trade network, linking Afghanistan with the head of the Gulf, both by land and sea

(Stech and Pigott 1986: 41-4)." (Moorey, 1994: 298-299). "Tin from 'Meluhha'...According to the Larsa texts, merchants were there (in Mari and Larsa) to purchase copper and tin: the copper came from Magan in Oman, via Tilmun (Bahrain), but the origin of the tin is left in question. Tin mines in north-west Iran or the Transcaucasus are highly unlikely. Fortunately, there is evidence for another tin source in texts from Lagash. Lagash, about 50 km east of Larsa, was of minor importance except under the governorship of Gudea (ca. 2143-2124 BC). His inscriptions indicate extensive trade: gold from Cilicia in Anatolia, marble from Amurra in Syria, and cedar wood from the Amanus Mountains between these two countries, while up through the Persian Gulf or 'Southern Sea' came more timber, porphyry (strictly a purplish rock), lapis lazuli and tin. (Muhly 1973: 404).

"...The mountains of Lūristan are also the location of the land of Barahs'e, known from the Neo-Sumerian period as Marhaśi...One of the texts from al-Rimah does refer to fifty minas of tin from the Nairi-lands. The Nairi-lands are now fairly well known, especially as they appear in the inscriptions of Tukulti-Ninurta I and Tiglath-Pileser I. They occupy the area northwest of Assyria, the region of Diyarbakir and the lands to the east of it, with a population said to be related to the later Urartaeans. The 'sea of the Nairi-lands' (*tamdi śa māt na-i-ri*) would then be identified with Lake Van...

On the west bank of the Tigris River...Ashur was the religious capital of ancient Assyria. Ashur was also the name of the the country and the main deity. The city was founded around 2500 BCE (during Fourth Dynasty) by settlers from Syria or from the south.

Tukulti-Ninurta I (1244-1207 BCE) fire-altar is for divinity Nuska.

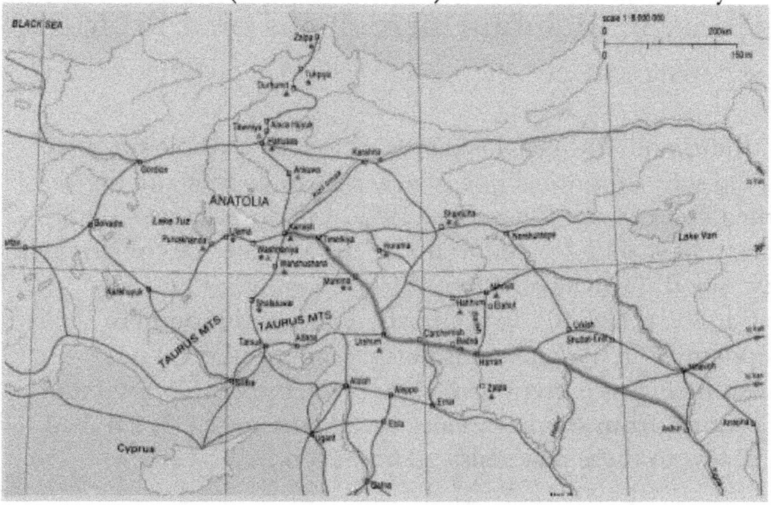

Some routes of the Old Assyrian Trade.[299]

Appendix P: Meluhha hieroglyphs on a Proto-Cuneiform tablet

"The Indus and Ghaggar-Hakra plains area as a whole possessed from the start substantial potential access to copper and tin ores (on their sources, see Dhavalikar 1995, 132-36; Kenoyer 1998, 94; Ratnagar 2004, 119-28) and to numerous varieties of construction-quality wood (Dhavalikar 1995, 150-51; Kenoyer 1998, 57; Ratnagar 2004, 128-40). In contrast, neither early southern Mesopotamia (in particular with respect to metal ores) nor predynastic Egypt (except with respect to copper imported into the far north from southern Palestine. [Harrison 1993, 83]) had such access to these materials." (Thompson 2006, 12).

Obverse: The hieroglyphs on obverse signify 'smelter, working in iron' (*koḷ*), copper metal (*lōha*) and worker in wood and iron (*badhoe*). The center-piece, stalk signifies: *kāṇḍā* 'metalware, tools, pots and pans' (Marathi); *kaṇḍa* 'stone (ore)(Gadba)'

1. a tiger, a fox on leashes held by a man: *kol* 'tiger' Rebus: *kol* 'working in iron, alloys' *lo* 'fox' (WPah.) Rebus: *lōha* 'copper metal' (Pali)

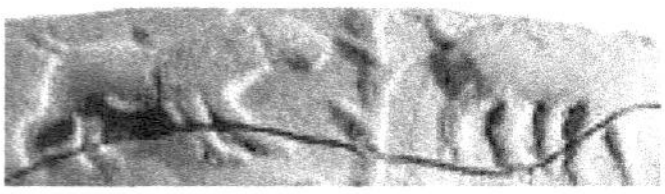

2. a procession of boars (rhinoceros?) and tiger in two rows *badhi* 'castrated boar', 'rhinoceros' Rebus: *badhoe* 'worker in wood and iron'.

kola 'tiger' Rebus: kol 'Kole, smeler of iron'; *kol* 'iron'.

3. *kaṇḍa* -- m.n. ' joint of stalk, stalk (Pali) *kāṇḍá* काण्डः m. the stalk or stem of a reed, grass, or the like, straw. Rebus 1: *kaṇḍa* 'stone (ore)(Gadba)' Ga. (Oll.) *kanḍ*, (S.) *kanḍu* (pl.

kanḍkil) stone (DEDR 1298). *gaḍa* 'large stone'. Rebus 2: *kāṇḍā* 'metalware, tools, pots and pans' (Marathi).

Reverse: The hieroglyphs on reverse signify products out of a smelting furnace and working with stone (ore).

Hieroglyph of a twig or sprout is repeated in three columns in top register. Hieroglyph of tiger + stalk in bottom register.

a twig, sprout (or tree branch) *kūdī, kūṭī* bunch of twigs (Sanskrit) Rebus: *kuṭhi* 'smelting furnace' (Santali)

kaṇḍa -- m.n. ' joint of stalk, stalk (Pali) Rebus 1: *kaṇḍa* 'stone (ore)(Gadba) Rebus 2: *kāṇḍā* 'metalware, tools, pots and pans' (Marathi).

The blurb of Metropolitan Museum of Art catalog says "The seal impression depicts a male figure guiding two dogs on a leash and hunting or herding boars in a marsh environment."

Line drawing showing the seal impression on this tablet. Illustration by Abdallah Kahil. Proto-Cuneiform tablet with seal impressions. Jemdet Nasr period, ca. 3100-2900 BCE. Mesopotamia. Clay H. 5.5 cm; W.7 cm.300.

Thanks to Abdallah Kahil for the line drawing which clearly demonstrates that the narrative is NOT 'a hunting with dogs or herding boars in a marsh environment.'

The hieroglyphs on the Proto-Cuneiform tablet records information. The hieroglyphs are signifiers together with some symbolic forms of cuneiform script. A male figure is guiding dogs (?Tigers) and herding boars in a reed marsh. Both tiger and boar are Meluhha hieroglyphs, together with the hieroglyph of a stalk on the top register (obverse). All these hieroglyphs are read rebus in Meluhha (mleccha) language, of Indian *sprachbund* in the context of metalware catalogs of bronze age.

Alternative 1: *Ka.* (Hav.) *aḍaru* twig (Bark.) *aḍïrï* small and thin branch of a tree; (Gowda) *aḍəri* small branches. *Tu.* aḍaru twig.(DEDR 67) Rebus: *aduru gan.iyinda tegadu karagade iruva aduru* = ore taken from the mine and not subjected to melting in a furnace (Ka. Siddhānti Subrahmaṇya Śastri, 1872, *New interpretation of the AmarakoŚa*, Bangalore, Vicaradarpana Press, p.330).

Alternative 2: *kūdī, kūṭī* bunch of twigs (Skt.lex.) kūdī (also written as kūṭī in manuscripts) occurs in the Atharvaveda (AV 5.19.12) and Kauśika Sūtra301 denotes it as a twig. This is identified as that of Badarī, the jujube tied to the body of the dead to efface their traces.[302] Rebus: *kuṭhi* 'smelting furnace' (Santali)

Alternative 3 Rebus: If the imagery of stalk connoted a palm-frond, the rebus readings are: Ku. N. tāmo (pl. ' young bamboo shoots '), A. tām, B. tā̃bā, tāmā, Or. tambā, Bi tā̃bā, Mth. tām, tāmā, Bhoj. tāmā, H. tām in cmpds., tā̃bā, tāmā m. (CDIAL 5779) Rebus: tāmrá ' dark red, copper -- coloured ' VS., n. ' copper ' Kauś., tāmraka -- n. Yājñ. [Cf. tamrá -- . -- √tam?] Pa. tamba -- ' red ', n. ' copper ', Pk. taṁba -- adj. and n.; Dm. trāmba -- ' red ' (in trāmba -- laċuk ' raspberry ' NTS xii 192); Bshk. lām ' copper, piece of bad pine -- wood (< ' *red wood '?); Phal. tāmba ' copper ' (→ Sh.koh. tāmbā), K. trām m. (→ Sh.gil. gur. trām m.), S. ṭrāmo m., L. trāmā, (Ju.) tarāmā̃ m., P. tāmbā m., WPah. bhad. ṭḷām n., kiũth. cāmbā, sod. cambo, jaun. tā̃bō (CDIAL 5779) tabāshīr तबाशीर् । त्वक्‌्क्षीरी f. the sugar of the bamboo, bamboo-manna (a siliceous deposit on the joints of the bamboo) (Kashmiri)

It is noteworthy that cuneiform which evolved in Mesopotamia (Elam) almost at the same time that Meluhha hieroglyph writing was evidenced on tablets, cylinder seals and other artifacts in Sarasvati civilization.

Harppa. Potsherd with incisions of three glyphs. "The earliest (Indus) inscriptions date back to 3500 BC." h1522A sherd.

Inscribed Ravi sherd. Hieroglyphs signifying *tabernae montana*, wilf fragrant tulip. It is not mere coincidence that evidence of early writing which has been discovered by the Harvard (HARP) project showing hieroglyphs on a potsherd were dated to ca. 3300 BCE – a date close to the date of the Jemdet-Nasr period Proto-Cuneiform tablet.

Traces of hieroglyphs are found on both sides of the Proto-Cuneiform tablet which also contains a proto-cuneiform wedge-shaped 'script' signs.

We wish every success for efforts at decoding proto-elamite script using Reflectance Transformation Imaging (RTI) System (see below).

A Proto-Cuneiform tablet with multiple seal impressions has the following Metmuseum catalog write-up: [quote] Administrative tablet with cylinder seal impression of a male figure, hunting dogs, and boars, 3100–2900 B.C.; Jemdet Nasr period (Uruk III script) Mesopotamia ClayH. 2 in. (5.3 cm) Purchase, Raymond and Beverly Sackler Gift, 1988 (1988.433.1) ON VIEW: GALLERY 402 Last Updated April 26, 2013 In about 3300 B.C., writing was invented in Mesopotamia, perhaps in the city of Uruk, where the earliest inscribed clay tablets have been found in abundance. This was not an isolated development but occurred during a period of profound transformation in politics, the economy, and representational art. During the Uruk period of the fourth millennium B.C., the first Mesopotamian cities were settled, the first kings were crowned, and a range of goods—from ceramic vessels to textiles—were mass-produced in state workshops. Early writing was used primarily as a means of recording and storing economic information, but from the beginning a significant component of the written tradition consisted of lists of words and names that scribes needed to know in order to keep their accounts. Signs were drawn with a reed stylus on pillow-shaped tablets, most of which were only a few inches wide. The stylus left small marks in the clay which we call cuneiform, or wedge-shaped, writing. This tablet most likely documents grain distributed by a large temple, although the absence of verbs in early texts makes them difficult to interpret with certainty. [unquote][303]

It is surmised that one of the animals being shown in a procession flanked by two stalks is a boar based on another, comparable, procession narrative on a serpentine seal of Uruk and Jemdet Nasr:

Late Uruk and Jemdet Nasr seal; ca. 3200-3000 BC; serpentine; cat.1; boar and bull in procession; terminal: stalk; heavily pitted surface beyond stalk of plant.

Boar or rhinoceros in procession. Cylinder seal impression:

642

Rhinoceros, elephant, lizard (gharial?).Tell Asmar (Eshnunna), Iraq. IM 14674; glazed steatite. Frankfort, 1955, No. 642; Collon, 1987, Fig. 610.

Cuneiform writing was most probably invented in Uruk in southern Mesopotamia (modern Iraq) about 3400 - 3300 BCE.[304] "It was invented to keep records of goods and services, and the language that was recorded was, as far as we can tell, Sumerian. The cuneiform script was later adopted by other people speaking languages as different as Akkadian, a Semitic language, and Hittite, an Indo-European language. Sumerian itself is, as far as we know, not related to any other living language. It is a language isolate."

Appendix Q: Archaeological context is a cultural context for symbolic forms of 'meanings'

The monograph of Prof. Massimo Vidale is a veritable masterpiece in explaining the archaeological context related to the Indus script and should be read by every aspiring anthropologist, archaeologist and student of languages.

It is not surprising that the authors of the illiterate harappan thesis have NOT responded to Vidale's powerful critique so far.

We can only quote Gould 2003: 47 as Vidale does at the beginning of the monograph: "Nothing matches the holiness and fascination of accurate and intricate detail. How can you appreciate a castle if you don't cherish all the building blocks, and don't understand the blood, toil, sweat, and tears underlying its construction?"

Indus writing hieroglyphs conveyed the sounds and words of an unidentified language: Meluhha. Hence, the writing is called Meluhha hieroglyphs.

A successful translation demonstrates the glosses of this Meluhha language.

The content is related to stone- and metal-work which is independently and reasonably tested using archaeological contexts.

Since the key, the cipher of the writing system is known to be rebus, the entire writing system is read as cipher texts of hieroglyphs deployed as sememe-graphs. This rebus cipher takes away the need for any guesses related to the information or knowledge communicated through the written language.

Length of a text is correlated to the information conveyed by the text. Length of a text can be short as on Greek ceramics very short texts were adequate to coney name (of owner, painter or potter), vessel' form, price and dedication to *amasioi* or lovers. "The words *kalos, kale* are 5 and 4 characters only, but written on serving and drinking cups in banquets they acquired specific and widely recognized meanings…An inscription of three characters incised on an Indus shipping jar, although short, might have conveyed as well in its functional contexts substantial information of key instructions…The early pictographic accounting tablets from Uruk may be as short as the texts of the Indus seals or those incised on some types of Indus vessels…inscriptions on Near Easter cylinder seals, in the second half of the 3rd millennium BCE, are frequently as long as the Indus ones, and nonetheless the short texts combine themselves with the iconography to convey some important messages about the identity of the bearer. The common assumption that the Indus texts, too, may report a combination of pictographic and syllabic signs, perhaps expressing – together with the standardized animal icons that figure below the inscriptions in the standard steatite seals – a system of social coordinates, attributions or functions and names stands unthreatened, as it remains compatible with the length of the sequences."(Vidale, Massimo, The collapse melts down, pp.335-336)

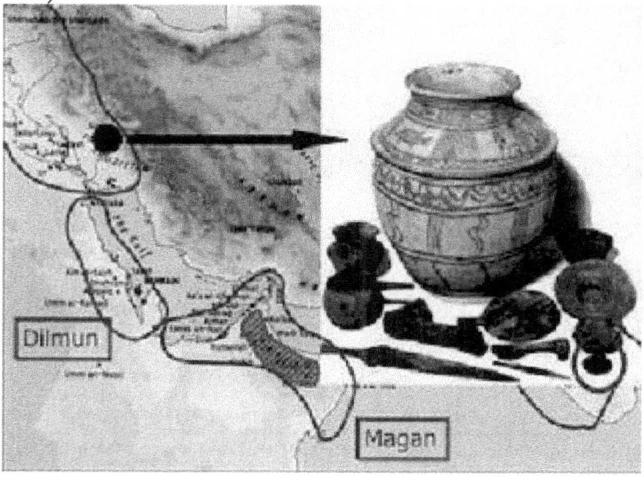

Susa pot, from Meluhha, with metal artifacts. The pot has an inscription, painted with 'fish' hieroglyph.

Is it not reasonable to relate the 'fish' hieroglyph painted on the rim of the pot, to the contents – metal artifacts, tools – contained in the pot?

"Actually, archaeological data show that Indus script was largely used as an important component of the information conveyed by steatite stamp seals, and that these seals were frequently impressed on special lumps of fine clay applied on doors, lids of vessels and chests, packages. At Mohenjo-daro stamp-sealed tags were found around the mouth of special vessels coated with straw and chaff, used to fire at high temperature in large vertical kilns stoneware bangles (Halim & Vidle 1984; Vidale 1994). This is one of the few direct proofs of the use of a seal for managing craft production so far identified in the whole archaeological territory of the ancient Near East and South Asia...Sealings with impressions of square steatite seals were used for monitoring the closure and opening of vessels, doors (with cylindrical pegs, and most probably with more complicated wooden sliding locks), perhaps animal cages, wooden boxes or chests, hales packed with light materials and secured with string, and special firing containers or saggars...That the use of steatite seals was somehow tied to management of craft production and trade of valuable goods, in the light of this archaeological evidence, is hardly questionable. Note also that there is no evidence, so far, that seals and sealings were used in centralized technologies of gathering, and redistribution of primary agricultural production, nor seals and sealings have been found, after more than 80 years of excavations, in any context suggesting performance of rituals and the like." (Vidale, Massimo, pp.354-355.)

These remarkable insights by Massimo Vidale point to the reliability of rebus readings of Meluhha hieroglyphs in the context of stone-ware and metal-ware activities and trade.

"Indus steatite stamp seals contain three orders of information: inscription, animalistic icon (realistic or imaginary) and often an object in front of the creature...Both at Harappa and Mohenjo-Daro, as well as in more important assemblages from other sites, the majority of the seals bears the image of the unicorn. The most complex administrative documents we have are clay sealings found at Mohenjo-Daro, Harappa, Lothal, Kalibangan and perhaps more recently at Bagasra, a site deeply involved in various specialized craft activities (Sonawane et al 2003), where unicorn seals were stamped one onto another, obliterating as a rule the common symbol of the unicorn, but carefully preserving, one below the other, the inscriptions – the expression and detailed recording of a chain of official responsibility."(Vidale, Massimo, p.356)

The rebus readings of Meluhha hieroglyphs covers all three orders of information: inscription, animalistic icon and often an object in front of the creature.

1. The inscription describes the bill of lading of a stone-ware or metal-ware consignment
2. The animalistic icon, say, unicorn describes that the consignment is coming out of a turner's or brazier's workshop.

sangaḍa 'lathe' (Marathi) *sangaḍa* 'portable furnace'. Rebus 1: : jangaḍ 'entrusted articles on approval basis'.Rebus 2: sangaḍa 'association' (guild). Rebus 2: sangatarāsu 'stone cutter' (Telugu). sang 2 संग् m. a stone (Rām. 199, 143, 1412; YZ. 557). L. 65 gives a list of the most common local stones used for ornaments, and other purposes. These are (in his spelling) *bilor,* a white crystal; *sang-i-baswatri,* a yellow stone used in medicine; *sang-i-dálam,* used by goldsmiths; *sang-i-farash* (p. 64), a kind of slate; *sang-i-Nadid,* of a dark coffee colour; *sang-i-Nalchan,* a kind of soap-stone, from which cups and plates are made; *sang-i-Musá,* of a black colour; *sang-i-Ratel,* of a chocolate colour; *sang-i-Shalamar,* of a green colour; *sang-i-sumák,* coloured blue or purple, with green spots; *Takht-i-Sulimán,* coloured black, with white streaks. (Kashmiri)

Rebus 3: sangar 'fortification wall' (Pushto). L. *sãgaṛh* m. ' line of entrenchments, stone walls for defence '.(CDIAL 12845) saṅgī सहचरः m. an associate, companion, comrade; confederate, ally, accomplice; a partner in business. (Kashmiri)

Hence, smith guild in a fortification, which is a characteristic architectural feature of hundreds of civilization sites. The object in front of the unicorn shown often refers to *sangatarāśi* = stone-cutting (Telugu), *sā̃gāḍā* m. ' frame of a building ' (M.)(CDIAL 12859) the citadel, *sangara* and the nature of the trade transaction, *jangad*, which means goods taken on approval, held by agent on behalf of owner. *Jangad* sale is 'a sale on approval and/or consignment basis' (that is taken without definite settlement of purchase). 'Entrustment Note': It is interesting to note that this traditional trade transaction process known as '*jangaḍa*' is traceable to hieroglyphs (secret, symbolic or picture writing = ರಹಸ್ಯ,ಸಂಕೇತ ಅಥವಾ ಚಿತ್ರ ಲಿಪಿ) of Indus Scripts. *Jangad* for trade transactions from Melhuhha constituted an improvement in documentation and control of guild (Corporation) transactions over earlier system of token, tallies and bullae It also connotes a cargo boat: sangaḍa 'pair' (Marathi) Jangal/Jangāl as: (a) A wooden plank fixed across the canoe to serve as seat for passengers, (b) Two canoes joined together with flat planks on them and used for transporting vehicles across the river, a barge. Military Guard: *jangaḍiyo* 'military guards who accompanies treasure into the treasury" (Gujarati) was one who delivered products into the treasury. The business tradition of '*Jangad*' is prevalent even today among diamond merchants/cutters of India. The derivative of '*Jangadiyo*' is '*Angadia*', that is a courier who carries goods from point to point, based on 'trust'. This is well explained in meaning of *Jangad* as 'Entrust Receipt' in Diamond Platform in Mumbai.

sangaḍa 'joined animals' (Marathi). Rebus: *sangāta* 'association, guild'.

sangaḍa 'bangles' (Pali).

san:gā̃ḍo a lathe (M.); cutting stone, gilding (G.) Kashmiri. sang 2 संग् m. a stone (Rām. 199, 143, 1412; YZ. 557).

Marathi. संगीन [saṅgīna] *a* (P) Built or made of stone.

Kashmiri. sang-sār संग्□-सार् । अवहारः (सामुद्रिकजन्तुविशेषः) m.(in Ksh.) public general abuse; a shark, a water-elephant, a Gangetic crocodile (the *ghaṛiyāl* of India).

mudrā́ f. ' seal, signet -- ring ' MBh. [Prob. ← Ir. EWA ii 654]Pa. muddā -- f. ' seal, stamp ', muddikā -- f. ' signetring '; NiDoc. mu(ṁ)dra, mutra ' seal '; Pk. muddā -- , °diā -- f., °daya -- m. ' seal, ring '; S. muṇḍra f. ' seal ', °rī f. ' finger -- ring with seal '; L. mundrī f. ' ring '; P. mundar m. ' earring ', mundī f. ' ring '; Ku. munṛo ' earring ', gng. mun*lṛ ' ring ', N. mun(d)ro, MB. mudaṛī; Or. muda ' seal ', mudi ' ring ', mudā ' act of sealing '; Bi. mū̃drī ' iron ring fastening blade of scraper '; G. mū̃drī f. ' ring ', M. mudī f., Ko. muddi; Si. mudda < muduva, st. mudu -- ' seal, ring '; Md. mudi ' ring '. mudrākara m. ' maker of seals ' Si muduvarayā ' goldsmith '. (CDIAL 10203, 10204).मुद्रा mudrā a seal or any instrument used for sealing or stamping , a seal-ring , signet-ring; the stamp or impression made by a seal ; any stamp or print or mark or impression (MBh.); a stamped coin , piece of money , rupee , cash , medal (Sanskrit)

मुद्रा mudrā (in rhetoric) the natural expression of things by words , calling things by their right names (Kuvlayānanda)मुद्रा mudrā a partic. branch of education (" reckoning by the fingers "); an image , sign , badge , token (esp. a token or mark of divine attributes impressed upon the body) (Divyāvadāna).

Appendix R: *ran:ga* ‘pewter or alloy of tin (*ran:ku*), lead (*nāga*) and antimony (*añjana*)’

'The earliest and most widespread of copper alloys is arsenical copper or arsenic bronze. This alloy commonly contains from c. 1-7 percent arsenic (As), although artifacts with over 20 percent As have been recorded. Objects of arsenical copper are reported from as early as the 5th millennium BCE in Anatolia, Mesopotamia and Iran and the alloy achieved particular prominence from the 4th millennium BCE across the Near East. Arsenical copper alloys show a very long technological continuity and continued to be used for more than 1,000 years after the introduction of tin-bronze in the 3rd millennium BCE...recent research at Tepe Hissar in Iran has highlighted the possibility that, already by the 4th millennium BCE, arsenic rich 'speiss' (an iron-arsenic compound) was intentionally smelted in order to be directly alloyed with copper to make arsenical copper...In addition to Cu-As and Cu-As-Ni alloys, ternary alloys of copper, antimony, and arsenic (Cu-Sb-As) have also been recorded in the ancient Near East. The best and most significant example is provided by the hoard of Chalcolithic (c. 3600 BCE) artifacts recovered from Nahal Mishmar, the 'Cave of the Treasure', near the Dead Sea. In addition to objects of hematite and ivory, 416 copper-based artifacts were recovered there. While 17 of the metal items are commonplace tools such as axes/adzes, chisels, and hammers, the vast majority are 'cultic' or prestige items such as mace heads (242), maces/standards/scepters (120), 'crowns' (10), vessels (5), and other items without an obvious utilitarian function. Analyses indicate that the 'cultic' items are made of a range of alloys rich in arsenic (up to 15 percent As), antimony (up to 26 percent Sb), and more, rarely, nickel (up to 9 percent Ni), whereas the tools in the hoard are made of very ure copper. The 'cultic' artifacts with high

As and Sb would have hade a very clear, silvery, or even purplish metallic appearance, strongly contrasting with the reddish color of the unalloyed copper. The complex and intricate cultic Cu-Sb-As alloy artifacts are amongst the earliest examples from the Near East of objects cast using the lost-wax (*cire perdue*) techique, a technological innovation that was no doubt facilitated by the lower melting temperature of such ternary alloys. In comparison, the pure copper tools from Nahal Mishmar were cast in simple, open (unifacial) molds...Cu-Sb-As alloy metal itself was almost certainly foreign to the region.'305

Metallic antimony was erroneously identified as lead.

Silvery, lustrous grey antimony.

The largest applications for metallic antimony are as alloying material for lead and tin. Alloying lead and tin with antimony improves the properties of the alloys which are used in solders, bullets and plain bearings. Black antimony is formed upon rapid cooling of vapor derived from metallic antimony.

Antimony forms a highly useful alloy with lead, increasing its hardness and mechanical strength. For most applications involving lead, varying amounts of antimony are used as alloying metal.

The ancient words for antimony mostly have, as their chief meaning, kohl, the sulfide of antimony. Pliny the Elder, however, distinguishes between male and female forms of antimony; the male form is probably the sulfide, while the female form, which is superior, heavier, and less friable, has been suspected to be native metallic antimony.[Pliny, Natural history, 33.33; W.H.S. Jones, the Loeb Classical Library translator, supplies a note suggesting the identifications.]

An artifact, said to be part of a vase, made of antimony dating to about 3000 BC was found at Telloh, Chaldea (part of present-day Iraq), and a copper object plated with antimony dating between 2500 BC and 2200 BC has been found in Egypt.(Kirk-Othmer Encyclopedia of Chemical Technology, 5th ed. 2004.)

Antimony(III) sulfide, Sb2S3, was recognized in predynastic Egypt as an eye cosmetic (kohl) as early as about 3100 BC, when the cosmetic palette was invented.[306]

Anjali mudrā is a salutation seal; an offering, a gesture of reverence, benediction, salutation. The root is: *anj* 'to honour or celebrate'.

Seated person in penance, *āsana mudrā*

h176b

m0304A

h1971B Harappa. Three tablets with identical glyphic compositions on both sides: h1970, h1971 and h1972. Seated figure or deity with reed house or shrine at one side. Left: H95-2524; Right: H95-2487.

m1181A 2222 Pict-80: Three-faced, horned person (with a three-leaved pipal branch on the crown), wearing bangles and armlets and seated on a hoofed platform.

m0453A m453B 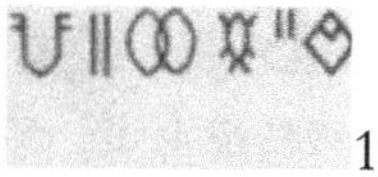 1629

Pict-82 Person seated on a pedestal flanked on either side by a kneeling adorant and a hooded serpent rearing up. The kneeling adorants in front of the hooded serpents are perhaps using Anjali mudrā.

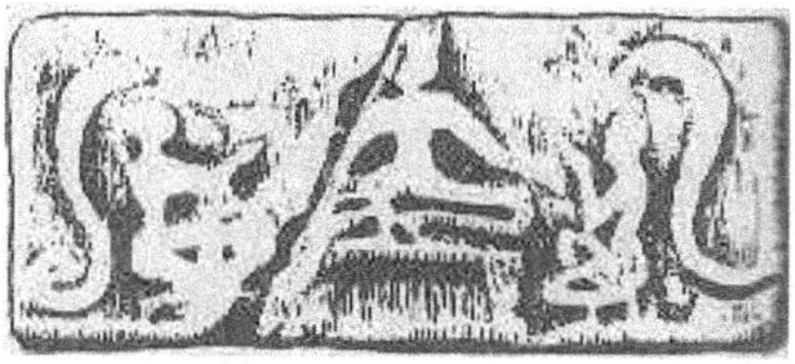

A drawing of the observe set of hieroglyphs which link it to Nahal Mishmar antimony-alloy artifacts with upto 26% antimony (Sb).

Three Meluhha hieroglyphs on this Mohenjo-Daro seal m0453 are: 1. Person seated in penance; 2. Adorants with folded hands (in *añjalí mudrā*) worship; 3. Hooded serpents: *kamaḍha* 'penance' (Prākṛt); *añci-* 'to reverence' (Tamil). *nāga* 'serpent' (Sanskrit). Rebus readings: *kamaṭa* 'coiner, mint' (Kannada); *añjana* 'antimony' (Sanskrit); *nāga* 'lead'. *paṭam* 'snake-hood' Rebus: *padm* 'Sharpness (of metal artifact)'. The message is that of an artisan working with copper, lead and antimony.

Hieroglyph: *añjalí* m. ' the hollowed hands placed together ' ŚBr.Pa. añjali -- m., añjalikā -- f., Pk. aṁjalī -- m.f.; Kho. anǰíl ' single or double handful, the hands put together palms up in salutation ', K. anzal f., P. añjlī f., Ku. ā̃julī, ā̃culī, ā̃jwāl ' double handful ', gng. ā̃jui, ā̃cui; N. ā̃juli, ā̃julo ' open palms placed together ', A. ā̃zâli, B. ā̃juli, ā̃jlā, Or. ā̃ñjuḷi, añj°, ā̃ñjuḷā, añj°, Bhoj. ā̃jurī, H. añjal, añjul, añjlā m., añjlī, añjulī f. ' double handful '; G. ā̃jḷī f. ' open palms together ', M. ā̃jḷī f., Si. ädilla; -- -- ul<-> from aṅgúli -- ; P. uñjal m. ' double handful ', Or. uñjlā, H. uñjal m., uñjlī f. with metathesis < añjul -- , or poss. < *upāñjali -- .WPah.kṭg. *andəl, ɔndəḷ* f. (poet. m.) ' both hands joined in greeting ' (obl. *anjli > andli Him.I 4), J. annal f.; Garh. ajūḷ (obl. pl. °ḷyõ) 'handful' (CDIAL 171). அஞ்சி añci, n. < añc. Chief, master; எசமானன். (யாழ். அக.)அஞ்சி[2]-த்தல் añci-, 11 v.tr. < añc. To reverence, worship; பூசித்தல். அஞ்சித்தல் சொற்ற பூசனை யடைவுமாம் (காஞ்சிப்பு. திருவே. 36). అంచితము [añcitamu] anchitamu. [Skt.] Ta. Worshipped, revered. అంచితముగా adv. Worshipfully, admirably.

అంజనరాయి [añjanarāyi] anjana-rāyi. [Skt. అంజనము+Tel. రాయి] n. Antimonium or black antimony. (Watts.) kajjala n. ' lamp -- black ' Suśr. [← Drav. or Mu. EWA 139 with lit. Former might account for N. g -- . J. Bloch BSOS v 738 puts it with kāla -- 1 as ← Drav.] Pa. Pk. kajjala -- n. ' lamp -- black (used as collyrium for the eyes) '; K. kazul, dat. °zalas m. ' lamp -- black ', S. kajalu m. (← L.); L. kajal, kajlā m. ' antimony for the eyes '; P. kajjal, kajlā m. ' lamp -- black for the eyes ' (→ WPah. bhal. kajjal m. ' collyrium '), Ku. kājal, gng. kā̃jaw, N. gājal; A. kāzal ' lamp -- black, a kind of bluish earth for marking the foreheads of women '; Or. kājal, kājara ' collyrium ', kajjaḷ, kajaḷa ' lamp -- black '; Bi. Mth. Bhoj. kājar ' collyrium '; H. kājal, kajjal, kajlā m., °lī f. ' lamp -- black, collyrium '; G. kājaḷ n. ' lampblack ', kājḷī f. ' soot ', M. kā̃jaḷ n., kā̃jḷī f.; Ko. kājjaḷa n. ' lamp -- black '. -- Deriv.: Pk. kajjalia -- ' blackened '; A. kāzalī ' dark red, purple '; M. kā̃jḷī ' made of soot '. WPah.kṭg. kä̃jəḷ m. ' lamp -- black, tattoo mark ', poet. kä̃jlu m. (Him.I 15); Garh. kājal ' lampblack, soot ' (l ← H.)(CDIAL 2622).

Ta. añcal relay, resting place on a journey, letter post; añci letter post. Ma. añcal id. Ka. añce a postal road, stage, relay, the post. Tu. añcal the post; añcidāye postman. Te. ance, anciya post, a relay of horses, palanquin-bearers, letter-carriers, etc.(DEDR 54). అంచె [añce] *anche.* [Tel. & Kan.] n. The post, a relay of horses or palankeen bearers. తపాలు, టపా. A row of things. అంచెల చెలందు at every station, మను. iv. 87. అంచెలుకట్టు v. n. To be at one's post: to wait as post runners one after another. అంచియ [añciya] anchiya. [Tel.] n. Another form of అంచె. అంచు [añcu] anṭsu. v. a. To send. To command. "అంచెలుకట్టు కాలితొడుసైచన నీవుగదమ్మ." మను. v. 72. See also అంచే. అంచ [añca] anṭsa. [Tel. & Kan.] Also అంచె. The post or mail for letters. అంచలంచలుగా పోయినారు they proceeded by relays. అంచలగుర్రాలమీద పోయిరా they rode post.

Bibliography

Asthana, S.P. 1976. History and archaeology of India's contacts with other countires: from earliest times to 300 BC, B.R. Publications Corp., Delhi.

Bibby, T.G., 1958. The 'ancient Indian Style' Seals from Bahrain, Antiquity 33: 243-246.

Chakrabarti D.K. (1982) "'Long-barrel-Cylinder' Beads and the Issue of Pre-Sargonic

Contact between the Harappan Civilization and Mesopotamia." In G.L. Possehl (ed.)

Harappan Civilization: a Contemporary Perspective. Delhi, 265-270.

Chakrabarti D.K. (1990) *The External Trade of the Indus Civilization.* New Delhi.

de Clercq, Louis. *Collection de Clercq: Catalogue Méthodique et Raisonné: Antiquités Assyriennes, Cylindres Orientauz, Cachets,Briques, Bronzes, Bas-Reliefs, Etc.* Paris: E. Leroux, 1888.

During Caspers, E.C.L. 1972. Harappan trade in the Arabian Gulf in the third millennium BC, Mesopotamia 7: 167-191.

During Caspers, E.C.L. 1982. Sumerian traders and businessmen residing in the Indus Valley cities: a critical assessment of archaeological evidence, Annali 42: 337-380.

Chakrabarti, D.K. 1977. India and West Asia--an alternative approach, Man and Environment 1:25-38.

Chakrabarti, D.K. 1978. Seals as evidence of Indus-West Asia Interrelations, in D. Chattopadhyaya, ed., History and Society, Essays in Honour of Prof. Niharranjan Ray, Calcutta, p. 93-116.

Corbiau, S. 1936. An Indo-Sumerian Cylinder, Iraq 3: 100-103.

During Caspers E.C.L. (1971) "Etched Carnelian Beads." *Bullettin of the Institute of Archaeology*, 10, 83-98.

Frankfort, H. 1934. The Indus Civilization and the Near East, Annual Bibliography of Indian Archaeology VII: 1-12.

Gadd, C.J. 1932. Seals of Ancient Indian Style found at Ur, Proc. of the British Academy, XVII: 191-210.

Gadd, C.J. and Smith, S. 1924. The new links between Indian and Babylonian Civilizations, Illus. London News, Oct. 4, p. 614-616.

Gibson, McG. 1976. The Nippur expedition, The Oriental Institute of the Univ. of Chicago Annual Report 1975/76: 26,28.

Kjaerum, P. 1980. Seals of Dilmun-Type from Failaka, Kuwait, PSAS 10: 45-53.

Kjaerum, P. 1983. *The Stamp and Cylinder Seals 1:1*, Failaka/Dilmun: The second millennium settlements, Jutland Arch. Soc. Publ. XVII:1, Aarhus.

Kramer, Samuel N. *The Sumerians: Their History, Culture and Character.* Chicago, IL: University of Chicago Press, 1963.

Lahiri N. (1992) *The Archaeology of Indian Trade Routes (upto c. 200 BC).* New Delhi.

Lamberg-Karlovsky C.C. (1972) "Trade Mechanisms in Indus-Mesopotamian Interrelations."

Journal of the American Oriental Society, 92, 2, April-June 1972, 222-229.

Mackay, E.J.H. 1925. Sumerian connections with Ancient India, JRAS: 696-701.

Mackay, E.J.H. 1931. Further Excavations at Mohenjo-daro, New Delhi.

Marshall, Sir J. 1931. Mohenjo-daro and the Indus Civilization, London.

Masson, V.M. and Sarianidi, V.I. 1972. Central Asia, Thames and Hudson, London.

Nissen, H.J. 1982. Linking distanct areas archaeologically, paper read at the 1st International Conference on Pakistan Archaeology, Peshawar.

Oppenheim, A. Leo. *Ancient Mesopotamia: Portrait of a Dead Civilization.* Chicago, IL: University of Chicago Press, 1964.

Parpola, A. 1984. New correspondences between Harappan and Near Eastern Glyptic Art, in B. Allchin, ed., South Asian Archaeology 1981, Univ. of Cambridge Oriental Publications 34, Cambridge.

Parpola, S., Parpola, A., and Brunswig, R.H. Jr. 1977. The Meluhha village: evidence of acculturation of Harappan traders in late third millennium Mesopotamia? JESHO XX: 129-165.

Pettinato G. (1972) "Il commercio con l'estero della Mesopotamia meridionale nel 3.

Millennio av. Cr. alla luce delle fonti letterarie e lessicali sumeriche." *Mesopotamia*, VII, 43-166.

Peyronel L. (2000) "Sigilli Harappani e Dilmuniti dalla Mesopotamia e dalla Susiana.

Note sul Commercio nel Golfo Arabo-Persico tra III e II Mill. a.C." *Vicino Oriente*,

12, pp. 175-240.

Possehl G.L. (1984) "Of Men." In J.M. Kenoyer (ed.) *From Sumer to Meluhha: contributions* to the archaeology of South and West Asia in memory of George F. Dales, Jr. Wisconsin Archaeological Reports, 3, pp. 179-186.

Possehl, Gregory L., 1996, *The Indus Age: The Writing System.* Philadelphia, PA: University of Pennsylvania Press.

Potts T. (1994) *Mesopotamia and the East.* Oxford.

Ratnagar, S. 1981. Encounters, the westerly trade of the Harappan Civilization, Oxford Univ. Press, Delhi.

Tosi, M. 1982. A possible Harappan Seaport in Eastern Arabia: Ra's Al Junayz in the Sultanate of Oman, paper read at the 1st International Conference on Pakistan Archaeology, Peshawar.

Tosi M. (1991) "The Indus Civilization beyond the Indian Subcontinent." In M. Jansen,M. Mulloy & G. Urban (eds.) *Forgotten cities on the Indus.* Mainz, 111-128.

Sollberger E. (1970) "The Problem of Magan and Meluhha." *Bulletin of the University*

of London, 8-9, pp. 247-250.

Vats, M.S. 1940. Excavations at Harappa, Calcutta.

Wheeler, Sir M. 1968. The Indus Civilization, Cambridge Univ. Press, Cambridge.

Yule, P. 1981. Zu den Beziehungen zwischen Mesopotamien und dem Indusgebiet im 3. und beginnenden 2. Jahrtausend.

153, 157, 158, 161, 162, 172, 185, 196, 198, 214, 225, 229, 230, 258, 260, 266, 283, 307, 316, 329, 338, 342, 350, 351, 353, 354, 356, 357, 359, 360, 369, 370, 374, 381, 382, 385, 386, 393, 394, 399, 409, 420, 423, 424, 435, 441, 452, 459, 460, 461, 465, 467, 485, 526, 528, 531, 565, 586, 591, 592, 593, 598, 599, 600, 604, 609, 620, 636, 657, 659, 665, 669, 676, 690, 691, 695, 699, 700, 702, 703, 705, 706, 707, 710, 712, 714, 715, 720, 730
buffalo, 82, 96, 125, 126, 127, 154, 155, 175, 178, 179, 180, 181, 206, 207, 212, 280, 282, 303, 341, 342, 343, 373, 396, 400, 423, 469, 524, 586, 587, 588, 589, 668
bull, 9, 25, 26, 28, 59, 71, 82, 100, 101, 102, 108, 110, 113, 116, 118, 122, 126, 127, 128, 155, 161, 165, 174, 176, 177, 180, 181, 183, 190, 192, 200, 201, 202, 204, 206, 207, 230, 231, 232, 236, 237, 238, 240, 243, 246, 247, 248, 250, 251, 252, 259, 265, 277, 278, 290, 309, 333, 334, 335, 337, 339, 340, 341, 342, 343, 345, 354, 361, 364, 368, 369, 373, 381, 385, 393, 394, 395, 396, 401, 405, 406, 407, 409, 410, 414, 415, 416, 417, 421, 423, 429, 430, 439, 442, 451, 453, 456, 457, 462, 468, 470, 471, 472, 473, 476, 478, 479, 484, 486, 487, 489, 492, 524, 538, 545, 562, 577, 587, 588, 596, 618, 620, 641, 655, 658, 659, 669, 676, 686, 688, 689, 696, 697, 709, 722
bush, 521, 632
carnelian, 13, 23, 27, 58, 83, 86, 87, 111, 166, 211, 221, 251, 258, 303, 388, 540, 605, 606, 608, 609, 611, 616, 656, 657, 701, 715
carpenter, 87, 397, 398, 399, 424, 477, 536, 631
cart, 362
cast, 190, 191, 594
casting, 3, 12, 25, 82, 146, 149, 260, 263, 264, 266, 299, 340, 359, 365, 369, 370, 372, 373, 375, 377, 378, 380, 383, 384, 385, 386, 390, 391, 409, 410, 583, 600, 634, 656, 657, 665, 674
chalcedony, 99, 111, 118, 340, 402, 403, 605

cipher, 5, 6, 7, 9, 11, 12, 21, 23, 24, 54, 132, 196, 197, 198, 205, 213, 234, 258, 265, 270, 274, 307, 485, 535, 539, 545, 546, 548, 557, 558, 559, 560, 562, 563, 575, 641, 657, 660, 663, 664, 665, 685, 724
circumgraph, 307
citadel, 263, 283, 413, 619, 620, 621, 624, 676, 728
city, 87, 233
cloth, 177, 362
comb, 182, 188, 196, 225, 229, 291, 292, 474, 592, 669
community, 46, 63, 85, 98, 172, 200, 201, 204, 216, 219, 234, 245, 352, 354, 363, 385, 400, 405, 414, 415, 424, 453, 476, 486, 548, 550, 572, 616, 687
composite animal, 24, 82, 231, 428, 468
conch, 25
copper, 3, 9, 12, 27, 28, 30, 32, 42, 60, 71, 72, 74, 79, 81, 83, 86, 87, 97, 98, 100, 101, 102, 106, 125, 128, 134, 135, 140, 141, 145, 146, 149, 150, 154, 157, 158, 159, 160, 161, 162, 165, 167, 171, 175, 176, 178, 179, 183, 187, 189, 193, 196, 198, 201, 202, 204, 205, 206, 209, 212, 215, 217, 219, 230, 231, 232, 234, 251, 258, 260, 266, 275, 276, 279, 280, 281, 283, 286, 287, 289, 290, 291, 300, 309, 329, 333, 334, 338, 340, 342, 349, 356, 357, 359, 360, 362, 364, 365, 368, 370, 373, 378, 380, 381, 386, 388, 390, 391, 392, 394, 395, 396, 397, 406, 408, 409, 410, 412, 413, 414, 420, 433, 434, 437, 439, 440, 441, 442, 443, 445, 446, 447, 449, 452, 454, 459, 461, 463, 465, 467, 472, 478, 480, 481, 483, 524, 527, 529, 546, 558, 563, 565, 584, 586, 587, 590, 591, 592, 593, 594, 595, 599, 600, 604, 605, 606, 608, 609, 610, 612, 614, 615, 617, 618, 620, 621, 622, 623, 624, 633, 634, 637, 638, 654, 657, 660, 665, 670, 674, 676, 684, 685, 690, 695, 696, 697, 698, 699, 700, 701, 702, 703, 704, 705, 706, 707, 708, 710, 711, 713, 714, 715, 716, 718, 720, 730, 732, 733
coppersmith, 30, 226
copulation, 252, 366, 396
crab, 198, 586, 622
crocodile, 204, 211, 212, 216, 267, 268, 280, 281, 282, 283, 366, 369, 371,

gold, 13, 14, 23, 26, 60, 71, 74, 76, 86, 87, 98, 102, 105, 111, 120, 142, 149, 157, 159, 162, 167, 171, 179, 207, 215, 219, 237, 251, 260, 262, 284, 290, 300, 301, 303, 309, 319, 333, 335, 356, 357, 358, 362, 366, 382, 385, 405, 406, 407, 440, 441, 443, 445, 461, 462, 463, 484, 526, 543, 579, 593, 597, 599, 600, 605, 611, 612, 638, 699, 700, 708, 710, 715, 716
goldsmith, 594
guild, 199, 200, 201, 204, 259, 260, 261, 283, 288, 311, 317, 318, 352, 354, 357, 363, 383, 385, 393, 394, 395, 396, 401, 408, 409, 410, 413, 414, 415, 453, 468, 476, 488, 577, 596, 617, 676, 685, 688, 727, 728
Haifa, 77, 184, 185, 213, 597, 604, 621, 657, 660, 663, 670, 690, 711
hair-knot, 331, 332
Harappa, 218
hare, 217
harrow, 101, 104, 221, 232, 249, 317, 318
haystack, 590
hermeneutics, 11, 678
hieroglyphic, 185, 413
hieroglyphs, 185
hill, 96, 97, 100, 164, 172, 178, 180, 239, 339, 340, 341, 376, 444, 446, 463, 529, 613, 695
hood, 203, 464, 555, 674, 733
horn, 40, 82, 110, 144, 165, 206, 230, 231, 232, 248, 265, 290, 309, 320, 338, 340, 344, 347, 378, 389, 406, 447, 462, 466, 482, 589, 596, 658, 662
horned, 473
ibex, 116, 125, 184, 333, 342, 389, 412, 429, 473
implements, 249, 374, 392, 426, 455, 457, 707
ingot, 27, 28, 81, 82, 101, 104, 134, 165, 177, 178, 184, 185, 188, 189, 193, 195, 210, 218, 229, 230, 239, 248, 250, 268, 281, 283, 293, 296, 308, 348, 351, 367, 371, 384, 397, 424, 461, 464, 481, 483, 484, 563, 589, 604, 636, 637, 638, 660, 697, 698, 714, 715
inscription, 88
iron, 9, 25, 27, 28, 29, 30, 31, 42, 74, 77, 81, 82, 97, 98, 100, 101, 102, 103, 104, 105, 106, 128, 134, 142, 143, 144, 149, 152, 155, 156, 157, 158, 159, 162, 163, 165, 168, 174, 176, 177, 178, 179, 183, 184,

serpent, 150, 278, 336, 449, 460, 461, 468, 481, 614, 635, 695, 699, 733
Shaffer, 715
shaggy, 362
shawl, 119
sign board, 620
silver, 13, 14, 24, 25, 59, 70, 71, 74, 76, 79, 82, 87, 97, 98, 101, 102, 104, 105, 135, 136, 142, 149, 157, 159, 160, 162, 164, 172, 179, 194, 203, 207, 211, 215, 284, 303, 333, 356, 357, 362, 382, 385, 389, 429, 440, 461, 473, 527, 605, 611, 638, 676, 683, 684, 698, 708, 709, 711, 712, 713
Sindhi, 87
slope, 351
sloping, 351
smelt, 218
smelter, 9, 28, 142, 143, 177, 178, 198, 205, 206, 212, 217, 219, 222, 229, 232, 266, 277, 278, 281, 282, 364, 378, 398, 436, 452, 453, 529, 586, 591, 593, 718
smelting, 185, 218
smith, 179, 185, 284, 362, 586, 590, 604
smithy, 7, 26, 60, 77, 96, 97, 98, 100, 102, 128, 155, 174, 176, 178, 182, 184, 189, 192, 193, 200, 204, 211, 216, 217, 218, 227, 231, 239, 240, 266, 269, 277, 280, 281, 282, 283, 287, 291, 310, 311, 312, 313, 315, 333, 351, 352, 357, 369, 370, 393, 394, 397, 398, 401, 409, 413, 415, 430, 435, 440, 442, 451, 452, 453, 454, 455, 456, 457, 461, 463, 467, 468, 472, 473, 476, 480, 481, 483, 587, 591, 612, 616, 617, 621, 622, 684, 685, 696, 697, 698, 699
Southworth, 64, 65, 295
sphōṭa, 5, 130, 131, 196, 216, 222, 270, 298, 299, 302, 541, 547, 557, 560, 566, 567, 568, 569, 570, 571, 572, 573, 574, 575, 577
spinner, 330
spokes, 206, 230, 231, 232, 394, 395, 407, 467, 620, 633, 676
spotted, 334
sprachbund, 18, 20, 21, 22, 35, 36, 60, 63, 64, 77, 82, 195, 216, 219, 258, 263, 267, 272, 274, 296, 298, 301, 350, 420, 485, 486, 539, 546, 548, 550, 558, 559, 562, 577, 621, 656, 658, 664, 668, 672, 676, 685, 687, 690, 691, 720
Sproat, 557, 673

372, 377, 390, 393, 394, 395, 396, 397, 398, 401, 408, 410, 414, 423, 424, 442, 462, 468, 471, 472, 480, 483, 484, 562, 577, 586, 588, 589, 591, 592, 594, 596, 597, 622, 624, 658, 676, 727
tusk, 658
twig, 281, 282, 420, 469, 482, 484, 618, 719, 720
unsmelted metal, 204, 253, 453, 476, 487, 688
upraised arm, 279, 363
Ur, 87
Uruk, 107, 187, 213, 333, 386, 418, 421, 428, 429, 430, 431, 449, 455, 457, 458, 479, 666, 667, 721, 722, 723, 725
vagina, 366
Vats, 291, 402, 403, 739
Vedic, 190
vessel, 225
warehouse, 27, 192, 195, 283, 352, 431, 637, 639
Warka, 3, 176, 177, 185, 187, 191, 192, 430, 461, 474
water-carrier, 219, 364
weapons, 595
wing, 119, 146, 149, 175, 338, 437, 442, 684, 685, 697
Wittgenstein, 547, 557, 558, 561, 568, 693
workshop, 186, 284, 310
writing, 217
zebu, 55, 183, 201, 202, 203, 204, 224, 240, 278, 336, 337, 385, 414, 453, 458, 468, 470, 479, 487, 615, 688
zinc, 3, 12, 25, 26, 134, 135, 136, 137, 139, 140, 141, 149, 154, 157, 165, 184, 201, 283, 367, 460, 463, 465, 473, 480, 526, 529, 590, 593, 599, 600, 634, 657, 665, 690, 696, 697, 698, 699

End Notes

1 In Karum-Kanesh over 20,000 tablets were discovered mostly related to records of trade transactions between Ashur-Kanesh along a section of the Tin Road.
2 Kongtrul, Jamgön; Trans. Guarisco, Elio; McLeod, Ingrid) (2005). The Treasury of Knowledge (*shes bya kun la khyab pa'i mdzod*). Book Six, Part Four: Systems of Buddhist Tantra, The Indestructibe Way of Secret Mantra. Bolder, Colorado, USA: Snow Lion Publications.

3 Kalyanaraman, S., 2013m *Meluhha – Tree of life*, Herndon, Sarasvati Research Center.
4 Huntington, John C. and Susan L., 1979, Scan numbers 0027221, 0001358.
5 http://creative.sulekha.com/temple-architecture-devalaya-vastu-part-six-6-of-7_338767_blog
6 Weidner, E., 1952, 'Das Reich Sargons von Akkad,' AfO 16 (1952): 6-11.)(cf. Gelb, IJ, 1970, 'Makkan and Meluhha in Early Mesopotamian Sources,' RA 64 (1970): 1-8). (Sollberger, E., 1969, 'The Problem of Magan and Meluhha,' Bull. Of the Institute of Archaeology 8-9 (1968-69): 247-50.
7 Gelb, I.J., 1970, Makkan and Meluhha in early Mesopotamian sources, RA LXIV, No. 1, pp.3-6.
8 Potts, DT, 1982,The road to Meluhha, The Journal of Nearestern Studies, Vol. 41, No. 4 (Oct., 1982), pp.279-288.
9 http://creative.sulekha.com/sanskrit-philia-and-indic-civilization_132117_blog
10 cf. Wilhelm Halbfass 1990, *India and Europe: an essay in philosophical understanding*, Delhi, Motilal Banarsidass, pp. 179, 185.
11 Gadamer 1976: xii). Gadamer, Hans-Georg. 1976, *Philosophical Hermeneutics*, ed. and trans. by David E. Linge, Berkeley: University of California Press.
12 Shendge, Malati, 1977, *The civilized demons: the Harappans in Rigveda, Rigveda*, Abhinav Publications.
13 AŚ XII.4.23; VII.10.16.
14 Manu I.23, tr. G. Buhler 1886: 33.
15 Parpola, Simo, Asko Parpola, and Robert H. Brunswig, Jr., 1977, "TheMeluhha Village — Evidence of Acculturation of Harappan Traders in Late Third Millenium Mesopotamia?", *Journal of the Economic and Social History of the Orient*, Volume 20, Part II.
16 Tr. CH Tawney, 1880, Calcutta; rep. New Delhi, 1991, I, p. 151
17
http://en.wikipedia.org/wiki/Invasion_of_India_by_Scythian_Tribes#Establishment_of_Mlechcha_Kingdoms_in_Northern_India

18 {Berger, H. Die Burushaski-Sprache von Hunza und Nagar. Vols. I-III. Wiesbaden: Harrassowitz 1988] [Tikkanen (2005)]}, [G.Morgenstierne, Irano-Dardica. Wiesbaden 1973], *The Munda Languages*. Edited by Gregory D. S. Anderson. London and New York: Routledge (Routledge Language Family Series), 2008.
19 Kalyanaraman, S., ed., 2008, *Indian Lexicon: A comparative dictionary of over 25 ancient Bharatiya (Indian) languages*, Manila. http://www.scribd.com/doc/2232617/Lexicon

20 http://sites.google.com/site/kalyan97/induswriting

21 Crawford, H., 2012, Meluhha. The Encyclopedia of Ancient History First Edition. Edited by Roger S. Bagnall, Kai Brodersen, Craige B. Champion, Andrew Erskine, and Sabine R. Huebner, print pages 4424–4425. http://onlinelibrary.wiley.com/doi/10.1002/9781444338386.wbeah24144/full

22 Possehl, Gregory and Gullapalli, Praveena; 1999; 'The Early Iron Age in South Asia'; in Vincent C. Piggott (ed.). *The Archaeometallurgy of the Asian Old World*; University Museum Monograph, MASCA Research Papers in Science and Archaeology, Volume 16; Pgs. 153-175; The University Museum, University of Pennsylvania; Philadelphia.

23 Translation based on http://www.valmikiramayan.net/sundara/sarga30/sundara_30_frame.htm See: Narayana Iyengar, 1938, Vanmeegarum Thamizhum; http://tashindu.blogspot.com/2006_12_01_archive.html In this work, Narayana Iyengar cites that the commentator interpret mānuṣam vākyam as the language spoken in Kosala.

24 Occurs in an ancient Vedic text Śatapathabrāhmaṇa 3.2.1; **mlt'se* (Tibeto-Burman); **muẓi/miẓi* 'say, speak, utter'(Proto-Dravidian?); *Nk. muṛ- (muṭṭ-)* to speak; *muṭṭa* language. *Konḍa miṛi-* to speak, utter.(DEDR 4989)

25 śatapatha Brāhmaṇa vol. 2 of 5, tr. By Julius Eggeling, 1885, in SBE Part 12; fn 78-81, p.39.

26 Paton, LB, 1908-27, ed., Ammonites, in Encyclopaedia of Religion & Ethics, Hastings, vol.I, 389; vol. 9, 892.

27 See S. K. Chatterji, Origin and Development of the Bengali Language, Calcutta, 1926 pp. 42,178. Source: Natya Shastra of Bharata Muni in english THE NATYASASTRA A Treatise on Hindu Dramaturgy and Histrionics Ascribed to B H A R A T A - M r X I Vol. I. (Chapters I-XXVII) Completely translated jor the jirst tune from the original Sanskrit tuttri «u Introduction and Various Notes, Royal Asiatic Society of Bengal, Calcutta http://archive.org/stream/NatyaShastraOfBharataMuniVolume1/NatyaShastraOfBharataMuniVolume1_djvu.txt

28 http://arxiv.org/ftp/arxiv/papers/1204/1204.3800.pdf

29 F.B.J. Kuiper, 1948, Proto-Munda Words in Sanskrit, Amsterdam, Verhandeling der Koninklijke Nederlandsche Akademie Van Wetenschappen, Afd.Letterkunde, Nieuwe Reeks Deel Li, No. 3, 1948, p.9 http://www.scribd.com/doc/12238039/mundalexemesinSanskrit

30 M.B.Emeneau, Linguistic Prehistory of India PAPS98 (1954). 282-92; Tamil Culture 5 (1956). 30-55; repr. In Collected papers: Dravidian Linguistics Ethnology and Folktales, Annamalai Nagar, Annamalai University, 1967, pp. 155-171.

31 K. V. Sarma, 1983, "Spread of Vedic Culture in Ancient. South India" in The *Adyar Library Bulletin, 1983*, 43:1.

32 Colin Masica, 1991, *Indo-Aryan Languages*, Cambridge Univ. Press.

33 Kalyanaraman, S., 2010, *Indus Script Cipher*, Herndon, Sarasvati Research Center

34 McAlpin, David W., *Proto Elamo Dravidian: The Evidence and Its Implications*, American Philosophy Society (1981).

35 Fuller, D.Q., 2007, Non-human genetics, agricultural origins and historical linguistics, in M. Petraglia & B. Allchin, ed., *The evolution and history of human populations in south Asia: interdisciplinary studies in archaeology, biological anthropology, linguistics and genetics*: 389-439, Dordrecht: Springer).

36 Robert Shafer, 1954, Ethnography of Ancient India, Otto Harras Sowitz, Wiesbaden, pp. 14,33.
http://archive.org/stream/ethnographyofanc033514mbp/ethnographyofanc033514mbp_djvu.txt
37 Mcintosh, Jane, 2008, *The Ancient Indus Valley: New Perspectives*, ABC-CLIO, pp.183-187
38 http://www.ling.hawaii.edu/faculty/stampe/aa.html

39 After Fig. 8.1 in: Charles Higham, 1996, *The Bronze Age of Southeast Asia*, Cambridge University Press.

40 Southworth, FC, The SARVA (South Asi Residual Vocabulary Assemblage), p. 58 Project website http://www.aa.tufs.ac.jp/sarva/ List of resources: (1) Turner's Comparative Dictionary of the Indo-Aryan languages (Oxford 1966)
(2) Burrow & Emeneau, A Dravidian etymological dictionary, revised edition (Oxford 1984)
(These two items are available by permission of Oxford University Press and the Digital South
Asia Library, University of Chicago.)
Additional items to be added as time permits include:
(3) Kuiper's famous list of 'foreign' words in RV (Kuiper 1991, see Witzel 1999b);
(4) Nahali words of unidentified origin (Kuiper 1962, Mundlay 1996);
(5) words listed in DEDR with etyma limited to a single branch of Dravidian;
(6) Munda materials from David Stampe's website
www.ling.hawaii.edu/Stampe/AA/ETYM/
Stampe&Munda, plus other materials in preparation at the University of Hawai'i;
(7) Sino-Tibetan materials from James Matisoff's Sino-Tibetan Etymological Dictionary and
Thesaurus (STEDT) Project (www.stedt.berkeley.edu/Matisoff/) when they become available;
(8) Materials from M. Witzel's articles (e.g. 1999a-c);
(9) Masica's list of agricultural words from "language X" (Masica 1979);
(10) Words of unknown origin found in OIA and Dravidian from Southworth 1979 & 2005a;
(11) Indo-Iranian words from Lubotsky 2001 (see also Witzel 2001, 1999b §5);
(12) words of unknown origin from Marathi (Kulkarni 1964), Khandeshi (Chitnis 1964), Katkari
(Kulkarni 1969), to be contributed by FCS;
(13) Vedda words from De Silva 1972;
(14) Residual words in the Dravidian Nilgiri languages (Emeneau 1997, v. Zvelebil 1990:63-72,
Witzel 1999b §2.4);
(14) Oriya vocabulary (AG);

(15) materials from Kusunda and Bangani languages (MW and colleagues),
(16) Comments on selected etyma from Mayrhofer 1986.
41 ***Language and Linguistic Area, Essays by Murray B. Emeneau,*** **(selected and introduced by Anwar S. Dil), 1980, Stanford University Press, California (which includes: Emeneau, MB, 1956, India as a linguistic area, in: Language, 32.3-16 Kuiper, FBJ, 1967, The genesis of a linguistic area,** ***Indo-Iranian Journal*** **10: 81-102 Masica, Colin P., 1976,** ***Defining a linguistic area, South Asia,*** **Chicago, University of Chicago Press (Based on the author's thesis, 1971).**
42 FBJ Kuiper, 1948, Proto-Munda words in Sanskrit, Amsterdam, Noord-Hollandsche Uitg.Mij., p. 9.
43 Parpola, Simo, A. Parpola and R.H. Brunswig, 1977 "The Meluhha Village: Evidence of Acculturation of Harappan Traders in Late Third Millennium Mesopotamia":*Journal of the Economic and Social History of the Orient* 20, 129-165
44 Sege Cleuziou 1978/79, 30ff.; Gerd Weisgerber 1980: 62-110; Gerd Weisgerber, 1981; Tosi, 1982; Gerd Weisgerber 1986: 135-142. Ozguc, Tahsin, 1962, *Mashat Hoyuk II: Bogazkoy un kuzeydogusund bir Hitit merkezi*, A Hittite center northeast of Bogazkoy, Ankara, Turk Tarih Kurumu Basimevi.

45 (*Cr. Ed.* VIII.30.79-80; Roy VIII.45.34-35)

46 Full text at:
http://ia700202.us.archive.org/23/items/prakritarupavata00simhuoft/prakritarupavata00simhuoft.pdf
47 Ed. Cowell, Edward Byles,1868, London, Trubner
48 See http://www.indianetzone.com/39/prakrit_language.htm
49 http://www.metmuseum.org/Collections/search-the-collections/328905
50
http://www.britishmuseum.org/explore/highlights/highlight_objects/me/c/cuneiform_tablet_and_envelope.aspx Clay tablet with a cuneiform letter and its envelopeEarly Colony Period, around 1850 BCE From Kültepe

51 http://www.metmuseum.org/collections/search-the-collections/325864
52 http://www.metmuseum.org/collections/search-the-collections/328900
53 Kulakoglu Fikri & Selmin Kangal, eds., 2010, *Anatolia's prologue, Kultepe Kanesh Karum, Assyrians in Istanbul*, Catalogue of the Kayseri Metropolitan Municipality.
http://hal.archives-ouvertes.fr/docs/00/78/14/10/PDF/Michel_2010_ANATOLIA_S_PROLOGUE_Writing_Computing.pdf

54 Giorgadze, GG, 1991, The Hittite kingdom, in: Diakonoff, IM, 1991, *Early Antiquity*, Univ. of Chicago Press, p.269).
55 http://azargoshnasp.net/history/Aryan/mitanniaryanpantheons.pdf Aryan gods of the Mitanni treaties by Paul Thieme JOAS Vol. 80, No. 4 (Oct. - Dec., 1960), pp. 301-317 evidencing an Indo-Aryan superstrate.] See: Elena eMallory, J. P (eds.), (2007), The Origin of the Indo-Iranians, Leiden-Boston.https://ia600600.us.archive.org/2/items/TheOriginOfTheIndo-iranians/TheOriginOfTheIndo-iranian.pdf

56 cf. S.S. Misra, 1992 *The Aryan Problem,* a linguistic approach.New Delhi: Munshiram Manoharlal Publishers, Delhi, p.10.

57 Gelb, IJ, 1970, Makkan and Meluhha in early Mesopotamian Sources, Revue d'Assyriologie et d'archaeologie Orientale, LXIV Volume No. 1, pp.1-6.

58 Harper, Prudence Oliver, 1995, Assyrian origins: discoveries at Ashur on the Tigris: Antiquities in the Vorderasiatisches Museum, Berlin, Metropolitan Museum of Art, New York, pp.23-24.

59 Vermaak, PS, 2008, Guabba, the Meluhhan village in Mesopotamia, in: *Journal for Semitics*, Vol. 17, No. 2: http://www.sabinet.co.za/abstracts/semit/semit_v17_n2_a12.html

60 MK Dhavalikar, 1997, Meluhha, the land of copper, *South Asian Studies*, 13:1, 275-279

61 Serge Cleuziou, Dilmun and Makkan during the third and early second millennia BC, 143-155 in: Shaikha Haya Ali Al Khalifa and Michael Rice (eds.) *Bahrain through the ages: the archaeology*, London, KPI, 1986.

62 Kirfel, W. Das *Purāṇa Pañcalakṣaṇa.*1927.Bonn : K. Schroeder.

63 S. Beal, 1973, *The Life of Hiuen Tsiang*, New Delhi, p 57; cf. NL Dey, *Geographical Dictionary of India*, p. 113 for an identification of Lamgham (Lampakā) 20 miles north-west of Jalalabad.

64 EJ Rapson, ed., 1922,*Cambridge History of India* , vol. I, Ancient India, Cambridge, p. 564.

65 NL Dey, *Geographical Dictionary*, p. 115.

66 SK Chatterji, 1950, Kirāta-jana-kṛti --The Indo-Mongoloids: Their contributions to the culture of India, Journal of Royal Asiatic Society of Bengal, Vol. XVI, pp.143-253.

67 Burrow, T., 1955, *The Sanskrit language*, UK, Faber & Faber Ltd., p.43, p.62.

68 WF Leemans, Foreign Trade in the Old Babylonian Period, 1960; 'Trade Relations on Babylonia', Journal of Economic and Social History of the Orient, vol. III, 1960, p.30 ff. 'Old Babylonian Letters and Economic History', Journal of Economic and Social History of the Orient, vol. XI, 1968, pp. 215-26; J. Hansam, 'A Periplus of Magan and Meluhha', Bulletin of the School of Oriental and African Studies, vol. 36, pt. III, 1973, pp. 554-83. Asko and Simo Parpola, 'On the Relationship of the Sumerian Toponym Meluhha and Sanskrit Mleccha', Studia Orientalia,vol. 46, 1975, pp. 205-38.

69 http://www.virtualsecrets.com/sumerian.html

70 Collon, Dominique, Catalogue of the Western Asiatic Seals in the British Museum: Cylinder Seals II: Akkadian, Post Akkadian, Ur III Periods, II, London, BMP, 1982, pl. XVII. Boehmer, R M, Die Entwicklung der Glyptik wahrend der Akkad-Zeit, 4, Berlin, 1965.

71 Apte, VS, *The Practical Sanskrit-English dictionary*, p. 1013.

72 Nagesa Bhatta, *Sphoṭavāda*, Tr. V. Krishnamacharya, 1977, Madras, Adyar Library, p.5.

73 *Paramalaghumanjūṣā* by K. Kunjunni Raja References are to the edition by Kalika Prasad Sukla, 1961, (with the editor's Jyotsnā commentary, Baroda. Karl H. Potter, Harold G. Coward, K. Kunjunni Raja, 1990, *Encyclopaedia of Indian philosophies: the philosophy of the Grammarians*, Delhi, Motilal Banarsidass Publ., pp. 324-325.

74 Mandana's answer to Kumarila, *Sphotasiddhi Kārikā* 3 as presented by G. Sastri, *Word*, p. 105.

75 http://community.dur.ac.uk/derek.kennet/samarra.htm

76 Frankfort, Henri, 1996, The art and architecture of the ancient orient, Yale University Press, p. 17.

77 http://s1.djyimg.com/i6/60105234343450.jpg

78 Ernst Herzfeld, Die vorgeschichtlichen Töpfereien von Samarra, Die Ausgrabungen von Samarra 5, Berlin 1930.
79 Stanley A. Freed, Research Pitfalls as a Result of the Restoration of Museum Specimens, Annals of the New York Academy of Sciences, Volume 376, The Research Potential of Anthropological Museum Collections pages 229–245, December 1981. Ernst Herzfeld, Die vorgeschichtlichen Töpfereien von Samarra, Die Ausgrabungen von Samarra 5, Berlin 1930.
80 http://en.wikipedia.org/wiki/Carbonate-hosted_lead-zinc_ore_deposits
81 Anderson, GM & RW Macqueen, 1982, Ore deposit models -6. Mississippi Valley-Type Lead-Zinc deposits, Geoscience Canada, Volume 9, Number 2, pp. 108-117. http://journals.hil.unb.ca/index.php/GC/article/download/3300/3817
82 Hindzinc Tech, HZL, V.1, No.1, 1989 http://www.portal.gsi.gov.in/portal/page?_pageid=127,745800&_dad=portal&_schema=PORTAL
83 Grierson, George Abraham, 1906, The Piśāca languages of north-western India, , Royal Aisatic Society.
84 Nappo, Salvatore. "*Pompey: Guide to the Lost City*", White Star, 2000.
85 Egyptian cults of Isis and Serapis in Roman Fleets. In: (Amenta. A-Luiselli, M. M.-Sordi, M. N (ed.) L'acqua nell'antico Egitto: vita, rigenerazione, incantesimo, medicamento - Proceedings of the First International Conference for Young Egyptologists (Chianciano Terme, 15-18 October 2003), Roma 2005: 241-253.
86 http://thedailybeagle.net/2013/09/08/the-pigna-and-the-apollo-belvedere-two-treasures-of-the-vatican/
87 http://www.cambridge...PC1617681e.html
88 http://www.flickr.com/photos/brankoab/7673434338/

89 Sarianidi 1981 b: 232-233, Fig. 7, 8. [Robert H. Brunswig, Jr. et al, New Indus Type and Related Seals from the Near East, 101-115 in: Daniel T. Potts (ed.), *Dilmun: New Studies in the Archaeology and Early History of Bahrain*, Berlin, Dietrich Reimer Verlag, 1983; each seal is referenced by a four-digit number which is registered in the Finnish concordance.]
90 British Museum website
91 http://www.shumei.org/art/miho/miho.html

92 George A. Grierson, George A., The Prakrit Vibhāṣās , Journal of the Royal Asiatic Society of Great Britain & Ireland (New Series) / Volume 50 / Issue 3-4 / October 1918, pp 489-517.
93 http://www.archaeologyonline.net/artifacts/iron-ore.html
94 http://www.harappa.com/indus4/e6.html
95 Uttarkashi Distt. http://asidehraduncircle.in/pagedisplay.php?tid=1531
96 http://rbedrosian.com/imyth.htm 1. G. M. Bongard-Levin, The Origin of the Aryans (New Delhi, 1980), pp. 48-49, 67, 99-101, 115.2. A. J. Carnoy, 1917, "Iranian Mythology", pp. 299-300. Metal imagery pervades the Avesta. According to the Bundahishn xxiv.1 when the first human Gaya Maretan ("Human Life") died, his body became molten brass, while the metals gold, silver, iron, tin, lead, quick-silver and adamant arose from his limbs. "Gold was Gaya's seed, which was entrusted to the earth

and carefully preserved by Spenta Armaiti, the guardian of earth. After forty years it brought forth the first human pair, Mashya and Mashyoi", Carnoy, p. 294; A flood of molten metal will burn up evil at the end of time, ibid. p. 262; K. D. Irani, "Socioeconomic Implications", p. 68 writes: "Metallurgy, though a technology, was in its early days associated with sacred lore and the invocation of occult forces. Its techniques, particularly the manufacture of steel arms, were for obvious reasons protected by shrouds of secrecy. Some of the technology, requiring the use of furnaces, became the speciality of fire-priests in temples that maintained fire-altars—particularly the techniques of generating fires of varying intensities". 3. A. J. Carnoy, p. 302.
97 http://www.flickr.com/photos/27305838@N04/4830444236/
http://www.iranicaonline.org/articles/simorg
http://en.wikipedia.org/wiki/Simurgh
98 See: http://bharatkalyan97.blogspot.in/2011/11/syena-orthography.html
99
http://www.italyforiraq.esteri.it/ItalyForIraq/documenti/Iraq_Museum_GUIDE_2012.pdf
100 http://oi.uchicago.edu/OI/IRAQ/Images/strom/strom_fig021al.jpg
101 http://oi.uchicago.edu/OI/IRAQ/dbfiles/objects/14.htm
102 After Fig. 7 Holly Pittman, 1984, *Art of the Bronze Age: Southeastern Iran, Western Central Asia, and the Indus Valley*, New York, The Metropolitan Museum of Art, pp. 29-30.

103 http://cdli.ox.ac.uk/wiki/doku.php?id=uruk_mod._warka

104
http://tc.templejc.edu/dept/Art/ASmith/ARTS1303/arts1303_2StoneAge2Sumer/Ston2Sumpage022.html

105 http://www.metmuseum.org/toah/hd/akka/hob_1999.325.4.htm

106 http://www.amazon.com/Indus-Writing-ancient-Near-East/dp/0982897189/ref=sr_1_1?ie=UTF8&qid=1371088202&sr=8-1&keywords=indus+writing
107 After Rice, M. ed., 2000, Traces of Paradise. The archaeology of Bahrain 2500 BCE-300 CE. London: The Dilmun Committee, 15.
108 Moorey, PRS, 1994, Ancient Mesopotamian Materials and Industries, Oxford, Clarendon Press.

109 http://indusscriptmore.blogspot.com/2011/08/problematic-13-stroke-signs-in-indus.html
110Cowell, 1973, Jatakas Book II, p. 172 ff.
111 Hunter, G.R., *JRAS*, 1932, 476
112 Gregory L. Possehl,Shu-ilishu's cylinder seal, Expedition, Vol. 48, Number 1, pp. 42-3. http://www.penn.museum/documents/publications/expedition/PDFs/48-1/What%20in%20the%20World.pdf
113
http://cdli.ucla.edu/cdlisearch/search/index.php?SearchMode=Text&txtID_Txt=P227514

114
http://www.archive.org/download/mmoires01franuoft/mmoires01franuoft.pdf Jacques de Morgan, Fouilles à Suse en 1897-1898 et 1898-1899, Mission archéologique en Iran, Mémoires I, 1990

115 Department des Antiquites Orienteles, Musee du Louvre, Paris.

http://www.louvre.fr/en/oeuvre-notices/statuette-man-carrying-goat

116 See: http://www.aakkl.helsinki.fi/melammu/pdf/vidale2004.pdf The Melammu project (In particular, Massimo Vidale, 2004, Growing in a foreign world: for a history of the 'Meluhha villages' in Mesopotamia in the 3rd millennium BCE. The article discusses archaeological and textual evidences; Plate XIX).
117 Laursen, Steffen Terp, 2010,, Westward transmission of Indus valley sealing technology: origin and development of 'Gulf type' seal and other administrative technologies in early Dilmun, ca. 2100-2000 BCE in: *Arabian Archaeology and Epigraphy* 2010: vol. 21: 96–134.

118 Ibid., p.105.
119 Kjaerum, 1994, fig. 1756/3-7, 9 and B-D.
120 Laurssen, opcit., p. 131.
121 Ibid., p. 96.
122 Rice, Michael,1994, *The archaeology of the Arabian Gulf*, c. 5000 to 323 BCE, Routledge p. 245.
123 Serge Cleuziou, Early bronze age trade in the gulf and the Arabian sea: the society behind boats, pp. 134-149 in: Daniel T. Potts, Hasan Al Naboodah, Peter Hellyer, 2003, *Archaeology of the United Arab Emirates*, Trident Press.
http://books.google.com/books?id=8Q6QnxfoRQ8C&source=gbs_navlinks_s
124 Gadd, CJ, 1932, Seals of Ancient Indian style found at Ur, *Proceedings of the British Academy* 18: 191-210.
125 Kjaerum, P., 1994, Stamp-seals, seal impressions and seal blanks, in: Hojlund, F & Andersen, H. eds., *Qala'at al-Bahrain – vol. 1. The northern city wall and the Islamic fortress*, Aarhus, JASP, pp.319-350. Kjaerum, P., 2007, The 'Charnelhouse' stamp seals, in Hojlund, F. ed., The burial mounds of Bahrain – Social complexity in early Dilmun, Aarhus, JASP, pp. 159-166. Al-Sindi, K., 1999, *Dilmun seals*. Manama, Ministry of Cabinet affairs & Information, State of Bahrain.
126 Laurssen, opcit., p. 97.
127 Hallo WW & Buchanan, B., 1965, A 'Persian Gulf seal on an Old Babylonian Mercantile Agreement. *Assyriological Studies* 16, p. 205
128 Vidale, M., 2005, opcit., p.156.
129 cf. T.C. Mitchell, 1986, Indus and Gulf type seals from Ur in: Shaikha Haya Ali. Cylinder (white shell) seal impression; Ur, Mesopotamia (IM 8028); white shell. height 1.7 cm., dia. 0.9 cm.; cf. Gadd, PBA 18 (1932), pp. 7-8, pl. I, no.7; Mitchell 1986: 280-1, no.8 and fig. 112; Parpola, 1994, p. 181; fish vertically in front of and horizontally above a unicorn; trefoil design. Al Khalifa and Michael Rice, 1986, *Bahrain through the ages: the archaeology*, London: 280-1, no.8 and fig. 112.
130 Gadd, CJ,Seals of Ancient Indian Style Found at Ur', in: G.L. Possehl, ed., 1979, *Ancient Cities of the Indus*, Delhi, Vikas Publishing House, p. 117.
131 *Deśīnāmamālā of Hemacandra* (ed. R. Pischel (1880), Bombay Sanskrit Series No. XVII; 1938, 2nd edn. by Paravastu Venkata Ramanujaswami)

132 David Kahn, David, *The Code-Breakers: The Story of Secret Writing*, New York, Macmillan, 1967, pp. 74-75.

133 Wells, Bryan, opcit., Table 3.1 Signs sorted by frequency

134 Parpola, A., New correspondences between Harappan and Near Eastern glyptic art, in: Bridget Allchin (ed.), *South Asian Archaeology, 1981*, Cambridge, Cambridge University Press, 1984.

135 JM Kenoyer, 1998, Ancient cities of the Indus Valley, Oxford University Press, p. 115.

136 Donkin, RA, 1998, *Beyond Price: pearls and pearl-fishing: origins of the age of discoveries*, Volume 224, Philadelphia, American Philosophical Society, 01 January 1998

137 Leemans, WF, 1968 'Old Babylonian letters and economic history: a review article with a digression on foreign trade', *Journal of the Economic and Social History of the Orient* XI: 171-226.

138 After Marie-Helene Pottier, 1984, Materiel funeraire de la Bactriane meridionale de l'age du bronze, Recherche sur les Civilizations, Memoire 36, Paris, fig. 21; Sarianidi, V.I., 1986, Le complexe culturel de Togolok 21 en Margiane, Arts Asiatiques 41: fig. 6,21; Potts, 1994, fig. 53,8; Amiet, 1986, fig. 132.

139 Denise Schmandt-Besserat, 2009, Tokens and writing: the cognitive development, *Scripta*, Vol. 1 (September 2009): 145-154. (Fig. 2).' (p.148, ibid.) Susa, ca. 3300 BCE.

140 cf. Dictionary and Thesaurus of Tocharian A. Volume 1: a-j. Compiled by Gerd Carling in collaboration with Georges-Jean Pinault and Werner Winter, Wiesbaden, Harrassowitz Verlag, 2009.

141 Papers presented at the international symposium, Tvarminne, 8-10 January, 1999), Helsinki, Suomalais-Ugrilainen Seura: 304, 310. 2001, The Indo-Iranian substratum in: Carpelan et al., eds., Early contacts between Uralic and Indo-European: linguistic and archaeological considerations.

142 Vidale, Massimo,Ravenna, 2004, Growing in a Foreign World:For a History of the "Meluhha Villages" in Mesopotamia in the 3rd Millennium BCE.

143 Donkin, R.A., 1998, Beyond price: pearls and pearl-fishing: origins to the age of discoveries, Philadelphia, American Philosophical Society, Memoir Volume 224, pp.49-50)Full text at http://tinyurl.com/y9zpb5n Note 109. For Sumerian words, see Delitzch, 1914: pp.18-19 (igi, eye), 125 (ku, fish), 195 (na, stone); and cf. Chicago Assyrian Dictionary I/J: 1960: pp.45 (iga), 153-158 (Akk. i_nu), N(2), 1980: p.340 (k), 'fish-eye stones'.Note 110. A.L. Oppenheim, 1954: pp.7-8; Leemans, 1960b: pp.24 f. (IGI-KU6). Followed by Kramer, 1963a: p.113, 1963b: p.283; Bibby, 1970: pp.189, 191-192: Ratnagar, 1981: pp.23-24,79, 188; M. Rice, 1985: p.181.Note 111. A.L. Oppenheim, 1954: p.11; Leemans, 1960b: p.37 (NA4 IGI-KU6, 'fish-eye stones').Note 112. Leemans, 1968: p.222 ('pearls from Meluhha'. Falkenstein (1963: pp.10-11 [12]) has 'augenformigen Perlen aus Meluhha'. (lit. shaped eyes beads from Meluhha).

144 http: //www.harappa.com/indus/Kenoyer-Meadow-2010-HARP.pdf

145 http://www.antiquity.ac.uk/projgall/agrawal323/Antiquity, D.P. Agrawal et al, Redefining the Harappan hinterland, *Anquity*, Vol. 84, Issue 323, March 2010.
146 http://tinyurl.com/bqvnkd4
147
http://www.britishmuseum.org/explore/highlights/highlight_objects/me/w/calcite_seal,_combat_scene.aspx
148
http://www.britishmuseum.org/explore/highlights/highlight_objects/me/w/white_and_cream_calcite_seal.aspx P. Amiet, *La glyptique Mesopotamienne ar* (Paris,Centre National de la Reherche Scientifique, 1980)
D.J. Wiseman, Catalogue *of the Western Asiat London*, 1962)
149 http://www.louvre.fr/en/oeuvre-notices/statue-queen-napirasu-wife-king-untash-napirisha
150 http://www.iranicaonline.org/articles/susa-i-excavations
151
http://www.louvre.fr/media/repository/ressources/sources/illustration/atlas/image_66481_v2_m56577569830704548.jpg
152
https://www.britishmuseum.org/explore/highlights/highlight_objects/me/b/bronze_fitting_seated_figure.aspx
153 Kuppuram, G., 1989. *Ancient Indian Mining, Metallurgy and Metal Industries*, Delhi: Ashish Singhal. Krishnan, M. V., 1976. *Cire Perdue Casting in India*, New Delhi: Kanak Publications.
http://en.wikipedia.org/wiki/Lost-wax_casting
154 http://en.wikipedia.org/wiki/Dhokra
155 http://anthromuseum.missouri.edu/minigalleries/lostwax/intro.shtml
156 Moorey, P. R. S., (1988). Early Metallurgy in Mesopotamia, in *The Beginning of the Use of Metals and Alloys. Papers from the Second International Conference on the Beginning of the Use of Metals and Alloys, Zhengzhou, China, 21–26 October 1986.*, ed. R. Maddin Cambridge, Massachusetts & London, England: The MIT Press. Muhly, J. D., (1988). The Beginnings of Metallurgy in the Old World, in *The Beginning of the Use of Metals and Alloys. Papers from the Second International Conference on the Beginning of the Use of Metals and Alloys, Zhengzhou, China, 21–26 October 1986.*, ed. R. Maddin Cambridge, Massachusetts & London, England: The MIT Press.
157 Azarpay, G. (1968). *Urartian Art and Artifacts. A Chronological Study*. Berkeley and Los Angeles: University of California Press.
158 Higham, C. (1988). Prehistoric Metallurgy in Southeast Asia: Some New Information from the Excavation of Ban Na Di, in *The Beginning of the Use of Metals and Alloys. Papers from the Second International Conference on the Beginning of the Use of Metals and Alloys, Zhengzhou, China, 21–26 October 1986.*, ed. R. Maddin Cambridge, Massachusetts & London, England: The MIT Press.
159 Agrawal, D. P. (2000). *Ancient Metal Technology and Archaeology of South Asia. A Pan-Asian Perspective*. New Delhi: Aryan Books International.
160 White, J. C. (1988). Early East Asian Metallurgy: The Southern Tradition, in *The Beginning of the Use of Metals and Alloys. Papers from the Second International Conference on the Beginning of the Use of Metals and Alloys, Zhengzhou, China, 21–26 October 1986.*, ed. R. Maddin Cambridge, Massachusetts & London, England: The MIT Press.)

161 Kenoyer in harappa.com slide description
http://www.harappa.com/indus2/162.html
162 Collections of IDAM Israel Museum(IDAM), Jerusalem, Israel
163 Davey, Christopher J., 2009, The early history of lost-wax casting, in J. Mei and Th. Rehren, eds., *Metallurgy and civilisation: Eurasia and beyond archetype*, London 2009, p.150.
http://www.aiarch.org.au/bios/cjd/147%20Davey%202009%20BUMA%20VI%20offprint.pdf
164 ibid., pp. 149-150.
165 Goren, Yuval, 2008, *The location of specialized copper production by the lost wax technique in the chalcolithic southern Levant*, in: Geoarchaeology: An international journal, Vol. 23, No. 3, pp. 374-397.
166 Vats, MS, 1940, Excavations at Harappa, Delhi, p. 370.

167 http://old.omda.bg/engl/history/varna_necropolis_treasure.htm
168 Janson, Horst Woldemar; Anthony F. Janson *History of Art: A Survey of the Major Visual Arts from the Dawn of History to the Present Day* Prentice Hall 1986.
169 Contenau G., Manuel d'archéologie orientale depuis les origines jusqu'à Alexandre : les découvertes archéologiques de 1930 à 1939, IV, Paris : Picard, 1947, pp. 2049-2051, fig. 1138 Parrot A., Les fouilles de Mari, première campagne (hiver 1933-1934), Extr. de : Syria, 16, 1935, paris : P. Geuthner, pp. 132-137, pl. XXVIII Parrot A., Mission archéologique de Mari : vol. I : le temple d'Ishtar, Bibliothèque archéologique et historique, LXV, Paris : Institut français d'archéologie du Proche-Orient, 1956, pp. 136-155, pls. LVI-LVII Author: Iselin Claire.

170 Contenau G., Manuel d'archéologie orientale depuis les origines jusqu'à Alexandre : les découvertes archéologiques de 1930 à 1939, IV, Paris : Picard, 1947, pp. 2049-2051, fig. 1138

Parrot A., Les fouilles de Mari, première campagne (hiver 1933-1934), Extr. de : Syria, 16, 1935, paris : P. Geuthner, pp. 132-137, pl. XXVIII

Parrot A., Mission archéologique de Mari : vol. I : le temple d'Ishtar, Bibliothèque archéologique et historique, LXV, Paris : Institut français d'archéologie du Proche-Orient, 1956, pp. 136-155, pls. LVI-LVII Author: Iselin Claire.

171 http://www.metmuseum.org/toah/works-of-art/1988.433.1
172 Kim Benzel, Sarah B. Graff, Yelena Rakic and Edith W. Watts, 2010, Art of the Ancient Near East, a resource for educators, New York, Metropolitan Museum of Art http://www.metmuseum.org/~/media/Files/Learn/For%20Educators/Publications%20for%20Educators/Art%20of%20the%20Ancient%20Near%20East.pdf
173 Tripathi, Vibha and Arun K. Mishra, 1997, Understanding iron technology: An ethnographic model, Man and Environment 22 (1): 59-67.
174 Ghosh, A., 2008, Prehistory of the Chotanagpur region, Part 4. Ethnoarchaeology, rock art, iron and he asuras in: The Internet Journal of Biological Anthropology, Volume

3, Number 1) http://ispub.com/IJBA/3/1/5134 See: Chakrabarti, Dilip K., 1993, Archaeology of Eastern India, Chotanagpur plateau and West Bengal, New Delhi, Munshiram Manoharlal. Chakrabarti, Dilip K. and Nayanjot Lahiri, 1993-1994. The iron age in India. The beginning and consequences, Puratattva No. 24: 12-33.
175 Amiet Pierre, Élam, Auvers-sur-Oise, Archée, 1966, p. 166, fig. 119.
Les quatre grandes civilisations mondiales. La Mésopotamie entre le Tigre et l'Euphrate, cat. exp., Setagaya, musée d'Art, 5 août-3 décembre 2000, Fukuoka, musée d'Art asiatique, 16 décembre 2000-4 mars 2001, Tokyo, NHK, 2000, pp. 214-215. Author: Herbin Nancie http://www.louvre.fr/en/oeuvre-notices/base-ritual-offering-carved-animals
176 http://www.penn.museum/documents/publications/expedition/PDFs/40-2/Life.pdf See also: *Expedition* 40:2 (1998), p. 33, fig. 5b
177 The Toda mund, from, Richard Barron, 1837, "View in India, chiefly among the Nilgiri Hills'. Oil on canvas.
178 Heuzey, Leon & Thureau-Dangin, 1910, *Nouvelles Fouilles de Tello*, Paris, Gaston Cros, Ernest Leroux, editeur, p.143.
http://ia600304.us.archive.org/14/items/nouvellesfouille00crosuoft/nouvellesfouille00crosuoft.pdf

179
http://www.academia.edu/2360254/Temple_Sacred_Prostitution_in_Ancient_Mesopotamia_RevisitedThat the hieroglyph of pot/vase overflowing with water is a recurring theme can be seen from other cylinder seals, including Ibni-Sharrum cylinder seal. Such an imagery also occurs on a fragment of a stele, showing part of a lion and vases.

180 http://bharatkalyan97.blogspot.in/2013/06/tablet-of-destinies.html
181 http://www.omilosmeleton.gr/pdf/en/indology/Vedic_and_Avestan.pdf
182 Legend of Anzu which stole the tablets of destiny and allegory of somahttp://bharatkalyan97.blogspot.in/2013/07/legend-of-anzu-which-stole-tablets-of.html The tablets of destiny may be a reference to Indus writing corpora which were veritable stone-, mineral-, metal-ware catalogs.
183 http://www.jtsa.edu/Documents/pagedocs/JANES/2009/Wazana_JANES31.pdf
184 Kannada. Siddhānti Subrahmaṇya śāstri's new interpretation of the Amarakośa, Bangalore,Vicaradarpana Press, 1872, p. 330.
185 The Toda mund, from, Richard Barron, 1837, "View in India, chiefly among the Nilgiri Hills'. Oil on canvas.
186 http://www.pinterest.com/lectrice79/honest-history-3000-2901-bce/
187 After Moorey, PRS, 1999, Ancient materials and industries: the archaeological evidence, Eisenbrauns.
188 Beck, Pirhiya, Notes on the style and iconography of the chalcolithic hoard from Nahal Mishmar (Chapter 3) in:Albert Leonard, Jr., & Bruce Beyer Williams, ed., 1989, Essays in ancient civilization presented to Helene J. Kantor, Studies in ancient oriental civilization No. 47, Oriental Institute of the University of Chicago, pp. 39-54 http://oi.uchicago.edu/pdf/saoc47.pdf
Ziffeer, Irit, 2007, A note on the Nahal Mishmar crown, in: Jack Cheng, Marian H.

Feldman, eds., Ancient near eastern art in context: studies in honor of Irene J. Winter by her students, BRILL., pp. 47-67.
189 JM Kenoyer, 1998, Ancient cities of the Indus Valley, Oxford University Press, p. 115.
190 http://oi.uchicago.edu/OI/IRAQ/dbfiles/objects/14.htm
191 Chatterjee, SK, The study of kol, *Calcutta Review*, 1923, p. 455
192 Przyluski, Non-aryan loans in Indo-Aryan, in: Bagchi, PC, *Pre-aryan and pre-dravidian*, pp.28-29
193 http://www.buddhanet.net/e-learning/buddhism/lifebuddha/1lbud.htm
194 Cunningham, Alexander, 1879, The stupa of Bharhut: a Buddhist monument ornamented with numerous sculptures illustrative of Buddhist legend and history in the 3rd century BCE, Published by order of the Secretary of State for India in Council, London, WH Allen and Co., p.184.
195 Davids, TW Rhys, Buddhist birth-stories (Jataka tales): the commentarial introduction entitled Nidaana Kathaa, the story of the lineage, translated from Prof. V. Fausboll's edition of the Pali text by TW Rhys Davids, London, George Rouledge and Sons, New York: EP Dutton and Co., p. 248.
196 Source: http://www.iranicaonline.org/articles/assyria-
J. Deshayes, "Marteaux de bronze iraniens," Syria 35, 1958, pp. 284-93.Idem, Les outils de bronze de l'Indus au Danube (IVe au IIe millénaire), Bibliothèque archéologique et historique 71, 2 vols., Paris, 1960.Idem, "Haches-herminettes iraniennes," Syria 40, 1963, pp. 273-76.Idem, "Nouveaux outils iraniens," Syria 42, 1965, pp. 91-108.Idem and J. Christophe, Index de l'outillage. Outils de métal de l'âge du bronze des Balkans à l'Indus II: Commentaires, Paris, 1964.
197 KTM Hegde and Ericson, J.E., 1985, Ancient Indian Copper Smelting Furnaces, in: *Furnaces and Smelting Technology in Antiquity*, ed. P.T. Craddock, Occasional Paper No. 48, British Museum, London, pp. 59-67.
198 http://www.hindunet.org/saraswati/trade1.htm
199 http://www.mpi.nl/people/levinson-stephen/research/figure_02.jpg
200 Nausharo NS 91.01.32.01. Dept. of Arch., Karachi. Jarrige 1988: 87, fig.41 (After fig. 2.19, Kenoyer, 2000).
201 http://en.wikipedia.org/wiki/File:Meghalaya_Khasi_Woman.jpg
202 Evans, Nicholas & Stephen C. Levison, 2009, The myth of language universals: language and diversity and its importance for cognitive science, *Behavioral and Brain Sciences*, ew, 429-492.
203 Derrida, J., 1976, *Of Grammatology*, The Johns Hopkins University Press, Baltimore.
204 Levelt, W. (1999). "The neurocognition of language", p.87 -117. Oxford Press.
205 *Philosphical Grammar*, R. Rhees (ed.), A. Kenny (trans.), Oxford University Press, Oxford, 1974, p. 161. See: *Philosophische Untersuchungen*, 2nd edn., GEM Anscombe and R. Rhees (eds.), GEM Anscombe (trans), Oxford University Press, Oxford, 1958. K. Kunjunni Raja, 1963, *Indian theories of meaning*, Adyar Library Series, vol. 91, pp. 360. Madras. Adyar Library and Research Centre, 1963. Reviewed by Murray Fowler, University of Wisconsin.
206 Harris, Roy, 1990, *Language, Saussure and Wittgenstein: how to play games with words*, London, Routledge, p. 5.
207 Harris, Roy, 1990, *Language, Saussure and Wittgenstein: how to play games with words*, London, Routledge, p. 28.

208 Harris, Roy, 1990, *Language, Saussure and Wittgenstein: how to play games with words*, London, Routledge, p. 28.
209 *Cours de linguistique generale*, 1922, reproduced in T. de Mauro's Edition critique, Payot, Paris, 1972. English translation by R. Harris, Duckworth, London, 1983, p.157.
210 *Cours de linguistique generale*, 1922, reproduced in T. de Mauro's Edition critique, Payot, Paris, 1972. English translation by R. Harris, Duckworth, London, 1983, p.155. loc.cit. Harris, Roy, 1990, *Language, Saussure and Wittgenstein: how to play games with words*, London, Routledge, p. 29.
211 Harris, Roy, 1995, *Signs of writing*, London, Routledge, p.4.
212 *ibid.*, p. 43, p. 45.
213 Anscombe, GEM and R. Rhees (eds.), GEM Anscombe (trans), *Philosophische Untersuchungen*, 2nd edn., Oxford University Press, Oxford, 1958, p. 174.
214 Gelb, Ignace J., 1952, *A Study of Writing, the foundations of grammatology*, Chicago, University of Chicago Press.
215 Ulmer, Gregory, 1985, *Applied Gramamtology, Post(e)-Pedagogy from Jacques Derrida to Joseph Beuys,* The Johns Hopkins University Press, Baltimore; Derrida,J., 1976, *Of Grammatology*, The Johns Hopkins University Press, Baltimore.
216 Marc Wilhelm Küster, 2006-7, *Geordnetes Weltbild. Die Tradition des alphabetischen Sortierens von der Keilschrift bis zur EDV. Eine Kulturgeschichte.* Niemeyer: Tübingen.
217 Buchler, J. ed., 1955, *Philosophical writings of Pierce,* New York, Dover, p. 99.
218 http://en.wikipedia.org/wiki/Polysemy
219 http://en.wikipedia.org/wiki/Polysemy Fillmore, C J; Atkins, B T S (2000). Describing polysemy: The case of "crawl". In Leacock, C. *Polysemy: Theoretical and computational approaches.* Oxford: Oxford University Press. pp. 91–110. p.100.
220 Lee, Penny, 1996, "The Logic and Development of the Linguistic Relativity Principle", *The Whorf Theory Complex: A Critical Reconstruction*, John Benjamins Publishing, p. 84.
221 Leavitt, John (2011), *Linguistic Relativities: Language Diversity and Modern Thought*, Cambridge, UK: Cambridge University Press.
222 Coward, Harold G.,1977, *The Sphōṭa Theory of Language: A Philosophical Analysis* , Delhi, Motilal Banarsidass; Gaurinath Sastri, 1981, *A Study in the Dialectics of Sphōṭa*, Delhi, Motilal Banarsidass.

223 Brough, J., (1952). "Audumbarayana's Theory of Language,". *Bulletin of the School of Oriental and African Studies, University of London,* 14 (1,): 73–77.
224 Dominik Wujastyk (1993). *Metarules of Pāṇinian Grammar, the Vyāḍīyaparibhāṣā.* Groningen: Forsten.
225 Bimal Krishna Matilal, 1990, *The word and the world: India's contribution to the study of language*, Oxford.
226 ^ 南海寄歸內法傳 *Account of Buddhism sent from the South Seas* http://www.buddhist-canon.com/history/T540204c.htm
大唐西域求法高僧傳 *Buddhist Monk's Pilgrimage of the Tang Dynasty* http://www.buddhist-canon.com/history/T510006c.htm

I-Tsing, *A Record of the Buddhist Religion : As Practised in India and the Malay Archipelago (A.D. 671-695)*, Translated by J. Takakusu, Clarendon press 1896. Reprint. New Delhi, AES, 2005, lxiv, 240 p. https://archive.org/details/arecordbuddhist00takagoog

I-Tsing, *Chinese Monks in India, Biography of Eminent Monks Who Went to the Western World in Search of the Law During the Great tang Dynasty*, Translated by Latika Lahiri, Delhi, etc.: Motilal Banarsidass, 1986.

227 AH Gardiner, *Speech and Language*, p. 70.

228 Brough, John, 1951, *Theories of General Linguistics in the Sanskrit Grammarians*, London, *Transactions of the Philological Society*, Vol. 50, Issue 1, pp. 27-46, November 1951, p. 33.

229 Gaurinath Sastri, 1959, *The philosophy of word and meaning, Some Indian approaches with special reference to the philosophy of Bhartrhari, Sanskrit College, Calcutta. Dept. of Post-graduate Training and Research Series, No. 5, Studies No.2*, pp. 102-103.

230 Aklujkar, Ashok, 1992, An Introduction to the study of Bhartṛhari, in: Bhate, Saroja & Johanes Bronkhorst, 1994, Bhartṛhari, Philosopher and Grammarian: Proceedings of the First International Conference on Bhartṛhari (University of Poona, January 6-8, 1992), Delhi, Motilal Banarsidass Publ., p.10.

231 Gottlob Frege, "Über Sinn und Bedeutung", in *Zeitschrift für Philosophie und philosophische Kritik C* (1892): 25–50; In English: "On Sense and Reference", alternatively translated (in later edition) as "On Sense and Meaning".

232 http://en.wikipedia.org/wiki/Reference

233 http://www.turkishhan.org/trade.htm

234 Charles, J.A. (1979). "The development of the usage of tin and tin-bronze: some problems". In Franklin, A.D.; Olin, J.S.; Wertime, T.A. The Search for Ancient Tin. Washington D.C.: A seminar organized by Theodore A. Wertime and held at the Smithsonian Institution and the National Bureau of Standards, Washington D.C. March 14–15, 1977. pp. 25–32.

235 Craddock, P.T. and Eckstein, K (2003) "Production of Brass in Antiquity by Direct Reduction" in Craddock, P.T. and Lang, J. (eds) Mining and Metal Production Through the Ages London: British Museum pp. 226–7.

236 http://www.infinityfoundation.com/mandala/t_es/t_es_agraw_zinc_frameset.htm

237 Lehto, R. S. (1968). "Zinc". In Clifford A. Hampel. The Encyclopedia of the Chemical Elements. New York: Reinhold Book Corporation. pp. 822–830.

238 Emsley, John (2001). "Zinc". Nature's Building Blocks: An A-Z Guide to the Elements. Oxford, England, UK: Oxford University Press. pp. 499–505.

239 Cierny, J.; Weisgerber, G. (2003). "The "Bronze Age tin mines in Central Asia". In Giumlia-Mair, A.; Lo Schiavo, F. The Problem of Early Tin. Oxford: Archaeopress. pp. 23–31.

240 Tosi, Maurizio, 1986, Early maritime cultures of the Arabian Gulf and the Indian Ocean in: Bahrain through the ages: the Archaeology, 1986, Rouledge, pp. 94ff.

241 J.D. Muhly, 1973, *Copper and Tin*, Hamden, Connecticut, Archon Books, pp.241-335.

242 Alster, Bendt, 1972, Nirnurta and the Turtle UET 6/1 2, *Journal of Cuneiform Studies* Vol. 24, No. 4 (1972), pp. 120-125.

243 http://bharatkalyan97.blogspot.in/2013/06/tablet-of-destinies.html

244 Legend of Anzu which stole the tablets of destiny and allegory of soma http://bharatkalyan97.blogspot.in/2013/07/legend-of-anzu-which-stole-tablets-of.html

The tablets of destiny may be a reference to Indus writing corpora which were veritable stone-, mineral-, metal-ware catalogs.

http://bharatkalyan97.blogspot.in/2011/11/syena-orthography.html śyena, orthography, Sasanian iconography. Continued use of Indus Script hieroglyphs.

http://www.jtsa.edu/documents/pagedocs/janes/2009/wazana_janes31.pdf

245 Vallat. F.,1985, Elements de geographic elamite (resume), *PO*.11, pp.49-54.
246 Witzel, M., 1999, Substrate languages in old Indo-Aryan (Rgvedic, Middle and Late Vedic), *Electronic Journal of Vedic Studies,* 5-1, pp. 1-67.
http://www.ejvs.laurasianacademy.com/ejvs0501/0501ART.PDF
247 Fox , Michael V. (1988). *Temple in society*. Eisenbrauns.
248 http://chandrashekharasandprints.wordpress.com/2013/05/08/kutch-and-kathiawar-a-tryst-with-history-part-vii/ Kutch and Kathiawar: A tryst with history

249 Hale, Wash Edward, 1986, *Asura in early Vedic religion*, Delhi, Motilal Banarsidass Publishers Pvt. Ltd.
250 Christensen, Arthus, 1932, *Les Kayanides* (The Kayanians), Copenhagen
251 Daiva, *Encyclopaedia Iranica*, p. 599.)
252 Kalyanaraman, S., 2013, *Meluhha—A visible language* Herndon, Sarasvati Research Center.
253 http://cdli.ucla.edu/Pubs/cdln/archives/000028.html CDLN 2014:001 Jacob L. Dahl: The proto-Elamite seal MDP 16, pl. XII fig. 198
254
http://cdli.ucla.edu/search/search_results.php?SearchMode=Text&ObjectID=P272825

255 Jean Perrot; Originally Published: December 15, 2008

http://www.iranicaonline.org/articles/jiroft-iv-iconography-of-chlorite-artifacts

256 Harris, Roy, 1995, *Signs of writing*, London, Routledge, p.52; loc.cit. F. de Saussure, *Cours de linguistique generale*, 2nd edn, Paris, Payot, 1922, p. 165.
257 F.R. Allchin, 1959, Upon the contextual significance of certain groups of ancient signs, *Bulletin of the School of Oriental and African Studies*, London.) (Kalyanaraman, S., 2010, The Bronze Age Writing System of Sarasvati Hieroglyphics as Evidenced by Two "Rosetta Stones" - Decoding Indus script as repertoire of the mints/smithy/mine-workers of Meluhha. Journal of Indo-Judaic Studies. Number 11. pp. 47–74.

258 *The Languages of China.* S. Robert Ramsey. Princeton University Press, 1987, p. 137.) See also: Woods, Christopher, 2010, *Visible language – inventions of writing in the ancient Middle East and Beyond*, Oriental Institute Museum Publications, Number 32, Chicago.
259 Houston, Stephen D., 1996, Sumerian and Akkadian, in: Peter T. and Bright, William, eds.,1996, *The world's writing systems*, OUP, p.53.
260 Houston, Stephen D., 2004, *The first writing: script invention as history and process*, Cambridge University Press, p. 64.
261 Daniels, Peter T., 1996, *The world's writing systems*, OUP, pp.42-43.

262 Cooper, Jerrold, 1996, Sumerian and Akkadian, p.42.
263 Sampson, Geoffrey, 1985, *Writing systems: a linguistic introduction*, Stanford, Stanford University Press, p.54.
264 Thompson, J. Eric S., Pictorial synonyms and homonyms in the Maya Dresden codex, p.148.
265 S. Kalyanaraman, 2010, The Bronze Age Writing System of Sarasvati Hieroglyphics as Evidenced by Two "Rosetta Stones" - Decoding Indus script as repertoire of the mints/smithy/mine-workers of Meluhha, Journal of Indo-Judaic Studies, Number 11, pp. 47-74.
266 Potts 2014 - Nomadism in Iran: From Antiquity to the Modern Era. New York: Oxford University Press, p. 75

267 Vidale, Massimo, 2004, "Growing in a Foreign World. For a History of the "Meluhha Villages" in Mesopotamia in the 3rd Millennium BCE" THE MELAMMU PROJECT Published in Melammu Symposia 4: A. Panaino and A. Piras (eds.), Schools of Oriental Studies and the Development of Modern Historiography. Proceedings of the Fourth Annual Symposium of the Assyrian and Babylonian Intellectual Heritage Project. Held in Ravenna, Italy, October 13-17, 2001 (Milan: Università di Bologna & IsIao 2004), pp. 261-80. Publisher:http://www.mimesisedizioni.it/

http://www.aakkl.helsinki.fi/melammu/
268 Massimo Vidale, 2007, 'The collapse melts down: a reply to Farmer, Sproat and Witzel', East and West, vol. 57, no. 1-4, pp. 333 to 366.
269 Freud, Sigmund, 1913, Trans. by AA Brill, Interpretation of Dreams, Chapter VI, The dream-work, New York, The Macmillan Company http://www.bartleby.com/285/6.html
270 Zainab Bahrani, 2011, The graven image: representation in Babylonia and Assyria, Univ. of Pennsylvania Press, p. 185-186.
271 http://www.louvre.fr/en/oeuvre-notices/base-ritual-offering-carved-animals

272 Chatterjee, SK, The study of kol, Calcutta Review, 1923, p. 455.

273 Przyluski, Non-aryan loans in Indo-Aryan, in: Bagchi, PC, *Pre-aryan and pre-dravidian*, pp.28-29.
274 Kannada. Siddhānti Subrahmaṇya śāstri, *New interpretation of the Amarakośa*, Bangalore,Vicaradarpana Press, 1872, p. 330.
275 George A. Lindbeck presents the nature of doctrine in his book, *The Nature of Doctrine: Religion and Theology in a Postliberal Age* (Louisville, KY: Westminster John Knox Press, 1984.
276 E.g. Wittgenstein, *Philosophical Investigations*, §245, §247, §252-3, §257, §278, §282.] For Wittgenstein's discussions on private language, see Ludwig Wittgenstein, *Philosophical Investigations*, trans. G. E. M. Anscombe (Malden, MA: Blackwell, 2005), §243-315
http://churchandpomo.typepad.com/conversation/2007/01/lindbeck_after_.html Eric Lee, 2007, Lindbeck After Wittgenstein?

277 This artwork is currently on display in Gallery 173 Said to be from Amathus, Cyprus. 1865–1872, found in Cyprus by General Luigi Palma di Cesnola; acquired by the Museum in 1874, purchased from General Luigi Palma di Cesnola http://www.metmuseum.org/collections/search-the-collections/30000008

278 http://en.wikipedia.org/wiki/Tin
279 Nissen, H.J., Damerow, P., Englund, R.K., 1993. *Archaic Bookkeeping*, Chicago: The University of Chicago Press, pp. 64-65.
280Vats 1940: 381; Marshall 1931: 488.
281 Chakrabari, DK, 1979, The problem of tin in early India--a preliminary survey, in: *Man and Environment*, Vol. 3, pp. 61-74.
282 Burney, 1977, 86; Muhly, 1973, 306-7, 449 note 542; Muhly, J.D., 1973, Tin trade routes of the Bronze Age, Scientific American, 1973, 61, 404-13.

283 Muhly, J.D., 1976, *Copper and Tin*, Hamden, Archon Books, pp. 306-7.

284 Pliny, *Naturalis Historia*, 34.2 and 37.44. The map and notes on Mesopotamian/Egyptian contacts are based on: D.T.Potts, 1995, Distant Shores: ancient near eastern trac with south Asia and northeast Africa, pp. 1451-1463, in: Jack M. Sasson, ed. 1995, *Civilizations of the Ancient Near East*, Vol. III, New York, Charles Scribner's Sons.

285 Copper-bronze artefacts from Mohenjodaro exhibited at the Mohenjodaro museum. Dr. Abdul Jabbar Junejo and Mohammad Qasim Bughio, 1988, Cultural Heritage of Sind, International Arabi Conference, University of Sind, Hyderabad, Sindhi Adabi Board.

286 Hegde, KTM, Sources of Ancient Tin in India, in: Alan D. Franklin, Jacqueline S. Olin and Theodore A. Wertime, eds., 1977, *The Search for Ancient Tin*, Washington D.C., US Government Printing Office.
287 Tylecote, R.F., 1976, A History of Metallurgy, The Metals Society, p. 11.
288 Penhallurick, R.D., 1986, Tin in Antiquity, London, Institute of Metals, pp. 18-32.
289 Muhly, J.D., 1973, *Copper and Tin: the distribution of mineral resources and the nature of the metals trade in the Bronze Age*, Hamden, Connecticut, Archon Books, p. 409.
290 Hirsch, H., 1963, Die Inschriften der Konige Von Agade, Afo, 20, pp. 37-38; Leemans, W.F., 1960, Foreign Trade in the Old Babylonian Period, p. 164; Oppenheim, A.L., 1954, The seafaring merchants of Ur, JAOS, 74, pp. 6-17.
291 Hansman, J. 'A Periplus of Magan and Meluhha', Bulletin of the School of Oriental and African Studies, vol. 36, pt. III, 1973, pp. 560.
292 Scheil, V., 1925, Un Nouvea Sceau Hindou Pseudo-Sumerian, RA, 22/3, pp. 55-56.
293 Wheeler, R.E.M., 1965, *Indus Civilization*; supplementary volume to the Cambridge History of India, 3rd edn., Cambridge, CUP, 1968.
294 Revue d'Assyriologie, Vol. 22: 56.
295 Oppenheim 1954: II, 15 n.24.
296 Oppenheim 1954: 6-12.

297 Raw, V. 27A, 25-7; loc.cit. Upenn University Museum, 1915, Publications of the Babylonian Section, Vol. 10' Stephen Langdon, Sumerian epic of paradise, flood and the fall of man, p.8 http://tinyurl.com/ybfhept

298 After Potts, 1995.

299 Roaf M. and Collon, D., 1990, *Cultural atlas of Mesopotamia and the Ancient Near East*, New York, Facts on File, p.113.

300 Kim Benzel, Sarah B. Graff, Yelena Rakic and Edith W. Watts, 2010, Art of the Ancient Near East, a resource for educators, New York, Metropolitan Museum of Art http://www.metmuseum.org/~/media/Files/Learn/For%20Educators/Publications%20for%20Educators/Art%20of%20the%20Ancient%20Near%20East.pdf

301 Bloomsfield's ed.n, xliv. Cf. Bloomsfield, *American Journal of Philology*, 11, 355; 12,416; Roth, Festgruss an Bohtlingk, 98.

302 See Vedic Index, I, p. 177.

303 http://www.metmuseum.org/toah/works-of-art/1988.433.1

304 Glassner, J-J. 2003. *The invention of cuneiform. Writing in Sumer.* Translated and edited by Zainab Bahrani and Marc van de Mieroop. Baltimore & London: The John Hopkins University Press, p. 45.

305 Potts, DT, 2012, *A companion to the archaeology of the ancient Near East*, John Wiley & Sons, pp. 307-308.

306 Shortland, A. J. (2006). "Application of Lead Isotope Analysis to a Wide Range of Late Bronze Age Egyptian Materials". Archaeometry 48 (4): 657.

www.ingramcontent.com/pod-product-compliance
Lightning Source LLC
Chambersburg PA
CBHW050326270326
41926CB00016B/3337
* 9 7 8 0 9 9 1 1 0 4 8 2 6 *